KU-755-137

For
Alex and Amy
who are learning to live in the exciting and bewildering world of complex organizations

David C. Wilson

For
My parents, Maurice and Toni
who guided me through an exciting and bewildering environment

Robert H. Rosenfeld

Contents

Contributors

David C. Wilson is a Senior Lecturer in Organizational Behaviour at the University of Warwick Business School.

Robert H. Rosenfeld is a Consultant for Financial Services Management Development Ltd, and a former Senior Research Fellow at the Centre for Corporate Strategy and Change, University of Warwick.

Nancy J. Adler is an Associate Professor of Organizational Behaviour and Cross-Cultural Management at the Faculty of Management, McGill University in Montreal, Canada. She also teaches executive and management seminars at INSEAD in France and at Bocconi University in Italy.

Christopher W. Allinson is a Lecturer in Organizational Behaviour at the School of Business and Economic Studies, University of Leeds, and a Chartered occupational psychologist.

P. D. Anthony is Visiting Reader in the Department of Behaviour in Organizations at the University of Lancaster.

Jean-Louis Barsoux is a Research Fellow at Loughborough University of Technology.

John G. Burgoyne is Professor of Management Learning in the School of Management at Lancaster University.

Richard J. Butler is Reader in Organizational Analysis at the University of Bradford Management Centre.

Elizabeth Chell is Director of the Centre for Small Business Research at the University of Salford.

Caroline Clark is Community Development Manager with Business in the Community, and a former Research Officer at Henley — The Management College.

Cary L. Cooper is Professor of Organizational Psychology at the Manchester School of Management, University of Manchester Institute of Science and Technology. He is currently President of the British Academy of Management and a Fellow of the British Psychological Society, and is editor of the Journal of Organizational Behaviour.

J. Martin Corbett is a Lecturer in Organizational Behaviour at the School of Industrial and Business Studies, University of Warwick.

Patrick Dawson is a Lecturer in Organizational Studies in the Graduate School of Management at the University of Adelaide. He is currently involved in a three year study of new technology and the management of expertise as part of the ESRC's initiative on New Technology and the Firm.

Arthur Francis is Head of the Business Policy and Marketing Group, and Senior Lecturer, at the Management School, London University. The case study for this text arose out of research funded by the ESRC's programme on the competitiveness of British Industry.

Hugh Gunz is Associate Professor of Organizational Behaviour at Erindale College and the Faculty of Management, University of Toronto, Canada.

Cynthia Hardy is Associate Professor in the Faculty of Management, McGill University.

David J. Hickson is Professor of International Management and Organization at the University of Bradford Management Centre. He is also the Eldon Foote Visiting Professor of International Business at the University of Alberta, Canada.

Geert Hofstede is Professor of Organizational Anthropology and International Management at the Department of Economics and Business Administration, the University of Limburg at Maastricht in The Netherlands. Professor Hofstede is also Director of the Institute for Research on Intercultural Cooperation at Limburg University.

Heather J. Hopkins is a Lecturer in Organizational Psychology in the Management School and a Research Fellow in the Legal and Policy Informatics Group at the University of Lancaster.

Dian-Marie Hosking is a Lecturer in the Applied Social Psychology of Organisations at the Aston Business School, Aston University.

Robert A. Lee is Senior Lecturer in Organizational Behaviour in the Department of Management Studies at Loughborough University.

Alan McKinlay is currently Colquhoun Lecturer in Business History at the Centre for Business History in Scotland, University of Glasgow.

Roger Mansfield is Professor of Business Administration and Director of the Cardiff Business School, University of Wales College of Cardiff.

Andrew M. Pettigrew is Professor of Organizational Behaviour and Director of the Centre for Corporate Strategy and Change, Warwick Business School, Warwick University.

David A. Preece is Senior Lecturer in Organization Analysis and Personnel Management at The Business School, Portsmouth Polytechnic.

Sheila Rothwell is Director of the Centre for Employment Policy Studies at Henley — The Management College.

Vicky Russell runs Walden Corporate Change Consultancy and is also a Research Fellow at London Business School. Previously she worked with Coopers & Lybrand Associates and Shell UK as a consultant in corporate strategy.

Paul R. Sparrow is a Consultant in Human Resource Strategy with PA Consulting Group, and a former Senior Research Fellow at the University of Warwick.

Ken Starkey is a Lecturer in Management in the Department of Industrial Economics at the University of Nottingham.

Valerie J. Sutherland is Honorary Lecturer in Organizational Psychology at the Manchester School of Management, University of Manchester Institute of Science and Technology.

Monir Tayeb is a Lecturer in International Business at the Heriot-Watt University in Edinburgh.

Terry Thornley is a Principal Lecturer in Management and Information Technology at Huddersfield Polytechnic.

Richard Thorpe is a Senior Lecturer in Management Development and an MBA Course Leader at Manchester Polytechnic.

Diana Winstanley is a Senior Lecturer in Organizational Behaviour and Personnel Management at the Kingston Business School, Kingston Polytechnic.

Acknowledgements

We would like to thank all the individual contributors to this book. Without the Readings and Cases, most of which were written especially for this text, the book would never have achieved the goals we had set ourselves as authors, namely: integration of theoretical perspectives, critical appraisal and an assessment of their utility in the context of complex organizations. The contributions have allowed us to address these issues within one volume.

The University of Warwick School of Industrial and Business Studies also provided a fruitful base from which to write the book. The many programmes in organizational behaviour taught across the range of undergraduate, postgraduate and executive courses provided us with useful ideas, perspectives, comments and suggestions in drafting this book. For example, some of the early sections of the book are developed from our experience of teaching material prepared for the distance-learning MBA at Warwick (previously administered through Wolsey Hall, Oxford and now administered by Warwick Business School). Feedback from our full-time MBA and executive courses helped to develop many of the middle and later sections. To them, and to the anonymous reviewers who made sound suggestions at many stages of drafting the text, and to Julie Ganner and her team at McGraw-Hill, we owe our thanks.

Finally, special thanks are due to Jo Wilson and Liz Martin-Rosenfeld for their sustained support of the whole project which inevitably ran substantially into 'family time' on many occasions.

Part I
Introduction

CHAPTER 1 About this book

Introduction

This book is aimed at addressing the contemporary issues which fall under the broad title of organizational behaviour. It is also designed with a view to incorporating text, readings and cases in one volume. The text is written to outline the topic areas. It shows to what extent our current theoretical and empirical knowledge can comment upon contemporary themes in organizations. In order to do this, the book contents spread across a wide range of topics.

Of course, there are topics which focus on the individual within the organization and the issues of working with others in groups or teams. We also look outside these areas towards more contextually based themes in the subject. In particular, this is the result of teaching and talking with managers, students of business and researching in the discipline. The book is thus led by research and guided by current issues. Therefore, themes of organizational change, control, decision-making and operating internationally are included as a natural part of organizational behaviour.

Organization of the book

Each section of the book corresponds to a set of different themes and approaches. Traditionally enough, we begin with you, the individual, in the organization. We look at some of the attributes of individuals and see to what extent these can be reflected in their behaviour in organizations. We also look at how organizations themselves behave toward their markets, their peers and their immediate environment. Linking these perspectives together are the underlying themes of continuity and change in organizations and what these imply both for working within them as well as for their management.

At the end of each section are both readings and cases. The intention is to achieve a further degree of thematic integration. Each reading is written by a leading researcher and academic in the specific topics in each section. The case studies present the reader with organizational scenarios and situations which illustrate the topics in practice as well as pose a set of problems for resolution. They ask: given your knowledge in this area, what would you recommend as a course of action and why? They are real problems from real organizations in Britain and Europe.

Why another text in organizational behaviour?

The broad ideas which went into compiling this book reflect the experience of the authors (as teachers and researchers) and also the experience, frustrations and suggestions of many of our peers. The teaching of theory and analysis in organizations has changed almost unrecognizably over the past five years. The growth of business-degree programmes at undergraduate and postgraduate level has placed the question of managing organizations and their human resources at centre stage. Coupled with this expansion comes a recognition of the importance of management education from practitioners. Organizations large and small, manufacturing and service, commercial and charitable, are now seeking education for their managers at all levels.

The role of business schools and management departments in higher education generally has been to supply this need, often at very short notice. The number of textbooks on organizational behaviour is extremely large, but predominantly North American in origin. There are some British and European texts available, but these are notable exceptions. Even these texts either cover the terrain partially (by design), or force the reader to go elsewhere for relevant case examples.

Examples which originate in North America and portray the experience of companies and managers in the United States and Canada have become rather less relevant to British and European organizations over the same time period. Examples of how it was done in General Motors America are not always helpful in looking at Jaguar or Austin Rover. At the very general level, of course, comparisons are possible. At any more detailed level, comparisons become strained, often to the point of irrelevance. The operating context, the fiscal economy, the regulatory environment, the values, attitudes and beliefs of individuals all differ between the two contexts. Managing organizational change in Britain, for example, necessitates attention to a whole set of characteristics which simply would not apply in North America. The history of the organization, its corporate culture, societal characteristics, levels of unionization are all different.

The intention with the current book is to capture theory and practice within one volume. The cases are intended to show how British and European organizations face problems, while the text is aimed at highlighting theories and research results as they apply in the Anglo-European context.

The book is divided into seven parts, all of which are self-contained. This means that the reader can also choose to sample particular parts if these are seen to be of particular relevance. We have also tried to make the text a coherent whole from beginning to end, so that the themes of the book can emerge through different perspectives and levels of analysis. Thus, a complete reading of the book should provide the framework and the foundations for the detailed study of organizational behaviour.

A framework for reading this book

This book spans a range of topics and levels of analysis. It is important, therefore, to know how to read it. The route map is summarized in Figure 1.1, which is intended to give a framework for analysis.

No one is likely to come into your office and say 'Look, have you got ten minutes, I think we've got an organizational behaviour problem!' It's going to

Figure 1.1
Studying organizations—a framework for analysis

Level of analysis	Example topics
Societal	nature of national context sector characteristics
Organizational	structure and process growth/development change/decline combine/divide
Group	human behaviour team working
Individual	people's needs/attitudes/values behaviour/learning

be far less specific and much more ambiguous. Perhaps it is a problem with one department which seems to be declining in performance, or is difficult for others to work alongside. A host of possible solutions and alternative interpretations is possible. As a first step, this book offers the chance to decide the level (or levels) of analysis from which to start. Is it a specific problem with specific individuals in the department? Is it the whole department which is tricky to deal with and there is no differentiation between individuals? Is the problem likely to be the location of the department in the organizational structure, or is it likely to be a much wider problem outside the scope and the control of any single organization?

Asking these questions provides us with four broad levels of analysis:

- societal
- organizational
- group
- individual

Taking the first letters of each gives the acronym SOGI and this is a useful way to think about analysing problems in organizations. This book is organized around the SOGI principle. Characteristics and attributes of individuals are dealt with in Part II, for example; the operation of groups in Part III and so on through the sections dealing first with organizations themselves and then the environment in which they are embedded. In addition, themes of change, control, effectiveness and competitiveness permeate all sections.

The book also takes the future as one of its themes. There are some changes of huge proportions which will face organizations and their staff over the next five years and beyond. Already, we can predict the likely occurrence of the single market after 1992 with the creation of an integrated European focus. Beyond this are questions such as the role of technology in taking organizations forward to new levels of efficiency and effectiveness. Or do technological advances such as Computer Integrated Manufacture (CIM) primarily result in the deskilling of a labour force which will be increasingly relegated to becoming baby-sitters for computer controlled machines? Major demographic changes are also predicted, coinciding with the integrated Europe date of 1992. There are a host of other questions which impact directly upon organizations and their design and management as we 'crystal-ball gaze' into the future. Much of the latter half of this book has been designed to examining these issues.

Behaviour and organizations

Introduction

All organizations are filled with people. They may occupy different positions. Some are managers, others workers; some are owners of their own businesses, others act as trustees of someone else's organization. Whichever is the case, one of the key aspects to understanding what is going on in any organization is to understand the people within it. Why did they choose to apply to that particular organization? How were they selected? What makes them work effectively and enjoy their life in the organization? And what makes them dissatisfied and looking for alternative jobs? The answers to these questions and a host of others are the central concerns of organizational behaviour.

What do we mean by behaviour?

Organizations are social collectivities. Behaviour refers to the nature of human interaction and conduct within them. This can be on a one-to-one basis or in groups. The discipline also refers to the behaviour *of organizations*. We talk of Cadbury's marketing strategy over the next five years, or the new strategies of organizations in the financial services sector (such as clearing banks and insurance companies). We know that organizations do not really act as if they were a person, yet we often perceive their actions as such. We talk of firms being aggressive or as fair employers and so on. Really, we mean that their managers and staff are moving the organization in these directions. As we shall see, people act on their perceptions, not on objective realities, so the concept of organizations 'behaving' is important. To talk of organizations in this way is called 'reification' (from the Latin word res—a thing). We talk of the firm as a thing.

Human behaviour is at the root of organizational behaviour. The discipline draws heavily from the behavioural and social sciences such as psychology, sociology, philosophy, politics and economics. It also shares each of these subjects' problems, doubts, questions and logics. However, organizational behaviour is more than just the sum total of these sciences. Because it is the study of human behaviour within specific settings (organizations which have a collective purpose) the aspects of common membership, the collective benefits and maintaining at least some forms of control and performance help to integrate knowledge so that organization behaviour becomes a study in its own right.

What sort of organizations do we mean?

At its broadest, the term organization can refer to any collective social arrangement. It is collective because individuals working alone could not possibly achieve the goals set or the task to be achieved. Thus, Imperial Chemical Industries (ICI) are just as much an organization as the darts team at the local pub. So are groups of musicians, railway enthusiasts' societies and women's institutes.

It is the purposive nature of social groups which makes them describable accurately as organizations. Organizations have to build in to their arrangements the means to achieve given aims (Pugh, 1974) and often have to ensure as far as possible the survival of the organization beyond the tenure of its present constituent individuals. Normally, organizations survive longer than most individuals, although there are exceptions.

This means that specific needs have to be met in these organizations. They must be able to perform effectively and this brings with it the need for some means of controlling what goes on in the organization. There are many criteria of effectiveness. Profit levels, return on investment and working capital are some of the more common measures for business organizations. Control mechanisms also cover a wide range of areas from selection of employees to corporate strategy and direction. These issues have been at the heart of organizational behaviour. In the next sections, we outline very briefly the early foundations of the subject.

What is organizational behaviour?

It is the study of the social arrangement of people in organizations. It is concerned with the application of key disciplines such as psychology and sociology specifically to organizations. The subject looks at how social processes are interwoven to form the fabric of organized society and how all these are reflected in the actions of organizations large and small.

The twin themes of control and performance allow us to examine how the subject has developed. What follows is necessarily a very brief and broad outline. For the reader interested in the detail of theoretical and empirical development in organizational behaviour, Nisbet (1973), Pugh (1974) and Zey-Ferrell and Aiken (1981) would be a fruitful source of ideas.

Scientific management: classical theories

Scientific management is possibly the first approach which set the course for the development of the subject. There are a number of key managers and academics who contributed to the development of scientific management and we refer to them together as the 'classical school' of organizational behaviour. Scientific management (which originated at the turn of the twentieth century) is founded on the principles of precision. There was a concerted effort to identify key aspects of work and organization which could be used to achieve efficiency through immutable principles.

The organization was viewed as a machine which could be made more efficient if universal principles could be applied. Historically, this search paralleled similar developments in the natural sciences. Perhaps the two foremost authors associated with the classical approach were Frederick Winslow Taylor (1911) and Henri Fayol (1949). The aim was to develop a 'one best way' of organizing.

In a famous address to the House of Representatives Committee in the United States, Taylor outlined the example of the science of shovelling. Having studied the process with respect to iron ore and having identified a 'normal' labourer (Schmidt, by name) Taylor argued that shovelling could be broken down into separate movements, each of which had an optimal level of mechanical efficiency. When applied, a consistently greater level of output was achieved.

Taylor also persuaded Frank Bunker Gilbreth (1908) to do the same to analysing the movements involved in bricklaying. By substituting shorter, faster movements for longer, slower ones the output of individual bricklayers was substantially increased. Gilbreth became notorious for being able to speed up almost any routine task. In an era of incentive and bonus schemes based upon productivity rates, his Therblig and Simo charts (which detailed every last movement) were hailed with enthusiasm.

It should be remembered that there were relatively few models of organization at this time which could act as comparators. The military, the railway companies and the Church were the most accessible for comparison. Fayol (1949) took Taylor's theories of individual working and efficiency and applied them to whole organizations. He wanted to standardize organizational efficiency. Based on a 'natural order' of centralization in which everything tends towards the brain in living organisms (and all directives come from it), Fayol listed his principles of organization:

- plan ahead
- keep records
- write down policies
- specialize labour and tasks
- ensure commensurate responsibility with authority
- keep managers' spans of control to approximately six people

Many of these principles remain pervasive in today's organizations in the guise of time and motion studies and general ergonomics. Classical theories were subjected to intense criticism on two fronts. First, they were argued to be open to abuse. They could be applied indiscriminately by unscrupulous managers (Gantt, 1919). Second, work organizations proliferated and became large and complex.

The adoption of scientific principles did not appear to work universally, and as general economic depression spread throughout the 1930s, many organizations became patently inefficient and poor performers. Taylor (and Taylorism) became the subject of a Congressional investigation and he was asked to account for himself and his theories. Before this, however, companies like Ford and many other manufacturing firms had adopted wholeheartedly the principles of scientific management and the impact of the whole classical movement can still be felt in modern organizations. Some of the key reasons which led to the demise of scientific management are listed in Table 2.1.

Table 2.1
Key factors in the demise of scientific management

Labour becomes a critical factor in the firm
As technology increased in complexity, labour became more specialized, taking longer to train in skills. The distinction made earlier by Taylor between manual and mental work became blurred. Labour cost more to recruit and train. Labour became more selective, the power of labour increased and unions and strikes began to appear as powerful antidotes to managerialism.

Increasing complexity of markets and products
The need for flexible and adaptive organizational structures became greater. The rigidity of the firm designed on Taylorist principles precluded subsequent change.

Political, social and cultural changes
Societal values were beginning to change. No longer were brutal supervision and unquestioned authority considered legitimate features of managerial behaviour.

Organizations became large and more complex
Firms could no longer be controlled under the direction of one person, such as the founding father. A search for good leaders and professional managers became pre-eminent. The focus of achieving good performance and maintaining control turned more towards human factors rather than towards principles of organizational design.

The human-relations school

This, as its name implies, was a theory of organizational behaviour which rested more upon human behaviour and less upon the mechanical efficiency of a productive unit. It was well timed. There was general labour unrest both in America and Britain and the shadow of economic depression was still large and long. Barnard (1938) marks the genesis of human-relations theories, although Elton Mayo (1949) and Roethlisberger and Dickson (1939) are equally famous for their experiments in the field and can also be considered founders of the movement.

The hallmark of human-relations theories is the primacy given to organizations as human cooperative systems rather than as mechanical contraptions. Barnard stressed:

1 *Natural groups* Humans tend to organize themselves into natural social groups which do not always coincide 'functionally specialized' workgroups. The social thus take precedence over the functional.
2 *Upward communication* Rather than flow 'naturally' from the top of the organization, information should be two-way, from workers to the chief executive. Relevant information comes from the workforce concerning both corporate and individual needs.
3 *Cohesive leadership* Is necessary for the development in executives of the long-run aims of the organization. Good leadership is necessary to communicate these goals to others in the organization. When achieved, this should ensure effective and coherent decision-making.

The following year (1939) saw the first large-scale investigations into productivity and social relations. These were the famous Hawthorne Studies which were conducted under the guidance of Elton Mayo. Initially set up to study the effects of illumination intensity on productivity, the studies revealed the importance of informal groups, work norms, the value of human leadership and the important role of psychology in counselling employees (Roethlisberger and Dickson, 1939).

The human-relations approach generated almost as many questions as it purported to solve. The most famous query has subsequently become known as the 'hawthorne' effect which is used commonly to describe the influence of experimentation itself as a factor in altering performance levels. The very fact that groups knew they were being studied led to an increase in output. Its assumptions were also subject to question. Did everyone desire freedom at work and the opportunity for self-development to the same extent? Is it possible to prescribe conditions under which groups will be happy? Does social happiness really lead to greater productivity, or are there hidden intervening variables? People also had a life outside the formal workplace. It was not their whole life. To many, a job could be viewed as strictly instrumental in securing money to spend on leisure time.

Debates still rage over these and other questions raised by the human-relations approach. It is not surprising, therefore, that subsequent schools of thought began to look outside the single unit of organization for explanations of both human behaviour and organizational performance. Open-systems theory, which views a single organization as enmeshed in a much wider environment which has an influence over its functioning and the people within it, is described in more detail in Chapter 18. Socio-technical theories also form part of this move away from particularism, human or organizational, and they are covered briefly in the next section. See the References at the end of this chapter for further reading that gives detailed coverage of these theories.

Socio-technical theories

The focus of these approaches to organization is the relationship between technology and the workgroup. These theories began to gather momentum following the rather wholesale and rapid adoption of the assembly line as an efficient and effective production method.

Socio-technical is a simple concept. It argues that there are two predominant elements to any organization which need management. These are the social and the technical. Bringing in new people or altering the pattern of work does not necessarily mean changing technology, nor does the introduction of new technology mean that social relations in the organization are fixed in one pattern.

Much has been written about the experiences of workers who are subjected to the rigours and restrictions of the assembly line (which was seen by management to be the answer to fast and high-volume production). Some of the best accounts can be read in Walker and Guest (1952) and Terkel (1974).

The results of working on an assembly line are well-known today, but they were not so well known in the 1950s and early 1960s. Workers would become numbed to the job. They would feel drained and lacking in any motivation to work at all. Work was purely instrumental. It paid the bills, or it was a job when the alternative was no job at all.

From a manager's viewpoint, the assembly line was a good idea. It made rational economic sense. Economies of scale were soon realized and mass production usually meant mass profits, so that pay levels could be at a higher rate in these plants than elsewhere.

From a worker's viewpoint, the assembly line meant no more seasonal variation in work (no worries about being laid off because of bad weather, etc.) and it also gave the security of working for a big company which was less likely to go broke. It also meant more stress and more illness, which were related to the pressures exerted by the assembly line.

The assembly line is just one way of organizing activities which are interrelated. The sub-tasks of the whole product are broken down into separate steps and related together so that when they are performed in sequence, the final step of the process produces the final product.

Mass production work is characterized by:

1 a mechanically controlled workpace
2 repetition
3 requiring minimum skill
4 giving no choice of tools or methods to the worker
5 requiring only surface mental attention

However, volume production of cars does not predetermine the adoption of the assembly line. The use of assembly lines was an overt management decision. At the time, managers gave little attention to considerations of whether the assembly lines were good or bad for employees. In fact, they assumed that the import of new technology made the production process fixed. It was humans who should change.

Fortunately, humans are extremely adaptable. For a time, it looked as if this was a good management decision. Employees adapted to the line and the car factories began to be profitable. Yet developments in the organization and management of coal mining in the UK were beginning to shed doubt on the efficacy of simple assembly-line production methods. These studies showed for the first time that managers had a choice in the way they organized the interrelated aspects of work. This kind of thinking was much broader than the human-relations school for it looked beyond the individual workplace towards a system of technology in which there was a social choice.

In studies of mechanization in coal mining in Britain (Trist and Bamforth, 1951) there were now ways of getting coal from the coal face using new technology. This could loosen more coal per hour than any individual or group of miners working by hand. Coal seams were opened up into what became known as Longwalls. A machine could travel along a huge expanse of coal face and hack out all the coal from up to a 100-metre straight run.

Management looked for a way to organize work around this new technology. Previously, miners did all the tasks of coal mining themselves. They:

1 cut the coal
2 loaded the coal on to wagons or conveyor
3 advanced the roof supports and roadways underground

With the new technology, it seemed obvious to borrow from the assembly line mass-production techniques for producing coal. This meant that the three stages above were now broken down into three separate jobs. Three shifts meant that it seemed natural to allocate one shift for each task. This soon created unforeseen problems for management:

1 Each shift began to develop different needs and wanted different rewards.
2 The cutters began to be the elite of the shifts with all the rest inferior to them.
3 The pay of each group was calculated on a different basis and each group negotiated separately with management.
4 Management's task was to coordinate the production cycle but this proved impossible. Sequencing activities might make sense in theory, but in practice it did not work in the coal mine.
5 The three-shift system led to all sorts of sabotage occurring between the shifts. In order to make the cutter's work doubly hard, for example, the shot-firers would often put only half-strength charges in the face. Or they might leave the odd undetonated charge for the cutters to find on their shift. It also led to social grievances being taken into the workplace. The shift system divided people in a way which facilitated getting your own back on someone.

In some mines, the work had to be organized differently since the physical conditions underground did not allow the longwall system to operate fully. Management resisted any changes to the sequential organization of work and tried to impose the longwall three-shift system. This failed. The miners grouped together and formed what we now know today as the Autonomous Working Group (AWG). Characteristics of the group were:

1 *One* group of workers performed all the tasks of the job.
2 Group composition was on a *self-selected* basis.
3 Production became continuous. Each group took over where the last one had finished. It did not matter where each group was on the production cycle.
4 Each individual did not have to possess all the skills required. It just mattered that the group as a whole had the full range of required skills within it.
5 Each group was paid on a common basis.

The function of management on these sites changed dramatically. The autonomous working groups began to operate in a self-regulating way. They effectively managed themselves. Instead of fragmenting the work task and organizing work specialization, the managerial task was now to integrate the activities of the various groups. It also gave managers the time to plan for the future and to look ahead. They were now free from managing the day-to-day activities of the plant and could concentrate on longer-term planning and strategies.

The socio-technical concept has since been developed and replicated all over the world in a whole range of firms. Scandinavian managers did not invent the autonomous working group, but they did invest in it in a big way in many of their manufacturing plants: Saab-Scania, Volvo, Electrolux, Atlas-Copco. Since then, a whole host of firms now uses autonomous working groups.

What is human-resource management?

As the rate of technological advance quickens, and the pace of change accelerates, organizations are increasingly becoming places where AWGs of experts in their field are gathered. The role of management is to integrate the various components of the firm and not to create fragmentation and specialization in the division of labour. Achieving coordination among sub-systems is likely to be the prime requirement of managers for many years to come. This skill rests upon the effective use of the human resource and has given rise to the recent term human-resource management.

Key themes of human-resource management (HRM) are responsible autonomy, involvement and commitment. This builds upon previous theories (such as human-relations) but differs markedly since HRM considers the total system of the organization. It asks the question: how can the organization be designed and its managers trained in order to utilize employees' skills fully and effectively?

This has led to a questioning of some of the basic principles upon which organizations have been historically designed. Countries such as Japan appear to treat their human organizational resources differently from most Western experience, for example. Japanese employees were given more trust, more autonomy, were treated as partners in the whole enterprise, enjoyed a lifetime's employment if they wanted and were subject to informal control mechanisms and consensual decision-making (Pascale and Athos, 1982).

Many of these aspects have been included in the agenda for re-energizing ailing and flagging organizations in the West. Ouchi and Jaeger (1978) argued that wholesale translation was improbable given the immense cultural and economic differences between Western countries and Japan, but agreed that a compromise could be reached which included many of the original features. This hybrid was termed by them the 'Type Z' organization. Features are:

- long-term (rather than lifetime) employment
- consensual decision-making
- individual responsibility
- informal control
- holistic concern for employees

(adapted from Ouchi and Jaeger, 1978: 311)

One of the end-products of HRM is aimed at securing competitive advantage for organizations which implement such strategies. In particular, the emphasis is upon instilling in each member of the organization a sense of strategic vision or holistic view of the direction of the whole organization (Johnston, 1986; Handy, 1987). Commitment is thus achieved through individuals' 'internalizing' the culture of their company, rather than through attempts to effect motivation from the 'outside' with the obvious disadvantages of artificiality these bring with them. Chapter 13 discusses the concepts of organizational culture in more detail.

The keynote themes of HRM practice have also been reflected in the research by Peters and Waterman (1982) and Kanter (1984). Excellent companies appeared to adopt particular configurations of HRM practice. These include:

- *Staying close to the customer*   Innovations arise from listening to the needs of customers. Key management skills here are communicating effectively and spanning the organizational boundary between it and its immediate operating environment.
- *Proactive and adaptive responses*   Change and innovation in the face of external developments must be fostered as a natural knee-jerk response by all individuals in the organization. Key skills are retaining core businesses and at the same time building in strategic flexibility and agility.
- *Clear focus for the business*   Reduces the level of complexity and ambiguity faced by managers. Sticking to what you know also pays off by allowing managers more time to think and to experiment.
- *Leadership vision*   Managers must be able to create a sense of purpose and instil commitment in their employees. Key skills require that the manager can also do the job of the employee, not as a substitute, but as a co-worker. Participation and communication are vital aspects.
- *A bias towards action*   Not talking problems so intensively that nothing ever is done. Doing something and taking action are essential. This requires a philosophy of accepting mistakes as inevitable, but as a significant learning process, not something to be penalized.
- *Simple form and lean staff*   Not to overdo formalization and rules. These should be just sufficient to cover activities and maintain control, but no more than this.
- *Simultaneous loose–tight properties*   Not quite the paradox it sounds. Basically, this means using tight controls in some areas and not in others. Tight control can be over market analysis and evaluation for example, while fairly loose control needs to be exercised over innovation and idea generation.
- *Productivity through people, consensus and trust*   This requires cross-functional thinking and collaboration not competition in decision-making, backed up by a highly efficient and over-utilized communication network.

It is likely that this represents only some of the key HRM strategies which successful companies will eventually incorporate as standard practice. Whether or not they all stand the test of time remains to be seen.

Not surprisingly, the HRM discipline has given rise to its ardent enthusiasts and its strong critics. Enthusiasts argue that adopting such principles as those outlined above are the only way to revive and revitalize organizations facing continual threats and increasing levels of competition. Critics argue that all HRM has done is to provide a set of normative recipes, untried in practice, with little theoretical foundation and with limited utility. Readings 1 and 2 (Lee and Anthony) at the end of Part I neatly summarize these debates, while Reading 3 (Burgoyne) explores the utility of these concepts for other areas of business education such as operational research.

Summary

We have explored the foundations of organizational behaviour in this chapter. The last twenty years have seen a massive increase both in theory generation and in research knowledge of many kinds of organizations.

The discipline presents a formidable challenge intellectually, for it requires a thorough understanding at many levels of analysis. We need to understand the motives and behaviour of individuals as well as the more global actions (and behaviours) of organizations themselves. Rhetoric and reality need careful distinction as the debates swing backward and forward across a whole array of academic disciplines (economics, psychology, sociology, philosophy to name only some) and cases of organizational practice. From its beginnings in scientific management to today's concerns with sustained competition and change, the subject can look forward to a challenging and stimulating future. The problems and opportunities facing modern organizations bear comparison to those with which Taylor, Mayo and Trist were grappling eighty, forty and twenty years ago respectively. They have given us a foundation of knowledge which we can develop and refine in future. The aim of this book is to highlight these developments and to alert the reader to the multitude of contemporary theories and debates.

References   Barnard, C. I. (1938) *The Function of the Executive*, Harvard University Press, Massachusetts.

Fayol, H. (1949) *General and Industrial Management*, transl. C. Storrs, Pitman, London.

Gantt, H. (1919) *Organizing For Work*, Harcourt, Brace & Hove, New York.

Gilbreth, F. B. (1908) *Field Systems*, Myron C. Clark, New York.

Handy, C. B. (1987) *The Making of Managers*, NEDO, London.

Johnston, J. S. (ed.) (1986) *Educating Managers*, Jossey-Bass, San Francisco.

Kanter, R. M. (1984) *The Change Masters: Corporate Entrepreneurs at Work*, Allen & Unwin, London.

Mayo, E. (1949) *Hawthorne and the Western Electric Company: The Social Problems of an Industrial Civilization*, Routledge, London.

Nisbet, R. A. (1973) *The Sociological Tradition*, Heinemann, London.

Ouchi, W. G. and A. M. Jaeger (1978) 'Type Z organizations: stability in the midst of mobility', *Academy of Management Review*, **3**, 305–14.

Pascale, R. T. and A. G. Athos (1982) *The Art of Japanese Management*, Penguin, Harmondsworth.

Peters, T. and R. Waterman (Jr) (1982) *In Search of Excellence: Lessons from America's Best Run Companies*, Harper & Row, New York.

Pugh, D. S. (ed.) (1974) *Organization Theory*, Penguin, Harmondsworth.

Roethlisberger, F. J. and W. J. Dickson (1939) *Management and the Worker*, Harvard University Press, Massachusetts.

Taylor, F. W. (1911) *Principles of Scientific Management*, Harper, New York.

Terkel, S. (1974) *Working*, Random House, New York.

Trist, E. and K. W. Bamforth (1951) 'Some social and psychological consequences of the longwall method of coal getting', *Human Relations*, **4**(1), 3–38.

Walker, C. and R. Guest (1952) *The Man on the Assembly Line*, Harvard University Press, Massachusetts.

Zey-Ferrell, M. and M. Aiken (1981) *Complex Organizations: Critical Perspectives*, Scott, Foresman & Co., Glenview, Illinois.

Organizations, management and you

Introduction

Since the fundamental building block of any organization rests in its people, the questions of selection, retention, training and development become crucial strategic issues for all managers (Manpower Services Commission/National Economic Development Office, 1987). This chapter deals with selection and training in particular, leaving questions of motivation and retention to be discussed in Chapters 5 and 6.

Human-resource planning

Massive changes in the political and economic content of all organizations have concentrated managers' minds on human-resource planning. The need to plan and invest in human resources as a means of creating and sustaining competitive performance is now recognized by virtually all organizations in Europe, USA and Britain. As yet, only a handful of British companies have any form of well-developed strategy towards human-resource planning. These include British Airways, Cadbury-Schweppes, Lucas Engineering and Systems, GKN, STC-ICL, Jaguar Cars, Sainsbury and Safeway. This is not an exhaustive list, yet current data indicate that most British companies do not have any formal planning strategy towards human resources (Torrington and Hall, 1987).

The topic of human-resource planning would require a separate textbook to do justice to its complexity. It has moved from the highly quantitative models of manpower planning to being much more qualitatively on the agenda of corporate strategy. Managing people is a key issue in the face of skill shortages, demographic changes, increased competition, decentralization and organizational change. We do not have space in this book to deal adequately with human-resource planning (see Hendry, Pettigrew and Sparrow, 1988 for detailed applications of planning) but we shall deal with the difficulties raised for managers within the context of such changes. Not least among these problems is recruitment (defining the need for personnel, advertising for staff and justifying their entry into the organization). For a detailed analysis of recruitment in Britain, see Watson (1989). We begin this chapter with selection.

Selection

As Watson (1989: 137) notes: 'selection techniques cannot overcome failures in recruitment, they merely make them evident'. Yet most managers will deal with the process of selection as a means of implementing the organization's human-resources plan (in whatever form this exists). Relatively few will be directly involved in recruitment other than corporate human-resource specialists. Most managers are involved in selection decisions.

Selection is a systematic attempt to make a very complex decision—filling the right jobs with the right people. There are a number of standard selection techniques which managers can use to help them reach a decision on the suitability of a candidate for a job. These include:

1 psychological testing

2 physical testing
3 interviews
4 assessment centres
5 familiarization courses

In order to use any of the above, the first step is to examine the characteristics of the post to be filled. This process is called job analysis.

Job analysis   This comprises a formal assessment of the skills, knowledge and experience needed to carry out a specific job effectively. For a job which already exists in the organization (i.e. is not a brand new post) this will comprise observation of a number of employees who are filling comparable roles. Detailed records can then be compiled about the nature of the job and the understanding of any technology involved.

This is usually achieved through observation and interviews, occasionally using specific techniques such as work-method study and measurement. The result of all this is a *job description*, which is the basis for the subsequent selection decision. Managers can now specify the characteristics and skill levels required by applicants for the job. For management posts, this usually specifies the number of employees supervised, the scope of authority and position in the hierarchy. For non-managerial posts this specifies the sequence of operations, the average time taken to carry out a task and the methods adopted to perform the task. Job descriptions will also spell out variables such as age, level of education, formal qualifications, level of previous training, experience, physical characteristics, dexterity, literacy and numeracy. Figure 3.1 shows a typical chart used to construct a job description.

Figure 3.1
A typical job
description chart
(supervisory role)

JOB		
Title	Production responsibility	
Location	....	
Number of subordinates	Budget responsibility	
POSITION/AUTHORITY		
Responsible to	Needs the permission of a senior to	
Responsible for	....	
RESPONSIBILITIES		
75% of time	....	
10% of time	....	
15% of time	....	
Working environment		
Sitting, standing, driving, combination Noise, heat, cold, dirt, risk, hours, holidays, etc.		

Psychological testing

These tests aim to be able to construct a profile of any candidate on such factors as personality, attitudes, values, intelligence and perception. The idea of them all is to assume that the results obtained on the day of the tests will accurately predict how the candidate will subsequently perform in the organization. According to Cronbach (1970: 26) a psychological test is one which enables a systematic procedure to be followed in assessing and observing a person's behaviour by using numerical scales or a category system. There are a battery of such tests. Most used are those accredited by the British Psychological Society.

Commonly used tests in Britain include the Thurstone Temperament Schedule, the Edwards Personal Preference Schedule, Cattell's 16PF (personality factor) test, and Rotter's (1966) Internal–External Locus of Control questionnaire. The first two tests measure personality traits on a number of dimensions (such as vigorous, dominant, aggressive, achieving, deferential). The latter two present statements and questions in a forced choice format. The individual has to choose one or other statement in all cases. In the event of ambiguity, the candidate is instructed to choose the statement with which he or she most agrees. The 16PF test comprises 187 questions; the Locus of Control test comprises 29 statements. Both rely on the trait theory of personality which examines the predilections of individuals to act or think in particular ways. These can be inherited or acquired (Chapter 4 outlines these theories in more detail and provides a criticism of them). Figures 3.2 and 3.3 show typical profiles for the 16PF and Locus of Control tests.

Figure 3.2
Personality profiles of female clerks and general managers (mixed sex) using Cattell's 16PF test

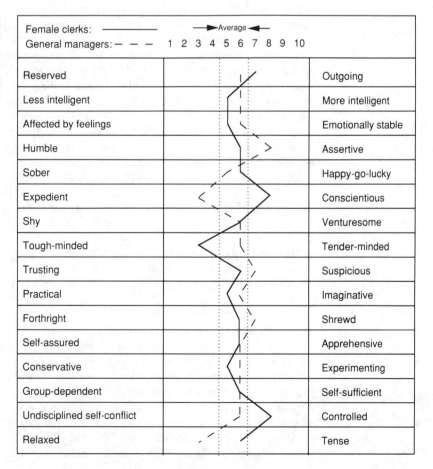

Figure 3.3
Locus of Control
profile using Rotter's
test (2nd year UK
Business Studies
undergraduates)

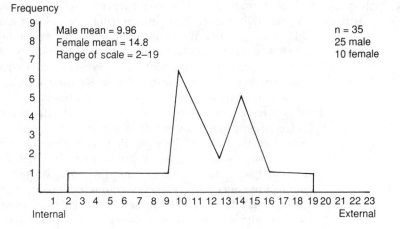

Frequency

Male mean = 9.96
Female mean = 14.8
Range of scale = 2–19

n = 35
25 male
10 female

Internal   External

A study conducted (by the authors) of forty female clerks and general managers (from a financial services organization) revealed the results shown in Figure 3.2. The female clerks tended to be conscientious, tough-minded, controlled and outgoing (persevering, moralistic, with a strong self-image, coupled with a no-nonsense attitude; they are generally self-reliant but are easy-going and warm to others). The general managers tended to be more assertive, expedient and relaxed than the clerks (more aggressive, stubborn, feel few obligations but are relatively easy about it all). Of course, this is just one sample. One could not assume that all clerks and general managers would display similar profiles.

Figure 3.3 shows some results from a small group of undergraduate students of management sciences from the University of Warwick (1988). Internals consider that they are in charge of their own destiny: whatever happens to them is a direct consequence of their own actions. Externals feel the reverse. Ill luck, chance and external circumstances will confound whatever they do. So outcomes are not attributable solely to individual actions. Most students clustered around the mean of 11.5, males being generally more internal than the females. Again, this result reflects just the characteristics of that sample and does not necessarily indicate a profile for all British undergraduates.

In all cases, tests should be both *reliable* and *valid*.

> **Reliability** of a test is the consistency with which it produces the same score throughout a series of measurements.
> **Validity** is the degree to which a test measures what it is intended to measure.

Although both the above tests have robust reliability and validity scores, doubts have still been raised concerning their consistency (see Ghiselli, 1966; Peck and Whitlow, 1975). Changes in the context in which the test is used can undermine validity despite attempts to standardize conditions and instructions. Many companies settle for what is called 'face-validity' (the extent to which the measure seems right). Finally, a study by Makin and Robertson (1986) revealed that out of 108 organizations drawn from the 'Times Top 1000' less than a third used *any* form of psychological tests. They relied instead on interviewing as a means of selection. Drenth (1978) indicates that in Europe even less emphasis is placed upon quantitative selection tests. They are, however, quite extensively used in North America (Beach, 1980).

Physical and competency tests

Most organizations will ask that the potential employee submits to a general health test to see if there are any major problems with cardio-vascular processes, eyesight and so forth. Tests which examine specific skills are relatively rare. Airline pilots, policemen and women, steeplejacks and some jobs in the armed forces are ones which specify and require certain physical characteristics (minimum height, fast reactions, above average stamina and physical fitness).

Other physical competencies include static strength, the maximum force that can be exerted against external objects (e.g. lifting weights), and stamina, the capacity to sustain maximum effort requiring cardio-vascular exertion (e.g. a hundred-yard dash). Once again, the relevance of these competencies varies from job to job. It is up to the manager to establish where and how a given competency becomes important.

Watson (1989: 145) points to the problems of reliability in physical tests. He cites cases of pilots who, having passed the Civil Aeronautics Administration fitness examination, displayed a 43 per cent disqualifying rate on re-examination! Neither do physical tests appear to predict future performance (at least not those tests which are medically oriented). Again, Watson reports the case of RAF pilots who showed no correlation between their accident rates over a ten-year period and whether or not they met the physical standards required.

Each of us is acquainted with various *competency* tests used to measure mental aptitudes and abilities. Some of these provide an overall IQ score, while others provide measures of more specific competencies required of people entering various educational programmes or career fields. All such tests seek to measure mental aptitude or ability and thereby facilitate the screening and selection of applicants. Of course, there is some controversy over the validity of such tests and of the significance accorded to test score trends over time. Table 3.1 gives an idea of the different kinds of competencies used in two well-known tests.

Table 3.1
Sample competency characteristics used in job selection and recruitment

NIIP Seven Point Test*	John Munro Fraser Fivefold Classification
1 Physical appearance and general physique	1 First impressions and physical make up
2 Attainments/general education	2 Qualifications
3 General intelligence	3 Abilities
4 Special aptitudes	4 Motivation
5 Interests (intellectual, practical, social)	5 Adjustment
6 Disposition	
7 Circumstances (age, marital status, mobility, dependants, domicile)	

*NIIP: the National Institute of Industrial Psychology.

Interviewing

This (combined with the use of written and verbal references) is the most frequently used selection test of British companies. As a technique it is cheap and easy to conduct, but full of potential problems. In this chapter we shall outline some of the more psychological problems associated with the interview. More structured approaches, such as assessing intelligence and aptitudes during the interview, are discussed in Chapter 4 (see particularly Table 4.1).

The interview is the time when the interviewer (usually a manager) meets the prospective candidate face to face. The manager can choose the setting to provide a variety of desired contexts. These can range from the threatening (sparsely furnished room with uncomfortable chairs and over-bright or bare lighting) through 'businesslike' to very informal and relaxed, where the candidate can be himself or herself. The crucial point is that the interview is a process where the manager makes a personal judgement about whether the prospective candidate is suitable and will 'fit-in'. This personal judgement relies heavily upon perceptual interpretation. This is how the interviewer perceives the interviewee.

Perception

Perception describes the process whereby people become aware of the outside world and themselves. The 'commonsense' view that perception simply registers what is 'out there' is wrong. A fundamental assumption of the psychology of perception is that an individual distorts his or her perceptions of the outside world to make it congruent with his or her set of beliefs.

While commonsense may argue that reality is mirrored in the mind, new ideas of perception have produced the insight that knowledge about the world enters the mind not as raw data, but already in highly abstracted forms—structures. This structure is known in psychology as a *gestalt*, which is the German word for configuration or shape. In the pre-conscious process of converting raw data into structures, information is inevitably lost. The creation of structures—the establishment of *gestalts*—is nothing less than the selective destruction of information to facilitate the recognition of patterns which have meaning for the perceiver.

This view of perception was pioneered by Jerome Bruner of Harvard University, who argues that perception involves an act of categorization. When we perceive something, we try to fit it into a classification system or frame of reference, and a trading process goes on between the perceived qualities of the thing and the hole in the classification system where we think it should fit (Asch, 1946).

Accurate perceptions?

There are, therefore, many barriers to the accuracy with which we perceive and understand the behaviour of others. Our interpretation can be quite wrong. This can be for any of the following reasons.

The halo effect

This occurs where the perceiver already has an overall impression of an individual. This may be favourable or unfavourable (i.e. good or bad). More specific traits or isolated events are then placed into this overall context of generalized perception. Thus, someone who is perceived by you as diligent and hardworking is unlikely to be perceived as lazy and cavalier if he or she 'plays truant' from work for a few days. Another person taking the same action (but who was someone whom you generally perceived unfavourably) would very likely be categorized as lazy. It would be 'typical' behaviour. Evaluation is thus influenced by an overall impression (the halo).

Logical error

Perception may also be confounded by the tendency to 'fill in the missing data' about a person. We learn to associate traits together (Asch, 1946). When we perceive some traits in a person, we naturally assume that he or she must also have other traits we associate with them. This is known as *logical error*. It is based on the notion that we tend to associate certain traits together.

Kelley (1950) demonstrated that if students were told a lecturer was 'cold' or 'warm' prior to his lecture, their perception of him or her was significantly different. Those who had been told the lecturer was cold also associated ruthlessness, lack of humour and selfishness with that description. Previously described as warm, associated traits were caring, interested in students and unselfish. Students would interact more readily with the 'warm' person. In situations of judgement, such as in a court of law, this effect can distort the verdicts of juries and judges. In the workplace, it can lead to prejudicial appraisal reviews and can result in scapegoating. When things go wrong, blame is attributed to the individuals who are overall perceived least favourably.

Projection and distortion

This is where an individual ascribes his or her own feelings to another person. It tends to be context-specific. For example, on a day when you are feeling particularly jaded or depressed, the tendency will be to perceive this in others too. Distortion of perception can also occur due to our perceptual set. The perceptual set configures the way we see all kinds of objects and make the individual more ready to perceive one thing rather than another. Figure 3.4 illustrates this by means of pictorial 'illusions'.

In the first set of three drawings (drawing A was originally based on a picture by the cartoonist W. E. Hill) individuals perceive either an old lady, a young woman looking over her shoulder or both. In a classic experiment, Leeper

Figure 3.4
Perceptual 'illusions'

Previous exposure to either
B or C will distort the subsequent
perception of A.

A simple illusion : Skeleton's head, or time for tea?

(1935) presented pictures B and C to two separate groups prior to showing them picture A. Pictures B and C remove the ambiguity of A. It is clearly either an old or a young woman. Leeper found that prior exposure to picture B or C predicted what respondents subsequently 'saw' in picture A. Between 95 and 100 per cent consistency was achieved in this experiment. Further aspects of personality and perception are described in Chapter 4.

The selection interview: advantages and disadvantages

The majority of jobs in British organizations are filled following at least one face-to-face interview. Advantages include:

1 It is relatively quick. It combines presenting the job to the candidate and the information-gathering process about the candidate's skills in social interaction, verbal fluency and technical knowledge.
2 Interviews are both 'expected' by candidates and are easy to arrange in most organizations.
3 It is not easy to specify an equally good alternative way of selecting candidates since most employers want to 'see' their prospective employees and to talk to them.

(See Robbins, 1989; and Arvey and Campion, 1982)

Disadvantages include:

1 All interviews are subject to perceptual biases. These may be inaccurate.
2 Interviewers often find it difficult to differentiate between relevant and irrelevant information in the interview process.
3 Multiple interviewers are likely to pick up on different aspects during the interview and so reach different conclusions about the candidate.
4 Early impressions (often gained in the first few minutes) are likely to colour subsequent judgements.

(See Wicks, 1984)

Assessment centres

These are used for the selection of management personnel, often from individuals already employed by the organization. They utilize simulation tests. These are designed to evaluate an individual's managerial potential. Behavioural simulations as well as written tests are used. Typically, two to four days will be spent going through psychological tests and exercises such as 'in-basket' and 'leaderless group discussions'.

An in-basket exercise is designed to simulate a large pile of correspondence with which a manager is likely to be faced after a few days' absence. The exercise assesses the candidate's ability to set priorities, to delegate and to use judgement in handling the information. Leaderless groups assess the candidate's ability to be part of and to lead a group in making a decision. Candidates are usually judged on how effectively they communicate orally, how persuasive they are, how sensitive they are to others' feelings and on their ability to lead a group.

Evidence suggests that assessment centres are extremely good predictors of future performance in managerial positions (see Gaugher et al., 1987: 510–11). They are more expensive than interviews, but perhaps their demonstrably better performance over interviews makes them cost-effective in the long run. Selecting the wrong managers can be very costly indeed.

Familiarization courses

The logical end of the selection process is the appointment of the most suitable candidate. Many organizations also use a formal orientation programme to introduce new members to the organization in which they are to work. Such courses typically provide individuals with a basic understanding of the organization, its culture and philosophies, its structure and its reward, appraisal and benefit schemes.

Training

Although selection is designed to recruit the most competent individual, he or she is unlikely to remain competent for the whole of their career. As changes take place in technology, knowledge and innovations, so too will the demands placed upon specific jobs. This is where training comes in. First, we need to differentiate between training and development which are often wrongly used as synonyms.

Training is a systematic process whereby an individual learns skills, abilities and knowledge to further both organizational and personal goals.

Development relies more upon the individual's initiative to ask questions and to bring out important points for consideration. More precisely, it should be called self-development since the impetus for development is very much grounded in self and not others.

On-site training

The belief here is that employees can best learn the specifics of a job through training in the actual work environment. This can be very effective in training specific techniques such as in apprenticeships. Skilled crafts such as plumbing, welding and building construction are learned from seasoned and skilled individuals in the organization. Often, the apprentice will have previously learned the basics of the trade at a college of further education. Training increases skill levels and tailors techniques to particular requirements (e.g. oil pipe welding, gas rig construction).

Off-site training

This includes any form of training which takes place away from the individual's workplace. One reason for off-site training can be to develop interpersonal or problem-solving skills (rather than technical expertise); another can be that training on site could be both expensive (by slowing production) and potentially dangerous (Robbins, 1989).

In some cases, organizations have training areas equipped with replica machines and tools away from the main production process. This is known as 'vestibule' training. It can also take the form of 'simulation' whereby individuals such as airline pilots can gain knowledge of particular situations without actually flying a real aircraft. Where individuals also have to learn a great deal of new information, then classroom training can also be used as an additional back-up. This includes films, lectures, computer-based training software and so on.

These latter techniques are relatively rare in Britain. Both Taylor (1980) and Keep (1989) point to the enormous preference for apprenticeships in most British companies. In the face of new initiatives to reform apprenticeships from the Manpower Services Commission following the recessions of the early 1980s, the number of new apprentices in manufacturing has decreased markedly (240 000 in 1964 compared with 7000 apprentices and 2000 new technicians in 1986). As Keep (1989: 181) says:

> Even allowing for the substantial reduction in employment in manufacturing and the changing demands of technology . . . the decline . . . is little short of astonishing.

However, it seems that other forms of training have not taken the place of apprenticeships in Britain (such as vocational education and training) and despite some arguments in the data, Britain compares very badly with European countries such as West Germany in adult training overall.

Management development

Alongside training, management development is a relatively new venture. For a concise history of management development from the 1940s see Sadler (1989). Not all of management development is strictly in line with the earlier definition of development. Much of it could be said to be training. There is on-site training (using more senior mentors) and off-site training using business schools, hotels management and conference centres. Alternatively, in-house management training programmes are conducted by professional trainers brought in specifically for the task.

Training managers, however, does require a great deal of development to take place if it is to be effective. The organization and all its resources can only help in achieving full potential for those in managerial positions. Two key reports (Constable and McCormick, 1987; Handy, 1987), emphasize this point. Although some organizations in Britain did offer training and the opportunity for development to their managers, the majority did not. Most managers lacked even basic formal educational training and, on average, received extra training approximately only one day per year. Opportunities for development were very limited indeed. According to Handy (1987) Britain lagged significantly behind competitor European countries and he suggested a 'development charter' for management development which includes a minimum of five days off-site training per year for every manager.

Whether or not management skills can be categorized and assessed in this way is open to question, particularly in the light of Mintzberg's (1973) account of what managers actually do. They interact frequently, deal with many issues per day, spend relatively short amounts of time on each issue and prefer verbal to written communication. It would seem that managerial activity might be too complex, changeable and ambiguous for the measurement of specific categories of achievement.

Lateral career movement

One commonly attempted development technique is job rotation. This involves moving managers from one department to another to familiarize them with the workings and the demands of each function. Development can occur on at least two fronts. First, managers gain an appreciation of the whole organization rather than just develop a perspective solely from their own function. Second, the 'generalist' experience thus gained can be of immense benefit in developing managers for senior positions in the organization.

Job rotation has had more success in non-managerial positions than with managers in Britain (see Buchanan, 1989). It can help relieve the boredom of monotonous jobs and can keep attention levels relatively higher on individual tasks. With British managers, job rotation has not met with the same broad levels of success. Recent studies indicate that managers often view working 'in another function' or alongside others in cross-functional teams with great suspicion. They tend to become protective about information and about their 'own' function (see Tunnicliff, 1988; Davies, 1988). This supports the political perspective of organizations which is outlined in Chapter 11. Chapter 7 gives greater detail on the topic of job redesign and rotation.

Age and career

Career is the usually linear sequence of steps taken by an individual through a number of organizational positions. Career correlates strongly with age (see Hall, 1976, for example) so the potential for development is likely to become less as the manager gets older, as follows.

Early career   During this stage, individuals are just completing their transition from education to occupation. Their personal lives are also subject to change—moving home, getting married, having children, etc. Career plans for this stage include mobility and the stretching of one's abilities.

Mid-life transition   Around late thirties and early forties career becomes an overwhelming concern. Often there is a conflict between demands of family and career for both men and women. Frustration and cynicism towards the 'system' (i.e. the organization) are often the result. Potential for development decreases.

Late career   Around the fifties and onward, the individual will more or less have become resolved to the demands and the operation of the 'system'. Ideals and objectives will have mellowed and cynicism may have increased to a point where development is virtually impossible.

The moral of the career stage analysis seems to be 'start developing managers as early as possible'. There is research evidence to support this view, also indicating that managers who receive particularly challenging jobs in their early career go on to be more successful, stay with the organization longer and carry on the process of self-development (Berlew and Hall, 1966; Van Maanen and Schein, 1977).

Summary

The importance of the individual as a resource for the organization has been the keynote of this chapter. We have concentrated upon how organizations can attract and select the kind of individuals they would like (or need). Examining this deceptively simple process reveals that a large number of psychological processes are likely to confound selection. Largely this is because humans tend to distort the information coming to them from the outside world and from other people. Perception in all its guises comes into play.

Once in an organization, the focus of attention becomes the progression of individuals both in terms of training and development. There are some predictable results from research in this area. For example, managers become increasingly harder to train and develop as they get older. There are some unpredictable results too. Britain does not fare very well in comparison to European competitors in the extent to which it invests in the training and development of its managers. Only a handful of organizations take this seriously and have formal, systematic programmes for their managers. This is despite government and private initiatives to increase the level and scope of training since 1980.

So far, we have not discussed the pool of labour from which even the imperfect selection processes and training methods we have described have to draw recruits. This is particularly poignant given demographic predictions for the 1990s. These indicate a drop in 20 per cent of young people available by 1995, particularly in the range 16–19 years old. The overall size of the available labour force is increasing, however, around 80 per cent of this net increase comprising women returning to work after having had a family. The 'balance' of the labour market will alter and will bring with it the need for recruitment and selection processes to be sensitive to these changes alongside changes in training and employment practices. These demands of the future are discussed in more detail in Part VII.

References

Arvey, R. D. and J. E. Campion (1982) 'The employment interview: a summary and review of recent research', *Personnel Psychology*, Summer, **35**, 281–322.

Asch, S. E. (1946) 'Forming impressions of personality', *Journal of Abnormal and Social Psychology*, **41**, 258–90.

Beach, D. S. (1980) *Personnel: the Management of People at Work*, 4th edn, Collier, Macmillan, New York.

Berlew, D. E. and D. T. Hall (1966) 'The socialization of managers: effects of expectation and performance', *Administrative Science Quarterly*, September (10), 207–23.

Buchanan, D. A. (1989) 'Principles and Practice in Work Design', in K. Sisson (ed.), *Personnel Management in Britain*, Blackwell, Oxford.

Constable, R. and R. J. McCormick (1987) *The Making of British Managers*, A Report for the BIM and CBI into Management Training, Education and Development, BIM, London.

Cronbach, L. J. (1970) *Essentials of Psychological Testing*, 3rd edn, Harper & Row, New York.

Davies, J. (1988) 'Organizational development and the management of change', MBA Dissertation, University of Warwick.

Drenth, P. (1978) 'Principles of selection', in P. B. Warr (ed.), *Psychology at Work*, 2nd edn, Penguin, Harmondsworth.

Gaugher, B. B., D. B. Rosenthal, G. C. Thornton and C. Bentson (1987) 'Meta-analysis of assessment center validity', *Journal of Applied Psychology*, **2**, 493–511.

Ghiselli, E. E. (1966) *The Validity of Occupational Aptitude Tests*, Wiley, New York.

Hall, D. T. (1976) *Careers in Organizations*, Goodyear, Santa Monica.

Handy, C. B. (1987) *The Making of Managers*, NEDO, London.

Hendry, C., A. M. Pettigrew and P. Sparrow (1988) 'Changing patterns of human resource management', *Personnel Management*, November, 37–41.

Keep, E. (1989) 'A training scandal?' in K. Sisson (ed.), *Personnel Management in Britain*, Blackwell, Oxford.

Kelley, H. H. (1950) 'The warm–cold variable in the first impressions of person', *Journal of Personality*, **18**, 431–9.

Leeper, R. (1935) 'The role of motivation in learning: a study of the phenomenon of differential motivation control of the utilization of habits', *Journal of Genetic Psychology*, **46**, 3–40.

Makin, P. and I. T. Robertson (1986) 'Selecting the best selection techniques', *Personnel Management*, November, 38–43.

Manpower Services Commission/NEDO (1987) *People: the Key to Success*, NEDO, London.

Mintzberg, H. (1973) *The Nature of Managerial Work*, Harper & Row, New York.

Peck, D. and D. Whitlow (1975) *Approaches to Personality Theory*, Methuen, London.

Robbins, S. P. (1989) *Organizational Behavior: Concepts, Controversies and Applications*, Prentice-Hall, Englewood Cliffs, New Jersey.

Rotter, J. B. (1966) 'Generalized expectancies for internal versus external control of reinforcement', *Psychological Monographs*, **1**(609), 80.

Sadler, P. (1989) 'Management development', in K. Sisson (ed.), *Personnel Management in Britain*, Blackwell, Oxford.

Taylor, R. (1980) 'The training scandal', *Management Today*, July, 46–51.

Torrington, D. and L. Hall (1987) *Personal Management: A New Approach*, Prentice-Hall, London.

Tunnicliff, A. (1988) 'A study into cross-functional awareness at British Sugar plc', MBA Dissertation, University of Warwick.

Van Maanen, J. and E. H. Schein (1977) 'Career development', in J. R. Hackman and J. L. Suttle (eds), *Improving Life at Work*, Goodyear, Santa Monica.

Watson, T. (1989) 'Recruitment and selection', in K. Sisson (ed.), *Personnel Management in Britain*, Blackwell, Oxford.

Wicks, R. P. (1984) 'Interviewing: practical aspects', in C. L. Cooper and P. J. Makin (eds), *Psychology for Managers*, BPS and Macmillan, Basingstoke, Hants.

There is nothing so useful as an 'appropriate theory'

R. A. Lee

An 'appropriate theory' is one which is used by an educator, even though it is known to have inadequacies in terms of the scientific supporting evidence underlying it and even though it is known to offer a simplified view of reality, because it is perceived as a useful way of encouraging insights which will help when coping with practical situations. This reading addresses issues relating to the use of 'appropriate theory' in management education. The reader is invited to consider the theories which are being taught on their current management programme and their 'appropriateness'.

Theories and theorists in management education

Anyone who teaches management, and anyone of even moderate intellect and experience who is subjected to such teaching, soon becomes aware that the theories used are often of limited scientific validity in terms of the explanations or predictions which they offer. At best they are partial; applied in the wrong way, without understanding of the necessary complementary ideas, caveats and provisos, they may even be misleading. Nevertheless they are essential for the proper education of managers. It is the widespread use of such theories which is responsible for many of the attacks from our peers directed at those of us who teach and study management. Our discipline is not seen as academically respectable by our colleagues who are concerned with more traditional areas.

It is almost possible to classify management lecturers into three groups, those who try to satisfy traditional academic criteria, those who are happy to develop and use any ideas provided they help to achieve their teaching objectives and, of course, a sizeable group who try, with varying degrees of success, to find an acceptable middle ground. In this paper it will be argued that any such schism within the broad church of management education is resolvable if appropriate theory is accorded its rightful place, worthy of equal respect, alongside efforts of a more strictly scientific nature. Lewin's dictum that 'there is nothing so practical as a good theory' is capable of more than one interpretation.

At a fundamental level it can be argued that all social-science theories have limitations. None is a total explanation of 'reality'. All are based on particular assumptions about such matters as nature of knowledge, the nature of people and the nature of reality itself. Nevertheless there are many researchers who are trying to develop what we may call 'scientific theory' which comes as close as possible to explaining reality within its own inherent assumptions. It can be argued that it is necessary when one is developing theory primarily for use by particular actors, rather than for traditional scholarly purposes, to accept that there will always be a gap between what any theory can offer and what the practitioner needs to know. This may render a different type of theory as appropriate for many educational purposes.

The gap between what theory can do to explain the practitioner's reality and what she or he needs to know may be called the 'experiential learning gap', it is represented in Figure R1.1.

Figure R1.1
The experiential
learning gap

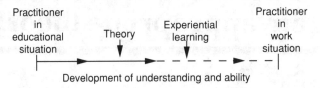

Development of understanding and ability

The 'experiential learning gap' is only partly explained by the simplifying assumptions inevitably underlying all theories. There are several other factors involved:

1 Theories are often designed within particular perspectives which do not conform to those of the practitioner. Any perspective, be it Marxist, Buddhist, Green, pluralist or whatever, may be of limited use to the practitioner if its fundamental tenets are rejected.
2 Theories are often not addressed at issues with which the practitioner is concerned. All theories will throw light on some aspects of reality but inevitably leave others in shadow.
3 The practitioner is concerned with unique situations which involve many variables that no general theory can accommodate; most significant among these will often be the practitioner and other actors who are engaged in a complex and dynamic social interaction.

To illustrate these points let us take the well-known subject of motivation. The would-be practitioner, away from the workplace, may be taught some simple ideas such as the hierarchy of needs developed by Maslow (1954) and the two factor theory of Herzberg (1966). None of us is naive enough to believe that on returning to work the practitioner would now have anything more than a very slightly improved understanding of the motivation of subordinates and perhaps an even more limited improvement in ability to effect change. The 'experiential gap' which the individual has to jump is very large. Referring to the factor above we can see that the theories taught may be less effective if the manager does not accept the motivation of subordinates as the major issue but rather influencing peers and senior colleagues. In any event the specific behaviours required of the practitioner will have to be tailored to a unique situation with a unique history and context and involving particular actors.

Experiential training of various types can be used to overcome some, perhaps all, of these problems. This is part of the strong case for experiential training. But what must not be forgotten is that the argument so far also has implications for the nature of theory itself, particularly where this is developed primarily to be used in conjunction with experiential work.

A supporter of the exclusive pursuit of 'scientific theory', on viewing Figure R1.1 may argue that what is required to bridge at least some of the gap is 'better' theory which can come closer to explaining the practitioner's 'reality'. There is merit in this point. To return to our earlier example, most management educators nowadays go way beyond Maslow and Herzberg and introduce ideas from, for example, the various cognitive process theories. Provided such theories can be introduced *in appropriate form* they offer valuable insights which will assist the experiential learning process. But they will never be sufficient in themselves to bridge the experiential learning gap and if they are not taught in appropriate form they may actually prevent the gap ever being crossed.

For example, if we apply 'scientific theory' related to snooker which is concerned primarily with applied mechanics, would it be useful to a practitioner to learn the detail of these theories? Probably not. Some simple 'appropriate' ideas about the use of cues and game tactics are sufficient.

It is argued that where theories are too complex or are designed for *ex post facto* explanation rather than for use by practitioners they may lead to confusion and the phenomenon which may be called *the paralysis of analysis*. There is always a danger, if the complexity of life is overemphasized, and if the need to understand fully is placed ahead of the need to act effectively, that managers can be turned into interested spectators rather than proactive participants.

Making scientific theories appropriate

Many of the theories currently used by management educators are appropriate versions of more complex theories which their originators intended to be scientific. The hierarchy of needs is an excellent example: Maslow himself would probably be disconcerted to see how his work is grossly simplified in order to provide some language and basic ideas in the middle of a conventional management programme. The same may be true of the human-relations theory of Roethlisberger and Dickson (1964), the leadership theory of Fielder (1967), the structural theory of Lawrence and Lorsch (1967), and the expectancy theory of Lawler (1973), to name but the tip of the iceberg.

In most cases the appropriate versions take the core ideas of their parent theory and present them in some simple way without too much jargon. There is clearly danger here. Important caveats may be dropped and attempts to increase impact and teachability may lose or distort the meaning of the underlying theory. Sometimes this is to be deplored; more often, when the educator is a skilled professional, the underlying ideas have been converted to something which is in effect a new, more appropriate, theory.

New appropriate theories

Much management theory is never intended to be scientific. Its *raison d'être* from the outset is that it is a reasonable reflection of reality as perceived by the practitioner and it can be used to assist in the development of personal conceptual frameworks which will be of value in the pursuit of practical goals. Support for appropriate theory can and often does include the existence of related scientific theory and the range of research sources which would be required for scientific validity but such support, whilst desirable, is not essential. The best kind of support for appropriate theory is its widespread acceptance by practitioners because of its high utility to them, but until that is achieved it is possible to argue for ideas on the basis of experience or other anecdotal evidence. What the theorist must beware of, in situations where there is no other support available, is any inclination to overlook counter-evidence or alternative approaches.

Clearly, theory which is supported in this way will always be disputable and subject to frequent development. It is fairly easy to be critical of what exists and to expound something new to replace it. Furthermore, each educator can have a personal variation around a few widely used core ideas. None of this is problematic if we remember that the aim of appropriate theory is not to be 'right' but to be useful. The context of management is changing so rapidly that new ideas are always required to help provide insights relevant to new issues. Each educator has a unique style and different conceptual variations will have different learning effects depending on how the learning situation is designed and also the particular participants involved.

A recent example of appropriate theory which unashamedly purports to be nothing else is that presented by Peters and Waterman (1982). Their 7-S

Framework (to understand and manage an organization effectively you have to understand and manage effectively: Staff, Style, Skills, Systems, Strategy, Structure and Shared values) is embodied in a simple figure in which each of the basic concepts is, with a bit of stretching, cutting and fitting made to begin with the letter 'S'. Their ideas are reduced to a handful of catchy guidelines in the form of appealing generalizations and the theory they represent is supported by a hotchpotch analysis of crudely researched and anecdotal data, sprinkled with a large amount of name-dropping and a small amount of discussion of relevant scientific research. And it is good stuff! Easily understood, exciting, and likely to stimulate the reader to some kind of rethink from which new insights about their own reality will emerge.

Peters and Waterman make no apology for their style, 'Anthony Athos at the Harvard Business School gave us the courage to do it that way, urging that without the memory hooks provided by alliteration, our stuff was just too hard to explain, too easily forgettable' (p. 9).

A recent critic of appropriate theory

At this point it seems necessary to acknowledge the arguments against the use of appropriate theory which have recently been put forward by Anthony (1986). Most of these arguments are summarized in Reading 2 of this book. He discusses issues related to teaching which he sees as having 'intellectual and academic respectability' as opposed to that which is aimed at enhancing 'vocational and practical skill'. He states that the latter involves 'some degree of slippage from the demands and standards of academic rigour' but does not accept that what is put in the place of these conventional academic virtues on programmes for experienced managers should be held in equal regard. This leads him to be highly critical of current MBA programmes in a manner which, if the thesis of this reading is accepted, is quite unjustified—'The conclusion is hard to avoid that postgraduate courses in management are designed for beginners rather than masters' (1986:119). He later states

> The rigorousness of academic work is valued because its results are more likely to be reliable. The alternative choice of what is called 'practical' is at best made by men who are too busy to insist upon reliability or, at worst, by those who are too stupid to understand the methods by which it is attained (p. 135).

Anthony discusses *In Search of Excellence* (Peters and Waterman, 1982) directly. 'The authors market ideas rather than examine them,' he states, 'memory hooks are necessary to the marketing of ideas to a managerial readership with serious intellectual deficiencies.' He concludes, 'The search for excellence continues a well-established tradition of management writing: it will not make its readers think' (p. 163).

Anthony's objectives are entirely laudable. He sets out to emphasize the need for managers to be encouraged to question their own values and to rethink the legitimacy of their position of influence over much of the nation's resources. He attacks the managerialist ideology which many management theories unquestioningly accept. This process, however, need not rely on perpetuating an undesirable academic snobbery; indeed it will probably be enhanced if Anthony produces an 'appropriate' form of his own ideas!

Conclusion

Those who use appropriate theories must be aware of the dangers beyond those discussed above. In the first place, there is the seduction of simplicity. It is one thing knowingly to make assumptions and to neglect certain complexities where their introduction would not serve the desired educational purpose but it is quite another to cling to an obviously unsatisfactory theory just because of its attractive simplicity. This is related to the danger of adopting theories because they are teachable rather than because they are effective. It is too easy to cobble together a programme based on a 'successful' combination of appealing ideas without considering the true nature of the 'experience gap' for the particular participants and tailoring theories to specific teaching objectives.

The existence of these dangers is not in any way an argument against the use of appropriate theories. This short reading is an attempt to show their vital importance to management education. There is just one more serious concern to express. It concerns the relationships between members of the management academic community and the lack of widespread acceptance of the need for both types of theory. This has several undesirable effects which can be highlighted by imagining management as a discipline without each in turn.

If the management academic community were to neglect the pursuit of full explanations of complexity then true academic progress would be impossible. Colleagues have been heard to bemoan the tedious treatment of narrow questions in certain journals and subsequently to dismiss totally the value of such endeavour. Rigorous research will always be essential; it will, among other things, serve to test and develop fundamental ideas from which appropriate theories can be developed.

Without appropriate theory there would be very little communication of the insights of scientific theory to practising managers. It will never be possible for busy practitioners to draw their own insights from the meticulous complexity of most research papers and it would not be possible to design management programmes around them.

The importance of appropriate theory should not, however, be seen entirely in terms of management development. Scientific theory itself can be improved by drawing on the many rich ideas within appropriate theory. Those who are at the sharp end of management education and management consultancy are likely to identify new issues of importance early and, by the nature of their work, they will often be exposing current ideas to the true test of application. It is easy to see the value of scientific theory for appropriate theory but the fact that this relationship can work in reverse must also be emphasized. It is desirable for exponents of both scientific and appropriate persuasions to keep abreast of developments in each other's wisdom.

References   Anthony, P. D. (1986) *The Foundation of Management*, Tavistock, London.

Fielder, F. F. (1967) *A Theory of Leadership Effectiveness*, McGraw-Hill, New York.

Herzberg, F. (1966) *Work and the Nature of Man*, World Publishing, Cleveland.

Lawler, E. E. (1973) *Motivation in Work Organisations*, Brooke/Cole, Monterey.

Lawrence, P. R. and J. W. Lorsch (1967) *Organisation and Environment*, Harvard Graduate School of Business Administration, Cambridge, Mass.

Maslow, A. (1954) *Motivation and Personality*, Harper, New York.

Peters, T. J. and R. H. Waterman (1982) *In Search of Excellence: Lessons from America's Best Run Companies*, Harper & Row, New York.

Roethlisberger, F. J. and W. J. Dickson (1964) *Management and the Worker*, Wiley, New York.

In defence of the appropriate

P. D. Anthony*

Any argument against appropriate theory is disadvantaged by its title, an illustration of the technique of influential naming in which opponents must espouse 'inappropriate' theory and begin by defending the apparently indefensible. A further difficulty is that 'appropriate' is used in two ways. Appropriate theory is theory which, despite scientific inadequacy, is useful for the development of insights in practitioners who are not themselves scientists (Lee, 1987), and it is theory which, although accurate, is complex so that it has to be introduced to practitioners in appropriate form. The first meaning might be termed the theory of useful error, the second of necessary simplification. Lee's argument confuses the two; inappropriate theory (damned by its appellation) becomes appropriate (and blessed) when its presentation changes so that those to whom it is presented come to understand it—but it may still be wrong and there is an alarming suggestion that it needs to be wrong to be understood. We are by now discussing both the theory, the students of it and their teachers. Stupid students, or inappropriate students, may not understand it if it is presented by good teachers who do understand it. Some may think they understand it when it is presented wrongly but with simplicity. Lee says this may not matter, may even be an advantage. We must hope that these students do not become practitioners although their error will be of more consequence in some areas of practice than others. Practitioners, for the most part, need to get it right, at least we must hope so if they are going to practise medicine upon us.

What do management practitioners need to get right? Well, if they are taking examinations in management they need to get the answers right. Generally speaking their teachers see to it that they have a fair chance of getting them right by asking them appropriate questions about appropriate material that they have been taught. The material does not change very much. Every year examination papers in personnel management regurgitate the proper conduct of selection procedures while acknowledging that they are not very appropriate to prediction of success. Every year students of Organizational Behaviour (OB) repeat the 'simple ideas' (Lee, 1987:249) of Maslow (1954) and Herzberg (1966). Every year students in organizational behaviour, organizational development, industrial relations (or all three) repeat that open participative systems are best and that industrial democracy works while decrying the lack of enthusiasm for such ideas of practitioners in management who are still stuck in bad old theory X. What happens to the students who give the appropriate answers about appropriate theory when they become practitioners of management?

What, indeed, do managers need to know? Who says what they need to know? Lee tells us that theories used in post-experience management

*Reprinted by permission: *Management Education and Development*, **18**(4), pp. 255–9.

education—even though they may be of limited validity, may be applied in the wrong way, and in fact may be downright misleading—are nevertheless:

> essential for the proper education of managers [but] it is the widespread use of such theories which is responsible for many of the attacks directed at those of us who teach management in the academic world. Our discipline is not seen as academically respectable by our colleagues who work in more traditional areas (Lee, Reading I:27).

My own case is not that these activities are not academically respectable; it is that they are not respectable at all, and that the disrespect for them that has accrued contributes to the low status of management, the weakness of its authority and the disinclination of good and intelligent young men and women to take it up—not because of a 'contempt for the useful' but because, on the whole, they would rather practise medicine.

The ultimate test of management theory is 'that it is a reasonable reflection of reality as perceived by the practitioner' and that it can 'assist in the development of personal conceptual frameworks which will be of value in the support of practical goals' (Lee, Reading I:29). We need not raise awkward and boring old questions of a traditional kind like: whose practical goals are the ultimate determinants of the usefulness of conceptual frameworks: the goals of the individual manager in getting on, of the shareholders, the directors, or satisfying, or surviving, of getting by or getting through? He, our practitioner hero, will know about practical goals (unless he is a foreman, God help him) and he will tell us what he needs to know. Well, not quite, according to Lee, because we, his teachers, know more than he does. Not about practical goals we don't, of course, but we know more about organization and social relationships and a great deal more about control techniques and an awful lot about motivational theory and conceptual frameworks. We have to go easy with all this because we must not confuse our practitioners by over-emphasizing the complexity of life lest they become interested spectators (Lee, Reading I:29). What we need is a useful dialogue between us clever chaps and the sturdy practitioners who know about their practical goals but could do with help in hitting them. The useful dialogue demands that we bridge the experiential learning gap.

This particular educational phenomenon is, according to Lee, explained by differences in the perspectives of the theorist and the practitioner, by lack of relevance of theory to particular issues which concern the practitioner and by his (*sic*) involvement in unique situations which 'no general theory can accommodate' particularly when he is engaged in a 'complex and dynamic social interaction'. These are revealing explanations. The argument about lack of relevance has confronted every management teacher and is often expressed in the form, 'It's all right in theory but it doesn't work in practice.' For the most part that old saw is nonsense; if it does not work in practice there is something wrong with the theory and its failure in practice is a classic case for theoretical verification and revision. Quite often, however, if the theory of metal fatigue is well founded it is the practice of box-girder bridge design that is at fault. There is an intimate and necessary relationship between good theory and good practice, except when you come to instances of theoretical perspectives which are rejected and of complex and dynamic social interactions. Here, I suggest, we are not dealing with theory at all.

In the first instance, where the practitioner rejects Marxist theory because he rejects the tenets of Marxism, the practitioner may be right (just as he would be to reject Thatcherism or managerialism). What confronts the practitioner in much (but not all) of Marxism is gross over-simplification, ideological loading and purposive prediction. The practising manager would be right to be gravely suspicious of a great deal of motivational or participative theory as a manipulative device at the length of a production line. In the second instance (the first and the second are often confused in practice) of complex social interactions, there is precious little theory of any level of generalization or predictive value. There is nothing to teach.

It depends, of course, on what kind of managers you are teaching and upon what they are being taught. If a manager needs to understand, in order to practice, the techniques of statistical analysis, you must ensure that he masters chi square theory. He or she may be required to understand the theory of cash-flow discounting, of multivariant analysis, of critical path analysis, of linear programming. If the theory is sufficiently simplified—made appropriate to his or her own experience to the extent that it is deliberately misinterpreted—our practising manager may end up bankrupt or in prison. If he is a colliery manager who was taught an 'appropriate' version of the theory of roof support or of gas suppression, he may well kill himself and his subordinates. The less he is dependent upon specific techniques and procedures, the more of a general manager he is, the more likely he is to need to exercise judgement, social and political skills. And it is in this, the most responsible and influential area of management, that there is precious little theory to help him to cope with confusion and complexity. What is available to him is a ready battery of consultants' advice, of educational programmes compounded of recipes and simplifications, distillations of general explanations of human behaviour, catalogues of the best ways to 'handle' people, select them, promote them, motivate and control them. None of it may relate to the constantly shifting situation and the arcane complexities that confront him but the advice is to hand, it is simple, it provides comfort and, above all, it is appropriate to his understanding. The 'theory' from which it was distantly derived was not, could not have been, appropriate, but the images in which it is presented must be acceptable and be deemed to be appropriate. The practitioner must and can be convinced that there is an appropriate mode of behaviour (Theory Y, 9.9: problem-solving, participative, supportive) that he can acquire which is not conceptually difficult; he just has to try.

What the management educator is trying to do in these areas is to change the behaviour of the practitioner-manager and that needs time—less, perhaps, if the practitioner is an idiot, more if he is a manager of intelligence and experience. But the time is not needed because complex theory has to be adapted, made appropriate, to the manager; it is needed to wear him down, to dull his critical senses, to condition him. It is not that the management 'educator' is wrestling with the explication of grand and complex theory to a practitioner who needs to understand it but rather that the educator is trying to convince him, to manipulate and mould him, much as Marx and Mrs Thatcher have tried and are trying to make us see the world as they do. They must all simplify, address us in terms and in language appropriate to our experience, ensure that they do not shock us into hostility. They are, all of them, engaged in the rhetoric of persuasion.

In a previous publication (Anthony, 1986), I suggested that this aspect of management education was mistaken in its conception and abortive in its consequence. What managers need is to apply critical and analytical intelligence to their environment; the ordinary expectation of education is to encourage and nurture these faculties; the function of management education is to suppress them.

Finally, Lee flatters me not only by the attention he gives to my views but by suggesting that I have advanced a theory that deserves an appropriate expression. That is kind of him but I must disclaim such ambitions. There *is* little or no theory and I have made no contribution to it. I have only submitted a polemic and an argument; my claim is that that is sufficient.

References   Anthony, P. D. (1986) *The Foundation of Management*, Tavistock, London.

Herzberg, F. (1966) *Work and the Nature of Man*, World Publishing, Cleveland.

Lee, R. (1987) 'The use of "appropriate theory" in management education', *Management Education and Development*, **18**, Pt 4, 247–54.

Maslow, A. (1954) *Motivation and Personality*, Harper, New York.

A behavioural science perspective on operational research practice

J. G. Burgoyne

Introduction

Organizational behaviour (OB) shares the business school curriculum with disciplines such as marketing, finance, accounting, corporate strategy, and operational research. It is often the belief by academics in these other disciplines that OB is the weak contender in this mixture. The uncertainty of the behavioural area does not appear to offer as much conviction, control, tools and techniques that some of these 'harder' disciplines appear to.

There is, therefore, the challenge of understanding not only how each of these competing disciplines relate to organization and management, but also the question of how they relate to each other.

The aim of this reading is to explore these connections in the case of the behavioural sciences and operational research (OR). The main argument is that the relationship may be thought about at three fundamentally different levels.

At the first level behavioural science can be conceived as a 'tool' discipline to OR, to help find ways of persuading clients to value, accept and implement OR solutions.

At the second level, behavioural science and OR can be thought of as intellectual and professional disciplines with overlapping interests. Each discipline may offer alternative accounts of the same phenomena. There may be genuine 'frontiers' between the two disciplines, of which artificial intelligence, managerial decision-making and expert systems may be examples. To the extent that both claim to be multidisciplinary, it is possible to consider the extent to which each incorporates some of the insights of the other, or draw on common academic and professional sources.

At the third level OR can be considered as a phenomenon that behavioural science can look at, interpret, and raise critical questions about. Thus questions can be asked about the social significance of the instigation, evolution and growth of OR, and the eras, cultures and organizational settings where this has and has not happened. Questions can be asked about the values and ideologies that are built into and supported by OR. Questions can be asked about the implicit and explicit assumptions concerning the nature of both people and organized activity which underline OR theory and practice. And, to the extent to which reality is, at least in part, 'socially constructed' (Berger and Luckman, 1967), then the question of the kind of personal and organizational realities created by OR practice can be asked. In addition, the behavioural scientist can pose questions about the kinds of people who become OR practitioners, the nature of their careers, how OR is organized within itself and within work organizations, and how its practitioners acquire and use power.

Each of these perspectives is valuable and useful. However, it is the author's observation that operational researchers tend to prefer the first of these levels, and behavioural scientists the last. This is an extension of the phenomenon where dialogue between the disciplines is based on claims such as 'my discipline includes/interprets your discipline'. Resisting this trap is a major challenge to interdisciplinary cooperation. This suggests that the middle level may be the most fruitful starting point from which to reach out to the other two.

The main aim of this reading is therefore to map some of the issues, ideas and dilemmas at each of these three levels, as an aid to thoughtful dialogue between behavioural scientists and operational researchers.

Assumptions about the nature of operational research (OR)

A reader approaching the OR literature to see what it is all about can get a reasonably consistent picture of what it consists of. Broadly speaking, it is concerned with bringing 'scientific' analysis to problems which exist in the 'real' world (Churchman, Ackoff and Arnoff, 1957).

The notion of what is 'scientific' is based on an image of empirical natural science, emphasizing objectively observable, preferably quantifiable, phenomena (Checkland, 1983).

An historical account of OR reveals two interesting points. First, there was an early emphasis on interdisciplinary work. Scientists were seen as providing method, while professionals and managers knew and had influence over the problem. More recently, the multidisciplinary feature has faded out of accounts of OR, in favour of a view of OR as a discipline in its own right, with applied mathematics, modelling and optimization as its substantive and methodological core.

The second point of interest is the early claim to find observable stable patterns of events even when these are 'rather unexpected in view of the large number of change events and individual personalities and abilities that are involved in even small operations' (Blackett, 1962). This statement, of observable mathematical regularities in aggregated events involving people, seems to constitute the standard OR justification for not needing to grapple with the confusing variety of behavioural-science thought.

Assumptions about the nature of behavioural science

Behavioural science presents no such unified central concepts, methods or history. The label itself is problematic both in terms of 'behavioural' and 'science'. The safest statement to make may be the most common sensical: that behavioural science is the study of people.

The traditional categories of approach remain the psychological and the sociological. Other established disciplines like anthropology also contribute. The development of the field has included 'intermediate' disciplines like social psychology, 'new' disciplines like linguistics and 'hybrids' like organizational behaviour—which has become the standard label in management and business school curricula. The field also encompasses areas of professional practice like organizational development (OD). The result is a complicated and messy picture.

One assumption or belief shared by much of behavioural/social science is that there is more to people and what they do than can be explained by their material make up and organic biological processes. It is because of this that the issue of what it means to be 'scientific' is more complicated and contentious in the behavioural sciences than it appears to be in OR. An extension of this, is a mutual non-acceptance of what the other regards as scientific.

The empirical model adopted by OR represents only one approach used in the behavioural sciences. Strong arguments have been mounted against this approach that this degenerates behavioural science back to the biological and material. Critics argue that an appropriate methodology must allow for the reality of the non-material, such as subjective experience, social process, patterns of meaning and symbolism (Reason and Rowan, 1981; Morgan, 1983; Harre and Secord, 1972). In some areas of the behavioural sciences, this argument has been well won; in others it has scarcely been heard.

If a general statement about what 'scientific' behavioural science means can be risked, it is perhaps that the method must be appropriate to the kinds of phenomena over and above the physical and physiological. This may involve a much broader conception of what is acceptable empirical evidence, and it may entail non-empirically based analysis (Burrell and Morgan, 1979).

Behavioural science as a tool for OR

The basic hypothesis of this reading is that OR is confident enough of its own general aim and approach to prefer to see behavioural science as a peripheral tool rather than a core interdisciplinary contributor.

There appear to be two areas of contribution for behavioural science within classical OR investigation: (1) contribution of concepts, models and measures within the investigation; and (2) dealing with the client system before, during and after the investigation.

Within an OR investigation, behavioural variables may be included while staying with the concept of a quantifiable model of causally related variables. For example, within a manpower-planning model, for example, it may be necessary to use such variables as 'morale' and 'job satisfaction' as determinants of labour turnover, 'skill' as a determinant of performance, 'learning curve' as a predictor of growth of performance over time. In such an investigation behavioural science might be looked at to: (1) suggest the variables; (2) provide hypotheses; and (3) offer empirical methodologies for measuring them.

A survey of the use of 'behavioural' variables in OR models is well beyond the scope of this reading, but two casual hypotheses might guide such an investigation: first, that OR will avoid behavioural variables wherever possible, and second, where they are used they will be borrowed most readily from areas of the behavioural sciences that have stayed closest to the 'natural science' model of doing research.

Shildon (1982) provides an example of the former: in a model to predict demand for train services he uses a variable Q for 'quality of service', which he defines operationally as a function of speed and frequency of service, rather than as a behavioural variable rooted in the experience of the railway passenger.

An example of the latter hypothesis is provided by Polding and Lockett (1982) in their attempt to study the implementation of OR projects. This study attempted to access the experiences of practitioners and clients through a questionnaire survey. However, the analytical methods of principle components and regression analysis were called in to give a reassuring, if possibly spurious, sense of order to this data. Such 'data-raking' techniques are used in those branches of the behavioural sciences that need to convert their data into quantitative expression of quasi-causal relationships. It is significant that such an approach was used in preference to in-depth qualitative case studies of a smaller number of OR studies from instigation to implementation.

Although, the conventional core of OR seems clear-cut, there is an apparent sense of 'crisis' (Checkland, 1983; Ackoff, 1979). This appears to be a crisis of mismatch between theory and practice, rather than within the theory itself. There seem to be two responses. First, is that OR needs to shift its theoretical base in a systems-oriented direction. The second reason is that the crisis derives from a mismatch between the rational logic of OR and the less rational processes involved in the acceptance and implementation of OR solutions. It is the applied behavioural science of the consultant which holds the key to overcoming the crisis. This is an area in which OR practitioners may be most ready to look for help from behavioural science tools.

Such help is on offer from some branches of the behavioural sciences, particularly those concerned in the broadest sense with organizational development (Lippitt and Lippitt, 1978; Schein, 1978). The general theme of such advice is that clients need to be regarded as people rather than rational decision-making machines simply needing a correct technical solution. Some of the behavioural issues which arise include:

1   Understand the problem the client sees, and how they see it, and talk to them in their language.
2   Recognize the nature and limits to the power and authority of the client.
3   Be sensitive to the pressures on the client, and their needs to maintain their own self-esteem.
4   Recognize that clients may be more able to take on new ideas at some times rather than others, and can sometimes do this only slowly.
5   Recognize that clients can either be 'complacent' about the problem or in a quiet state of panic about it—the former need the reality bringing home to them, the latter need encouraging to see that there are solutions and ways out.
6   In attempting to get a problem recognized and a solution accepted, consider the questions: *who knows* about the problem, *who cares* whether it is solved or not, and *who can* do anything about it? If an overlap between these categories exists or can be brought about, then this may define a fruitful client to work with.
7   Try to put forward solutions and recommendations that are not only *technically sound* but also *politically acceptable* and *administratively feasible*.
8   For a client to take action he or she needs *to recognize a problem*, have a *vision of its solution*, see a *path to this solution*, and know in detail the *first step* in this journey (this 'list' can provide a framework for a presentation).
9   Clients are likely to grow to trust consultants only slowly, as they prove trustworthy, reliable, helpful and sensitive—initially over small matters.
10 A consultant can usefully give a client a balance of *support* through listening and sympathy about a problem and *confrontation* with evidence of new aspects of the problem, analyses or interpretations of it and ideas for ways to solve it.

Such 'practical guidelines' offered by the behavioural sciences may well be criticized by others as untested folklore, manipulative, or undermining the true role of behavioural science. However, since any consultant is likely to be a 'behavioural-scientist-in-practice', the ten points above may at least provide a starting point for greater awareness of the processes involved.

The underlying principle is about understanding the psycho- and sociologics of the client. Where this problem has been addressed from within the OR tradition, it has been on the basis of the concept of 'mutual understanding'. Polding and Lockett (1982) marshal a certain amount of evidence to support the view that when 'mutual understanding' is interpreted to mean getting clients to think and understand solutions in OR terms, then this is counter-productive in terms of implementation. They conclude that 'there is possibly a need for mutual understanding more in a sociological than an intellectual sense'.

Behavioural science and OR as adjacent disciplines

Given the pluralistic nature of the behavioural sciences, the easiest areas for substantive dialogue appear to occur where there are similar methodological assumptions.

The 'natural science' OR model would see prediction and control as major aims, aligning it closely with technical objectives of manipulating material entities to the aims of humankind. Much of behavioural science can be seen as concerned with explanation rather than prediction and control. Explanation can serve as illumination and emancipation rather than control.

Areas of common interest between behavioural science and OR appear to be limited to:

1 behavioural science concepts that can translate into variables of the kind acceptable to OR models;
2 methodological issues, at the level of research design and statistical, particularly multivariate, analysis;
3 the substantive area of decision-making.

Concepts and variables like 'morale', 'job-satisfaction', 'skill' and 'learning curve' were given as examples of areas of 'behavioural science tools' earlier. Such concepts, their meaning and interpretation, can potentially be an area of interdisciplinary discussion. Other branches of the behavioural sciences, like managerial effectiveness, and leadership style (Campbell *et al.*, 1970) seek to develop models in the OR style which identify and measure independent variables, like 'participativeness', and relate them to measures of 'productivity' and 'performance'.

Methodological common interests may be more obvious, but occur in those parts of the behavioural science scene which overlap the home territory of OR theory and practice. Overlaps occur at the levels of research design, and of analytical technique. Issues like experimental design (Campbell and Stanley, 1964) may represent common ground. Equally, at the level of analytical technique, some behavioural scientists, particularly psychometricians, would find much common ground with operational researchers on issues of regression analysis, factor analysis and so on.

OR is defined by its methodology rather than the phenomena it investigates. It is presented as a practical, problem-solving activity. For phenomena of mutual interest such as decision-making the perspective adopted by the OR researcher differs from the behavioural scientist. OR interest in decision-making is rooted in the normative and rational, whereas the behavioural science interest is likely to be more descriptive and psychological. The situation may be similar to the common but different interests of the computer scientists and psychologist in artificial intelligence. Both parties are interested in an operational clarification of the concept of intelligence, and both look to the other for hypotheses about process and mechanisms underlying it.

Studies like those by Newall and Simon (1972) and Clarkson (1962) approach decision-making from the descriptive, behavioural side, but seek to develop models in the systematic form characteristic of the OR researcher. With the emergence of 'expert systems' there appears to be a genuine area of common interest, and a practical incentive to explore it, between the computer scientist, operational researcher and psychologist.

It is possible that areas such as this will allow a renaissance of multidisciplinary OR.

At a theoretical level, a number of strands of thinking in the behavioural sciences are converging on the issue of 'human agency' — that people can create new meanings, make free choices and initiate actions rather than act out parts in a deterministic story (Giddens, 1976). This suggests that the traditional OR view of regularities in aggregate events could usefully be reconsidered.

In summary, therefore, it seems that:

1 The multidisciplinary base of OR never had a high behavioural science content.
2 What there was has eroded away as OR has become a discipline in its own right.
3 Areas of common interest are:
   (a) methodological, (b) in decision-making.
4 The emergence of 'expert systems' may provide the practical incentive and pressure to address behavioural issues directly.
5 The evolution of thought in the behavioural sciences suggests that this could be a good time to look at the question of individual 'free' choice and regularities in aggregate behaviour.

Behaviour science views of OR as a phenomenon

Behavioural science views of OR can be organized under two headings: (1) views of OR as an institution and social phenomenon; and (2) views of operational researchers as people, and the way they are organized as a profession.

Considering OR in a historical context, it can be asked why OR sprang up and grew when it did, where it did, and what its significance is in social history? The two or three decades following the Second World War can now be discerned to have been an era of 'scientific rationality', corresponding to a decline in religious and spiritual values, an increase in materialistic values, and increasing influence of formal organization on everyday life—all supported by the belief that science would produce solutions to all human problems. The 'crisis' in OR (Checkland, 1983) can be interpreted as the beginning of the end of that particular era, and the beginning of the current one (of which the pattern is not yet clear), which seems to contain a recognition that matters are decided by political process, reference to ideology and dogma, and various forms of fundamentalism, either religious or secular (Peters and Waterman, 1984). The interesting question is: how is OR reacting to this new era?

The OR approach fits best with a systems views of organizations, as opposed to an 'interactionist' humanist perspective (Burrell and Morgan, 1979; Silverman, 1970). Thus organizations are seen as 'designed mechanisms' with unitary objectives and structures independent of people, rather than evolving social structures emerging from human interaction, satisfying multiple needs and objectives for multiple stakeholders. Most OR studies involve the notion of a collective objective which can be optimized for maximum payoff by the right arrangement of the sub-systems.

It can be argued that systems view of the nature of organizations are self-fulfilling—organizations behave in this manner if enough of the people in them see them this way. OR practice can be seen to support this process, and add to the centralization of power inasmuch as OR projects are sponsored by, and serve the ends of, those most powerful in defining objectives, functions and structures.

At more micro levels, OR can be seen to favour objective material criteria rather than possibly meaningful subjective ones, and thus has an effect on organizational life. For example, OR studies of hospitals are more likely to address themselves to bed-occupancy rate, cure-rate and waiting-list time, than to attempt to assess human suffering and well-being.

From a behavioural science point of view, OR, considered across the spectrum from macro to micro issues concerning its practice, represents a value position, has its own ideology, reinforces certain material, structural and power realities in organizations, and thus has a moral and ethical content.

Behavioural science can offer interpretations of phenomena to do with operational researchers, and the ways they are organized. The personalities, careers, professionalization and education of operational researchers, the way in which the profession is organized, and the way in which OR consultancies and departments are organized are examples of some of the issues that could be addressed.

The extent to which OR as an occupation attracts and selects people with certain personalities, the extent to which OR provides lifelong careers, and the 'career anchors' (Schein, 1978) of OR practitioners could be investigated. The extent to which OR is a profession and exhibits the phenomena of professionalization: claims to protect the public, maintenance of ethical standards, regulation of entry to the profession, exploitation of monopoly power, operation of a labour market, and the fixing of fees, could also be explored.

The organization of OR consultancies, and the extent to which they are organized as commercial companies or on the model of professional partnerships, is of interest, as is the issue of how OR departments are organized and located within work organizations.

The education and training of operational researchers suggests itself as a topic of some interest. The question of a gap between theoretical and practical OR is pertinent here, as are questions of the role of education in licensing (formally or informally) practitioners. Finally, the education of operational researchers could be considered from the point of view of its role in creating and maintaining the value systems and ideologies implicit and explicit in OR practice.

Summary and conclusions

The aim of this reading has been to map some of the ways in which behavioural science and operational research can be thought about in relationship to each other, rather than to draw any strong specific conclusions.

It has been argued that behavioural science can be thought of across a broad spectrum from 'technical servant' through 'intellectual partner' to 'radical critic', in relation to OR theory and practice.

The survey has suggested that the existing linkages at all three levels are weak, and such linkages as were promised by the early interdisciplinary nature of OR have eroded as OR has developed as a discipline in its own right.

It is suggested that the middle level, of 'intellectual partner', is the best ground for fruitful debate. Within this, the most promising areas for discussion include: methodology, human free will and agency and the study of human decision-making in relation to expert systems. Exploration of these issues is likely to establish the ground from which to reach out to the other two levels.

References

Ackoff, R. L. (1979) 'The future of operational research is past', *Journal Operational Research Society*, **30**, 93–104.

Berger, T. L. and T. Luckman (1967) *The Social Construction of Reality*, Penguin, Harmondsworth.

Blackett, P. M. S. (1962) *Studies of War: Nuclear and Conventional*, Oliver & Boyd, Edinburgh.

Burrell, G. and G. Morgan (1979) *Sociological Paradigms and Organizational Analysis*, Heinemann, London.

Campbell, D. T. and J. C. Stanley (1964) 'Experimental and quasi-experimental design for research in training', in *Handbook of Educational Research*, Rand McNally, Chicago.

Campbell, J. P., M. D. Dunnette, E. E. Lawler and K. E. Weik (1970) *Managerial Behavior Performance and Effectiveness*, McGraw-Hill, New York.

Checkland, P. (1983) 'OR and the systems movement: mapping the conflicts', *Journal of the Operational Research Society*, **34**(8), 661–76.

Churchman, C. W., R. L. Ackoff and E. L. Arnoff (1957) *Introduction to Operational Research*, Wiley, New York.

Clarkson, G. (1962) *Portfolio Selection: A Simulation of Trust Investment*, Prentice-Hall, Englewood Cliffs, New Jersey.

Giddens, A. (1976) *New Rules of Sociological Method*, Hutchinson, London.

Harre, R. and P. F. Secord (1972) *The Explanation of Social Behaviour*, Blackwell, Oxford.

Lippett, G. and R. Lippett (1978) *The Consulting Process in Action*, University Associates, San Diego, California.

Morgan, G. (1983) *Beyond Method: Strategies for Social Research*, Sage, Beverly Hills, California.

Newall, A. and H. A. Simon (1972) *Human Problem Solving*, Prentice-Hall, Englewood Cliffs, New Jersey.

Peters, T. S. and R. H. Waterman (1984) *In Search of Excellence: Lessons from America's Best Run Companies*, Harper & Row, New York.

Polding, E. and G. Lockett (1982) 'Attitudes and perceptions relating to implementation and success in operational research', *Journal of Operational Research*, **33**, 733–44.

Reason, P. and J. Rowan (1981) *Human Enquiry: A Sourcebook of New Paradigm Research*, Wiley, London.

Schein, E. H. (1978) *Career Dynamics*, Addison-Wesley, Reading, Mass.

Shildon, D. C. (1982) 'Modelling the demand for high speed train services', *Journal of Operational Research*, **4**, 713–22.

Silverman, D. (1970) *The Theory of Organisations*, Heinemann, London.

Part II
The Individual

CHAPTER 4 Attributes of individuals

Introduction

In this chapter two key themes which predominate in organizational behaviour will be examined. First, are people different? Do they have separate, unique characteristics which make them the kind of person they are? Second, is the really important thing how we perceive others? It is not really so crucial if individuals differ if we perceive them in different ways ourselves. Since we act upon our perceptions, then the study of perception rather than personality should be our focus.

This perception–personality debate is one of the many which permeate psychology. There is insufficient space in this chapter to reveal the complexities of these debates, but the interested reader should follow up the literature cited in the references at the end of this chapter (see particularly McKenna, 1987). Many aspects of perception (e.g. first impressions, the halo effect and logical error) were dealt with in Chapter 3. Here, we look at values, attitudes, needs, expectations and personality.

Values, Attitudes, Needs and Expectations

Dealing with aspects of the individual in organizational behaviour leads naturally into an examination of values, attitudes, needs and expectations. Put simply, these fundamental building blocks of human behaviour explain why individuals are motivated to strive for certain things and why they try to satisfy themselves in certain ways.

Values

According to Rokeach (1972) values are concerned with conduct and desired end states:

> To say that a person 'has a value' is to say that he has an enduring belief that a specific mode of conduct or end-state of existence is personally and socially preferable . . . once a value is internalized, it becomes, consciously or unconsciously, a standard or criterion for guiding action . . . for morally judging self and others.
>
> (Rokeach, 1972: 160)

The value system of classical, traditional organization theory represents an individualistic, rational approach to life which sets the highest values on achievement, aggression, and affluence. Historically derived from Calvinism, this Protestant ethic system presumes that an individual is predestined either to heaven or hell and that the ticket is made out according to how well he or she manages the stewardship of worldly goods that come his or her way. Values provide the yardstick by which that stewardship might be judged.

This pervasive value system seeped into every aspect of life, defining attitudes towards everything, particularly anything that smacked of enjoyment (payday was on Friday, which was favoured as a drinking night for the working classes because it provided the least chance of upsetting the work week). Even the name Protestant ethic is misleading, for the value system pervaded every religious and ethnic culture to some extent.

Attitudes   Attitude may be defined as the predisposition or tendency of a person to evaluate some symbol, person, place, or thing in a favourable or unfavourable manner. The person's opinion constitutes the verbal expression of an attitude. In essence, an attitude is a state of mind which people carry around in their heads, through which they focus on particular objects in the environment, such as foreigners, Communists, pornography, the unions, men or women, students or academics.

Attitudes are made up of three elements:

1 cognitive
2 affective
3 conative

The dimensions of an attitude are presumed to follow a sequence such as (1) cognition ('I see the Communists as a threat to the free world'), (2) emotion ('I feel strongly about the Red threat'), and (3) behaviour ('I would rather be dead than Red'). This sequence, or train of cognition, emotion, and behaviour, may be followed in some circumstances, but not in all, as the three elements interlock and interact (see Lovejoy, 1950; Hilliard, 1950). For example, by changing people's behaviour patterns, it is also possible to change their attitude (see Chapter 5).

Needs   The most uncomplicated behaviour is found in infants. When they are hungry, thirsty, or uncomfortable, they cry; when they are happy, they smile or giggle; and when they are sleepy, they sleep. Through observing and studying infants, psychologists have learned a great deal about the forces governing behaviour. Not many adults cry when hungry or thirsty. Whether or not they cry when in pain depends upon what was learned as children. Many people still smile and laugh when they are happy, and some people go to sleep when they are sleepy. Although people can complicate the ways of meeting these basic human needs, the needs must still be met—survival depends on it.

In order to survive, one must have enough air, water, food, protection from physical dangers, and so forth. The infant obviously is dependent upon others to have survival needs met—the best it can do is give some signals of hunger, thirst, or discomfort. Survival needs can be met in fairly universal ways. Even as they grow and mature, people develop fairly similar methods of meeting these needs. Tastes and preferences develop, but the basic ingredients for survival are more or less universal.

Humans are also social beings and therefore require interaction with others. For infants, this need is initially met by the immediate family. The important ingredient is a kind of support base which provides a sense of belonging and the beginnings of feelings of personal worth. Although the individual might survive the absence of such a support base, it is not likely to be a very healthy existence and can set the stage for a lifetime of desperately seeking a state of social belonging or of apathetic withdrawal from human contact.

Like survival needs, the social needs do not disappear from the scene once they are provided for. They continue to exert important influences on individuals' behaviour throughout their entire lives. When threatened they tend to prompt people into some kind of definite action. When you have felt alone, isolated, or deprived of the kinds of warmth and support that human contact alone can offer, you are likely to seek out your friends or your family or even casual acquaintances. When it gets really bad, you may go to a public place just to be in the presence of others.

Unlike the survival needs, the social needs do not seem to demand immediate gratification, at least among most adults. When necessary a person can await the return of a valued friend, although a letter or even just thinking about the other can provide some degree of comfort. Also, social needs are satisfied in a greater number of ways than are the more basic survival needs. Look at the variety of social systems people live in, the differences in family relationships, and the varying patterns of friendship and social groupings. In short, the social needs of people seem to have some relation to survival but not quite the critical character associated with air, water, food, safety, etc. And while they exert powerful influences on all our behaviour, they are subject to wide variations in style. We explore the motivational aspects of these needs in Chapter 5.

Expectations

Usually before you make a choice you appraise the situation and decide which alternatives are likely to result in self-enhancement. Few people like to waste their efforts and even fewer wish to engage in behaviour that goes against their values, attitudes, and needs. To deal with the matter of choosing the best course of action in a situation your appraisal takes the form of a kind of prediction — 'the chances are that if I do this, I will achieve what I want.' You make a statement (implicit or explicit) of your expectancy regarding the probable outcome. It is like being your own personal scientist, making hypotheses, testing them out, revising them when they prove wrong, and holding on to the ones that prove accurate. Outcomes that are rewarding tend to create and reinforce the expectancies that are positive. Conversely, outcomes that are unrewarding or punishing lead to expectancies that are neutral or negative.

In general, the behaviour most likely to occur is that which the person expects to enhance self-concept most (Nadler and Lawler, 1977). When the expectancy and the self-concept fit together no dilemma is experienced. But what happens when an anticipated outcome involves some risk to self, yet no alternatives exist to meet goals? For example, suppose you see yourself as bright and as capable of putting your ideas into words very clearly.

Your goal is to be outspoken in departmental meetings at work so that you can have some reaction to your ideas from your supervisors. You now find yourself in a department in which the supervisor refuses to entertain questions until the reports are given; but you also find that there is no time left for discussion at the end of the meetings. You can choose to keep your mouth shut, expecting a negative reaction should you speak up, or your can say something anyway in order to move towards your goal. In order for anyone to predict what you are likely to do would require that they know:

1 the strength of your goal to speak out;
2 your expectancy regarding the negative consequences of speaking out; and
3 your expectancy regarding the positive and negative consequences for your self-concept in not speaking out.

Trait approaches to personality

Personality

Personality can be summarized as the pattern of traits and dispositions which distinguish one individual from another and determines how he or she adjusts to their environment. Such traits and dispositions are enduring and some psychologists have argued that they are almost impossible to change except for some fine turning at the edges (see, for example, Wiggins, 1973; Rokeach 1972). Others have argued that personality is predominantly a function of heredity which then is subject to change depending upon the environment in which the individual works and lives (Gilmer, 1984; Holden 1980). Holden's work demonstrated that genetics appeared to play a central part in determining personality. He studied a number of pairs of identical twins, separated at birth, who were all placed in different environments yet displayed strong similarities and traits. Their pattern appeared to be the same or very similar. They married spouses often with the same first name; they liked to wear similar kinds of clothes; if one of a pair smoked, then so did the other and they tended to favour similar or the same names for their children.

The structure of personality

Systematic ways in which psychologists have looked at personality include a wide range of psychoanalytical approaches, typologies and trait theories.

Psychoanalytical theories highlight the tension between nature and nurture (i.e. the dynamic interplay of ourselves with our immediate environment). Freud (1933) is perhaps the most well-known theorist who adopted this approach. Freud concentrated on the conflicts which arose between what he termed 'libido' (the basic nature of us all to seek pleasure in all its forms) and the norms, values and mores of wider society. Technically, this is the conflict between the 'ego' (self) and the 'superego' (societal values). Freud also proposed the concept of the 'id' which is generally held to describe the variety of impulses and desires which we seek to gratify often subconsciously.

Erich Fromm (1941) argued that personality structures were the product of man's interaction with society. Despair, pessimism, aggression for Fromm all stemmed ultimately from man's inability to cope with the expectations and demands of wider society.

Typologies and trait theories both attempt to classify different personalities based on a set of factors or characteristics on which we can all be compared. Freud described the 'obsessional' type of personality (critical and sceptical), the 'erotic' (sociable and self-dramatizing) and the 'narcissistic' (concerned with self and self-satisfied). Based on the work of Carl Jung, a German psychologist, Eysenck proposed two dimensions of personality:

Introversion—Extroversion

Neuroticism—Stability

(Eysenck and Wilson, 1975)

Based on the idea that personality is essentially genetic in origin, Eysenck describes a number of *personal dispositions* which correspond to his two dimensions. For example:

Extroversion   Comprises expressiveness/impulsiveness/risk-taking behaviour/sociability/ practicality/expressiveness and irresponsibility.

Introversion   Comprises carefulness/reflectiveness/unsociability/inhibition/control/ inactivity and responsibility.

Neuroticism   Comprises low self-esteem/little autonomy/unhappiness/anxiety/ obsessiveness/hypochondria and guilt.

Stability   Comprises self-esteem/autonomy/happiness/tranquillity/health and well-being/calmness and quiescence.

None of these is an exclusive category and most individuals fall between the extremes outlined above. The structure of personality is hierarchical according to Eysenck. Individuals who exhibit particular traits (such as anxiety or obsessiveness) are also likely to possess other predictable traits (such as hypochondria and guilt). You can find the questionnaire test designed by Eysenck in a book by Eysenck and Wilson (1975).

There is no 'good' or 'poor' pattern of personality as measured by Eysenck's traits, although some personalities are likely to be more socially acceptable in particular settings. A neurotic extrovert, for example, would possibly be considered out of place in an environment which favoured solitude and reflective behaviours (such as a library or monastic orders).

Apart from the questionnaires (see Chapter 3), personality can be tapped by a number of other methods. Based on the assumption that each individual will interpret ambiguous stimuli in a different and unique way, the Rorschach test examines the interpretation of ink-blots and similar blotches of indefinable shape (see Rabin, 1958). A Swiss psychiatrist, Rorschach recorded both why individuals interpreted the ink blot as they did as well as precisely what it was they saw. The test is ridden with difficulties in scoring and it is neither reliable nor standardized.

The Thematic Apperception Test (TAT) relies upon the idea that we all project situations into the future in our own separate ways. The most common form of this test is for the candidate to make up a story having been shown a picture which portrays a person (or people) in an ambiguous setting. Twenty such pictures are thus shown and the twenty stories are examined for themes and consistently held personality traits. The test is widely used and is more reliable than the ink-blot tests, although it too is subject to rigging by candidates taking the test.

Some of the major factors which comprise personality are shown in Figure 4.1.

Figure 4.1
The major components of individual personality

Demographic characteristics	Competency characteristics	Psychological characteristics
e.g. age	e.g. abilities	e.g. values
sex	aptitudes	attitudes
race	skills	interests
		traits

Individual
personality

Environmental approaches to personality

The structural/trait approaches to personality neglect to consider the impact of the environment or situation on individuals. The role played by the environment includes socialization, imitation and ideology. The culture in which we grow up (e.g. family, social groupings and friends) influences personality. What is considered to be ideologically acceptable behaviour in one culture does not always easily translate to another culture. Mead's (1935) work in primitive societies illustrates that differences in child socialization led to differences in subsequent behaviour (the males took on what we would consider female roles in Western cultures). This would not easily translate to 'traditional' Western cultures which instil in the male aggressive, competitive and independent behaviour.

Mischel (1973) argued that the situation played an important part in shaping personality. While there may be underlying stability in personality (through traits, for example) it was open to change in different situations. Each situation demands a different personality response. Mischel argued that the same situation can provoke different responses from different individuals and that different situations can bring out similar responses from the same individual.

Although compelling, we do not know enough about these theories to say if they have any kind of substance. Problems include:

1 a lack of substantial empirical work;
2 difficulty in classifying the enormous number of situational variables;
3 problems in isolating and controlling for an individual's previous experience with similar situations, or prior knowledge of a forthcoming situation.

Following point 3 above, the effect of stereotyping begins to emerge.

Stereotyping and prejudices

In news bulletins and magazine articles, the terms prejudice and discrimination are generally used as synonyms. More analytically, prejudice can be defined in the following way: it is an attitude (usually negative) towards the members of some specific group (racial, ethnic, sexual, etc.) which causes the person holding it to evaluate others solely on the basis of their membership in that group. When an individual is prejudiced against the members of some group, we mean that he or she tends to evaluate such persons in a negative manner simply because they belong to that group—not because of their individual characteristics or behaviour.

The cognitive component of prejudice refers to beliefs and expectations held about the members of a particular group. Often, these beliefs form clusters of preconceived notions known as stereotypes. Stereotypes are of major importance, for once formed, they exert several powerful effects. First, they lead individuals to assume consistencies which do not really exist. For example, they can give rise to the belief that all members of a given racial, ethnic or other group possess similar traits or invariably. Second, they exert a powerful impact upon the processing of new social information. They shape the interpretation of such information so that it is perceived as offering support for the stereotyped beliefs, even if this is not actually so.

Unfortunately, stereotypes are both common and persistent. They change very slowly, even over the course of several decades. They exist with respect to racial groups, sex, occupational groups, geographical upbringing, age, education, social class, and even physical beauty (Cash, Gillen and Burns, 1977). Burrell (1984: 97) argues that the field of organizational behaviour itself stereotypes organizations as sexless places. He argues that novels and biographies possibly reflect a more rounded reality of organizational life. Hearn *et al.* (1989) develop this theme, concluding that most organizations reflect a set of dominantly masculine prejudices.

In discovering the origins of prejudice, several different answers have been offered. Among the ones receiving most attention have been the suggestions that prejudice stems mainly from:

1 intergroup contact;
2 the presence of certain personality traits;
3 learning experiences occurring early in life.

With respect to intergroup conflict, it has been proposed that prejudice often arises when different groups strive for the same jobs, housing, and other resources. Since their contacts under these conditions are largely hostile and competitive, it is not surprising that these interactions give rise to strong, negative attitudes. Research evidence has been obtained from a number of different studies which suggests that when groups must compete, negative feelings akin to prejudice often emerge (see Sherif *et al.*, 1961; Kerrington, 1981). Conversely, when contacts between various groups are largely friendly and cooperative in nature, such reactions are reduced.

It has been proposed that certain personality traits predispose individuals toward prejudices. It has been suggested that prejudice is often related to a cluster of personality traits termed the 'authoritarian personality' (Adorno *et al.*, 1950). Briefly, authoritarian individuals are persons showing a pattern of submissive obedience to authority, punitive rejection of groups other than their own, and rigid thinking. Either you are a member of the group and are for them, or you are a member of some other rejected group, and must be against them. Authoritarian individuals are far from rare, and you will probably encounter many during your career.

A final view is that stereotypes are learned. Basically, it suggests that children acquire negative attitudes towards various social groups either simply by observing such reactions on the part of their parents or through direct reward and training for expressing such views. While parents, teachers, and peers are probably most important in this respect, the mass media, too, may play a role. Until recently, members of racial and ethnic minorities appeared only rarely on television and in films. Further, when they did, they were often shown as holding low-status jobs, as living in slums, and as speaking with a heavy and incomprehensible accent. Given repeated exposure to such material, it is far from surprising that many children soon acquire negative attitudes towards such persons, even if they had never met any in real-life situations.

Cognitive theories of personality

Psychological characteristics of individuals

Another category of individual attributes is psychological characteristics. While there is a wide range of these characteristics, they share a common tendency to predispose an individual to behave in predictable ways. These predispositions have a substantial influence on behaviour. Extroverted salespersons, for example, are likely to see things differently than introverts and to be seen differently by others. These differences will influence their behaviour and the sales they are able to generate.

There is not enough space in this book to deal with the many psychological and cognitive studies of individuals. Two broad dimensions which have important implications in work organizations are internal–external orientation and problem-solving style.

Locus of control: internal–external orientation

The internal–external orientation measures the extent to which a person feels able to affect his or her life (Rotter, 1966). Chapter 3 dealt with locus of control with respect to using its results for selection. Here, we are more concerned with its cognitive aspects. People have general expectancies about whether events are controlled primarily by themselves, which indicates an internal orientation, or by outside forces, characteristic of an external orientation. 'Internals' believe they control their own fate or destiny. 'Externals' believe much of what happens to them is uncontrolled and determined by outside forces. Two examples of questionnaire items which have been shown to distinguish internals from externals are:

1 a Many of the unhappy things in people's lives are partly due to bad luck.
  b People's misfortunes result from the mistakes they make.
2 a As far as world affairs are concerned, most of us are the victims of forces we can neither understand nor control.
  b By taking an active part in political and social affairs, people can control world events.

(Rotter, 1966)

Answers 1a and 2a reflect an external orientation while individuals responding with 1b and 2b show an internal orientation. Rotter's scale of locus of control is produced by asking 29 such forced choice pairs of statements. Given six 'filler' pairs, the scale ranges from 0 (purely internal) to 23 (purely external). Most populations score around the mean although closer study of particular groups can reveal marked differences in locus of control. Table 4.1 shows some of the ways in which internals and externals have been found to differ.

Table 4.1
Some ways in which internals differ from externals

Information processing	Internals make more attempts to acquire information, are better at information retention, are less satisfied with amount of information they possess, are better at utilizing information and devising processing rules.
Job satisfaction	Internals are more satisfied, less alienated, and less rootless.
Self-control and risk behaviour	Internals exhibit greater self-control, are more cautious, and engage in less risky behaviour.
Expectancies and results	Internals see a stronger relationship between what they do and what happens to them, expect working hard leads to good performance, feel more control over how to spend time, perform better.
Preference for skill versus chance achievements	Internals prefer skill-achievement outcomes; externals prefer chance achievements.
Use of rewards	Internals are more likely to use personally persuasive rewards and power bases; less likely to use coercion.
Response to others	Internals are more independent, more reliant on own judgement, less susceptible to influence of others, they resist subtle influence attempts and are more discriminating in information acceptance. Information is more likely to be accepted on own merits rather than based upon prestige of its source.
Leader behaviour	Internals prefer participative leadership; externals prefer directive.

Source: Schemerhorn, Hunt and Osborn (1982: 90). Reprinted by permission.

Problem-solving style

This examines the way in which a person goes about gathering and evaluating information in solving problems and making decisions (Hellriegel and Slocum, 1976). In the problem-solving process, information gathering and evaluating are separate activities. Information gathering is the process by which a person organizes stimuli or data for use. Styles of information gathering vary from sensation to intuitive. Sensation-type individuals prefer routine and order, and emphasize well-defined details in gathering information. Intuitive-type persons prefer the big picture, like solving new problems, and dislike routine.

Evaluation involves making judgements about how to deal with information once it has been collected. Styles of information evaluation vary, from an emphasis on feeling to an emphasis on thinking. Feeling type individuals are oriented towards conformity and try to accommodate themselves to other people. They try to avoid problems that might result in disagreements. Thinking-type people use reason and intellect to deal with problems. They down-play emotional aspects in the problem situation.

It is likely that people with particular problem-solving styles may be better suited to certain jobs than others. For instance, intuitive-feeling or intuitive-thinking individuals are likely to be better counsellors than sensation-feeling or sensation-thinking individuals. Given a fit between the problem-solving style and the information-processing requirements of a job, it is plausible that a person should be more productive and satisfied than when there is a lack of fit.

Job satisfaction

Work plays a dominant role in our lives. It occupies more of our time than any other single activity. For most of us, it is central to our self-concept: we define ourselves, in part, by our careers or professions. We say we are an accountant or an operations manager when asked 'What do you do?' Rarely do we answer 'I play the piano or I'm quite a good painter' if these are our hobbies. The definition of work takes precedence in our self-description.

Most people can readily report feelings, beliefs, and behaviour tendencies relating to their jobs. In short, they hold strong and well-established attitudes towards their work and specific aspects of it. Such attitudes are generally known as job satisfaction.

Job satisfaction is of central concern to organizational behaviour researchers. One major reason for the continuing interest in job satisfaction is that positive and negative attitudes towards work may exert powerful effects upon many forms of organizational behaviour. However, while job satisfaction is closely related to some forms of work-related behaviour, it does not seem to play a direct role in others.

As is true of other attitudes, job satisfaction can be measured by several different techniques. By far the most common approach is by administering to individuals a set of rating scales on which the respondents simply report their reactions to their jobs. A large number of different scales have been developed. Items similar to those used on one (the Minnesota Satisfaction Questionnaire) are presented in Table 4.2.

Table 4.2
On type of attitude scale

In my present job, this is how I feel about:	Not at all satisfied	Slightly satisfied	Satisfied	Very satisfied	Extremely satisfied
The variety of tasks I perform	1	2	3	4	5
My responsibility for planning my work	1	2	3	4	5
Opportunities for advancement	1	2	3	4	5
My rate of pay	1	2	3	4	5

The Job Descriptive Index (JDI) is a similar scale. Individuals completing this scale are presented with lists of adjectives and asked to indicate whether each does or does not describe a particular aspect of their work. (Respondents indicate their reactions by placing a 'Y' for yes, 'N' for no, or '?' for undecided next to each adjective.) One interesting feature of the JDI is that it assesses reactions to five distinct aspects of the job: the work itself, pay, promotional opportunities, supervision, and people (co-workers). Items similar to those included on the JDI are shown in Table 4.3.

Table 4.3
Items similar
to those
on the JDI

Place a Y (for yes), an N (for no), or a ? (for undecided) next to each word to indicate whether it does or does not describe your job:	
Work	*Pay*
____Interesting	____Fair
____Unpleasant	____Appropriate to my level
____Useful	____More than I deserve
____Simple	____Adequate for my current lifestyle
____Tiring	____Related to my performance

Another technique for assessing job satisfaction is the critical incident procedure. Here, individuals are asked to describe incidents relating to their work that they found particularly satisfying or dissatisfying. Their replies are then carefully analysed to uncover underlying themes and reactions. Finally, job satisfaction can also be assessed through interviews. Unfortunately, such procedures are often long and costly; therefore they have not been used for this purpose very often. Regardless of the specific approach adopted, the goal in assessing job satisfaction remains the same: uncovering the feelings, beliefs and behaviour tendencies of employees towards various aspects of their work. Further details of attempts to increase job satisfaction by redesigning or enriching jobs are outlined in Chapter 7.

One of the key features of any job is its ability to be stressful to the individual. All jobs have the potential to be stressful rather than give satisfaction. We explore stress in the next section.

Stress

Have you ever found yourself in a situation that seemed to be more than you could handle? If you have ever driven in frenzied commuter traffic, delivered a speech to a large, unfriendly audience, or looked frantically for your flight a few minutes before take-off in a bustling airport, your answer is certain to be yes. These situations share a common feature: they threaten literally to overwhelm our ability to handle or cope with them. When conditions of this type exist, we experience stress. As McGrath (1976) argues:

> there is a potential for stress when an environmental situation is perceived as presenting a demand which threatens to exceed the person's capabilities and resources for meeting it.

While our reactions to stress vary greatly (everything from damp palms and shaking knees to intense feelings of despair), most fall under three major categories. First, we respond to stress physiologically. This includes a rise in heart rate and blood pressure, increased respiration, and a diversion of blood to skeletal muscles—the ones used in fight or flight situations.

In addition, we react psychologically. We experience such feelings as fear, anxiety and tension. We actively seek to evaluate or appraise the stress-inducing situation, to determine just how dangerous it really is. Finally, we also respond to stress overtly, with a variety of coping behaviours. These range from attempts to gather more information about the stressful situation through direct steps to deal with it, and may also include intra-psychic strategies—ones designed simply to make us feel better (e.g. taking a drink or convincing ourselves that there really is not much danger).

Stress can emerge from every aspect of our daily lives. In this brief discussion of the topic, we will focus on two groups of factors that produce or influence stress: ones relating to aspects of organizations and ones involving the personal characteristics of individuals. It is important to emphasize that trying to detail objective situations and variables to describe a situation as stressful is fraught with difficulty.

Stress is largely a *perceived phenomenon* (Lazarus, 1966). Only the individual experiencing the stress can identify the specific set of factors which are causing stress. They may not, however, be aware of all of them and we begin this section by looking at common situational causes of stress found in the organization. Reading 4 by Valerie Sutherland and Cary Cooper fleshes out some of these ideas, particularly with respect to the characteristics of individuals with regard to perceived stress.

Organizational causes of stress

Occupational demands   Some jobs seem potentially more stressful than others. It is tempting to equate the harried job of a waiter or waitress in a busy restaurant with high levels of stress, while the relatively staid occupation of a bank clerk, for example, could be interpreted as being far less stressful. This may not be the case, however. The perception of the individual and the characteristics of the job within the organisational structure will all mediate the levels of stress. Some of these factors are described below.

Role conflict   Stress from conflicting and often irreconcilable demands. When individuals join an organization, they are generally expected to behave in certain ways. Such expectations constitute a role—a general set of guidelines indicating how persons holding certain positions should behave. In many cases, the presence of roles is beneficial: they save you the trouble of deciding what constitutes appropriate behaviour in many situations. Often though, roles can be the source of considerable discomfort and stress. This is especially likely in situations where different groups of people with whom an individual interacts hold contradictory expectations about how he or she should behave. Under these conditions, role conflict exists, and the person in question may find him or herself being pulled in different and incompatible directions.

Role ambiguity   This is stress from uncertainty. Even if an individual manages to avoid the strain associated with role conflict, he or she may still encounter this even more common source of on-the-job stress. It occurs under conditions where individuals are uncertain about several matters pertaining to their jobs: the scope of their responsibilities, the limits of their authority and that of others, company rules, job security, and the methods used to evaluate their work.

Overload and underload   Doing too much and doing too little. When the phrase 'job stress' is mentioned, many people imagine a harried executive who is attempting to dictate a letter, talk on three telephones, conduct an interview, and write a report simultaneously! This is referred to as 'overload', and while it rarely reaches this extreme, more than half of all white-collar workers report experiencing it to some degree in their jobs (French and Caplan, 1972).

Conversely, being asked to do too little in one's work can also be quite stressful. Such 'underutilization' generally results in monotony and intense boredom. Stress occurs since most persons wish to feel useful and needed, and by doing nothing in their job their self-esteem is threatened. Individuals also appear to have a strong need for stimulation, and their preferred state is definitely not that of staring blankly into space (Katz and Kahn, 1978).

Responsibility for others   This is often perceived by individuals as a heavy burden, although it is often encouraged in organizations as a part of career development. In general, being responsible for other people (dealing with them, motivating and making decisions about them) creates potentially higher levels of stress than positions in which such responsibility is absent (McLean, 1980). Such persons are more likely to report feelings of tension and anxiety. And they are also more likely to develop the 'classic' symptoms of stress, such as ulcers and hypertension.

The basis for this difference is easily discerned. Supervisors and managers must often deal with the human costs of their decisions. They must witness the anguish of persons who are fired or passed over for promotion, as well as witness the reactions of those given negative feedback on their work. In families, the same stress due to responsibility can be seen in both mothers and fathers (over children's schooling, nurturing them for some preconceived future, etc.).

Lack of participation   This situation can cause stress from a perceived absence of input. Lack of employee participation in decisions which affect them and their job can serve as a source of tension and stress for two reasons. First, many employees feel 'left out'. Second, individuals may also experience feelings of helplessness or loss of control. These reactions often intensify the impact of other stressful events. Stressors are *additive*. An individual experiencing all six of the above situational conditions would be more prone to suffer the symptoms of stress than an individual experiencing one of the above situations. However, we must not neglect the interpretive nature of the stress–individual relationship. Certain individuals may not feel stressed at all, but will be in perhaps two or three of the above situations (see Sutherland and Cooper, Reading 4).

The individual and stress

Lazarus (1966) argues that a better way to study stress and its effects is to study both situational events and their respective perception by different individuals. Much work has been conducted in this area. In this section we concentrate on three major fields of study:

1 *Impact of life change*, such as the death of a loved one, divorce, etc. (Holmes and Rahe, 1967).
2 *Maintaining a hard-driving, high-pressure life style*   This is sometimes referred to as 'Type A' behaviour (Pittner and Houston, 1980).
3 *Perceived control and reactions to stress*   Events which are under your control (in terms of scheduling, etc.) cause less stress than those externally set (Rotter, 1966).

Life events and the individual

'Whenever a major change in state takes place the need arises for the individual to re-structure his ways of looking at the world and his plans for living in it' (Murray Parkes, 1971). The idea that we all have to adapt and change to various events has been a keystone of much research linking the onset of stress-induced illness to life changes.

The most well-known research into life changes is that of Holmes and Rahe (1967) who devised the Social Readjustment Rating Scale. Respondents are asked to rate a series of life events according to their relative degrees of perceived necessary readjustment. It is argued that the greater the level of adjustment required, the greater is the level of stress, accompanied by a high possibility of subsequent illness (physical and/or mental). The scale is shown in Table 4.4. The rank order was derived from a total of 394 American subjects, equally split male–female, predominantly Caucasian and between 20 and 60 years old.

Table 4.4
The Social Readjustment Rating Scale (Results for 394 Americans)

Rank	Life event	Mean value
1	Death of spouse	100
2	Divorce	73
3	Marital separation	65
4	Jail term	63
5	Death of close family member	63
6	Personal injury or illness	53
7	Marriage	50
8	Sacked from work	47
9	Marital reconciliation	45
10	Retirement	45
11	Change in health of family member	44
12	Pregnancy	40
13	Sexual difficulties	39
14	Gain of new family member	39
15	Business readjustment	39
16	Change in financial state	38
17	Death of close friend	37
18	Change to a different line of work	36
19	Change in number of arguments with spouse	35
20	Mortgage over £5000*	31
21	Foreclosure of mortgage or loan	30
22	Change in responsibilities at work	29
23	Son or daughter leaving home	29
24	Trouble with in-laws	29
25	Outstanding personal achievement	28
26	Wife beginning or ceasing work	26
27	Begin or end school (formal education)	26
28	Change in living conditions	25
29	Revision of personal habits (dress, etc)	24
30	Trouble with the boss	23
31	Change in work hours or conditions	20
32	Change in residence	20
33	Change in schools	20
34	Change in recreation	19
35	Change in church activities	19
36	Change in social activities	18
37	Mortgage or loan less than £5000*	17
38	Change in sleeping habits	16
39	Change in number of family get-togethers	15
40	Change in eating habits	15
41	Holidays	13
42	Christmas	12
43	Minor violations of the law	11

*Figures at 1966 prices!
Source: Adapted from Holmes and Rahe (1967) by permission of Pergamon Press plc.

For the respondents, marriage was given the arbitrary value of 500, and they were asked to complete the remaining 42 life events allocating scores to the extent that they believed the event needed more or less readjustment than marriage. Mean values such as those in Table 4.4. can then be calculated across any sample.

Holmes and Masuda (1973) categorized the life-change units (LCUs) as:

1 Mild life crisis (mild stress) 150–99 LCU
2 Moderate life crisis (moderate stress) 200–99 LCU
3 Major life crisis (high levels of stress) 300+LCU.

It would appear that there is consistency across different nations using the Social Readjustment Rating Scale. Rank order correlation coefficients are shown in Table 4.5.

Table 4.5
Cross-cultural comparisons of rank ordering using the Social Readjustment Rating Scale*

Culture group	Japanese	West European	Spanish	Negro American	Mexican
American	0.752	0.884	0.847	0.798	0.735
Japanese		0.884	0.836	0.816	0.724
W. European			0.849	0.772	0.754
Spanish				0.848	0.767
Negro American					0.892

*Spearman's Rank Order Correlation Coefficient.
Source: adapted from Masuda and Holmes (1967); Komaroff (1967); and Celdran (1970).

In this research area, cross-national research supports similarities rather than differences. The correlation coefficients in Table 4.5 are consistently high. This is quite remarkable. Western Europeans, for example, have a culture embedded in the democratic ethic, bolstered by internalized Christian moral values for the most part. Japanese eastern culture is embedded in a particularistic hierarchical system which emphasizes family-oriented, externally sanctioned rules of ethical conduct. Yet perception of stressful life events is very similar.

Of course, this does not mean that every individual who scores over 300 LCUs will definitely suffer stress to the point where illness will inevitably result. There are many intervening factors such as personality, locus of control and Type A behaviours. We have covered personality in this chapter and Chapter 3. Locus of control is summarized in Table 4.1. We discuss Type A behaviours briefly in the next section.

Type A behaviours

These can be classified as individuals who are:

1 extremely competitive: always striving for achievement;
2 always doing things in a hurry (walking, working, eating);
3 aggressive and restless: are impatient at the pace of most things around them;
4 keen to take on responsibility: leisure time is difficult to cope with;
5 often setting themselves objectives to achieve both in domestic and working life.

Some cultures (such as North America and, to a lesser extent, Britain) value such behaviour highly in managers and thus reinforces Type A traits. A study of 236 managers revealed a connection between Type A behaviours and symptoms of stress, such as high blood pressure and high cholesterol levels (Howard, Cunningham and Rechnitzer, 1976). Other studies, however, have found little support for this association (see Brief, Schuler and Van Sell, 1981). It is certain nevertheless that Type A individuals experience more stress both at work and at home.

Type B behaviours are the opposite of Type A. They will experience much lower levels of stress. Type B characteristics are:

1 little sense of urgency or impatience;
2 enjoy leisure and do not feel guilty about it;
3 can play sports and games without always being competitive;
4 feel little need to advertise their achievements.

Personal strategies for coping with stress

Self-improvement and self-help have been popular themes during the past two decades. Many techniques for coping with the harmful impact of stress (and for creating 'wellness') have been suggested. Some of these focus on physical strategies and others on psychological or behavioural approaches. Examples are:

1 *Physical strategies*
   - exercise
   - good diet
2 *Psychological strategies*
   - develop networks of social support within the organization
   - plan ahead, be prepared with alternative proposals
   - take a holiday
   - try meditation and relaxation training

Organizational strategies for reducing stress

While personal strategies for coping with stress differ greatly, all rely on giving individuals techniques they can use for dealing with stress when it occurs. Organizational strategies for managing stress seek to minimize it by removing factors which are potentially stress-inducing in the work setting. Many of these involve changes in structure. Others focus primarily on changes in the nature of specific jobs. These include:

1 *Changes in organizational structure or function*
   - decentralization
   - adjustments to the reward system
   - improved techniques of training and placement of employees
   - arranging for employee participation in the decision-making process
   - improved lines of communication in the organization
2 *Changes in the nature of specific jobs*
   - job enlargement (see Chapter 7)
   - job enrichment (see Chapter 7)

Summary

This chapter has introduced a number of key issues in the study of organizational behaviour. In particular, the question of whether behaviour is situationally determined, or is largely determined by perception, is important. For example, all jobs have the potential to create a stressful situation, so we would expect all individuals to experience stress. Yet, people's perceptions differ. They appraise the same situation in different ways. From this perspective, some people may experience very little stress, while others experience a great deal.

There are no hard and fast answers to these questions. There is empirical support for both *social-action* explanations (everything can only explained in terms of how any one individual perceives his or her world) and for *environmental determinism* (where the characteristics of the situation are argued to take primacy in explaining behaviour). Although introduced here at the individual level of analysis, this debate will be seen to run centrally through many of the following chapters.

References

Adorno, T. W., E. Frenkel-Brunswik, D. J. Levinson and R. N. Sanford (1950) *The Authoritarian Personality*, Harper, New York.

Asch, S. E. (1946) 'Forming impressions of personality', *Journal of Abnormal and Social Psychology*, **41**, 258–90.

Brief, A. P., R. S. Schuler and M. Van Sell (1981) *Managing Job Stress*, Little, Brown & Co., Boston.

Burrell, G. (1984) 'Sex and organizational analysis', *Organization Studies*, **5**(2), 97–118.

Cash, T. F., B. Gillen and D. S. Burns (1977) 'Sexism and "Beautyism" in personnel consultant decision making', *Journal of Applied Psychology*, **2**, 301–10.

Celdran, H. H. (1970) 'The cross-cultural consistency of two social consensus scales: the Seriousness of Illness Rating Scale and the Social Readjustment Rating Scale in Spain', University of Washington Medical Thesis.

Dunnette, M. D. (1976) 'Basic attributes of individuals in relation to their behavior in organizations', in M. D. Dunnette (ed.), *Handbook of Industrial and Organizational Psychology*, Rand McNally, Chicago, pp. 469–520.

Eysenck, H. J. and G. Wilson (1975) *Know Your Own Personality*, Penguin, Harmondsworth.

French, J. R. P. and R. D. Caplan (1972) 'Organizational stress and individual strain', in A. J. Morrow (ed.), *The Failure of Success*, Amacom, New York.

Freud, S. (1933) *New Introductory Lectures on Psychoanalysis*, Norton, New York.

Fromm, E. (1941) *Escape from Freedom*, Rinehart, New York.

Gilmer, B. von H. (1984) *Applied Psychology: Adjustments in Living and Work*, 2nd edn, Tata McGraw-Hill, New Delhi.

Hamilton, D. L. (1983) 'Person perception', in J. R. Hackman, E. E. Lawler and L. W. Porter (eds), *Perspectives on Behavior in Organizations*, McGraw-Hill, New York, pp. 41–56.

Hearn, J., D. L. Sheppard, P. Tancred-Sheriff, and G. Burrell (eds) (1989) *The Sexuality of Organization*, Sage, London.

Hellriegel, D. and J. W. Slocum (1976) *Organizational Behaviour*, 2nd edn, West Publishing, Minneapolis.

Hilliard, A. L. (1950) *The Forms of Value*, Columbia University Press, New York.

Holden, C. (1980) 'Identical twins reared apart', *Science*, March, 1323–4.

Holmes, R. H. and M. Masuda (1973) 'Life change and illness susceptibility', *Separation and Depression*, **12**, 43–65.

Holmes, T. H. and R. J. Rahe (1967) 'Social Readjustment Rating Scale', *Journal of Psychosomatic Research*, **11**, 213–18.

Howard, J. H., D. A. Cunningham and P. A. Rechnitzer (1976) 'Health patterns associated with Type A behaviour: a managerial population', *Journal of Human Stress*, **4**, 24–31.

Katz, D. and R. Kahn (1978) *The Social Psychology of Organizations*, 2nd edn, Wiley, New York.

Kerrington, S. M. (1981) 'Intergroup relations and nursing', *European Journal of Social Psychology*, **11**, 43–59.

Komaroff, A. L. (1967) 'A comparative study of Negro, Mexican and White Americans', *Journal of Psychosomatic Research*, **12**, 25–36.

Lawler, E. E. (1983) 'Satisfaction and behavior', in J. R. Hackman, E. E. Lawler and L. W. Porter (eds), *Perspectives on Behavior in Organizations*, McGraw-Hill, New York, pp. 78–87.

Lazarus, R. S. (1966) *Psychological Stress and the Coping Process*, McGraw-Hill, New York.

Leeper, R. (1935) 'The role of motivation in learning: a study of the phenomenon of differential motivation control of the utilization of habits', *Journal of Genetic Psychology*, **46**, 3–40.

Lovejoy, A. O. (1950) 'Terminal and adjectival values', *Journal of Philosophy*, **47**, 593–608.

Masuda, M. and R. H. Holmes (1967) 'The Social Readjustment Rating Scale: A cross-cultural study of Japanese and Americans', *Journal of Psychosomatic Research*, **12**, 10–24.

McGrath, J. E. (1976) 'Stress and behavior in organizations', in M. D. Dunnette (ed.), *Handbook of Industrial and Organizational Psychology*, Rand McNally, Chicago, p. 1352.

McKenna, E. F. (1987) *Psychology in Business: Theory and Applications*, Lawrence Erlbaum Associates, Sussex.

McLean, A. A. (1980) *Work Stress*, Addison-Wesley, Reading, Mass.

Mead, M. (1935) *Sex and Temperament in Three Primitive Societies*, William Morrow, New York.

Mischel, W. (1973) 'Toward a cognitive social learning re-conceptualization of personality', *Psychological Review*, **80**, 252–83.

Murray Parkes, C. (1971) 'Psycho-social transitions: a field for study', *Social Science and Medicine*, **5**, 21–45.

Nadler, D. and E. Lawler (1977) 'Motivation: a diagnostic approach', L. W. Porter (eds), *Perspectives on Behavior in Organizations*, McGraw-Hill, New York.

Pittner, M. S. and B. K. Houston (1980) 'Response to stress, cognitive coping strategies, and the Type A behavior pattern', *Journal of Personality and Social Psychology*, **39**, 147–57.

Rabin, A. I. (ed.) (1958) *Projective Techniques in Personality Assessment*, Springer, New York.

Rokeach, M. (1972) *Beliefs Attitudes and Values: A Theory of Organization and Change*, Jossey-Bass, San Francisco.

Rotter, J. B. (1966) 'Generalized expectancies for internal versus external control of reinforcement', *Psychological Monographs*, **80**, issue 609.

Schemerhorn, J. R., J. G. Hunt and R. N. Osborn (1982) *Managing Organizational Behavior*, Wiley, New York.

Sherif, M., O. J. Harvey, B. J. White, W. R. Hood and C. W. Sherif (1961) *Intergroup Conflict and Co-operation: The Robbers' Cave Experiment*, University of Oklahoma Press, Norman.

Wiggins, J. S. (1973) *Personality and Prediction: Principles of Personality Assessment*, Addison-Wesley, Reading, Mass.

CHAPTER 5   Theories of motivation

Introduction   Motivation is one of the earliest concerns of organizational behaviour. Links between a motivated workforce and increased performance (often assumed, and with surprisingly little empirical support) led managers to strive toward 'motivating' their workforces in an attempt to reduce alienation.

> *Alienation*   is where the individual feels that work is a necessity imposed upon him or her. Working under such conditions means abandoning one's control over doing the job or of developing it.
>
> *Motivation*   is where the individual feels that work is sometimes good and sometimes bad, but that it is fulfilling, satisfying and capable of development in all ways.

A precise definition of motivation is elusive since the concept comprises both the characteristics of individuals, characteristics of the situation, and the perception of that situation by the individual. Yet we can usually spot the motivated individual with relative ease. He or she usually works harder, is interested in the task, is alert, bright and full of enthusiasm and ideas. Motivation then is characterized by a certain level of willingness on the part of an individual to increase effort, to the extent that this exertion also satisfies some need. In using this definition, we must distinguish between *motives* and *needs*.

> *Motives*   are the internal drives and energies of an individual. They direct behaviour. This behaviour results in outcomes. Any single outcome (such as the purchase of a sports car) may be the result of multiple motives (I like the speed; I like the image I think it portrays; I only need two seats in my car; I like being my own mechanic, etc.).
>
> *Needs*   are also internal to the individual. They can be physiological (I need sleep, warmth, food) or social (I like working with others and talking to them) or self-esteem needs (I need to gain the respect of others for what I do).

It is the interaction between the situation and needs and motives which forms the basis of most theories of motivation. In this book we shall be concerned with this interaction in the workplace, although clearly motivation is not limited solely to life in work organizations.

Theories of work motivation are largely grounded in the field of psychology. Psychologists, in turn, rely substantially upon the philosophical tradition of hedonism in their theory-building efforts—people seek to maximize pleasure and minimize pain in their day-to-day lives. Two categories of motivation theories evolve from this starting point: *content* theories and *process* theories.

Content theories

Content theories provide a link between individual needs and work rewards. They offer a perspective based upon the relative value people place upon various rewards. Content theorists make a number of important assumptions about the relationship between an individual's motivation and job satisfaction (Maslow, 1943, 1970; and McClelland, 1961). The first assumption is that needs are both physiological and psychological in origin. Second, that managers have the facility to alter rewards to suit individual preferences — thereby satisfying individual needs. Figure 5.1 illustrates the key factors which concern the content theorists.

Figure 5.1
Assumptions which form the basis for content theory

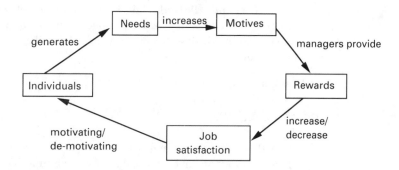

Maslow's Hierarchy of Needs

This theory assumes that man is basically a wanting animal seeking to satisfy needs both in social and working life. Man is motivated towards satisfying these needs and does so in a predisposed and logical order. This hierarchy is listed in Figure 5.2.

Figure 5.2
Maslow's Hierarchy of Needs

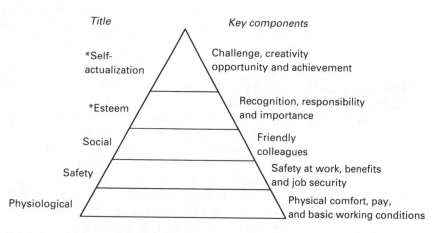

* denotes a 'higher order' need

Source: Adapted from Maslow (1943)

According to Abraham Maslow, needs which are satisfied are no longer motivators. This means that managers who constantly provide the same rewards cannot expect increasing levels of motivation from their staff.

Individuals are only driven by needs which remain unattained. Maslow's Hierarchy of Needs assumes that an individual can only progress through the five levels by satisfying each one in turn. For example, until one's safety and security needs are satisfied, status-based rewards would have little effect.

The highest level in Maslow's hierarchy is self-actualization. Given the somewhat 'existential' nature of this highest-order need, Maslow argued that it could never be completely satisfied. That is, individuals would continue to be motivated by challenging jobs and creative task demands. This is what would happen in an ideal situation according to Maslow. In most organizations and other aspects of social life this ideal is rarely attained. In practice, individuals trade off needs rather than pursue them in a strictly ordered hierarchy. For example, it is possible to self-actualize, but at the expense of safety, the love of others and higher levels of pay.

McClelland (1961) also falls into the category of content theorists. His acquired-needs theory focused on needs similar to the higher-order needs identified by Maslow. Specifically, McClelland argued that individuals have needs for:

1 achievement (nAch)
2 affiliation (nAff)
3 power (nPow)

Although each person has all of these needs to some extent, only one of them tends to motivate an individual at any given time. To give you a rough idea of how these needs are determined, Figure 5.3 helps you to identify your own predominant need at any given time.

In contrast to Maslow's view that individuals are born with a well-ordered hierarchy of needs. McClelland argued that individual needs vary over time and as a result of their life history. From a practical point of view, McClelland felt that by manipulating the work environment, managers could satisfy different distributions of employee needs for achievement, affiliation and power.

As can be seen from Table 5.1, McClelland's approach allows a potential linkage between different individual needs and idealized job attributes.

Herzberg's dual-factor theory of motivation

This theory was derived in the 1950s by Frederick Herzberg and his associates at the University of Pittsburgh (Herzberg, Mausner and Snyderman, 1959) where they examined the models and assumptions proposed by Abraham Maslow. In a research study involving 200 engineers and accountants, the subjects were asked to describe times when they felt especially satisfied or dissatisfied with their jobs. Careful analysis of the incidents described yielded an intriguing pattern of findings. Incidents involving the work itself, achievement, promotion, recognition, and responsibility, were often mentioned as sources of satisfaction, but rarely as a source of dissatisfaction. In contrast, incidents involving interpersonal relations, working conditions, supervisors, salary, and company policies were frequently mentioned as causes of job dissatisfaction, but rarely as a cause of satisfaction. The result of Herzberg's

Figure 5.3
Identification of
McClelland's needs

> 1 Do you like situations where you personally must find solutions to problems?
> 2 Do you tend to set moderate goals and take moderate, thought-out risks?
> 3 Do you want specific feedback about how well you are doing?
> 4 Do you spend time considering how to advance your career, how to do your job better, or how to accomplish something important?
>
> If you responded yes to questions 1–4, then you probably have a *high need for achievement*.
>
> 5 Do you look for jobs or seek situations that provide an opportunity for social relationships?
> 6 Do you often think about the personal relationships you have?
> 7 Do you consider the feelings of others very important?
> 8 Do you try to restore disrupted relationships when they occur?
>
> If you responded yes to questions 5–8, then you probably have a *high need for affiliation*.
>
> 9 Do you try to influence and control others?
> 10 Do you seek leadership positions in groups?
> 11 Do you enjoy persuading others?
> 12 Are you perceived by others as outspoken, forceful and demanding?
>
> If you responded yes to questions 9–12, then you probably have a *high need for power*.

Source: based on Steers and Porter (1979: 57–64).

Table 5.1
Idealized job
attributes and
individual needs

Individual need	Job attributes	Typical jobs
High nAch	Greater responsibility. Challenging goals.	Commission-based, self-reliance, e.g. stockbroker, insurance salesperson.
High nAff	Friendship, team work.	Social workers, sporting teams, volunteer worker.
High nPow	Clear structure, authority and influence over others.	Military ranks, politicians, plant managers.

Source: Schermerhorn, Hunt and Osborn (1982).

work was termed the Motivation–Hygiene (M–H) Theory. The basic attributes of this theory are:

1 There are two types of motivators, one type which results in satisfaction with the job (called motivators), and the other one which merely prevents dissatisfaction (called hygiene factors). These two types of factors are quite separate and distinct from each other.
2 The factors that lead to job satisfaction (motivators) are:
  - achievement
  - recognition
  - work itself

- responsibility
- advancement

3 The factors which prevent dissatisfaction (hygienes) are:
- company policy and administration
- supervision
- interpersonal relations
- money
- status
- security

Criticisms of content theories

Both Herzberg's and Maslow's findings were soon investigated in a large number of studies conducted by other academics. Unfortunately, these replicative studies failed to offer strong support for the content theories. While some studies did yield findings similar to those reported by Herzberg, many others reported sharply contrasting results (see, for example, Schneider and Locke, 1971). In this study it was found that hygienes and motivators exerted powerful effects upon both satisfaction and dissatisfaction—contrary to Herzberg's basic assertion that these positive and negative reactions stem from different distinct clusters of variables. Several studies which sought to substantiate Maslow's theory also failed to find support for the needs hierarchy (see Lawler and Suttle, 1972; Rauschenberger, Schmitt and Hunter, 1980).

In view of this evidence, acceptance of Maslow's Hierarchy of Needs and Herzberg's theory as fully adequate theoretical frameworks does not seem justified. This is not to say that they are of no value. The M–H Theory served to call attention to the importance of psychological growth as a basic condition for lasting job satisfaction. Attention to this fact led in turn to much work concerned with the question of how jobs might be designed to foster such growth. This led to models such as the Job Characteristics Model (Hackman *et al.*, 1975). This is discussed in detail in Chapter 7 (see Figure 7.1). In terms of motivation, the model provides a framework for enriching jobs to cater for the needs of individual workers, especially to give autonomy, feedback of performance and results and a sense of accomplishment (it is perceived as significant by the worker).

Maslow's theory has been criticized as being static, descriptive and ideologically biased. Like Herzberg, it cannot predict behaviour through analysing needs. Needs could be argued to reflect a cosy set of middle-class values rather than a rigorous theory (see Chapter 4). Both theories are full of methodological problems and they would not meet the criteria demanded by modern social-science research.

Research was not conducted under controlled conditions. Respondents' data were evaluated by numerous researchers so that immense amounts of subjectivity permeated the results. Respondents themselves compounded this subjectivity. When asked to think of a time when they felt very good or very bad about their jobs, respondents tended to attribute the good things to themselves, and the bad things to the situation. We will revisit this attribution of blame to external factors in Chapter 10, where groups also display the same phenomenon. Finally, not all individuals respond in the same way to having more challenging work or a greater sense of accomplishment (see House and Wigdor, 1967 for a review of critiques of the M—H Theory).

Process theories

Process theories attempt a more dynamic approach by striving to understand the thought processes of individuals which act to influence their behaviour. They are thus more linked to the process of developing motives rather than to a static analysis of needs. Two process theories which offer significant implications for motivation in work organizations are *equity theory* and *expectancy theory*.

Equity theory

The basis of equity theory lies in the process of individual comparison. If individuals feel that they are being rewarded unfairly for what they do, the result is likely to be alienation or de-motivation. This process is very similar to the more general sociological theory of social comparison (Adams, 1963). Figure 5.4 outlines the major stages in the comparison process.

Figure 5.4
The equity theory of motivation: the comparison process

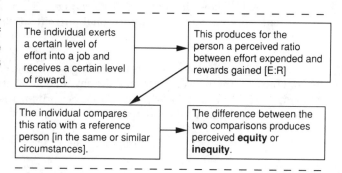

The most obvious form of inequity exists when a person doing a particular job compares what he or she earns with another person doing the same job in another but similar organization. If they receive different levels of pay or benefit, for example, the person who receives less will feel negative inequity (see Figure 5.4). Equally, an individual who receives significantly more pay and benefits than others doing the same job will also experience inequity. This time, positive inequity exists. Both states represent an imbalance which is perceived by the individual who strives to achieve a balance (i.e. to achieve equity). The relevance of equity theory to studies of motivation is that it explains a rationale for human behaviour which is not tied into need hierarchies or to specific kinds of individual drives. On the positive side, equity theory helps explain a potentially limitless list of factors which can lead toward motivating behaviour. More negatively, its basis as a theory of motivation places great emphasis upon managers whose task becomes that of changing the levels of rewards in order to satisfy others' perceptions of equity. This is no easy task both physically and mentally. It means that managers must infer inequity from the behaviour (or complaints) of others and must choose the most appropriate form of changes to achieve stability.

The behaviours of individuals which result from perceived inequities cover a wide range. Some of the more common responses include:

- negotiating for higher rewards
- altering the bases on which comparisons are made
- looking for alternative employment

Managerial action designed to overcome negative inequity amongst staff might include:

- better communication regarding how rewards are calculated
- a commitment to rectify any real inequities brought to light
- constant monitoring of the comparisons which most matter to individuals.

Fundamentally, managers must be sensitive to how others perceive their working environment. For example, I might recognize that I am in an inequitable position with regard to my peers in other organizations. They may be promoted faster, earn more money, or work fewer hours. Nevertheless, I may not perceive this inequity as a motivational drive since I derive satisfaction from other factors (where I live, loyalty to the organization, etc.). The argument that every employee in a work unit will view their annual pay rise as fair is simplistic. It is not how a manager feels about the allocation of rewards that counts, it is how the individuals receiving their rewards feel or perceive them that will determine the motivational outcome of the equity dynamic.

Expectancy theory

Expectancy theory, also known as the path–goal (P–G) concept, received its initial thrust from the work of Victor Vroom, an organizational psychologist at Yale University. Vroom (1964) argues that performance is a multiplicative function of motivation (M) and ability (A):

$$Performance = f(M, A)$$

Motivation to perform a task can be assumed to vary with:

1 the utilities of outcomes associated with the performance of that particular task (*valence*);
2 the *instrumentality* (belief that performance and outcome are linked) of performance for the achievement or avoidance of particular outcomes;
3 the *expectancy*, which determines the amount of effort expended by the individual in pursuit of a number of desired outcomes (such as gaining money to spend on a new car or house).

Basically, this is a hypothesis about decision-making. The presumption is that people can make intelligent and rational estimates about the consequences of particular choices and how such consequences will affect their own interests. Thus, the P–G model presupposes that people can estimate expectancies (in terms of probabilities that range from 0 to 1) in regard to both whether they can carry through particular tasks and the likelihood that their efforts will be noticed and rewarded accordingly. This 'logic' is illustrated in Figure 5.5.

Vroom's theory is important because it avoids the general error of the previous approaches which put the cart before the horse by arguing that enhancing human satisfaction always leads to improved task performance. The P–G/expectancy model gets the horse and cart in the right order by arguing that getting the task right determines human satisfaction. In application of P–G theory, the emphasis must be on carefully investigating what employees' expectancies, utilities and instrumentalities are; and then, setting out to change the structure of the situation to provide what management and workers want. This may be very difficult to achieve in practice. A brief summary follows:

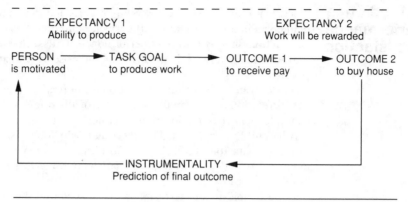

Figure 5.5
The path–goal
sequence

EXPECTANCY 1
Ability to produce

EXPECTANCY 2
Work will be rewarded

PERSON ——→ TASK GOAL ——→ OUTCOME 1 ——→ OUTCOME 2
is motivated   to produce work   to receive pay   to buy house

INSTRUMENTALITY ◄———
Prediction of final outcome

Content theories
- are based on the concept of hedonism
- assume individuals seek to satisfy all needs
- assume homogeneity of needs and individuals

Process theories
- focus particularly on choice behaviours
- rely on assuming a strong causality between means and ends
- are often impractical to implement in practice
- often are over-simplified since they neglect intervening factors such as egocentric behaviour and differences in individuals' perceptions

Reinforcement theory: a situational approach to motivation

The reinforcement theory of motivation is based upon the notion that the likelihood of a particular behaviour being repeated is a function of its expected consequences (Thorndike, 1911). If you do something which results in a pleasant reward, you are more likely to do it again. Similarly, if you undertake something which has an unpleasant consequence (negative reinforcement), you may be less likely to repeat it.

A simple illustration could be if a new employee joins your work group. To welcome this new member, you might go out of your way to be friendly and jovial with him or her. However, if the individual does not respond by similar friendly behaviour, it is unlikely that you would continue going out of your way for very long. By not receiving any positive reinforcement, you would not be motivated to continue your behaviour.

Essentially, there are four kinds of reinforcement. *Positive reinforcement* is to provide a pleasurable reward following a desired behaviour. *Negative reinforcement* is a way of increasing a particularly desired behaviour by offering an individual an opportunity to avoid an unpleasant consequence. For example, to avoid criticism from your manager, you might adopt those behaviours which he or she wishes to see. *Extinction* is the withdrawal of reinforcement which was previously provided to encourage behaviours. An example would be if a manager would make it a point to strongly criticize employees who arrived late for work. If, for some reason, the boss was no longer able to provide this negative reinforcement, the gradual extinction of the desired behaviour, i.e. arriving on time, might result. The final type of reinforcement is *punishment*. Rather than award good behaviour, punishment is the imposition of some unpleasant consequence as a result of undesirable behaviour.

Predicting performance and satisfaction

There is no simple relation between job satisfaction and performance. A widely held belief in human-relations theory (see Chapter 2) is that improving job satisfaction directly improves performance. Thus, improving employee morale is argued to cut down labour turnover and absenteeism and to increase production.

The current view is that satisfaction is not related to performance or, if it is, the correlation is very small. Some statistically oriented psychologists, for example, believe that a low, but consistent relationship exists (for example Lawler and Porter, 1978). The question is why job satisfaction is such an important variable. Probably the most important reason is that there is some evidence to suggest that high job satisfaction reduces absenteeism and employee turnover.

In path–goal-theory terms, it can be argued that the satisfied individual is motivated to work where her or his important needs are met. Lawler and Porter (1978) state:

It may well be that a high general level of job satisfaction of needs like self-actualization may be a sign of organizational effectiveness. Such a level of satisfaction would indicate, for instance, that most employees have interesting and involving jobs and that they are probably performing them well. One of the obvious advantages of providing employees with intrinsically interesting jobs is that good performance is rewarding in and of itself. Furthermore, being rewarded for good performance is likely to encourage further good performance.

Managing pay as an extrinsic reward

The development and maintenance of a fair and appropriate system for providing pay for work performed can be a major, and often frustrating, challenge for organizations. If it is not well-managed, pay dissatisfaction can lead to some potentially troublesome consequences (see Figure 5.6).

Figure 5.6
The consequences of pay dissatisfaction

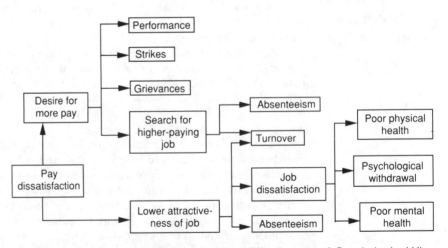

Source: Lawler, E. E. *Pay and Organizational Effectiveness: A Psychological View,* McGraw-Hill Book Company, New York.

Dissatisfaction with pay received can seriously affect the longer-term ability of an organization to survive. If the better employees start to leave or work less,

Table 5.2
The multiple meanings of pay as viewed from a job satisfaction perspective

What is Pay?	According to . . .
Pay is a flexible reward which can satisfy a number of needs. First, it can overcome immediate 'lower-level' needs. Second, it provides the medium through which 'higher-level' needs are addressed.	Abraham Maslow
Pay is, primarily, a hygiene factor. When it is seen as too low, an individual would feel dissatisfied. Under certain circumstances, pay can also be a motivator since it can be seen as a form of recognition for merit, etc.	Frederick Herzberg
For high nAch individuals, pay increases are a form of feedback. For high nAffil people, elements of pay which are derived from meeting group targets can be a source of motivation. For individuals with high nPow, pay might be viewed as a function of their position in the organizational firmament.	David McClelland
Pay is one of the more important 'yardsticks' people use in organizations to assess their position vis à vis others. Based on their assessment, work effort may be altered accordingly.	J. S. Adams
When an individual believes that improved performance will lead to more pay (instrumentality), higher levels of motivation will result. Similarly, if an individual understands how much extra effort must be expended to attract more pay (expectancy), then the individual can make a decision whether or not to work harder.	Victor Vroom
Providing pay can be a positive reinforcement of desired behaviour. Alternatively, pay on a piece-rate or commission basis can be seen as having elements of negative reinforcement.	E. L. Thorndike

coupled perhaps with difficulties in recruiting new, qualified staff, then the organization's ability to regenerate itself is thrown into question. Thus the motivation of employees via pay can have a direct effect on organizational survival.

Earlier in this chapter, we outlined six of the major theories of motivation. Each have their own unique interpretation of why people perform the way they do. In each theory, pay is seen as an important element of the reward system. Nevertheless, it is interesting to note the different interpretations offered by each theory as to why pay is important. Table 5.2 illustrates the concept of pay according to the various schools of thought.

Summary   Theories of motivation are appealing at the intuitive level but, when subject to analysis, none appears to offer substantial empirical evidence as to their efficacy. Content theories are possibly more useful at identifying basic values and needs in human beings than as theories of motivation. Even here, there is an untenable assumption of homogeneity in all content theories. All people do not have identical needs in an identical pattern. Recourse to Sayles's (1963) study of a variety of work groups points out that Herzberg's theories might well apply to many managers and to achievement-oriented work groups, but it is inapplicable to apathetic or conservative work groups which want to remain as they are.

Extending motivation theories into choice behaviours, rather than studying individual needs, merely complicates the issue even further. Expectancy theory and its derivatives make sweeping assumptions about causality and about individuals' capacities to specify future desired states clearly, in rank order and without ambiguity. Furthermore, even if this were possible, the degree of change or restructuring required in both organizations and individuals which would have to take place to accommodate motivation through process theories is unrealistic to achieve in practice.

It is likely that any single or unified theory of motivation is impossible to articulate. Individuals themselves are complex enough in their needs, values, beliefs, perceptions and attitudes. Add to these the additional factors of an individual's interaction with an organization and the analysis of what motivates him or her becomes very complex indeed.

Nevertheless, theories of motivation lie at the heart of much organizational practice. Equity theory can be seen in action in the guise of pay bargaining, for example. It is often assumed by both trades unions and management that achieving parity in pay across various sectors will achieve equity and will lead to increased productivity and performance. Herzberg underpins virtually every job enrichment or satisfaction approach, while Maslow has permeated at all levels from health and safety at work to the self-actualizing need of creative leaders, currently fashionable in the management literature.

References   Adams, J. S. (1963) 'Toward an understanding of inequity', *Journal of Abnormal and Social Psychology*, **67**, 422–36.

Hackman, J. R., G. Oldham, R. Janson and K. Purdy (1975) 'A new strategy for job enrichment', *California Management Review*, **15**(3), 96–7.

Herzberg, F., Mausner, B. and B. Snyderman (1959) *The Motivation to Work*, Wiley, New York.

House, R. J. and L. A. Wigdor (1967) 'Herzberg's dual factor theory of job satisfaction and motivation: a review of the evidence and a criticism', *Personnel Psychology*, **20**(4), 369–89.

Lawler, E. E. and L. W. Porter (1978) 'The effect of performance on job satisfaction', in D. W. Organ (ed.), *The Applied Psychology of Work Behavior: A Book of Readings*, Business Publications, Dallas, Texas.

Lawler, E. E. and J. L. Suttle (1972) 'A causal correlational test of the need hierarchy concept', *Organizational Behavior and Human Performance*, April, 265–87.

McClelland, D. C. (1961) *The Achieving Society*, Free Press, New York.

Maslow, A. H. (1943) 'A theory of human motivation', *Psychological Review*, **50**(4), 370–96.

Maslow, A. H. (1970) *Motivation and Personality*, 2nd edn, Harper & Row, New York.

Rauschenberger, J., N. Schmitt and J. Hunter (1980) 'A test of the need hierarchy concept by a Markov model of change in need strength', *Administrative Science Quarterly*, **25**(4), 654–70.

Sayles, L. R. (1963) *Behavior of Industrial Workgroups*, Wiley, New York.

Schermerhorn, J. R., Hunt, J. G. and R. N. Osborn (1982) *Managing Organizational Behavior*, Wiley, New York.

Schneider, J. and E. A. Locke (1971) 'A critique of Herzberg's incident classification system', *Organizational Behavior and Human Performance* **6**, 441–57.

Steers, R. M. and L. W. Porter (1979) *Motivation and Work Behavior*, McGraw-Hill, New York.

Thorndike, E. L. (1911) *Animal Intelligence*, Macmillan, New York.

Vroom, V. H. (1964) *Work and Motivation*, Wiley, New York.

CHAPTER 6

Applying concepts of learning and motivation: behaviour modification

Introduction

Behaviour modification (BM) is the attempt to try and control individual behaviour by systematically reinforcing those behaviours deemed to be desirable. It thus draws heavily upon concepts of learning, reinforcement and conditioning. Many texts in psychology deal in depth with these concepts (see, for example, Hilgard, Atkinson and Atkinson, 1975). In this chapter we shall only touch upon these debates. Our major concern is to illustrate the role of BM in work organizations. First, we must examine the basic building blocks of BM, learning, reinforcement and conditioning.

Learning, reinforcement and conditioning

The concept of learning is so common that many people take it for granted and rarely stop to think about how it is accomplished. Learning is a crucial component of BM. Without learning, there would be no reason to expend energy on changing behaviour patterns. In very general terms, it is through learning that behaviour is modified. As one would expect there are countless definitions for learning. One working definition is that: *learning is a relatively permanent change in behaviour that results from reinforced practice or experience.* The implication is that if the reinforcement process can be controlled, then learning can also be controlled. Learning can be subdivided into two distinct processes: learning through insights and latent learning.

Learning through insights

Learning through insights involves three stages. First, one must understand a particular situation and identify what the problem is which needs to be solved. The second stage requires some thinking about the problem and its context. During this time, no learning may be apparent as one searches for a potential solution. The third stage is the brilliant flash when a solution becomes evident. A feature of learning through insights is that solutions derived in this manner are frequently used in a variety of other situations as well. Once a solution has been found, it is continually tried to resolve other problems. This can also have important negative effects upon creativity in decision-making (see Chapter 10).

Latent learning

Latent learning is slightly more complex. It derives from the ability to use knowledge from past experience to guide behaviour in a totally new situation. Latent learning is the accumulation of knowledge which does not have any immediate regard but which, in a particular context, can be recalled to guide behaviour.

Reinforcement

Reinforcement is the process through which certain consequences strengthen behaviour. Consequences which encourage particular behaviour are called reinforcers. Behaviour is *positively reinforced* when positive consequences are applied or accepted. Behaviour is *negatively reinforced* when negative consequences are applied or accepted. In a similar manner, behaviour can be *extinguished* when positive consequences are withheld.

Positive reinforcement is a strategy of accentuating the positive in order to eliminate the negative. By complimenting an individual on a success and/or providing some other form of recognition, the successful behaviour may be strengthened and be more likely to re-occur. Positive reinforcement can be material (pay, promotion, privileges), verbal (compliments) and non-verbal (a smile, paying attention).

Negative reinforcement means inducing desired behaviour by withdrawing a particular undesirable condition upon improved performance. For example, if an employee works harder to prevent his or her boss from nagging, then negative reinforcement has occurred (Luthans and Kreitner, 1974). One way to consider negative reinforcement is as a type of 'blackmail' (Luthans, 1981). The principle is that people will behave in a particular way to avoid punishment.

Extinction means that an identifiable behaviour can be stopped if a particular reinforcement is withheld. For example, if a crying child is ignored and the behaviour eventually stops, then extinction has occurred. If people refuse to laugh at off-colour or racist jokes, then the behaviour of telling such jokes will eventually be extinguished. In work organizations, it is difficult to incorporate extinction as any deliberate policy. The problem is that by withholding reinforcement, the undesired behaviour may increase in the hope of regaining attention. A result could simply be further escalation of the situation.

Punishment should not be confused with negative reinforcement. Negative reinforcement increases the frequency of a desired behaviour, while punishment is intended to decrease the frequency of undesired behaviour. Punishment involves the imposition of a negative consequence upon a particular response. Since negative outcomes tend to be avoided, this should reduce the likelihood that the undesired behaviour will re-occur. Alternatively, punishment can also mean the withdrawal of a pleasant consequence. The theory is that if an individual values a particular consequence, the withholding of it is a punishment and has the effect of decreasing the likelihood of the undesired behaviour happening again. To be effective, punishment tactics should observe the following five points (Hellreigel, Slocum and Woodman, 1983):

1 Tell the person what he or she has specifically done wrong.
2 Tell the person what is right. This is an attempt positively to reinforce correct behaviour.
3 The punishment should follow as soon after the undesired behaviour as possible.
4 Punish in private, praise in public.
5 Be fair, make the punishment fit the 'crime'.

Conditioning

Though the two terms are frequently interchanged, conditioning is not the same thing as learning. Conditioning is the *process* by which learning occurs. Learning is the *result* of conditioning. Conditioning describes the various reactions to an individual's behaviour, and the modifying effect these reactions have upon the individual's behaviour in the future. If the person's behaviour changes, then we can say that the individual has been conditioned. There are two basic types of conditioning process, *classical* and *operant* conditioning.

Classical conditioning

The most famous demonstration of classical conditioning was conducted by the Russian physiologist Ivan Pavlov in the 1880s. Pavlov had noticed that dogs began to salivate at the sight of food. To test this reaction, Pavlov constructed an experiment in which a bell was rung shortly before the dog was given food. After this procedure had been followed for a number of times, Pavlov found that he was able to trigger the dog's salivation just by ringing the bell. The conclusion was that Pavlov was able to induce a reflex action by providing a particular stimulus. In terms of classical conditioning, this can be expressed as:

Prior to conditioning

An unconditioned stimulus (i.e. food)
caused
an unconditioned response (i.e. salivation)
At this stage, ringing a bell would be a neutral stimulus
(i.e. it would have no effect at all)

After conditioning

A conditioned stimulus (i.e. ringing the bell)
caused
a conditioned response of salivation
(irrespective of food being present)

Classical conditioning appears to explain a number of behaviours. For example, phobias can be argued to be the conditioned response to an early childhood trauma. In advertising, many television commercials use imagery which has less to do with the product and more to do with implanting a favourable image into the consumer's mind. For example, the strikingly beautiful scenery used in many automobile advertisements triggers a subconscious connection between the car (the product) and scenic beauty (image) even if the majority of driving will be along congested urban roads!

Generalization can also occur. A similar, though unrelated stimulus brings out a conditioned response. With Pavlov's hungry hound, it was found that salivation occurred (to a lesser extent) at the sound of a metronome as well as a bell. Commercially, this occurs regularly. For example, individuals have a response to particular product brand names. A good (or bad) experience with a product made by one manufacturer would very likely provide the consumer with a conditioned response to the manufacturer's entire product range.

Operant conditioning

Classical conditioning is the study of how particular stimuli affect responses, S→R. Operant conditioning looks at the process of responses affecting stimuli, R→S. This has become known as the 'Skinnerian' approach after the work of the psychologist B. F. Skinner (see Skinner, 1961, for example).

Operant conditioning imitates the process of evolution. This is achieved by patiently waiting for a particular response (R) and then rewarding the person with a stimulus (S) to reinforce the continued behaviour. The underlying theory is that behaviour is strengthened or weakened by its consequences. The classic experiment used by Skinner to demonstrate this effect was to place a hungry rat in a box which contained a lever. When the lever was pressed, a pellet of food would drop into the box. When first placed in the box, the rat would explore and eventually, by chance, it would press the lever. Skinner found that the rat would then press the lever more and more frequently to obtain the food.

In work organizations, Skinner's work has specific implications. By controlling the consequences of particular actions, it is possible to change people's behaviour. By strengthening, maintaining or reducing the consequences of particular activities, the likelihood of a behaviour can be altered. Hamner and Hamner (1976) and Luthans and Kreitner (1974; 1975) have related Skinner's ideas to a number of work organizations in North America and results are significant. Both approaches are very similar. They involve a step-by-step analysis of performance-related behaviours and the application of a managerial strategy to motivate and to reinforce changes in individuals' behaviour.

Hamner and Hamner's positive reinforcement programme

1 Management sets organizational goals for each worker. These are reasonable, attainable, focus on behaviour and are measurable.
2 Each individual keeps a record of job performance so that the relationship between the organizational goal and actual performance is clear.
3 The manager identifies behaviour which appears to be associated with positive performance and rewards this (by praise, for example). Negative behaviour/performance links are not criticized. The absence of praise is sufficient for negative reinforcement and is argued to prevent the individual feeling overly controlled. The key to this approach is the extrinsic approach to applying concepts of motivation. Praise leads to a desire for more praise and to the further achievement of performance-related goals.

Luthans and Kreitner's behavioural contingency management model

1 Identify the particular behaviours which are necessary for good job performance. These are those behaviours which may take up relatively little effort or time for an individual, but which are very effective for performance. These are called critical behaviours.
2 Measure both the strength and the frequency of such behaviours by keeping a record.
3 Where changes are necessary, managers should design an intervention strategy to achieve the desired behaviours. This will involve the explicit giving of rewards to individuals or groups and may also involve changes to work design, organizational structure, etc. This model applies rewards as motivators. It thus pays little attention to the more perceptually based theories of expectancy in motivation (see Chapter 5). Typical rewards are shown in Table 6.1.
4 The new state should be subject to constant monitoring to sustain the behaviour modification.

Table 6.1
Typical rewards to support behaviour modification in work organizations

Work Design	Social	Institutional
Private office	Free lunches	Preferential services (e.g. cheap loans)
Redecoration	Pub/wine bar get-togethers	Profit sharing
Provision of windows/music	Friendly greetings	Free membership of private schemes (e.g. health insurance)
Action on suggestions	Informal recognition	Share ownership schemes
Job rotation	Public praise	Use of firm's recreation facilities (e.g. sport's grounds)

The above methods of modification rely heavily upon the processes of *shaping* and *modelling*.

Shaping

Shaping involves taking a large, complex task and breaking it down into small components. Each of the components can then be taught separately until the entire sequence has been learned. Shaping is the way we learn to walk, ride bicycles, play tennis, etc.

In organizations, shaping involves the application of positive reinforcements as the individual becomes increasingly adept at each step of the learning process. The role of a manager in a shaping process is that of a teacher, a coach or helper. Rather than saying what was wrong, the 'shaping' manager will clarify how to do a task correctly. When the individual has completed the task, some appropriate reinforcement is provided (praise or other reward) and then the next sequential step is attempted.

Modelling

Though related to the concept of shaping, modelling adopts a different method of communicating the desired behaviour to the individual. The basis of modelling is to illustrate the 'ideal' form of behaviour and then ask individuals to model themselves along the same lines. Positive reinforcement is provided as individuals become more adept at imitating the desired behaviour.

There are a wide number of ways to use modelling in organizations. Training exercises which involve role-playing as well as other forms of feedback-oriented exercises (such as experiential learning) all incorporate some form of modelling.

Applications and limitations of behaviour modification

To many people, the term behaviour modification implies manipulation, coercive control and other 'Orwellian' management methods (see Robertson and Cooper, 1983). Others have argued that theories based upon simple stimulus–response relationships (getting dogs to salivate at the sound of a bell, chickens to ring bells and mice to run mazes) are overly simplistic and inapplicable in organizations.

Behaviourists and cognitive psychologists fundamentally disagree about putting BM into practice in organizations.

Behavioural psychologists   argue that all behaviour is learned through a process of experiencing rewards and punishments. Individuals can learn to do something without necessarily being motivated to act voluntarily.

Cognitive psychologists   argue that individuals think before they act. Therefore the key to modifying behaviour lies in motivation. Learning can be achieved by motivating individuals to act in particular ways (see Locke, 1977).

It is likely that neither of the above views are right, but that the truth is contained in both statements. We know from Chapters 3 and 4 that we can better understand behaviour from examining both the individual and the context or situation. Behaviour modification is central to this interaction between person and context.

Despite academic scepticism, behaviour modification seems to have been extremely successful, especially in North American organizations such as B. F. Goodrich, General Electric, Collins Food, Standard Oil Ohio and Emery Air Freight. In Britain, behaviour modification has seen some success in safety and hygiene applications. Getting people to wear protective clothing and masks both for their own safety and for the safety of others has never been easy, especially where there are no direct penalties for not conforming. By changing management styles and giving rewards for wearing protective clothing, etc., its acceptance has become far more widespread. In the food industry, this was also reinforced by increased legislation on cleanliness in the workplace, so differentiating cause and effect in this case becomes difficult.

Summary   Behaviour modification in work organizations is the process in which performance-related behaviours are identified and managed; desirable behaviours are strengthened and undesirable behaviours are weakened. This process is contingent upon reinforcement and conditioning.

The controversy surrounding the use of BM techniques in organizational settings has become intense in recent years (see Locke, 1977; Gray, 1979; Locke, 1979). Views on BM tend to be at either of two extremes: for it or against it. The cognitive theorists propose that individuals engage in complex thought processes before behaviour occurs. Behaviourists have tended to exclude the issue of thinking from their model. Another criticism is that BM focuses attention on explaining behaviour rather than predicting it. Champions of BM respond that the observation of how people respond to environmental stimulus provides the most important clues to how they will respond in the future.

There are four primary concerns upon which critics of BM have focused their energies. They are:

1 *Control*   These are the ethical issues raised when managers are provided with tools designed to control subordinates. Managers themselves can often feel uncomfortable with the thought of having control over someone else's behaviour. There is a large element of authoritarianism built into BM. It presumes that the controllers of behaviour (the shapers, the modellers, the reinforcers and the punishers) all have unquestioned control and authority.

2 *Reinforcements*   Successful BM is limited by the degree to which the manager can control the reinforcements. If a manager can not influence events which the employee finds rewarding, then the manager will not have much influence over employee behaviour. Managers are often restricted in the extent to which they can alter the level of pay scales and benefits, or make decisions about promotions or disciplinary procedures, for example.

3 *Group behaviour*   BM tends to focus on the level of the individual. However, group demands may conflict. For example, suppose an employee's job is altered to provide for greater responsibility and it is expected that this will result in the individual's working harder and achieving greater job satisfaction. This outcome may conflict with a workgroup norm which might exist that restricts the actual amount of work which someone does. From the employee's perspective, a decision has to be made regarding the relative attractiveness of the two conflicting reinforcements—job satisfaction or group acceptance.

4 *Identification*   BM has consistently focused upon lower hierarchical levels. Little research has been conducted at more senior managerial levels. Also, managers are often unable to identify what employees find reinforcing (Kerr, 1975). While there are many things which might be favoured by the employee (more pay, benefits, etc.), it is possible that these do not function to reinforce the desired behaviour. Unfortunately, a manager cannot just ask the employee what the best reinforcer might be—there is no guarantee that the answer will be complete or even correct. There are many reasons why this is so. Individuals may feel foolish to admit the things that they most desire or they may distrust the manager's motives. In the final analysis, the best way to isolate effective reinforcers is to deduce what the employee has responded to in the past. To do so consistently requires managers to be acutely aware of the problems of cause and effect—which is, essentially, the problem in the first place!

References   Gray, J. L. (1979) 'The myths of the myths about behaviour mod in organizations: a reply to Locke's criticisms of behaviour modification', *Academy of Management Review*, **4**(1), 121–9.

Hamner, W. C. and E. P. Hamner (1976) 'Behaviour modification on the bottom line', *Organizational Dynamics*, **4**, 3–21.

Hellriegel, D., J. Slocum and R. Woodman (1983) *Organizational Behavior*, 3rd edn, West Publishing, St Paul, Minn.

Hilgard, E. R., R. C. S. Atkinson and R. L. Atkinson (1975) *Introduction to Psychology*, 6th edn, Harcourt Brace, New York.

Kerr, S. (1975) 'On the folly of rewarding A, while hoping for B', *Academy of Management Journal*, **18**(4), 769–83.

Locke, E. A. (1977) 'The myth of behaviour modelling in organizations', *Academy of Management Review*, **2**(4), 543–53.

Locke, E. A. (1979) 'Myths in the myths of the myths of behaviour mod in organizations', *Academy of Management Review*, **4**(1), 131–6.

Luthans, F. (1981) *Organizational Behaviour*, 3rd edn, McGraw-Hill, New York.

Luthans, F. and R. Kreitner (1974) 'The management of behavioural contingencies', *Personnel*, July–August, 7–16.

Luthans, F. and R. Kreitner (1975) *Organizational Behavior Modification*, Scott, Foresman, Glenview, Illinois.

Robertson, I. T. and C. L. Cooper (1983) *Human Behavior in Organisations*, MacDonald & Evans, Plymouth.

Skinner, B. F. (1961) *Analysis of Behavior*, McGraw-Hill, New York.

CHAPTER 7
Structural modification: job design, goal setting and work scheduling

Introduction

In contrast to *ex*trinsic rewards which are the central focus of most motivation theories, structural modification refers to those rewards which are *in*trinsic. That is, they come from the job itself. The ways in which jobs are organized, therefore, will also have an effect upon whether they motivate or de-motivate individuals. Although, whether or not a job provides adequate rewards for an individual will depend ultimately on perception to a great extent, there have been a number of attempts to alter the structure of jobs in an attempt to increase intrinsic rewards and to increase job satisfaction. These include the design of jobs, job simplification, job enlargement and enrichment as well as work scheduling. We explore each of these in turn in this chapter.

There appear to be two broad distinctions in the literature on structural modification. Early theories were concerned with individual tasks (typically routine or shop floor jobs) and focused on increasing both efficiency and the level of reward from individual tasks. Later theories were more concerned with examining how jobs fitted into the wider context of individual's lifestyles (typically flexible working hours to suit family and other commitments). Both approaches argue that motivation arises primarily from doing the job itself, rather than for any external incentive controlled by management. Aldag and Brief (1977) note how individuals may receive quite low salary levels, but receive immense satisfaction from their jobs. Teachers or some volunteer workers would fit into this category. Other intrinsic rewards could come from taking pride in doing a good job. Some craftsmen are an example of this. Finally, helping others without expecting commensurate rewards oneself (altruism) may account for intrinsic work rewards above all other motivating factors. However, managing structural modification is neither easy in itself nor is it free from ideological bias. Managers who view labour antagonistically and as needing to be controlled will manage staff very differently to the humanistic, egalitarian manager, (Braverman, 1974).

Job design: a theory of intrinsic rewards

As Umstot, Bell and Mitchell (1976) note, job design involves the deliberate, purposeful planning of the job. This means not only perhaps re-arranging how tasks are done (their sequence, for example) but also involves examining how more social or informal aspects of the job might affect perceived rewards and satisfaction. The question of who designs and plans particular jobs has long been a central question in organization theory. Leaving this solely to management implies that workers should have little say over how their jobs are organized. Empirical evidence points to the ability of many workers to organize and design their own jobs (see Socio-technical systems, Chapter 2) with varying degrees of help from management. Results appear to indicate that where individuals have the autonomy to design their own jobs (within the limits of feasibility) then both job satisfaction and job performance levels increase.

Yet, early days of job design took a different view, arguing that jobs should be standardized and mechanized as far as possible. This was called job simplification.

Job simplification: Taylorism

Job simplification emphasizes the reduction of a job to its component parts, and then a reassembly of these parts into an optimally efficient work process. Deeply rooted in the tradition of scientific management (Taylor, 1911; see Chapter 2), job simplification emphasizes the following features:

1 mechanical pacing, or the use of an automated assembly line to monitor the speed of production (Walker and Guest, 1952);
2 repetitive work processes, or designing the work so that individuals replicate the same tasks;
3 concentration on only a fraction of the product; for example, in automobile manufacturing, one individual might mount the wheel of the stub axle assembly, while another might place the hub cap on the wheel;
4 predetermination of tools and techniques; that is, describing and prescribing the work process as precisely as possible;
5 limited social interaction among the labour force;
6 low skill requirements, or breaking the job down into specific and relatively simple tasks that require minimal training.

Typically, the implementation of work simplification uses industrial-engineering methods. To begin, industrial engineers study the exact series of motions in a job, using detailed observation records and drawing extensive diagrams of the work process. Next, they monitor the time required for each part of the job. Third, they identify and then attempt to eliminate all false, slow and useless movements. Finally, they redesign the job by collecting into a series the quickest and best movements. To accomplish the last step, work simplification typically involves a high use of machines, maximum spacing of rest periods, high specialization of work activities, and matching of workers to jobs best suited to their abilities, experience and aptitudes.

Jobs which stand to gain most from simplification tend to be those influenced by rapidly changing technology. It is likely that some fully automated manufacturing processes will simplify jobs in the extreme. Workers will become machine minders, baby-sitters of the factory floor. On the other hand, some workers (but by no means all) prefer less complex jobs. Only diagnosis of a specific situation can determine the functional or dysfunctional nature of job simplification.

Typical dysfunctions are: worker boredom, limited opportunities for individual growth, and mechanization for its own sake. The costs of task segmentation that must be overcome include:

1 moving and repositioning items between operations;
2 assembling separate tasks into a more efficient total process;
3 balancing the line to reduce down-time; and
4 providing additional external supervision and work pacing (Emery, 1975).

Table 7.1 summarizes some of the advantages and disadvantages commonly associated with job simplification.

Job enlargement

Taylorism and job simplification was to have an immense influence over the organization of jobs which lasted virtually throughout two world wars. It was in the immediate post-Second World War period that the implications of boredom and repetition became increasingly apparent especially in machine-

Table 7.1
Expected advantages
and disadvantages of
machine-paced
assembly lines

Potential advantages	Potential disadvantages
Increased economy because: • Jobs require little training • Jobs staffed by low-skilled people • Workers interchangeable among jobs • Production quality and quantity easily controlled	Economy gains not realized because: • Absenteeism high • Turnover high • High wages required to attract workers • Production quality suffers because workers become bored and frustrated

Source: adapted from Lawler (1973).

paced technologies (see Table 7.1). In place of job simplification, enlarging jobs involved the re-combination of what were previously separate tasks. This proved popular with managers of the era, especially since it effected quite substantial changes in the jobs carried out by workers but largely left the rest of the organization unchanged (e.g. its overall structure, the number of functions etc.).

Where jobs proved difficult to enlarge, perhaps because technologies such as assembly lines prevented re-combining tasks, the solution of job rotation was a second alternative. This involved workers performing a variety of tasks rather than just one and switching between them at pre-set intervals. Again, this had the advantage of keeping the structure of the organization constant whilst changing the ways in which tasks were performed within it. The practice persists today in the guise of cross-functional work, especially for managers. Yet, one outcome of job rotation experiments was to demoralize staff further, since it often only added one meaningless job to another (Herzberg, 1968).

Job enrichment

Widespread demoralization of staff led to a further search for alternative ways to make work more interesting and intrinsically satisfying. Recourse to motivation theories appeared to come up with the answer. Expectancy theories (see Chapter 5) were to be the basis for the *job characteristics model* widely reported by Hackman *et al.* (1975). Herzberg's (1968) theory of motivation was to provide a second source of enriching jobs by allowing workers more autonomy and responsibility in their daily tasks (see Table 7.2). First, we list the main features of the job characteristics model.

This model focuses on the features of the job itself, identifying five core characteristics relevant to motivation and satisfying workers who perform the task. The characteristics include aspects of the job itself (the task) as well as the processes by which the job is carried out (e.g. responsibility and autonomy). A job high on all the core characteristics is argued to be enriched. The five characteristics are:

The task
1 *Identity* The extent to which the task is one meaningful piece of work. The worker can see tangible beginning and end points to his or her job.
2 *Significance* The extent to which the task directly affects the jobs of others within or outside the organization.
3 *Variety* The extent to which the task employs different skills and abilities of each worker. In common parlance, the job becomes challenging.

The Worker
4 *Autonomy* The extent to which the individual can exercise discretion over how the job is performed (e.g. in time scheduling or over which tools to use).

Table 7.2
The principles of job enrichment

Principle	Motivators involved
1 Remove some controls while retaining accountability.	Responsibility and achievement.
2 Increase the accountability for individuals for their own work.	Responsibility and recognition.
3 Give a person a complete natural unit of work (module, division, area).	Responsibility, achievement and recognition.
4 Grant additional authority to an employee in his/her activity, provide job freedom.	Responsibility, recognition and achievement.
5 Make periodic reports directly available to the worker rather than the supervisor.	Recognition
6 Introduce new and more difficult tasks not previously handled.	Growth and learning
7 Assign individuals specific tasks, enable them to become experts.	Responsibility, growth, and advancement

Source: Herzberg (1968).

5 *Feedback* The extent to which the individual receives direct information concerning how effectively the task has been performed.

According to the job characteristics model, high scores on the core characteristics lead to conditions which promote high levels of task motivation, performance and satisfaction. Designing in the five features to jobs, therefore, increases the likelihood that performance and job satisfaction will benefit (Hackman *et al.*, 1975). Table 7.1 depicts extreme cases of job enrichment and their effects upon individuals.

The basis of these assumptions is that the more individuals experience that their work is meaningful, the greater is their motivation to work and the more satisfaction they receive from working. This is achieved by creating a job over which they have responsibility and can see a tangible outcome from their efforts. Empirical evidence to support the theory is relatively scarce. Brief and

Figure 7.1
Growth needs and the 'core' job characteristics

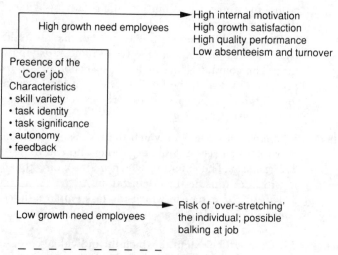

Source: adapted from: Hackman *et al.* (1975)

Aldag (1975) summarize job enrichment studies which had been carried out in a variety of organizational settings (perhaps the most well known involved the jobs of female telephone operators). Others included studies of financial service organizations and dental practices. The results, however, indicated that whilst some success was achieved along the predicted dimensions, other factors led to confound the results. Individuals became anxious about their job security, for example, and unforeseen difficulties arose because other people's jobs not in the experiment were affected. In general, more managers than workers agreed that job enrichment had been successful.

Implications of job design

No single job design is ideal for every person. Any effort at redesign, therefore, must take into account individual differences. A blanket approach to redesign is unlikely to be effective since:

> The object of job redesign is to ensure a closer fit between individuals and their jobs, and to meet both the needs of the individual and those of the organization.

Efforts towards achieving this integration are evident in the job characteristics model—it states explicitly that the impact of the core job dimensions on personal and work outcomes is moderated by employee-growth need strength. The greater this need, the more likely it is that the employee will obtain meaningfulness from the job when the core job dimensions are present.

However, a number of other individual difference factors have been suggested which influence the potential success of job redesign (Wanous, 1974). The age of the employees should be considered. Younger workers tend to accept change more readily. Older employees tend to prefer more repetitive jobs because they have made the adjustment to them and know how to do them well. Education may also be relevant. Generally, the higher the employee's education, the greater the preference for autonomous and challenging jobs. Similarly, self-assurance has shown success as a moderator. The greater the self-confidence, the greater assurance the employee has that he or she can learn more exciting tasks. Individuals who favour the Protestant work ethic—hard work, efficient time utilization, assumption of responsibility—can also be expected to accept redesign options more readily.

Although often overlooked by zealous advocates of job redesign, some individuals are actually happier with repetitive and monotonous jobs. When given the opportunity to assume a job with demanding and rewarding tasks, some individuals will opt to remain in their highly repetitive and low-skill jobs. These individuals do not have the strong needs for growth and autonomy or have chosen to satisfy their needs away from the workplace. Many workers look to their jobs as providing the means to allow them to do more gratifying activities outside the work context (Terkel, 1972). To ignore this diversity in the workforce is foolhardy. Efforts to redesign everyone's job in an organization to improve its motivation potential will undoubtedly lead to making some people less happy and less productive.

Goal-setting

Much management time is spent on determining what are appropriate organizational goals and how to get individuals to work towards their achievements. Edwin Locke (1968) is one of the organizational researchers who has devoted a substantial effort in understanding the various components of goal-setting. Locke argued that well-selected and communicated goals can, in themselves, be a motivating factor for employees. This principle underlies much of the work done on such techniques as Management By Objectives (MBO).

According to Locke, effort expended by individuals in undertaking a desired set of behaviours is a function of four properties of the goals themselves:

1   *Difficulty*   This is the extent to which an individual sees goals as challenging but achievable.
2   *Specificity*   The greater the precision in defining the goals, the more likely it is that individuals will understand how (and when) they should achieve them.
3   *Acceptance*   The degree to which an individual accepts the goals as ones which they would like to achieve.
4   *Commitment*   The individual is committed to achieving these goals and undertakes, on their own initiative, actions to fulfil this aim.

The principles of goal-setting are closely aligned to theories of motivation. For example, expectancy theory suggests that goals are more likely to be accepted if they are seen as attainable (high expectancy) and that the desired outcome for the individual will clearly result (high instrumentality) (Latham and Ukl, 1975).

Working in groups: self-regulation and autonomy

This aspect of job redesign owes a lot to the work of researchers in the socio-technical school of organization theory (see Chapter 2). Socio-technical redesign complements the other approaches described so far. It responds specifically to the difficulty of introducing new technology into a work system effectively. Researchers at the Tavistock Institute were among the first to note the negative impact of new technology on worker productivity and satisfaction. In both the coal-mining (Trist and Bamforth, 1951) and textile weaving industries (Rice, 1958), the introduction of a new technology conflicted with a strong work culture and social system. Automobile manufacturers experienced similar resistance to the increasing automation of the assembly line, resulting in greater absenteeism, increased sabotage, and lowered productivity (Gyllenhammar, 1977).

To combat such problems, Scandinavian automobile manufacturers (Saab and Volvo), introduced the concept of autonomous workgroups for meeting workers' social needs while introducing technological innovation into work. These workgroups controlled their own task assignments and the division of labour within the group.

Volvo and Saab also introduced self-regulating groups, in which employees who perform interdependent tasks work in a common unit (Cummings, 1978). Such work design requires that the workers have the ability to regulate and control their tasks to influence their transaction with the environment, and to differentiate themselves from other groups sufficiently to form a whole. Self-regulating groups perform many roles traditionally assigned to management, such as making job assignments and determining work processes.

The introduction of autonomous or self-regulating work groups had a significant impact. In 1975, for example, a specially built Volvo plant operated at 100 per cent efficiency, as compared to 80 per cent in other plants which were not so redesigned (Huse, 1980). In the mining industry, productivity rose from 78 per cent to 95 per cent (Trist and Bamforth, 1951) and in the weaving industry, from 80 per cent to 95 per cent with a substantial drop in labour turnover in both cases.

Alternative work schedules

Another way work settings may be modified is to rearrange work schedules. There are a variety of different ways to do so. Four of the more common alternatives to the traditional eight hours per day/five days per week working are provided below:

1 Restructured work week
2 Flexible work hours
3 Job sharing
4 Career breaks

Each of these approaches shares a common concern for making the work day and its time requirements more compatible with individual needs and non-work activities.

For many people, one of the more attractive attributes of the increased flexibility in work schedules is the opportunity to restructure the required amount of work hours over as many or as few days in the week as one would like. Most academic attention in this area has gone towards the consideration of the effects of compressing five days of work into a shorter period (Cohen and Gadon, 1978). Most often this is referred to as the 4–40 week. This signifies that the standard forty hours of work per week is squeezed into four days instead of five. Such a reduction in the number of working days in a week can have both positive and negative consequences, as Table 7.3 illustrates.

Table 7.3
Benefits and disadvantages of a compressed working-week schedule

	Organizations	Individuals
Benefits	Reduced employee turnover Improved productivity Attractiveness to recruits	Job satisfaction Greater opportunity for leisure
Disadvantages	'Who works Friday' syndrome Fulfilling customer requirements Trade union suspicion	Tiredness Safety at risk Family difficulties

Source: Adapted from Cohen and Gadon (1978).

The alternative to a shortened work week is an extended one. This occurs when an individual makes a commitment to work a particular number of hours (or complete a particular task) within an agreed time. Within these constraints, the individual can spread the work over as many or as few days as he or she likes. One example of this is with homeworkers. These are individuals who essentially work from home for their employer. These individuals are free to work whatever hours and days they might wish — as long as the job is done on time. This is most frequently seen in occupations where computers play a large part in completing the job and in communicating with others, i.e. programmers, word processors, etc.

Flexible work hours also offer employees a degree of control over their hours worked. *Flexitime*, as it has come to be called, essentially shares responsibility for defining appropriate hours of work in a day between the employee and the organization. By offering individual employees some scope for control over their work hours, an organization is also offering a higher degree of job autonomy. Research undertaken in the United States has indicated that flexitime is an effective motivation strategy (Cohen and Gadon, 1978). Figure 7.2 illustrates a typical implementation of the practice.

To implement flexitime, a working day is broken down into two types:

Figure 7.2
A sample flexible
working hours
scheme

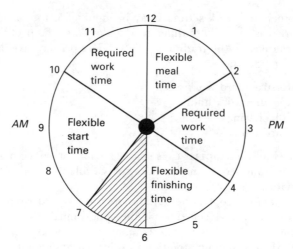

flexible and core. The organization may set a condition that all employees must be at their stations during the core times, but they can select a personal schedule within the flexible time periods to suit themselves. There are numerous advantages accruing to this form of work scheduling (Golembiewski and Priehl, 1978). For the organization, allowing for greater employee flexibility could reduce absenteeism and turnover as well as improve job motivation. For the individual, advantages include flexibility to accommodate any personal needs, ability to avoid travelling through peak commuting times, and a greater sense of control over the job itself.

Job sharing occurs when two (or more) people decide to take on a full-time job, splitting the hours worked between themselves. For example, an office receptionist's job might be split so that one person comes in at 8.00 am to do the task until 12.30 pm. Then a second person takes over and continues the job until 5.00 pm. Such sharing of a work schedule could appeal to people who only wish to work part-time. The organization can then benefit from the contribution of people who may not otherwise have worked for them. In addition to the potential sharing within a single working day, it is also feasible to share a job over longer time periods:

Split day	One job sharer works in the morning, another in the afternoon
Half-week	Both sharers work for two and a half days per week
3 day/2 day	Each job sharer works 3 days one week, two days next week
Week on/off	Each job sharer alternates work weeks

Job sharing is becoming more widespread in Britain, particularly in the public sector. In the private sector, the pressure of demographic trends is likely to increase its use. Some of the organizations which have begun to use such flexible working practices are shown in Table 7.4.

Work schedules and demographic trends

It is likely that most organizations will be forced to think about alternative job schedules. A report by the NEDO/Training Commission (1988) indicates that by 1995 the number of young people in the British labour market will have fallen by 1.2 million, a drop of 20 per cent. The overall size of the labour force will increase by 900 000 (to 1995) with 80 per cent of this being women, many of

Table 7.4
Organizations which
have recently
introduced flexible
working schemes

Part-time working	Job sharing
Boots plc	Boots plc
Fisons	British Telecom
London Weekend Television	Irish Civil Service
Racal Defence Systems	BBC
Stearns Catalytic International	Pedigree Pet Foods
Selfridges	Fox's Biscuits
Borough of Islington	GEC Telecommunications
Royal Bank of Scotland	Dixons
Freemans	
Burtons	
Radio Televis Eirean	
Norvik Press	
Roberts and Partners	
CPM Sales and Promotion	
Term-time contracts	Homeworking (data processing)
Boots plc	Rank Xerox
Dixons	ICL
Carlsberg Brewery	
Crest Hotels	
Royal Bank of Scotland	
Midland Bank	

whom will be seeking re-entry into the labour market having had their families. Job schedules will now have to accommodate the needs of a mother with young children. Firms which neglect to do this will face a severe competitive disadvantage. Career breaks are one way of re-scheduling work to these ends and has been successfully implemented by a number of companies.

Career breaks

This allows employees to take a break from a job for a specific time (usually 2 to 5 years). They then return to work at the same level or grade. Employment is guaranteed on return, but is supported by a training programme which brings knowledge and experience up to date. This scheme needs a good level of communication between the organization and the individual throughout the career break, especially to keep in touch with organizational changes. Advantages include:

- savings on recruitment and selection by obviating the need to advertise for staff who, without the scheme, would have left the organization permanently;
- reduction in skill shortages;
- retention of skilled and experienced staff;
- maintains a smoother flow of potential successors to senior positions;
- provides the opportunity of getting good quality applicants in the first place. Firms which offer career break schemes will be more competitively placed to attract good staff;
- can help reduce stress and absenteeism;
- provides a role model for other females in the organization for the successful combination of career and family.

Table 7.5 lists eight examples of career-break schemes in British organizations.

Table 7.5 Career break schemes in eight organizations

Organization (No. employed) Date scheme started	Eligibility	Terms	Contact during break	Payment	Comment/additional features
Barclays Bank (85 000) 1986 amended 30.11.88	5 years' service, with satisfactory performance; promotion potential, grade 3 and above (junior to middle clerical).	Full break for up to 2 years or part-time work for 2-year period, 14 hours or more per week. Two breaks possible with 1 year minimum work in between.	Expected to work 2 weeks per year. Participants receive monthly information packs to help keep in touch with organization changes.	Both groups retain grade rate for work done. Part-timers: work counts towards pension and they retain housing/loan discounts.	Also provides flexible start times and will consider informal job sharing arrangements.
BP core scheme	At individual company's discretion to apply service qualifications, standards of performance.	Management discretion to offer complete break, part-time work, flexible hours, work spread between home and office, job sharing. Company discretion on terms, length, etc.	Recommendation to encourage the employee to maintain contact with her manager—brief visits to the office to discuss updating skills, etc.	Not a contractual right but all reasonable effort should be made to resume work in same or similar job with equivalent grade or status.	Responsibility for detailed conditions is up to individual companies—apart from treatment of common benefits, ie pension, share plans, loan plans and cars.
BP Oil (4600) Dec. 1987	3 years' service, good performance record, further career potential. At management discretion.	As above. For complete break, unpaid leave is for max of 1 year, for part-time work—max of 1 year subject to review.	As above.	As above.	

Table 7.5 Career break schemes in eight organizations – (cont.)

Organization (No. employed) Date scheme started	Eligibility	Terms	Contact during break	Payment	Comment/additional features
British Gas (89 000) 1.5.88	Women expecting babies, men if both partners work for BG. 3 years' service at end of maternity leave. Grade S.4 and above (1st line supervisor) or manual craft grades.	Up to 2 years from end of 29-week maternity leave. 3 months' written notice of intention to return, BG will 'make every effort' for return to be at same grade and work pattern.	Employees sent house journal, employees' annual report. Encouraged to attend briefing/training sessions – expenses paid. May be offered paid temporary work.	8 weeks' half pay on top of maternity – reclaimed by company if employee does not return. After 3 months' return, extra 4 weeks' half pay.	Also operates reservists scheme for up to 5 years. No guarantee of suitable work but loose contact maintained – house journal, annual reports sent plus vacancy notices.
British Rail (166 000) 1.9.88	Men/women with 5 years' service, satisfactory performance record, leaving to look after children, only one per family. Service qualification may be waived in exceptional circumstances. Skills, etc required (see next col.).	*Guarantee scheme* Up to 3 years' absence part-time work at same grade on re-entry. Applies to those with skills, qualifications, expertise – at management discretion. 3 months' notice of return required. Option of part-time work for same period.	At least 4 weeks' work per year, regular monthly contact with local personnel manager. Annual seminar to be held, unpaid, but childcare expenses and travel facilities provided.	Grade rates paid for work done during complete break. Part-timers paid appropriate rate for work, not necessarily as before.	Non-guarantee scheme up to 10 years for child carers – details of suitable vacancies sent. Reservists scheme – pool of experienced staff who resign to take care of children, can take up temp. work – cover for absence, sick leave, etc. Up to 10 years.

Table 7.5 Career break schemes in eight organizations – (cont.)

Organization (No. employed) Date scheme started	Eligibility	Terms	Contact during break	Payment	Comment/additional features
Leicester City Council (4500) Feb. 1988	All employees leaving for domestic reasons (childcare, dependant relative) after satisfactory probationary period, and former employees who left after 1.10.81 for domestic reasons. Must have satisfactory medical assessment.	From a minimum of 2 years to 5 years (extension possible). Re-entry programme of 6 weeks' re-induction course, training, support groups and/or mentors. Reviews 3, 6 and 12 months after return. Satisfactory medical assessment needed on return. Re-employment is at same point.	10 days' employment per year minimum, plus 2½ day refresher course to establish training needs for annual 10 days.	Payment for employment and training during scheme and on re-entry is at same point as when the employee left. No other paid work for any other organization can be done during break without permission.	The council also provides job sharing, a workplace nursery and specific training schemes for women and ethnic minorities.
Lloyds Bank (51 000) 1982, amended 1.12.88	5 years' service men and women, grade 2 and above. (Grade 1 is probationary grade for first year.)	Employees guaranteed a job on return within 5 years. Eight weeks' notice of return required.	At least 10 days' work per year (cover for holidays, etc.), mutually agreed time.	Salary for 10 days per year, work during break and on return, grade rate plus across-the-board increases.	Old scheme was only 'for those considered suitable' — now applies to almost all staff and guarantees re-employment.

Table 7.5 Career break schemes in eight organizations – (cont.)

Organization (No. employed) Date scheme started	Eligibility	Terms	Contact during break	Payment	Comment/additional features
Midland Bank (49 000) 1985	Men/women with 5 years' service, managers, appointed officers, management trainees with AIB. Consideration given to management trainees without AIB and those with potential to become management trainees. Fully effective performance also required.	Maximum of 5 years. Eight weeks' notice of return necessary. Re-entry on grade held before, if possible at same or similar work.	At least 10 days' work per year mutually agreed. Group newspaper and other appropriate publications sent. Annual discussion with personnel manager, one day programme for updating.	Pay for 10 days' work, etc. at same grade rate, on return at same grade rate.	The bank is also setting up 2 workplace nurseries and planning a third.

Source: adapted from *IRS Employment Trends*, January 1989.

Summary

The design of jobs in any organization is not a simple and straightforward task. It involves examining both the organization itself (its structure and its system of operation) and the individuals within it (their motivation to work, the values they hold and their other psychological attributes). There is little research in the area which categorically can suggest 'recipes' for job design, although some authors have presented their results in perhaps too enthusiastic a way. Some aspects of redesign (such as the creation of autonomous working groups or the introduction of flexitime) are also simply not possible in some organizations.

On the positive side, research evidence to date provides a set of choices for the design and the redesign of jobs. Given the increasing rate of technological change in virtually every facet of organizational life coupled with large shifts in the demography of the available workforce, it would seem vitally important not to lose sight of the concept of choice in job design, so that jobs are not unthinkingly subsumed under the banners of rigid work hours, automation and computerized technologies.

References

Aldag, R. J. and A. P. Brief (1977) 'The intrinsic–extrinsic dichotomy: toward conceptual clarity', *Academy of Management Review*, **2**, 497–8.

Braverman, H. (1974) *Labour and Monopoly Capital: The Degradation of Work in the Twentieth Century*, Monthly Review Press, New York.

Brief, A. P. and R. J. Aldag (1975) 'Employee reactions to job characteristics: a constructive replication', *Journal of Applied Psychology*, **60**, 182–6.

Cohen, A. R. and H. Gadon (1978) *Alternative Work Schedules: Integrating Individual and Organizational Needs*, Addison-Wesley, Reading, Mass.

Cummings, T. G. (1978) 'Self-regulating work groups: a socio-technical synthesis', *Academy of Management Review*, **3**, 625–34.

Emery, F. E. (1975) 'The assembly line—its logic and our future', *National Labour Institute Bulletin* (US), **1**, 1–19.

Golembiewski, R. T. and C. W. Prehl (1978) 'A survey of the empirical literature on flexible work hours: character and consequences of a major innovation', *Academy of Management Review*, **3**, 853–73.

Gyllenhammar, P. G. (1977) *People at Work*, Addison-Wesley, Reading, Mass.

Hackman, J. R., G. Oldham, R. Janson and K. Purdy (1975) 'A new strategy for job enrichment', *California Management Review*, **15**(3), 96–7.

Herzberg, F. (1968) 'One more time: how do you motivate employees?', *Harvard Business Review*, **46**, Jan.–Feb., 53–62.

Huse, E. F. (1980) *Organizational Development*, 2nd edn, West, St Paul, Minnesota.

Latham, G. P. and G. A. Ukl (1975) 'A review of research on the application of goal-setting in organizations', *Academy of Management Journal*, **18**, 824–45.

Lawler, E. E. (1973) *Motivation in Work Organizations*, Wadsworth, Monterey, Calif.

Locke, E. A. (1968) 'Toward a theory of task motivation and incentives', *Organizational Behavior and Human Performance*, **3**, 157–84.

NEDO/Training Commission (1988) *Young People and the Labour Market: a Challenge for the 1990s*, NEDO/Training Commission, London.

Rice, A. K. (1958) *Productivity and Social Organization: The Ahmedabad Experiment*, Tavistock, London.

Taylor, F. W. (1911) *The Principles of Scientific Management*, Harper, New York.

Terkel, S. (1972) *Working*, Wildwood House, London.

Trist, E. and K. W. Bamforth (1951) 'Some social and psychological consequences of the long wall method of coal getting', *Human Relations*, **4**, 3–38.

Umstot, D., C. H. Bell and T. R. Mitchell (1976) 'Effects of job enrichment and task goals on satisfaction and productivity: implications for job design', *Journal of Applied Psychology*, **61**, 367–79.

Walker, C. R. and R. H. Guest (1952) *The Man on the Assembly Line*, Harvard University Press, Mass.

Wanous, J. P. (1974) 'Individual differences and reactions to job characteristics', *Journal of Applied Psychology*, Oct., 616–22.

Attributes of the individual as moderators of work stress

Valerie J. Sutherland and Cary L. Cooper

Understanding stress at work

Our understanding of the nature of stress at work increases as data from research into many different occupations form consistent patterns. There have been at least six sources of potential stressors identified with an extensive range of occupations. Although the relative importance of each category varies according to a particular job, stressor categories may be defined as: *intrinsic to the job* (e.g. physical conditions); associated with ones *role in the organization* (e.g. role conflict); *career development* (e.g. over- or under-promotion); caused by *relationships at work* (e.g. a difficult boss); or associated with the *organizational structure and climate* (e.g. simply being in the organization; office politics, etc.). These factors cannot be understood unless the stressors identified with the *interface between work and home* are also taken into account (e.g. life crises; death in the family, divorce, etc.).

Sources of stress of a particular occupation, together with certain personality characteristics, are predictive of stress manifestation. Symptoms of occupational ill health include absenteeism, high labour turnover, poor industrial relations, job dissatisfaction, escapist drinking, and increased cigarette smoking. Job 'burn-out', physical and psychological ill health, accident involvement, and poor performance are consequences of exposure to mismanaged stress.

This interpretation oversimplifies the problem. Although our understanding of potential sources of stress at work is comprehensive, it is less understood why some individuals thrive and cope in an acknowledged, high stress situation, while others have less resilience to stressful events.

Response to stress—an interactive process

An interactive view of stress is that situations are not inherently stressful. The consequences of occupational stressors are the product of particular situations derived from the individual's personality, behaviour pattern and life circumstances. The judgement of threat is dependent on many attributes of the individual. For example, demographics (age, sex, education), attitudes, past experience, values, needs and personality characteristics, influence and affect the perception of a source of stress at work. A situation will only be perceived as stressful when an imbalance exists between perceived demands and perceived abilities. Continuous monitoring of the situation and feedback alters our perceptions and response to a potential stressor. Thus, the effect of a potential source of stress varies between individuals (Cassel, 1976).

Personality, behaviour patterns, needs and values as mediators of the response to stress

The area of study to receive the most attention appears to be that of 'personality characteristics'. This will be discussed first, together with 'behaviour pattern' factors, and the issues of 'needs and values'. Second, the individual qualities of ability and experience will be reviewed as a conditioning variable in the response to stressors in the environment. Third, the issue of ethnicity will be briefly discussed, given the more heterogeneous working population of the 1980s and beyond. Last, the factors of 'age' and 'physical condition' will be considered.

Many personality variables are implicated in the mediation of stress. Table R4.1 indicates some of the attributes that are implicated in the way stress is perceived by the individual.

Table R4.1
Personality characteristics and behaviour patterns as mediators of response to stress

neuroticism	anxiety
emotional instability	rigid versus flexible
high conformity	self-esteem
submissiveness	locus of control
seriousness	the 'hardy' personality
self-sufficiency	Type A coronary-prone behaviour
introversion/extroversion	sensation seeking

Using personality tests

Most research in this area has focused on personality differences between high- and low-stressed individuals. This examines the relationship between various psychometric measures, for example, the Minnesota Multiphasic Personality Inventory (MMPI) or Cattell's 16 Personality Factors Scale (16PF), with stress-related diseases such as coronary heart disease (CHD). Findings from several studies (Jenkins, 1971) indicate that patients with fatal CHD tend to show greater neuroticism in MMPI scores than those who incur and survive coronary disease. Studies using the 16PF report findings of emotional instability; high conformity and submissiveness; de-urgency/seriousness and high self-sufficiency. However, most of the studies were retrospective and, thus, the characteristics reported may be a reaction to CHD and not a precursor of it.

Introvert/extrovert

Other dimensions of personality which are likely to interact with stress include introversion/extroversion (Brebner and Cooper, 1979). The extrovert is viewed as 'geared to respond' and will attempt to respond when given an opportunity whereas the introvert may inhibit a response and seek more information. An important point to consider here is the 'self-selection' of individuals into a particular occupation. For example, offshore oil workers could be sensation-seeking extroverts who are attracted to this unique, relatively new situation of the self-contained, hostile environment of a drilling rig in the North Sea or the China Sea. Workers who are compatible will survive best, or longer than others, who will move away or function poorly (McMichael, 1978).

Rigidity and flexibility

The investigation by Kahn et al. (1964) into role conflict and role ambiguity also includes personality measures from a full range of occupations (first-time supervisors and upwards). Response to role conflict was found to be mediated or 'conditioned' by the personality of the individual. For example, anxiety-prone people experienced the conflict as more intense; introverts suffered more tensions and reported more deterioration in interpersonal relations; 'flexibles' (as opposed to 'rigids') were more open to influence from other people and were more likely to become overloaded, but 'rigids' were more susceptible to rush jobs from above (Brief *et al.*, 1981; Chan, 1977; Ivancevich and Matteson, 1980).

Self-esteem

Self-esteem also appears to be an important individual trait in the workplace. Mueller (1965) suggests that individuals with self-reported low esteem were also more likely to perceive greater work overload. Kasl and Cobb (1970) believe that self-esteem acts as a buffer against adverse stress reaction, and CHD risk increases as self-esteem declines.

Locus of control

Another characteristic of the individual which may be an important moderator of stressors in the environment is 'locus of control' (Rotter, 1966). This refers to the extent to which individuals perceive that they have control over a given situation. People who are characterized as 'internals' believe that their decisions and actions will influence what happens to them. The belief that they play a role in determining the events that impinge upon them is viewed as a factor in the expectation of coping with a stressful situation; thus they suffer less threat and fewer adverse reactions than the externally orientated individuals who tend to believe in luck or fate, and that they do not have any control over their environment. However, 'internals' will experience more anxiety in a situation in which they perceive that they have no control.

The issue of *perceived* level of control in the work situation has been extensively studied in relationship to noise as a stressor in the environment. The work of Glass and Singer (1972) highlights the importance of the individual's perception of noise in a given situation. The extent to which the worker believes that he or she is in control of the noise, and the ability to predict or govern its onset, appears to be crucial in mediating disruption of both mood and performance (Graeven, 1975; Jones, 1983). The importance of categorization of individuals as 'internals' or 'externals' may therefore be relevant in that it is acknowledged that subjective experience of noise may be more crucial than the objective measurement of environmental noise.

However, Lefcourt (1976) warns that locus of control is not a trait nor a typology and people are not totally 'internals' or 'externals'.

The 'hardy' personality

Kobasa *et al.* (1982) have included some elements of 'control' as part of the 'hardy' personality. This is a *conditioner* of the effects of stressful life events. Prospective data from a growing body of research indicates that the 'hardy type' is less likely to suffer illness as a consequence of exposure to stressful situations.

Hardiness incorporates the quality of 'commitment' versus alienation, 'control' versus powerlessness, and 'challenge' versus threat. This cluster of personality dispositions is, thus, viewed as a resistance source. *Commitment* is the tendency to involve oneself in whatever one is doing, whether it appears negative or positive, rather than disengaging. *Control* involves believing and acting as if one can influence the course of events, rather than being a passive victim of events. *Challenge* involves the expectations that it is normal for life to change, and that changes will stimulate personal growth.

Person– Environment fit

This 'subjective-experience' factor is the focal point for assessing a job stress measure known as 'person–environment fit' (P–E fit) (Caplan, 1983). P–E fit is assessed by asking subjects to indicate 'desired' and 'actual' levels of work-related factors, such as role ambiguity, workload and responsibility, and looking at the differences between the scores. Misfit is defined as either exceeding a person's capability/capacity or if capability/capacity exceeds what the role requires. Resultant stress manifests in problems such as depression, job dissatisfaction and anxiety (Caplan, 1983).

Type A coronary-prone behaviour

The most frequent cause of death in Western society today is from coronary heart disease and related circulatory disorders. As such, the Type A versus Type B differentiation and its association with an increased risk of heart disease has received a great deal of attention. The 'Western Collaborative Group Study' (WCGS) (Rosenmann *et al.*, 1975) began in 1959 and has examined 35 000 men over the years to produce data of an epidemiological, pathological and biochemical nature, relating aggressive emotion with a high risk of getting CHD (Carruthers, 1980). The study confirms the importance of other factors such as family history of CHD, cigarette smoking, level of education, elevated systolic and diastolic blood pressures, and higher serum levels of cholesterol, beta lipoproteins and neutral fat.

The study classified individuals as 'A' or 'B' types on the basis of structured interviews; none had any prior record of heart disease. Results of follow-up investigations at regular intervals have confirmed the Type A behaviour pattern as a precursor of CHD, independent of the standard risk factor (Rosenmann *et al.*, 1975). Those judged to be Type A at the onset of the study had twice the rate of clinical coronary diseases, were five times as likely to have a second myocardial infarction and had twice the rate of fatal heart attacks experienced by the Type B subjects at follow-up (8.5 year point).

Modification of Type A behaviour patterns

Research continually shows that Type A behaviour may be reliably rated as a deeply ingrained, enduring trait. Beehr and Newman (1978) also discuss the issue of Type A/B as a personality characteristic or a behaviour; however, McMichael (1978) maintains that it is not a trait, but a style of behaviour and a habitual response to circumstance. The assumption is that behaviour can be changed. The extent to which an individual can change, to prevent heart disease, is not fully understood. It should be remembered that neat categorizations are dangerous in that they over-simplify. Often, only individuals exhibiting extremes of behaviour are at risk, whereas most individuals are somewhere in the middle along a continuum of the Type A/Type B behaviour pattern. Categorizations may therefore not be very useful.

The issue of 'self-selection' into jobs that entail a greater exposure to stimulation or stressors needs to be considered. Those with particular personality and behaviour characteristics may seek out a certain type of work environment (Caplan *et al.*, 1975). Type A individuals are more prone to perceive stress in an exaggerated fashion, and experience more stress at work and more CHD, with the latter due partially to the former (House, 1974).

Personality—Innate or learned? Needs and Values—Innate or learned?

Implicit in this discussion is that personality results in a predisposition to respond in a certain way. Therefore personality is an important moderator in responding to a stressor in the environment. The presence or absence of behaviour pattern can increase or decrease the likelihood that a particular event or condition will be perceived as stressful (Quick and Quick, 1984). This also applies to the needs and values of an individual which help to determine the perception of opportunity, constraint and demands of the environment, and the relative importance of the outcomes (Schuler, 1980).

Needs and values identified as mediators in the response to organizational stressors include:

- achievement (McClelland, 1965);
- self-control, certainty and predictability (Zaleznik *et al.*, 1977);

- feedback (Corson, 1971);
- fairness and justice (Adams, 1965);
- interpersonal recognition and acceptance;
- ethical conduct (Kahn *et al.*, 1964);
- responsibility, meaningfulness and purpose (Hackman and Oldham, 1975);
- personal space and ownership (Sundstrom, 1977);
- stimulation (Levi, 1967)
- intrinsic satisfaction (Harrison, 1975).

Knowing an individual's needs and values, whether innate or learned, is necessary in understanding whether the individual will experience stress from his or her perception of the working environment.

Abilities and experience

Research on 'ability' and 'experience' as moderators of the response to organizational stress is scarce, but are seen as important in that they influence perception of opportunity, demand and constraint and, consequently, the choice of strategy to deal with a stressor (Schuler, 1980).

Ability

The factor of 'ability' is incorporated in the research on role/work overload (Kahn *et al.*, 1964). Quantitative overload (French and Caplan, 1973) may be interpreted in terms of the ability of the employee, as well as the time available to do the job. A worker with more ability can accomplish more work in less time than an employee with less ability for the job. Sales (1970) has shown that quantitative overload is negatively related to self-esteem, and positively to tension and heart rate. Qualitative work overload as a source of stress (French and Caplan, 1973) is also related to the moderator variable, 'ability', in that some employees could not complete the work successfully, regardless of the time allowed, because they do not have the skill required to do the job and would thus experience qualitative work overload as stressful.

Experience

McGrath (1970) suggests that 'experience' should also be considered as a moderator of the response to stressors in the work environment. This is in terms of 'familiarity' with the situation. Past exposure, practice and training to deal with a situation can effect the level of and thus modify the reaction to that stressor. This may perhaps explain why the method of role-play is more successful in attitude/behaviour change in training situations (e.g. educational and safety campaigns) than lectures, posters or discussions alone.

Ethnicity

Membership of a particular racial or minority group can have an effect on an individual's response to a stressor in the environment, in addition to being a source of stress itself. Expectations and aspirations of the individual will affect the perception of opportunity, constraint and demand, and may be more acute for members of a minority group where different cultural and social factors may magnify the source of stress; for example, status incongruence in interpersonal relationships at work.

Age and physical condition

Age

Age is an important consideration as a moderator variable of stress. Each stage of life has its own particular vulnerability and coping mechanism (McLean, 1979). For example, career development, over- and under-promotion and thwarted ambition, can only be fully understood in relation to the stage of life of the individual concerned. As Levinson (1978) states, 'there are seasons of a man's life which when documented will point to likely periods of stress and why they occur'. A study of middle-aged construction workers (Theorell, 1976) found the measure of 'discord' among employees to be much higher in the 41–56 age group than the 55–65 age group. This suggests that age may perform a moderator role in the experience of job stress, and is linked perhaps, to factors such as expectation and aspiration.

Physical condition

An individual's biological condition may determine how a stressor response is manifested. Physical condition is viewed as part of the process and a logical predictor of illness. Hennigan and Wortham (1975) have demonstrated that individuals in good physical condition, and who are not cigarette smokers, are able to maintain a low heart rate during the normal stress of the work day, whereas stress is more likely to increase the heart rate of others less physically fit.

Conclusion

Individual qualities or characteristics can help to explain the level of stress that an individual might experience. Yet much of the research to date is correlational and leaves questions of causation unanswered (Beehr and Newman, 1978).

Discussion that seeks to review individual attributes as mediators in the response to stress is misleading in that discrete categorization is not possible, and may not be appropriate. Overlap exists and many variables cannot be viewed in isolation. The problem of clarity of discussion is minimal in comparison to the complexity which confronts the stress researcher. Most studies are limited to the investigation of relatively few individual attributes of the individual that may mediate in the response to stress; it simply would not be possible to consider all potential moderating variables in one study.

Acceptance of this may explain the current strategy adopted in stress management programmes. It is not possible to change the environment to suit all personnel, nor is it possible to eliminate all sources of stress. At some stage, individuals in organizations will be required to work under pressure or strain. Response to pressure and coping strategies vary significantly. It is more productive to identify individual strengths and weaknesses and where necessary teach the vulnerable members of the organization to cope more effectively.

References

Adams, J. S. (1965) 'Inequity in social exchange', in L. Berkowitz (ed.), *Advances in Experimental Social Psychology*, **2**, Academic Press, New York.

Beehr, T. A. and J. E. Newman (1978) 'Job stress, employee health and organisational effectiveness: a facet analysis model and literature review', *Personnel Psychology*, **31**, 665–99.

Brebner, J. and C. Cooper (1979) 'Stimulus or response induced excitation: a comparison of behaviour of introverts and extraverts', *Journal of Research into Personality*, **12**, 306–11.

Brief, A. P., R. S. Schuler and M. Van Self (1981) *Managing Job Stress*, Little, Brown & Co., Boston.

Caplan, R. D. (1983) 'Person–environment fit: past, present and future', in C. L. Cooper (ed.), *Stress Research, Issues for the Eighties*, Wiley, Chichester and New York.

Caplan, R. D., S. Cobb, J. R. P. French, R. Van Harrison and S. R. Pinneau (1975) 'Job demands and worker health: main effects and occupational differences', NIOSH Research Report.

Carruthers, M. (1980) 'Hazardous occupations and the heart', in C. L. Cooper and R. Payne (eds), *Current Concerns in Occupational Stress*, Wiley, London.

Cassel, J. C. (1976) 'The contribution of the social environment to host resistance', *American Journal of Epidemiology*, **104**, 107–23.

Chan, K. B. (1977) 'Individual differences in reactions to stress and their personality and situational determinants', *Social Science and Medicine*, **11**, 89–103.

Corson, S. A. (1971) 'The lack of feedback in today's societies—a psychosocial stressor', in L. Levi (ed.), *Society, Stress and Disease*, **1**, Oxford University Press, London.

French, J. R. P. and R. D. Caplan (1973) 'Organizational stress and individual strain', in Marrow (ed.), *The Failure of Success*, Amacon, New York, pp. 30–66.

Glass, D. C. and J. E. Singer (1972) *Urban Stress: Experiments on Noise and Social Stressors*, Academic Press, New York.

Graeven, D. B. (1975) 'Necessity control and predictability of noise annoyance', *Journal of Social Psychology*, **95**, 85–90.

Hackman, J. R. and G. R. Oldham (1975) 'Development of the job diagnostic survey', *Journal of Applied Psychology*, **60**, 159–70.

Harrison, R. V. (1975) 'Job stress and worker health: person–environment misfit', paper presented to the American Public Health Association Convention, Chicago.

Hennigan, J. K. and A. W. Wortham (1975) 'Analysis of workday stress on industrial managers using heart rate as a criterion', *Ergonomics*, **18**, 675–81.

House, J. S. (1974) 'Occupational stress and coronary heart disease: a review and theoretical integration', *Journal of Health and Social Behaviour*, **5**, 12–27.

Ivancevich, J. M. and M. T. Matteson (1980) *Stress at Work*, Scott, Foresman, Glenview, Ill.

Jenkins, C. D. (1971) 'Psychological and social precursors of coronary disease', *New England Journal of Medicine*, **284**(5), 244–55.

Jones, D. M. (1983) 'Noise', in R. Hockey (ed.), *Stress and Fatigue in Human Performance*, Wiley, London.

Kahn, R. L., D. M. Wolfe, R. P. Quinn, J. D. Snoek and R. A. Rosenthal (1964) *Organizational Stress: Studies in Role Conflict & Ambiguity*, Wiley, London, p. 41.

Kasl, S. V. and S. Cobb (1970) 'Blood pressure changes in men undergoing job loss: a preliminary report', *Psychomatic Medicine*, **32**, 19–38.

Kobasa, S. C., S. R. Maddi and S. Kahn (1982) Hardiness and health: a prospective study', *Journal of Personality and Social Psychology*, **42**, 168–77.

Lefcourt, H. M. (1976) *Locus of Control*, Wiley, London.

Levi, L. (1967) *Stress: Sources, Management and Prevention; Medical and Psychological Aspects of the Stress of Everyday Life*, Liveright, New York.

Levinson, D. J. (1978) *The Seasons of a Man's Life*, Knopf, New York.

McClelland, D. C. N. (1965) 'Achievement and entrepreneurship: a longitudinal study', *Journal of Personality and Social Psychology*, **1**, 389–92.

McGrath, J. E. (1970) 'A conceptual formulation for research on stress', in J. E. McGrath (ed.), *Social and Psychological Factors on Stress*, Holt, Rinehart & Winston, New York, pp. 10–21.

McLean, A. A. (1979) *Work Stress*, Addison-Wesley, Reading, Mass.

McMichael, A. J. (1978) 'Personality, behavioural and situational modifiers of work stressors', in C. L. Cooper and R. Payne (eds), *Stress at Work*, Wiley, London.

Mueller, E. F. (1965) 'Psychological and physiological correlates of work overload among university professors', unpublished doctoral dissertation. University of Michigan, Ann Arbor.

Quick, J. C. and J. D. Quick (1984) *Organizational Stress & Preventive Management*, McGraw-Hill, New York.

Rosenmann, R. H., R. H. Brand, D. Jenkins, M. Friedman, R. Strauss and M. Wurm (1975) 'Coronary heart disease in the Western Collaborative Group Study. Final follow up experience of 8.5 years', *Occupational Health*, **32**(11), 524–27.

Rosenmann, R. H., M. Friedman and R. Strauss (1966) 'C.H.D. in the Western Collaborative Group Study', *Journal of the American Medical Association*, **195**, 86–92.

Rotter, J. B. (1966) 'Generalized expectancies for internal versus external control of reinforcement', *Psychological Monographs*, **80**, (1) whole no. 609.

Sales, S. M. (1970) 'Some effects of role overload and role underload', *Organizational Behaviour and Human Performance*, **5**, 592–608.

Schuler, R. S. (1980) 'Definition and conceptualization of stress in organizations', *Organizational Behaviour and Human Performance*, **25**, 184–215.

Sundstrom, E. (1977) 'Interpersonal Behaviour and the physical environment', in L. Wrightsman (ed.), *Social Psychology*, Brooks Cole.

Theorell, T. (1976) 'Selected illness and somatic factors in relation to two psychosocial stress indices — a prospective study on middle aged construction building workers', *Journal of Psychosomatic Research*, **20**, 7–20.

Zaleznik, A., M. F. R. Kets de Vries and J. Howard (1977) Stress reactions in organizations: syndromes, causes and consequences, *Behavioural Science*, **22**, 151–61.

Personality and Bureaucracy

Christopher W. Allinson

Psychologists have never really agreed on what determines human personality. Some believe it is largely inherited, others that it is a product of environmental influence. Most accept that while mental characteristics are passed on genetically, important developments occur later as individuals learn to respond to cultural and social factors. This learning, or 'socialization', results from role changes throughout life. Although many take place relatively early on, significant shifts in personality may be observed well into adulthood.

Particularly important after adolescence is the influence of the work organization. Organizational socialization has been defined as 'the process by which an individual acquires the social knowledge and skills necessary to assume an organizational role' (Van Maanen and Schein, 1979). It occurs at all stages in the work career, but the first year is crucial (Berlew and Hall, 1966). Former expectations may need to be revised as the newcomer adapts to prevailing conditions. Through its culture, task assignments and supervisory practices, the organization shapes individual attitudes and behaviour (Jones, 1983). After this 'breaking in', changes associated with career progress and technological advancement lead to further socialization, each prompting the development of personality characteristics (Kolb and Plovnick, 1977).

Evidence of organizational socialization is strong. One of the best known is Kohn and Schooler's (1983) survey of over 3000 American men. Their study revealed a marked relationship between 'occupational self-direction' and several psychological dimensions such as social orientation, self-concept and work values. Subsequent examination suggested 'that job affects man more than man affects job'.

Bureaucratic personality

A major concern in the study of the effects of different kinds of organization on personality has been the impact of bureaucracy. The idea that this type of work environment is responsible for a characteristic pattern of attitudes and behaviour has a long tradition. The most convincing theoretical interpretation remains that of Robert Merton, an American sociologist writing almost half a century ago. Merton (1940), though acknowledging the positive attainments of bureaucracy, regarded the emergence of what has become known as the 'bureaucratic personality' as a serious threat to efficiency. It develops essentially as a result of over-socialization. The attitudes and values necessary for the employee to make an effective contribution are adopted with such intensity that the needs of the organization become subordinated to the mechanics of the bureaucracy itself:

> that state of affairs in which one's abilities function as inadequacies or blind
> spots. Actions based upon training and skills which have been successfully

applied in the past may result in inappropriate responses under changed conditions (Merton, 1940).

This is much the same as Dewey's concept of 'occupational psychosis':

> As the result of the day-to-day routines, people develop special preferences, antipathies, discriminations and emphases . . . These psychoses develop through demands put upon the individual by the particular organization of his occupational role (Merton, 1940).

Attention is diverted from the objectives of the organization to the details of its control system; rules become ends in themselves rather than means to an end. Strict compliance with regulations becomes a ritual, regardless of its appropriateness for particular circumstances. Rigid adherence to formal procedures, and a fastidious insistence on 'going by the book', may cause the bureaucrat to lose sight of the real task in hand. Behaviour becomes so rule-bound that it is often impossible to meet the needs of clients. Acar and Aupperle (1984) cite a case in point:

> Newspapers throughout the United States reported that, on 7 March 1984, Lilian Boff died of a heart attack while a Dallas fire department dispatcher wasted precious minutes delaying the prompt dispatch of an ambulance to the Boff residence as requested by Larry Boff, Lilian's stepson. This dispatcher had been a nurse for 17 years. The delay was caused by her insistence to speak to Mrs. Boff before sending an ambulance. She paid no attention to Larry Boff's pleas that his stepmother could not possibly be expected to carry on a coherent or even audible conversation with the ambulance dispatcher while she was gasping for air! Such pleas went unheeded in spite of the dispatcher's medical knowledge, and the woman died while her stepson was undergoing this Orwellian or Kafkaesque experience.

Little wonder that bureaucracy is saddled with pejorative connotations of red tape and small-minded officialdom. But what is at the root of this syndrome? Merton claimed that it derives from various structural sources:

Career structure   The working life of the bureaucrat is defined in terms of a career plan. Reluctance to lose associated benefits, such as regular salary increases, pension schemes and fixed promotion opportunities, can lead to overconformity, conservatism and timidity.

Esprit de corps   There is a feeling of common destiny among members of the bureaucracy; interests are shared, and since promotion is based on seniority, competition is almost nonexistent. This results in a defensive informal system surfacing whenever the entrenched interests of the group are threatened, possibly at the expense of assisting higher officials or the clients of the organization.

Sanctification   Employees' emotional involvement may lead to bureaucratic norms which were originally intended to encourage administrative efficiency becoming rigidified and sacred. They emerge as values in their own right, divorced from the technical purposes for which they were designed.

Impersonality   Bureaucracy emphasizes the depersonalization of relationships and categorization of cases with which it deals. This norm of impersonality, and the consequent refusal to provide clients with personalized, individual consideration, gives rise to charges of arrogance and high-handedness.

Authority   Sometimes officials allow the authority associated with their position to influence behaviour towards clients, leading to the impression of a domineering attitude. Recourse by the client to other staff is often unsuccessful owing to the prevailing *esprit de corps*. Although customers in the private sector can always turn to another organization, there is no such alternative for the client of a monopolistic public-sector institution.

March and Simon (1958) have provided a diagrammatic summary of Merton's model (see Figure R5.1).

Figure R5.1
The Merton model.
Copyright © 1958 by
John Wiley & Souslne
Source: adapted
from J. G. March and
H. A. Simon (1958)
Organizations, Wiley,
New York, p. 41.

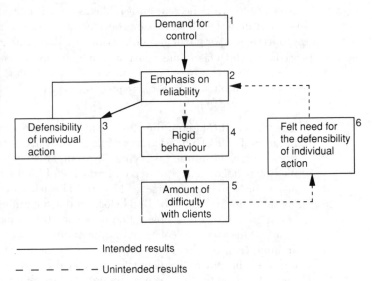

The process begins with a *demand for control* (1) from those at the top. This is met by an *emphasis on reliability* (2) of behaviour. Techniques for achieving this include the establishment of standard operating procedures and a monitoring of their implementation. This leads, on the one hand, to the intended consequence of reliable *individual action* which is *defensible* (3). On the other hand, however, for the reasons described above, there is the unintended effect of *rigid behaviour* (4) unsuited to dynamic conditions. Officials fail to respond to the peculiarities of individual cases and the *amount of difficulty with clients* (5) grows. As performance suffers, management responds with an even greater stress on control and reliability. This tends to increase the *felt need for defensibility of individual action* (6). Thus there is a renewed *emphasis on reliability* (2), and the 'vicious circle' is complete.

The role of anxiety

Presthus (1979) has argued that 'anxiety is probably the most critical variable in organizational behavior'. The sheer size and impersonality of the modern corporation is largely to blame:

> Fear is always prevalent . . . even if you're the topman, even if you're hard, even if you do your job—there's always insecurity. You're always fearful of the big mistake (Terkel, 1974).

Several sources of anxiety can be identified. Although they overlap, it is convenient to consider the main ones separately.

Fear of superiors   When things go wrong, blame can always be attached to those who have violated the regulations whether they are responsible or not. Afraid of this possibility, bureaucrats frequently choose to apply rules to the letter, even when discretion is called for:

> Bureaucratic superiors cannot generally censure a subordinate for following official regulations exactly, regardless of how inefficient or ridiculous such action may be in a particular case . . . feelings of dependency on superiors and anxiety over their reactions engender ritualistic tendencies (Blau and Meyer, 1971).

Fear of specialists   Managers in bureaucracies find themselves increasingly reliant upon specialists for the achievement of goals. The specialists, who may be subordinates, have to be trusted to apply skills properly which are often little understood by others in the organization. Thompson (1961) points out that the anxieties which managers suffer as a result may lead to an exaggerated need to control and a consequent tendency towards ritualism. The problem is compounded by the fact that insecure superiors invariably generate pressures on those who are accountable to them, hence the creation of more anxiety among subordinates with the attendant behavioural consequences.

Fear of inadequacy   Bureaucrats may be acutely aware of their failings in performing certain tasks. For many, the resultant anxiety can be calmed by a ritual performance of more straightforward activities. This explains the often irrational resistance of officials to improvements in procedure; they prefer to cling to the old routines with their comfortable familiarity (Blau and Meyer, 1971).

Fear of uncertainty   The main anxiety of many bureaucrats stems from their uncertainty about how to behave. They are afraid of being caught in error and losing their jobs or at least being shunted off into isolated and unpleasant positions. Presthus (1979) described people afflicted in this way as 'indifferents'. Commitment to the organization is low and their most significant rewards are obtained away from work. Their main defence is 'going along' with the system: following the rules and documenting that they have done so, avoiding risks, offloading responsibilities and, on occasion, doing nothing (Benveniste, 1977).

Fear of Failure   Another kind of anxiety is associated with the pursuit of career success. Presthus (1979) has identified what he calls the 'upward mobiles' whose big fear is failure. Their anxiety, according to Thompson (1961), is like Calvinism in that it creates doubt as to who is 'chosen'. As with Calvinism, this doubt can be reduced by excessive activity, a businesslike demeanour and conformity. Their middle-class upbringing has taught them that conformity is a means to status and power, the ends which they value most.

Kanter (1977), in her study of an American industrial supply corporation, confirms the 'rules mindedness' of those who seek power. The rule book becomes a 'power tool' since it is the one thing over which superiors can be guaranteed to give their backing. This applies especially to officials who, though lacking significant power, hold managerial responsibility. To secure their position or impress superiors, they sacrifice subordinates' freedom for a desire to play safe and 'get it right'. Thus ritualistic conformity from subordinates is all important. Proper form rather than a good outcome is the main concern.

In search of the ritualists

In what kind of organization is the bureaucratic personality most prevalent? To begin to answer this question it is necessary to understand what bureaucracy really means. Its modern technical definition derives mainly from Weber's

(1947) classic description. For him, bureaucracy in its ideal form is characterized by a hierarchical authority structure, specialist functions, strict separation of work from non-work activities, and control by written rules. Recruitment is on the basis of technical qualifications, and the formal requirements of the job are clearly distinguished from the qualities of the person who does it.

It seems logical to suggest that an organization is bureaucratized to the extent that it resembles Weber's archetype. Attempts at assessing bureaucratization have invariably revealed two fundamental dimensions of organization structure: the degree to which rules are formalized, procedures standardized and jobs specialized and the extent to which authority is centralized (Pugh and Hickson, 1976). A number of investigators (e.g. Child, 1972) have shown that these have a negative relationship with each other. This is not to say that there is a strict tendency for activities always to become more structured as authority is less concentrated, or vice versa. But it does indicate that bureaucracy in its purest form, as described by Weber, is likely to be structured and decentralized; once behaviour has been programmed through rules, standard procedures and job descriptions, decision-making can be delegated to lower levels with confidence.

What is surprising is the fact that research studies have consistently shown that this model is exemplified not by public-sector administrative organizations as popularly imagined, but by large industrial corporations in the private sector (Pugh and Hickson, 1976). So much for the idea that civil-service and local-government departments are the very epitome of bureaucracy in Weber's terms. The evidence suggests that, if anything, they represent its antithesis, relying on direct management of subordinates rather than structuring to achieve control.

The implication is that the bureaucratic personality seems more likely to be encountered in the administrative sections of big business than anywhere else. This is borne out by the author's own findings (Allinson, 1984, 1986). Over 300 employees at all job levels of six differently structured organizations were questioned about their 'bureaucratic orientation' (an index of bureaucratic personality) and job satisfaction. Questions relating to bureaucratic orientation concerned willingness to comply with commands, preference for impersonal work relationships, acceptance of rules and regulations and need for security provided by conformity. Questions relating to job satisfaction asked employees how well they liked their job, how much of the time they felt satisfied with it, whether or not they would consider changing it for another and how they thought their satisfaction compared with that of others. The results were consistent and interesting.

First, employees in large industrial bureaucracies (structured and decentralized) had a higher bureaucratic orientation than those in the other organizations. Second, the relationship of bureaucratic orientation with age and length of service was stronger in the industrial companies than elsewhere, suggesting the particular socializing effect of that kind of work environment. Third, employees in local-government departments (unstructured and centralized) had a lower bureaucratic orientation than those in the other organizations. And finally, the rate of increase in job satisfaction with bureaucratic orientation was higher in the industrial bureaucracies, and lower in local government, than anywhere else.

Looking ahead

Despite predictions of its demise, bureaucracy continues to flourish. More flexible structures have had to be adopted under volatile conditions, but organizing along the lines of Weber's model still appears to bring the best results for the large-scale operation in a relatively stable environment. The fact remains that:

> bureaucracy is a form of organization superior to all others we know or can hope to afford in the near and middle future; the chances of doing away with it or changing it are probably nonexistent in the West in this century (Perrow, 1972).

So the bureaucratic personality seems unlikely to disappear completely. As long as organizations seek to regulate behaviour through formal rules and standard procedures, the excesses described by Merton will probably persist to some degree.

It is important, however, that the problem is not exaggerated. By no means all bureaucrats are ritualists. Many are notable for their innovation and creativity (Blau and Meyer, 1971; Williams, Sjoberg and Sjoberg, 1980) while others, especially those of a neurotic disposition, are more likely to resist formal rules or rebel against them (Thompson, 1961; Presthus, 1979). Furthermore, there may be ways in which the effects of the bureaucratic personality can be reduced or even eliminated.

One possibility is that modern methods of alleviating occupational stress and anxiety will strike at its very roots. Another is that organizations may, through appropriate training, resocialize employees so that they are able to understand better the purpose of regulations, properly use their discretion and develop a willingness to treat each individual case on its merits. In conclusion, therefore, it seems reasonable to suggest that while the bureaucratic personality may represent an unfortunate side-effect of bureaucracy, it does not in itself justify the denigration or wholesale rejection of that mode of organization.

References

Acar, W. and K. E. Aupperle (1984) 'Bureaucracy as organizational pathology', *Systems Research*, **1**, 157–66.

Allinson, C. W. (1984) *Bureaucratic Personality and Organization Structure*, Gower, Aldershot.

Allinson, C. W. (1986) 'The industrial bureaucrat', *Journal of General Management*, **11**, 47–55.

Benveniste, G. (1977) *Bureaucracy*, Boyd and Fraser, San Francisco.

Berlew, D. E. and D. T. Hall (1966) 'The socialization of managers: effects of expectations on performance', *Administrative Science Quarterly*, **11**, 207–23.

Blau, P. M. and M. W. Meyer (1971) *Bureaucracy in Modern Society*, 2nd edn, Random House, New York.

Child, J. (1972) 'Organization structure and strategies of control: a replication of the Aston study', *Administrative Science Quarterly*, **17**, 163–77.

Jones, G. R. (1983) 'Psychological orientation and the process of organizational socialization: an interactionist perspective', *Academy of Management Review*, **8**, 464–74.

Kanter, R. M. (1977) *Men and Women of the Corporation*, Basic Books, New York.

Kohn, M. L. and C. Schooler (1983) *Work and Personality: An Inquiry into the Impact of Social Stratification*, Ablex, Norwood, New Jersey.

Kolb, D. A. and M. S. Plovnick (1977) 'The experiential learning theory of career development', in J. Van Maanen (ed.), *Organizational Careers: Some New Perspectives*, Wiley, New York, pp. 65–87.

March, J. G. and H. A. Simon (1958) *Organizations*, Wiley, New York.

Merton, R. K. (1940) 'Bureaucratic structure and personality', *Social Forces*, **18**, 560–8.

Perrow, C. (1972) *Complex Organizations: A Critical Essay*, Scott, Foresman, Glenview, Ill.

Presthus, R. (1979) *The Organizational Society*, rev. edn, Macmillan, London.

Pugh, D. S. and D. J. Hickson (eds) (1976) *Organizational Structure in its Context: The Aston Programme I*, Saxon House, Westmead.

Terkel, S. (1974) *Working*, Avon, New York.

Thompson, V. A. (1961) *Modern Organization*, Knopf, New York.

Van Maanen, J. and E. H. Schein (1979) 'Toward a theory of organizational socialization', in B. M. Staw (ed.), *Research in Organizational Behavior*, Vol. 1, JAI Press, Greenwich, Conn., pp. 209–64.

Weber, M. (1947) *The Theory of Social and Economic Organization* A. M. Henderson and T. Parsons (eds), Free Press, Glenview, Ill.

Williams, N. M., G. Sjoberg and A. F. Sjoberg (1980) 'The bureaucratic personality: an alternative view', *Journal of Applied Behavioral Science*, **16**, 389–405.

County General: a question of gender, power or good business?

Sheila Rothwell

County General is a medium-sized financial services firm which is beginning to expand rapidly. There are currently about 5000 employees—a fifth of whom work at the Head Office in London, a similar proportion are employed at the five regional offices, and the rest are in the 300 branches spread across England and Wales.

The General Manager (James Stevens) is coming to the final item on the agenda of the monthly Management Executive Committee meeting, which is attended by the directors of Finance (Frank Walker), Marketing (Mark Reed), Business Operations (Brian Lewis), Personnel (Peter Baker) and Management Services (Simon Morris), as well as the Company Secretary (Marjorie Stone).

JAMES   Well, gentlemen, we've reached some important agreements about our future strategy for expansion into new areas outside our traditional business. I'm pretty sure the full Board will approve it but there might be some questions about our ability to resource it—in people rather than money alone. We know we will have to recruit specialists in new areas of expertise but we're going to need a lot more managers and professionals generally and its not going to be easy—we could be doubling our total numbers within 5–10 years. The outside competition for bright young whizzkids is hotting up and I don't know whether we've got enough home-grown talent to develop further—we're stretched for branch managers already in some areas. The trouble is that the majority of our staff are female clericals and we've never been able to attract many women managers—except yourself of course, Marjorie, a stalwart of the Company, can't imagine the place without your hard work! The Chairman's often on at me to get some ladies—give a bit of substance to his speeches about social responsibility I suppose—so I'd like us to consider what, if anything, we should do about the situation. Peter, this is really a Personnel matter, so it's your patch, what do you think?

PETER BAKER (*Personnel Director*)   Well, I'm not sure whether you're asking me to go out and recruit some women managers or suddenly to promote some clerical supervisors. It's not easy and either way could be discriminatory—we've done all we can already but nothing much seems to have happened. As you know, we've always prided ourselves on treating everyone fairly and equally and we didn't have to make more than minor changes (about cheap home loans and time off for shopping) when the Equal Pay and Sex Discrimination Acts came into force. It was mainly cosmetic—like taking the 'his' out of some of our recruitment publicity, although I suppose there's still some around in our internal job descriptions. There's an outside chance of an odd-ball claim under the new equal-value regulations, I suppose, but the clerical, technical and managerial job evaluation schemes are all separate so it's not very likely.

BRIAN LEWIS (*Business Operations*)   Well, pay's your area of course, but I've often thought some of those clerical supervisors in the regional or big branch offices have a harder job than the managers of small branches. Not that I can see women handling difficult customers and negotiating loan deals of course. Most of them prefer to be in the background with the other girls; the customers prefer it that way too.

MARK REED (*Marketing*)   I must say, a few more women on the Executive floor in this place would damn well brighten up the place a bit. Could even humanize our hardliners.

BRIAN   Might have to watch your language a bit then, Mark. But it wouldn't be the same really would it—what about the Director's Dining Room and the bar—turn the whole place into a boudoir, eh? Don't mean you Marjorie, of course, you've never rocked the boat, and with your mother to get home to you've never had time for much socializing. Which reminds me, what about another spot of coffee, my dear?

MARK   Well at my last firm, which was in retailing, we had some really bright professional women. Those in marketing and sales were running rings round some of the older salesmen. It's the same in most of the advertising agencies I deal with these days. I know I haven't brought in any new women managers here yet because I just can't see them fitting in; it's not easy for any outsider in fact. We've got a few field saleswomen now—and we need to tap the female market much more as there's plenty of money there these days—but it's not simple. The male representatives don't feel easy with the women at our conferences (probably because their wives are suspicious) and although one saleswoman is doing a particularly good job she's costing us a bomb in travel expenses because she prefers to drive home at night, saying she (or her husband) objects to the 'sexual harassment' she gets at hotels.

BRIAN   That's the real trouble—husbands and families—even if we recruit more women managers they'd be off as soon as they got pregnant or else when we tried to move them. You all know we've got to be able to move people around the country as part of their management development to give them experience of different parts of the business and gradually enlarge their areas of responsibility in larger branches or head office departments. I can see that need getting greater not smaller as we expand. Anyway, that's why we've got a mobility clause in our contracts and why I put a lot of emphasis on that in interviewing the few women who apply to us for these sort of positions. The ones inside mostly have the message already.

SIMON MORRIS (*Management Services*)   Come on, I've got several women computer programmers and systems analysts who have moved around the country a lot—I'm only afraid they'll be off again soon, although I'm glad to say the married ones don't swap as quickly as the young men. I rely on them to keep the systems running and put out a lot of the new development to contract staff. I've got one woman on maternity leave now, finishing off one project from home, as I have arranged for a terminal there. There's no reason why we couldn't do a lot more of that, if the managers could learn to cope with not having everyone sitting around them all the time.

JAMES   Don't talk to me about maternity leave—I've lost one of the best women planners I've ever had and there's always a collection for someone in the office who is getting married or leaving to have a baby.

PETER   What should we do then? Start a crèche here? I believe one or two use the one run by the council, but I can't see many of them wanting to bring kids in and out of the city centre every day. Anyway most of them would rather look after them at home themselves while they're small, and I must say I think that's right.

MARJORIE STONE (*Company Secretary*)   So do I. Children are a responsibility and you can't do two jobs properly. I knew I had to choose between career and family so I decided accordingly. And I paid or arranged for most of my own training.

FRANK WALKER (*Finance*)   Yes, Marjorie, and we know your legal brain is twice as good as most of the men who've ever done your job. But times are changing and I must admit I'm beginning to see things differently now my daughters are growing up. I've paid a lot for their education, they've all got good qualifications and I'm damned if I want to see those wasted. My eldest got married last year and intends to have a nanny for her baby when it arrives so she can continue as a solicitor. I expect her mother will still have to help out to take the pressure off sometimes. Come to that, we're getting some promising young girl accountants in the business now and we're investing a lot in them—time off for study and examination fees, etc. The department can't afford to lose them, and it won't be easy to replace them either.

PETER   Those are the graduates—there's still the problem that most of our women have left school at fifteen and just haven't enough educational background to cope with professional management jobs today, even if they didn't have families to look after.

MARK   Well, I don't know that we're all highly qualified around this table, we've just had the experience. Had a bit of sales training in my case.

SIMON   It was different when you could learn most of it on the job. Now a lot of it's in the system and many of the tasks that once took years of experience can now be done by anyone after a few weeks. That's why we've got to do extra management training anyway, and we could easily do a bit more on top of that for some women that have been here a while.

JAMES   None of this positive discrimination. It's a dangerous path—just creates more inequality. Anyway, why do we recruit women who don't even have 'O' levels? Most of the men we take on seem to have 'A' levels or degrees. I thought both sexes got roughly equally qualified these days?

MARK   The women are not always unqualified in fact. I was talking to one in the office who was apparently a trained teacher and she knows another who has a Diploma in Art and Design, but they didn't think there was any point in putting them in their applications for part-time clerical work. They could handle more responsibility easily if they had the confidence.

BRIAN   Well, no one could do my job part-time—double time more likely. But there's not much point in looking at elderly part-timers for our future young managers. We want people with real drive and commitment.

PETER   Come off it, some of them are only thirty and their kids are almost at secondary school already. They'll soon be looking for a bit of career fulfilment themselves—or else they'll be looking for something else and letting their marriages break up.

MARK   Some will break up anyway, but once the trauma's over divorcees often put a tremendous amount of energy into their work—you know that woman in

Swansea: one of those rare creatures, a female branch manager. She's doing extremely well. Possibly would have been promoted already if she'd been a man. Perhaps someone's afraid she's after his job.

BRIAN   Well, her regional manager hasn't said anything as far as I know and it would be up to him to put her name forward in the first place. Of course he's a bit traditional; probably would never imagine her going any higher, even if he gives her good annual reviews.

SIMON   He's one of those who'd rather resign than work for a woman himself from what I've heard. I'm probably the only one here who has ever done so in my early career. Is that what we're really afraid of?

JAMES   What I'm afraid of is spending the rest of the night chewing this over without deciding anything. Supposing we start with an audit of the current situation—how many women, which department, which skills, qualifications, salary levels, etc. and then make some decisions on the basis of fact?

PETER   Well we know the general picture of course. Roughly 65:35 female to male overall, but of the 800 managers it's about 95:5 male to female or 85:15 if we include professionals. I gave those figures to the Staff Association when the Chairman asked last year: I don't think he was too bothered but some of the women were pushing him. We could have the detailed picture if Management Services had given us the data I'm after, but as it is we would have to get consultants in to do a detailed study.

SIMON   I could give you most of what you want—not the qualifications of course—just from an analysis of pay-roll data but you've never asked for it. Most of us know our departments—I've got plenty of women professionals but hardly any over £15,000 a year; there just aren't enough management posts in my patch to promote them. I think it's a waste of time and money getting consultants in to tell us that—we ought to bring them in to start making some changes now—not delay them another year. Or we could do that ourselves anyway—some short pilot schemes—and monitor results.

FRANK   I'm sure we don't want to rush into anything that's not properly planned. Stirs up expectations from women's libbers and a lot of opposition and backlash from those who don't want change anyway.

MARK   Seems to me a survey would be a good idea, if we made it an attitude audit. Then we could test out reactions to change proposals, see whether women want training or promotion or whatever—we'd probably need some discussion panels too for exploring reasons and feelings. Rather like we would test market a new product—and then we'd need publicity . . .

JAMES   Well, before we get too carried away, I propose we bring in some consultants with a brief to review the opportunities for women's career development here and make recommendations for improvements. I think you should talk to two or three different outfits first, Peter, give them a flavour of our discussion and see how they would propose to go about the job, how much staff involvement they would want and that sort of thing. Then you and I will meet again to decide who should do it. Agreed, gentlemen?

Question   Imagine you are a consultant brought in to County General. What would you propose to do and how might you go about implementing it? Take account of the strengths and weaknesses in the situation, the culture and the likely sources of opposition or support, in discussing your plans.

Payment systems: control to commitment in Newtons' Ingredients

Richard Thorpe

Introduction

This case describes a highly successful company operating a continuous process plant. As competition has increased there has been a gradual move towards automation of many aspects of the work. The process is capital-intensive, with labour costs currently accounting for less than 5 per cent of the total cost. However, it is recognized that the way in which labour is used will be crucial to maximizing the use of capital.

The company also recognize the important part that payment systems play in meeting its objectives—how, through design, they can not only ensure that employees produce the correct forms of effort, but also serve as important catalysts for change.

Newtons' Ingredients

Background of the company

Newtons is a large, diversified, international company operating in the food industry. The group of companies of which Newtons is a part has a turnover of £105m, £3m being contributed by the ingredients division. This contribution represents 2 per cent of both turnover and cost.

The industry

The ingredients industry is fragmented, and although there are few direct competitors (the industry being oligopolistic) there is fierce competition, not only in relation to the price of existing products but also in terms of new market segments.

The products

Basically Newtons has two types of product—baked and blended. Taken together they break down into 1500 individual products involving some 800 different ingredients, and they service some 2200 customers worldwide.

The processes

Both types of product require process technology of varying degrees of sophistication. The baked products, for example, require a fair amount of technical input from the operators, while the blended products need little technical intervention in the process and relatively unskilled labour is required.

The market place— change and uncertainty

Both types of products have enjoyed a stable, although steadily expanding, market share. In marketing terms it could be described as mature. The other manufacturers of the same types of commodity have begun to compete by expanding and fragmenting the product range.

The customer is essentially the retailer (i.e. someone making cakes or other food items). Branding is therefore unimportant, except for public-relations purposes. Emphasis is placed on price, quality and customer service.

A current requirement in order to remain competitive has been to push existing capacity to the limit of present resources, including people. With competition it is expected that volumes will decline and the upgrading of skills of machine-minders and technicians will become even more important.

To achieve this, staff at all levels will need to be both better trained and able to perform a much wider range of tasks, particularly when further technology is applied to existing processes.

Additional new market opportunities— baked products

The company has recently acquired a new, rapidly growing segment of the food ingredient market. Currently, it is the market leader with 70 per cent of the market. Investment has already been made in new plant and there are other possibilities for expansion. A green field site has been acquired and there is the opportunity to develop completely new systems of plant operation and systems of remuneration. The latter, it is thought, would materially assist a move to more responsibility and flexibility on the part of the operatives.

Threats to blended products

There is a steadily growing demand for the blended products. However product quality is seen to be of paramount importance, with customer service a close second. The factor of the labour force is important in meeting these objectives, not because superior technical knowledge will improve the process but because it is felt that superior product knowledge will improve the quality. In this area of the business, automation is being increasingly applied to improve throughput; however increased throughput will not involve increased manpower. There is consequently a requirement for operatives to accept new skills and working practices if performance is to be improved.

Organization structure

The current organization is run on 'traditional' structured lines. Brief reporting lines are set out in Figure CS2.1. These include the factory manager, departmental managers, foremen, chargehands and mixers, classes 1 and 2.

Figure CS2.1
Traditional organizational structure

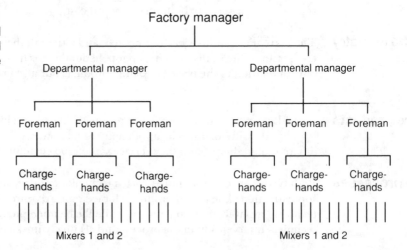

Motivation and manpower problems

The management recognized the following problems engendered by the 'traditional' structure:

- Brighter younger workers became frustrated. Once they had achieved mastery of their tasks, promotion could be slow. Many waited for 'dead men's' shoes.
- Senior managers often acted as 'gatekeepers' in the structure preventing

junior employees from undertaking tasks for which they were perfectly capable. Delegation was not seen as a moral imperative and as a result junior employees became disillusioned. Failure of senior managers to develop subordinates was poor management practice, storing up problems for the future.

- In consequence, both managers and their subordinates underperformed. People were viewed as less important than roles, status and structure, with the result that there was inflexibility and a general reduction in the performance of the organization as a whole.

Union organization and affiliation

Working relationships with the unions were harmonious. Unions were strongly supported in the plant, with three unions representing the majority of the workforce (Table CS2.1).

Table CS2.1
Background to the payment system

Section of workforce	Union	Membership (%)
Manufacturing and warehousemen	USDOR	100
Drivers	T&G	100
Managers and ancillaries	M&F	52–60

The current senior management had begun to consider that the wage payment system was working against the changing priorities of the organization.

Employees were paid a fixed sum based on the demands of the job as set out in their job description. No system of job evaluation was used and differentials between job titles and responsibilities were purely on the basis of custom and practice, with differentials maintained or not as the case may be by the separate agreements made in the annual collective bargaining agreements.

No bonuses were paid although on various occasions in the past differentials had been altered by productivity bargaining agreements (mid 1960s) and time and attendance bonuses (1970s). These had long been consolidated. All that remained outside the basic wage figures were some short shift payments.

The proposed new system — integrated pay

A radical plan has been proposed to alter completely the wage-payment system. It is hoped that the new system will promote two aspects of performance thought to be important for the company's continued success—flexibility and commitment. The basis of the system is flexible teamwork. Not only will multi-skilled teams work together, occasionally taking on a limited amount of each others' work, but they will also work flexibly as a whole. The new factory site is to be divided into a number of fairly large working areas. The group of workers in each area will be responsible for a discrete aspect of the process. Each group will include all current grades of employee and through a process of job evaluation it is hoped that all jobs will be accommodated into a single common wage structure. This structure with the hourly rate allotted to each grade is shown in Figure CS2.2.

Grade 1 is seen as a probationary grade. All new employees would be placed there for the first six months. Allocation to other grades would be strictly based on the range of testable skills which an employee can demonstrate that he or she has.

In order to attract employees to the new system the company would reduce the working week from 40 hours to $37\frac{1}{2}$ hours. It is considered that the effect would be to increase the average pay by 11 per cent to all workers. Jobs falling outside the grades would be red-circled so that annual pay increases would eventually bring them into line.

Figure CS2.2
New organizational
structure

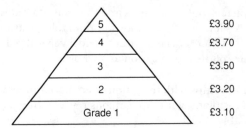

Perhaps the boldest aspect of the proposed new system is that employees would have to accept work at the same pay level in work specialisms outside their traditional discipline or skill. For this to be possible the company would guarantee to provide training in all personal and testable skills compatible with the proposed scheme. This should serve to prove the competence of employees to undertake the variety of work required.

Promotion through the grades will necessitate the demonstration of a wider range of skills, not only in their main discipline, but also to a limited extent in other disciplines. The aim is that ultimately employees will not only work flexibly within their own teams, but also with the overall group.

So, for example, Grade 1 workers in the manufacturing function will be expected to undertake a variety of manufacturing functions as well as a limited number of quality functions, such as sampling, and engineering functions, such as greasing (see Figure CS2.3, Employee A).

Figure CS2.3
Example of
functional flexibility

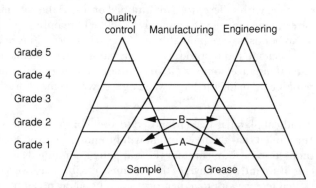

As individuals rise throughout the hierarchy, management would reserve the right to deploy them wherever they might be required provided they were qualified (sideways and down), regardless of their pay grade (see Figure CS2.3, Employee B). It would therefore be mangement's responsibility to achieve the maximum potential from their labour force. For the labour force, anyone would be free to advance up the grades provided their individual competence level can be increased. The company would be pledged to take individuals as far as the individuals can achieve and the responsibility thus placed on the company for training is recognized.

Questions

1 How might such a revolutionary new scheme be designed and implemented so that it has the best possible chance of success? Design an implementation plan.

2 What disadvantages do you foresee in the proposed new structure? Comment on how you might alleviate or reduce any disadvantages.

3 In exactly what ways will the new system improve the motivation of individuals and groups? Locate your discussion in theories of motivation.

Part III
The Group

Group behaviour

The group as the unit of analysis

So far, in Parts I and II, we have been looking at the behaviour of individuals in organizations. The principles of scientific management, for example, were focused on the performance of individuals at work. But this perspective is too simplistic to handle the complexity of most organizations. For most individuals, a great deal of organizational time is spent in groups. Groups make recommendations; groups make decisions; groups inherit the decisions of other groups, and groups form, re-form and split up, often in a relatively short time. We shall look at the different types of groups later in this chapter. For the moment, we need to be clear about certain aspects of behaviour which are common to all groups and which must be understood if poor performance, conflict, misunderstandings and bad communication are to be avoided.

The behaviour patterns which occur within any group are directly related to its performance or its task achievement (Shaw, 1981). Groups which are badly managed, or which manage themselves badly, will be less effective in getting tasks accomplished and in making accurate and sensible decisions. Chapter 10 details how decision-making processes can be heavily influenced by the characteristics of a group and many other organizational processes can be similarly affected.

Small groups can be defined as two or more individuals who interact with one another and where there is a psychological interrelationship between them. There must be a significant level of interdependence between group members to the extent that members of the group perceive the group to be 'real' and to the extent that members can readily distinguish themselves from non-members (Alderfer, 1977). Within the group, members take on specific roles or tasks and these too are recognized by the group as a whole. Such roles build in expectations of behaviour from individuals and thus a certain measure of predictability can also emerge.

We can distinguish between *formal* groups and *informal* groups in organizations.

Formal groups   These are designed and created around specific tasks. Membership is often assigned to individuals in an organization and they may serve the group for a specified length of time (for example, one year or six months). In general, formal groups would show up on the organization chart. They are mostly specified by functional differentiation. A standing committee is an example of a formal group. Most people in an organization are members of at least one formal group. It is through this that they achieve a formal role in the company.

Other kinds of formal groups are task groups which are rather more temporary than standing groups. Task groups form around a specific need at a particular point in time. Product development groups, some research groups and some marketing or sales teams are examples of task groups. Likert (1961) showed that often individuals could be members of many formal groups in an organization. Structurally, coordination between formal groups is achieved through 'linking pins' created by multiple membership. Figure 8.1 shows a typical linking-pin structure.

Figure 8.1
Multiple group
membership through
a 'linking-pin'
structure

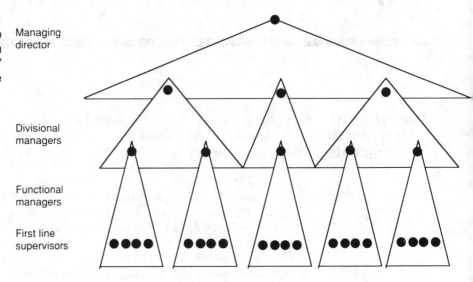

Managing
director

Divisional
managers

Functional
managers

First line
supervisors

Informal groups   These occur because organizations are social places as well as functional purposive structures. People like to talk to one another. The groups of friends which arise in this way cross functional as well as hierarchical boundaries. Membership of informal groups is voluntary, although access into one of these groups can be less than easy, since such groups can quickly develop their own ways of doing things. This includes an implicit or explicit description of the kind of person who is acceptable to the group and who is not.

Informal groups are the focus of information-sharing, allow the testing out of new ideas and schemes, act as sounding boards for all kinds of information and they can mobilize considerable resistance to formal schemes and plans. The weight of resistance is likely to increase to the extent that the informal group contains mostly co-workers from similar levels in the hierarchy. It is too easy to concentrate only on the negative side of formal groups. Much has been written about their resistance to reorganization schemes, new designs of jobs and the adoption of new technologies. However, the coherence and psychological solidarity that characterize informal groups can also be a great asset to the organization when management goals and those of the informal group are in line. If the informal group wants to streamline inventory processing or wants to improve product or service quality, then this is probably the fastest way of achieving these goals! It will certainly be quicker than most formal routes.

Operating problems and opportunities of the group

Like individuals, groups develop and change over time. There are some predictable stages through which most groups will progress although the strict sequence of these stages may vary. The stages are:

1 *Forming*   Testing by group members to try and determine acceptable behaviour and attitudes. Life in this stage of the group is mostly about taking and giving cues about expected behaviour.
2 *Storming*   Identifies the pecking order of members in the group. A time of negotiation and sometimes outright conflict as power and status are allocated to individuals around the group. Group leaders tend to emerge at this stage

although their tenure of office may be short-lived if the group continues to storm.

3 *Norming*   This is the stage at which group rules are made. Tasks of the group are clear and are freely articulated by all group members. The group is developing norms.

4 *Performing*   A mature group psychologically which will impart considerable effort into achieving goals and successful performance generally. Levels of within-group conflict are very low and further sub-grouping of specialisms is likely as the level of task flexibility increases.

Not all groups go through all stages. Each stage, however, has some overall implications for management styles which may be appropriate. For example, the process of storming can be avoided entirely by autocratic leadership styles. A group created by a hierarchically superior manager will be in no doubt about the question of who is boss. The feelings of cohesiveness which develop at the next stage (norming) are not, however, likely always to be in line with what the autocratic manager initially intended and the group can adopt a position which is defensive or antagonistic. This raises the question of whether an appropriate management style would be to let the group get on with its formation without much overt interference (with the benefit of ultimately achieving a cohesive and good performing group, balanced against the time cost of the group going through all its developmental stages).

Roles and role behaviour

The division of labour within any organization between its maintenance, its productive and other support functions necessitates the creation of *roles*. Put simply, roles ensure that the life of any organization is capable of outlasting its present sum total of individuals. Formal roles are created in organizations so that different individuals can be selected to carry out specified tasks. When a selection panel chooses an individual for a job in an organization, they are really matching what they know about that individual to a role description. Just as there can be formal and informal groups, so too are roles both formal and informal. Formal roles are those such as job descriptions, and task specifications. They can be clearly specified quite independently of any single individual. We talk of people holding 'office' in an organization when we refer to the role they currently perform. The organization is thus (in formal terms) a system of multiple roles.

Informal roles are those actions and behaviours of individuals which are not specified or expected by their formal role position. We all take on multiple roles in organizations as well as in the wider society. For example, how would you describe all the roles you undertake during a typical day? Your formal role might be Production Controller. You might also be fairly handy with computers and software because that is one of your hobbies. So an informal role might be that of fixer and possibly trainer for your colleagues in regard to their personal computers. You might also be well experienced in the school of life and interpersonally sympathetic, so another informal role you might take on would be that of 'agony aunt' or counsellor to your organizational colleagues. In wider society, you will also occupy a number of formal and informal roles: wife, father, mother, friend, cricketer, golfer, squash player, do-it-yourself expert are examples. Together, these multiple roles are called a 'role-set' (Katz and Kahn, 1978).

The application of role theory and the taking up of roles in groups has a long and disputed history in social science. As far back as 1936, Linton began to give primacy to the concept of role in social sciences and Parsons (1951) and Merton

(1957) pronounced roles and role behaviour central to the understanding of action and structure in organizations. Others have argued that the concept of role is of little analytical or practical value (see Bittner, 1965; Garfinkel 1967; Goffman 1956). The argument against roles hinges upon the difficulty of trying to understand human behaviour in organizations. To talk about roles is merely to impose a construct which is not 'real' in an objective sense. Behaviour is only understandable in the descriptions and the terminology of those individuals who do the behaving. It is argued that this has little to do with roles or role behaviour.

The implications of roles for the study of organizational behaviour cannot be ignored, however, despite the continuing academic debates. Roles are based upon expected behaviours and performances from individuals in the group. These multiple expectations form the basis of judgements (can this person do the job?) and the basis of appraisal and rewards (how well did the person occupy the role?). Gross (1968) has identified a list of roles which are most commonly taken on in a work group. It is not an exhaustive list, but it is instructive in that it gives illustrations of specific roles and their associated behaviours in the group. See how many in Table 8.1 you recognize from your last work group meeting.

Table 8.1
Common roles in a work group

Task-oriented individuals	Those who predominantly try to get the job done and get some output from the group.
People-oriented individuals	Those who are concerned with interpersonal relationships in the group and who work hard to maintain a good social climate.
No-sayers	Those who consistently oppose most proposals; have thick skins; find fault with virtually everything.
Yes-sayers	Those who try to get round opposition, are enthusiastic and counter the no-sayers.
Regulars	Those who are obviously accepted by the group. These are the 'in people' who accept and project the group's norms and values.
Deviants	Mavericks who depart from group values.
Isolates	'Lone wolves' who often depart even further from expected values and behaviour than the deviants.
Newcomers	New entrants to the group who need to be guided by others; are expected to be seen but not heard.
Old timers	Those who have been in the group for a long time and who know the ropes.
Climbers	Individuals who are commonly expected to get ahead often on the basis of assumed potential rather than any concrete demonstration of ability.
Cosmopolitans	Group members who view themselves as part of a wider professional or cultural community and who often consider the group and its members inferior to this wider community.
Locals	Those who are firmly rooted in the group and in the organizational community.

Multiple roles: conflict and ambiguity

An organization consists of sets of multiple roles, all of which overlap in some form or other. Some roles will be directly related while others will only be tangential to one another. We examine the interrelationships between groups in the next chapter. Here, we are concerned with the multiple roles which any one individual might occupy simultaneously and which can give rise to conflict and ambiguity. Multiple roles are not easy to manage either for the individual or for the manager of individuals in organizations. For example, multiple activities (i.e. tasks) might comprise one role description. Alternatively, any organizational task may involve the individual taking on multiple roles. Finally, a single individual might be responsible for multiple tasks in the organization. The possible permutation of multiple roles, tasks and people is thus complex. However, the symptoms of things going wrong as a result of multiple roles are known as conflict and ambiguity. We explain these in the following sections.

Role conflict   is heightened when multiple role expectations are mutually exclusive. That is, any attempt to fulfil one set of role expectations automatically makes satisfying other expectations difficult or impossible. There are four types of role conflict which occur in organizations (see Table 8.2).

Role conflict is a serious issue for both organizations and for individuals. Most evidence on role conflict is unambiguous. The greater the level of conflict, the less effective is the organization overall and the less satisfied are the individuals within it (see Mitchell and Larson, 1987, who discuss the extensive study carried out by Fisher and Gitelson, 1983).

One of the aspects of reorganization which is frequently overlooked is that any form of structural change in an organization will bring with it different levels and intensities of role conflict. Structural change may reduce some existing conflicts, but it may equally create new role expectations which are incompatible. Since reorganization appears to be a common response by managers to a range of organizational difficulties (falling market share, lack of profitability, feelings of stagnation and human resource problems) the implications that this is likely to have for creating conflicts should not be dismissed lightly. Future performance may not be as good as expected (Hickson *et al.*, 1986).

Role ambiguity   is more simple to identify than role conflict. It describes the situation where individuals are unsure what to do when they occupy a role (Katz and Kahn, 1978). There can be two aspects to this ambiguity, the means and the ends. An individual can be unsure what is expected or which tasks are to be achieved (the ends). Equally, there can be ambiguity over how to achieve tasks, even though they may be specified quite clearly (the means). Selection and promotion procedures in organizations can inadvertently increase levels of role ambiguity. If the aim is to retain a key individual—for example, by creating a new post or by promotion—it is unlikely that anyone in the organization including the role occupant will have a clear idea of what is expected. An organization facing rapid and far-reaching changes will also create an environment of high role ambiguity for its staff.

Since both role conflict and ambiguity have deleterious consequences for both organizational and individual performance, it is important that they are recognized and managed effectively. This is more complex than simply identifying the problem and trying to remove the ambiguity or conflict. The confounding factors are:

1 position in hierarchy;
2 the design of jobs;
3 variable abilities of the individual in their ability to handle conflict and ambiguity.

Research indicates that role conflict is most often experienced by more junior managers and in other relatively lower positions in the firm (McClelland, 1985). Conversely, role ambiguity is likely to increase at more senior levels of management. Senior management tasks simply cannot be broken down into specific and identifiable features which would obviate ambiguity. In many respects, a definition of the key elements of senior management tasks would

Table 8.2
Types of role conflict

Type of role conflict	Description
Intrasender role conflict	Occurs when your boss tells you to do two or more things which are impossible. For example, you might be asked to give a job top priority and be told simultaneously not to neglect any other task. Obviously, doing one task will be at the expense of the other. Conflict occurs because you have to decide what to do in the knowledge that one or more jobs will be neglected and the task allocated will not be fully accomplished.
Inter-sender role conflict	Occurs when two or more people in your role set sent messages which conflict. You cannot meet both sets of expectations. This is a common managerial problem. Conflicting demands might be from sales functions to produce multiple products or variants to satisfy customer demand versus demands from production functions to stick to one or two product variants to smooth the production process and inventory processing.
Inter-role conflict	Occurs when a single person occupies multiple roles. Fulfilling one role automatically obviates the other. In organizations, managers frequently experience role conflict in this way. They may be expected to make decisions which are for the good of the organization overall, and at the same time be expected by their subordinates to make decisions and fight for the good of the department. Both are likely to be incompatible, just as conflicts between being a full-time mother and a full-time manager cannot easily be resolved.
Person–role conflict	Occurs when the person and the expected behaviours of the role do not coincide. For example, you might be recruited to a position in which the expected role behaviour is to adopt an aloof, distant and aggressive management style. If this conflicts with your own feelings about how other people in the organization should be treated, then conflict will occur. Many of us look to our 'principles' to sort out this conflict, by which we mean what we feel fundamentally is right. Many resignations and requests for transfers are directly related to this conflict.

place role ambiguity at centre stage. Selection of senior managers is often based upon the predicted ability of the role occupant to handle (even welcome) ambiguity. For example, Brian Corby, the recently retired Chief Executive of the Prudential Corporation outlined a number of key factors which his organization sought as indicative of senior management potential. These included the ability to see beyond and around day-to-day problems, to demonstrate creativity in problem-solving and to handle complex and often contradictory data in decision-making (*Sunday Times*, 11 December 1988).

Role conflict and ambiguity can create a situation which individuals find stressful (see Chapter 4). However, just as in the studies of stress, the perception of conflict and ambiguity will differ between individuals. Some individuals can handle quite high levels of conflict and ambiguity and feel at ease in their organizational position. Others suffer quite marked degrees of stress because they do not enjoy, and possibly cannot cope with, the levels of ambiguity and conflict (Cooper and Marshall, 1976). Trying to match individual characteristics with the ability to cope with conflict and ambiguity has been the focus of empirical research. Those individuals with a high need to achieve, for example, have been identified as those who experience most difficulty with role ambiguity (McClelland, 1985). Ambiguity frustrates the clear identification of factors which will lead to the fulfilment of their achieving goals. On the other hand, extroverts appear to feel quite at home in the same situation.

Even though the relationships between personality variables and perceived ease with role conflict and ambiguity are persuasive, they are only partially useful. They ignore the dynamic context of organizational life. Individuals change as they progress through organizations and as they get older. The ability to handle problems encountered through role changes also. It is likely that an individual's ability to handle conflict and ambiguity increases positively with experience but only to a point. After that, as maturity sets in, the ability may reduce. Since different individuals will reach such a hypothetical maturity point at different rates, matching individual characteristics and role conflict and ambiguity becomes tenuous.

Training in handling situations which exhibit conflict and ambiguity can also help individuals to cope better with existing levels and even actively to seek such positions. Managers also may benefit from training in role conflict and ambiguity even though they may not experience it themselves (or are able to cope with it 'naturally'). This is because it is all too easy to equate poor performance with specific individuals or aspects of personality rather than with characteristics of the role. The person gets blamed, not the role. An understanding of why conflict and ambiguity can arise, often from seemingly unrelated decisions, can be of immense help in alleviating problems.

Socialization and the pressure to conform in groups

Anyone who has ever joined a group will have experienced pressures to conform and will have undergone a process of socialization. All social groups develop *norms* about expected behaviours from group members and they can exert considerable pressure upon new members to conform. The word conformity is important here, because it emphasizes the rather one-way nature of the change process which occurs. The group expects a certain kind of behaviour. The new member conforms by changing his or her earlier preferences to those of the group.

If any one is in doubt about the strength of the pressure to conform in groups, try arguing for a position which you know is counter to that held by the group. You will be subjected to the most intense pressure to conform. *You* should change and not the group. Leavitt (1972) has identified some discrete stages which will occur in the above scenario of the group and its individual 'deviant':

1 *Reason*   The group attempts to question the 'data base' of the deviant. What evidence do you have for your position? At this stage, the group appears reasonable and rational in its behaviour.
2 *Seduction*   The group now tries to appeal to loyalty values. You're a valued member of this team, they say. We've been through a lot together, so why are you going against us now? The group is trying to get the deviant to see sense (its sense).
3 *Iron fist is revealed*   The group attempts to beat submission out of the deviant. They gang up on him or her. They shout, they harass and harangue and they disbelieve any further data revealed by the deviant.
4 *Amputation*   If the deviant can withstand the first three stages, then continued deviance will result in the group excommunicating him or her. They will no longer be held as a valued member of the team. This, of course, has tremendous implications for a group which meets regularly with the same members. The next time the group meets, the deviant will start by being perceived as hostile no matter what the topic and the group will be suspicious of all behaviour.

The potency of group pressure can be found in the classic study of Solomon Asch (1951). Stanley Milgram's (1974) empirical work also revealed a strong tendency for individuals to conform because the concept of obedience is ingrained in us from a very early age. The study by Asch demonstrates the power of a group to elicit *conformity* of opinion and judgement among its members. Milgram's study illustrates the power of *obedience* in achieving conformity. Each study is described briefly in the next sections.

The Asch experiment in conformity

The Asch experiment took place in a laboratory setting. In the laboratory was a group of six subjects (college students). All were shown drawings of lines and were asked in turn to comment on the relative length of each. For example, they were asked which of the lines drawn in Figure 8.2 was the same length as line 'A'.

Figure 8.2
The Asch experiment in conformity

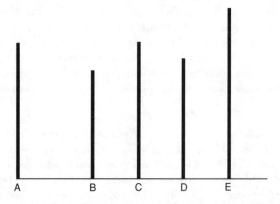

In the experiment, Asch had engineered who was in the group. Really, there was only one volunteer. The confederates and the one volunteer then said which line was the longest, the next longest and so on. At the first session, all group members correctly identified the lines. At a second session, the confederates consistently gave an incorrect answer. They would say, within hearing of the true volunteer, that a line blatantly shorter than 'A' was equal to it in length! In 32 per cent of cases, the volunteer went along with this opinion despite initially showing hesitancy because the answer was obviously wrong. It seemed to be important to achieve unanimity of opinion from the group. Some volunteers did resist group pressure although the film record of the study shows how obviously uncomfortable and hesitant many of them felt in this.

In a further similar study, Asch was able to demonstrate that if the volunteer had an 'ally' whereby one of the confederates consistently defied the group and gave the correct answer, the ability of the volunteer to withstand group pressure was greatly increased. Now the 'deviant' was no longer alone, the potency of group pressure was substantially eroded. The Asch experiment is important and relevant to today's managers for it shows what can happen in any group given a task to make a decision on data which are absolute by any standards of common sense. Given that most organizational problems are not so well defined, group pressure on conformity to feelings, hunches and other subjective data is greatly increased. Further pressures on conformity are also produced if the group is one which meets regularly and considers a range of issues (see Chapter 10).

Compliance and conformity

While compliance and conformity will produce the same end result (obedience to group pressure) it is important to distinguish between them. Compliance differs from conformity in that it reflects conformity through ulterior motives (such as the desire to please the boss, pragmatism — you are new and the rest of the group are long serving — or the recognition of greater power bases on the group). Asch's study revealed three ways in which individuals conformed to, or complied with, group pressure:

1 *Distortion of perception*   Individuals in the group are aware that the group is 'wrong' but they suppress their disagreement while the group is in session. Later, they believe the group was correct after all. Here is obedience through *compliance followed by conformity* (although this kind of conformity happens outside the confines of the group meeting, it can occur as the same group subsequently meets on separate issues).

2 *Distortion of judgement*   Individuals think the group is correct and that they must be wrong. Any doubts they may have are extinguished during the process of the group meeting. This is obedience *solely through conformity*.

3 *Distortion of action*   Individuals are aware that the group is 'wrong'. However, they suppress their deviation from the prevailing opinion. They never subsequently believe that the group was correct. This is *obedience solely through compliance*.

Asch's experiments indicated that distortion of judgement was the major reason for obedience. In other words, individuals tend to conform more than they tend to comply. While this is a surprising finding in a laboratory experiment, it is likely that in work organizations such factors as different hierarchical levels in a group will increase the tendency for individuals to comply rather than to conform. Compliance is thus the recognition of strong power bases (such as the chairperson who is the most senior manager) and compliance may be largely because of political or pragmatic motives (see Chapter 11).

The Milgram studies of obedience to authority

Even the most democratic organizations rely ultimately upon one set of persons following the directions of another group because they are perceived to have the *authority* to give that direction. Managers have to rely on their staff following their directions. If this were not so, organizations would become chaotic places which would never achieve any targets or goals. Most of us recognize authority (although it eludes precise definition) and readily react to it when we think its exercise is reasonable. Of course, the definition of what is reasonable is also not amenable to precise definition, although it is worth noting that the basis of the British and many other legal systems is founded upon the judgement of what a 'reasonable' person would have done in a particular set of circumstances.

In a wider society, too, there is a rule system based upon the acknowledgement of authority. Driving on the public highway requires that drivers and pedestrians follow rules laid down by another authority. The majority of us follow those rules since they allow traffic to flow relatively smoothly and are designed to avoid accidents and collisions. We also talk of 'blind obedience' to authority and of 'authoritarian regimes' wherein the populace of a country are subjected to extremes of dictate. Here, we are making value judgements about the appropriate exercise of authority.

Milgram wanted to show that individuals are socialized to obey. In a group, this tendency can induce people to obey and carry out tasks which, outside the group, would be considered evil or malicious. One of Milgram's intentions was to demonstrate why so many soldiers in the Second World War had apparently followed without question the orders of their officers and inflicted horrendous torture upon prisoners. Such barbarism, said Milgram, could largely be explained by group pressure.

The study consisted of volunteers who took part in a learning experiment. The experiment took place in the early 1960s. Forty adult males from a wide range of social and economic backgrounds were paid to volunteer to be subjects in the experiment. They were told that they were part of an experiment in learning, education and punishment. Each volunteer was then asked to assist another (who was actually a confederate) to learn sets of word pairs. Both individuals faced each other divided by a thick glass screen much as you would find in most recording studios, so that communication between the two was only possible by microphone and loudspeaker.

In front of the volunteer was a machine which administered electric shocks to the 'learner'. On hearing a wrong answer, the volunteer was to administer an electric shock to the learner in order to assist learning by a small punishment. A correct answer resulted in no electric shock being given. The voltage of the shock varied on a scale which ran between 15 and 450 volts. Each time the learner gave a wrong answer, the voltage was to increase to the next higher voltage and so on. The voltage scale was labelled clearly from 'slight shock' through 'extreme intensity shock' to 'XXX'.

As the voltages increased, the learner would protest about the pain being inflicted and that he no longer wanted to take part in the experiment. The volunteer was told to continue by the researcher running the experiment. This continued until severe electric shocks were given. It needed the volunteer to protest three times to the researcher for the experiment to be abandoned. Screams of pain and sometimes ominous silences were clearly audible by the volunteer each time a severe shock was administered. The results indicated that:

1 Sixty-five per cent of the volunteers administered the maximum severity electric shock. This represented 26 out of 40 volunteers.

2 Most volunteers, when pressed to continue by the researcher, exhibited signs of tension and stress such as nervous laughter and trembling. Nevertheless, they continued often on the cajoling of the researcher who insisted that the experiment would be spoiled if they did not continue.

3 At the end of the experiment, all volunteers were told the true nature of the research and that in fact no electric shocks had been administered.

4 The extremely high percentage of conformity by the volunteers gives very strong indications that individuals will obey those they consider to be authoritative and responsible. Even in the case where obvious pain was being inflicted on another individual, the tendency was dominantly to follow directions which came from the source of authority.

Since the time of the Milgram study, virtually no further replications or similar studies have been conducted. Concern for ethics in social-science research have precluded this. Milgram's study is thus an isolated but very powerful example. Whether differences in the propensity towards obeying authority exist between different nations or in different periods in history is debatable. However, the number of mass atrocities in wider society (such as those in Uganda, Cambodia, etc.) and mass devotion to group causes (such as the Moonies and the mass suicide pact of the religious group 'The People's Temple' in Jonestown, Guyana in 1978) lend substantial support to Milgram's findings. Led by the Reverend Jim Jones, an estimated 912 of his People's Temple followers died by taking cyanide or apparently shooting themselves (*The Times*, 26 November 1978).

In organizations, group structures can impose authority and legitimacy upon member individuals in the same way that authority can be used or abused by managers more senior in the hierarchy. The dangers in not recognizing the potency of conformity and obedience to authority are twofold. First, authority can be abused or misused. Secondly, individuals will feel pressured to follow the directions of that authority irrespective of whether such actions would be considered immoral or questionable in the wider context. It is likely that some of these pressures were brought to bear on individuals in the recent 'insider trading' on the British stockmarket in order to make them play the illegal games conducted by others in the financial hierarchy. Within organizations, there is great potential for the abuse of authority both by groups and individuals. Recognition of this by both the authority figure and the recipient can act as some kind of counterweight, although it is unlikely completely to rule out immoral acts in business organizations.

Team building

This approach has been popular in the management development literature for some years as a way of getting individuals to think positively about groups and to avoid some of the pitfalls of compliance, conflict and conformity outlined in this chapter.

Team building relies on alerting all group members to the processes which occur in groups and argues that these processes can be managed to the advantage of the group and ultimately to the performance of the organization (see Dyer, 1987). There is insufficient space in this book to deal with this specialized subject in the necessary depth to do it justice. Team building involves specific techniques which lie outside the scope of this text. Dyer (1987) is an accessible and thorough text of this field.

Summary   When looking at groups rather than individuals in organizations, we recognize that group behaviour has its own set of issues which need to be recognized and managed. In particular, the notion of *roles* is central to understanding the operating problems of groups and the difficulties that individuals can encounter in participating in organizational groups. Roles can cause severe conflict and can create high levels of ambiguity for individuals.

Groups also exert a great deal of influence over constituent members. They can be considered greater than the sum total of their parts, as if they had a life of their own. This is most prevalent in *group norms* and in *socialization processes*. New and existing members of groups will consistently be required to conform to the collective norms and expectations of the group. Those who refuse become *deviants* who are given a few chances to come back into the fold but who are excommunicated if they continue their deviance.

The pressure to *conform* or *comply* (and thus the intense difficulty in resisting) to group authority and group norms is immense. Both the experiments by Asch (1951) and by Milgram (1974) are powerful landmarks which bear witness to the levels of obedience which are attributable to group pressure. *Moral and ideological commitment* by individuals can also be *subverted* by group pressure which can persuade individuals to conform to certain aspects of behaviour they would consider unthinkable in another context. Thus the abuse of this pressure by individuals in organizations is a constant threat. Illegal acts such as deception and deliberate deceit can occur (Staw and Swajowski, 1975) as well as self-interested actions by managers such as insider trading and other illegal financial dealings.

References

Alderfer, C. P. (1977) 'Groups and intergroup relations', in J. R. Hackman and J. L. Suttle (eds) *Improving Life at Work*, Goodyear, Santa Monica, California.

Asch, S. E. (1951) 'Effects of group pressure upon the modification and distortion of judgement', in H. Guetzkow (ed.), *Groups, Leadership and Men*, Carnegie Press, New York.

Bittner, E. (1965) 'The concept of organization', *Social Research*, **32**, 239–55.

Cooper, C. L. and J. Marshall (1976) 'Occupational sources of stress: a review of the literature relating to coronary heart disease and mental health', *Journal of Occupational Psychology*, **49**, 11–28.

Dyer, W. G. (1987) *Team Building: Issues and Alternatives*, 2nd edn, Addison-Wesley, Reading, Mass.

Fisher, C. D. and R. Gitelson (1983) 'A meta-analysis of the correlates of role conflict and ambiguity', *Journal of Applied Psychology*, **68**, 320–33.

Garfinkel, H. (1967) *Studies in Ethnomethodology*, Prentice-Hall, New York.

Goffman, E. (1956) *The Presentation of Self in Everyday Life*, Edinburgh University Press, Edinburgh.

Gross, B. M. (1968) *Organizations and Their Managing*, Free Press, New York.

Hickson, D. J., R. J. Butler, D. Cray, G. R. Mallory and D. C. Wilson (1986) *Top Decisions: Strategic Decision Making in Organizations*, Jossey-Bass, San Francisco and Blackwell, Oxford.

Katz, D. and R. L. Kahn (1978) *The Social Psychology of Organizations*, 2nd edn, Wiley, New York.

Leavitt, H. (1972) *Managerial Psychology: An Introduction to Individuals, Pairs and Groups in Organizations*, 3rd edn, University of Chicago Press, Chicago and London.

Likert, R. (1961) *New Patterns of Management*, McGraw-Hill, New York.

Linton, R. (1936) *The Study of Man*, Appleton-Century, New York.

McClelland, D. C. (1985) *Human Motivation*, Scott, Foresman, Glenview, Ill.

Merton, R. K. (1957) *Social Theory and Social Structure*, Free Press, New York.

Milgram, S. (1974) *Obedience and Authority*, Tavistock, London.

Mitchell, T. R. and J. R. Larson, Jr. (1987) *People in Organizations: An Introduction to Organizational Behavior*, McGraw-Hill, New York.

Parsons, T. (1951) *The Social System*, Free Press, New York.

Shaw, M. E. (1981) *Group Dynamics*, 3rd edn, McGraw-Hill, New York.

Staw, B. and E. Swajowski (1975) 'The scarcity-munificence component of organizational environments and the commission of illegal acts', *Administrative Science Quarterly*, **20**, 345–54.

CHAPTER 9 Intergroup behaviour

Multiple groups as the unit of analysis

Understanding behaviour within any one group can be a significant aid to the management process. However, most organizations consist of multiple groups, each of which interacts with another in order to achieve common organizational tasks. The kinds of behaviours which occur between groups are very different from those which occur within them. They have their own dynamic and their own characteristics which require a different set of management skills to handle them.

Organizations consist of multiple groups each of which is interdependent. This interdependence can take a number of specific forms. It can be *sequential*, *pooled* or *reciprocal* (Thompson, 1967). Each form of interdependence has implications for the nature of the interaction between the various groups and for the management of this interaction.

Sequential inter-dependence

Describes where one group always initiates action for subsequent groups. For example, in an assembly line, production groups initiate action for other groups such as the paintshop or the trim assembly. The production line is the most pure example of sequential interdependence in organizations. The output of group A becomes the input of group B and so on until the last group is reached. The output of this last group (or set of groups) is the final product of the organization (see Figure 9.1).

Pooled inter-dependence

Occurs when two or more groups carry out their tasks independently. The output of these groups is then coordinated by another group (or set of groups) before a final output is produced. In some organizations, such as universities, pooled interdependence is commonplace and a relatively enduring feature of organizational life. In other organizations, such as manufacturing firms, pooled interdependence often occurs at specific times in the production cycle or during the development of new products where research, design and piloting can go on without being linked in to the rest of the organization (such as finance and quality control). Figure 9.2 illustrates a simple form of pooled interdependence.

Reciprocal inter-dependence

This is the most highly interlinked relationship between groups. The output of one or more groups is passed to and fro between a number of groups until final output is achieved. Some hospitals work on this principle as well as some firms in the high-technology industries. Figure 9.3 depicts the arrangement of reciprocal interdependence.

Each of these forms of interlinking between groups has a fundamental impact upon the need for high levels of mutual assistance, information gathering and availability, agreement and compliance between groups, feedback and general coordination. The management task is to ensure maximum effectiveness in intergroup coordination whatever the nature of their interdependence. This is

Figure 9.1
Sequential
interdependence

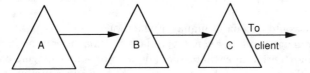

Figure 9.2
Pooled
interdependence

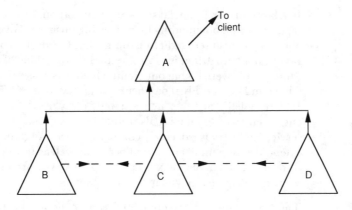

Figure 9.3
Reciprocal
interdependence

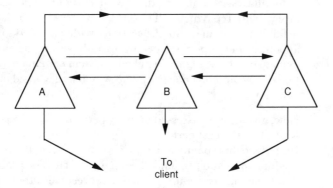

confounded by a number of factors, the net result of which is to make intergroup relations problematic, hostile and uncooperative.

This is not always the case, however. Miller (1976) has noted that certain types of interdependence can effectively act as a self-regulating influence on intergroup activities and promote effective and efficient functioning. For example, high reciprocal interdependence between groups coupled with an inability to distinguish precisely between individual group contribution and a reward system which is equally broad, will tend to unite groups in a common purpose. On the other hand, where groups are required to interact intensively, yet are not bound up in common reward or joint problem-solving activities, the propensity for them to conflict or compete is significantly increased (Dutton and Walton, 1966). Since organizations can never achieve the ideal of total self-regulation between groups, the management task becomes one of handling intergroup competition and conflict. The first step to achieving this, is to understand the *nature* of conflict and competition. There are a number of identifiable factors and stages through which conflicting groups progress. We examine these in the following section.

Intergroup competition and conflict

It would be a naïve manager who thought that no part of his or her job was to manage conflict. Even if it is a largely subconscious activity, a great deal of managerial time will be spent organizing and achieving coherence among different parts of the organization. Even fairly common and seemingly innocuous managerial techniques can backfire and fail because of the severity of intergroup competition. The following example gives an illustration:

In a large British financial services organization, recovery of debts and poor repayments on outstanding loans was big business. Given the relative ease of obtaining consumer credit in Britain since the election of the Thatcher government in 1979, it was also becoming something of a growing problem. More people were taking out credit which was easier to obtain and easier to fall behind in monthly repayments. A survey by the Office of Fair Trading in 1988 revealed that debts incurred in this way were relatively common. Nearly one in ten loans to individuals resulted in poor repayment. Since the financial services industry is extremely competitive, each organization is both trying to extend the amount of credit it allocates as well as trying to achieve efficient recovery of bad debts. Successful competitive performance comes from securing effective repayments from debtors.

The organization had a number of teams of debt collecting clerks all of whom reported to a manager of the section. At first, all clerks were organized on an individual basis. Each one dealt with a set number of clients who were in arrears with repayments. The level of success in securing repayments began to fall. So the manager of the section divided his clerks into four groups, appointed one supervisor per group and, because he had read his management text books, installed a system of management by objectives (MBO) a common enough system which had worked in a number of similar situations.

Now, groups were assessed on their performance. Every month, the group which had the best performance (measured by debts) received a cash bonus. Initially, debt repayment levels got better. Then, the level slid back to its original point and gradually began to worsen. The problem turned out to be that the manager of the section did not recognize that each of the groups was increasingly in competition with the others and that levels of intergroup conflict were extremely high.

Individual clerks would now work to achieve the cash bonus for their group. They would contact a much greater number of clients than before, trying to secure a repayment. This led to a situation where clerks would contact a client who would secure a repayment for a single month without having much regard to whether that client continued payment. There were high levels of competition between group members to secure clients who would pay up for a single month and poaching of each others' clients became common.

Of course, some groups were better at this than others, and one group consistently won the cash bonus. The other groups became disenchanted and ceased working as hard as they had done previously. The net result was a feeling of extreme hostility between group members (where none had occurred before) coupled with an increase in debt levels to the organization. Clients were only being asked to repay for one month to secure performance figures for the clerks. Subsequent payments were of secondary importance.

Given the high number of clients who were in debt, clerks could 'shop around' different individuals to achieve repayment.

Thus, setting up a seemingly effective management system can result in the creation of intergroup competition and conflict which actually reduces performance rather than enhances it (as in the example above). We discuss at what levels conflict becomes dysfunctional later in this chapter. For the present, we try to define conflict before we elaborate on its management.

Attempting a definition is difficult enough. Some common themes are identifiable, however.

1 Conflict exists only in so far as it is perceived by the parties it is deemed to concern. If a person or a group is unaware of the conflict, they generally agree that no conflict exists. Others in the organization may suggest that there is conflict between two parties who themselves do not perceive this.
2 There must be evidence of overt or covert opposition or blockage to particular stances adopted by various individuals or groups in the organization.
3 There must be two or more parties whose interests or goals appear to be incompatible.

Traditional management approaches to conflict

For many managers, the assumption is that all conflict in their organization is bad. It detracts from the efficient functioning of the organization. *Conflict becomes described in terms of violence, destruction or irrationality*. Since conflict is assumed to result in ineffective and inefficient organization, 'good' managers aim to avoid it altogether. Avoidance of conflict thus becomes the major role of managerial responsibilities. This traditional philosophy, that agreement is good and that conflict is bad, still holds true in many organizations today.

This is hardly surprising if we examine some of the values which are prevalent in our developed societies. From early schooling we have all been encouraged to 'get along with others and to avoid conflict even if you do not like them'—and domestic life most likely reinforced this philosophy. In national philosophies, the anti-conflict message is strong. America and Britain are often described as peace loving nations no matter what their actions might imply. They buy offensive weapons and act aggressively toward other countries in the name of peacekeeping and defence. Many of the aggressive acts conducted by Britain in the Northern Ireland situation are described as peacekeeping acts despite the recent adoption of a shoot-first, ask-questions-afterwards philosophy toward IRA terrorists. This is not intended as a political statement. It just describes how we as individuals react more favourably to the language of peacekeeping rather than to the vocabulary of conflict.

Much of the management literature which deals with conflict takes a particular orientation to it. Conflict should be resolved. That is the manager's job. Part of the salary is 'combat pay' for attending to all the aggravation the manager faces in the process of conflict resolution. This is particularly true of the literature which sprung up around and developed from the human relations school (see Chapter 2).

The interactionist management approach to conflict

This management approach says that *conflict management* and *conflict resolution* are not the same thing. Certain levels of conflict are seen as a good thing in the organization. Managers should encourage the occurrence of some conflict in their organizations. Of course, beyond a certain level, conflict does become destructive or dysfunctional, but up to that point conflict is good for helping to achieve sustainable organizational performance:

1 It keeps the organization on its toes.
2 It avoids the organization getting too routinized and its members becoming apathetic to change.
3 It results in better decisions since ready made solutions are not immediately applied unquestioningly to problems. There is the possibility of collecting a greater number and diversity of alternative.
4 It provides a forum for all members of the organization to be self-critical, and to be critical of the organization as a whole.

The main characteristics of the traditional and the interactionist management approaches are summarized in Table 9.1.

Table 9.1
Traditional and interactionist models of conflict

Traditional	Interactionists
Conflict is avoidable	Conflict is inevitable
Conflict is caused by troublemakers, primadonnas and deviants	Conflict is determined by structural factors such as the physical shape or the hierarchical design of an organization, the design of a career structure or the nature of a class system
Managerial forms of authority tend to emphasize the rational elements, e.g. going through the appropriate channels or sticking to the rules	Conflict is seen as integral to the nature of organizational change
Allocation of blame to scapegoats is accepted as inevitable	A particular level of conflict is optimal. Individuals are not blamed for engaging in conflict

Figure 9.4 shows the relationship between levels of conflict and organizational performance.

Of course, defining the level at which conflict is optimal is an extremely difficult task for a manager but it is safe to say that most of us would begin to feel distinctly uncomfortable in organizations in which very high levels of

Figure 9.4
Organizational performance and conflict

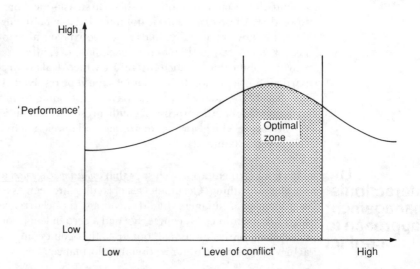

conflict were being approached. Equally, most of us would feel bored and unfulfilled in organizations which had little or no intergroup conflict in them. They would be very bland places indeed. There is, therefore, a large safety margin in between these two extremes.

This feeling of comfort with certain levels of conflict is dependent upon assuming the archetypal 'reasonable person'. All organizations are not staffed with such reasonable people. Take, for example, the situation of hijackers of airliners. Ordinary aircrew find themselves in intense conflict with terrorists and the like. Such hijacking organizations operate outside the bounds of what most of us would consider reasonable. Other terrorist organizations and some religious organizations are also staffed with individuals for whom intense conflict is a way of life.

Managing these conflict situations successfully requires recognition that for terrorists the idea of death is something that is often quite attractive to them. Confrontational styles of management would not be particular appropriate! If you think that these are extreme examples, many apparently 'normal' managers from ordinary groups in ordinary organizations appear at least initially to engage in near self-destructive levels of conflict. They:

1 threaten to resign and take key staff with them;
2 have open confrontations with their bosses;
3 ignore their immediate bosses and go over their heads to the chief executive.

Some are successful at maintaining and managing these high conflict situations, although others in the company are likely to feel under threat or under stress. Others are not so successful and stumble on in the firm very unhappily, or are forced to resign.

Managing intergroup conflict

The manager who begins to tackle conflict by adopting any of the above behaviours is taking a high-risk strategy which is likely to fail fairly quickly as resentment and frustration at these behaviours grows. *Most intergroup conflict is a product of organizational structure.* Managing conflict requires the identification of the underlying and predictable structural causes before attending to particular groups or individuals who are only a part of the structural jigsaw puzzle. We have seen already how various configurations of interdependence can heighten or contain intergroup conflict. The following is a well-known experiment which describes intergroup conflict. It shows how levels of conflict can be managed by paying attention to structural variables rather than interpersonal ones. It also shows how conflict can be managed into becoming cooperation.

The Sherif and Sherif studies of intergroup conflict

A study conducted by the psychologists Muzafar and Carolyn Sherif (1953) in North America consisted of a series of experiments relating to group formation, group conflict and cooperation. They tell us a great deal about conflict and its origins in organizational structure.

The experiment

Summer camps for boys were the setting. This was so that sample conditions could be controlled and reproduced exactly in the future. The groups were informal and comprised boys previously unacquainted prior to the experiment. All the boys came from similar socio-economic backgrounds. They were all healthy, well-adjusted and from white, Protestant, middle-class homes. Experimental situations were kept lifelike by choosing activities characteristic of such camps (such as making camp and canoeing) but usually requiring obstacles to be overcome first. Data-collection methods were disguised or made a natural part of the setting. Several methods were used at all the stages so that results could be cross-validated.

The experiment was designed to be in three stages of one week each. The stages for the whole experiment comprised:

Stage 1 group formation
Stage 2 the development of conflict between the groups
Stage 3 the reduction of conflict and the development of cooperation

Stage 1 *Group formation*   This was characterized by the formation of group norms and status and role relations. Leaders and their assistants emerged. As the groups established themselves, rituals, nicknames, group names and secret symbols were adopted.

Stage 2 *Intergroup conflict*   Now, there were activities where only one group could achieve an outcome at the expense of all the other groups. Games were placed such as tug-of-war and baseball. This created animosity between the groups (intergroup conflict). The level of conflict was sufficiently high that a boy who previously nominated another a 'best friend' rating (in another group) now gave him a negative rating. The effect of intergroup conflict was to *increase the solidarity, cooperativeness and morale within each group.*

Stage 3 *Cooperation*   At first, events were introduced which required the groups to meet for pleasant contacts such as the sharing in prizes or other benefits. There was no need for the groups to be interdependent or to compete. However, these events heightened conflict rather than reduced it. Further hostilities ensued between the groups.

Activities which required mutual assistance between groups were then introduced. These 'superordinate goals' were extremely appealing to both groups but necessitated their cooperation if they were to achieve their goal. For example a lorry was to go for food, but it 'broke down'. Everyone was hungry, so the groups had to work together and pool resources to get the lorry started (e.g. some rope, some cables, tools, etc). At the end of this week, the groups became increasingly friendly and positive ratings began to develop across group lines. Best friends once again were found frequently between individuals in different groups.

Conclusions to be drawn out of the Sherif study

1 The occurrence of conflict is not solely attributable to the characteristics of individuals. It arises under given structural conditions. The fact that individuals within the groups are 'well-adjusted' and otherwise normal appears not to matter.
2 Cooperative and democratic procedures created within any one group are not transferable directly to intergroup relations.
3 Solidarity within a group is most pronounced when conflict between groups is at its highest.
4 Interaction between rival groups in pleasant circumstances does not itself eliminate conflict.
5 Interaction between groups towards a commonly desired superordinate goal helps to create good relations between groups. This needs to occur more than just once to secure cooperation out of previous conflict. A sense of teamwork is thus created towards a common goal. Peters and Waterman (1982) have argued that it is possible to create just one such sense of teamwork in a complex organization of thousands of people. While this may be true of the organizations they studied, it is more likely that multiple visions occur

throughout the organization at various levels and between various functions. The management task thus becomes one of identifying goals at which the majority of these groups can aim and which they find broadly acceptable (Cyert and March, 1963).

There are two further aspects of intergroup conflict which are not so readily observable from the Sherif studies. One is that the use of superordinate goals can be promoted by managers as a genuine attempt to achieve cooperation between groups. This will only be a successful strategy if:

1 the conflicting groups share the same goal;
2 individuals are of equal status;
3 the goal is actually attained.

If not, the likely result is an increase in both conflict and mutual prejudices (e.g. stereotyping members of the other group).

The second is that the use of superordinate goals can be an overtly manipulative ploy, aimed at serving the self-interest of the manager rather than solving any intergroup conflict. Machiavelli in *The Prince* knew this well. He argued that an effective manipulative strategy for handling internal dissent between factions within one nation was to go to war (or appear to do so) with another nation. The once-divided country now became united in its hostility towards the supposedly hostile nation. Governmental policies towards the domestic population can be rather less than generous or even unfair, since the population will be willing to endure hardship in the face of external threat and pull together in a national effort. This aspect of handling conflict in organizations is covered in some detail by Kelly (1974) and Jay (1967).

Another less obvious facet of the Sherif studies is that the 'Hawthorne Effect' has to be borne in mind, as it does in most experiments in social science. This effect describes how changes can occur in the experimental situation more because of the novelty of the enterprise and the desire by participants to please or achieve the goals of the researcher, and less because of the variables at play in the experiment (see Adair, 1984 for an extended discussion of this effect).

Finally, it is all too easy to identify the structural underpinnings of intergroup conflict and argue that a solution to any such intergroup problem is to change the structure of the organization. Most organizations have structural arrangements that are unlikely to be changed radically by any individual or any group of managers. The restructuring of a complex organization is usually a ponderous and a painful process and many managers would rather settle for handling dysfunctional conflict by 'finger-in-the-dyke' management rather than undergo the stresses and strains of structural change (see Miller and Friesen, 1984).

Miller and Friesen (1984: ch. 4) show that many firms display characteristics of makeshift changes to their structures, attending to the detail of the present day but neglecting to think more broadly about the nature of smooth, integrated intergroup relations. Many managers seemed to be willing to let bureaucracy take the blame for intergroup disharmonies. The firm had a structure, the structure had its rules and if groups disagreed with one another, the solution was to consult the rules or to create new ones to accommodate the present conflict. In an assessment of successful organizational performance, Miller and Friesen (1984) empirically supported the adoption of proactive and anticipatory strategies by managers. That is, they did not try and tackle problems such as dysfunctional levels of conflict between groups in a piecemeal fashion, but tried to avoid its occurrence in the first place by attention to the structural rather than inter-personal causes of conflict in organizations.

Implementing strategies to handle intergroup conflict

This takes us back to the points made at the beginning of this chapter. In order to implement changes to reduce intergroup conflict when it occurs, first we have to identify the *locus of the conflict*. For example it might fall into one or more of the following categories:

1	*hierarchical conflict*	e.g. senior management versus middle management
2	*functional conflict*	e.g. work study versus personnel, or sales versus production
3	*professional versus functional conflict*	e.g. accountants versus production, or more complex conflicts for example between management, workforce and shop stewards
4	*management versus the shop floor*	e.g. management versus the workforce directly
5	*union versus union*	e.g. craft unions versus a general workers' union, or more general multiple union conflict

Having established the *locus* of the conflict, it is then necessary to examine *the nature of the conflict*. There are three broad types. Any intergroup conflict can be one of these types. Over time, the nature of the conflict can change from one to the other.

1	*A fight*	The aim is to injure or destroy, subdue or drive away the perceived source of conflict by the group. One group wants to get rid of the other group/s permanently.
2	*A game*	The source of conflict is accepted as being integral to the situation. Other conflicting groups are not exact mirror images of one another, fighting for scarce resources in an irreconcilable fashion. Compromise can be reached, although this will mean some groups appear to benefit more than others. The situation can be structured over time so that different groups benefit over a set time frame.
3	*A debate*	The aim of all groups is to convince one another of their logic. This is not usually detrimental to organizational functioning since the aim is neither to destroy other groups nor to score points from them.

The nature of the conflict will determine to some extent the strategy for its resolution. A debate, for example, will possibly not need resolution at all. It probably represents around the ideal level of conflict for securing good performance from groups. A game is more likely to require intervention. An assessment of the structural context and the range of mutually acceptable compromise positions by the groups would likely be a productive way of handling this kind of conflict. A fight, on the other hand, needs instant attention, otherwise irreparable damage may be done both to the organization in terms of loss of production, profits and personnel and in terms of psychological damage inflicted upon group members. This can be one of the prime causes of stress encountered by individuals in organizations (Albrecht, 1979; French, Caplan and Harrison, 1982).

Adapted from much of the literature on industrial relations, many current managerial strategies towards handling intergroup conflict rely on one or more of the following:

1 negotiation
2 mediation
3 arbitration

Negotiation Disputing parties come together to determine the terms of the exchange which will be acceptable to both parties. Essentially, negotiation is about the quid pro quo which is acceptable to all parties. Negotiation tests the power balance in an organization. It is conducted on a face-to-face basis and the terms of the dispute are hammered out person to person.

Mediation A third party is involved in trying to resolve the conflict between two parties. This is a useful strategy to employ when face-to-face contact (negotiation) has failed. Usually negotiation fails because in the process of testing the power balance, the parties become polarized into positions which preclude further face-to-face contact. There is no common ground whatsoever.

The mediator is usually able to keep contact between the factions and can effect neutral communication between them. But even this can go wrong or can be ineffective at resolving disputes. In this case, arbitration may be the next step.

Arbitration The dispute goes to a third party, but in this case the third party has the power to formulate and implement a settlement which is binding on both parties. Arbitration can be compulsory by law. This is the kind of arbitration which trades unions often use when negotiations break down using other means of conflict resolution. Other kinds of arbitration are not legally necessary, but can be effected in organizations by voluntary agreement.

None of the above strategies will preclude the outbreak of further intergroup conflicts since the underlying structural causes are not changed. They have been shown to be successful, however, in a number of disputes so their efficacy is not to be dismissed lightly. In many cases, sufficient degrees of necessary structural change are either not possible or are too time-consuming, so other strategies have to be pursued. Thomas (1977) has outlined five possible strategies for handling conflict which build upon the rather stark negotiation, mediation and arbitration framework. These are shown in Table 9.2.

Summary This chapter has highlighted the importance of understanding the behaviours which occur between groups in organizations. Since most complex firms cannot achieve the provision of goods or services without functional differentiation, certain interdependencies are inevitably created between groups. The nature of these interdependencies can vary. They can be sequential, pooled or reciprocally related, although many intergroup relations are complex mixtures of all three types. These interdependencies are the source of intergroup conflict, competition and cooperation.

Conflict between groups is usually much less attributable to the personalities who inhabit the group and much more related to the ways in which multiple groups are structured together. The nature of their interdependencies will give a clue to the likely levels of conflict between groups.

For most managers, effecting radical changes in the structure of their organizations is not a feasible proposition although fine tuning within the limits

Table 9.2
Five conflict
management
strategies

Strategy	Useful when
Competition	• Other groups take advantage of non-competitive behaviour. • Very quick decisions need to be made. • The organization's survival is at stake.
Collaboration	• The goal is to learn more information/skills. • Commitment and consensus are needed above all else. • Feelings and emotions need exploring.
Avoidance	• An immediate decision is not needed. • More information is required. • There is no chance of winning in a competition. • People are angry and need to cool down before they can talk and think rationally again.
Accommodation	• Losses need minimizing. • You discover you were wrong. • The impact on other groups is more important than on your own. • Credit is needed for future situations.
Compromise	• The issue needs breaking down into manageable pieces. • A temporary settlement is needed. • Collaboration and/or competition do not work. • When stalemate is achieved between groups of equal power.

Source: adapted from Thomas (1977: 487).

of feasibility can reduce intergroup conflict markedly. Other strategies adopted rely on correctly identifying *the source* of the conflict, *its nature* and *its intensity*. With this information, resolution of intense conflicts can occur. Among these are: the creation of superordinate goals to unite groups, the reduction of interdependence (where feasible), expanding the resource base (to avoid fighting for slices of a small cake), resorting to systems of problem solving such as arbitration and mediation (Robbins, 1983).

All organizations need a certain level of conflict within them to spur on performance and to provide the impetus for change and innovation. Without this driving force, most organizations would become stifled by becoming over-institutionalized and resistant to any form of change. Part of the management process is therefore to keep the balance between effective and ineffective levels of conflict. This is all the more difficult since there are no fixed guidelines to gauge the 'level' of conflict which is appropriate. Other factors such as the incidence of stress, feelings of discomfort, incidence of complaints and stereotyping behaviours have to serve as guides in this respect.

It is equally likely that a manager will be in a position where the *creation* rather than the reduction of intergroup conflict might be required. Complacency and rigorous adherence to the status quo are typical contexts in which this might be necessary.

References

Adair, J. (1984) 'The Hawthorne Effect: a reconsideration of the methodological artifact', *Journal of Applied Psychology*, **69**, 334–45.
Albrecht, K. (1979) *Stress and the Manager*, Prentice-Hall, Englewood Cliffs, New Jersey.

Cyert, R. and J. G. March (1963) *A Behavioral Theory of the Firm*, Prentice-Hall, Englewood Cliffs, New Jersey.

Dutton, J. M. and R. E. Walton (1966) 'Interdepartmental conflict and cooperation: two contrasting studies', *Human Organization*, **25**, 207–20.

French, J. R. P., R. D. Caplan and R. V. Harrison (1982) *The Mechanism of Job Stress and Strain*, Wiley, London.

Jay, A. (1967) *Management and Machiavelli*, Holt, New York.

Kelly, J. (1974) *Organizational Behavior*, Irwin, Illinois.

Miller, D. and P. H. Friesen (1984) *Organizations: A Quantum View*, Prentice-Hall, Englewood Cliffs, New Jersey.

Miller, E. J. (ed.) (1976) *Task and Organization*, Wiley, New York.

Peters, T. J. and R. H. Waterman, Jr. (1982) *In Search of Excellence: Lessons from America's Best Run Companies*, Harper & Row, New York.

Robbins, S. P. (1983) *Organization Theory: The Structure and Design of Organizations*, Prentice-Hall, Englewood Cliffs, New Jersey.

Sherif, M. and C. W. Sherif (1953) *Groups in Harmony and Tension*, Harper and Bros., New York.

Thomas, K. W. (1977) 'Toward multidimensional values in teaching: the example of conflict behaviours', *Academy of Management Review*, July, 472–91.

Thompson, J. D. (1967) *Organizations in Action*, McGraw-Hill, New York.

Decision-making in groups

Introduction

If any single task is central to the management function, decision-making would be the main activity of virtually all managers in all organizations. It is arguably this process which distinguishes managerial activity from that of other functional responsibilities and tasks in the organization.

At first sight, descision-making appears deceptively simple. To decide means to make up your mind by choosing among alternative courses of action. Such actions do not necessarily have to be concrete or tangible. One can decide to become a better or more educated and informed person. One can decide to eat a healthier diet some time in the future.

In business organizations, managers do make decisions about tangible organizational problems. They make decisions about new products or new services. Managers decide upon the size and scope of existing operations and can choose to add or subtract from these as conditions are deemed to suggest. Some of these decisions are taken regularly in organizations by individual managers. Other decision topics are taken by groups of them. Over time, organizations develop accustomed and predictable ways of making these decisions. This routinization of decision-making allows for shorthand ways of making decisions since many of the arguments and rationalizations can be encoded in very precise and predictable form. This is called 'programmed' decision-making (Simon, 1960).

Programming is evident, for example, in standard operating procedures or in the computerization of regularly occurring decisions or situations. Beyond these parameters or guidelines, however, there lies an almost infinite scope for how decisions are to be made. When choosing among alternatives is not guided by precedent or by standard procedure, the focus of managerial activity is centred upon managing the decision-making process and achieving a set of outcomes on which action can be taken.

One popular stereotype of the manager is that of the creative, energetic individual decision-maker. While this may be true of some senior executives or the owners of small family businesses, most managers will find themselves most of the time involved with other managers discussing a wide range of decision topics. The role each individual manager plays in these group decisions will vary from topic to topic. Sometimes, the manager will be representing the collective feeling or viewpoint of his or her department. At other times, the manager will be called into a group (or may form one) because of specialist knowledge or because what is to be decided will have implications for most areas of the organization. In either case, the topics under discussion are usually beyond the scope of any one individual in the organization. A single manager would lack sufficient information, technical skill, or both, to make the decision alone.

We have already seen in Chapters 8 and 9 that groups of individuals can be characterized by a number of aspects which are specific to group rather than individual processes. Decision-making in groups is no exception. Not only do the overall group process characteristics arise, but also the act of trying to make a decision can result in very specific kinds of behaviours from group members. So much is this a recognized part of organizational life that a number of aphorisms have arisen around the topic of committees, working parties, boards of directors and other decision-making groups:

- 'A camel is a racehorse designed by a committee.'
- 'The best committee is a five-man group where four of them are absent.'
- 'A committee is a collection of the unfit appointed by the unwilling to perform the unnecessary.'

These humorous, but often all too accurate, descriptions of decision processes in groups, find their grains of truth in what can happen in group decisions if not actively recognized and managed. They describe what happens when the decision process deviates for whatever reason from the rational or theoretically ideal process. This ideal process is called 'synoptic' by Lindblom (1959). It can be modelled thus:

Identify problem
↓
Generate alternative solutions
↓
Evaluate and choose between alternatives
↓
Implement the chosen solution
↓
Maintain the solution via monitoring,
review and appraisal

Humans make decisions trying to be rational but they rarely succeed in practice. They are *intended* to be rational. This is why Herbert Simon has made the distinction between economic man and administrative man. Economic man tries to maximize—i.e. selects the best possible course open to him. Administrative man tries to achieve outcomes which are satisfactory and sufficient. Combining these two words together gives us the portmanteau word—*satisficing*—which is how Cyert and March (1963) described the bulk of organizational decision-making activity.

Man cannot, or will not, spend time looking for optimal alternatives. He is happy with and can only deal with gross simplifications and only a few limited variables at any one time. In business organizations, this means going for adequate rather than optimal market share—or going for sufficient rather than optimal profit.

Since humans are notoriously inefficient decision-makers in the above ways, this is why it makes sense to have at least some decisions in organizations programmed by standard procedures so that people are not making all decisions from scratch each time. People can and do make new or novel decisions, of course, but they are usually very bad at it when compared to the theoretically rational process.

The rational model appears accurate and robust, especially if we add in feedback loops to it at all the various stages in the process which is what occurs in computer modelling of decision processes. The problem is that the model assumes two things:

1 perfect knowledge
2 perfect rationality

Perfect knowledge implies that any one person or group of people making a decision have all the information available to them that they need and exactly when they want it. Perfect rationality means that, once in possession of the information, the individual or the group will act in sequence, without prejudice, emotion, or without any of the characteristics of being 'human'. Of course, these are unrealistic expectations. In practice, a number of things can contribute to decisions in groups being rather less than rational both in terms of the process (what happens in the interactions between the group members) and the outcome (what the group eventually decides). We have highlighted three major areas, conformity, culture and power.

Conformity

Because groups tend to foster conformity behaviour (see Asch, 1955; Milgram, 1974; Leavitt, 1972), they equally put this pressure upon participants in decision-making. While it might appear useful to have a group comprising the same individuals meeting regularly on a number of topics (because they represent the whole organization, they free up time for others, they are considered 'good' judges and are fair-minded) the reverse is often true. The outcomes and processes of this group are likely to be defective in the following respects:

- Information is not actively sought beyond that which is to hand, or information is only partial or biased.
- Only a handful of alternatives are considered.
- Those alternatives which are considered are then only evaluated partially and some are not really evaluated at all.
- There is a strong tendency among the group members to keep things as they are and not to speak or recommend change.
- Once an outcome is reached, there is little or no consideration of planning for any other future contingencies which might occur.

(Adapted from Janis and Mann, 1977)

The appearance of this group from the outside is one of unanimity and it is this which often tempts other managers to leave the group alone by equating the group's ability to achieve consensus with its apparent effectiveness. This conformity is called 'groupthink' by Janis (1972). He describes groupthink as:

a deterioration of mental efficiency, reality testing and moral judgement that is the result of in-group pressures.

Janis examined some famous cases of decision-making by groups in world history. He looked at the decision to invade Cuba (Bay of Pigs), the Pearl Harbor attack and the escalation of the Vietnam war. He concluded that all these decisions or events were characterized by the propensity of the group just to drift along. Such drift builds in false consensus in the group. Individuals who might feel that they disagree with the group's decision rarely voice that opinion inside the group.

Symptoms of groupthink

1 The group feels invulnerable. There is excessive optimism and risk-taking.
2 Warnings that things might be going awry are discounted by the group members in the name of rationality.
3 There is an unquestioned belief in the group's morality. The group will ignore questionable stances on moral or ethical issues.

4 Those who dare to oppose the group are called evil, weak, or stupid.
5 There is direct pressure on anyone who opposes the prevailing mood of the
   group.
6 Individuals in the group censor if they feel that they are deviating from group
   norms.
7 There is an illusion of unanimity. Silence is interpreted as consent.
8 There are often self-appointed people in the group who protect it from
   adverse information. These people are referred to as 'mindguards'.

Janis's work has important implications. All of the above can commonly
occur in committees or board meetings. Organizations can very quickly
become helpless, with managerial decisions drifting towards goals which are
either inappropriate or are left unquestioned. Once decline has set in through
groupthink, its reversal is tremendously difficult.

**Risky shift
decisions**

Another group effect upon decision process is risky shift. This is the tendency
for individuals to accept higher levels of risk when taking decisions in groups.
Stoner (1968) found that there was a significant tendency for groups to go for
relatively risky but high pay-off decisions, while individuals favour relatively
safe decisions with moderate payoffs. Thus, groups do not represent the
'average' risk of their constituent individuals. One explanation of risky shift is
the diffusion of responsibility. You can blame it on the group if things go
wrong. Other explanations focus on the conformity effect of group processes
(like groupthink). If an individual favours moderate risk, the group will take
this as a base line and shift towards greater risks. The reverse trend towards
safe decisions can also occur.

Culture

There can also be conformity between group decision-making and overall
organizational culture. Meyer and Rowan (1977) and Mitchell, Rediker and
Beach (1986) show how images, values and ideas that are held *corporately* are
used as guidelines for decision-making. Organizations in which bold,
adventurous risk-taking is predominant will inevitably hold these cultural
attributes against any group decision outcome as a measure of its worth.
Decisions will be seen as good or as acceptable to the extent that they fit with
the prevailing cultural values of the organization.

Wilson *et al.* (1986) also demonstrate that decision-making is 'bounded' by
what is considered organizationally legitimate or acceptable. This is different to
the fit of culture and decision criteria because it refers to the rules and structures
of organizations which are set up *before decision-making begins*. As long as decision
processes are in line with what is prescribed in the organization, then decisions
will be fairly trouble-free. Even the most important, strategic decisions will be
made fairly routinely. This phenomenon has been described at length by Lukes
(1974) and is derived from earlier work by Schattsneider (1960) which refers to
this process as the 'mobilization of bias'.

Of course, decisions made by groups which conform to the bias of
organization may be effective and contribute to organizational success. This in
turn reinforces the rules and procedures by which decisions are made. On the
other hand, decisions may not yield such good results, but it is the decision-
makers themselves who are targeted as the source of failure and rarely the
overall system. Decision-making is likely to go on in the same old way and thus
contribute to an ever-increasing spiral of decline (Whetten, 1980).

Power   We shall deal with power as a separate topic in Chapter 11 of this book. Here, we shall just highlight some aspects of power as it relates to group decision-making. Groups in organizations generally comprise individuals who come from various parts of the firm. They are likely to be from finance, and production, from sales and/or marketing and in a group they are all expected to agree on common organizational policy which should bring them equal benefits. Of course, this is not what happens in practice.

Each individual brings to the group his or her own perspective on how the problem should be solved. Each person views the organization they are in not as a global overall being, but from a very 'local' view which is essentially coloured by the particular department they are in. Sales managers will tend to see all organizational problems and opportunities from a sales point of view and production managers likewise from a production point of view. One will be interested in the sales-volume aspects of any decision, while the other will focus on efficient and trouble-free inventory processing.

'Local rationalities' is the term given by Cyert and March (1963) for these often conflicting perspectives. Taken to an extreme, these conflicts can be disruptive and can lead eventually to organizational failure. Usually, it does not reach this level. This is because humans work on the principle of *satisficing*. We will accept what is satisfactory rather than go full out for exactly what we want. In this way, a level of compromise can be achieved between parties rather than total conflict. Achieving this compromise, however, can involve managers in the most intense political activity where achieving success in the political battles for power can seem more important than achieving an acceptable decision outcome (see Pettigrew, 1973; Wilson, 1982 for cases which vividly describe such processes).

Groups of managers also rarely try and solve all the pressing decision issues at once. This would be impossible given their complexity and the level of conflict they would generate. What happens in practice is that groups commit themselves to solving problems in sequence. First they try to satisfy market demand and then they try to keep production and stocking levels smooth, for example.

Managers will also try to avoid making decisions with very long-term implications. A decision group would be unable to handle the complexity involved. Decision-making thus becomes an activity to solve pressing problems and not to discuss long-range strategies. This is called 'uncertainty avoidance' (Cyert and March, 1963).

Information search is generally only carried out in the face of a problem. It does not occur all the time. Search for information is motivated—it rarely occurs naturally. As we already know, search is also never optimal, since decision-makers satisfice. The search is also for recipes or solutions which have worked previously and which now look appropriate to the present problem.

The implications are that organizations will develop slowly and in piecemeal rather than radical steps since their decision-makers will tend to act reactively to demands and will seek solutions to their current problems by seeing what the group or the organization did in the past. Three major theories of decision process describe this. These are:

1 *Incrementalism*, or the science of muddling through (Lindblom, 1959; Braybrooke and Lindblom, 1963).
2 *Garbage can theory* (Cohen, March and Olsen, 1972; March and Olsen, 1976).
3 *Process typology* (Mintzberg, Raisinghani and Theuret, 1976; Hickson *et al.*, 1986).

Incrementalism

According to Lindblom (1959) this is the way most decisions are handled in organizations most of the time. The history of actions in the past dominate current and future decisions. Only a limited number of alternatives are considered and decision outcomes are nearly always piecemeal steps forward from current practice. Lustick (1980) notes that even when problems arise which are so large that they cannot be tackled piecemeal, managers still attempt to muddle through by taking bits at a time and by relying on history for guidance and inspiration.

In a study of nine American firms, Quinn (1980) reinforced the finding that incrementalism was a dominant mode of process. He also suggested that perhaps incrementalism was a logical way forward for decision-makers and organizations, arguing that it was a useful recipe for achieving progressive change. The other side of incrementalism is that both managers and organizations will become locked in to particular frames of reference which are inherently conservative. Decisions will always be made, some even appearing quite efficient processes, but it may also be that the wrong set of decisions are being made and the organization is in danger of sliding incrementally out of business.

Garbage can theory

First proposed by Cohen, March and Olsen, (1972), this theory argued that the linear, rational model of decision-making was both unrealistic and useless to practising managers. What happened instead, they argued, was that organizations were really collections of solutions. Solutions represent an individual's or, more likely, a group's view of what ought to be done in a given set of circumstances. These solutions were a product of organizational culture and the outcomes of previous decision processes. As soon as a fresh problem faced decision-maker, one of these pre-existing solutions was attached to it. Organizations are thus:

> 'a collection of choices looking for problems . . . solutions looking for issues to which they might be the answer, and decision makers looking for work (Cohen, March and Olsen, 1972: 2).

The term garbage can (or dustbin, to Anglicize the terminology) is a colourfully chosen symbol which describes the decision-making forum (for example a committee) as a rubbish bin. Anything gets thrown in and any number of people can use the same or multiple rubbish bins. Trying to sort out the rubbish into a coherent whole is useless since its contents are initially unrelated anyway. The only way decisions are made, therefore, is by individuals or groups trying to get their preferred solution implemented. The key factor here is that chosen solutions are not necessarily logically connected to the current decision topic. They are merely stimulated by its occurrence.

March and Olsen (1976) have taken this analogy a stage further by suggesting that choices, ready-made solutions, the occurrence of problems, what information is wanted and who should make the decision are almost totally unconnected! That is, organizations are places in which groups and individuals have multiple and conflicting interests and goals. These are not pieced together in any 'rational' way. It may be, for example, that someone's view is proposed, accepted and implemented even if this is unrelated to prior discussions or information.

The picture is one of an organization which appears not to know what it is doing, for it is impossible to uncover any single strand of logic to decision processes. There are multiple garbage cans into which multiple topics for decision are placed. There is, however, no apparent logic to who gets involved, who proposes solutions and which solution is eventually chosen. This situation is termed 'organizational anarchy' by March and Olsen (1976).

Process typology

It is unlikely that 'organized anarchy' occurs in all organizations. Two large-scale empirical studies of decision-making suggest that only a handful of organizations might be like this and an even smaller handful of topics. In a study of 25 decision topics, Mintzberg, Raisinghani and Theuret (1976) found that quasi-linear processes were the norm in Canadian organizations. They were characterized by many interruptions (lack of information or political blocking) and many recycles, especially from phases of the process where alternatives were being considered and the nature of the problem came in for some redefinition. So, while processes are complicated, there does appear to be an attempt by decision-makers at achieving some linear sequences.

In the largest study of strategic decision-making so far, Hickson *et al.* (1986) examined 150 cases of decision process in 30 UK organizations. Details of this study can be found later in this chapter and in Reading 6 by Professor David Hickson. It is sufficient to record here that all the decision processes could be described as characteristically, *sporadic, fluid* and *constricted*. Each process type is co-related to two factors, the level of complexity facing decision-makers through a topic and the level of political activity each arouses (see Figure 10.1).

Managing decision-making processes

The study of decision-making requires a detailed analysis on many levels, ranging from organizational to individual. Managing the process, therefore, is complex but not impossible. Empirical studies have demonstrated that there do seem to be patterns of process which are mediated by group and organizational factors as well as by the topic under scrutiny (for example, a reorganization topic or a new product decision).

Here, we differentiate between managing the group of individuals making the decision, and managing the more abstract processes of decisions at the organizational level.

Managing groups

Although groups do generally outperform individuals in decision-making (they are consistently less creative, however, see Van de Ven and Delbecq, 1974), the first question to answer is 'Do we need to resolve this problem by using a group, or would an individual be more effective?'

Research by Vroom and Yetton (1973) indicates that groups have clear advantages over individual decision-makers according to situation, time and leadership. When information is scarce, deadlines are medium-term, the nature of the problem is unclear and many individuals need to accept the decision outcome, groups are more effective and offer more advantages than individuals. If the group also shares its leader's preferred outcomes, then the group will be all the more effective.

Making groups work once they are together is another matter. There have been a number of techniques introduced which attempt to do this, although all have had limited success.

Brainstorming

Developed as far back as 1939 (see Osborn, 1963) this is still the most prevalent use of groups by managers who are looking for a creative solution or new ideas. Members of the group suggest ideas or solutions to the topic or problem which

Figure 10.1
Three decision-
making process
types: constricted,
sporadic and fluid
Source: Hickson *et al.* (1986: 117).

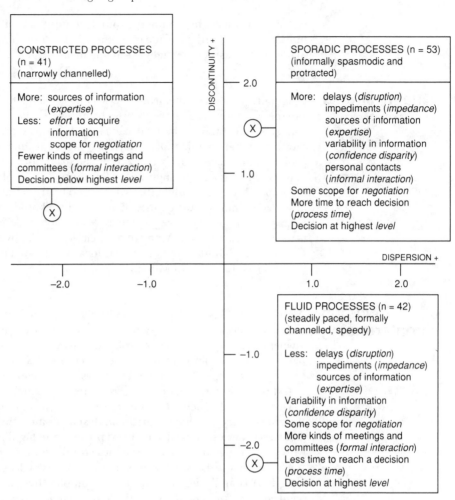

immediately come to mind. They can be as innovative, seemingly 'silly' or unrelated as people want. The aim of brainstorming is thus to break through conventional thinking and, through creativity, chance or serendipity, come up with a comparatively superior solution. Unfortunately, the bulk of empirical research does not support claims of superior creative performance from brainstorming groups. Individual decision-makers are better (see Van de Ven and Delbecq, 1974).

Delphi technique

Introduced in the 1970s by the Rand Corporation, this method avoids face-to-face contact, but uses multiple ideas and inputs from individuals. Anonymous suggestions are centrally recorded, members are sent each others' ideas and subsequently give their feedback. A centrally placed manager collects and recirculates written notes and ideas. These steps recycle until consensus is reached. The idea is to try and obtain all the benefits of a group decision (multiple ideas, suggestions, more expertise, and greater amounts of information) without also having the disadvantages of group processes (such as groupthink and interpersonal conflict). This technique is time-consuming and can feel artificial or forced to managers, but is more effective than brainstorming (Jewell and Reitz, 1981). It is not yet known to what extent the technique is more or less effective than using conventional face-to-face group decision-making. The Nominal Group technique is similar, except that individuals rank order the ideas of others in the 'group'. The decision is then made on the basis of the highest ranking idea.

Quality circles

Originally developed in North America and often mistakenly attributed to the Japanese, quality circles are groups of employees who meet together on company time (about a half day each month) to generate solutions to problems they face in the organization. They are designed to enable people to talk over problems they face in the organization (such as poor quality of some manufactured goods, or suggestions for improving production processing) and to discuss day-to-day difficulties which crop up from time to time. Originally designed to improve the quality of manufactured products, they are now extensively used to achieve participative decision-making throughout the entire firm. Results are mixed. Many quality circles end up by being characterized by plenty of talk but little action on their ideas which are not taken up by others in the firm (see Lawler and Moreman, 1985).

Decision conferencing

A recent idea of the 1980s, decision conferencing finds its genesis in high-technology decisions. It is a two- or three-day decision-making session in which 'owners' of a problem or set of problems participate. Different viewpoints of the participants are combined into a computer model which is generated on the spot by the group. The model then allows experimentation of the 'what if?' kind, to test the consequences of preferred courses of action.

Decision conferencing requires three specialist staff. A facilitator looks after the group processes that occur; an analyst looks after the computer modelling; and a recorder uses a projected word processor to highlight to the group the words it is using and to determine the central issues.

This technique is likely to spread into all kinds of decision activity. It is designed to handle decisions which are complex, over which there are different points of view already known and where the objective is to reach consensus. The group has support from other staff who feed in information. The decision process is deliberately phased (identify the problem, generate data, analyses data and discuss solution towards consensus) so that group members are clear where they are in the decision process. The process is intensive. Again, this is resource costly, but initial results look promising, especially in larger organizations which can afford to have their senior managers away for such lengthy periods (Rowe, Boulgarides and McGrath, 1984).

Overcoming groupthink

Specific techniques which have been developed to overcome groupthink are also worth mentioning since their efficacy extends into the central core of organizational life. As Furtado (1988: 43) states 'clearly defining a vision, getting the organization behind it, encouraging risk taking and participative involvement of all the workforce are not incompatible with the basic management skills'. These are the very aims of earlier attempts by researchers to overcome the phenomenon of groupthink.

The manager must be sensitive to the various roles that can be played in any group decision. In any group, there are identifiable positions which individuals adopt during the decision-making process. For a 'balanced group' to allow full discussion and avoid some of the pitfalls of groupthink, all the following roles should be represented (Belbin 1981):

1 *chairman*   the co-ordinator
2 *team leader*   the shaper: gives the process direction
3 *innovator*   creative thinker
4 *monitor*   the critical thinker
5 *company worker*   getting the task done for the firm
6 *team worker*   manages the interpersonal interaction in the group
7 *the completer*   keeps the team on its toes by always making
                          reference to the end goal of the decision
8 *resource investigator* keeps the team in touch with others in the
                          organization

Individuals tend to adopt one or maybe two of these roles quite consistently. All these roles are necessary, so a well-balanced group will contain all roles. Note that this might mean individuals adopting more than two roles in a very small group.

Having identified the various roles at play in group decision-making, the manager can also take further steps to achieve commitment from members of decision-making groups. They are:

1 The leader encourages each member to be a critical evaluator.
2 The leader and the key members should be impartial in the early stages of the decision.
3 The same problem is assigned to outside groups who input their results.
4 Before a consensus is reached, each member tests proposals on subordinates and reports the results.
5 Outside members are invited in to challenge the views of key group members.
6 At every meeting, someone is assigned the role of devil's advocate.
7 Split big groups into subgroups to get more involvement and address any differences in the big group.
8 Explore and anticipate the actions of any rival groups.
9 After reaching consensus, hold a follow-up meeting to air any residual doubts or second thoughts.

Managing group decisions: summary

1 Look at the composition of the group. Who is in it and what roles do they take?
2 What is the nature of the problem to be solved?
3 What kind of decision quality do we want? An interim incremental step, or a radical shift decision?
4 Decision content and process must be examined together.

Managing decisions in the organizational context

Placing the group in the context of the organization

Creating efficient and participative workgroups is a central part of the manager's task. Equally central is to recognize that all decisions by such groups are made in the wider context of the organization. As Hickson *et al.* (1986) show, there appear to be three major kinds of process through which decisions will travel irrespective of organization type (public or private ownership, service or manufacturing firm).

Decisions also appear to be deliberate managerial strategies rather than the more chaotic model of decision anarchy proposed by Cohen *et al.* (1972). Deliberation, however, does not always mean a smooth, rational process. We summarize in Table 10.1 the major aspects of the Hickson *et al.* (1986) study.

The bulk of decision processes take between 4 and 24 months to process through an organization. The sample mean for 150 cases was 12.4 months. Of course, there were some outliers. One decision took four years to get to the authorization stage, while another took only 2 months, which occurred in a

Table 10.1
Major features of
decision-making in
organizations (The
Bradford Studies)

Type of process	Examples of typical decision topics	Mean duration (months)
Sporadic	New products	22
	Location of headquarters or of plant	13
Fluid	Sources of inputs	6
	Major share issues	6
	Some reorganizations	13
	Some technology issues	20
Constricted	Budget decisions	10
	Some personnel issues	11
	Some domain issues	10
	Some service provision decisions	12

Source: adapted from Hickson *et al.* (1986).

public-administration organization belying the stereotype that public bureaucracies are necessarily slower than their commercial counterparts.

Neither do committees slow down decision processes. Again this is counter-intuitive, but strongly supported by empirical evidence from all 150 cases of the Bradford Study. They take more individual time of the group members, but overall decisions taken through the committee or group route take no longer than those which are taken individually by managers. This highlights the point that it all depends which perspective you take when looking at decision-making.

If you were one of the managers in the decisions which used committees, you would say that they were time-consuming, lengthy processes which probably took up a lot of your valuable time when you could be more productive. Yet if you were to take an organizational perspective, those decisions take no longer in the long run, so by concentrating your management effort and channelling it into committees you were possibly saving yourself time on the same issue at subsequent stages.

Summary

Groups are essential mechanisms for making organizational decisions, even though individual managers are often considered or consider themselves to be effective decision-makers. When groups get together, some predictable group effects occur which, if not managed, will detract from the efficacy of using groups to solve organizational problems.

The major group problem is that of conformity, which raises its head in a number of guises ranging from groupthink—where within the group there is excessive conformity to method and content of decision—or organizational culture, where there is pressure from outside the group to make decisions in such a way to fit in with what is considered acceptable by the wider organization.

Both individuals and groups are unable to achieve anything close to the rational model of decision-making. They invariably compromise because of:

1 cognitive limits on their capacity to process information;
2 competing demands from different parts of the organization which have to be met in order to achieve an outcome.

There are a number of techniques which can overcome some of the problems of group decision-making but none is wholly effective. The most common, brainstorming, is the least effective of other techniques such as the Delphi method and its derivatives such as the nominal group, and decision conferencing.

Decision-making should also be considered from the organizational perspective. There are some predictions that can be made at this level. Ownership of the organization, for example, appears to make little difference to any aspect of the decision process. Most strategic decisions take, on average, twelve months from first idea to authorization. Committees do not slow things down at this level of analysis, although they do take more time in concentrated bouts from individual managers.

References

Asch, S. E. (1955) 'Studies of independence and conformity: A minority of one against unanimous majority', *Psychological Monographs*, **20**, (whole No. 416).

Belbin, R. M. (1981) *Management Teams: Why They Succeed or Fail*, Heinemann, London.

Braybrooke, D. and C. E. Lindblom (1963) *A Strategy of Decision*, Free Press, New York.

Cohen, M. D., J. G. March, and J. P. Olsen (1972) 'A garbage can model of organizational choice', *Administrative Science Quarterly*, **17**, 1–25.

Cyert, R. and J. G. March (1963) *A Behavioral Theory of the Firm*, Prentice-Hall, Englewood Cliffs, New Jersey.

Furtado, T. (1988) 'Training for a different management style', *Personnel Management*, March, 40–3.

Hickson, D. J., R. J. Butler, D. Cray, G. R. Mallory, and D. C. Wilson (1986) *Top Decisions: Strategic Decision-Making in Organizations*, Blackwell, Oxford, Jossey-Bass, San Francisco.

Janis, I. L. (1972) *Victims of Groupthink: A Psychological Study of Foreign Policy Decisions and Fiascos*, Houghton Mifflin, Boston.

Janis, I. L. and L. Mann (1972) *Decision-Making*, Free Press, New York.

Jewell, L. N. and H. J. Reitz (1981) *Group Effectiveness in Organizations*, Scott, Foresman, Glenview, Illinois.

Lawler [III], E. E. and S. A. Moreman (1985) 'Quality circles after the fad', *Harvard Business Review*, Jan.–Feb., 65–71.

Leavitt, H. J. (1972) *Managerial Psychology*, 2nd edn, Chicago University Press, Chicago.

Lindblom, C. E. (1959) 'The science of muddling through', *Public Administration Review*, XIX (2), 79–88.

Lukes, S. (1974) *Power: A Radical View*, Macmillan, London.

Lustick, I. (1980) 'Explaining the variable utility of disjointed incrementalism', *American Political Science Review*, **74**, 342–53.

March, J. G. and J. P. Olsen (1976) *Ambiguity and Choice in Organizations*, Universitetsforlaget, Bergen.

Meyer, J. M. and B. Rowan (1977) 'Institutionalized organization: formal structures as myth and ceremony', *American Journal of Sociology*, **83**(2), 340–63.

Milgram, S. (1974) *Obedience and Authority*, Tavistock, London.

Mintzberg, H., D. Raisinghani and A. Theuret (1976) 'The structure of "unstructured" decision processes', *Administrative Science Quarterly*, **21**, 246–75.

Mitchell, T. R., K. J. Rediker and L. R. Beach (1986) 'Image theory and organizational decision-making', in H. P. Sims, Jr and D. A. Gioia (eds), *The Thinking Organization: Dynamics of Organizational Social Cognition*, Jossey-Bass, San Francisco.

Osborn, A. F. (1963) *Applied Imagination: Principles and Procedures of Creative Thinking*, Scribner's, New York.

Pettigrew, A. M. (1973) *The Politics of Organizational Decision Making*, Tavistock, London.

Quinn, J. B. (1980) *Strategies for Change: Logical Incrementalism*, Irwin, Homewood, Illinois.

Rowe, A. J., J. D. Boulgarides and M. R. McGrath (1984) *Managerial Decision-Making*, Science Research Associates, Chicago.

Schattsneider, E. E. (1960) *The Semi-Sovereign People: A Realists' View of Democracy in America*, Holt, Rinehart and Winston, New York.

Simon, H. A. (1960) *The New Science of Management Decision*, Harper & Row, New York.

Stoner, J. (1968) 'Risky and cautious shifts in group decision: the influence of widely held values', *Journal of Experimental Social Psychology*, **4**, 442–59.

Van de Ven, A. H. and A. Delbecq (1974) 'The effectiveness of nominal, Delphi and interaction group decision-making processes', *Academy of Management Journal*, **17**, 605–32.

Vroom, V. H. and P. W. Yetton (1973) *Leadership and Decision-Making*, University of Pittsburgh Press, Pittsburgh.

Whetten, D. (1980) 'Sources, responses and effects of organizational decline', in J. R. Kimberly and R. H. Miles (eds), *The Organizational Life Cycle*, Jossey-Bass, San Francisco, pp. 342–74.

Wilson, D. C. (1982) 'Electricity and resistance: a case study of innovation and politics', *Organizational Studies*, **3**(2), 119–40.

Wilson, D. C., R. J. Butler, D. Cray, D. J. Hickson and G. R. Mallory (1986) 'Breaking the bounds of organization in strategic decision-making', *Human Relations*, **39**(4), 309–31.

Power and leadership in organizations

Introduction

Leadership, power and position are not always equated with one another in any organization. It would be folly for any individual to assume that position in the hierarchy necessarily meant the commensurate possession of power and influence. Sometimes, seniority and power do go hand in hand. More often, power is also to be found elsewhere in the organization, sometimes in the most surprising places.

One of the most evident areas in organizations where power is exercised is in the question of leadership. We have seen in earlier chapters that a typical work group, if left alone to solve a problem, will be characterized by the emergence of a leader. This would be an informal role, but one which could influence other roles in the group. The leader will have some power to influence the behaviour of others in the group.

First we must decide exactly what power is. Its definition has caused some problems, since achieving an all-embracing, precise and workable, social-scientific definition has proved elusive. All of us can recognize when power is exercised, especially when it is exercised against us! Defining where that power came from, or why our own power seemed somehow *less* than that of our peers is not so easy. In this chapter, we shall use a broad but workable definition:

Power is the ability of one social unit to influence the behaviour of another social unit and to achieve preferred situation or outcomes.

A social unit can be an individual, a group, an organization or a group of organizations.

Usually, the exercise of power occurs over specific issues, such as in decision-making processes where at its simplest one manager wants one outcome while another manager wants something very different. We could predict the likely outcome of this power struggle if the managers were of different levels of seniority and if we equated hierarchical position and power. We would say that one manager has the *authority* to exercise power over the other. As we shall see, authority is only one aspect of power and can be relatively impotent in relation to other bases (or sources) of power.

Certainly, there are some skilled individuals who manage power relationships very well. One popular example can be found in the British television series *Yes, Minister* where Sir Humphrey, the Permanent Secretary, is able to influence both the decisions and the behaviour of his hierarchical superior, the Prime Minister. Before we discuss power in greater detail, we turn to the question of leadership as one explicit aspect of exercising influence in organizations.

Leadership: managing power and influence

Analysing the manager as leader is perhaps the most explicit recognition that a part of the management process concerns exercising power and influence. Of course, the management task overall is much wider than this in its scope. It contains many tasks which could be described as non-political (planning, thinking and co-ordinating for example) although these too may have substantial elements of managing power within them.

The potency of the leader to influence other people and even whole organizations is a common theme which prevades the history of many industries. Based on the assumption that the ability to lead and influence was embodied in certain characteristics (or traits) of the individual, many key positions in government and in all kinds of organizations have been filled with dynamic, enthusiastic and arguably highly competent individuals. Certain characteristics (or traits) defined effective leaders. For example, the appointments of Sir Ian MacGregor as Chairman of the British Steel Corporation, Sir Michael Edwardes as Chief Executive of British Leyland (as it was then called), Arthur Scargill as leader of the National Union of Mineworkers and Margaret Thatcher as leader of the Conservative government are all examples of leadership positions appointed through a faith in traits. Effective leaders could exercise influence and bring about changes.

Initial studies aimed at identifying these traits all failed to come up with any conclusive evidence over what they were, or which were the most important. Nevertheless, some current selection criteria for senior management positions seem to reflect a prevailing belief in some traits. Examples include:

- the ability to solve problems and see how they fit into the wider scheme of things;
- a strong desire to achieve;
- self-confidence and self-discipline;
- the ability to listen and to communicate effectively;
- stability of emotion and a positive attitude towards other members of the organization, especially subordinates;
- being analytical and intelligent (but not *too* intelligent).

Contingency approaches to leadership began to uncover factors other than traits which had an impact not only on the leader but also on the followers, especially their job performance and levels of satisfaction. Power exercised through leadership was argued to be mediated by a number of other characteristics. Key contingency researchers are Fiedler, Chemers and Mahar (1978); House (1971); and Vroom and Yetton (1973).

Contingency approaches to leadership

Fiedler's model of leadership effectiveness

Fiedler argued that leadership styles could vary. The effectiveness of any work group was dependent upon achieving a *match between leadership style and context* (the situation in which leadership was exercised). He argued that certain situations determined the amount of control and influence open to the leader.

There were two measures which Fiedler used to assess the match between leadership style and situation. These were Assumed Similarity between Opposites (ASO) and Least Preferred Co-Worker (LPC):

ASO scale   measured how similar were the most and the least preferred co-workers as perceived by leaders;

LPC scale   measured the degree to which leaders favourably perceive their least preferred co-worker.

The idea was for respondents to think of all the individuals with whom they had worked, and to rank the persons whom they perceived to be the most and least difficult to work with in terms of getting the job done. This was not to measure like or dislike of a person. It was to identify the person with whom accomplishing a task proved most difficult and most easy. The results from Fiedler's research indicated that the LPC scale was a significantly better predictor of match in leadership style than the ASO scale.

Three styles of leadership were identified:

Relationship-motivated (human relations leadership style)	High similarity in ASO. A favourable co-worker description. LPC score above 64.
Task directed (hard-nosed leadership style)	Great difference in ASO. Unfavourable co-worker description. LPC score below 57.
Choice of task/relationship style	ASO does not distinguish. LPC lies between 58 and 63. Manager has to decide the type of blend between task- and relationship-orientated styles.

Fiedler argued that the appropriate style of leadership could be predicted from ASO and LPC scores. To the extent that there was a match between situation and style, the effectiveness of the workgroup would be enhanced. There was no one best style, and neither the task-directed or relationship-motivated styles were 'better' than one another.

To put the LPC scores into a more complex contingency framework, Fiedler also assessed the amount of *control* available to a manager under particular situations. These 'situational variables' are:

1 *the leader–member relationship* (the acceptability of the leader to the members of a group);
2 *the degree of structure in the task to be accomplished* (whether everything is spelled out or is ambiguous);
3 *the degree of position power of the leader* (whether the leader has formal authority endowed to him or her by virtue of position in the hierarchy).

A context of high favourability towards the leader would comprise, for example, being readily acceptable to the group; a task which is structured and unambiguous; coupled with a position of high formal authority. This would be a situation which was highly favourable to the leader since it allowed him or her a large degree of control. Matching favourability of context and leadership style, Fiedler found that the best match of style to situation was achieved where the task-directed style was adopted under *both* favourable and unfavourable conditions, with the human-relations style most effective in the mid ranges of favourability (see Figure 11.1).

Fiedler's theory of leadership and influence may be summarized thus:

1 Appropriate styles of leadership are contingent upon the degree of control pertaining to various situations.
2 The exercise of influence through leadership is likely to be most successful when there is a match between situation and style.
3 In the event of a mismatch, Fiedler suggests that it is easier to try and change the situation rather than to attempt to change style.

Figure 11.1
Style and situational
context: Fiedler's
effectiveness model

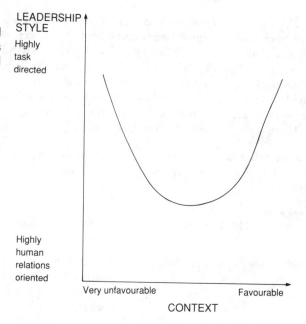

House's path–goal
theory of leadership

Well rooted in the contingency approach, House argues that the role of influence through leadership is to compensate for things lacking in the work context. Leaders are both more influential and more effective when they complement the context. He identifies four styles of leadership and three contingency variables.

1 *Leader directiveness*
   - letting subordinates know what is expected
   - saying what should be done and how
   - clearly defining the role of the leader
   - maintaining standards of performance and work scheduling
2 *Leader supportiveness*
   - being interpersonally aware of the needs of others
   - treating group members as equals
   - being friendly and approachable
3 *Leader achievement-orientedness*
   - setting goals which are challenging
   - continuously seeking performance improvements
   - having a high degree of faith in others to perform to the best of their ability
   - continually emphasizing the achievement of excellence
4 *Leader participativeness*
   - consulting others regularly
   - asking for suggestions and advice from others over specific decisions.
   - taking all suggestions into account when taking a decision
   (Adapted from House and Mitchell, 1974)

Each of the four styles is dependent upon three contingency variables, each of which has an impact on the effectiveness of the style employed. The three variables relate to the characteristics of subordinates. They are:

1 Whether subordinates are close-minded and rigid, or are open and flexible to how they operate.
2 Whether subordinates are internally or externally oriented. Internals believe

broadly that any event is a consequence of their own actions. Externals believe that what happens to them is largely a matter of luck, chance or fate (Rotter, 1966).

3 The ability of subordinates to handle the current task and to develop and learn how to handle future tasks.

In general, House's results confirm those of Fiedler. Directiveness is positively related to subordinates' satisfactions and expectations when the task is ambiguous. The leader absorbs uncertainty for the group. The reverse is true when tasks are clear and well-defined. Supportiveness is an appropriate style for highly repetitive tasks, or those which are frustrating or physically unpleasant. Being one of the crowd helps to compensate for situational conditions. Achievement-orientedness is appropriate for groups who face non-repetitive tasks which are also ambiguous. This style is argued to maintain a constant striving for excellence in performance. Participativeness is appropriate in situations where the group comprises largely internally oriented individuals who are engaged in non-repetitive tasks.

Vroom and Yetton's normative theory of leadership effectiveness

Vroom and Yetton (1973) concentrate upon decision-making in their studies of leadership. They argue that leaders should be flexible and change their styles to match situations. This, of course, is the reverse of Fiedler's argument, who proposed that leadership style was less amenable to change than the situation.

Two criteria of decision effectiveness are used by Vroom and Yetton to indicate the kind of appropriate leadership style. These are decision *quality* and *acceptance*. The argument is that some decision topics are more directly related to performance from a workgroup than others. Those topics which centrally affect the working conditions and environment of a group (such as job design or responsibilities) should require the leader to adopt a participative decision process.

Where a decision is relatively peripheral to the concerns of a group, then the manager can adopt either an authoritative or participative style. It has little effect upon performance. Vroom and Yetton identified five alternative styles open to the manager. These are summarized in Table 11.1. The five styles range from autocratic to collaborative. As subordinate commitment to the decision increases, then the appropriate style should become more collaborative. This is based on the assumption that a decision, even if technically correct, can be blocked and caused to fail because of resistance from those who have to carry it out, or live with its results.

Both Likert (1967) and Reddin (1970) offer similar models, arguing that autocratic power exercised through leadership is likely to result in poor performance and non-acceptance by others. Likert's results indicated that significantly greater levels of performance came from groups in which the power of the leader was articulated through a participative and democratic style.

Hosking (1988) argues that the exercise of power through leadership is more complex than either simple trait models or complex contingency theories. She argues that to understand leadership completely, one must understand it as a negotiated process worked out between leader, group and situation. Reading 7 summarizes this argument succinctly. Any analysis of leadership should include 'people, processes, and contexts' (Hosking 1988: 164).

Table 11.1
Vroom and Yetton's
five decision styles

Autocratic styles
1 You solve the problem or make the decision yourself, using information available to you at the time.
2 You obtain the information required from your subordinates, then decide yourself. You may or may not let your subordinates know the nature of the decision problem. Subordinates are treated solely as information-givers, not as generators of alternative courses of action or of solutions.

Consultative styles
1 You share the problem with subordinates on an individual basis. Having collected together their ideas and suggestions, you then make the decision yourself. This may or may not reflect subordinates' influence.
2 You collect together subordinates as a group. They generate alternatives and suggest solutions in discussion with you. Then you make the decision individually (as above).

Collective or group style
1 You share the problems with a group of subordinates. Together you try and reach consensus on the problem and its solution. You act much as a chairperson of the group, not trying to influence the group to adopt your preferred solution. You are also willing to accept and to implement any solution which has the support of the entire group.

Source: adapted and reprinted from *Leadership and decision-making*, by Victor H. Vroom and Philip W. Yetton, by permission of the University of Pittsburgh Press. © 1973 by University of Pittsburgh Press.

Understanding the nature of power in organizations

An initial framework for the study of the bases of power was described by French and Raven (1960). This represents something of a classic analysis of the sources of power. There are five key *bases* of power:

1 *Reward*   To the extent that one individual has the capacity to reward another, and to the extent that this is recognized by both parties, then there is an imbalance of power. For example, if one manager has the capacity to promote, appraise or otherwise reward then he or she has this source of power.
2 *Coercive*   If individual A has the capacity to operate sanctions or punishments against B for behaviour unwanted by A, then A has a coercive base of power. The giving of unpopular task, firing and reprimanding are all illustrations of this kind of power.
3 *Legitimate*   To the extent that individual B feels that it is right for A to make a request then A has power over B. This is the concept of authority described earlier.
4 *Expert*   If one individual perceives another to have key knowledge or specialized technical skill, then the 'expert' will have a significantly more potent source of power.
5 *Referent*   To the extent that others in the organization wish to identify with a single individual, for example in leadership style, manner of dress, or manner of handling difficult clients, then that individual will have a substantial power base.

All of these can occur in a work organization and they are not necessarily correlated with seniority. The possession of all five power bases would make an individual very powerful indeed, so the bases are also additive. Some of the bases can occur outside formal organizations. Referent power can be seen in the relationship between a rock star and fans or sporting heroes and their supporters. Other bases can occur in family life, between parent and child for example. It is easy to see how reward and coercive power might operate in this context.

All of this only begins the analysis of power. It is a necessary, but not sufficient description of what happens in organizations. There are a number of other factors which will contribute to (or erode) power. Broadly, these can be found in:

1 organizational structure;
2 the operating environment of the organization.

If we were to try and find where power lies in any organization, we would probably gain most insight by keeping structure and environment uppermost in our minds. For example, it is common business parlance to describe organizations as 'production-led' or as 'market-led'. This means that one differentiated part of the organization's functions has become dominant outside the scope of its own functional area. In a production-led company, we would predict that the production director would be more influential and more successful in achieving desired outcomes over a range of decisions than the sales director, even though hierarchy may not differentiate between their positions.

As Mangham (1986: 9–15) notes, this use of managerial language assumes and subsumes a number of aspects of power which are rarely made explicit in day-to-day managerial activity. The aim of this chapter is to uncover these assumptions and identify sources of power.

Power and organizational structure

The most explicit and precise analysis of power through structure was outlined in by Hickson *et al.* (1971). Termed a *Strategic contingencies theory* of power, it built upon and brought together a number of previous studies (see, for example, Emerson, 1962; Crozier, 1964) into a self-contained and testable theory of power. To acquire power, individuals in organizations needed to be indispensable, in the right place at the right time and considered by others in the organization to be doing a critically important job. The formal theory is set out in Table 11.2.

Just like French and Raven's bases of power, the three elements of strategic contingency theory are additive. The key single contingency is that of coping with uncertainty (see Hinings *et al.*, 1974 for an empirical test of this theory) followed in turn by immediacy, non-substitutability and pervasiveness. In the Canadian Brewery studied by Hinings *et al.* (1974) for example, the four departments of this firm were ranked in order thus, from greatest to least powerful over a range of key decisions:

1 production
2 marketing
3 engineers
4 accounting

Production department was most powerful since brewing is a relatively simple process in engineering terms. Once the plant is designed and running, the crucial aspect of the organization is its product which is in the hands of production (quality and quantity of output, coupled with the special, non-substitutable 'brewers' expertise).

The division of labour into specialized departments and sub-groups and their relative dependence upon one another to keep the organization viable is a persuasive argument in favour of analysing key contingencies. It is not in the

Table 11.2
Strategic
contingencies
theory of
power bases

Power source	Description
Coping with uncertainty	Specialization allows some departments or individuals to cope with ambiguous and unpredictable circumstances. They create certainty for others in the organization and are thus more influential and powerful.
Non-substitutable	Dependence of other parts of the organization on those which cope with uncertainty can be reduced if there are alternative sources of information or service. The power of any part of a firm is lessened if it can be substituted.

Centrality	Being well-networked into the whole organization will confer power. This has two apects:
	1 pervasiveness
	  where the number of links with other groups in the firm are many.
	2 immediacy
	  where the cessation of activity by a person or a group would impede the workflow of the organization straight away.

interests of any of the parts of the organization to engage in behaviour which is destructive to the firm as a whole, since if it founders so do they. It is in sub-groups' interests to fight for their particular stake in the scarce resource allocation process which is the fact of life for most organizations. Those which are most contingently placed will have the loudest and more influential voice over all decisions and will have primary access to resources.

This kind of analysis gives only a partial analysis and flavour of the exercise of power. 'Most middle managers know only too well . . . that hunches, inspiration and politicking are often what gives a company its shape' (*The Economist,* July 1988: 68). In other words, it is the *individual* exercise of power, the process of exercising power, which is the key to its understanding. We look at these aspects in the next section.

The individual in the structure   Not surprisingly, power studies which have emphasized the case-study method for its analysis have concentrated mostly on the role of the individual manager as fighter, manipulator, as terrier in the system and as gallant knight to save the day against all odds. Not too much here about strategic contingencies (see Pettigrew, 1973; 1985; Wilson, 1982). Yet a common contingent theme can be found at least in some of these more detailed studies of individual activities.

Control of information, through gatekeeping, through filtering between parties, through manipulation and deceit figures large in many cases. In Pettigrew's (1973) description of the decision by a retail firm to purchase a new computer, Kenny, the 'gatekeeper' who had access to computer suppliers and all associated information, was able to sway the final decision in whichever way he saw beneficial to himself. Wilson's (1982) study of a chemical manufacturing company which took the decision to generate its own supply of electricity and become independent of the Central Electricity Generating Board, also focused on the role of individual power processes. Alwyn, one of the key individuals in the process, and who got what he wanted via the final decision (promotion to managing director) again used information and data to his own advantage, keeping some back from general view and publicly questioning other people's data on the topic.

Later empirical studies seem to reinforce *the primacy of individual action* within the organizational structure, rather than structural configuration itself as a source of power. Kenny and Wilson (1984) studied 188 managers from 60 Australian organizations and found that managers ranked managerial expertise (knowledge of the system) and access to and control of information above the sub-unit contingency of coping with uncertainty. Distinguishing between person, position and sub-unit sources of power, the study revealed the relative importance of person and position over the importance of the manager's department to the organization in endowing power over a wide range of decisions. Factors studied were:

Person based
- expertise (knowledge of technical process or equivalent)
- managerial expertise (knowledge of the organization and people — 'the system')
- personality (the ability to get on with and persuade others)

Position based
- formal authority
- access to and control over information
- access to senior management and other senior staff

Sub-unit based
- the importance of the department to the organization (e.g. coping with uncertainty, non-substitutable etc.)

(from Kenny and Wilson, 1984: 414)

Managers from this sample consistently ranked managerial expertise as the most important power base, followed by access to and control over information. Sub-unit contingencies came third. These findings concur with many of the detailed case studies of power in organizations (see, for example, Pettigrew, 1973; Wilson, 1982). Hickson *et al.* (1971) in proposing the contingencies' view also suggested that individual actions of managers may take primacy over structural contingencies.

Thus we are at a stage in the understanding of power where the individual manager is pivotal. The exercise of power is best seen first as the outcome of individual action and individual characteristics. If these are supported by favourable *structural* configurations the power base is increased significantly. Power is thus a blend of individual person-based factors, and particular configurations of structure in the organization. However, even integrating the individual and organizational structure makes some unwarranted assumptions about the political nature of organizations and individuals.

The environment and inter-organizational relations [the operating environment of the organization]

As Mintzberg (1973) showed, a great deal of managerial activity is spent interacting and liaising with the managers of other organizations. This is no accident, nor is it representative of a desire by managers for more business lunches. It is reflecting the fact that no organization exists in a vacuum. Virtually all organizations have suppliers, customers, competitors, government agencies and a host of other organizations to deal with in the everyday pursuit of their business.

This complex interaction between organizations comprises the operating environment of any firm, and it also has the capacity to develop and sustain power relationships. As a first step, one could simply convert the factors of the strategic contingencies' model to apply to external organizations in contact. Contingencies then become analysable across the immediate operating environment of the firm. For example, a supplier which is non-substitutable from the perspective of the focal organization will be more powerful and will have potentially more say in what that organization does than just one of many undifferentiated customers. Key customers who buy a lot of products or services are also likely to be more central than those who are small or only occasional customers.

Further analysis reveals that we can go beyond this important but over-simplified perspective. As Pfeffer and Salancik (1978) argue, the overall system of inter-organizational relations has its own dynamic. Linkages between external organizations and the focal firm can either be 'loose' or 'tight'. While networks of organizations can also be characterized as loosely or tightly coupled, it may be that only *some* and *not all* of the actions by a supplier, a government agency or a customer impinge upon the operation of the focal firm. The network of inter-organizational relations is thus loosely coupled.

On the other hand, a single firm can be 'paralysed' in its strategic actions by a tightly coupled network of organizations in contact. Butler *et al.* (1977) distinguish between organizations which are almost completely held in check by outside interests and those which can extend their actions beyond their formal boundaries and themselves exert influence over customers, regulatory bodies and suppliers. An example of a completely paralysed organization is an Electricity Board, the regional supplier of electricity in England. The organization is forced by regulation to buy all of its electricity from one supplier, the Central Electricity Generating Board, and sell to whoever requires electricity. Organizations which can extend their influence beyond their formal boundaries into their operating environment are very powerful indeed. This was achieved by Jaguar, the British motor car manufacturer, in the early 1980s when plagued with an increasing number of component breakdowns in their cars. Jaguar insisted on their suppliers taking responsibility for quality control and component failure.

It would be tempting to account for these differences in strategic autonomy by ownership. State-owned organizations are likely to be far more constrained in their 'strategic choice' than those which are privately owned (Child, 1972). This does not appear to be the case. In a study of thirty British firms, Hickson *et al.* (1986) found no evidence at all to support differentiation of power distribution on ownership or manufacturing or service criteria. Public and private, manufacturing and service organizations were not characterized by significant differences in external control.

The task of addressing these power relations is thus the same in all organizations. There are a number of ways in which we can see organizations attempting to reduce the impact or the potency of external influences. The boards of many companies contain directors who also sit on the boards of other related companies. These interlocking directorates help smooth out dependencies. They can also present excellent opportunities for control by these directors (see Useem and McCormack, 1981). Used in this way, directors can use a number of organizations in the network to satisfy their own personal ambitions.

When the external control of organizations becomes too far balanced towards one or two external constituencies, then 'organizational drift' is a likely result. This process was described by Engwall (1978). Giving the example of a newspaper company, Engwall shows how the initial aims of an organization to be a fair, liberal and analytical newspaper were confounded when financial dependence on politically motivated external sources forced the editors to follow a particular political line.

Mintzberg (1983; 1984) also argues that the nature of the power balance in the operating environment (its 'configuration') will differ according to the type of firm and its strategic history. For example, in a large mature firm it is likely that no single external interest has sufficient power to exert pressure on the managers in the focal organization. Such a configuration will hold until major changes in strategic direction occur (or are forced by demand or fiscal exigencies) and then the opportunity for a re-establishment of the power balance is created once more. This is one of the reasons why many large, mature organizations resist change to such a degree since the potential political threats to which they may become exposed are enormous (see Chapter 14).

Joint ventures are another way in which managers handle power imbalances in the wider environment and keep influence in check. The problem with this approach as Harrigan (1986) illustrates, is that all parties to a joint venture have to be convinced that there is at least an equal split of benefits to be obtained from entering the partnership. Since this is not always easy to demonstrate, the number of joint ventures is relatively low. There is also the suspicion that one party may hold about the other, that information detrimental to one party is being deliberately withheld by the other (see the next section).

Reciprocal trade agreements, representation of multiple firms in trade associations and verbal agreements on good business practice are other examples of managing the wider political environment. Even this level of analysis still misses some important aspects of the nature of power in organizations. We explore these in the next section.

Power beyond the individual, organizational structure and operating environments

Power can be exercised in far more subtle ways than the analysis currently reveals. So far, the analysis relies upon observing or accounting for the relative influence of managers (or organizations in the wider context) over decisions or organizational problems. At first sight this looks promising, especially if the spread of decision topics studied is representative of managerial reality. Certainly, studies by Hickson *et al.* (1971; 1986), Tannenbaum (1968) and Hinings *et al.* (1974) cover all the issues a manager is likely to meet in any organization. So it is not that the situation is unrepresentative.

Closer inspection reveals another side to power. It is not just overt influence over identifiable decisions which is an important indication of power. Those who influence what is *not* open to decision are at least of equal (and probably greater) power. These are the issues which are not debated in any wider managerial decision arena. They are called '*non-decisions*' (Bachrach and Baratz, 1970) and they can arise in a number of ways.

It is useful at this stage to distinguish two separate arguments. One is that *non-decisions arise because of limited participation opportunities in the decision-making process*. Senior management, for example, might take a particular view over the future strategic direction of the organization. In turn, this will involve substantial investment programmes, constant introduction of new or revised products, the nature of which has already been decided by the time middle management come to debate such issues. Because middle management did not participate in the initial decisions, any subsequent decisions that they take will be framed in a particular context set outside their own control. A great many alternatives, therefore, are not open to debate. This process of power framing (or context setting) can be a deliberate action which can span across many levels in the organization. It is a fairly sophisticated version of 'agenda setting', something familiar to all who sit through committees and working groups.

Another form in which non-decisions can arise is more *a product of the kind of organization in question and its history*. As Daudi (1986) notes, all power relations in organizations take place within a context that has characteristics and dynamics of its own. Over time, organizational customs and practices take on a life of their own and these can also shape power relations in any firm. Such customs and practices are the result of organizations coping with the uncertainty they face in their operating environment. Particular forms of interdependencies and reporting relationships develop, as well as particular degrees of centralization or decentralization, and formal or informal practice (see, for example, Pfeffer and Salancik, 1978; Brooke, 1984). This develops over time and sediments much in the same way as alluvial silt builds up along the course of a river. The effects on power relations are twofold:

1 The creation of myth and ceremony

Argued in detail by Meyer and Rowan (1977), the creation of myth and ceremony means that the process of institutionalization effectively acts as an unrecognized control mechanism. Certain behaviours and practices are taken for granted or encouraged, often without anyone reflecting on their efficacy or even why they are there in the first place. For example, organizations which have developed with the 'ceremony' of ensuring that all functional managers keep within budgets which are strictly controlled outside their domain will produce predictable patterns of behaviour in their managers. All decision-making will be directed at keeping within the financial control procedures. Functions will become territorial, since the primary way to demonstrate managerial performance will be on financial data for the department or section (Burchell *et al.*, 1980).

Other kinds of behaviour are inertia, resistance to change, the non-recognition of opportunities and the conviction that the organization is already doing things right. Pettigrew's (1985) case study of ICI showed graphically how the conceptions of senior management were constrained by the tremendous weight of institutionalization in the company. Certain alternatives were just not open to debate and it took an era of leadership from a very different perspective to break the mould and effect changes. The resistance which met John Harvey-Jones and his predecessors who tried to effect changes is a sobering illustration of the enormous strength of such institutionalized power.

2 The creation of knowledge elites

This is really the other side of the myth and ceremony argument. Power will accrue to those individuals who understand how the system works. Those who can accurately predict outcomes for a given set of circumstances in their firm are in a relatively more powerful position than their peers who cannot recognize cause and effect. Knowledge of the system has been illustrated in a number of case studies. In Pettigrew's (1973) study of a retail organization's computer purchase, Kenny recognized that his organization's system focused on the role of the 'gatekeeper'. Those who interfaced with external organizations (in this case, computer suppliers) could effectively control much of what subsequently happened within their own organization.

In Wilson's (1982) case study of a chemical company, Alwyn recognized that a decision taken against his interests could be reopened by his subsequently casting doubt on the data produced to support the arguments. In an organization where the culture was to favour fast action on quantifiable data, undermining the empirical arguments was a sure route to ensuring continued debate, which was what Alwyn wanted (see Mangham, 1986: ch. 4).

In the exercise of upward influence, knowing how your boss operates, reasons and thinks has been described in some detail. This kind of knowledge can foster or protect self-interest in subordinates. Knowing your boss's preferences on a set of issues enables effective screening mechanisms to be set up which can operate in your self-interest. For example, you would only pass on certain kinds of information and withhold that which you knew would be detrimental to your interests. You might also pass information upward in a particular form, missing out some selected facts perhaps, or preserving ambiguity in the presentation of data, allowing the boss to interpret them in whichever way was thought desirable (see Leavitt, 1972; Sayles, 1979; Gabarro and Kotter, 1980).

Summary

Power can accrue to individuals in organizations in a number of ways, many of which do not lend themselves to direct empirical observation. Power is primarily a concept of action. It is a process which is acted out in a particular setting and what we usually see, or experience, as members of any organization are the effects of power being exercised rather than the source of that power.

The sources or bases of power can result from the characteristics of individuals. More likely is that a combination of individual characteristics and the interrelationships which occur in complex organizations go towards explaining the locus of any individual or group influence. Extending the focus of the discussion further, we can view power as residing in networks of organizations and the managerial task becomes one of not only managing internal organizational processes, but also involves managing the wider environment of organizations in contact such as suppliers, customers, competitors and regulatory agencies.

Going beyond structural analyses of contingencies and coping with uncertainties, we uncover more insidious sides to power. Those issues which are never recognized or which never come up for open debate really indicate that power is being exercised outside the arena of overt decision-making. There are a number of non-issues (non-decisions) which the very powerful can keep for themselves and which shape the subsequent choices of everyone else. To discover power at this level means we must analyse the history and the development of any organization as well as refer to the context in which it currently operates. This naturally makes the study of power in this depth extremely difficult. Nevertheless, the isolated case studies of power and non-decisions which do exist demonstrate the potency of influence at this level and show that organizations can be the result of conscious political design rather than of any other criteria such as efficiency, public good or utility.

References

Bachrach, P. and M. S. Baratz (1970) *Power and Poverty: Theory and Practice*, Oxford University Press, London.

Brooke, M. Z. (1984) *Centralization and Autonomy: A Study in Organizational Behaviour*, Holt, Rinehart and Winston, London.

Burchell, S., C. Clubb, A. Hopwood, J. Hughes and J. Nahapiet (1980) 'The role of accounting in organizations and society', *Accounting, Organizations and Society*, **5**(1), 5–27.

Butler, R. J., D. J. Hickson, D. C. Wilson and R. Axelsson (1977) 'Organizational power, politicking and paralysis', in M. Warner (ed.), *Organizational Choice and Constraint*, Sage, London.

Child, J. (1972) 'Organizational structure, environment and performance: the role of strategic choice', *Sociology*, **6**(1), 1–22.

Crozier, M. (1964) *The Bureaucratic Phenomenon*, Tavistock, London.

Daudi, P. (1986) *Power in the Organization: The Discourse of Power in Managerial Practice*, Blackwell, Oxford.

Emerson, R. M. (1962) 'Power-dependence relations', *American Sociological Review*, **27**(1), 31–41.

Engwall, L. (1978) *Newspapers as Organizations*, Saxon House, Farnborough.

Fiedler, F. E., Chemers, M. M. and L. Mahar (1978) *The Leadership Match Concept*, Wiley, New York.

French, J. R. P. Jr and B. Raven (1960) 'The bases of social power', in D. Cartwright and A. F. Zander (eds), *Group Dynamics*, 2nd edn, Row, Peterson, Evanston, Illinois.

Gabarro, J. and J. Kotter (1980) 'Managing your boss', *Harvard Business Review*, **58**, Jan.–Feb., 92–100.

Harrigan, K. R. (1986) *Managing for Joint Venture Success*, D. C. Heath, Lexington, Mass.

Hickson, D. J., R. J. Butler, D. Cray, G. R. Mallory and D. C. Wilson (1986) *Top Decisions: Strategic Decision Making in Organizations*, Blackwell, Oxford, Jossey-Bass, San Francisco.

Hickson, D. J., C. R. Hinnings, C. A. Lee, R. E. Schneck and J. M. Pennings (1971) 'A strategic contingencies' theory of intraorganizational power', *Administrative Science Quarterly*, **16**(2), 216–29.

Hinings, C. R., D. J. Hickson, J. M. Pennings and R. E. Schneck (1974) 'Structural conditions of intraorganizational power', *Administrative Science Quarterly*, **19**, 22–44.

Hosking, D. M. (1988) 'Organizing, leadership and skilful processes', *Journal of Management Studies*, **25**(2), 147–66.

House, R. J. (1971) 'A path–goal theory of leader effectiveness', *Administrative Sciences Quarterly*, **16**, 321–38.

House, R. J. and T. R. Mitchell (1974) 'Path–goal theory of leadership', *Journal of Contemporary Business*, Autumn, 81–97.

Kenny, G. K. and D. C. Wilson (1984) 'The interdepartmental influence of managers: individual and sub-unit perspectives', *Journal of Management Studies*, **21**(4), 409–27.

Leavitt, H. (1972) *Managerial Psychology: An Introduction to Individuals, Pairs, and Groups in Organizations*, 3rd edn, University of Chicago Press, Chicago and London.

Likert, R. (1967) *The Human Organization*, McGraw-Hill, New York.

Mangham, I. L. (1986) *Power and Performance in Organizations: An Exploration of Executive Process*, Blackwell, Oxford.

Meyer, J. M. and B. Rowan (1977) 'Institutionalized Organization: Formal Structures as myth and ceremony', *American Journal of Sociology*, **83**(2), 340–63.

Mintzberg, H. (1973) *The Nature of Managerial Work*, Harper & Row, New York.

Mintzberg, H. (1983) *Power in and around Organizations*, Prentice-Hall, Englewood Cliffs, New Jersey.

Mintzberg, H. (1984) 'Power and organizational life cycles', *Academy of Management Review*, April, 207–24.

Pettigrew, A. M. (1973) *The Politics of Organizational Decision-Making*, Tavistock, London.

Pettigrew, A. M. (1985) *The Awakening Giant: Continuity and Change in ICI*, Blackwell, Oxford.

Pfeffer, J. and G. R. Salancik (1978) *The External Control of Organizations: A Resource Dependence Perspective*, Harper & Row, New York.

Reddin, W. J. (1970) *Managerial Effectiveness*, McGraw-Hill, New York.

Rotter, J. B. (1966) 'Generalized expectancies for internal versus external control of reinforcement', *Psychological Monographs*, no. 609, 80.

Sayles, L. (1979) *Leadership: What Effective Managers Really Do, and How They Do It*, McGraw-Hill, New York.

Tannenbaum, A. S. (1968) *Control in Organizations*, McGraw-Hill, New York.

Useem, M. and A. McCormack (1981) 'The dominant segment of the British business elite', *Sociology*, **15**, 381–406.

Vroom, V. H. and P. Yetton (1973) *Leadership and Decision-Making*, University of Pittsburgh Press, Pittsburgh.

Wilson, D. C. (1982) 'Electricity and Resistance: A Case Study of Innovation and Politics', *Organization Studies*, **3**(2), 119–40.

Politics permeate

David J. Hickson

Politics permeate organizations because organizations are collections of people who have differing past experiences, differing current circumstances and therefore potentially differing interests. Each person is interested in sustaining or improving his or her own job and future prospects, his or her own department and its future, as well as that of the organization on which both job and department depend. One highly politicized view of organizations is that of Crozier and Friedberg (1980) who see them as '*ensembles des jeux*' — groups of players vying for position in organizational games of self-interest. It may be that such a definition reflects a cultural bias. American executives seem to find over-politicized situations distasteful (Lyles, 1987).

Notwithstanding national differences, the task of accommodating everyone's interests when something is being decided is, to some extent, a political one. The instant thought 'to whose advantage?' is evidence of the political sensitivity of the managerial world. People influence one another to make sure that others are aware of their needs and problems, to make their views known and to reach some degree of consensus. Politics in this sense need not and should not have a negative connotation (Dror and Romm, 1988).

The interests implicated

Once a matter does come up for decision, numerous participants are drawn in along the way. They embody numerous affected interests. Each matter for decision impinges upon an assortment of such interests. They give the process its political character. Some may be involved in most major decisions, others only in a few. Production departments and their equivalents in service organizations (such as the medical and nursing staff in hospitals or administrative sections in insurance companies) are almost always in on the action. As are sales and the finance people. Production, sales and finance, by whichever titles they may be known in different forms of organization, are a core trio through whose hands most big decisions must pass. Others involved in many decisions are government departments and agencies, and suppliers, both of these from outside the organization itself. Personnel, research, purchasing and maintenance functions are drawn in on some decisions.

This assortment of interests coming in at one stage and exiting at another stage of the process of moving towards a decision has been called the 'decision-set' of interests (Hickson *et al.*, 1986). Some of them appear many times while a particular decision is being taken, others only once.

For those wishing to influence the course of events, the timing of the part they play can be crucial. Everyone cannot attend to everything at once. Timing when to join in and when to speak up requires political judgement. It has been suggested that even though most of the action takes place during the middle phase of a decision-making process, it is especially vital to influence the start and the finish (Heller *et al.*, 1987).

Influential interests

Pfeffer and Salancik (1978) see organizations as 'markets for influence and control'. As each interested party has something to gain and something to give, influence is created in the constant exchanges between them. In a study of British manufacturing and service organizations, trades unions influenced decisions on organization-wide personnel regrading and reallocation proposals but not decisions on investment in new technology (despite the effects these eventually may have upon their members). Customers influenced decisions on new products but not decisions on supplies of money (raising capital) or raw materials. Accounting departments influenced corporate budgets and plans but not decisions on new services where relatively little financial expenditure was required. Research or design departments influenced decisions on new products but not takeover bids, and so on (Hickson *et al.*, 1986: 138).

Those internal units which exercise the greatest influence do so by influencing a range of matters not only within their own spheres but beyond that in matters that would be thought to be the primary concern of other specialist units. Research conducted among small Canadian breweries (Hinings *et al.*, 1974) found that the production departments (the most influential of the departments) strongly influenced: (1) marketing and product packaging (primary concern of the sales departments); (2) capital budgets and personnel training (primary concerns of the small accounting-cum-personnel departments) as well as decisions on production volume, quality and efficiency within their own realm.

The set of interest units involved in the process of making a decision contains some heavyweights and lightweights. Some are involved in most decision-making and when involved are strongly influential—the heavyweights. Some are rarely involved and even if involved do not count for much—the lightweights. Then there are those who, although rarely involved, do have quite a say on those occasions when they come in, and those who although often involved have little say nevertheless. Those four groups are shown in Table R6.1. They are from the 1021 internal and external units named as having each been involved in one or more of the 150 cases of decision-making in the thirty organizations studied by Hickson *et al.* (1986).

The heavyweights are all internal, namely production and its equivalents in

Table R6.1
Heavyweight and lightweight interest units

	Involvements infrequently	Involvements frequently
	Fringe lightweights Trade unions	**External lightweights** Auditors, trade associations, shareholders
Influential infrequently	Competitors Purchasing	Government departments and agencies
	Maintenance, personnel, etc.	Suppliers
	Fringe heavyweights Customers, clients	**Internal heavyweights** Production 'workflow'
Influential frequently	Research, design Liaison and claims	Sales, marketing Accounting, Divisions

Source: Hickson *et al.*, 1986.

service organizations, sales and accounting (and other control departments such as inspection), and also large divisions where an organization has a divisional rather than a function form. The lightweights include purchasing, maintenance, and personnel as well as external interests such as unions and competitors. Unions were not invited to take part in decision-making nor did they seek to do so lest managerial entanglement should compromise their position. Occasionally, they would have a say on the bigger personnel grading issues, but mostly their role was to attempt to protect their members from disadvantage after the decisions had been taken (Wilson *et al.*, 1982). Competitors are important for the strategy of an organization, of course, but they were taken account of more through considering customers or clients.

Customers had substantial influence on decisions regarding new products, technology, and market-related matters such as distribution and prices. As such matters were only a minority of total strategic decisions, they were not often concerned in decision-making. Nor were research and design departments, though they were influential on matters within their own sphere. The liaison and claims category covers sections within local government and insurance companies, for example. Top right in Table R6.1 comes a group of interests all of which are external, including financial auditors, trade associations, shareholders, national and local government in all its forms, and suppliers. These become involved in many decision-making processes, but do not have much influence even so.

Solutions precede decisions

During the period it may take to reach a decision, many of those involved in the discussions will form their own ideas regarding the appropriate outcome. They are ideas that are likely to have been in their minds long before the particular matter for decision took shape, even if only dimly so. Someone may have felt that coordination would be improved if several departments were merged, especially if this enhanced their own career chances. Someone else has recently become convinced that the company's future lies in overseas markets. Hence when a decision-making process gets underway, those involved bring a wide array of preconceived 'solutions'. Perhaps what they want may not fit into what this decision is about, but if not it may do so next time. Hence the notion of such a process as a 'garbage can' into which tumble streams of problems while participants dump in their many ready-made solutions (March and Olsen, 1976). When solutions coincide with problems that fit them, a decision is possible.

This reverses the conventional view of decision-making. Instead of an orderly process moving towards a decision, the decision is seen as 'uncoupled' from the process. This explains some of the peculiarities of the process. People do things for reasons other than making a decision. They fight for the right to participate, and then do not bother to do so. They ignore information already there, call for more, and then ignore that too. In service organizations, in particular in universities and hospitals, the process can itself be as important as the decision. Success tends to be judged more by who took part than in whether the means are available to implement a decision once taken (Rodrigues, 1980). How a decision is made can be more important than whether it is carried out.

As different 'solutions' surface during the process, there is potential for conflict. A production director and his supporters want equipment purchased, the purchasing director and those who think like him argue that money would be better put to other uses (Wilson, 1982). The production director's 'solution' comes from his long-term inclinations as an engineer to find the answer to a problem in new or better technology, whereas the purchasing director typifies his self-image as a champion of wise spending. Such views do not go away with the resolving of this particular controversy. They will remain to be voiced during other decision-making processes. So in each process there is only 'quasi-resolution of conflict' (Cyert and March, 1963), not real resolution.

The reasons for influence

Some individuals or groups have more influence than others in putting forward 'solutions' and knocking others. This results from a combination of factors which provide greater 'control of strategic contingencies' (Hickson et al., 1971). By virtue of a position in the organization, others become dependent upon them and susceptible to their influence. Three reasons for this are: (1) if a department or other grouping within an organization is central to the workflows between sub-units (so the work of others waits upon what it does); (2) when its work is non-substitutable (no one else either inside or outside the organization can do what it does); and (3) when what it does effectively reduces the overall level of uncertainty felt within the organization.

In the Canadian breweries illustration (Hinings et al., 1974), the production units were in every case the most influential because they coped with the main uncertainty. Markets were predictable and closely regulated by government, down to the details of advertising, distribution, sales territories and numbers of sales staff; the technology of heating and cooling liquid and passing it from vessel to vessel was simple and stable; accounting was little more than routine bookkeeping. But the quality of the hops was not under control. It varied seasonally and year to year. Thus the quality of what went into the bottles, and therefore the reputation on which all else rested, depended on the skill of the brewers in blending so as to produce a uniform output from a non-uniform input.

Crozier (1964) noticed the same phenomenon in tobacco factories in France where engineers coped with the only uncertainty in an otherwise routinized situation—the breaking down of the machinery, and wielded corresponding influence. In Israel, Cohen and Lachman (1988) found the same phenomenon in health-care clinics where the professional standing of the physicians was not sufficient of itself for predominant influence. Only by coping with primary uncertainties did they emerge as the most influential group in a clinic.

With varying influence, executives in the higher echelons of organizations strive to make what they can of the social pressures of decision-making. They may be successful, as in the story of the turn-round of Imperial Chemical Industries from a downward to an upward spiral (Pettigrew, 1985). They may fail, as the managers of a textile company whose decisions were studied by Hickson et al. (1986) did when they decided to resist a takeover but were unable to prevent it.

The most political processes

The overall characters of the processes differ a great deal. The making of one strategic decision may be a most political affair, the next much less so, a third least political of all. This does not denote their importance. All will be strategic with costly and far-reaching consequences, yet some will be more political than others. The processes most likely to be politically charged have been termed 'sporadic', those less so 'constricted', those least so 'fluid' (Hickson et al., 1986; Cray et al., 1988).

Sporadic processes

These are most likely to be highly politically charged as they concern particularly 'weighty and controversial' matters (Hickson et al., 1986: 174).

These are matters with potentially serious consequences, drawing in a multiplicity of information and views from numerous departments and external sources. Many of those involved have interests which come from differing objectives. In short, such a matter is diversely involving, contentious, with external influences, from which come its political nature. Typical examples would be decisions on novel new products and on takeover bids.

What happens then is an 'informally spasmodic and protracted' process (see Chapter 10) swirling with activity. Comparatively more of the action takes place informally around the office desk or over lunch, and less in arranged meetings of committees and the like. There are flurries of action between delays, rather than smooth movement, and all this tends to take longer than otherwise. The politics of it demand time and attention.

For example, the management of a British nationalized industry had to decide what to do about a firm that was a large purchaser of its products (Hickson *et al.*, 1986: 118). A situation arose where either the firm might go out of business or it might be bought by other interested parties. The firm itself hoped for an injection of capital to revive it, but the local authorities were opposed to any expansion on ecological grounds. Here was a vital matter which involved not only internal departments but a range of powerful external bodies whose interests had to be accommodated. Spasms of work to produce and agree upon forecasts of cost and output, and to prepare proposals to the other organizations concerned and appraise their counter-proposals, were broken by pauses as their next moves were awaited. After eighteen months of careful negotiations the board decided to take a one-third share in its customer firm. A tricky, political process came to an end.

A constricted process

This is likely to be less politically loaded. It will probably concern a relatively 'normal and recurrent' matter that has some familiarity about it. Something similar has been dealt with before, and the way in which it will be handled is widely understood and accepted. Its consequences do not concern everyone, and in particular they do not implicate external interests. If strong influences have to be reckoned with they will be from inside the organization. In short, such a matter is comparatively well known, with consequences that are more limited, influenced by internal interests only.

So usually the process can be held within bounds. The matter moves along a 'narrowly channelled' course without too many interests becoming directly involved all at once since those concerned 'know the form' and they allow it to proceed as usual. Appropriate departmental experts contribute, but there is a minimum of committee work as most things can be settled informally. The process stays within accustomed channels around a central figure, such as a financial director or a managing director who may be able to conclude the decision without reference to any higher authority.

Yet there can be political undercurrents, always liable to surge to the surface and divert the flow of events in a sporadic direction. A corporate plan or budget is a good example. It can be prepared from the information used for the previous annual plan or budget, departments putting in their sectional estimates as usual with no need to go further for information nor anyone outside taking an interest in the decision. At the same time a plan or budget is a latent statement of the pattern of power which no one can afford to lose out. It is politically delicate.

An example of another kind was a decision to modernize an insurance company. On the surface, it was a commitment to update and centralize data processing for the main line of business, vehicle insurance. But its underlying significance was much greater. The company had been taken over by a larger firm and its management feared obliteration by the new owners. They set out to defend the company by demonstating that it was such a good profit-earner that it would be best left undisturbed. Their decision to rationalize administration and organization was a political move to this end.

Fluid processes

Least politically prone are *fluid processes* since they are unlikely to encounter controversy. Most often they focus on 'unusual but non-controversial' matters. Although the consequences will be widely felt they are not likely to be as serious as those of the weighty kind of question which excites a sporadic process. Moreover, fewer interests are implicated, and their objectives are compatible. Influence is evenly spread, no one interest having sufficient influence to attempt to push its proposals forward in a way that could arouse controversy and resistance. In short, though such a matter can be quite novel and have diffuse consequences, it is not excessively serious nor contentious. So it is likely to be dealt with in a relatively smooth 'steadily paced, formally channelled, speedy' way.

For example, the management of a retail financial services supplier was pursuing an expansionist strategy. The question arose whether they should take this as far as offering current-account facilities in direct competition to the clearing banks or continue with merely paying out cash to depositors in person. The decision-making was straightforward. It revolved around the deliberations of a special managerial Working Committee set up to consider the matter. They met regularly to collate and assess information on costs and competition, and a year later, the main Board accepted its recommendation to take the risk. It was a smooth committee-coordinated process.

Interests, influence, and the resulting politics are, then, the very stuff of decision-making in organizations. How else could it be when organizations are made up of so many people with diverse viewpoints and are surrounded by so many others who have a stake in what they do? Highly politically charged matters, the sort which energize sporadic processes, arise most often in manufacturing and in publicly owned organizations (Hickson *et al.*, 1986). But evidence suggests that they arise sooner or later in every kind of organization. Managers are constantly making and remaking the decisions that shape the future of an organization. What they decide is shaped by interests within and without, and subsequent events may change what they intend to happen. Nevertheless, most of the time they are more in control than anyone else is, and their decisions affect not only their own lives but the lives of many others.

References

Cohen, I. and R. Lachman (1988) 'The generality of the strategic contingencies approach to subunit power', *Organization Studies*, **9**, 371–91.

Cray, D., G. R. Mallory, R. J. Butler, D. J. Hickson and D. C. Wilson (1988) 'Sporadic fluid and constricted processes: three types of strategic decision-making in organizations', *Journal of Management Studies*, **25**(1), 13–39.

Crozier, M. (1964) *The Bureaucratic Phenomenon*, Tavistock, London.

Crozier, M. and E. Friedberg (1980) *Actors and Systems*, University of Chicago Press, Chicago.

Cyert, R. M. and J. G. March (1963) *A Behavioral Theory of the Firm*, Prentice Hall, Englewood Cliffs, New Jersey.

Dror, Y. and T. Romm (1988) 'Politics in organizations and its perception within the organization', *Organization Studies*, **9**(2), 165–80.

Heller, F., P. Drenth, P. Koopman and V. Rus (1987) *Decisions in Organizations: A Three Country Longitudinal Study*, Wiley, New York.

Hickson, D. J., R. J. Butler, D. Cray, G. R. Mallory and D. C. Wilson (1986) *Top Decisions: Strategic Decision-Making in Organizations*, Blackwell, Oxford; Jossey-Bass, San Francisco.

Hickson, D. J., C. R. Hinings, C. A. Lee, R. E. Schneck and J. M. Pennings (1971) 'A strategic contingencies' theory of intra-organizational power', *Administrative Science Quarterly*, **16**(2), 216–29.

Hinings, C. R., D. J. Hickson, J. M. Pennings and R. E. Schneck (1974) 'Structural conditions of intraorganizational power', *Administrative Science Quarterly*, **19**(1), 22–44.

Lyles, M. (1987) 'Defining strategic problems: subjective criteria of executives', *Organization Studies*, **8**(3), 263–80.

March, J. G. and J. P. Olsen (1976) *Ambiguity and Choice in Organizations*, Universitesforlaget, Oslo and Tormso.

Pettigrew, A. (1985) *The Awakening Giant*, Blackwell, Oxford.

Pfeffer, J. and G. R. Salancik (1978) *The External Control of Organizations: A Resolute Dependence Perspective*, Harper & Row, London.

Rodrigues, S. B. (1980) 'Processes of successful managerial decision-making in organizations', PhD Thesis, University of Bradford, Yorkshire.

Wilson, D. C. (1982) 'Electricity and resistance: a case study of innovation and politics', *Organization Studies*, **3**(2), 119–40.

Wilson, D. C., R. J. Butler, D. Cray, D. J. Hickson and G. R. Mallory (1982) 'The limits of trade union power in organizational decision-making', *British Journal of Industrial Relations*, **20**(3), 322–41.

READING
7

Leadership processes: the skills of political decision-making

Dian Marie Hosking

Introduction   'Leadership' has returned to the boutique of management fashion. Leaders again are celebrated. Attention has shifted from junior managers, to chief executives (CEOs), and consequently, from groups 'in' organizations, to organizations as 'wholes'. No longer are we called on to abandon the concept of leadership as unhelpful. Instead, tributes are trumpeted to the designers of 'excellence': organizations are treated as designer goods, more or less effectively fashioned by CEOs who have learned 'human handling skills' (Bennis and Nanus, 1985) or learned how to motivate through 'beautiful values' (Peters and Waterman, 1982).

The purpose of this reading is not to review the vast literatures on leadership; thorough treatments of this kind may be found elsewhere (Bryman, 1986; Smith and Peterson, 1988). Rather, the intention is to indicate what a truly *social-psychological perspective* must look like and why. Arguments are also laid out for a model in which the concepts of leadership and organization are integrated using the concept of skill; a more detailed description can be found in Hosking and Morley (1988).

Leadership is argued to be central to the dynamics of organizations (Hosking, 1983; Hosking and Morley, 1988). The concept of 'organization' is here being used as a verb, not a noun, as is more usual. Few have attempted to develop the concept of 'organizing' as an alternative for the concept of organization. Work of this kind has much to recommend it.

It will be argued that the skills of leadership are the skills of organizing: the concept of *skill* will be offered as a way of integrating the analysis of leadership and organization. The skills are claimed to be those implicated in the processes of *political decision-making*, very broadly defined. Processes of this sort are viewed as fundamental to the creation and maintenance of social order within and between groups. Broadly speaking, a perspective is adopted in which leadership processes are understood to define and implement understandings concerning the status quo, or rather, potential changes which imply either losses or gains for a given group (see Chapter 11).

It should be said that the model is intended to facilitate analysis of leadership and organization regardless of whether there are appointed managers, contracts of employment, or a written charter. So, for example, it has been employed to analyse more or less effective strategies for organizing women's groups (Brown and Hosking, 1986), and the 'domestic portfolio' of tasks (Hosking, 1989), as well as design teams, and chief executive action (Hosking and Mann, 1988).

The model is intended to be neither predictive, nor causal. It is offered as an 'appreciation', emphasizing the crucial ways in which organization is a matter, not just of 'fact', but also, value. Leadership and organization are infused with value. To understand this requires knowing something of the skills involved.

Contexts of leadership: managers and managerial processes

A great deal of 'leadership' research has concentrated on managers: on persons charged, through formal appointment, with responsibility for the work of others. Such persons have been deemed to be leaders on the grounds of their appointed responsibilities; alternatively, they are assumed to meet some analytical criterion such as being the prime source of influence over the work of others (e.g. Hosking, 1981).

This said, leadership typically has been abstracted from the broader context of managerial work and organizing activity. It was partly through an examination of the literatures on managerial work that the 'organizing skills' model emerged. These will be reviewed briefly to show what is important for the understanding of leadership.

Managerial work: activities, contacts and content

Studies of managerial work can broadly be summarized under three headings: activities, contacts, and content.

Managerial activities

There exists a long tradition of studies designed to document the 'observable' aspects of what managers do. Through methods such as diary completion, and activity sampling, there has emerged a picture of what seems to be typical. It seems clear that any attempt seriously to discuss leadership in the context of management has to recognize that 'live action', usually face to face, is the norm; quiet reflection, and solitary action is relatively rare (Mintzberg, 1973; Whitely, 1984).

Live action is very significant, but not for the reasons commonly supposed. The model shortly to be outlined emphasizes that leadership is effected through 'live action', or more precisely, through social relationships; relationships are a basic resource in the definition, negotiation, and implementation of strategy.

Contacts

Managers have very large contact networks (Kotter, 1982; Stewart, 1976). These may be (a) authority relationships as might be formalized by an organization chart; (b) 'lateral' contacts, where neither has formal authority over the other; and (c) contact may be with someone 'outside' the manager's own workplace. The extent and significance of non-authority relations (b) and (c) has largely been ignored. It is these that suggest networking (rather than hierarchy), negotiations and exchange (rather than authority) are central to organizing processes and leadership. The model shortly to be outlined argues that leadership is more effective in protecting and promoting particular values and projects when *relationships* are used as medium for strategic action (Grieco and Hosking, 1987; Brown and Hosking, 1986).

Content

Authors such as Stewart, and Mintzberg, have written of their attempts to get at the 'content' of managerial behaviour. They have remarked on the difficulties involved in getting at the 'deep structure' and purposes of activities. The interest is in understanding what is 'going on' at a 'deeper level' when, for example, a manager is on the phone, participating in an unplanned meeting, or extending a network of contacts.

The kinds of questions that might be posed include: what is being learned and why; what knowledge bases are being drawn on, and contributed to; what are the essential human competences implicated in such activity; are the activities strategic, and if so, in pursuit of whose values and whose active interests (projects)? Questions such as these focus on the strategic aspects of *social* processes and their interrelated *cognitive* and *political* elements; questions such as these seldom have been asked; they are addressed in the 'organizing skills' model.

Implications

What we know about managerial activities and contacts suggests the need further to investigate social processes—interactions and relationships— particularly their strategic and negotiated qualities. The prevalence of social action should be taken, not as evidence of the absence of planning, but rather, as the context of 'cognition'. The processes of social action are recognized as the means by which individuals seek to protect their values and promote their projects. Similarly, the processes of leadership, management, and organization, can be 'joined' and 'ordered' through influence, in relation to value.

Contexts of leadership: organization

It is relatively uncontroversial to suggest that the concept of organization implies the following three elements. First, people must be 'included'—or some subset of their values, knowledge, and actions repertoires (Lewin, 1951). Second, organization implies relationships which have cognitive, social and political aspects. Third, relationships will show a degree of stability such that actions and interactions can be grounded in 'explanations' of the past, and anticipations of the future.

Writings on organization can broadly be distinguished by two traditions. These emphasize: on the one hand, organization as a noun—as a state, entity, or 'condition'; and on the other, organization as a verb—as activity and process (see Hosking, 1988).

There is a need for increased attention to organization as a verb. Such an approach offers a general framework for the study of organizing, whether or not the actors are legally contracted to the same, or indeed any, employer. What is important is that organizing is performed in interrelated social, cognitive, and political processes. These processes (a) reflect and effect differing values and interests; (b) reflect and create interdependence and inequalities of influence; (c) require leadership to facilitate their flexibility and effective long-term promotion of core values.

Leaders and leadership

Three elements seem common to most definitions of leadership. *First*, leadership is a fundamentally social phenomenon, and some form of social interaction, usually face to face, is required. *Second*, leadership has the effect of structuring activities and relationships. *Third*, to be defined as a *leader*, a participant must be perceived as salient, relative to others: in particular, they will be recognized as of higher status in terms of their contributions to influence.

Person or process

The bulk of research claimed to concern leadership has, in fact, focused on appointed officials—managers and the like. The approach has largely been 'top-down', attention being directed to those role occupants who are either assumed to be active in leadership processes, or who are assumed to meet some other conceptual requirement. As a result, a considerable portion of research has investigated *leaders'* characteristics, leadership being treated as though it were one.

In contrast, a 'bottom-up' approach does not conflate the concepts of leaders and leadership. Leadership *processes* are the focus of interest, leaders being identified as those who make especially salient contributions. This is the approach advocated here. Leadership acts are contributed by participants who 'influence their fellows more than they are influenced by them' (Gibb, 1969: 212). However, to be defined as leadership acts, it is essential that such influence is acceptable. Leaders are defined as those who 'consistently make effective contributions to social order, and who are expected and perceived to do so' (Hosking and Morley, 1988).

It is for these reasons that leadership here is claimed as a certain kind of 'organizing' activity. When leadership is defined in this way it implies: first, that leaders may or may not be appointed officials; second, that there may be one or more of them; third, that they can be identified only through the analysis of leadership processes; and last, that leadership processes, like organizing processes, cannot usefully be restricted within the arbitrary bounds of 'formal' organizations.

Physical and social realities

Those who have focused on leaders, and leadership as a personal characteristic, have paid little attention to the social realities of leaders or those with whom they interact. 'Situational' and 'organizational' characteristics have generally been treated as contextual variables, independent of the activities and sense-making of participants. This approach has dominated work on leadership, just as it has dominated work on organizations. This reflects in a person–situation split which treats: leaders as entities; leadership as their relatively unbounded acts; and contexts as conditions independent of partcipants' cognitive–social processes.

An emphasis on social realities directs attention to the sense-making activities of *all* participants; indeed, this is how leaders are identified. Sense-making identifies: acts which influence social constructions; those perceived to make the most consistent and significant contributions; and why they are perceived to do so.

Unitary or pluralist perspective

The unitary approach minimizes differences in values and interests as they might exist between groups 'within' an organization. When investigating leadership contributions such differences cannot be ignored (Hosking, 1984). Values and interests cannot be ignored for the reason that they are central to participants' constructions of their social order and the terms on which they will 'do business'.

A pluralist approach recognizes that political processes are endemic to leadership. Leadership is a political matter for the reason that participants differ in their projects and in their influence. Leadership is political for the reason that some values are likely to be promoted at the expense of others.

Choices and constraints

A bottom-up approach makes no assumptions about who necessarily exercises choice, or who are necessarily constrained: leaders are identified by the effects of their acts, not by the fact of their appointment. Leadership is considered as a process in which social order is negotiated, sometimes tacitly, and sometimes explicitly. Those who achieve most influence in the course of negotiations, who do so most consistently, and who come to be expected and perceived to do so, are defined as leaders.

Leadership processes: summary

Leaders emerge in the course of political decision processes. These 'organizing processes' involve the collective negotiation of social order, including recipes for action, and the terms of exchange. To have any degree of permanence, social order must be flexible to the degree that relatively enduring changes can be both created and handled. This is a 'dilemma' intrinsic to all social organization (Brown and Hosking, 1986). It is a dilemma because an 'uncommitted potentiality for change' (Bateson, 1972) must be achieved without sacrificing stability sufficient for participants to experience a sense of identity and continuity. There are various ways of trying to reconcile these conflicting demands, however, only some are effective in the longer term (Weick, 1979: 217). The handling of this dilemma is what leadership is all about. The processes required to achieve this must be very skilful indeed.

Leadership, skill, and the negotiation of order

It is now possible to outline an integrative model which combines these findings about management, leadership, and organization. Such a model requires adequate concepts of participants, processes, and contexts theorized in terms which are commensurate with the model.

Decision-making processes

The skills of leadership are the skills of complex decision-making. Decision-making is understood to begin when one or more participants conclude that the status quo is changing, is likely to change, or is in need of change, and takes action on that basis. Actual and potential changes are interpreted in relation to values and interests, and in relation to beliefs about causal connections. Changes may be interpreted as either 'threats' or 'opportunities', that is, as potential losses or gains in relation to particular projects.

Decision-making is complex when the consequences of a given course of action or policy are unclear. It is complex to the extent that some consequences seem desirable while others do not. It is complex when it is political: when participants disagree about 'the values at stake, the weight to be given to them, and the resolution of major uncertainties' (Steinbruner, 1974: 18). The skills in decision-making can be discussed using the terms summarized in Figure R7.1. Through their 'networking' actors effect the 'core processes' of search, interpretation, influence and choice. In so doing, they both build and mobilize 'knowledge bases' and other resources for influence. Through these processes, the 'core problems' of the social order are organized in relation to 'value'. Figure R7.1 shows each element to be connected with each other element. This is consistent with the argument that relations between persons and contexts are 'two'-way.

Networking, core processes, and core problems

Decision-makers may be more or less active in making social contacts and in building relationships. They may do so within their social order, and with persons 'outside' it. Social contacts provide information, sponsorship, and other

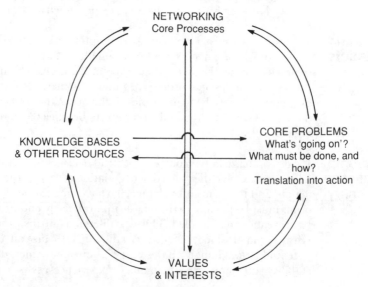

Figure R7.1
Schematic representation of organizing processes

resources, depending on factors such as the strength of direct and indirect relationships, and whether the participants share the same sense of social order.

'Networking' is a major organizing activity which may make all the difference to whether or not changes in the status quo are understood and handled. Networking may be performed by only a few, or by many participants in organizing. Networking has strategic implications, whether or not it is practised consciously. Leadership processes are more likely to be skilful when one or more participants is active in networking with those on whom the interests of the order most depend.

Through networking participants: (a) build up their knowledge bases, (b) understand the processes through which they can promote their values and interests; and (c) translate their understanding into action. Through these processes, they handle the 'core problems' of working out what is going on, what can and must be done, and how to implement these understandings.

Networking and knowledge

Networking is the social vehicle for cognition. 'Cognition' is a generic term used to refer to the totality of processes which affect appreciations of the 'outside' world, and the ways these are represented (Forgas, 1983). Networking is a more or less continuous process of building and implementing what recently has become known as 'practical intelligence' (Sternberg and Wagner, 1986). If managers, or indeed anyone else, learns the 'how' and 'why' of organizing and leadership, they do so, not by 'academic' means (Scribner, 1986) but through the social processes of networking.

Networking contributes to knowledge building through its relationship with 'ordinary seeing' (Neisser, 1976). In moving around, participants are less likely to distort, deny, or remain unaware of contradictions (Nisbett and Ross, 1980; Steinbruner, 1974). Networking reduces the likelihood of inflexible, categorical judgements, and by facilitating the recognition and accommodation of change, facilitates social learning (Figure R7.1).

Skilful organizing is a matter of getting the 'right' description of changes in the status quo. Given the arguments about the social construction of realities, 'right' does not have to mean 'real'. Instead, views about what is right are judgements that a particular description is reasonable, sensible, and agreeable. By 'moving around', participants can float ideas and get feedback to help them determine what agreements will work and which will be acceptable (Huff, 1984).

Some people 'move around' more than others; what is more, some are better than others in networking with those on whom they are, or could be, dependent. Similarly, groups differ in the degree to which one or more participants are active in these ways, and are expected to be so (Brown and Hosking, 1986).

Networking and influence

Networking helps to achieve influence, both within the social order, and with those 'outside'. Whether inside or 'outside' the group, relationships provide the medium for achieving direct and indirect influence, that is, for structuring the interpretations and choices of those on whom the values and interests of the group depend.

One of the ways in which influence is achieved follows from reasons already given: networking facilitates the development of 'knowledge bases'. Through networking 'information' is invested with value; it is in these processes that leadership is evidenced, since leadership acts are those which most influence what information is used and how. When particular individuals consistently make contributions of this kind, and are expected to do so, the term 'leader' is appropriate. For these reasons, leaders have a major impact on the creation of 'social knowledge' (Trujillo, 1983).

Networking, negotiation, and exchange

Negotiation characterizes relationships because: *different people sponsor different 'scripts'*, and influence has to be acceptable. Some participants are more influential than others because they know what, why and how to negotiate. Generally, negotiation characterizes processes within and between groups so that understandings are built and translated into action. These are organizing processes in which particular acts achieve influence and come to be associated with particular individuals, e.g. leaders emerge.

Organizing processes are processes of *exchange*. The term 'exchange' here is used broadly to include fairly tangible resources of the sort emphasized in *economic* perspectives, and in discussions of 'transactional leadership' (Burns, 1978). However, importance is also attached to *symbolic* resources as contributed by acts which give meaning and perspective to events. A major reason why participants gain power in a system of relationships is because others come to rely on them for contributions of this kind. It seems to be popular to exclude such processes from the range of the exchange concept, defining them as something unusual, as 'transformational leadership' (Burns, 1978). However, the more general concept of exchange is essential for the understanding of leadership and organizing of long-term relationships and to the understanding of 'flexible' social order.

Knowledge bases

The processes developing and sharing knowledge has also been called 'organizational learning' (see Shrivastava, 1983). Those who are active in networking are more likely to be skilled 'perceivers' and skilled in the achievement of influence. What follows is a description of the knowledge bases they build and deploy.

Threats and opportunities

Those active in networking have more than one account of events and are more likely to understand which issues require action. They also will have a better understanding of these issues as potential threats and opportunities. When threats and opportunities are skilfully handled, the values and interests of the group are more likely to be protected and promoted.

Capacities and demands

Skill lies in the use of 'efficient strategies' to link the '*demands*' of tasks with the '*capacities*' of performers (Welford, 1980). 'Demands' are core problems; 'capacities' are resources, which are limited. These limitations have important implications for understanding threats and opportunities, and for mobilizing relationships to achieve influence.

'Efficient strategies' are likely to be more consistently practised by those who are active in networking. This is because they have more diverse and/or accurate 'scripts', but also because they have built relationships within which they can negotiate acceptance of their influence. 'Demands' are met through the development and mobilisation of capacities, that is, network resources.

Dilemmas

Dilemmas are endemic to the process of complex decision-making and, therefore, to organizational processes. Dilemmas make decision-making difficult, and often stressful. They characterize situations of choice whereby selection of a policy—concerning means or ends—rules out an alternative, and in so doing, *leaves a problem unresolved*.

Perhaps the most fundamental dilemma is that which underlies the achievement of 'flexible social order'. The dilemma is how to achieve a degree of order which is *sufficient* for core problems to continue to be solved, while at the same time *not too much*—perpetuating a rigid way of doing things as they have always been done.

Other kinds of knowledge

A number of authors have noted the extent and significance of knowledge bases in achieving effective organization. For example, certain general managers have been observed to be 'incredibly knowledgeable' about various aspects of their business (Kotter, 1982: 126). In particular, they have been found to have a high degree of 'organizational familiarity' and 'industry familiarity' (Gupta, 1984). Knowledge bases of this kind are an essential feature of flexible social orders.

What is important here is that the relevant knowledge is both *available* and *able to be mobilized*. Those most active in networking are most likely to contribute to, and make sense of, the network's knowledge bases, to have the relationships which will facilitate their mobilization and, therefore, to be most consistently influential in the structuring of social order. It is in this sense that leaders contribute most to skilful leadership processes.

Summary

Substantial literatures are to be found on 'leadership' and 'organization'; these literatures are almost entirely independent of each other. The concepts can, and should, be theorized in relation to one another. A model has been described which does just this. It is believed to represent a truly social psychological approach; combining arguments about persons, processes and contexts. This has been achieved through taking the view that leadership cannot be abstracted from the organizational processes of which it is a part. The study of leadership, properly conceived, is the study of the processes in which flexible social order is negotiated and practised so as to protect and promote the values and interests in which it is grounded. The skills here described are endemic to these processes such that if they are at a low level, the social order will be unlikely long to survive. Equally, to the extent that organizing processes reflect high levels of these skills, the values and interests of the social order are likely to be protected and promoted. To the extent that particular participants are expected and perceived to make consistent, influential, contributions, it is argued that leaders are to make especially important contributions to skilful organizing.

References

Bateson, G. (1972) *Steps to an Ecology of Mind*, Intertext, London.

Bennis, W. and B. Nanus (1985) *Leaders: Strategies for Taking Charge*. Harper & Row, New York.

Brown, H. and D. Hosking (1986) 'Distributed leadership and skilled performance as successful organization in social movements', *Human Relations*, **39**(1), 65–79.

Bryman, A. (1986) *Leadership and Organizations*, RKP, London.

Burns, J. (1978) *Leadership*, Harper & Row, New York.

Forgas, J. P. (1983) 'Social skills and the perception of interaction episodes', *British Journal of Clinical Psychology*, **22**, 195–207.

Gibb, C. (1969) 'Leadership', in G. Lindzey and E. Aronson (eds), *The Handbook of Social Psychology*, **4**, 2nd, Addison-Wesley, Mass.

Grieco, M. S. and D. M. Hosking (1987) 'Networking, exchange and skill', *International Studies of Management and Organization*, XVII, No. 1, 75–87.

Gupta, A. (1984) 'Contingency linkages between strategy and general manager characteristics: a conceptual examination', *Academy of Management Review*, **9**, 299–412.

Hosking, D. M. (1981) 'A Critical Evaluation of Fiedler's Contingency Hypothesis', *Progress in Applied Social Psychology*, **1**, G. Stephenson and J. Davis (eds), Wiley, New York.

Hosking, D. M. (1983) 'Leadership skills and organizational forms: the management of uncertainty', Paper Presented to the Sixth EGOS Colloquin, Florence.

Hosking, D. M. (1984) 'On paradigms and pigs', in J. Hunt, D. Hosking, C. Schriesheim and R. Stewart (eds), *Leaders and Managers: International Perspectives on Managerial Behaviour and Leadership*, Pergamon, Oxford.

Hosking, D. M. (1988) *Organizing, Leadership and Skilful Process*, Journal of Management Studies, **25**(2) 147–66.

Hosking, D. M. (1989) 'Organizing the domestic portfolio', in M. Grieco, L. Pickup and R. Whipp, *Gender, Transport and Employment*, Gower, Aldershot.

Hosking, D. M. and L. Mann (1988) 'The Organizing Skills of CEO's: A strategic Decision-Making Perspective', XXIV International Congress of Psychology, Sydney, Australia, August.

Hosking, D. M. and I. E. Morley (1988) 'The skills of leadership', in J. G. Hunt, R. Baliga, P. Dachler and G. Shriesheim, *Emerging Leadership Vistas*, Arlington Heights, Lexington, Mass.

Huff, A. (1984) 'Situation interpretation, leader behaviour, and effectiveness', in J. Hunt, D. Hosking, D. Schriesheim and R. Stewart (eds), *Leaders and Managers: International Perspectives on Managerial Behaviour and Leadership*, Pergamon, Oxford.

Kotter, J. (1982) The General Manager, Free Press, London.

Lewin, K. (1951) *Field Theory in Social Science*, Harper & Row, New York.

Mintzberg, H. (1973) *The Nature of Managerial Work*, Harper & Row, New York.

Neisser, U. (1976) *Cognition and Reality*, Freeman, San Francisco.

Nisbett, R. and L. Ross (1980) *Human Inference: Strategies and Shortcomings of Social Judgement*, Prentice Hall, Englewood Cliffs, New Jersey.

Peters, T. J. and R. H. Waterman, Jr (1982) *In Search of Excellence: Lessons from America's Best Run Companies*, Harper & Row, New York.

Pugh, S. and I. E. Morley (1988) *Total Design*, University of Strathclyde, Monograph.

Scribner, S. (1986) 'Thinking in action: some characteristics of practical thought', in R. J. Sternberg and R. K. Wagner (eds), *Practical Intelligence: Nature and Origins of Competence in the Everyday World*, CUP, Cambridge.

Shrivastava, P. (1983) 'A typology of organizational learning systems', *Journal of Management Studies*, **20**, 7–28.

Smith, P. B. and M. F. Peterson (1988) *Leadership, Organizations, and Culture*, Sage, London.

Steinbruner, J. (1974) 'The cybernetic theory of decision', Princeton University Press, New Jersey.

Sternberg, R. J. and R. K. Wagner (1986) *Practical Intelligence: Nature and Origins of Competence in the Everyday World*, CUP, Cambridge.

Stewart, R. (1976) *Contrasts in Management*, McGraw-Hill, New York.

Trujillo, N. (1983) 'Performing Mintzberg's roles: the nature of managerial communication', in L. Putnam and M. Pacanowsky (eds) *Communication in Organizations: An Interpretive Approach*, Sage, London.

Vickers, G. (1968) *Value Systems and Social Process*, Tavistock Publications, London.

Weick, K. (1979) *The Social Psychology of Organizing*, Addison-Wesley, Mass.

Welford, A. (1980) 'The concept of skill and its application to social performance', in W. Singleton, P. Spurgeon and R. Stammers (eds), *The Analysis of Social Skill*, Plenum Press, London.

Whitely, W. (1984) 'An exploratory study of managers reactions to properties of verbal communication', *Personal Psychology*, **33**, 77–89.

The Abbeystead disaster

Heather J. Hopkins

On the evening of Wednesday, 23 May 1984, a group of 44 people, including 8 employees of the North West Water Authority, assembled in a valve house at the outfall end of the Lune–Wyre Transfer Scheme at Abbeystead. At 7.30pm a massive explosion ripped through the building; 16 people were killed and 28 were seriously injured. This case study examines some of the organizational factors which led to this disaster.

The River Lune–Wyre Transfer Scheme had originally been conceived in the 1960s when it had been expected that the expansion of population in the industrial conurbations of South Lancashire would create a substantial increase in the demand for water. The then Lancaster River Authority commissioned a firm of engineering consultants, Binnie and Partners, to design a system to transfer water from the rivers of the northern part of the country to south Lancashire. The Wyresdale Transfer Scheme was designed in the early 1970s. It was to be the initial stage of a larger scheme and its purpose was to transfer water over a distance of 11.6 km between the River Lune at Lancaster to the River Wyre at Abbeystead. The designers, Binnie and Partners, had to take into account a number of design considerations. As might be expected, cost was a significant factor. At the same time, the scheme was to be located in an area of natural beauty, and therefore the design had to take into account environmental concerns related to its preservation. Binnies also had to design for the security of the installation and to protect the valves themselves from adverse weather conditions. In 1974 there was a Public Enquiry by the Department of the Environment and in 1975 planning approval was given. The construction contract was awarded to Edmund Nuttall Ltd and work began at the end of the year. Work was completed in early 1979 and water transfer began in 1979 under the organizational control of what was now the North West Water Authority (NWWA). The Factory Inspectorate visited the installation in July 1981 and effectively designated it a 'low-risk' establishment.

From the time the scheme became operational, there was increasing concern in the village of St Michaels-on-Wyre, downstream from Abbeystead. Heavy flooding in the village had led villagers to wonder if the problem may have been caused by the transfer system. The NWWA were anxious to demonstrate that this was not the case and, therefore, invited a group of villagers to inspect the Abbeystead scheme and to see a demonstration of the pumping system in operation. The events of that fateful evening are as follows: at 7.00pm the visitors were admitted to the valve house, a concrete building set into the hillside; at 7.12pm pumping was started. The visitors waited to see the water come through. By 7.22pm no water had yet reached the valve house. A phone call was made to the pump operator to double the speed of the flow.

At 7.30pm the building was blown apart by a huge explosion. Those who were not killed instantly were badly injured from explosion injuries, burns and

the collapse of the heavy cement roof. At 7.40pm the first flow of water reached
the valve house. Local residents who had heard the explosion reached the scene
and alerted the emergency services. At 7.48pm the first ambulances arrived at
the scene of the disaster and at 7.50pm the pump operator was contacted by
telephone and told to check the water flow because of the explosion. The pump
operator thought the call was a hoax and rang back for confirmation. At 8.05pm
the pumps were turned off. The dead and injured were taken to hospitals in
Lancaster and Preston and by 6.00am the following morning salvage operations
were completed.

Later that day (24 May 1984) the first inspection of the site of the disaster
was made and preliminary investigations concluded that the explosion was
caused by the ignition of methane present in the valve house. It was thought
that methane had collected in a void in the tunnel and that when pumping
started, the volume of water in the tunnel pushed the methane into the valve
house. A match or a spark was thought to have been the immediate cause of the
explosion.

The Times, on 25 May 1984 also speculated on methane as the cause arguing
that 'the location of the pumping station in the Forest of Bowland suggests a
likelihood of methane'. The article continued, 'Some coal was known to exist in
parts of the underground area through which the station's pipeline ran at
depths of as much as 500ft.' An official inquiry was started almost immediately
with the two-fold objective of discovering the cause of the disaster in order to
avoid future similar accidents and, secondly, to attempt to determine who was
to blame for the accident. The Health and Safety Executive brought in a team of
ten specialists to work at the Abbeystead site and consulted very many more
experts in the preparation of background reports. NWWA carried out its own
internal investigation to which Binnie and Partners were asked to report.

In October 1984 the Inspector of Factories produced a report indicating that
the methane found at the site of the disaster was of 'ancient origin', that is, was
millions of years old. In the same month, an inquest on the victims concluded
that the explosion of methane had been an unforeseeable accident. The Health
and Safety Executive (HSE) Report in the early part of 1985 confirmed this
conclusion. The report found that methane and air had accumulated in the
tunnel void over the period of seventeen days immediately before the explosion
when the tunnel was not in use.

When operations commenced on the evening of 23 May and water entered
the tunnel the lethal mixture was pushed into the valve house where it had been
ignited. The report drew attention to shortcomings in the design which allowed
gases from the water tunnel to be vented into an enclosed valve house and not to
the open air. This had been done partly to satisfy environmental considerations
and partly because the presence of methane had not been suspected. The
presence of ventilation grids in the outside wall of the valve house had not been
adequate to the task of dispersing the large amount of gas which had
accumulated on the night of the explosion.

A further factor was brought about by the fact that the NWWA had failed to
keep the tunnel full of water as the designers had originally intended. This
practice was outside the specifications of the operating manual supplied by
Binnies but had been introduced for environmental reasons by those NWWA
workers directly responsible for the operation of the scheme. Basically, they had
a problem with a wash-out valve at the outfall-end of the tunnel at Abbeystead.
This was intended by the designers to be opened from time to time to flush out
the system. When the system was operated properly silt was able to build up
which discoloured the River Wyre when the valve was flushed. Consequently,

water authority workers had adopted the practice of leaving the valve partly open to permit a constant trickle of water into the river.

Senior management were unaware of this practice. The consequences of these informal methods had not been considered by those involved. These two factors, design and operational practice, taken together had allowed a large volume of methane to develop. The immediate cause of ignition was not identified. However, smoking by visitors or staff had not been prohibited and this may have triggered the explosion. At the same time, it could have been caused by a static spark, as for example, when someone removed a garment made of man-made fibre.

The inquiry did not allocate blame. The report argued that the solubility of methane in water had not been fully understood by the parties involved nor by the water industry in general. The civil engineering profession had not benefited from reports on the dangers of methane. Where reports had been published they had not been widely circulated or publicized. The HSE recommended that in future this should happen and argued for venting in similar water transfer schemes to be to a safe place, for regular monitoring for gas during construction, for safe systems of working to be laid down and for all procedures to be regularly monitored.

For the victims of the disaster, the distressing outcome of the inquiry was the decision not to press criminal charges against the designers, constructors or operators of the scheme. Mr John Rimmington, director-general of the executive, commented, 'It is for the water authority to consider the question of their responsibility—morally, humanly, and civilly' (*Guardian*, 8 Feb. 1985).

As a result of this outcome, the victims of the disaster had to take civil action against the designers, the constructors and the NWWA. The case took two years to prepare and resulted in charges of negligence being brought against each of the defendants. These were as follows.

Binnie and Partners were charged with negligence in not making adequate provision against the possibility of methane entering the tunnel, in not venting the tunnel directly into the open air, through not sinking sufficient boreholes to detect the possibility of methane along the tunnel route, and through not warning the contractors or NWWA about the dangers of methane. Edmund Nuttall Ltd were charged with negligence in making adequate tests for methane during construction and through not taking sufficient notice of an employee who repeatedly suffered headaches during the tunnelling work. The NWWA were charged with negligence through failing to check the flow of water in the valve house or to ensure that the tunnel was always full of water; employees ignored internal requirements regarding safety and their duty of care to visitors. The NWWA was also charged with negligence in failing to take precautions over the possibility of gas being present in the valve house and not treating it as a confined space and with neglecting their duty to have an up-to-date knowledge of safety measures at the installation, especially regarding the possibility of methane.

Broadly, the arguments brought against the designers were that they carried out an inadequate site investigation to cut costs, despite the fact that geological conditions suggested that methane was a possibility. Problems had been dealt with on an ad hoc basis and, consequently, the designers had not tried to identify potential problems. The designers contested that this was not an unusual approach and that the ground was so fractured that more boreholes would not have improved their level of information. They, therefore, argued that their failure to provide more adequate ventilation was not an act of negligence. Binnie and Partners argued that the design of the scheme had been unique and that they had been under pressure from environmentalists and local landowners and that this had meant that they had been unable to use high ventilation stacks. The case against the designers and contractors together was that testing and monitoring for gas had not been given sufficient attention. The designers claimed that it was the responsibility of the contractors to test for gas.

However, the contractors claimed that their responsibility was to provide safe conditions for their workers during tunnelling and that they had done this. The case against NWWA was that they should have foreseen the danger of voids in the system by checking the water flow and making sure that the tunnel was not empty. They had created a void through the unauthorized use of the wash-out valve and disregarded internal safety broadsheets. They had neglected their duty of care to visitors. The NWWA claimed that they relied on the expertise of the designers they employed and that, as clients, they were entitled to expect that the design would be safe. They had not been warned of any dangers or the need for close monitoring of the system. Moreover, NWWA argued that the deviation from laid-down practice in cracking open the wash-out valve was a reasonable solution to the specific problem of silting and not, therefore, negligent.

The trial, which was held at the High Court sitting in Lancaster, lasted for some eight weeks. On 13 March 1987, the judge, Mr Justice Christopher Rose, after listening to some 138 hours of evidence from thirty-seven witnesses, found all three defendants guilty of negligence and apportioned the liability as follows: Binnie and Partners were found to be primarily responsible and with 55 per cent of the blame, Edmund Nuttall Ltd 15 per cent, and NWWA 30 per cent. The judge made clear that pleas of ignorance were no defence against the charge of negligence. He concluded that sufficient knowledge to have avoided the disaster was generally available to the defendants if they had availed themselves of it. Interim payments of £3500 were awarded to each of the twenty-two survivors but these payments were not be to made until after a five-week period during which time the defendants were able to initiate an appeal.

They did appeal and in February 1988 the Court of Appeal held that Binnie and Partners were totally liable for the disaster. Binnie and Partners appealed to the House of Lords and on Thursday 9 June 1988, their appeal was rejected by the Law Lords. The company's counsel, David Graham, said that if the judgment stood, legal fees and payments to the victims and water authority would cost Binnie and Partners at least £7.25m. For the victims and villagers who had raised the cost of fighting the case the ruling was an enormous relief. However, there could be further delays and more court cases if Binnie and Partners contest the estimated claims for compensation. A spokesperson for Binnie and Partners said that Parliament needed to consider who was liable for compensation when there was no one to blame for an accident.

Is it true, however, to say that no one was to blame for the Abbeystead Disaster?

Questions

1 Imagine that you are a consultant hired by the NWWA to advise on procedures for the future design and development of new installations. You are required by your client to examine and report on deficiencies in current practice and make recommendations which attempt to safeguard against future disasters. What would your list contain and what would be your recommendations?

2 Disregarding the legal implications of the term, consider the extent to which

the disaster was 'foreseeable' from the point of view of organizational behaviour, concepts and knowledge. How might 'disasters' fit into the knowledge base of organizational behaviour?

3 What lessons can be learned from the disaster and what are their implications for the future organizations of similar projects?

The information presented above gives only a broad outline of the Abbeystead disaster. Further information can be obtained from press reports of the accident, articles in technical journals especially *New Civil Engineer*. See also *The Health and Safety Executive Report, The Abbeystead Explosion* (1985). However, you should approach the question of identifying the relationships between the parties, making explicit the assumptions which each organization made in pursuing its own objectives and by isolating issues which need to be addressed. In particular, the article by J. Reason (1987) 'The Chernobyl errors', *Bulletin of the British Psychological Society*, **40**, 201–6 provides a useful analytical framework.

The writer is indebted to Lyn Hague, Department of Independent Studies, University of Lancaster, who collected and collated information about the Abbeystead Disaster for her own research and made much of her material available for this case study.

The management of a software writing team

Terry Thornley

The software team's project

The project was concerned with the development of a management planning system. The system held large amounts of financial and accounting data and used COBOL programs to access and dissect the data in order to adapt it and produce reports. The users ran the system interactively from a terminal receiving output either to the terminal or as hard copy. The system had proved very popular within the company and had become a potentially viable commercial product.

The project had been running for about two years under the control of the system designer. Various people had worked on it but the team concerned in the research had been together for approximately eighteen months. The project had been developed in 'releases' and was in fact completed at the time of writing. New releases were concerned with improvements and amendments aimed at making the product of the project more flexible and improving its general capability. As the demand for the product increased it grew too large to be controlled by the team. More forward planning and direction was needed. Control was passing from the team to individuals higher up in the organization.

Team members

The project leader, for analysis and design, was Caroline. She was also the troubleshooter and spent quite a lot of time with the users in London. The rest of the time she was mainly with the rest of the team in the North of the UK. She was the only permanent company employee in the team. Elizabeth was originally employed as a contract programmer/analyst but took over as team leader when the person originally appointed as team leader proved unsuccessful. Her appointment was made by Caroline. Andrew and Peter were contract programmers. Both were appointed by Caroline. Janet was the industrial trainee who joined the team when the previous trainee left to go back to college.

The five people identified above formed the software team. Above them were Stuart and Alan, who were concerned with forward planning and the general progression of the project. Alan was subordinate to Stuart and was supposed to be the link between the team and Stuart. This presented few problems for most of the life of the project because Stuart was an absent external manager, leaving Caroline as de facto manager. In the months immediately prior to the research, however, Stuart had started to play a larger part in the management of the project—a development that was strongly resented by the team.

In the early stages of the project Sally and June were employed as home programmers. The women worked at home, part-time, so it took longer for their programs to be completed. Consequently, they were always behind the rest of the team and communication between them and the team was not very good. Their mode of work did not fit in with that of the team and their level of commitment seemed lower. After they had completed an initial batch of work

Caroline terminated their employment, which met with the approval of the rest of the team.

The internal organization of the team

The members of the team did not enter it with predetermined responsibilities. They entered as programmers or programmer/analysts and little was known of the industrial trainee's abilities. The allocation of tasks occurred partly through Caroline's assessment of the strengths and weaknesses of the team members and partly through negotiation and mutual agreement:

> We all sat down and agreed about the splitting of the work. It's the same sort of idea when new work comes in—we talk about it and ideas are thrown around until there is a volunteer or someone is volunteered!

Although this had led to the allocation of tasks to specific individuals such allocations were not seen as final. Tasks could be reallocated depending on workloads and timescales.

The level of standardization of tasks and procedures in the team had largely been determined by the members themselves. For example, they had their own programming standards which they applied as experienced professionals. Where it was felt necessary, such as the ordering of stationery and manuals, standard routines were used. In other areas, however, such as complaints about the computer service, standard procedures were not maintained. On the whole, few rules and standards had been imposed on the team by the larger organization.

There was little emphasis on formalization within the team. For example, program designs were usually agreed verbally rather than programmers being issued with specific instructions. Each contractor had a formal contract with the organization but the work he or she did bore little relationship to the job description associated with the post. Caroline did not have a job description: 'I don't exist!' There was little formal communication with higher management in the form of rules and regulations but the team communicated formally through memoranda with individuals and departments concerned with the project. Communication between the members of the team was largely verbal.

A formal hierarchy existed to the extent that Caroline was in charge of the project and Elizabeth was team leader but there were few signs of superior/subordinate relationships in the day-to-day activities of the team. Authority largely resided with the individual who possessed the requisite skill, knowledge and expertise.

Leadership of the team

Caroline acted as the leader of the team. Although Elizabeth was designated team leader she largely played a passive role, being seen by the other members as Caroline's deputy. Elizabeth filled an enabling role, for example, performing liaison and co-ordinative duties, though she also held the team together on a day-to-day basis.

Caroline was the driving force behind the project and the team. She was very committed to the project and was acknowledged as a hard worker:

> She wants to develop a very high standard product.

She had a good understanding of the stengths and weaknesses of the individuals in the team and had helped to shape their roles, though she expected roles to change in a dynamic way and viewed the process of reformulation of tasks, etc. as being a matter of negotiation between members of the team rather than direction by her. Similarly, she imposed few controls on the team with regard to either work or general behaviour.

Caroline was the designer of the systems and as such led the team at a general technical level. She often worked with individual members on the solution of problems. She had a high level of technical expertise but not always in the same areas as individual team members. Caroline's main impact on the level of the team's performance was through her ability to motivate by example:

> She makes you stay and work when normally you would have gone home.

Although payment was made for overtime working, many hours of overtime were worked which were not claimed for. The working of unpaid overtime had, in fact, become an established norm of behaviour. All the team had great respect for Caroline and were very loyal to her:

> There is a loyalty to her—she has earned it. She makes the project work. She brought us together. She has drive, energy and ability and an excellent circle of contacts.

> I wouldn't have renewed my contract if it hadn't been for her. I still don't want to let her down even though I don't like the situation with the new management.

> She is very good at judging character and attitudes. She chose a very good team.

> She is easy to work with—good-tempered when you make silly mistakes. She just doesn't leave you with the manual—she takes time to help you.

Caroline had a very participative approach to decision-making. She kept the team informed of developments and looked to them for advice and help. Decision-making was largely a team effort, based on discussion and a frank exchange of views.

The social activities and task activities of the team

The team was sited in an office which contained two other people. The terminal room, which was an extension to the office, was used by other staff. So, although there was communication with other staff, the most frequent opportunities for communication were with team members. Caroline, when not dealing with users, spent most of her time with the team. The close proximity of the members of the team to each other and their common interest in the project had led to the emergence of a task and a social system to which all the team belonged.

As a task group, the members of the team worked well together. This cohesion appeared to be partly a function of Caroline's leadership style, partly because they found the work interesting and fulfilling and partly because they considered themselves to be 'professionals' and expected high standards of performance from each other:

> We all work hard—you wouldn't be able to get away with not pulling your weight, unlike some teams I've worked with.

The team was highly task-orientated. Each member filled in Fiedler's Least Preferred Co-Worker questionnaire (which gives a measure of task orientation) and achieved low scores (the lower the score, the higher the task orientation). Another indicator of task orientation was the team's reaction to the person who filled the team leader role in the early stages of the project and to the two home programmers. The leader could not keep pace with the group nor provide the support which was needed. He did not fit into the fast-moving task system:

> Whatever he did he was always lagging behind—he was pedestrian.

Similarly, the two home programmers were seen as falling below the standard of performance required by the group:

> They just weren't organized enough. They worked two days a week always out of phase. They needed to be able to take twice as long as everyone else over a task and because they did not work with us they needed an organized environment. In the end we just couldn't give it to them and because we couldn't plan forward to give them a buffer they had to go.

The social system had emerged through the team working together and through their common concern for the project—the task system. There was a good, friendly atmosphere, with frequent interaction and communication. All the members of the team got on well with each other and socialized during working hours. Social practices had emerged such as doing the crossword in the paper every day and going to the pub on special occasions such as birthdays. Work was often the topic of conversation, however, during social activities.

Caroline was the leader of both the task and the social system. When she was present both social and task activities took place around her. The social relationships were invaluable to the achievement of task activities:

> You enjoy what you are doing so you get on with it.

The atmosphere was also conducive to learning and development and there was little feeling of competition between members:

> Everyone helps you, nobody tries to put you down.

Generally speaking, the social system was not as important as the task system to the members of the team. Although each member expressed disappointment at the prospect of the team eventually splitting up they took the view that transient relationships were inevitable in contracting work. However, they expressed great satisfaction from working with people for whom there was liking and respect stemming from shared commitment to a common task:

> It's a good working environment—the people are friendly yet know when to back off. Everyone is interested and helps with problems.

> It is good experience—it will be a bit of a shock when it ends, but it will. That's how it goes in this business.

Although the team had a large degree of autonomy there was obviously a need for contact with other groups and individuals. Most of the contacts were maintained by Caroline. These included contact with administration, typists, higher management and the computer service. It was very important that the team remained on good terms with the operations staff. If there were problems on the operations side the service could be lost for long periods. The computer was located near London, which further complicated this aspect of communications. Elizabeth had fewer contacts but her contribution was nevertheless important, especially her contact with other technical staff. There was strong competition for their services, and as a result, Elizabeth had to be resolute in her demands but tactful and diplomatic when her requests for help were turned down.

The team's performance and effectiveness

The life of the project had three distinct stages. The first stage was essentially concerned with the selection, assessment and organization of the team by the project leader, Caroline. She was very task-orientated and recruited people whom she thought would have a similar orientation. She knew Andrew and Peter had this quality from their work on other projects. The other members of the team were selected on the basis of their performance at interview. During the first six months three personnel were replaced. Caroline actually had a budget for six contractors but chose what she considered were high-quality staff rather than spread the money over six workers at lower quality.

Caroline's relationship with higher management at this point was an autonomous one. She was given the brief and the budget and allowed to make decisions and allocate resources in the way she thought best. For example, hard decisions such as the removal of staff were not avoided, with the result that a hard-working, able team was established.

In the second stage the product was developed and put into operation. During this stage the team again worked in an autonomous way, with control largely being in Caroline's hands. She in turn adopted a democratic and participative style of leadership.

The members of the team were asked if they thought they were effective. Their responses fell into two categories. One set of responses concerned methodological problems associated with the measurement of effectiveness. The other set produced a number of indicators of the concept. Four indicators of effectiveness were identified by the team:

1 Was the team staying within its budget?
2 Were deadlines being met?
3 Was the product of a high quality?
4 Were the users happy?

The cost of the project was quite small in relation to many other projects run by the firm. Money had always been available when needed and overtime had always been freely allowed. Caroline thought the project had stayed within budget but acknowledged the subjective nature of the determination of a budget figure and the assessment of variations from it:

If people want something they will pay for it.

Subjective judgement also caused problems regarding the team's assessment of their ability to keep to deadlines:

When originally deciding, one doesn't always see everything that has to be done. All knowledge is not there and one has to learn.

There have always been problems reaching release dates but that's part and parcel of any job.

We wouldn't manage if we only worked normal hours, but I don't think we are expected to go home at five with everyone else.

The team also pointed to the fact that failure to meet deadlines was often due to factors outside their control:

We have continual problems with the computer. We should have gone live yesterday but we hadn't got a service at all.

It's the second time we've been shifted to a new computer these last few months. The management doesn't seem to consider the implications and repercussions of what they do. It's wasted us days and made meeting the deadlines impossible.

The lack of secretarial services has caused us no end of problems. All our specifications and documents are in my handwriting and no one can read them! Reissues take months to do properly. Handwritten texts get so thick that photocopying becomes a problem—it's a ridiculous situation.

The team did acknowledge, however, that they themselves were partly the cause of some of the delays:

> We are not particularly efficient. I think of things afterwards and have to backtrack. We've had our criticisms when we were late. I suppose most of the internal things could be controlled—we change our minds too much, but then who can design a perfect system and methods? We are a development team not robots and we are trying to innovate.

> Stuart says I don't control the project properly. I don't do proper designs and I don't know exactly what is going on all the time, but I think what we are trying to achieve is more important—it's like that in other departments.

The members of the team were quite strong in their belief that they were producing what the users wanted:

> It's the only project I've worked on where the users think it is wonderful and the developers are never satisfied!

> I'm sure our users think we are effective. They get more help, support, information and assistance out of us than they do anyone else—we are their favourite people!

> We might be late in getting a release out of the door but once it was gone we don't expect to see it again. We don't wait for the users to find errors—we find them ourselves!

> We don't get dragged in at three in the morning.

A number of the responses to the questions of effectiveness were of a general nature:

> We need a better designer but I don't think there is one in the firm. I'm not a professional designer. I try my best but someone else could do it better. I have all the good ideas but I can't write good specifications. Luckily I've got a very perceptive team!

> Yes we are effective but we are against the grain—that's why we are always in trouble. We are told that we need analysts and proper specifications but we short cut all that. We could do with an overall structure, but if we can work straight from the users' needs we don't need separate analysts.

> It is the company's big new baby. There are queues both inside and outside waiting for it. Mind you, it is our main user who has sold it. He has got a lot staked in it—he designed it by telling me what he wanted.

The third stage of the project was concerned with the product's further development and expansion. Higher management decided that it would be necessary to put the project into the wider organizational structure of the firm. This was achieved by appointing Stuart project leader over Caroline. The decision was greeted with dismay, resentment and anxiety by the team. They realized that more planning and management were needed but did not like Stuart's leadership style nor his intentions to make sweeping changes in the membership of the team. Additionally, they were professionally concerned that the standards of the product would be lowered and its future threatened by its exposure to the various political machinations of the organization:

> Stuart isn't interested in the project and the software product—it is going to cause problems.

Stuart wants to move the project to a site where there is notoriously little care over standards and performance. Others could do the job as well as we can once they got used to it but it seems that there is little interest in doing a good job—it's a shame but it is the typical attitude. He will tie up the package and let it stagnate.

No wonder this company is in such a mess, nobody can see beyond internal power politics.

That's what's so good about this project. It hasn't got tangled up in the politics and power struggles up 'til now. Once a project does it is doomed. So many good ideas and money-makers have been suffocated.

It's a potentially big money-maker, especially as we could sell hardware to run it on, but it will not be taken to its full potential because the guys at the top haven't got the same aims.

Until recently we had no visible management. We have now been assigned to new management and they are taking an active and interfering role. Decisions have been thrust upon us.

He [Stuart] seems to take notice and be on your side then goes behind your back.

Stuart will not back up the team. He just harasses everybody.

He [Stuart] doesn't care about not getting things done. If he can account for being eighteen months late and not be blamed then he is an effective manager. He isn't interested in making the right decisions—as long as he is seen to be making the right decisions by his superiors.

The morale of the team fell in the third stage. This appeared to have an adverse affect on the members' motivation to work:

We now don't work as hard or as single-mindedly. Our direction and purpose has been lost. Left alone we would have progressed much further, but there's nothing we can do. We will all be out of the picture soon anyway.

We would have worked much better if people had just backed off. So many people have jumped on the bandwagon and are telling us what to do that we are getting nowhere and won't unless those that stay with it have got enough push to cut out the garbage.

The third stage of the project had only just begun at the time of writing but there had already been a marked change in the attitude and behaviour of the team. In terms of the dimensions of organizational climate, the following changes had occurred.

The task structure had become more pronounced and the direction and control of activities had increased. Rewards and punishments were now seen to be more related to organizational politics than to the development of the product. Centralization had increased, with decision-making passing from the team to the new project leader. The emphasis on achievement had fallen. There had been a noticeable increase in the level of stress in the team. The team members were still open with each other but there was resentment, suspicion and distrust of the new project leader. The morale and status of the team had fallen. Feedback from the users had started to fall and the feedback from the management was viewed with suspicion. There was still a desire to achieve the project's goals but the team saw these changing and being replaced by political goals.

(This case was prepared by Dr Terry Thornley, Principal Lecturer in Management Studies, Huddersfield Polytechnic, and is based on a study undertaken by Elizabeth Beddall, a fourth-year student on the Polytechnic's BA Computing in Business Course. The case is not designed to illustrate either the effective or ineffective management of a team but as a basis for analysis and discussion.)

Questions

1 What can Stuart do to alleviate some of the problems the team is facing? What actions would you recommend he take and why?

2 How would you have managed the software team in its early stages to prevent the negative aspects occurring as described in the case?

Organization of aero engine manufacturing: Jet Propulsion PLC — Part I

Richard J. Butler

Introduction

In principle, a jet (or gas turbine) engine is simple. It consists of a multi-stage fan (the compressor) which accelerates a large volume of air rearwards at high velocity thereby generating a forward thrust, according to Newton's law stating that every action has an equal but opposite reaction.

Turbines, connected by a shaft, drive the compressor; energy to drive the turbine is injected into the air stream by burning fuel at high temperatures in combustion chambers which further accelerates the air stream rearward. The whole is contained in a series of casings to make a kind of tube.

Manufacturing a jet engine is complex. Stresses are high due to high rotational speeds (30,000 revs per minute), temperatures and pressures. Weight has to be minimized and there is a constant search for new materials to cope with these conditions. The cost of failure is very high both in terms of money and human life.

Consequently safety and quality standards and checks have to be written in to every stage of research, design and manufacture and closely adhered to. Materials have to be inspected and major components identified by serial numbers throughout manufacture and their working lives. This allows a life history to be developed so that components can be replaced after so many operating hours or, if there is a failure, a component can be traced back throughout its stages of manufacture.

Engines (as with aircraft) have to be approved by the Air Registration Board (ARB) for civil planes, or the Air Investigation Department (AID) for military planes. These government agencies have resident on-site engineers who have powers of access to the whole organization for inspection purposes.

Complexity also derives from the need to match a basic engine type to customer specifications. Here the customer usually means a combination of air-frame manufacturer (Boeing, Douglas, BAC, etc.) and the final purchaser of the aircraft, either an airline or a government. Every engine type has to be adapted to a particular airframe and every aircraft is often adapted to purchaser needs. In general this means that major components are made for a particular order rather than for a general inventory from which components are taken for mass assembly. Batches of components than have to be tracked throughout manufacture and tied to a final engine order for assembly.

There is also a constant search for improved materials, ways of improving performance and ways of manufacture. When a new engine type is introduced it will provide a number of innovations (materials, etc.) which may require learning of new manufacturing techniques.

The organization of production

The major components of an engine are the blades (turbine and compressor), shafts, discs (for turbines and compressors), gears, casings (the main framework of an engine). Each of these are manufactured in self-contained shops within the area known as main works. There is also a separate forge, stores, and heat treatment area; assembly is carried out at another site. Each of these components presents special problems of manufacture.

The blade shop is one such self-contained manufacturing unit. Each compressor and turbine stage may require up to 100 blades of a particular size and design, there being perhaps 3 or 4 turbine stages and 9 or 10 compressor stages in an engine. There are 5 current basic engine types but spare parts have to be made for any gas turbine engine ever made by the company. Further, the blades required for a basic engine type can vary on certain features according to the specific customer order.

Manufacture starts with bought-in forgings and castings from one of two main suppliers. Inspection of these forgings is carried out on a 100 per cent basis by the manufacturer to tight standards and using approved methods laid down by Jet Propulsion. These manufacturers are frequently visited by the purchasing superintendent for blades who has responsibility to ensure the required quality level.

Blades travel round the blade shop in batches through a fixed sequence of operations. Critical operations are the machining of the aerofoil sections and 'roots' for fixing blades into the discs. Batch sizes are usually about 100–200. One hundred per cent inspection is carried out at each operation. A batch number enables quality to link a particular component back to a batch of forgings. This identity remains with a blade throughout its operating life.

The blade shop has 4 production foremen and 200 operators. There is also the purchasing superintendent, a production controller (whose job it is to ensure that production keeps to schedule; he has one assistant) and a quality superintendent who manages the 20 inspectors and has responsibility for ensuring quality standards. This requires frequent liaison with design (on another site), purchasing, production control and foremen.

These managers have a dual reporting responsibility. They are functionally responsible, respectively, to a procurement manager, product controller and quality controller for the whole works. These managers are in turn responsible to a works manager. There is also a line of responsibility to the blade shop manager. This arrangement is replicated across the other production shops (discs, shafts, gears, casings). Each shop operates as a cost centre.

There is a further grouping of other production works managers and various research, design and development groups who report to directors. At the works level there are also a number of central staff groupings, personnel, accounts and administration.

The organization is supposed to work as follows. The production plan comes down from the order book through the production director. Here, there is broad agreement, in discussion with works managers and production controllers, as to what is made where and what is bought in. This overall production plan is broken down at the works level to a production schedule on a week-by-week basis for each production shop. This production schedule becomes the plan for a shop manager who then has to assess requisite resources, labour, machines, tooling, jigs and fixtures, etc. It is his responsibility to plan for these resources, to produce cost estimates; on a week-by-week basis he is held responsible for so many units of (in the case of the blade shop) specific blades, or shafts, gears, etc., for the other shops.

For the blade shop this production plan ultimately results in batches of forgings arriving to be made into specific finished blades for delivery to a finished component stores which is a temporary holding place for components on the way to assembly. Production control's job within the shop is to develop a route card detailing the specific operation each batch has to encounter and to set a schedule. This has to be done in discussion with the shop manager, foremen, purchasing (who have to ensure the supply of materials) and quality (who have to advise on any possible hold-ups due to quality standards).

All shop managers in the works have an early Monday morning meeting with the works manager, works production controller and works purchasing and quality managers to plan the week's production. Following this meeting, the blade shop manager meets his superintendents to plan the week's production within his shop. On Thursday morning, these meetings are repeated, but in reverse order, as the shop manager meets his superintendents to find out any hold-ups and then attends a works production meeting in which snags are discussed across the works.

Within the blade shop all components follow approximately the same sequence. Machines have to be adapted and set to different sized components, usually using jigs and fixtures which are located on to machines. Blade production is not yet a precise technology, however, especially in the final stages. The aerofoil section is checked but often has to be slightly altered to remove high spots. This is done by hand polishing. The extent to which this has to be done frequently causes disruptions which can only be sorted out by the superintendents getting together in a huddle on the shop floor and hammering out a problem. This is always done against the knowledge that there is a production schedule to be met.

Problems often come to light if a batch fails inspection at a particular stage of production. Why this has happened is not usually immediately obvious. It may be operator error, a fault with the machine, an incorrect instruction given to an operator, a faulty forging or tolerances which cannot be met. To solve problems like this needs a team effort between shop management. However, they often have to go outside the shop to resolve these problems. Quality may need to discuss tolerances with design, production control may need to re-examine their production plan, purchasing may need to discuss a batch with suppliers. These discussions may often involve the functional managers for quality, production control and purchasing if a problem threatens to disrupt the overall production plan. If the blade shop is having particular problems over producing for a particular engine, adjustments to the production schedule may have to be made, but this can only be done at the works-manager level. If disruptions become sufficiently severe to threaten the engine-building programmes, this can only be resolved at the next level up, the director level.

Problems of this severity are rare; generally problems are resolved by discussion within the relevant shop with some advice sought from outside. Production problems often come down to the need to resolve a tension between what design want and what production can routinely achieve.

When tolerances stated on engineering drawings are exceeded, components can be accepted through the official 'concession' system instead of being scrapped. A concession is a granting of permission to pass jobs outside these tolerances and requires approval of engineering design (perhaps more than one department), production, quality and AID or ARB. There is an official form, giving a concession number for this which gives details of the deviations and requires signatures from the appropriate interests. Copies of these forms are filed and the concession number is tied to the particular batch or even specific component in the case of larger components. If problems become apparent in service the concession may be referred to and it is important that the proper procedure is adhered to. Gaining a concession can often be an involved procedure. Production may pressure for quick passing of a batch to make up their schedule but design may be hesitant on the grounds that the performance and even safety of the engine may be affected. AID and ARB likewise may impose stringent restrictions upon the granting of concessions. Spontaneous meetings of design, quality, production control, purchasing, a foreman and perhaps the shop manager would often gather around a batch of components on the shop floor to see if a batch could be passed.

Questions

1 Draw an organization chart showing line relationships in solid lines, functional relationships in broken lines.

2 How would you describe the technology of the blade shop?

3 Describe the organization of production in terms of the main interdependencies. Where are the main reciprocal interdependencies located and why?

4 What is the difference in relationship between the functional superintendent in the blade shop and the shop managers and between the superintendents and their functional managers? What role do the functional managers play?

5 Can you predict some possible problems with this type of organization?

Organization of aero engine manufacturing: Jet Propulsion PLC—Part II

Richard J. Butler

Day-to-day operating problems in the blade shop at Jet Propulsion were generally worked out in discussions between the superintendent and the foremen, sometimes drawing upon the shop manager and functional heads to resolve conflicts. Variability in production arose because of variability in blades needed for particular engine orders and because the production processes, especially as regards the aerofoil section, were far from perfect.

Quite frequently, however, a problem would turn into a major crisis having ramifications beyond the blade shop. John Barker, the quality-control superintendent, always found himself at the centre of these crises. Quality occupied a rather uncomfortable position between design and production. For production, the weekly schedule was the 'Bible'; foremen were harassed by production control and eventually the shop manager, Uriah Humperdinck, for unfulfilled quotas. For design, engineering specifications and drawings were the 'Bible'; if they agreed to wider tolerances an engine could fail to achieve performance on test before dispatch to a customer. In pursuing a concession John Barker was sometimes pushed by production who wanted to achieve their schedule. His credibility as a good engineer was at stake with design if he tried too hard to gain a concession from design. Quality's role was to adjudicate in these disputes; this required an understanding of production processes and of the design requirements of engines and a considerable amount of tact and diplomacy.

One such crisis illustrates this problem well. John Barker was in his office one Thursday afternoon, reading some material sent to him by his boss, Cyril Smith, the quality control manager for the works. The material concerned a conference on non-destructive testing techniques the following week. Cyril had suggested that John attend since he was becoming the works expert on the subject.

The door burst open and there was Bert Buster, the production control superintendent for the blade shop.

'That blooming fusspot inspector of yours, Tony Tinker, has failed a whole batch of blades at final inspection again. These are a rush job needed tomorrow by assembly for the Saudi order. Humperdinck will have my hide if these are not through—and yours and your damn Tinker.'

'Here we go again,' thought John. After being in the blade shop for a year he could by now always recognize a first-rate crisis brewing. They went to find the inspector to investigate. True enough, every blade of a batch of 200 was no less than one thousandth of an inch (one 'thou') undersize on a tolerance of 5 thou for the aerofoil section. Many were out by 5 thou, i.e. 10 thou less than the specified dimension.

'They are definitely outside the limits,' said John, looking at the inspection limit.

'I want those through today,' demanded Bert. 'I'm going to get Humperdinck.'

While Bert stormed off, John asked Tony Tinker to remeasure the blades. Then John saw Buster and Humperdinck approaching at a rapid pace. Humperdinck took one look at the inspection record, turned to John with a charming smile, and said: 'Not too bad, eh lad. We can get those through the boffins can't we? Just you go up to design now and explain—they'll understand.'

John said that most of the blades appeared too seriously at fault and in no way would design wear it.

Humperdinck's smile vanished. 'I need those, otherwise I'll be eating you for breakfast,' he snapped. 'See to it, and report to me at 5.30.' He walked off.

Both Buster and Uriah Humperdinck were long-service employees of vast experience in their own empires, who had worked their way up from the shop floor. Uriah was a large, bald man in his fifties with a stentorian, booming voice which could be heard across the noise of machinery. He struck fear into any young engineer. On the surface he showed a contempt for graduate 'whizzkids and boffins' as he called them, although John had noted that both his sons had gone to Cambridge. One had to be very careful and sure of one's facts before crossing Uriah Humperdinck.

John noted that it was now 3 o'clock. He phoned Charlie Butterworth, his main link man in design. Over the past year John had managed to gain quite a lot of respect among the design team dealing with blades as somebody who understood the problems of getting an engine to the required performance. John knew that a certain proportion of blades would be accepted outside the tolerances, but errors were cumulative and too high a proportion of blades with the wrong aerofoil section would reduce performance. At the limit, safety could be jeopardized since an engine with compressor stages not matching properly would 'stall'. This meant that a turbulent airflow could be caused and eventually blades could snap off and wreck the engine. In an extreme case, blades could burst through the engine casing and endanger the aircraft. News of an air crash anywhere in the world would immediately create interest in Jet Propulsion. Questions asked would be: was the aircraft fitted with air engines? was the crash a result of engine failure? Every engineer and inspector appreciated that failure in service could eventually be traced back to what they were doing many years previously.

When Charlie heard the numbers of blades involved he whistled and said, 'No way—we let on some under-tolerance blades on that engine only last week as a concession, as you know. Already that engine is going to be struggling.' John had expected this answer so did not argue, but asked that Charlie might come to the blade shop to see for himself.

'I'm not sure what good that will do,' said Charlie, but reluctantly agreed.

By the time Charlie arrived, Tony Tinker had completed the remeasuring. It was now 3.45. The picture had not substantially changed. 'I don't see what I can do,' said Charlie. 'I checked before coming down. We are already to our limit on fitting and of tolerance blades. Anyway, there's no possibility of accepting blades 10 thou under.' John noted that about one-third of the batch were badly outside the tolerances; two-thirds were only 2 thou outside. So he asked if this two-thirds might be acceptable. 'Now you're putting pressure on me,' said Charlie. 'You know better than that, John. You've seen how performance can be affected. We're also getting near the stall limit. I don't like it and it won't do you any good if you're seen to side with production.' John knew there was no joy to be had here and for the moment did not pressurize any more.

John thought he should let Cyril Smith know about the situation; things were looking bleak. Next he contacted the quality superintendent on assembly, Ralph Debenham. 'You know that Saudi order, what's the position on that?' he asked.

'It's urgent and they're short of blades,' said Ralph. 'Are there any spare around?' asked John. Ralph promised to have a look. The time was 4.45. He knew there would be no news from that quarter before he was due to see Humperdinck. He prepared himself.

'Well, lad, have you got 'em?' was Uriah's greeting. He received the news stonily. 'I'll get Pat Childs [works manager] in on this,' he said. 'We'd better get Cyril as well.' Uriah knew the limits of bluster and had quietened down.

There followed a meeting in Uriah's office of John, Uriah, Bert Buster, Pat Childs and Cyril Smith. John outlined the engineering problems and his discussion with design. Bert outlined the seriousness of the hold-up in production. Pat Childs asked a few questions. John told him about his enquiry to assembly.

By now it was 6 o'clock and Pat said there was nothing more they could do that day. He asked that John should follow up his enquiries with assembly and have further discussions with design first thing in the morning. Bert should find out if any work in progress in the blade shop could be adapted or speeded up to replace the faulty batch. They were all to reconvene next morning at 10.30 in Uriah Humperdinck's office. Pat concluded by stressing the importance of the Saudi Arabian order to the company.

'We've been wanting to get our engines fitted for the Saudi Arabian air force. The Americans have had their own way there for too long,' he said. 'This will have to go to Harvey King [managing director] if there is any hiccup,' he concluded.

John was in his office in the blade shop by 7.45 next morning when the production operators started. He wanted to check the inspection figures and get some more precise breakdown of the measurements. He was now working on the theory that design might be able to accept some of the blades that were only a small margin outside tolerance. Maybe some other blades could be brought to light from other sources.

He also had a word with Bert Buster to see what progress he had made in finding suitable material on the shop floor. Although Bert was a bit abrupt this morning, John and Bert usually got on quite well; Bert was beginning to accept that John knew something about production.

At 8.30 he contacted Ralph Debenham at assembly. The news was that there were about 250 blades of the same type awaiting fitment in another engine not due for delivery for another two months. He now contacted Charlie Butterworth and asked if it would be possible to take 50 of the least faulty blades from the batch which were all only one thou beyond tolerance. This would give the requisite 250 blades. Charlie said he would look into it and arrange to meet John in assembly at 9.15.

There they consulted the inspection record of the blades awaiting fitment to the other engine and found that they were all well within tolerances. Charlie said he would consult his colleagues to judge the effect on performance.

It was now time to attend the meeting in Uriah Humperdinck's office. Harvey King was also there. John emphasized the possibility that design might accept 50 of the faulty batch if they could be mixed with 200 from the batch in assembly. There was concern that this would then make the other engine late, but Bert Buster reported that there were probably sufficient of this blade type as work in progress to make this unlikely. At last a solution was appearing on the horizon.

Shortly after this, design phoned to say that 50 of the faulty blades within one thou tolerance could be mixed with some of the other batch of blades. A concession was written out and accepted by all parties. Assembly had been held up for one day. The engine eventually passed its running test.

Questions

1 Analyse the way in which this decision was made, how information was used and influence exerted.

2 Would you call this effective decision-making? Is there anything that might improve it?

Part IV
The Organization

CHAPTER
12

The structure of organizations

Introduction Probably the most immediate and accessible way to describe any formal organization is to outline its structure. For the student of organizations, knowledge of its structure is indispensable as a first step to understanding the processes which occur within it. When asked to describe their organization, individuals will frequently first sketch out an organization chart to show how their organization 'works'.

They do not really mean this is how the organization functions. That would be too simplistic. The organization chart merely gives some tangible evidence of who reports to whom, how many levels of senior, middle and junior management there are in the firm and how the whole organization is assembled together. The chart gives the formal authority and communications structure of the organization. It tells you nothing about the informal processes which occur within any organization. Nevertheless, an understanding of organizational structure is fundamental for both the manager and the student of organization, for structure can cast its influence in a number of key areas. Problems with organizational structure, such as might be found in an inappropriate design for example, are likely to overshadow all other problems the organization may face.

This chapter is chiefly about the structure and design of formal organizations. We may define structure as:

> **the established pattern of relationships between the component parts of an organization, outlining both communication, control and authority patterns. Structure distinguishes the parts of an organization and delineates the relationship between them**

The level of analysis has moved on from Part III (which looked at multiple groups as its focus) to looking at organizations as entities in themselves. When talking about organizational structure in this chapter, we are generally going to be describing a unit which *is* the whole organization.

There are antecedents for examining organizational structure in both individual and group levels of analysis. From the earlier parts of this book, we know that the classical school of management theory was closely concerned with job design, administrative efficiency and overall structure (Taylor, 1911; Gilbreth, 1908; Urwick, 1943). Equally, the human-relations school of management theory had something to say about appropriate structures for effective performance from organizations (Mayo, 1949; Roethlisberger and Dickson, 1939). Essentially, the argument was that organizations should be structured around the needs and desires of its individuals. If these needs were 'blocked' through the adoption of a particular structure, then the structure should change. In this way, greater levels of sustained commitment were argued to be achieved from individuals.

The problems with both the classical and the human-relations approaches to organizational structure was that the links between organizational performance and preferred structure remained tenuous and ambiguous. For example, Blain

(1964) demonstrated that there was no simple causal relation between limiting the spans of control of managers as proposed by Graicunas (see Urwick, 1943) and effectiveness. Other tenets of the classical school were equally shown to be questionable in securing effective performance from organizations. The aims of these researchers of the 1930s and 1940s to try and identify effective universal organizational structures were not realized.

Later work, beginning in the late 1950s and developing rapidly through the 1960s, stressed that the adoption of a particular structure by an organization was no accident. Appropriate structures all depended on a number of identifiable factors such as size of the organization, what kind of technology it used, and whether it was in stable or unpredictable market conditions. This approach has been classified by Lupton (1971) and many others as the *contingency* approach to organizational structure and design.

Contingency approaches to organizational structure

Unlike the classical and human-relations schools, contingency theorists argued that there was no one best way of structuring an organization. It all depends on circumstances, they said. In order to narrow this approach down a little, we have selected those aspects of structure from a wide literature base which appear to occur most frequently and which seem to have commonalities between them. The first distinction to be made along these lines is between *differentiation* and *integration*.

Differentiation and integration

Differentiation

Vertical	**1**	The extent to which an organization is divided into specific levels of decision-making authority.
Horizontal	**2**	The extent to which overall tasks are performed in specialized task units across the organization.

Integration

Vertical	**1**	The extent to which there is coordination and control in the organizational hierarchy.
Horizontal	**2**	The extent to which there are coordination and control procedures across different functions of the organization.

Both differentiation and integration are keynote factors in any understanding of organizational structure. Before we see how they are argued to vary with situational factors, it is necessary to expand each concept a little further.

Both concepts can be regarded from the vertical or the horizontal perspectives. Vertical, simply means viewing how much variation occurs at different levels hierarchically in the organization. Horizontal refers to variation across the organization at the same hierarchical level. Vertical and horizontal differentiation is self-explanatory, but integration can be both vertical and horizontal because in the majority of organizations ownership, formal authority and ultimate responsibility tend to be located at the top of the hierarchy.

Problems in vertical integration can be resolved by resorting to power endowed by the formal authority of a senior position (see Chapter 11). Achieving problem-free horizontal integration is less easy since no formal authority can force it to work. Many organizations design elaborate integration procedures to cope with this situation. These include management-information systems, networked data bases, the creation of liaison roles between functions, decision conferencing (see Chapter 10) and other operating procedures. It is by no means certain that implementing such procedures leads necessarily to effective integration (Galbraith, 1973).

Differentiation   A manager who lets decisions be made away from his or her authority at
lower levels in the hierarchy is creating vertical differentiation. Of course, recall
of this decision-making authority by senior management alone would result in
lower levels of vertical differentiation. Therefore, we could look solely at the
number of levels that occur within an organization as an indicator of
differentiation. This would give us a guide, but it would not tell us *how
decentralized* is decision-making authority in that firm. Both measures are
required to provide an index of vertical differentiation.

Figure 12.1
Tall and flat
organization
structures
(a) Tall structure with
high vertical
differentiation
(b) Flat structure with
low differentiation

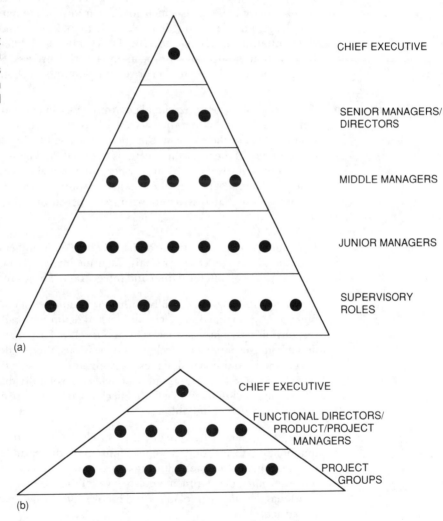

Integration   Integration is closely linked with differentiation. An organization which is
highly differentiated will need a greater number and intensity of integration
mechanisms. Generally, three contingencies impact upon integration and
differentiation. These are:

1 Size of   As long as organizations remain small, there is really little need for large levels
organization   of differentiation and little consequent need for complex or sophisticated
integration devices. As organizations grow, the need to differentiate and to set

up integration procedures becomes a greater priority. The organization is no longer under the control of one person or group of persons. It is also likely that the number of product or service lines will have expanded, each requiring its own mini-organization internally to cope with operating conditions for each product or service.

2 Technology   The kind of technology (or technologies) employed by an organization will also affect the extent of possible integration and differentiation. In modern manufacturing processes, such as in car design and manufacture for example, integration by computer networks has become relatively commonplace. The number of different units which go into car design and manufacture may be very large indeed resulting in a relatively high degree of horizontal differentiation. To change degrees of integration and differentiation would bring with it implications for the manufacturing process. So, to this extent, integration and differentiation are contingent upon technology.

3 Environment   The nature of the organizational environment will also have an effect upon differentiation and integration. We shall discuss environments more fully in Chapter 17. For the moment, the greater the complexity of the operating environment of the firm, the greater is the need for a highly differentiated organizational structure. That is, where an organization faces a large number of different demands from its immediate environment, then it is appropriate to adopt a differentiated structure with specialist sub-units to cope with these demands.

In a pioneering study relating demands of the environment to organizational structure, Burns and Stalker (1961) identified two extreme types of combinations of differentiation and integration. These are:

Mechanistic structures   Typically with a great number of tasks broken down into functional specializations, clear and formal definitions of duties and responsibilities, a precise hierarchy and levels of formal authority, information flowing up the organization chart and decisions filtering down. The continued development and survival of these organizations rests on the assumption that sets of rules and procedures outlast the lifespan of individual human beings. Thus, each well-defined role in the mechanistic structure can be filled with a number of different individuals.

Organic structures   Tasks are not so precisely defined with relatively little functional specialization, flexible definitions of duties and responsibilities, information and decisions flowing across and up and down the organization. The continued development and survival of these organizations lies in the continual development of ideas and innovations rather than in the formality of the structure itself.

Burns and Stalker studied the adaptation processes of English and Scottish organizations from the beginnings of the Second World War to the late 1950s. A number of British firms had been successful since the taking up of defence contract work for the government, requiring the adoption of new technologies and the close interlinking of scientific research and organizational practice. These firms were both successful and had adopted an organic structure. Scottish firms had not entered this market. They were largely concentrated in heavy industries based on iron and coal. By the end of the Second World War, the British government tried to persuade selected Scottish firms to join the new electronics industry which was expanding, rather than persist in heavy industry which was declining.

According to Burns and Stalker, the majority of the Scottish firms which did take up the new challenge retained their 'old' mechanistic structures rather than adopt the more organic structures of their English counterparts. They all failed to be profitable and many were forced into irreversible decline.

Thus, firms which face changeable and unforeseen circumstances are best suited to cope with this environment by adopting an organic structure. Similarly, firms facing routine demands which are predictable should adopt a more mechanistic structure to be effective. In a later study conducted in North America, Lawrence and Lorsch (1967) appeared to confirm Burns and Stalker's earlier findings. There seemed strong evidence to suggest that an appropriate organizational structure could be divined from looking at the characteristics of the immediate environment of the firm. The more stable the environment, the more mechanistic the structure should be (and vice versa). It should be noted that this relationship between environment and structure has come in for a lot of criticism and many of the explanations for organizational successes are laid at the door of political manoeuvrings by governments, rather than be attributed to appropriate structural design (see Hughes, 1985, for example).

However, the finding by Lawrence and Lorsch (1967) and the current experiences of British organizations suggest that Burns and Stalker's findings appear to hold some truth. Organizations such as Jaguar, Ferranti, the TI Group and Glaxo Holdings have consistently put into practice organic, flexible structures and have survived and thrived in difficult and turbulent environments. All these organizations were previously mechanistic and all faced extreme threats to their survival when markets and operating environments changed in the early 1980s.

The remaining two important contingent factors, size and technology, have had a wealth of studies devoted to them to assess their relative influence upon organizational structure. The work of Joan Woodward and the Aston School are the keynote British studies here. We look at each in the next sections.

Technology and organizational structure

Technological complexity

Joan Woodward's (1965) research represents one of the first systematic studies of organization carried out in Britain. Like many scientific studies, the key findings that technology and structure were closely related emerged almost by chance.

Together with a team of researchers from Southeast Essex Technical College, Woodward tried to verify that a certain kind of organizational structure or style of management was universally the most effective. The influence of the classical and human relations schools can be seen at work here, assuming that there must be one best way to organize. Woodward's sample of organizations studies was impressive. She covered 91 per cent of all firms in south-east Essex which employed a hundred people or more. In this way, a large spread of organizational types and sizes were examined, although engineering, chemical and electronic firms were better represented than others. Using interviews, documentary data such as company records and observation techniques, the research examined the success of the firm related to:

1 market share, the corporate vision of chief executives, and financial strategies;
2 style of management; for example, was it formal associated with specific task descriptions and duties?

3 the number of levels in the hierarchy, the relative size of the administrative component of the firm and the average span of control of managers;

4 the kind of manufacturing process used by the firm (its technology).

Finding initially no common patterns in the data, Woodward continued to re-analyse the large and unique data base at her disposal. It was not until she had reduced the number of categories of organizations in the sample to three, based upon their *complexity of production processes*, that the relationships between organizational structure and technology emerged. From this, she argued that: *the complexity of the production process determined the structural characteristics of the firm.*

Woodward's three categories of production process were: unit or small batch; large batch or mass production; and process production.

Unit or small batch production

Production is designed to handle different customer requirements. Such processes typically produce custom-made goods or specialized equipment. Predictability and control over the production process are low. The key department or sub-unit is product development.

Mass or large batch production

Production is designed to handle volume output with production runs of over a week. Examples include assembly lines and large bakeries. Because the majority of the production process is standardized, control and predictability are much greater than in unit production. The key department or sub-unit is production.

Process production

Production processes are organized on a continuous basis, unlike a production line which can be stopped intermittently. Procedures are both standardized and repetitive. Control and predictability are at their highest with marketing as the key function. Examples of firms with process production are: chemical manufacture, oil refining and some pharmaceutical firms.

The primary relationships between the three production process types and structural variation are shown in Figure 12.2.

Technological predictability

Charles Perrow (1967) examined the same questions as Woodward. He, too, came to the conclusion that technology was a key determinant of organizational structure. One obvious omission from Woodward's work was that it only covered a dominantly manufacturing set of technologies. As this kind of manufacturing technology became substituted by other technologies (microchips, computer-aided manufacture and design, artificial intelligence systems and so on) the relevance of Woodward's work declined.

Perrow argued that new and emerging technologies could be analysed along a simple dimension. It was *the extent to which the technology was predictable* which was the key factor in assessing the impact of technology on organizational structure, rather than complexity. The second dimension concerns the nature of the search process when exceptions do arise (see Table 12.1).

The routine quality of a firm's technology determined how many specialist roles were needed to handle events which were unpredictable or which needed constant monitoring. This is the case with many manufacturing firms which use mass production, assembly-line methods and many standardized service outlets, such as fast food chains. At the non-routine end of the spectrum are firms which specialize in research and development work, or which adopt and adapt technologies which are still developing, such as aerospace industries, some firms in nuclear technologies, modern architecture firms, and some

Figure 12.2
Structure and
technology: a
summary of
Woodward's findings

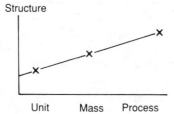

Structure

Number of levels of management.
Span of control of chief executive.
Ratio of managers to other staff.

Unit   Mass   Process

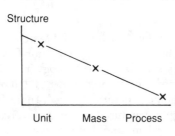

Structure

Ratio of direct to indirect staff.
Ratio of manual workers to administrative
and clerical posts.
Total cost of labour.

Unit   Mass   Process

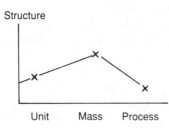

Structure

Number of written communications.
Line/staff differentiation.
Number of sanction procedures.
Span of control of first level
production supervisor.

Unit   Mass   Process

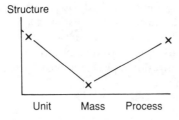

Structure

Number of verbal communications.
Number of skilled employees.
Level of role ambiguity.

Unit   Mass   Process

predominantly computer-based firms such as design and financial services organizations.

Perrow's classification of technologies is summarized in Table 12.1. Some technologies present greater problems than others if things go wrong or there is a breakdown. Even getting a common level of understanding of how the manufacturing process works is extremely difficult if you cannot see, feel or touch it! More routine technologies permit more bureaucratic organizational structures to be employed. The reverse is true for firms with non-routine, ill-defined technologies. They need structural flexibility to cope with the demands made by using such complex technologies and to accommodate the fast pace of change and development which usually goes hand in hand with modern technologies.

It was not until the 1980s that Perrow shed some empirical light on his typology of technology, although other researchers had used his model and had produced a high level of support for it. One such study was by Hage and Aiken (1969), who found that the more routine the task, the more decision-making is centralized and vice versa.

Table 12.1
Perrow's
classification of
technologies

Problem/solution search processes	Few exceptions	Many exceptions
Well defined and analysable problems	Routine	Engineering
Problems are ill defined and difficult to analyse	Craft	Non-routine

Perrow (1984) looked at the occurrence of disasters or accidents in organizations, arguing that one seemingly common factor was the mismatch between organizational structure and technology in use. Among many of the examples he describes, possibly the best known is that of the horrific explosion in the Union Carbide chemical plant in Bhopal, India. The firm had grown over the years into a highly structured, mechanistic organization. Technology in the mean time had moved on from the early days of chemical manufacture. Organizational structure remained the same.

When a fault occurred in the Bhopal plant, it was not immediately noticed since the specialization of roles coupled with the remoteness of the manufacturing process (control at a distance, located at a console, and heavy reliance on automatic safety checks) did not foresee the need for inter-role communication (as in the organic structure). When a switch was accidentally thrown which had the effect of giving a false 'all systems OK' reading, role specialization was such that there was no facility for checking this, even though there were signs that something was amiss. By the time the problem was recognized it was too late. No individual had the capacity to stop the inevitable explosion which ensued, causing widespread and long-term chemical damage to human and plant life. Organizational structure and technology in use were mismatched according to Perrow. In this case, the results were far worse than the loss of effective organizational performance which is inevitably associated with inappropriate structure.

Size and organizational structure

The Aston studies

Although based in the 1960s, the research conducted at the University of Aston still has a strong influence over current research and managerial practice. The research did two things. It identified the basic dimensions of organizational structure and looked at what factors were important 'in influencing the structure and functioning of an organization' (Pugh et al., 1969: 91). In a study of 46 organizations in the Birmingham area, ranging from family-owned firms to large manufacturing and service organizations, six initial dimensions of structure were identified:

1 *specialization*   the number of different specialist roles in an organization and their distribution;
2 *standardization*   the number of regularly occurring procedures which are supported by bureaucratic procedures of invariable rules and processes;
3 *formalization*   the number of written rules, procedures, instructions and communications;
4 *centralization*   where authority lies in the hierarchy to make decisions that have an impact for the whole organization;
5 *configuration*   the width and the height of the role structure. Height describes the number of roles from the lowest-paid worker to the chief executive. Width

describes the reporting relationships of roles. For example, the number of people reporting directly to a supervisor, other managers and the chief executive;

6 *traditionalism* often forgotten, this dimension predates much of the work which was to follow on organizational cultures. It examined how many procedures in the firm were standardized but not written down. That is, the commonly accepted version of the ways things are done around this organization.

Since some of the above dimensions were found to be interrelated, four major features of organizational structure were identified as separate features:

1 *structuring of activities* the extent to which there is formal regulation of the roles of individuals; it includes some aspects of specialization, formalization, standardization and span of control;
2 *concentration of authority* to what extent the authority for decision-making rests in bodies outside the organization (e.g. headquarters in a divisional organization) and is centralized at the higher levels within it;
3 *line control of the workflow* to what extent throughputs were controlled directly by line management as opposed to standard procedures or recording processes of staff functions;
4 *supportive component* the relative size of administrative and other non-workflow personnel.

The key aspect of technology examined by the Aston group was *workflow integration* — the extent to which operations were continuous, in a fixed sequence and automated (Hickson, Pugh and Pheysey, 1969), where workflow refers to the production and distribution of outputs. Manufacturing firms showed much greater levels of workflow integration than service organizations. Also, the more the technology was automated, continuous and in a fixed sequence, the more likely it was that the structure of the firm would be mechanistic. It would have, for example, highly specialized and differentiated roles, a large number of standard procedures and a high percentage of staff (non-workflow) employees. These results concur with the findings of Woodward and Perrow. However, the Aston Group also showed that *organizational size* appeared to have a strong relationship with organizational structure.

In larger organizations (measured by the total number of employees) the impact of technology on organizational structure was less. It was rather the size of the organization which seemed to create some structural imperatives for organizational design. Larger organizations were more specialized and formalized. They were also relatively decentralized. Increased size seemed to increase the likelihood of recurrent events and predictable decision problems. Thus, standardization becomes almost inevitable. Many other researchers have conducted supportive studies of the size/structure relationship (see Blau and Schoenherr, 1971; Child and Mansfield, 1972; Meyer, 1972).

There has been some discussion of the direction of the size/structure relationship. For example it is possible that rather than size causing structure, the relationship is the other way around. Organizations become large because their structure predisposes them to grow. Aldrich (1972) presents this alternative interpretation. However, Meyer's (1972) study, conducted over time to allow for causal inferences to be made, supports the finding that size causes structure (and not the other way round). The practical implications here are that size and structure are closely interrelated. Equally, unless active steps are taken to manage organization design specifically, the firm will become bureaucratic in structure as it grows in size. This may be a good thing in environments which are stable and predictable, but in rapidly changing contexts it may result in an inflexible, bureaucratic dinosaur of an organization, efficient for yesterday's business and ill-equipped for current operations.

In smaller firms, the Aston group found that technology had a substantial impact upon structure along the lines Woodward had suggested. Finally, those parts of the organization which were immediately impinged upon by the production process were more likely to be designed along the lines of the technological imperative suggested by Woodward and Perrow.

A further set of studies on organizational structure needs mention here, for they are both very different in tenor and tone from any studies which have preceded them. They also have important implications for managers who must look to what their organization is doing strategically if they are to understand the appropriateness of structure.

The link between strategy and structure

Although we shall discuss some aspects of strategy later in this book (see Chapters 19 and 22), here we shall concentrate on the relationships between organizational strategy and its structure. Chandler (1962) was one of the pioneers in forging the link between strategy and structure. He defined strategy as:

> the determination of the basic long-term goals and objectives of an enterprise, and the adoption of courses of action and the allocation of resources necessary for carrying out these goals.   (Chandler, 1962: 13)

A business historian, Chandler was one of the first analysts to examine the structure of organizations over time in order to see what factors affected structure and in which causal sequence. In his study of nearly one hundred American firms (such as DuPont, Standard Oil and Sears) he found a consistent pattern:

- The structure of an organization was related to its strategy.
- Structural adaptation always seemed to follow the pursuit of a chosen strategy.
- Thus, structure follows strategy.

Nearly all firms in the sample began as centralized bureaucracies offering limited product lines. As they grew, in line with increasing demand for their products, each firm changed its structure dramatically. They bought suppliers (vertical integration), they increased the number of different sources of supply and they began to diversify their product range. To cope with this, they created a *divisionalized structure* instead of the former centralized bureaucracy (see Figure 12.3). So common were these patterns that Chandler asserted:

> growth without structural adjustment can lead only to economic inefficiency. Unless new structures are developed to meet new administrative needs . . . the technological, financial, and personnel economies of growth and size cannot be realized.   (Chandler, 1962: 16)

Further studies appeared to confirm that structure follows strategy, and those firms which expand and do not progress towards more decentralized and ultimately divisionalized structures risk almost certain inefficiencies in economic performance (see Stopford and Wells, 1972; Rumelt, 1974). A similar study to Chandler's was conducted in Britain by Channon (1973). He also found support for the structure-follows-strategy thesis. The only major difference between British and American firms appeared to be that managers in

Figure 12.3
A typical
divisionalized
structure

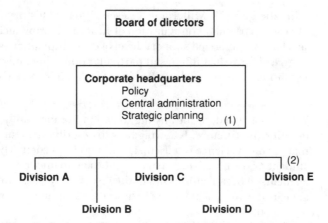

(1) Overall policy and financial control are from centralized
    headquarters. This facilitates corporate integration across the
    wide range of products and services provided by the divisions.

(2) At the division level, each is treated as a profit centre in
    its own right. Each will have a chief executive and its own
    administrative support systems.

British firms were more reluctant to decentralize to the same extent as their
North American counterparts. It was common to find structural progression to
the divisionalized form, but often one division would be carrying on a closely
related business to the original firm and could account for up to 80 per cent of
total business. These structures were termed 'hybrids' and were argued to be
less efficient than a fully decentralized divisional structure (see Figure 12.4).
    Other studies of strategy and structure were to reveal that while structure
virtually always follows strategy, managers do have a limited choice in the kind
of structures they adopt. Child (1972) called this area of discretion 'strategic
choice'. The argument was that some structural adaptation must occur if
changes in strategy are to be fully effective, but the nature of the adaptation
allows for some level of choice away from the purely divisionalized form (see

Figure 12.4
A 'hybrid' divisional
structure

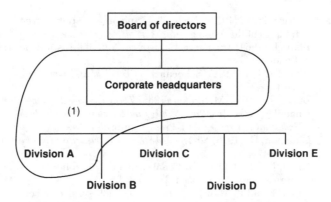

(1) The 'hybrid' refers to the relation between headquarters and
    one of the divisions. This division will be in the same business
    area which was pursued prior to divisionalization. It is not
    unusual for the division to account for up to 80 per cent of total
    business.

Mintzberg, 1979; Miller and Friesen, 1984). This means that managers can choose a particular configuration of structural forms such as planning systems, level of computerized support, level of decentralization, spans of control and degree of formalization to suit particular operating and environmental conditions. These are described in more detail in Part V of this book.

Summary

When we try to describe any organization, we inevitably make an attempt to describe its structure. Knowing how to describe structure in the terminology of management science is a useful start, but not particularly edifying for the student or the practising manager. The key to understanding structural elements in organizations lies in the research by the Aston researchers, who gave us the analytical factors to describe structures as formalized, specialized and so on.

The real contributions of research into organizational structure, however, are to be found in the attempts to relate appropriate structural forms to identifiable operating conditions of the firm. This was attempted by the Aston researchers and many others who, if nothing else, revealed that structure was most likely related to multi-variate phenomena. The major established relationships are with:

1 *Types of technology* (a large category covering the work of Woodward and Perrow);
2 *Size* of Organization;
3 *Strategy* pursued by the organization (for example, a consistent strategy of growth is best served by adopting a structure which is decentralized and divisionalized in a multi-product company).

One problem is that all the different elements of the research on structure are virtually incompatible, so any additive knowledge is difficult to achieve. Perrow's use and definitions of technology for example are not completely compatible with those of Woodward. We do know, however, that technology, size and strategy are going to have fundamental implications for the operations of a firm and that adopting changes in organizational structure without regard to contingencies can bolster the probability of success or can exacerbate failure.

References

Aldrich, H. E. (1972) 'Technology and organizational structure: a re-examination of the findings of the Aston group, '*Administrative Science Quarterly*, March, 26–43.

Blain, I. (1964) *Structure in Management*, National Institute for Industrial Psychology, London.

Blau, P. M. and R. A. Schoenherr (1971) *The Structure of Organizations*, Basic Books, New York.

Burns, T. and G. M. Stalker (1961) *The Management of Innovation*, Tavistock, London.

Chandler, A. E., Jr (1962) *Strategy and Structure: Chapters in the History of the American Industrial Enterprise*, MIT Press, Cambridge, Mass.

Channon, D. (1973) *Strategy and Structure in the British Enterprise*, Harvard University Press, Boston.

Child, J. (1972) 'Organizational structure, environment and performance: the role of strategic choice', *Sociology*, Jan., 1–22.

Child, J. and R. Mansfield (1972) 'Technology, size and organization structure', *Sociology*, Sept., 369–93.

Galbraith, J. R. (1973) *Designing Complex Organizations*, Addison-Wesley, Reading, Mass.

Gilbreth, F. B. (1908) *Field System*, Myron C. Clark, New York and Chicago.

Hage, J. and M. Aiken (1969) 'Routine technology, social structure and organizational goals', *Administrative Science Quarterly*, **14**, 366–77.

Hickson, D. J., D. S. Pugh and D. C. Pheysey (1969) 'Operations technology and organizational structure: an empirical reappraisal', *Administrative Science Quarterly*, **14**, 378–98.

Hughes, M. (1985) 'Debureaucratization and private interest government: the British state and economic development policy', in W. Streeck and P. C. Schmitter (eds), *Private Interest Government: Beyond Market and State*, Sage, London.

Lawrence, P. R. and J. W. Lorsch (1967) *Organization and Environment*, Harvard University Press, Cambridge, Mass.

Lupton, T. (1971) *Management and the Social Sciences*, Penguin, Harmondsworth.

Mayo, E. (1949) *Hawthorne and the Western Electric Company: The Social Problems of an Industrial Civilization*, Routledge, London.

Meyer, M. W. (1972) 'Size and the structure of organizations: a causal analysis', *American Sociological Review*, Aug., 434–41.

Miller, D. and P. H. Friesen (1984) *Organizations: A Quantum View*, Prentice-Hall, Englewood Cliffs, New Jersey.

Mintzberg, H. (1979) *The Structuring of Organizations: A Synthesis of the Research*, Prentice-Hall, Englewood Cliffs, New Jersey.

Perrow, C. (1967) *Organizational Analysis: A Sociological View*, Tavistock, London.

Perrow, C. (1984) *Normal Accidents: Living With High Risk Technologies*, Basic Books, New York.

Pugh, D. S., D. J. Hickson, C. R. Hinings and C. Turner (1969) 'The context of organizational structures', *Administrative Science Quarterly*, **14**, 378–98.

Roethlisberger, F. J. and W. J. Dickson (1939): *Management and the Worker*, Harvard University Press, Cambridge, Mass.

Rumelt, R. P. (1974) *Strategy, Structure and Economic Performance*, Harvard University Press, Cambridge, Mass.

Stopford, J. M. and L. T. Wells, Jr (1972) *Managing the Multi-National Enterprise: Organization of the Firm and Ownership of the Subsidiaries*, Basic Books, New York.

Taylor, F. W. (1911) *Principles of Scientific Management*, Harper, New York.

Urwick, L. (1943) *The Elements of Administration*, Harper, New York

Woodward, J. (1965) *Industrial organization: Theory and Practice*, Oxford University Press, London.

Organizational culture

Introduction

While we may describe an organization by referring to its formal structure, it tells us little about what it feels like to work in such organizations. Such formal descriptions of organizations rarely capture the *essence* of life in the company, what it feels like to be part of a large or small firm, what the other employees are like, whether you are expected to treat the boss with some deference, or whether a more egalitarian relationship is preferred.

If a friend asks you to describe the new organization you have joined, it is highly likely that you will begin to describe the *culture* of the organization. You might say that the office appears friendly, your peers are approachable, no-one is pressurizing you for completion of your work, so long as the job gets done you can fill your work hours as you like, and the new firm has a pleasant 'feel' to it. All of these aspects describe aspects of organizational culture. They are often intangible. You cannot see or touch culture, but you can describe its manifestations and its effects upon you as a member of an organization.

The word culture has been traditionally used in common parlance to describe a particular characteristic or characteristics of nations in the world. The word is highly descriptive of the kind of feelings most of us recognize when we are in a particular territory (organization or country) for we can express whether we feel it to be 'foreign or alien' to us and so can express to what extent we feel at ease or uncomfortable in its environment.

Anyone who has worked for, or been a member of, a number of different organizations, will immediately recognize that the mix and type of cultures within them varies widely. We will feel happier in some cultures than others and we will each perform and contribute to the organization differently depending upon how 'at home' we feel. An organization in which all the staff feel that the culture is alien to them is unlikely to be staffed with willing and highly motivated individuals. Given the right opportunities, such staff are also very likely to leave quickly to join organizations in which they feel more comfortable. So culture has some fundamental implications for both individual and corporate performance. We will address these issues later in this chapter and they are also discussed in Reading 8 by Andrew Pettigrew. For the moment, we must try and identify precisely the nature of culture in organizations.

What is organizational culture?

Roger Harrison (1972) describes organizational culture as:

> the ideologies, beliefs and deep-set values which occur in all firms . . ., and are the prescriptions for the ways in which people should work in those organizations.

An earlier definition, which also serves to show that the concept of culture has been with the discipline of organizational behaviour for some considerable time, comes from Elliot Jaques over thirty-five years ago. He describes the culture of the firm as:

its customary and traditional way of thinking and of doing things, which is shared to a greater or lesser degree by all members, and which the new members must learn and at least partially accept, in order to be accepted into the services of the firm.

(Jaques, 1952: 251).

A more modern definition, characterized by its brevity, comes from an in-house publication distributed around International Computers Ltd. It was entitled 'The ICL Way: The Way We Do Things Around Here' (Beattie, 1987: 5).

The document contained a set of commitments for all ICL staff and outlined the obligations for ICL managers. It set out the way in which the firm wanted to run its business and the things ICL staff had to do if they were to be part of this culture. The definition is brief, certainly does not claim to be original, but is commonly used in a number of British and European firms to encompass the notion of organizational culture. GKN, Cadbury–Schweppes, Rowntree–Mackintosh, British Airways, British Steel and Rank, Hovis, McDougall are examples. These are all organizations which have an explicit statement of their culture. Commonly, an identification of organizational culture precedes an attempt (or series of attempts) to effect changes in it (see Chapter 14). Here, we are concerned with isolating and identifying culture itself. Synthesizing the above definitions, we can say that culture means:

The basic values, ideologies and assumptions which guide and fashion individual and business behaviour. These values are evident in more tangible factors such as stories, ritual, language and jargon, office decoration and layout, and prevailing modes of dress among the staff.

Identifiable and tangible examples of culture at work in the organization include:

1　What combinations of *obedience* and *individual initiative* are expected from staff?
2　Do *formal work hours* matter or does it only matter that the work gets done in time and not when it is done?
3　*Do committees control* the organization or are individuals relatively autonomous to make decisions?
4　What about *dress or personal eccentricities*? Will the organization tolerate a wide range of these or does it prescribe rigid limits? It is not very long ago that the wearing of trousers by women was not allowed in British banking organizations, for example. At the other extreme, the development of the Apple range of personal computers was achieved by a workforce where eccentricity and personalized dress sense were encouraged.

These four examples give us a flavour of the kind of beliefs and values which might prevail in a particular organization. In addition to these, we might also see culture reflected in the *physical appearance of a firm's buildings, shops or offices*. The open-plan offices of a new commercial or financial firm give us an immediate impression from which we take a very different message to the separate office 'closed-door' office layout of the older more traditional firm. It would be wise, however, not to take the physical aspects of firms as infallible indicators of corporate culture since what looks initially as though it might be a rather stuffy or snooty organization—if we only infer this from its buildings or offices—could turn out to be a very informal and flexible place in which to work.

A single organization is also likely to display more than just one culture. This is particularly likely if the organization is large, or is structured into separate divisions. Different departments in any one large organization are likely to exhibit different cultures as are the different divisions of a multinational corporation.

To describe organizational culture thus means that we are describing a relatively enduring 'pattern of basic assumptions' (Schein, 1984) which act as parameters for the considered correct way to think, feel and act. As a first step, we look briefly at four ways of classifying organizational culture. These are described more fully in Handy (1986).

(a)   Power cultures

This culture depends upon a single source of influence and is often referred to as the spider's web with the all-powerful spider at its centre. Such an organization is typically a family firm of a small business. In the extreme case, the central influence and prevailing culture might be centred upon just one person, although it is more likely to be a power clique comprising a small number of persons.

Working in such organizations requires that employees correctly anticipate what is expected of them from the power holders and perform accordingly. Getting this right can mean a happy and satisfied organization which in turn can breed quite intense commitment to corporate goals. Anticipating wrongly can lead to intense dissatisfaction and to high labour turnover as well as a general lack of effort and enthusiasm. *The advantages* which can accrue to an organization which displays this kind of culture include:

(a) A flexible organization with the ability to react quickly to changing circumstances or to seize opportunities as they arise. There are few rules and procedures, and decisions are really taken by influence processes. Outcomes really are the results of power plays.

(b) If the power-holders correctly anticipate the strategic direction of the organization, then they can effect quite marked competitive advantage over their peer organizations. Managers can move quickly, without the encumbrance of having to satisfy procedure. Individuals in the company can prosper financially as well as personally and to the extent that they do not value job security as supreme, they will tend to adopt this culture as natural over time and will try to perpetuate it in this and other organizations. When they are on course and successful, these organizations can be stimulating and exciting places in which to work.

The disadvantages of this kind of organization include:

(a) These cultures put a great deal of faith in the worth and abilities of the individual. There is little or no back-up from committees or groups to decide upon policy and/or corporate strategy. If the individuals get it wrong then the whole organization tends to suffer.

(b) If some effort is not put into maintaining and sustaining the firm beyond the lifespan of its current spider/s, then it will only survive in its present form for a very short time. Many family businesses make this mistake and very quickly lose direction or stagnate.

(c) When these firms grow, further difficulties of maintaining control at the centre arise. It is very difficult to retain this kind of culture in a large firm. Organizations which want to retain power cultures must make a concerted managerial decision to keep units small, leaving unit heads maximum independence.

(b) The role culture

This culture shares a number of factors in common with Weber's description of the 'ideal-type' bureaucracy. The role culture is one which attempts to achieve logic and reason in the same highly specified way as Weber (1947) detailed bureaucratic organizational structure. It is called a role culture because roles (or positions in the firm) are given primacy over the individuals who fill them. The firm is best described by its role set. In this way, the firm can sustain its existence beyond the contribution of specific individuals and can recruit people successively into preset roles.

Rules abound in this kind of culture. These are rules for jobs, recruitment, the settlement of disputes, hierarchical and authority definitions all of which are coordinated by a relatively small and narrow band of senior managers. Performance of staff is only required up to the formal description of the role. Better performance can, in some cases, be dysfunctional. Power in these cultures is predominantly endowed by position in the hierarchy rather than by any other bases.

The advantages of this culture are the predictability and stability can be attributed to the firm both from external observers looking in and from those employed within. This is a strength only in so far as the environment which the organization faces is both predictable and relatively stable. Since efficiency can be achieved by one year being like the next, these kind of firms can become extremely efficient over time if they face a benign and unchanging environment. Firms with long product life-cycles and those with programmed work can operate on being role cultures quite successfully. In particular, the role culture is appropriate for organizations where economies of scale are far more important than innovation and flexibility.

The disadvantages of the role cultures lie in their in-built inertia. Because cultural norms cover most organizational situations, the complexity produced when situations need to change is immense. These cultures cannot easily adapt to changing circumstances, nor can they handle experimentation to any large degree. They are cultures founded upon predictability and represent the sedimentation of many years' organizational practice. Role cultures are often efficient organizations for yesterday's business.

(c) The task culture

This culture has no single source of power endowed by hierarchical location. Senior management allocates projects to the various parts of the organization, and projects are worked on and developed autonomously by teams of staff who often get together for that project alone. The culture is inherently cross-functional, mixing different levels of expertise together in project teams and deliberately subjugating hierarchical authority to the development of the project or task.

This culture is often associated with organizations which adopt matrix or project-based structural designs (Knight, 1977). These are discussed in greater detail in Chapter 15 of this book. The task culture depends upon the right people being brought together at the right time in order to assemble the relevant resources for the completion of a particular project. The culture is one of teamwork rather than individual effort and reward. Like many teams, however, individual members can fall into the frame of mind of assuming they have greater expertise or power than the rest and the culture is likely to be critically damaged.

The advantages of role cultures are *flexibility and fashion*. They are flexible because response to changes in the environment can be extremely swift. In a market where products change quickly, organizations with these cultures can help sustain competitive advantage. Given their project basis, they can also develop quite quickly into market leaders if they get the project and its development right.

They are also fashionable, for they display many of the criteria which organizational behaviour currently advocates (e.g. combining groups and individuals through common goals; reducing overall hierarchy; allowing personal space and freedom and a change from humdrum and predictable long-term routine).

The disadvantages of role cultures are that it is almost impossible to produce economies of scale or any great depth of technical knowledge since projects and products have short life-cycles. Where organizations need creativity, lateral thinking and speed of reaction, they often build in elements of this culture into departments or areas such as advertising product innovation groups and other task forces. Transferring this culture to other parts of the organization, or even the whole of it, is likely to have negative implications, however, not the least of which is that the efforts which have to go into managing and maintaining a task culture often outweigh the strategic advantages of flexibility associated with it (Child, 1984).

Task groups are very difficult to control once they are under way, and projects generally depend upon a purse of limitless money which can underwrite any task or mission the group feels necessary. Failure to provide this money across all projects can lead to demotivation among those who fail to get money and to competition between those who do receive some funding.

(d) The person culture

This is the least common form of culture found in complex organizations in Britain, North America and continental Western Europe. It is, however, a culture commonly desired by individuals who work in other kinds of cultures, since it often accords with their personal wishes and values.

The individual is the keynote of the firm. The firm is there to serve the interests of the individuals who form it. Professionals such as lawyers, architects and some consultants initially organize themselves into this kind of culture. The reason for them getting together at all is so that they can enhance and develop their personal aims and ambitions by teaming up with others of a like mind and sharing the benefits of organization (such as common administration, a central office location, or some central equipment such as a computer).

Such cultures rarely persist for long. Very quickly the organization begins to take on a life of its own beyond its members' purely personal ambitions. It can very quickly shift into a role or a power culture as soon as this happens. It is possible for this culture to be found in pockets within large organizations where other cultures predominate. Some specialist groups, such as computer experts or experimental laboratory staff often feel little allegiance to their organization but feel very strongly about doing their own thing, and thus they develop a form of person culture.

Culture and structure

The four broad cultural types outlined above are useful as a first step in looking as this subject. Handy (1986) argues that each culture is usually represented by or associated with a particular structural form. In other words, organizational design and culture are related (see Chapter 12). Power cultures are designed like a spider's web around the power clique, role cultures are reflected in functionally differentiated structures, task cultures are reflected in matrix forms and person cultures have virtually no formal structure at all. Figure 13.1 shows the dominant structural and cultural relationships as described by Handy (1986).

Figure 13.1 Culture and structure: likely combinations*

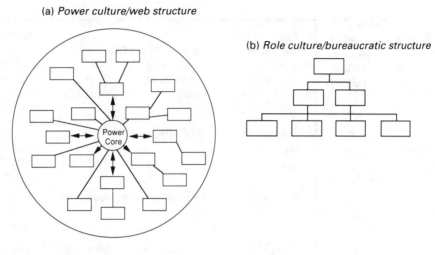

(a) *Power culture/web structure*

(b) *Role culture/bureaucratic structure*

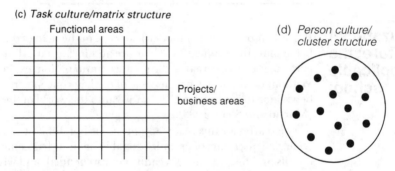

(c) *Task culture/matrix structure*

(d) *Person culture/ cluster structure*

*The person culture is virtually free of a formal structure. Handy (1986) characterizes it as a 'cluster' of individuals.

It would be a fallacy, however, to assume that organizational design and organizational culture were inseparable. They are two important facets of organization which may be related as Handy suggests, but there is no reason to assume that they are always related, or that the one always causes the other.

Organizational culture: two important dimensions

Since organizational culture is a broad-brush concept without precise definition, its interpretation has been equally broad. To many, culture has provided the long-elusive link between corporate success and effective and efficient organization. To others, the concept of culture has provided an intellectual challenge to try and distil the essence of its various component factors and levels of analysis.

We distinguish between these two approaches by calling the first the *applicable school* and the second the *analytical school*. This does not mean that there are only two schools of thought, of course. There are countless approaches in between.

The utility of highlighting the two extreme ends of a continuum lies in being able to show the very marked differences in the ways in which the notion of organizational culture has been applied. Table 13.1 illustrates the extremes of the applicable and the analytical approaches and gives some examples of the related disciplines upon which each draws.

Table 13.1
Four broad ways of viewing organizational culture

Applicable/ analytical	Culture viewed as	Related concepts (examples)
Applicable	**Commitment** to a firm's values and corporate goals	Motivation theories, decision theories, leadership
Applicable	**A recipe** for success	Strategic management, organizational change, organization structure and design
Analytical	**Context and history** of the organization	Business history, anthropology, the sociology of language
Analytical	The **control** of individual and group behaviours, approving some and not others	Social psychology, socialization, studies of informal organization

Organizational culture: the applicable school

Possibly more than any modern concept in the field of organizational behaviour, the application of culture and its arguable links with corporate performance have created the greatest anticipation, excitement and debate. Without doubt, it has become one of the key concepts from organizational behaviour to be translated so readily into the world of the practising manager (Martin and Siehl, 1983).

The reason for this ready acceptance is not difficult to see. For once, it would seem, the discipline of organizational behaviour has come up with a topic with few 'ifs and buts', which is readily comprehended, and which can be applied immediately. The terminology of organizational culture has also found ready acceptance among managers. It can be found, for example, in a number of biographies of very recent leaders of British industry (see, for example, Edwardes, 1983; Harvey-Jones, 1988). The seeming lack of ambiguity of the concept, coupled with its apparently successful application by some of the key figures in British industry, has placed culture as a central concept.

Getting organizational culture 'right' has widespread implications for both corporate success and for effective human resource management by achieving widespread commitment throughout staff to organizational goals and strategies. Nowhere is this more evident than in some of the recent literature on the subject from North America. Peters and Waterman (1982), and Kanter (1984) write as staunch advocates of attention to organizational culture as a way of achieving success and sustainable competitive advantage (Porter, 1980). Peters and Waterman distilled the essence of corporate success into eight areas, all of which stem from getting the culture 'right'. In the right combination (and in the right organization) business success seems likely to follow. Table 13.2 lists the eight areas of organizational culture identified by Peters and Waterman.

Kanter (1984) similarly argued that there were combinations of cultural

Table 13.2
The core of
excellence: Peters
and Waterman's
eight basic attributes
of success

1 Bias for action	Getting on with it. The organization is not paralysed by analysis. Managers think about decisions then get on with implementing them.
2 Close to the customer	Learning from clients. Key concepts are quality, service and reliability.
3 Autonomy and entrepreneurship	Foster many leaders and innovators throughout the organization.
4 Productivity through people	The labour force is the root of quality and productivity. We/they attitudes are dysfunctional.
5 Hands-on, value driven	Top management keeps in touch with all areas of organization. An emphasis on managing by walking about.
6 Stick to the knitting	The odds for excellent performance seem to favour those organizations which stay close to the businesses they know.
7 Simple form, lean staff	Keep structure simple and top management levels lean.
8 Simultaneous loose-tight properties	Organizations are both centralized and decentralized. Autonomy and product development are decentralized. Core values are centralized.

factors which predisposed an organization to be able to cope more easily with changes, and which secured current and future successes. Broadly, she concluded from a study of both successful and less successful companies that sustainable success stemmed from an organizational culture which favoured corporate entrepreneurship coupled with heavy investment in human resources. For example, the value system of an organization should be committed to promoting people early in order to stretch them (ready for the next job), providing easily available seed capital for projects suggested by individuals throughout the organization, and rewarding the *attempt* at innovation rather than its subsequent success or failure.

Schwartz and Davies (1981) and Silverzweig and Allen (1976) have also produced evidence from companies in North America which seems to suggest that particular cultural configurations support and sustain success. The addition they make to the points already made by Peters and Waterman and Kanter focus upon creating a culture which favours experimentation to which all staff are committed. In this way, innovations can be tested, tried out in the organization and experienced. Where this leads to improved performance, the experiment can then be incorporated into the organization in the knowledge that staff have already experienced the 'new' culture and are committed to it.

The impact of this research has been fundamental for many British organizations. Firms in the private, public and voluntary sectors have begun to look seriously at their organizational culture and how changes might be brought about to improve and secure strategic success. British Gas, Imperial Chemical Industries, British Sugar Corporation, many building societies, banks and non-profit-making organizations such as Oxfam, World Wildlife Fund and Christian Aid are among the long list of companies currently wrestling with the problem of trying to adopt an 'appropriate' culture. Much of the attention focuses on human-resource-management issues in British organizations (see Hendry and Pettigrew, 1986; Hendry, Pettigrew and Sparrow, 1988), rather than on the more product-innovation centred changes favoured by North American firms. This is primarily because it seems that British firms have lagged far behind their North American and European counterparts in the training and development of their managers (see Hayes, Anderson and Fonda, 1984; Sorge and Warner, 1986). In particular British firms seem historically to have espoused a culture towards human-resource management where it is viewed as an add-on extra, rather than as an integral part of organizational strategy. The relatively poor record of qualifications in business and related disciplines by British managers is also a key part of this pattern (Sorge and Warner, 1986).

Solid empirical evidence that certain cultural recipes lead to strategic success is limited. This is particularly so if we confine our attention to the links between cultural change and corporate successes in British and European organizations. Some companies, like ICL, are currently trying to modify and change their cultures (see Beattie, 1987). Only time will tell if such changes result in improved organizational performance. Other companies, such as British Gas, British Steel, GKN and many financial service organizations, are working alongside researchers and consultants towards the same end. Because of the long-term nature both of achieving and implementing cultural change, the discipline will be found wanting in empirical evidence for some time yet. The indications of what we know so far, however, seem to suggest that there may be some kind of link between the strategic performance of an organization and its corporate culture, although the number of intervening variables and the potency of their effects remain unknown.

Organizational culture: the analytical school

The analytical approaches to culture are far less ready to establish direct linkages between culture and organizational success. Instead, researchers argue that organizational culture is a multi-variate phenomenon and first we must isolate and identify the various factors which comprise the umbrella term 'organizational culture'.

There are those researchers who argue that organizational culture is a product of both corporate and national history. Organizations are as they are because of the way they have developed over time and because of the way they have grown alongside the dominant ideologies and mores of their nation. Any organization thus becomes a reflection of the wider context in which it is (and, historically, has been) located. The beliefs, attitudes and values of managers are thus little different from, and are supported by, the dominant belief systems of a wider national context. This continuity has been termed 'living history' by Malinowski (1945), and it has formed the framework for much recent research.

Other researchers acknowledge the impact of history, but argue that the situation is less deterministic than the picture presented above. Bate (1984) and Pettigrew (1979) for example, both view organizational culture as essentially an interactive phenomenon. Individuals observe, mix within and interact with the world around them. Through this process, an individual can symbolize and attribute meaning to events and objects. This is the basis of the philosophy of interactionism (see, for example, Blumer, 1965). The dominant factor (and the most recognizable) in this interaction is that of language.

Pettigrew (1979) argues that language embodies the most important and the most obvious way in which culture is transmitted within organizations. There are accepted ways of doing things in an organization, and its spirit, character and overall philosophy are captured in the language spoken in its boardrooms, offices, corridors, and shop floors. It is by means of this language that new individuals to the culture learn its 'rules'. They learn what fits in and what is considered heretical. They also learn stories and myths about both the organization and some of its participants (Mitroff and Kilmann, 1976). Expressions of language can also be reinforced by rituals and procedures such as those which might accompany the installation of a new director or company chairman. There will be dinners and banquets, formal toasts, the informal interaction of party-goers. The language which emanates from such rituals is important, for it shapes the social architecture of the organizational as surely as any formal structure or design (see Deal and Kennedy, 1982; Trice and Beyer, 1984).

The development and persistence of organizational cultures via language depends upon the notion of collective sharing. Listeners to the tellers of organizational stories all create and maintain a language which is only fully understandable within the organizational context. This is very much in the tradition of bygone village stories and story-telling as an oral tradition of communication. It is also doubtful whether social and organizational scientists will be able to label precisely the vast variability of cultures created by this shared interaction of structure, meaning and language over time. Descriptions by individuals in organizations which outline the 'taken for granted' and 'common-sense' views which prevail are possibly the best keys we have as yet to understanding and categorizing organizational cultures (Silverman, 1970).

Implications of organizational culture for organizations and management

The pervasive nature of organizational culture cannot be stressed too much. It is likely to affect virtually all aspects of organizational life. Because it is more often implicit in its articulation by members of an organization (rather than a set of explicit statements), managing the culture is both a difficult and imprecise task. Managing the culture requires that managers are relatively clear about the various cultures which exist in their organizations and can decipher or interpret what others tell them about the culture.

Attempts to manage culture can be both painful and rewarding. Pettigrew's (1985) detailed account of attempts to change the culture at ICI rests very much on the ability and facility of John Harvey-Jones and others to 'think the unthinkable and to say the unsayable'. That is, cultural change only became possible when an extremely strong and well-articulated counter-culture began to foster in the organization. In this case, understanding and then changing the culture brought with it corporate success. Becoming more open in management style, decentralization, the extensive use of organizational development and management training and streamlining and simplifying the management structure were all part of this cultural management process.

Many organizations, such as Jaguar and STC-ICL, have taken the route of implementing cultures which reflect responsible autonomy on the part of their middle and junior managers. In Handy's terms, they have moved significantly towards becoming dominantly task cultures.

It would be unwise, however, to associate corporate success solely with task cultures. The very recent experiences at Sulzer Brothers based in Switzerland seem to bear this out. Faced with declining profits (66 million Sfr. in 1983 and two further years of losses) the new President of the Board, Fritz Fahrini, began to attack the corporate culture of Sulzer Brothers. For many years, the organization had been essentially a task culture. Decisions were decentralized, managers at all levels were given a great deal of autonomy, and decision-making was predominantly by consensus. In less than two years, Fahrini has begun to change the culture of Sulzer. Vocabularies of managers now include describing management by consensus as on the scrapheap. The structure of the organization has also come in for some major changes. The division of labour, previously blurred and cross-functional, has now been very clearly demarcated. Job descriptions and responsibilities have been redrawn and are much more precise. The ultimate aim is eventually to split the organization into separate product divisions, each run as a separate company bound by common bureaucratic rules.

Here, we have the adoption of what Handy would term a role culture. It appears to have been successful. Despite poor financial exchange rates, group sales rose 2 per cent in 1987 and group orders increased by 4 per cent in the same year. The first quarter of 1988 saw a 14 per cent increase in orders (Wicks, 1988: 6–12). A role culture being successful in a rapidly changing corporate environment is not something that many authors in the applicable tradition of organizational culture (outlined earlier in this chapter) would predict or advocate. It might, however, be attributable to the national context in which Swiss businesses operate.

Most Swiss managers will have a relatively higher level of education (particularly in comparison to UK managers), and loans and capital are relatively abundant and cheap. Coupled with an extremely stable political economy, the *national* culture of Switzerland differs markedly from Britain and many other European countries. In addition, around 12 of the top 26 Swiss companies are *family-owned*, so the propensity towards more centralized role cultures is perhaps not too surprising.

So, although corporate culture can take multiple forms, such is the complexity of its character that simple relationships with organizational effectiveness and performance are unlikely. Empirical evidence suggests that a link is likely but there are plenty of cases, such as that of Sulzer described above, which do not support the thesis.

Summary

We have seen that corporate culture is an all-embracing concept, highly complex but essential for a clear understanding of how most organizations operate both internally and towards their wider environment. We can view culture as:

1 *A control mechanism*   By making explicit what are the prevailing values, norms and vocabularies in the organization, managers can instigate powerful control over others by demarcating what are the acceptable and unacceptable ways in which things are done in their organization.

2 *Organizational history*   The context through which the organization has developed and progressed: the hallmarks of the past and the heavy hand of past actions over present beliefs, values and attitudes.

3 *Commitment to the firm and its values*   The process through which individuals are motivated and committed to the prevailing beliefs in the organization. Achieving commitment by getting individuals to incorporate the firm's value systems into their own personal beliefs.

4 *A recipe for success*   A presumed matching of corporate culture and strategic success: especially the argued ability of certain cultures to cope more easily with the change process in organizations.

Critics of the 'culture school' point out that many of the theories and assumptions are simplistic and often mutually exclusive (see Turner, 1986;

Johnson, 1987; Young, 1989). One assumption is that culture is concerned primarily with corporate solidarity and common values. Another is concerned with corporate division into separate political factions. Common to both views is that culture enables a fixed set of meanings and motivations to organizational events. Culture allows very convenient single interpretations of multiple events which, according to Weick (1979), are likely to have multiple causes including fate and chance.

Even though we have as yet little empirical proof for the culture and performance link, there are far more data which suggest that organizations can easily become locked into their respective culture (or set of cultures). We approach the question of change and organizational culture in the next chapter.

References

Bate, P. (1984) 'The impact of organizational culture on approaches to organizational problem solving', *Organization Studies*, **5**(1), 43–66.

Beattie, D. (1987) 'Integrating human resources and business plans at ICL', *Institute of Personnel Management*, National Conference.

Blumer, H. (1965) 'Sociological implications of the thought of George Herbert Mead', *American Journal of Sociology*, **71**, 535–48.

Child, J. (1984) *Organization: a guide to Problems and Practice*, Harper & Row, London.

Deal, T. E. and A. A. Kennedy (1982) *Corporate Cultures*, Addison-Wesley, Reading, Mass.

Edwardes, M. (1983) *Back from the brink: An Apocalyptic Experience*, Collins, London.

Handy, C. B. (1986) *Understanding Organizations*, Penguin, Harmondsworth.

Harrison, R. (1972) 'How to describe your organization', *Harvard Business Review*, Sept.–Oct.

Harvey-Jones, J. (1988) *Making it Happen: Reflections on Leadership*, Collins, London.

Hayes, C., A. Anderson and N. Fonda (1984) *Competence and Competition: Training and Education in the Federal Republic of Germany, the United States and Japan*, NEDO/MSC, London.

Hendry, C. and A. M. Pettigrew (1986) 'The practice of strategic human resource management', *Personnel Review*, **15**(5), 3–8.

Hendry, C., A. M. Pettigrew and P. Sparrow (1988) 'Changing patterns of human resource management', *Personnel Management*, November, 37–41.

Jaques, E. (1952) *The Changing Culture of a Factory*, Tavistock, London.

Johnson, G. (1987) *Strategic Change and the Management Process*, Blackwell, Oxford.

Kanter, R. M. (1984) *The Change Masters: Corporate Entrepreneurs at Work*, Counterpoint, London.

Knight, K. (1977) *Matrix Management*, Gower, Farnborough.

Malinowski B. (1945) *The Dynamics of Culture Change*, Yale University Press, New Haven.

Martin, J. and C. Siehl (1983) 'Organization culture and counter culture: an uneasy symbiosis', *Organization Dynamics*, 52–65.

Mitroff, I. I. and R. H. Kilmann (1976) 'On organization stories: an approach to the design and analysis of organizations through myths and stories', in R. H. Kilmann, L. R. Pondy and D. P. Slevin (eds), *The Management of Organization Design: Strategies and Implementation*, North Holland, New York.

Peters, T. and R. Waterman, Jr (1982) *In Search of Excellence: Lessons from America's Best Run Companies*, Harper & Row, New York.

Pettigrew, A M. (1979) 'On studying organizational cultures', *Administrative Science Quarterly*, **24**, 570–81.

Pettigrew, A. M. (1985) *The Awakening Giant: Continuity and Change in ICI*, Blackwell, Oxford.

Porter, M. E. (1980) *Competitive Strategy*, Free Press, New York.

Schein, E. (1984) 'Coming to a new awareness of organizational culture', *Sloan Management Review*, **25**, 3–16.

Schwartz, H. and S. M. Davies (1981) 'Matching corporate culture and business strategy', *Organization Dynamics*, **2**, 30–49.

Silverman, D. (1970) *Theories of Organizations*, Heinemann, London.

Silverzweig, S. and R. F. Allen (1976) 'Changing the corporate culture', *Sloan management review*, **17**(3), 33–49.

Sorge, A. and M. Warner (1986) *Comparative Factory Organization: An Anglo-German Comparison of Management and Manpower in Manufacturing*, Gower, Wissenschaftszentrum Publications, Berlin.

Trice, H. M. and J. M. Beyer (1984) 'Studying organizational cultures through rites and ceremonials', *Academy of Management Review*, **9**, 653–69.

Turner, B. (1986) 'Sociological aspects of organizational symbolism', *Organization Studies*, **7**(1), 101–15.

Weber, M. (1947) *The Theory of Social and Economic Organization*, transl. T. Parsons and A. M. Henderson, introduction by T. Parsons, Free Press, Chicago.

Weick, K. (1979) *The Social Psychology of Organizing*, Addison-Wesley, Reading, Mass.

Wicks, J. (1988) 'Fritz Fahrini sees chances and changes for Sulzer', *Swiss Business*, Sept., 6–12.

Young, E. (1989) 'On the naming of the rose: interests and multiple meanings as elements of organizational culture', *Organization Studies*, **10**(2), 187–206.

CHAPTER 14 Change in organizations

Introduction

The topic of change in organizations has currently become very fashionable. It has become a central concern with managers and organization theorists alike. Both groups recognize the crucial importance of managing the change process successfully but, equally, lack precise guidelines or frameworks for its study. In this chapter, we shall look at some of these frameworks. First, we should see why the topic has recently become central on the management agenda.

One reason lies in the massive impact brought about by social, technological and economic factors. All have witnessed substantial transformation in recent years. Particularly since 1979 in Britain, with the socio-economic policies of Conservative government, the business community has had to undergo a great deal of reorientation. Competition from producers abroad have forced us to re-assess the ways in which we organize our domestic output. In technology, for example, fears that Japanese organizations might be 'doing it right' has prompted a great deal of emphasis on studying and copying their manufacturing processes. Many British organizations such as Lucas, the Rover Group and many other manufacturing organizations have recently abandoned their traditional production processes in favour of the Japanese based system of inventory processing including Just-in-Time production sequencing in an attempt to save time, money and materials.

Just-in-Time inventory processing is a different way of organizing the manufacturing process. No longer is the manufacturing cycle based upon a fixed quantity of throughput determined by a pre-set volume. Each stage of the manufacturing process becomes semi-autonomous, taking in only what it **needs** from the previous stage in the process, not what it is given. The overall aim is to reduce stockpiling, waste and increase quality of the throughput.

The implementation of these and other changes has not always been easy. Nor has it always resulted in the expected benefits of increased quality and reduced production costs.

Socio-economic changes within Britain (especially in the role of the state) have also had a great impact on all organizations in the private, public and voluntary sectors. There has been a substantial erosion of state support (via state agencies) both for individuals and organizations in favour of a more individualistic or independent orientation. Today, individuals and organizations are expected to be masters and mistresses of their own fates. There is a tremendous emphasis on survival and development based upon individual action and independence.

It is popular to assume that the degree of change facing organizations today is greater than ever before. At the beginning of the 1970s, Alvin Toffler prophesied that 'things are moving faster' and that to many there was a feeling that 'change is out of control' (Toffler, 1970: 27). It may feel that way to those involved in the process, but recourse to recent industrial history assures us that change has been the hallmark of organizations past, present and future.

Rapid industrialization at the turn of the century brought with it a whole host of changes focusing not only on the development of new technological processes for the emerging organizations, but also on the social and economic transformation of a previously rural-based community to an urban-based labour force. The introduction of the assembly line was another major change (Walker and Guest, 1952) and rapid advances in technology throughout the Second World War were soon making their impact in industrial organizations during the immediate post-war period.

The manager has always had to cope with and handle change. It is endemic to organizational life. Possibly the reason for the greater emphasis on managing change today lies in its increased pervasiveness into all aspects of our lives. Not only is technological change taking place, but also there are changes occurring at all levels of social and institutional practice. Personal values are questioned. Work is no longer a 'natural' part of individuals' lives. Managers are no longer accepted as 'natural' leaders. They have to earn and justify their position. And, at the bottom of all this is the almost inevitable link between change and organizational survival. Those organizations which do not respond to the challenges and changes facing them are likely to become dinosaurs in the evolution of modern society. They will become old-fashioned, uneconomic and, ultimately, will close down. The shedding of labour which this will inevitably produce will add yet another tragic tale to the story of managing (or rather mismanaging) change.

The change process

Change is about achieving a future desired state of affairs. In part, it is the act of crystal-ball gazing, looking into the future to predict what will be the context in which organizations and individuals will exist. Another part of the change process lies in the need for individuals to react and adapt to changed situations. This is possibly the most commonly experienced aspect of change in many organizations. Market share drops, or a new product comes out of a competitor organization and forces a reaction. The organization has to change and adapt to these new pressures.

The first part of the change process, looking into the future, is called *planned change*. Targets are set, timetables for achieving intermediate goals are drawn up and the process is constantly monitored. The second aspect of change, adapting to an already changed situation, is called *reactive change*. As we shall see, both are beset with difficulties for organizations. Many commentators have argued that organizations spend too much time in reactive change and not enough time in planning change programmes to cope with future contingencies (Peters and Waterman, 1982; Kanter, 1983). In order to minimize the disruptive and uneconomic process of reacting, organization should anticipate change and be proactive. These authors also argue that substantial gains in performance are likely to ensue from such proactivity. Empirical support for this is limited and it is too early to say with any certainty that there is a direct correlation.

Although ideally it would be beneficial always to be able to predict the future, in practice this is impossible. It is also by no means proven that organizations which do actively scan the future and plan and change accordingly out-perform those which react to a changing environment. We do know, however, that organizations that rarely change at all suffer a significantly higher mortality rate. So, one lesson for the practice of running any organization is always to build in the capacity for some level of change.

The key to all this lies in people. Individuals create and maintain change.

Organizations are incapable of initiating change although they can sometimes block it. Creating change through people represents the focus of what follows. It is the *how* of the change process. It is all too easy to equate the *what* of change (the goal or the target) with the process of its achievement. Unless people are involved, committed and prepared to adapt and learn, objectives, plans and future desired states will inevitably founder on the rocks of resistance (which is often viewed as a negative response, but is one which can be quite legitimate where people are excluded or where commitment is not sought). We start our analysis with the fundamental building block of change—the individual.

Change and the individual

A common response to the question of change is that 'of course change is necessary: it's just that we can tell you who will resist any proposals before we even begin'. Here is the first fallacy. The tendency to stereotype or to articulate beliefs is not usually based upon any systematic analysis of the situation. Often it is guided by what happened in the past in similar circumstances or from folklore (what someone else in the organization said a certain individual or group would do). This *may* be accurate in present circumstances, but it is more likely to be full of inaccuracies. Resistance to change from an individual's perspective needs careful analysis, not glib myth and stereotyping.

According to Kotter, Schlesinger and Sathe (1986), there are four common reasons for resistance to change from individuals. These are:

1 self-interest
2 a lack of trust coupled with misunderstanding
3 different viewpoints or assessments of the benefits of change
4 a low tolerance for change

They are based on *history* (what happened in the past in a similar situation) on *emotion* (how individuals feel about the proposed scenario) and *fact* (what individuals actually know about the change). Self-interest refers to the sense of loss that individuals feel they will encounter in future states of change and the actions they will take to avoid this happening. The feeling is that the aspects of the job they hold dear at present will be eroded or threatened under the new regime. The actions they take will be to try and 'block' the change, often by forming opposing camps or sections in the organization. They may argue that no one really understands their concerns; that this is change just for the sake of it; that more analysis is required and so on. What they are doing is to act parochially and politically to defend their territory or to defend what they consider are their 'rights' in the organization (see Pettigrew, 1985 for an extended example of these kinds of resistance in Imperial Chemical Industries).

A lack of trust can quite easily arise when the intentions of the proposed change are wrongly interpreted by one or more individuals. This can occur because mistrust exists already through previous experience, or can occur through a lack of effective communication. The initiator of the change may assume that others are aware of the details and the rationale for the proposal, but in reality they are probably only half-informed. Subsequent actions can become wrongly interpreted and resistance is inevitable. If there is a simple maxim to be derived for this, it is that managing the change process needs a great deal of effort to secure a greater level and more effective communication throughout the organization (Plant, 1987).

Resistance to change is also inevitable when individuals perceive the situation in very different ways. Many managers assume that everyone in the organization sees the problem and their proposed solution in the same way. They also assume that everyone has the same level of access to the information which they have at their disposal. This is almost never true. Shop-floor workers, functional managers, people in other divisions of the company will all be privy to different sources of information. In turn, this will colour their view of the organization. Since people act on their perceptions (rather than on any rational set of 'facts') there will be a wide range of viewpoints towards a proposed change.

Some members of the organization will undoubtedly see the proposals as detrimental to their current position, others will be neutrally disposed and some will support them. Which group is 'correct' in their assessment is vital knowledge. It may be that the individual proposing the change feels confident in his or her prediction of the likely benefits of the change. Resisting others who oppose the change is thus a good strategy to pursue. However, it may be that those resisting are in a position to predict more accurately the likely outcomes. They may have access to more information, for example.

In this case, standing up to resistance would not be an effective strategy. There are two difficulties which now become apparent. One is, how do we know in advance who has the most correct interpretation of likely outcomes? The other is that trying to fend off or block resistance is virtually always seen as a good thing for managers to do, irrespective of who is right or wrong. That is part of their job and they get paid for handling the inevitable aggravation which ensues. Handling the first issue can only begin with increasing communication throughout the organization, but it also requires a great deal of further work to secure commitment to the change. The second problem is even harder to address since it requires a change in the way the organization is currently operating. It needs some degree of cultural change or shift. We shall deal with this in more detail later in the chapter.

A low tolerance for change means that some individuals who are less able than others to adapt to change and to new circumstances are likely to resist proposals for future changes irrespective of whether the change is likely to benefit them or not. As Drucker (1981) notes, the capacity for individuals to handle change is limited. This varies, of course, from person to person, but even the most receptive individual can easily reach the limits of their tolerance. In addition, some individuals will resist any kind of change simply because they think that to support it would be to admit that their present position or viewpoint is wrong. They have a vested interest in maintaining the status quo.

In a wider perspective, organizations can appear from the outside to be changing and adapting to current demands, but on the inside they are in turmoil. Much of this turmoil can come from a severe reduction in individuals' tolerance to change. For example, in 1988 Cadbury-Schweppes were having problems in gaining commitment to change programmes from their managers. Long-term change had been taking place over the previous ten years or so, aimed at flattening out the managerial hierarchy and decentralizing the organization generally. The problem was described by one of the senior managers as 'change fatigue'. People had become fed up constantly coping with and managing change. Because change had been a constant feature of most managers' lives, and because there had been an incremental 'inching' towards decentralization, many individuals had lost sight of the advantages or the goals of the overall change programme. They could no longer attribute tangible benefits to change. Their tolerance for change was thus significantly reduced.

People in groups and the change process

Groups, too, can become formidable obstacles to achieving change. They can also be powerful promoters and supporters of the change process if they lend their weight to its promotion. Pettigrew (1985) showed this graphically in his study of corporate changes in Imperial Chemical Industries. It was not until a small group had mobilized itself around John Harvey-Jones and his proposals for change that any progress was made. Indeed, previous attempts to achieve the same kind and level of change had failed primarily because the individual proposer of the change (Lord Beeching) had met solidly with group resistance from all the other directors.

Patterns of institutionalized behaviour in groups such as conformity to group pressure and 'groupthink' (Janis, 1972; Milgram, 1974) can also be powerful barriers to achieving change. Groups can develop extremely rigid patterns of behaviour which are not only difficult to change themselves, but which are also considered 'correct' by group members. Their way of doing things is the right way. Others in the organization are out of step with them if they choose to see things differently.

Organizations and the change process

Moving to the organizational level of analysis we can immediately cement a link between the question of organizational culture (described in Chapter 13) and change. Just as patterns of behaviour in groups can block or enhance change, so too can the wider patterns of behaviour, values and beliefs prevalent in the organization overall (Hall, 1977). If we consider the role culture outlined in Chapter 13, one of its noticeable features is the precision with which the most detailed aspects of organization are spelled out. Rules, regulations and procedures are mostly formalized by writing them down. This, of course, allows an organization to be supremely predictable. Promotion routes, entry points and salary scales are closely documented so that all members are clear of their place in the overall structure. There are documented plans for action in the face of most contingencies. Organizations such as the Civil Service, the National Health Service, many manufacturing firms and many other large companies are dominantly role cultures with precise and formal specification of roles and duties.

These organizations are like this because of their history. Each time new problems or contingencies arose, rules and procedures were created to cope with them. This process continued until the organization became a very complex set of formal procedures. In a *perfectly stable environment*, these organizations are virtually unbeatable. There is a procedure for every eventuality. They will out-perform almost any other organization designed on different principles. Create change in the immediate environment, however, and these organizations display extreme agonies in trying to change and adapt. This is because they are efficient organizational solutions to yesterday's problems. They are not designed to change and adapt to today's problems.

Changing the culture of an organization is one of the most difficult tasks facing all its constituent individuals. It is very much like trying to change all that you as an individual believe in, or have been brought up to believe in. To energize change requires an 'unfreezing' of the status quo, change to be effected, and a 'refreezing' or consolidation of the new state. This pattern was first identified by Kurt Lewin in 1951, and is still pertinent today. Lewin argued that organizations existed in a state of equilibrium which was not itself conducive to change. This equilibrium was the result of opposing forces which constantly acted upon the organization and its individuals. These were forces for change (driving forces) and forces against change (restraining forces). Table 14.1 shows a typical set of these forces.

Table 14.1
Lewin's equilibrium:
driving and
restraining forces
for organizational
change

Driving forces (forces for change)	Restraining forces (forces against change)
	From individuals
	Fear of failure
Changing markets	Loss of status
Shorter product life-cycles	Inertia (habit)
Changing values towards work	Fear of the unknown
Internationalization	Loss of friends
Global markets	
Social transformations	*From organizations*
Increased competition	Strength of culture
New technology	Rigidity of structure
New personnel	Sunk costs
	Lack of resources
	Contractual agreements
	Strongly held beliefs and recipes for evaluating corporate activities

Lewin called the process of balancing driving and restraining forces a '*quasi-stationary equilibrium*'. This is because a true equilibrium assumes that no change takes place at all given a perfect balance between opposing forces. In the world of organizations, of course, this is unrealistic. There is change happening all the time. The point is that the opposing pressures of driving and restraining forces will combine to constrain change to a minimum and mitigate against any degree of further and future changes.

In order to promote the right conditions for change there has to be an unfreezing of this situation. An imbalance must be created between the driving and restraining forces. This means removing restraint or fuelling driving forces. Lewin argued that there was an optimal way of configuring this process. First, the restraining forces should be attended to, and selectively removed. The driving forces will automatically push change forward since removing the restraining forces has created an imbalance in the quasi-stationary equilibrium. Ideally, an increase in the number of driving forces or an increase in the potency of the existing set will achieve a greater degree of change. Refreezing the new situation is the final stage.

This sequence is essential according to Lewin. If attention is first given to driving forces, then the result will be a commensurate increase in the number or the potency of restraining forces, and the status quo will remain. No change will occur.

Organizational culture and change

The prevailing culture of any organization can present a formidable challenge to those attempting to implement change. The sunk costs of individuals and groups in creating and maintaining the present culture are considerable. In order to achieve a significant shift in organizational culture most of the following key aspects of organization will have to be subject to attention.

Changing the culture: key aspects of the organization

- *The balance of power* (includes political imbalances between individuals, groups and at the organizational level)
- *Organizational structure* (this will undoubtedly be designed around sustaining the present culture and not to accommodate new scenarios)
- *Management and leadership styles* (these too will be a product of the culture which will have supported certain styles and screened out others)
- *Organizational history* (antecedents of practice. If it worked in the past there is little reason to change it. Those who suggest change are considered to be abandoning tradition, flying in the face of history, or just plain heretical).

Changing organizational culture means achieving a significant and lasting change in the philosophy of management and the adoption of suitable and supportive organizational structures to consolidate and support the change. Not surprisingly, achieving cultural change is extremely complex and difficult.

As Bate (1984) and Miller and Friesen (1984) note, organizations can very easily become prisoners of their own cultures. They 'learn to become helpless' in the face of change (Bate, 1984). From a more dynamic perspective, organizations also tend towards more extreme forms of their existing culture. For example, organizations which are predominantly role cultures will tend to become more obviously bureaucratic over time, while more task-oriented cultures will tend towards becoming more project-centred (Miller and Friesen, 1984). The task facing managers in these organizations is not to create conditions for change. This is happening all the time. The difficulty is in reversing or in changing the direction of the pattern of learned behaviours.

Even seemingly small changes which are counter-cultural can be extremely difficult to achieve. For example, changing reward systems in an organization from those which give rewards for visible successes to those which also reward experimentation are relatively easy to design in theory. In practice, they are beset with difficulties. Even 'excellent' organizations such as the 3-M Corporation described by Peters and Waterman (1982) find it difficult to sustain a culture which encourages experimentation. This has to be done out of sight, away from the mainstream activities of the organization. Innovating behaviour occurs in time 'borrowed' from the organization.

Rewards are also not based on trying out new ideas, or even developing them, but are solely focused on success. The possibility here is that experimentation and innovation can become stifled through a fear of failure. An individual who has had one idea defined as a failure in public is unlikely to try again unless he or she is rewarded for the process of experimentation rather than just on results.

This is quite a trivial example in relation to the enormity of the task of changing organizational culture, or cultures. However, it shows the extreme complexities that will face individuals in the process of cultural change. The key question remaining for all levels of organizational change (personal, group and organizational) is *who* effects the change? These individuals are known as change agents and we discuss their role in the next section.

Change agents

Change agents are the individuals or groups of individuals whose task is to effect the desired change. They can be internal or external to the organization. Internal change agents are usually employees of the organization, while external change agents usually are advisers or consultants. On any change programme, internal and external change agents can work together.

The role of the change agent is to act as intermediary and as a spur to effecting change. The role of intermediary occurs between the forces which are promoting the change (see Table 14.1) and choosing a strategy for the change to take place. The change agent depicts a future scenario and outlines the roles and positions individuals will occupy in the future state. It is also necessary for the change agent to spell out his or her own role clearly. This can range from complete collaboration with internal staff to adopting a role of absolute authority as the expert.

It is not surprising that the role of the change agent is extremely difficult. Not only is the role likely to cross and challenge existing power networks in any organization, but also the threats imposed by the change itself will be transferred personally to the change agent. He or she will be held responsible for any perceived threats.

Internal change agents are almost always credible as 'experts' within their own organizations. However, they also need a substantial power base in order to develop and sustain their efforts. Such political potency is often denied to the internal role.

External change agents almost always have political credibility, but often lack the detailed knowledge of the organization which can undermine their role of 'expert'. Hesitation on the part of the external change agent over which route to take in the change effort can also lead to an undermining of expertise. Since the process of change rarely lends itself to precise mapping of future states, this problem is extremely common where external change agents are involved.

Some reasons why external change agents decide to go and do something else!

The level of difficulty inherent in the role of the external change agent often persuades individuals who are in the profession to go and do something less complex with a greater degree of certainty of success. We outline below some of the issues which contribute to this difficulty.

The majority of consultants (external agents) operate towards the *micro level of change*. They are involved in specific 'one-shot' change efforts which are targeted at specific individuals or specific groups. This can range from management development training to T-groups and personal-growth workshops. Quite often, these take place outside the premises of the organization in concentrated bursts of activity. Participants thus tend to view the whole experience as special or transitory and soon fall back into the old ways on return to their organization. Such change efforts are likely to have limitations in their scope and are likely to fade quickly.

Attempts at macro-level changes by external consultants are relatively rare. Two factors mitigate against macro-level changes by external agents—power and complexity (Astley *et al.*, 1982). Inevitably, change will present real or imagined threats to the existing power structure of an organization. Resistance from those who perceive they will have some of their power eroded in the future desired state will exert very strong resistance to the change. Often, access is required by the external agent at a level senior to the organization in question (the board of a company, or a government ministry) and this can present obvious problems since the consultant will rarely have been initially called in at this level.

Another factor is that external change agents are sometimes limited in the amount of access they have across the focal organization. It is quite common for access to be restricted to staff or human-resource functions, thus placing immediate limits on applicability and generalizability. It also usually places severe budgetary limitations on the whole process.

External change agents are rarely presented with a well-specified problem to solve. The initial 'problem' itself can be spurious and misleading or, at best, only partially true. Consultants are also rarely called in by individuals from the focal organization. This could arouse accusations towards the individual of acting beyond their legitimate authority, being high-handed, or simply incompetent. It could also raise suspicion by others in the organization as to the motives of calling in a change agent to a dysfunctional level.

Therefore, the problem facing the external change agent is really:

1 ambiguous and ill-defined;
2 the outcome of a process of group negotiation or consensus from within the focal organization.

There is no longer any clear point of ownership of the problems in the change process, and the external change agent has little chance of isolating and identifying specific, unambiguous issues. It is more likely that he or she will produce a set of further issues and problems rather than any solutions to current problems.

As noted in Chapter 11, organizations cannot be considered in isolation from the political dimension of stakes and stake-holders, interests and interest groups. The change process is no stranger to the political arena. External change agents are often called in to bolster one side or the other in an internal political conflict. The change agent acts in a legitimating capacity to interests and issues in the focal organization.

It would be wrong, however, to assume that change through external change agents was never possible given the formidable array of problems outlined above. There are some distinct advantages to the role of external change agent which can contribute towards successful change programmes. External change agents can:

1 *act as 'court jesters'* They can poke fun at practices in the organization which others, who are employed within it, cannot voice without fear of repercussions for themselves or their department.

2 *act freely, not tied to partisan politics*

3 *gain access to a wider range of individuals and departments than is afforded members of the organization*

4 *use a wider 'vocabulary' than most organizational members* They can express organizational events and processes in a new way, expressed in terms unfamiliar to those in the organization. This alone can be a powerful stimulant for promoting analytical thinking and a first step to unfreezing the status quo.

5 *send information around the organization which would be impossible or prohibited to others*

6 *avoid responsibility, to some extent, if things subsequently go wrong*

Significant organizational change is rarely achieved by external change agents alone. To ensure the greatest chance of success, internal and external change agents must work together. The creation of a special internal cross-functional team would be one way in which internal change agents could be organized. This team acts as an invaluable source of information for the external change agent. They are also a forum in which ideas can be piloted, discussed and subsequently spread to the rest of the organization. They will also need to have at least some access to powerful groups around the organization in order to mobilize support for their ideas (Pettigrew, 1985). It needs a significant, critical mass to push most changes through organizations. Political support is also vital to deal with many opposition which might arise, since the internal team will be unable to take on this role and simultaneously assess the proposals for change objectively.

The final step in this collaborative process between internal and external change agents is to cement the change, or to 'refreeze' it in Lewin's terminology. There are a number of ways of achieving this. The creation of a new set of terminology, or working vocabulary, can be very effective since it distinguishes a clear break from the 'old' and the 'new'. The old state of affairs cannot be described adequately using existing vocabulary. The changed state is thus not a case of what we used to do before (plus a few amendments). It is described and rationalized using new words, new phrases and with fresh aims. In this way, the change process is consolidated and the need for the external change agent dwindles to nothing. It now becomes the task of internal members of the organization to monitor the change and assess its efficacy in the light of current and future practice. Large firms, such as ICL and the Royal Dutch/Shell Group, create teams of internal consultants and change agents specifically to carry out the task of monitoring and suggesting future modifications to change processes.

Summary

The question of organization change is central to all kinds of organizations. It is the way in which organizations thrive, grow and stabilize rather than wither and decline. Yet achieving change presents one of the most intransigent problems for both organizations and individuals.

Resistance to change seems endemic to both organizations and individuals. At the level of the organization, resistance is likely to come from accepted ways of doing things, the powerful hand of history (we've always done this in the past . . . so why not now?) and sunk costs invested in strategic recipes towards their own sector of operations and towards other organizations. Individuals resist change for reasons of apprehension, possible loss of influence, a predisposition to stability and sheer conservatism. These are just a few of the barriers facing the people who try and effect change in organizations—the change agents.

References

Astley, W. G., R. Axelsson, R. J. Butler, D. J. Hickson and D. C. Wilson (1982) 'Complexity and cleavage: dual explanations of strategic decision-making', *Journal of Management Studies*, **19**(4), 357–75.

Bate, P. (1984) 'The impact of organizational culture on approaches to organizational problem-solving', *Organization Studies* **5**(1), 43–66.

Drucker, P. (1981) *Managing in Turbulent Times*, Pan, London.

Hall, R. H. (1977) *Organizations: Structure and Process*, 2nd edn, Prentice-Hall, Englewood Cliffs, New Jersey.

Janis, I. L. (1972) *Victims of Groupthink: A Psychological Study of Foreign Policy Decisions and Fiascos*, Houghton Mifflin, Boston.

Kanter, R. M. (1983) *The Change Masters: Corporate Entrepreneurs at Work*, Allen & Unwin, London.

Kotter, J., L. A. Schlesinger and V. Sathe (1986) *Organization: Text, Cases and Readings on the Management of Organizational Design and Change*, Irwin, Homewood, Illinois.

Lewin, K. (1951) *Field Theory in Social Science*, Harper & Row, New York.

Milgram, S. (1974) *Obedience and Authority*, Tavistock, London.

Miller, D. and P. H. Friesen (1984) *Organizations: A Quantum View*, Prentice-Hall, New York.

Peters, T. and R. Waterman, Jr. (1982) *In Search of Excellence: Lessons from America's Best Run Companies*, Harper & Row, New York.

Pettigrew, A. M. (1985) *The Awakening Giant: Continuity and Change in ICI*, Blackwell, Oxford.

Plant, R. (1987) *Managing Change and Making it Stick*, Fontana, London.

Toffler, A. (1970) *Future Shock*, Pan, London.

Walker, C. R. and R. H. Guest (1952) *The Man on the Assembly Line*, Harvard University Press, Cambridge, Mass.

CHAPTER 15 Alternative forms of organization

Using different means to achieve ends

It would only be a partial analysis to assume that we had covered all types of organizational structures in Chapter 12. Those we have already discussed can be broadly classified as variants on a theme of formal, functionally differentiated, bureaucratic organizational structures. They are designed to reinforce functional expertise, to maintain control using rules and regulations, with decision-making centralized at senior levels.

The structures we are going to examine in this chapter are very different from functional organizations. They are a diverse group of organizations, including matrix structures, voluntary and non-profit organizations, cooperatives and other alternative organizational forms. We explore the characteristics of each in the following sections.

Matrix organization structures

There is no precise definition of the matrix form of organization since, in practice, there are a number of variants. All matrix structures have a common theme, however. They are all traditional hierarchical structures which also have a formally recognized *lateral dimension*. That is, communication, authority, influence and control are structured as much laterally across the organization as they are vertically. Matrix organizations take the functional structure of traditional organization and superimpose a set of project areas or business operations which cut laterally across the functions (Knight, 1976). Figure 15.1 depicts a typical matrix organization structure.

Functional areas are delineated vertically, while project operations or business areas cut across all functions laterally. The overall structure of a matrix organization thus resembles a 'cell' or a honeycomb. One key property of this kind of structure is that unity of command no longer applies. Individuals in the organization have two bosses. One will be the project team boss, and the other will be the functionally based manager. Both function and project thus produce authority figures.

Although we have used function and product as two dimensions of the matrix, other combinations can exist (such as national versus international responsibility in a multi-national firm, or between existing product profitability and new product innovation). The key to the matrix lies in its polarization of two dimensions creating a vertical and a horizontal information flow.

A number of well-known organizations are designed around the matrix principle. Many of these are North American, such as Monsanto Chemical, Texas Instruments and the 3-M Corporation, but matrices are not confined to American practice. In the United Kingdom a number of organizations in all sectors of operations also use matrix structures. These include Prudential Assurance plc, International Computers Ltd, and Christian Aid in the voluntary sector. Matrix structures can also be found widely throughout secondary and tertiary education organizations in Britain. Organizing into faculties, for example, represents the idea of a business area, while literacy

Figure 15.1
A 'typical' matrix
structure

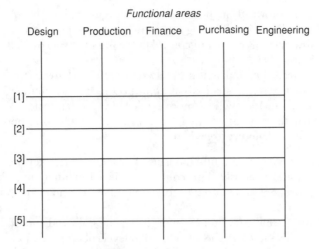

(1)–(5) represent projects or business areas.

Project groups occur at the points where the grid intersects.

Representatives from any function can be part of many projects
at the same time.

schemes and introducing new technologies (such as information technology) in schools are examples of projects which span a number of functional areas.

The potential problems posed by individuals reporting to two managers simultaneously (such as divided loyalties, conflict and competition) can usually be reduced to manageable levels by segregating domains of authority. For example, project managers have authority over those members of the project team and functional managers retain authority over more general organizational areas such as promotion, appraisal and staffing. As Galbraith (1971; 1973) notes, matrix organizations are decentralized, horizontally differentiated structures, designed to combine the advantages of both functional and project forms of organization. But they can only achieve these aims if authority and responsibility are clearly differentiated and understood between function and project in the first place.

The benefits of functional differentiation are largely rooted in the efficient use of specialists. By grouping specialists together in functions (such as marketing, production, product development, or sales) clear economies of scale are achieved. The organization needs less specialists (who are expensive to employ) and clear areas of responsibility are demarcated. As we have noted in previous chapters, there are also disadvantages inherent in the functional structure. The most problematic lies in the development of 'local' interests (see Chapter 11). Functional goals and perspectives dominate wider organizational goals. Coordinating functions to work together, or to view the wider perspective, becomes difficult to the extent that special liaison roles may have to be created. Matrix structures achieve, at least in theory, integration between functional specialists and multiple projects. In this respect they are *strategically flexible, open to change, and centred very much on the needs of their clients.*

It is rare, however, to find an organization which can be described wholly as a matrix. More frequently, only parts of an organization adopt the matrix form. It is common for certain activities such as research and development or marketing and sales staff to be organized along matrix lines while the rest of the organization is singularly functional. Broadly, the greater the extent of the matrix towards including the whole organization, the greater is the level of complexity in achieving integration between project areas and maintaining strategic direction and control of the organization overall (see Child, 1984; Hunt, 1986).

According to Davis and Lawrence (1977) there are specific conditions under which a matrix structure is appropriate. Implicit in their arguments (and those of Child, 1984, who is more explicit) in all other conditions, the matrix structure will be wholly inappropriate. Suitable conditions which favour a matrix structure are where:

1 There is an unambiguous need to act upon two key organizational areas simultaneously. This could be project and function; technical quality and product innovation; product manufacture and development of customer services.
2 External environmental pressures are high and conditions are turbulent. This increases the need for high levels of internal interdependence. It also has the secondary effect of creating a 'common enemy' for internal projects, and this acts as an integrating mechanism.
3 Technology in use does not involve substantial 'sunk costs'. That is, the overall technical characteristics of the organization are variable, flexible and usable in multiple sites. Thus, centralized computer integrative systems, for example, are likely to mitigate against the adoption of a matrix organization, simply because they force centralized rather than dispersed integration.
4 It is apparent to the majority of organization members that multi-function, multi-skill linkages are both necessary and appropriate.
5 Part of this becoming apparent will rest with any obvious economies of scale which can be achieved through the shared use of people, skills and the development of project rather than functional culture.

According to Galbraith (1974), the matrix structure affords a number of strategic advantages to an organization. These are very much in line with the advantages claimed by Lawrence and Lorsch (1967) and Burns and Stalker (1961) for 'organic' organizational design (see Chapter 18). Because lateral communication and integration are increased in the matrix structure, the organization has the following advantages:

• *strategically flexible*   Information can be processed quickly and efficiently and difficult or rapidly changing environmental conditions can be analysed and responded to very rapidly.
• *high standards of technical excellence maintained*   Since specialists interact frequently with both their own functional areas of knowledge as well as with other specialist knowledge domains, they maintain a state-of-the-art orientation to projects.
• *clear differentiation between strategic and operating decisions*   Top management is clearly charged with responsibility for strategic or policy decisions. Senior managers also have more time to concentrate on policy since they are no longer required to manage project teams or to oversee them closely. The financial and accounting systems of the organization are tailored to suit budgeting for projects and new products and services (rather than being functionally based). There are specific systems in place to support cost centres, profit centres, revenue and investment centres.
• *enhanced aspects of social organization*   Motivation, commitment and personal development are enhanced. Individuals are not totally bound by status or level in the hierarchy. Project teams ensure that all who are members are

there because they want to be and that all members will be able to have their views heard. Participation in the day-to-day running of the organization is also increased. Personal development is enhanced because working in project teams allows individuals to broaden their experience both in the technical sense as well as in the wider organizational perspective (i.e. the broader aspects and implications of what is decided).

(Adapted from Galbraith, 1974; Knight, 1976)

Disadvantages of matrix organization, apart from the obvious issue of individuals coping with dual authority, lie chiefly in the area of coordination. This covers both interpersonal coordination (learning how to work in groups, how to handle and live with conflict) and organizational coordination (administrative costs of integrating projects, ensuring efficient and effective communication). A further disadvantage can arise in conditions of resource scarcity. Where people or finance are no longer freely available throughout the organization, decisions have to be made about which projects will be supported and which projects will have to be put on ice for a while. Inevitably, this raises questions concerning exactly who makes these decisions between various projects as well as raises conflict and competition between project members themselves.

From a financial perspective, the creation of profit centres cannot be taken to be synonymous with a matrix structure. Individual profit centres can exist in the most centralized organizations. The key to financial coordination in the matrix is to allow managers as much leeway as possible in capital expenditure and sourcing of products and services (Horngren and Foster, 1987).

From a behavioural perspective, individuals must be able to handle role conflict and ambiguity as a natural part of everyday organizational life. They must become effective members of task groups. For many individuals who may be technical specialists used to working alone (or solely with a few other specialists in the same field) this can be a daunting prospect. A substantial amount of human-resource investment in learning to work effectively in groups is required before matrix organization can realize its operating advantages over more mechanistic forms.

Voluntary and non-profit organizations

Voluntary and non-profit organizations are mostly absent from the concerns of most organizational analysis. Textbooks covering organizational behaviour rarely deal with these kinds of organizations other than perhaps to give them a passing mention as alternative forms of organization. Williamson and Ouchi (1981: 366) argue that such organizations are obscure, defy systematic analysis and cannot be studied easily by the conventional analytical tools of organizational analysis.

This is both surprising and not strictly true. First, voluntary organizations form a significant part of many economies in Britain and in Europe. Recent campaigns such as Band Aid and Comic Relief have become headline news throughout the European community. Although the Band Aid Trust raised some £70 million, the knowledge that this represented only a fraction of the total voluntary income of charities in the UK gives some idea of the extent of this important third sector of the economy. In the same year (1985), Oxfam received virtually £60 million, Save the Children Fund received £43 million and the National Trust nearly £70 million (source: *Charity Statistics* 1985/86). Voluntary organizations have also been around for a long time. They are an established part of most economies, many with roots going back to the eleventh and twelfth centuries.

If we took a purely structural analysis of present-day voluntary and non-profit organizations, we would see initially very little difference between them and their 'for-profit' cousins. Most voluntary organizations have functions, a hierarchy, a reporting structure and a communication and integrating network (although these may not be described in this language which is borrowed from business organization). In most other respects voluntary and non-profit organizations are very different. So what are these organizations, and how might we define them?

Definitions of these organizations are particularly imprecise given the broad spectrum of types which comprise voluntary and non-profit organizations. Any attempt at definition must also recognize that it is culturally bound. The following broad descriptions apply for Britain only. Both North America and Europe generally differ widely in their use of terminology.

1 In Britain, a voluntary organization is one which provides goods and services on a non-commercial basis. Revenue is sourced from donations and other gifts rather than from the sale of products. Well-known examples would be Oxfam, Mencap or the Royal National Lifeboat Institution. A considerable proportion of the labour force is voluntary and, hence, unpaid. The voluntary title is not lost if some of its members are paid or if the organization receives most of its funding through government agencies. Membership of the organization is not through inheritance, nor through family or society connections. Membership is not directly aimed at securing economic benefits for its members.

2 A non-profit organization is similar in many respects to a voluntary organization except that its aims are almost always explicitly aimed toward the economic or social betterment of its members. Examples include professional associations and labour unions. Membership is voluntary and much of the work of the organization is carried out by volunteers in addition to full-time paid staff.

3 Not all voluntary organizations are legally constituted charities. Charitable status is endowed by the Charity Commission, an independent body which is charged with the task of ensuring that the activities of a voluntary organization conform with the laws of charitable trusts. Broadly, voluntary organizations which are political, or are pressure groups aimed at effecting changes in current practice, or are self-help groups, cannot be legally registered charities. The benefits of being a registered charity are discussed in detail in Chesterman (1979) and Wilson (1984). They include tangible benefits of fiscal advantage (charities can claim tax relief and rate relief) and less tangible benefits of organization image (which appears legitimated by its inclusion on the charities' register).

The above organizations are quite distinct and specifically different from their commercial counterparts. For example, a key aspect of their survival rests on the contract each individual has with the organization. This is dependent on notions of altruism and self-help. Volunteers join an organization because they want to help others. Titmuss (1970) examined the motives of 3325 blood donors in Britain, asking them why they gave blood. The predominant category of responses cited altruism, a general desire to help people or society without seeking extrinsic reward for such help.

Many voluntary organizations act as 'brokers', relying on individuals giving money and services to the organization which are then translated into service provision for the needy, the elderly or the handicapped, for example. An extreme form of this kind of brokerage can be seen in an organization such as Oxfam which collects money from people in Britain and distributes its services in Third World countries. Donors thus rely on the organization being an 'honest broker', translating their resources efficiently and effectively into disaster relief.

These interrelationships between giver, organization and receiver have been described by Mauss (1954) and Titmuss (1970) as the *gift relationship*. It is this relationship which forms the foundation for the host of concerns which arise in voluntary and non-profit organizations and their management. Butler and Wilson (1989) and Wilson (1989) argue that the interdependencies of the gift relationship coupled with the concept of organizational membership based on voluntarism have brought two key areas into sharp focus. These are:

1 The need to formulate strategies which place equal emphasis on gaining inputs as on providing services. Alongside this comes the need to adopt a more professional style of management, often based upon or copied from models in the commercial sector.

2 A concern with organizational structure. In particular, a propensity to decentralize and to adopt a more project centred or matrix structure. This is usually coupled with an attempt to change or to improve organizational image.

Managers of voluntary organizations face a vast number of interdependencies. They must simultaneously manage inputs, outputs and internal organization. This task is very different from managing the same activities in commercial organizations. First, there are very few instances of contracts with suppliers which are common in other forms of for-profit organization. Second, there are usually a vast number of suppliers ranging from thousands of individuals who give money into tins held by street collectors, to donations by corporate bodies such as government agencies or commercial firms. Both these factors make managing the external environment of the organization complex. Third, internal control is difficult to secure. Much of the labour force is voluntary and is therefore not amenable to many of the leadership and motivation theories culled from commercial practice. Nor are precise job definitions, descriptions and other aspects of formalized organization wholly appropriate.

We can understand the complexities of managing voluntary and non-profit organizations if we examine first of all their position in the overall economy. As Butler (1983) suggests, the present-day economy consists of a mix of three broad areas. These are:

- *The market*   Survives on the generation of surplus value. Revenue created primarily through the sale of goods and services and secondarily through various patterns of investment. Resources are allocated primarily by the price mechanism. This alerts entrepreneurial activity into selecting areas of provision of goods and services which are most profitable for them and to move away from less profitable areas.

- *The statutory sector*   Includes central and local government agencies. Survives primarily through revenue produced through various systems of taxation. Resources are primarily allocated by means of central planning.

Some price mechanism may be used (such as in nationalized industries like the railways) but these are really pseudo-prices which are aimed at reducing the overall level of government subsidy.

- *The voluntary sector* Includes registered charities and non-charities. Survives primarily through donations of time, money and other resources from thousands of individual donors and volunteers. Revenue also gained from some statutory grants and to a much less extent from commercial organizations. Charges for services are very rare. Some revenue raised through limited trading such as retail outlets or mail-order services for Christmas cards and similar goods.

As a third way of providing services, the voluntary sector is becoming increasingly popular. One reason is that if a voluntary organization performs a function which was previously provided by the state, then this allows state spending to be allocated to other areas (or allows an overall reduction in state spending). Current income to just the top 200 registered charities passed £300 million in 1987 in the UK. There are no reliable data for the income of other charities, non-charities and non-profit organizations, but their combined income will at least have equalled that of the top 200 charities. Non-profit and voluntary organizations are big business.

Efficient and effective management of voluntary organizations requires attention to a number of criteria. The gift relationship must be managed. At its simplest, this means some form of specialization in order to deal with securing inputs. More complex scenarios occur where funds come from government agencies or from commercial organizations which are earmarked for a particular purpose. Managers of voluntary organizations in receipt of such funds are now no longer being recipients of altruistic behaviour. They have to manage a dependence relationship between giver and their organization (Pfeffer and Salancik, 1978). As the external environment changes, voluntary organizations will have to respond and adapt. This will mean managers spending some considerable time managing the political economy of the voluntary sector, liaising with government agencies, checking on the activities of competitor sister organizations and trying to secure a stable funding base.

As far as internal organization is concerned, pressure will be felt by managers in an attempt to increase efficiency, rationalize services, secure distinctive competence and generally to professionalize management of the organization (Handy, 1988; Wilson, 1989). Some key behaviour issues will have to be addressed in this process. For example, given the ideology of voluntarism which lies at the heart of voluntary and non-profit organizations, one would expect that decentralized structures with a minimum of hierarchy, formalization and standard procedures would be the norm.

To a large extent, decentralization has been a common feature, with organizations such as Christian Aid adopting a matrix structure. Others, such as Oxfam, have decentralized without reaching the stage of implementing a total matrix structure. Oxfam is a project organization. Other voluntary organizations such as the Royal National Institute for the Blind have recruited managers from commercial organizations as a deliberate strategy to 'import' the benefits of efficient commercial practice (see Butler and Wilson, 1989).

The overall need for precision in everything from job descriptions and responsibilities to standardized accounting procedures has not been a natural process of transition for organizations in the non-profit and voluntary sectors. For example, volunteers who feel that they do good jobs and who can expand their activities into a number of organizational activities, quite naturally resent the imposition of job demarcations. Historically, volunteers have been able to fit in where required and to expand or contract their role as necessary. Job descriptions and role responsibilities preclude this to a large extent.

The need for coordination in a decentralized organization has sometimes been overlooked. A danger here is one of creating a decentralized organization, comprising a set of different projects, but without the facility to integrate and coordinate the overall organization. The importation of managers from the commercial sector has done little to ameliorate these difficulties, since their message of professionalisation equally clashes with the individualistic culture of most voluntary organizations. The culture itself presents a barrier to attempts at corporate integration.

In countries such as Britain where the role of the state has been consistently one of reducing the number of services offered and provided by statutory agencies, the strategic importance of the voluntary sector is likely to increase substantially. Data on income, level of investments and the number of voluntary organizations in operation support this view. In countries such as Sweden, where the activities of statutory agencies are far more comprehensive and complete, the need for a healthy, efficient voluntary sector is less pressing.

Where there is a demonstrable need for a strong voluntary sector, the pressures toward professionalization and achieving distinctive competence (as competition increases) are likely to result in the operation of fewer, larger charities. Those which cannot or will not change are likely not to gain long-term support and will thus find continued operation difficult or impossible.

Cooperatives

Just as with voluntary organizations, cooperatives are organizations which are structured to reflect particular assumptions about human needs, social organization, the requirements of organizational life and material reward and motivation (Kanter, 1972). They are heavily value-laden work organizations. Cooperatives may be defined as organizations with the following characteristics:

1 Management, objectives and the procurement and disposal of assets are controlled by the workforce.
2 To achieve worker control, the organization is designed around a voting system whereby a majority or a high proportion of votes is decisive.
3 Reward for capital and reward for labour are kept distinct on the principle that labour hires capital. Capital does not hire labour in cooperative organizations.

Worker owned and controlled cooperatives may be subdivided into two major types, the *consumer cooperative* and the *producer cooperative*.

Consumer cooperatives

These cooperatives are designed around two interdependent principles:

1 there is to be no exploitation of members (in economic terms);
2 the commitment and loyalty of members to the organization are a function of the feelings of fairness and good value which it is felt the cooperative has achieved for this and future generations.

The best-known British example of a consumer cooperative began as the British Rochdale Co-operative. This organization was founded in the middle of the nineteenth century by factory workers who were trying to overcome economic exploitation by shop-owners who commanded a virtual monopoly over goods and prices. They began by opening a cooperative shop, selling goods to members of the cooperative at first (rather than to general customers). In this way, workers and their families became members of the cooperative organization. Their return was in the form of a dividend which represented a share of the profits. As the organization grew, goods were sold to the wider public who, in turn, became members of the cooperative and also received a dividend.

This type of cooperative grew rapidly throughout the nineteenth and twentieth centuries. Their activities spread to different markets such as property and finance, building societes, agriculture, food and general merchandise retailing. Growth brought with it the need for full-time administrators and managers. Member-owners could no longer do everything. Directors were appointed to handle the management task. They could be voted out of office by the members, thus preserving one of the central tenets of cooperative operation. Writers such as Braverman (1974), however, argued that this process saw the demise of consumer cooperatives since the link between trust and assured value through a democratic structure were lost by the imposition of a hierarchy which mediated between the two concepts.

Producer cooperatives

Producer cooperatives are profit-oriented organizations, often designed (but not always) along the lines of traditional capitalist modes of organization. The primary difference between capitalist organizations and producer cooperatives is the requirement in the cooperative for everyone to own a share of the organization and to participate in decision-making processes which affect the overall direction and policies of the cooperative.

These types of cooperatives are very different from consumer cooperatives. Many originated as attempts to fill gaps left by commercial organizations which have found certain areas unprofitable. In some cases, producer cooperatives have been formed principally as an alternative to the total closure of a larger commercial enterprise. The cooperative to produce motor cycles at the Meriden factory in the West Midlands, Britain, was of this kind. It did not survive, however, ultimately hitting the same problem as its commercial, non-cooperative predecessor. The motor cycle just did not sell in sufficient quantities to sustain the organization.

Another way in which producer cooperatives can emerge would be as alternative forms of social and organizational structure. For example, the formation of a cooperative could achieve some level of integration and some benefits of economies of scale to groups of artisans, musicians or agricultural workers. Here, the cooperative acts as an umbrella organization for previously separate related businesses.

Producer cooperatives tend to be more capital-intensive than their consumer counterparts. This is because many require machinery and other manufacturing equipment in order to sustain production. Because the members of the cooperative are also the owners of these capital assets, a problem can arise if the members are unwilling to finance the purchase of a fixed asset, or permit the organization to mortgage any of its existing assets to acquire loan capital. In Britain, the number of producer cooperatives is increasing steadily (see Table 15.1). Growth has occurred in most sectors, apparently regardless of varying levels of capital intensity. Footwear and textiles show the biggest increase overall.

Not all producer cooperatives emerge in well-developed economies. Indeed,

Table 15.1
Number of worker
cooperatives in the
UK by sector

	August 1980	August 1982
Crafts	19	40
Consultancy	21	33
Construction	33	69
Engineering/chemicals	26	41
Footwear/textiles	19	82
Printing/publishing	61	75
Transport hire	11	13
Films, music, theatre	28	46
Retail/catering	112	151
'Workspa ces'	0	15
Totals:	330	565

Note: 25 cooperatives in 1980, and 17 in 1982 are included in more than one trading category.
Source: The Times, Monday, 8 August 1983.

another of their characteristics is that they often emerge in situations of marginal or difficult economies. This is particularly true of cooperatives which have emerged in the Third World, where they are not additions to a well-established economy (as in Britain, Europe and North America) but are the sole representation of organization in many sectors of the economy. This can also occur in well-developed economies where other factors make organization into producer cooperatives as attractive or necessary venture. An example of this is the development and growth of the Mondragon cooperative in Spain, which was formed by the inhabitants of this Basque region of Spain in the face of political oppression. The cooperative has grown to include not only manufacturing organizations (producing refrigerators and other consumer durables) but also banks and other institutions to support the whole network of organizations throughout the cooperative (see Bradley and Gelb, 1982; Thomas and Logan, 1982).

Both consumer and producer cooperatives share certain characteristics and value patterns among their membership and in their *raison d'être*. We summarize some of these in Table 15.2.

How sustainable is the cooperative organization?

Much in the same way as voluntary organizations, the genesis of cooperatives owes a large part to the fostering of a strong community spirit among its members. If we look at the formation of the Mondragon cooperative in Spain, we can see in extreme form the kind of solidarity which acts as the cement to bond the organization together in the first place.

The spirit of community was fostered in the people of the region following the atrocities inflicted by the German Airforce upon the town of Guernica just before the Second World War.

> The rhythm of this bombing of an open town was, therefore, a logical one: first, hand grenades and heavy bombs to stampede the population, then machine gunning to drive them below, next heavy and incendiary bombs to wreck the houses and burn them on top of their victims . . . the whole town of 7,000 inhabitants, plus 3,000 refugees was slowly and systematically pounded to pieces (*The Times*, 28 April 1937).

Table 15.2
Key organizational
features of
cooperative and
capitalist
organizations

	Cooperative organization	*Capitalist organization*
Ownership	By producers/members. Assets can be withdrawn when they leave the organization	By outside shareholders who can sell assets in the wider market
Control	By members/producers or their representatives	By managers who are salaried employees and who are mobile between firms
Power	Symmetrical throughout the organization	Deliberately asymmetrical. Power is spread throughout the firm dependent upon level in hierarchy, access to and control over information and other contingencies
Communication	Initially by mutual adjustment	Initially by bureaucratic routines
	Representation on committees, an assembly, etc.	Commands, parameters and schedules used as much as possible
	As size of coop increases and as issues become more ambiguous considerable bureaucracy can occur	As ambiguity increases, mutual adjustment may be used
Decision-making	Decentralized, with consensus as the ideal. In producer coops, the producers are always involved	Centralized usually with possible consultation of producers. Majorities favoured rather than always trying to achieve consensus
Labour force	Sensitive to turnover. No means of firing staff	Often designed around coping with high turnover. Firing of staff made possible through formal procedure
	Selected on level of commitment, ability to pay a financial stake, and attitudes toward the cooperative	Selection on formal qualification and placed on a point in the salary structure. Advancement through specified grades
	Motivation often from a sense of solidarity and ideology	Motivation often instrumentally economic

The spirit of community which this created made the subsequent formation of communal and community-based forms of organization almost inevitable (Kanter, 1972). Other events, less widely atrocious and traumatic, can also spur the formation of cooperative ventures. The impending closure of the motorcycle works at Meriden, for example, was the impetus for employees to continue to run the company as a cooperative.

Once set up, can cooperatives survive in the long term? There appear to be a number of factors which mitigate against their long-term survival. Cooperatives must maintain the commitment of its members beyond the initial impetus and they must do this often in the face of extreme competition from other organizations and turbulent or hostile environments. Direct market forces can be alleviated to some extent if the cooperative sells its products to the same community from which it draws its labour supply (producers). Communal solidarity is thus increased and the cooperative can be afforded some shelter from the pure economic standards that would apply in wider markets. Sympathetic customers may be prepared to pay a premium or to accept a restricted range or quality of product from their own cooperative. If this cannot be achieved, the cooperative must compete directly in the open marketplace alongside traditional commercial organizations.

The supply of finance to cooperatives is nearly always a problem in the longer term (Bradley and Gelb, 1982). Using equity issuance to raise capital would be in danger of compromising cooperative principles. The Mondragon cooperative recognized this and a bank was set up to act as a 'buffer' organization to supply finance to the wider cooperative. Others, such as the ill-fated Meriden Motorcycle Cooperative were unable to do this. The cooperative was forced to compete in the open market and, in the long term, failed.

The human resource aspects of cooperatives can be both a strength and a weakness. Since job rotation and minimal job specialization is encouraged, this can achieve substantial benefits of corporate awareness in all individuals in the cooperative. This is something that we have noticed is unlikely to occur in traditional functionally differentiated organizations. However, cooperatives can thus become staffed by 'jacks-of-all-trades' rather than groups of individual specialists. The acquisition of specialist skills and knowledge may become central to organizational survival, since without managerial skills, productive and technical knowledge, sustaining operations against even the most benign competition is likely to be very difficult.

Organizational growth also poses potential problems for the cooperative. As size increases not every member of the organization can participate directly in decision-making (one of the central tenets of cooperative organization). In large cooperatives this can be handled by dividing decisions into policy topics and operating topics. For major policy decisions, an elected representative group is empowered to decided. In operating decisions, similar sub-groups can act as task and problem-solving decision arenas. This runs the risk of creating bodies of 'professional' specialized decision-makers, which, once established, would take the cooperative far from its original ideal.

Representative decision-making committees run the risk of fragmenting cooperatives. They may have to meet outside formal working hours or require extra work from individuals. Thus they can easily be composed of the more zealous cooperative members whose interests may not necessarily be those of the wider cooperative. Once in a position of decision-making power, such individuals can exercise discretionary influence if they wish (see Pettigrew, 1973; 1985; Hickson et al., 1986). Rojek and Wilson (1987) illustrated how this fragmentation had occurred in Yugoslavia with respect to systems of self-management. They also argued that cooperatives in Yugoslavia were pressured to adopt more bureaucratic ways of operating because they had to interact with the wider capitalist system of world trade and world markets. While such fragmentation of power and influence is typical of formal, traditional capitalist organizations, its occurrence in cooperatives can rapidly lead to their demise.

Other alternative forms of organization

At the most extreme end of any centralized/decentralized continuum lie acephalous organizations. Quite literally, these are organizations without a head, without a leader, and without the necessary supporting structures to sustain either centralization or decentralization. Space limits us to little other than mentioning such organizations in this book. They are alternatives to hierarchies (heterarchies). Examples include the Women's Movement in Britain, some conservationist groups and peace movements. Some hippy communes, convoys and temporary social organizations (some festivals) could also be included as heterarchies.

Summary

In this chapter we have looked at ways of structuring and designing organizations beyond the traditional, the formal, and the bureaucratic. Making organizations more project-centred and overlaying a lateral as well as a vertical dimension gives us the matrix structure. The fostering of a task culture and a project or matrix structure has been argued to create a flexible organization, capable of rapid and proactive change in the face of hostile or unpredictable environments (Handy, 1986).

Flexibility is also the keyword for describing voluntary organizations. Because of their position in the economy (relatively independent and non-profit-seeking) these organizations can also adapt easily. Since they tend to be staffed with individuals who work through motives which are altruistic rather than instrumental or economic, motivating staff and achieving loyalty to the organization are of little problem. Cooperatives also have some of this ideological overlay, but in this case, they are explicitly profit-seeking.

All three forms of organization pose problems of achieving integration and coordination. Traditional systems of management and the application of well-worn management theories are unlikely to be effective. They are more likely to be counter-productive to effectiveness. These kinds of organization need very different styles of management if they are to succeed in the long term. Yet there is always the pressure upon all 'alternative' structures to revert to traditional, formal bureaucractic structures. Once this has happened, the beliefs, ideologies and values of alternative organization will disappear. One challenge for the future will be to find new styles of management appropriate to alternative organizations, new styles which are not just borrowed and adapted from traditional management theory, but which are designed explicitly with matrices, voluntary organizations and cooperatives in mind.

References

Bradley, K. and A. Gelb (1982) 'The replication and sustainability of the Mondragon experiment', *British Journal of Industrial Relations*, **10**(1), 20–3.

Braverman, H. (1974) *Labour and Monopoly Capital*, Monthly Review Press, New York.

Burns, T. and G. R. Stalker (1961) *The Management of Innovation*, Tavistock, London.

Butler, R. J. (1983) 'Control through markets, hierarchies and communes: a transactional approach to organizational analysis', in A. Francis, J. Turk and P. Willman (eds), *Power, Efficiency and Institutions*, Heinemann, London.

Butler, R. J. and D. C. Wilson (1989) *Managing Voluntary and Non-Profit Organizations: Strategy and Structure*, Routledge, London.

Charities Aid Foundation (1985/86) *Charity Statistics*, CAF, London.

Chesterman, M. (1979) *Charities, Trusts and Social Welfare*, Weidenfeld & Nicholson, London.

Child, J. (1984) *Organization: A Guide to Problems and Practice*, Harper & Row, London.

Davis, S. M. and P. R. Lawrence (1977) *Matrix*, Addison-Wesley, Reading, Mass.

Galbraith, J. K. (1973) *Designing Complex Organizations*, Addison-Wesley, Reading, Mass.

Galbraith, J. R. (1974) 'Organizational design: an information processing view', *Interfaces*, **4**, 28–36.

Galbraith, J. K. (1977) 'Matrix organization design: how to combine functional and project forms', *Business Horizons*, 29–40.

Handy, C. B. (1986) *Understanding Organizations*, Penguin, Harmondsworth.

Handy, C. B. (1988) *Understanding Voluntary Organizations*, Penguin, Harmondsworth.

Hickson, D. J., R. J. Butler, D. Cray, G. R. Mallory and D. C. Wilson (1986) *Top Decisions: Strategic Decision-Making in Organizations*, Blackwell, Oxford; Jossey-Bass, San Francisco.

Horngren, C. T. and G. Foster (1987) *Cost Accounting: A Managerial Perspective*, 6th edn, Prentice-Hall, Englewood Cliffs, New Jersey.

Hunt, J. (1986) *Managing People at Work: A Manager's Guide to Behaviour in Organizations*, McGraw-Hill, London.

Kanter, R. M. (1972) *Commitment and Community: Communes and Utopias in Sociological Perspective*, Harvard University Press, Cambridge, Mass.

Knight, K. (1976) 'Matrix organizations: a review', *Journal of Management Studies*, **13**(2), 111–30.

Lawrence, P. and J. W. Lorsch (1967) *Organization and Environment*, Harvard University Press, Cambridge, Mass.

Mauss, M. (1954) *The Gift*, Norton, New York.

Pettigrew, A. M. (1973) *The Politics of Organizational Decision Making*, Tavistock, London.

Pettigrew, A. M. (1985) *The Awakening Giant: Continuity and Change in ICI*, Blackwell, Oxford.

Pfeffer, J. and G. R. Salancik (1978) *The External Control of Organizations: A Resource Dependence Perspective*, Harper & Row, New York.

Rojek, C. and D. C. Wilson (1987) 'Workers' self-management in the world system', *Organizational Studies*, **8**(4), 297–308.

Thomas, H. and C. Logan (1982) *Mondragon: An Economic Analysis*, Allen & Unwin, London.

Titmuss, R. (1970) *The Gift Relationship: From Human Blood to Social Policy*, Penguin, Harmondsworth.

Williamson, O. E. and W. Ouchi (1981) 'The markets, hierarchies and visible hand perspectives', in A. H. Van de Ven and W. F. Joyce (eds), *Perspectives on Organizational Design and Behavior*, Wiley, New York.

Wilson, D. C. (1984) 'Charity law and the politics of regulation in the voluntary sector', *King's Counsel*, **34**, 36–41.

Wilson, D. C. (1989) 'New trends in the funding of charities: the tripartite system of funding', in A. Ware (ed.), *Charities and Government*, Manchester University Press, Manchester.

Is corporate culture manageable?

Andrew M. Pettigrew

Is corporate culture manageable? The straightforward answer to that question is—with the greatest difficulty! The more academic answer to the question depends on what is meant by corporate culture and management.

Let me be clear first of all what I mean by management, and in particular management process. Management is much more than just a process of analytical reasoning. A search through many of the basis textbooks in business strategy in the 1960s and 1970s gives the impression that the development of strategy is a rational analytical process. Seeing the process of management in such rational terms is not a helpful starting point for answering the question: is corporate culture manageable?

The rational approach to strategic management has tended to describe and prescribe techniques for identifying current strategy, analysing environments, resources, and gaps, revealing and assessing strategic alternatives, and choosing and implementing carefully analysed and well-thought-through outcomes. Depending on the author, explicity or implicitly, the firm speaks with a unitary voice or can be composed of omnipotent, even heroic general managers or chief executives, looking at known and consistent preferences and assessing them with voluminous and presumably apposite information, which can be organized into clear input–output relationships.

More recently the empirical process research by authors such as Bower (1970), Pettigrew (1973; 1985a; 1985b), and Mintzberg (1978) has introduced a rather different and more realistic language for thinking about management processes of change. Strategic change is now to be viewed as a complex human process in which differential perception, quests for efficiency and power, visionary leadership skills, the vicariousness of chance, and subtle processes of additively building up a momentum of support for change, and then vigorously implementing change, all play their part.

If the process of management is conceived in such social and political terms, what is the working definition of corporate culture used to develop the arguments in this paper? Following Pettigrew (1979), Schein (1985), Barney (1986), and others, corporate culture is understood as a phenomenon which exists at a variety of different levels. At the deepest level, culture is thought of as the complex set of values, beliefs, and assumptions that define the ways in which a firm conducts its business. Such core beliefs and assumptions are, of course, manifested in the structures, systems, symbols, myths and patterns of reward inside the organization. The basic proposition of this reading is that it is rather easier to adjust the manifestations of culture than it is to change the core beliefs and assumptions within an organization. However, any practical strategy for changing corporate culture has to involve thought and action both at the level of core beliefs, and of the cultural manifestations of those core beliefs.

This reading has six parts. After this introduction, there is a section outlining the analytical framework used to understand processes of cultural change in organizations. There then follows a section which explores why corporate culture is so difficult to manage. The following section focuses on one of the central problems of strategic change, how to change the core beliefs of top decision-makers in the organization. We then move on to briefly describe some of the range of empirical studies going on at the Centre for Corporate Strategy and Change, University of Warwick, exploring the context, content, and processes of strategic change in a number of different firms in a variety of different sectors. This work is exemplified by brief reference to a completed study of Imperial Chemical Industries (Pettigrew, 1985a) and an on-going study of Jaguar Cars. The reading ends by cataloguing some of the key management tasks and mechanisms used to change corporate cultures.

Context, content and process in studying strategic change

In this writer's view, theoretically sound and practically useful research on strategic decision-making and change should involve the continuous interplay among ideas about the *context* of change, the *process* of change and the *content* of change, together with skill in regulating the relations among the three. Figure R8.1 outlines the broad analytical framework used at Warwick for guiding our empirical research.

Figure R8.1
Corporate culture and change: an analytical framework

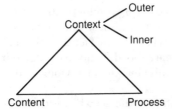

The starting point for this analysis of strategic change is the notion that formulating the content of any new strategy inevitably entails managing its context and process. Outer context refers to the social, economic, political and competitive environment in which the firm operates. Inner context refers to the structure, corporate culture and political context within the firm through which ideas for change have to proceed. Content refers to the particular areas of change under examination. Thus the firm may be seeking to change technology, manpower, products, geographical positioning, or indeed corporate culture. The process of change refers to the actions, reactions, and interactions from the various interested parties as they seek to move the firm from its present to its future state. Thus the *what* of change is encapsulated under the label content, much of the *why* of change is derived from an analysis of inner and outer context, and the *how* of change can be understood from an analysis of process.

One of the weaknesses of the existing literature on business strategy is its focus on the link between outer context and content. The singular and exclusive analytical concern with outer context and content has led to the planners' nightmare of the lack of acceptance of planning solutions. A major practical suggestion of this reading is that action to change the strategies and cultures of firms is much dependent on the ability not only to link the *what* of change to the outer context of the firm, but also to link and fashion such suggestions to the internal political and context of the firm, and to manage such connections through the firm by adroit considerations about the process of management.

Why is corporate culture difficult to manage?

Listed below are seven major factors which make corporate culture difficult to manage. These are:

1 the levels issue
2 the pervasiveness issue
3 the implicitness issue
4 the imprinting issue
5 the political issue
6 the plurality issue
7 the interdependence issue

Briefly put, the levels issue relates to the fact that corporate culture exists at a variety of different levels in the firm. Thus at the deepest level it refers to the beliefs and assumptions of people inside the organization both about the internal workings of the organization and the way the organization faces its external environment. As I have already suggested, it is rather more difficult to change the core beliefs and assumptions within the organization than it is to change some of the manifestations of culture in, for example, the organization's structure and systems.

The pervasiveness issue is a corollary of the points made above about different levels of culture. Culture is not only deep, it is also broad. Thus corporate culture refers not just to people, their relationships and beliefs; it also refers to their views about company products, structures, systems, corporate purpose, and modes of recruitment, socialization, and reward.

The implicitness issue pertains to the fact that much of corporate culture is taken for granted. It is remarkably difficult to change things which are implicitly part of people's thinking and behaviour, and are rarely brought out explicitly for consideration.

Imprinting draws attention to the deep historical roots of much of corporate culture. History weighs a very heavy hand in the present and future management of most corporations.

The political issue refers to the connections between corporate culture and the power distribution in the firm. Certain power groups in the organization have a vested interest in the beliefs and assumptions which may have primacy at any point in time in the firm's development. Those power groups are unlikely to be willing to discard those beliefs and assumptions without persistent and consistent challenge.

The plurality issue is a close cousin of politics and culture. Most firms do not just have a single corporate culture but at any point in time may have a variety of different sets of beliefs and assumptions—in effect a series of sub-cultures. Tension about the future development of the firm is often expressed in terms of the language and political positioning of these different sub-cultures.

Finally, the interdependency issue focuses on the fact that culture is interconnected not only with the politics of the firm, but also with the structure, systems, people and priorities of the firm. Between them the above seven issues make corporate culture remarkably difficult to manage, and certainly to change.

A key aspect of strategic change: changing the core beliefs of the top decision-makers

The point has been made that corporate culture exists at a variety of different levels in the firm. The deepest of these levels is the core beliefs and assumptions of the organization's top decision-makers. Such beliefs are obviously critical, for they not only define what key people perceive as is important in the organization's environment; such beliefs also help to determine areas for management attention, choice, and change within the firm. Studies by, for example, Grinyer and Spender (1979), Pettigrew (1985a), and Johnson (1987) all reveal the critical role of top management beliefs in inhibiting and facilitating change in the firm.

Research at the Centre for Corporate Strategy and Change at the University of Warwick is seeking to explore some of the key problems of strategy and change in private- and public-sector organizations in the UK. Longitudinal empirical studies are under way in firms in the automobile, merchant banking, publishing, engineering, commercial banking, office automation and computing and retailing sectors. A large empirical project has just begun in 8 of the 14 regions in the NHS in the UK. In this reading, the briefest reference can only be made to a completed study of the long-term processes of strategic change in Imperical Chemicals Industries (ICI), and a study under way in Jaguar Cars.

The ICI Study of Strategic Change

The ICI study of strategic change uses extensive high-level and longitudinal data to explore processes of strategic and operational change on the Main Board of ICI, and in ICI's four largest divisions over the period 1960–83. The full results of this study are now available in Pettigrew (1985a). Some of the key findings of the study relevant to the question: is culture manageable?, can be stated as follows:

1   Change in ICI did not occur as a continuous incremental process.
2   The pattern of change over a 25-year period in the company was for radical periods of change to occur at certain critical points in time. Such radical periods were interspersed with long periods of incremental adjustment. These radical periods featured changes in the core beliefs, structure and business strategy of ICI.
3   The timing of these radical packages of a change were associated with:
    (a)   Real and constructed business crises. In other words, ICI made substantial changes only when it was in severe economic difficulties. The two great eras of change over the last two or three decades have been between 1960 and 1964 and between 1980 and 1986. A critical facet of these change periods was not only the association with business crisis but also the active strategies by the managers in ICI to construct a climate for change around these business crises. Mobilizing the context in order to provide the legitimacy and justification for change was a critical part of the process of managing change.
    (b)   Such radical packages were also connected with changes in leadership and power in ICI. The era of change in the early 1960s was associated with the appearance of Paul Chambers, later Sir Paul Chambers as Chairman of ICI. More recently John Harvey-Jones, now Sir John Harvey-Jones, has provided substantial change leadership in the company. Both Chambers and Harvey-Jones supplied quite different business leadership in the company. They were both men who had not spent their whole career in the ICI culture.
    (c)   Finally the timing of these radical packages of a change were much

associated with the transformation in the beliefs of the top decision-makers in ICI.

A crucial finding in the ICI study relates to the sequencing in the pattern of change in the company. The sequencing of change did not follow the conventional wisdom in the business policy literature that changes in organizational structure should follow changes in business strategy. Rather the pattern of change in ICI was a complex mixture of adjustments of core beliefs of the top decision-makers, followed by changes in beliefs, and out of those changes in beliefs and structure began to emerge the new business strategy of the firm. If this pattern is clearly established in other case studies, it makes the issue of first challenging and then changing the core beliefs of the top decision-makers a critical factor in the theory and practice of managing strategic change.

For a discussion of how the ICI process of change occurred, see Pettigrew (1985a). In addition, the final section of this paper draws on the ICI case to reveal some of the key management tasks and mechanisms used to effect changes in corporate culture.

Changes in corporate culture in Jaguar Cars

In ICI the change problem was how to break down the core beliefs of the top decision-makers as ICI faced a rapidly changing external environment. As the old beliefs were questioned, so a new ideology was introduced by Harvey-Jones and others which emphasized a sharpening in market focus, a greater entrepreneurial emphasis to more decentralized units, a lessening of bureaucracy and central control, and a change in the mode and style of operation of the Main Board. These attempts at cultural change were linked to major changes in structure and manpower. The business strategy changes which emerged emphasized a move from heavy to speciality chemicals and a continuation of attempts to reposition ICI in North America and to move increasingly into the markets of the Pacific Basin.

Paradoxically, in Jaguar Cars the problem of cultural change has been the revival and revamping of an old culture in line with the business and competitive conditions of the 1980s. What the chairman and chief executive of Jaguar Cars, Sir John Egan, has attempted to do is best understood in relationship to the three main phases of Jaguar's development. These phases are the Lyons' era, 1928–72; the BL era, 1972–80; and the Egan era from 1980 onwards.

In broad terms the Jaguar culture under Lyons was one of the intense personal loyalty to 'Sir William' linked to a marked identification with a distinctive product ('grace, pace, space'). This culture also rested on a clear commitment to engineering excellence which was routinely expressed in a 'can do' mentality (for example the meeting of exceptional project deadlines) which became famous within the industry. There was an absence of elaborate management control.

Under BL the strengths of this culture and approach to building luxury and racing cars withered. As BL removed key functions (sales, purchasing) to central office or other plants, those who remained at Jaguar's main manufacturing plants concentrated on surviving a hostile corporate overload and a series of senior managers who did not respect the Jaguar culture.

John Egan, however, saw the Jaguar culture, albeit the remnants in 1980, as a vital resource in rebuilding the company. The Chairman and other senior executives, as part of the process of establishing a 'stand-alone company', have attempted to revive and extend that culture which had all but died under BL. The Chairman and Board have demonstrated that the new stand-alone company was to be built on both the accepted qualities of the old Jaguar culture, together with an infusion of outside expertise (for example, university engineers, sales and marketing heads from Lotus).

The core beliefs of the newly created senior management were examined by Egan at an early stage in 1980 as part of his securing their total commitment to saving the company. Once that commitment was forthcoming it then became a question of reviewing the traditional features of adherence to engineering excellence and product loyalty on a wider basis, as well as extending those features to embrace the highest standards of competitiveness in quality, reliability and productivity recognized in the 1980s. In effect Jaguar decided they had to emulate Daimler-Benz.

Since 1980/81 the task of changing Jaguar's culture has centred on the inculcation of this commitment among middle management, workforce, suppliers, and contractors. This task is very much in progress but some important examples of structures and symbols within the company emerge. They include:

1 Regular US dealer visits to the major Jaguar manufacturing plants and confrontations with factory sections responsible for quality defects. These visits are also backed-up by monthly dealer award schemes, and successful employees have their names put on a plaque in the reception area adjacent to the Queen's Awards to Industry which have been presented to Jaguar.
2 New contractoral relationships with suppliers are reinforced by an annual Jaguar award ceremony for the best performers, held at prestige locations in London.
3 The creation of weekly 'washing-up' meetings on the manufacturing tracks. These washing-up meetings tackle problems as they arise and are linked via parallel engineering meetings to the monthly board.
4 Many of these symptoms of cultural change have been recognized by outsiders. One city analyst connected with Jaguar observed that the new head of communications and corporate affairs is now 'more Jaguar than some of the people who have been there for 25 years'.

Changing corporate culture: key management tasks and mechanisms

The ICI, Jaguar, and related Warwick studies reveal the following factors as important in facilitating changes in corporate culture:

1 A receptive outer context, together with managerial skill in mobilizing that context in order to create an overall climate for change to occur.
2 Leadership behaviour either from individuals recently brought into the organization from outside, or from individuals who have been pushing for change from a powerful internal position for some time. Most of the cases of change reveal a very clear and consistent drive from the top.
3 The existence of inarticulate and imprecise visions from the agents of change at the very top.
4 The use of discrepant action by key figures in the new guard in order to raise the level of tension in the organization for change.
5 Using deviants and heretics, both external and internal to the organization in order to say the unsayable and think the unthinkable. External and internal consultants are regularly used for this purpose.
6 Releasing avenues and energy for change by moving people and portfolios.
7 Creating new meetings and other arenas where problems can be articulated and shares and energy focused around the need for change.
8 Altering the management process at the very top. A key aspect of this seems

to be the need to change top management processes from being highly divisive in character to being much more coherent and cohesive.

9 Reinforcing any embryonic cultural shifts through closely matched structural changes, then strengthening such cultural and structural changes through the public use of the organization's reward systems.

10 Finding and using 'role models' who can through their own public behaviour display key aspects of the new culture. The identification of people who can 'walk and talk' seems to be a key aspect of making concrete and public the desire cultural changes. These role models of the new era also help the continuing reinforcement of change.

11 Carrying the message deep into the organization through the use of training and development strategies.

12 Transmitting the new beliefs and behaviour down into the organization by revamping employee communication mechanisms.

13 Finally there is the old-fashioned but critical need for persistence and patience. All of the studies of strategic change we are looking at emphasize the complexity and difficulty of effecting such changes, even where the change is eventually triggered by major environmental disturbances. Persistence and patience is critically important at the difficult stage of breaking down the core beliefs of the old guard, getting new problems sensed and articulated in the organization, developing a sense of concern that those problems are worthy or analytical and political attention, and then articulating the new order often through highly inarticulate and impressive visions of the future.

References

Barney, J. B. (1986) 'Organizational culture: can it be a source of sustained competitive advantage?' *Academy of Management Review* **11**(3), 656–65.

Bower, J. L. (1970) *Managing the Resource Allocation Process*, Harvard University Press, Cambridge, Mass.

Grinyer, P. H. and J. C. Spender (1979) 'Recipes, crises, and adaptation in mature businesses', *International Journal of Management and Organization*, ix, (3), 113–25.

Johnson, G. (1987) *The Process of Strategic Change: A Management Perspective*, Basil Blackwell, Oxford.

Mintzberg, H. (1978) 'Patterns in strategy formation', *Management Science*, **24**, 934–48.

Pettigrew, A. M. (1973) *The Politics of Organizational Decision-Making*, Tavistock, London.

Pettigrew, A. M. (1979) 'On studying organizational cultures' *Administrative Science Quarterly*, **24**, 570–581.

Pettigrew, A. M. (1985a) *The Awakening Giant: Continuity and Change in ICI*, Basil Blackwell, Oxford.

Pettigrew, A. M. (1985b) 'Culture and politics in strategic decision-making and change', in J. M. Pennings (ed.), *Organizational Strategy and Change*, Jossey Bass, San Francisco.

Schein, E. H. (1985) *Organizational Culture and Leadership*, Jossey Bass, San Francisco.

Managing turnaround: the politics of change

Cynthia Hardy

Introduction

Managing turnaround means managing change under the most difficult of circumstances. Turnaround is preceded, by definition, by decline—profits have fallen, revenues have been reduced, and the viability of the enterprise may be at stake, threatening jobs and livelihoods. Clearly, such a turbulent time is not the ideal one in which to be introducing major changes, and yet it is the time when they are most needed.

Much of the literature views turnaround as, primarily, an economic process—a view with which managers often inadvertently concur. Long-term survival will, however, depend on the human dimension—the continued commitment and motivation of the workforce. Management can ill afford to allow productivity to fall, strikes to occur, unfavourable publicity to deter customers, or people with critical skills to leave. Turnaround is a political, as much as an economic problem since it depends upon the cooperation of various interest groups; many of which will have been threatened by the preceding decline, and all of which will have a stake in the future plans of the organization (Hardy, 1989).

This reading examines the case of turnaround in universities. Their experience illustrates a number of issues that are relevant to other organizations, in both the public and private sectors.

Turnaround: the economic view

The discussion of turnaround in the business literature (Schendel and Patton, 1976; Schendel, Patton and Riggs, 1976; Hofer, 1980; Hambrick and Schecter, 1983) defines decline in terms of reduced profitability, sales or revenues. It has been associated with a variety of causes—higher wage and raw material costs, increased competition, strikes, inefficient production, technological change, substitute products, lower prices and depressed demand. The key to a successful turnaround, according to this literature, lies in choosing appropriately between operating and strategic turnaround—an inappropriate response usually exacerbates the decline. Faced with decline, one must either 'do different things' or 'do things differently'. The former relates to stategic turnaround, the latter to operating turnaround.

The choice depends on the cause of decline: if the underlying cause is structural market change, the response should be strategic; if internal inefficiency is the problem, operating turnaround will suffice. Managers need, then, to consider carefully the causes of decline and its effect on the shape and size of the organization's niche (Zammuto and Cameron, 1985, Zammuto, 1988). The niche refers to the environment or domain in which the organization operates. If the size of the niche decreases, the level of activity that can be sustained also decreases. Thus, competition heightens and organizations have to perform more efficiently. If decline modifies the shape of the niche because the nature of demand changes, new forms of activity will be required.

Turnaround: the political view

Economic solutions ignore the practical difficulties of implementing their chosen solutions and do not consider the adverse effects they may have on organizational members, Turnaround depends on the continued commitment of all levels of employees (Bilbeault, 1982; Khandwalla, 1983/84), who are expected to be creative and productive, even though they may have seen colleagues lose their jobs, and may face an uncertain future themselves. Employees quickly learn how their peers have been dismissed and, if they perceive them to have been unfairly treated, their own commitment will suffer. Union resistance also has to be taken into consideration—union disapproval may take the form of overt confrontation, sabotage, and non-cooperation (Hardy, 1985a).

As many writers have pointed out, the environment alone does not determine strategy. In effect, an element of strategic choice exists (Child, 1972; Hrebiniak and Joyce, 1985), which may be shaped by the internal organizational setting— the structure and culture of an institution (Melin, 1985). Managers may think twice about which are the most acceptable changes and the best ways of introducing them.

There is a second political component—turnaround may depend on the cooperation, not only of internal, but also external interest groups (Dowling and Pfeffer, 1983; Pfeffer and Salancik, 1978; Keim, Zeitham and Baysinger, 1984). External intervention is often clear in the case of public agencies, which are accountable to outside bodies and dependent upon them for funding. Business organizations are, however, often less autonomous than might otherwise appear (Randall, 1973; Bozeman and Straussman, 1984). Companies operating in regulated industries, subject to takeovers will find themselves dependent on external interest groups (Hardy, 1989). As a result, all types of organization will engage in collective strategies (Astley and Fombrun, 1983) to defend themselves against external threats. Such externally directed actions are all the more important when the industry is under threat and attempts are being made to resist decline (for example, Levine, 1979; Jick and Murray, 1982; Miles and Cameron, 1982; Hardy, 1985b).

Thus the political dimension of turnaround is managers' ability to manage conflict and generate commitment. The key to successful turnaround lies in balancing this political component with appropriate economic responses to decline.

The economics of university decline

The causes of decline have long been documented in the higher education literature (Parker and Zammuto, 1986). It has resulted from reductions in public funding and/or enrolment. For example, US universities have suffered primarily from declining birthrates, although some state schools have also had to contend with, in some cases substantial, funding cuts. The impetus for decline in Canada has come from a relatively gradual compression in government funding, at a time of growing enrolment. Many UK and European universities have had to cope with large decreases in public funding (for example, Mortimer and Tierney, 1979; Walford, 1987).

Funding cuts in North America have tended to change the size rather than the shape of the niche, since they usually involve a reduction in the lump sum awarded to the university for operating expenses—overall revenues may be reduced but universities are not forced to curtail specific activities. In the UK, cutbacks have been more targeted and have resulted in changes in the shape of niche in some universities, as certain programmes have been phased out. Enrolment decline has changed drastically the niche of some small, specialist institutions in the US. In the 1970s many liberal arts colleges were forced to offer totally new programmes such as MBAs, continuing education programmes, and executive development in order to survive shifts in enrolment and demand (Zammuto and Cameron, 1985).

The politics of university decline

Universities are particularly interesting arenas in which to study the political side of decline, for two reasons. First, they contain a wide variety of different interest groups that possess the power to influence decision-making. Power is diffuse and decentralized, as a result of professional values and academic freedom (Hardy *et al.*, 1983). Moreover, because of the loosely coupled nature of faculties and departments (Weick, 1976), groups may have vastly differing interests. In a situation where scarcity exists, such as declining enrolments or funding, one can expect a political situation to develop as these interest groups compete for the available resources (Pettigrew, 1973; Hardy *et al.*, 1983). Thus, turnaround becomes impossible without the commitment of the *professoriate*, since few decisions fall under the rubric of administrative fiat. Attempts to introduce major changes may provoke a political backlash if professors try to block and influence decisions. Any attempt to impose decisions runs the risk of jeopardizing the loyalty and commitment of the staff (Davis and Morgan, 1981). Since excellence depends largely on a committed *professoriate* (Pearson, 1986), the commitment and cooperation of individuals are paramount to successful turnaround.

Second, political issues also arise because universities depend on a variety of external interest groups. In many cases, universities are publicly funded and, hence, depend heavily on government agencies. They also rely on donors, business, and granting agencies for funds. Thus, universities face a variety of external political pressures, the management of which will be crucial in the event of decline.

Managing turnaround

Traditionally, the turnaround literature works from the outside in, and from formulation to implementation. In other words, environmental analysis leads to the formulation or choice of strategy, the implementation of which then changes the organization in various ways. The recommendations below work in the reverse order—they suggest that managers should start by thinking about their organization and its culture, an analysis of which will help them determine how change can be implemented.

Cultural turnaround

Successful turnaround in universities involves the maintenance of morale, motivation and commitment, and the reduction of conflict. In general, it requires a culture in which there is a sense of shared mission. Administrators must take care to protect the culture during decline because of the potential damage that can be rendered by a period of scarce resources, particularly since it has been suggested that a sense of shared mission is more important than either operating or strategic turnaround in determining recovery (Parker, 1987). If this is the case, we might expect administrators to avoid actions that will endanger the commitment and loyalty of their staff and engender political conflict.

The importance of protecting culture reinforces the argument that turnaround is not purely an economic activity; it involves an interpretative strategy in which the focus is on symbolic management, communication, and cooperation (Chaffee, 1984). Since universities have different cultures (Chaffee and Tierney, 1988; Tierney, 1988), every institution must formulate a strategy which meets its individual needs (Parker, 1987). A study of retrenchment strategies in two Canadian universities found that cultural variations led to different strategies. One university had highly decentralized decision-making in a relatively collegial culture, the second was more centralized, with a history of quantitative studies of resource allocation, successful participation and ostensibly 'fair' cuts. In the second, it required finding a methodology for making selective cuts that was deemed legitimate by the university community. Thus, successful turnaround may look different in different institutions (Hardy, 1987a; 1989).

Incremental vs quantum turnaround

The economic literature conceives of turnaround as a quantum phenomenon, in which a global solution is imposed in one fell swoop. In reality, a series of incremental steps towards turnaround may be less disruptive and more likely to engender acceptance. Managers need to realize that turnaround of any kind is a difficult process. Even the 'limited' changes associated with operating turnaround will be difficult to implement in a university—cutting cost, collecting operational information, challenging tenure decisions, making professors more accountable—threaten traditional academic norms. Change brings about opportunities to secure additional sources of power and threats to existing positions. Interest groups engage in political activity as they attempt to influence the direction of the changes (Pettigrew, 1976; Huff, 1980). Administrators must learn how to influence the change process. It will require powerful change agents, credibility building, and the mobilization of the rank and file (Quinn, 1980; Kanter, 1983; Khandwalla, 1983/84; Pettigrew, 1984; 1985).

These political realities will play a part in deciding how to respond to decline, as will the desire to protect culture. Managers may decide to exercise their degree of strategic choice in favour of incremental turnaround, rather than unilaterally imposing a quantum change. They may also lack the power to impose quantum change—the initial 'choice' of administrator may bear little resemblance to the strategy that is put into action. Thus, quantum turnaround may not only be undesirable, but also infeasible. Incremental turnaround allows administrators to combine environmental analysis and political acumen to work, gradually and incrementally, towards the long-term changes that are required (Lindblom, 1959; Quinn, 1978). It enables administrators to act opportunistically instead of heavy-handedly. It allows universities to respond to environmental changes and work towards new priorities, albeit at a sedate pace. In this way, the plans of administrators mesh with the culture of the university rather than jeopardize it, and the plans which finally emerge are in a more viable form.

Political turnaround

Political turnaround involves attempts to pressure or external groups to provide support for the institution which, in turn, helps it resist decline (for example, Levine, 1979; Jick and Murray, 1982; Hardy, 1985b). This defence of the organization's domain (Miles and Cameron, 1982; Zammuto and Cameron, 1985) creates slack, which buys time to implement incremental turnaround, and reduces the magnitude of cutbacks. Political turnaround helps to increase the degree of strategic choice, thus enabling administrators to take the necessary steps to protect culture and engage in incrementalism.

Political strategies involve the mobilization of power, which exists because one actor is dependent on another for certain resources—the person or group controlling those resources is then able to exercise power over the other

(Emerson, 1962; Pettigrew, 1973; Pfeffer, 1981). In this situation, however, the organization wants to exercise power over the groups on which it is dependent and will, therefore, find it difficult to exercise direct power. There is, however, a second, unobtrusive side to power where actors use the symbolic sources of power to produce more favourable and supportive sentiments (Hardy, 1985a; 1985c; 1986). This section discusses some of the ways in which Canadian universities have used unobtrusive power to win favour from the government, or influence it indirectly by creating media and public support (see Hardy, 1987b).

Playing the visibility game
Universities need to impress upon interest groups that they are providing expert services which are essential to society and which are threatened by budget cuts, penalizing the public because there is no other way of providing them. They are using expert power (Pettigrew, 1973) to win the support of their clientele, attract media attention, and mobilize public opinion, all of which may help influence the government. One way of making this point clear is to make cuts in the most visible services (Levine, 1979; Jick and Murray, 1982). Another tactic is to run up a large deficit, which can then be cited as a clear indication that, in providing much-needed services, the organization has been unable to balance its budget. This strategy has been used with some success by Quebec hospitals. Quebec universities have also incurred large deficits and used them to argue that the entire system is underfunded — projected deficits for May 1987 of a total of $128.7 million, more than 10 per cent of their government revenues. It appears to bring in, at least, promises of future relief.

Playing the PR game
Interest groups must believe in the organization's credibility (Pettigrew, 1973) if requests for support are to be successful. They need to be convinced that the university has served a valuable purpose that is jeopardized by budget cuts. Managing credibility requires a careful balance between the reputation of the institution and the damage being inflicted on it by budget cuts: administrators want to draw attention to the latter, but they do not want to cast doubt on the former. Consequently, Canadian universities usually make statements to the effect that quality has not yet been compromised by cuts, but will be if they continue — declining standards are always 'just around the corner' (Skolnik and Rowen, 1984). In this way, administrators hope to avoid alienating their clientele by suggesting that quality has already suffered.

Playing the numbers game
Information control is an important power source since it allows the selective release of supportive information (Pettigrew, 1973). Managing visibility and public relations primarily involves the effective use of the media. Universities will, however, also need some 'objective' data to support their case, particularly in negotiations with funding agencies. Political decisions are validated with reference to the 'facts' — data that are marshalled to justify the outcome. Institutions are therefore advised to collect the statistics which support their cause and use them in negotiations (Hardy, 1985b). In this case, it involves details on the magnitude of cuts, cost, and numbers of students over time — tangible evidence of the damage done by cutbacks. Universities in different Canadian provinces tend to use different comparative statistics, relying on those that 'prove' their arguments of underfunding most effectively.

Playing the networking game
Universities also need political access to individuals who wield power (Pettigrew, 1973). Publicly funded universities have to deal with various levels of government and have to identify the key interest groups (Hardy, 1985b). In effect, they need to discern where the power lies — with the civil servants,

ministers, or a mediating body such as the University Grants Committee (now the UFC) in Britain. Political strategies and lobbying should be directed at wherever the power lies.

Playing the conspiracy game

Universities must solicit the involvement of other interest groups by coalition building (Hardy, 1985b) to obtain group support (Pettigrew, 1973). A campaign that incorporates a group of universities emphasizing the detrimental effects of cuts on the system as a whole tends to carry more weight than a single institution. Consensus may be difficult to engineer, however, if declining resources put institutions in competition with each other and create conflict rather than cooperation (Hardy, 1985b). Interviews with university and government officials in three Canadian provinces support the view that cooperation has been relatively weak—universities tend to be split by conflicting self-interests and find it difficult to build enduring or effective coalitions.

Political turnaround alone does not solve the problems associated with declining resources. It is, however, particularly appropriate in publicly funded universities since it increases the degree of strategic choice. It has also been used by private universities to attract donors and students.

Summary and conclusions

This reading has argued that managing turnaround is both an economic and a political process. It has used the example of universities because they represent a form of 'ideal type', in which both the economic and political pressures can be seen. In order to balance these pressures and effect a successful turnaround, it has been argued that university administrators need to pay attention to culture, incremental change, and their externally oriented defence. Universities are not unique organizations. All managers in all spheres, including business, face similar pressures during turnaround.

Recent research in the business literature has drawn attention to the link between an effective organizational culture and success. In which case, managers need to think carefully about actions that will damage that culture and, in the long term, threaten the viability of the enterprise. Second, while some businesses will have to move quickly to impose quantum solutions to decline because of the prevalence of economic pressures, there are other situations where managers have some economic room for manoeuvre, which they can use to reduce the negative effects of change (Hardy, 1989). Third, the political defence of a threatened domain is equally applicable to the business sector—one of the best documented cases is that of the tobacco firms (Miles and Cameron, 1982). By using these defensive measures proactively, managers can increase their options to introduce change gradually and protect culture.

All of these actions will require political skills. The problem with the economic approach to turnaround is that it emphasizes analytic skills, and devalues the importance of social and political expertise (Lyles and Lenz, 1982). If managers are to manage turnaround successfully, they will need to combine both political and economic considerations, and learn how to manage culture, overcome resistance, maintain morale and commitment, and resolve conflict.

References

Astley, W. G. and C. J. Fombrun (1983) 'Collective strategy: social ecology of organizational environments', *Academy of Management Review*, **8**(4), 576–87.
Bilbeault, D. B. (1982) *Corporate Turnaround*, McGraw-Hill, New York.

Bozeman, B. and J. D. Straussman (1984) 'Publicness and resource management strategies' in R. H. Hall and R. G. Quinn (eds) *Organizational Theory and Public Policy*, Sage, Beverly Hills.

Chaffee, E. E. (1984) 'Successful strategic management in small private colleges', *Journal of Higher Education*, **55**(2) (March/April), 212–41.

Chaffee, E. E. and W. G. Tierney (1988) *Collegiate Culture and Leadership Strategies*, Macmillan, New York.

Child, J. (1972) 'Organizational structure, environment and performance: the role of strategic choice', *Sociology*, **6**(1), 1–22.

Davis, J. L. and A. W. Morgan (1981) *Institutional Change Under Conditions of Instability and Contraction*, Leverhulme Project on the Future of British Higher Education.

Dowling, J. and J. Pfeffer (1983) 'Organizational legitimacy: social values and organizational behaviour', *Pacific Sociological Review*, **18**(1), 122–35.

Emerson, R. M. (1962) 'Power-dependence relations', *American Sociological Review*, **27**, 31–41.

Hambrick, D. C. and S. M. Schecter (1983) 'Turnaround strategies for mature industrial-product business units', *Academy of Management Journal*, **26**(2), 231–48.

Hardy, C. (1983) 'The management of university cutbacks: politics, planning and participation', *Canadian Journal of Higher Education*, **6**(4), 407–33.

Hardy, C. (1985a) *Managing Organizational Closure*, Gower, Aldershot.

Hardy, C. (1985b) 'Resisting cutbacks: some issues facing public administrators', *Canadian Public Administration*, **18**(4), 531–49.

Hardy, C. (1985c) 'The nature of unobtrusive power', *Journal of Management Studies*, **22**(4), 384–99.

Hardy, C. (1986) 'The contribution of political science to organizational behaviour', in J. Lorsch (ed.), *The Handbook of Organizational Behavior*, Prentice-Hall, Englewood Cliffs, New Jersey.

Hardy, C. (1987a) 'Using content, context and process to manage university cutbacks', *Canadian Journal of Higher Education*, **17**(1), 65–82.

Hardy, C. (1987b) 'Turnaround strategies in universities', *Planning for Higher Education*, **16**(1), 9–23.

Hardy, C. (1989) *Strategies for Retrenchment and Turnaround*, De Gruyter, Berlin.

Hardy, C., A. Langley, H. Mintzberg and J. Rose (1983) 'Strategy formation in the university setting', *The Review of Higher Education*, **6**(4), 407–33.

Hofer, C. W. (1980) 'Turnaround strategies', *Journal of Business Strategy*, **1**, 19–31.

Hrebiniak, L. G. and W. F. Joyce (1985) 'Organizational adaptation: strategic choice and environmental determinism', *Administrative Science Quarterly*, **30**, 336–49.

Huff, A. S. (1980) 'Organizations as political systems: implications for diagnosis, change and stability', in T. G. Cummings (ed.), *Systems Theory for Organization Development*, Wiley, London.

Jick, T. D. and V. V. Murray (1982) 'The management of hard times: budget cutbacks in public sector organizations', *Organizational Studies*, **3**, 141–69.

Kanter, R. M. (1983) *The Change Masters: Innovation for Productivity in the American Corporation*, New York: Simon and Schuster, 1983.

Keim, G. D., C. P. Zeithaml and B. D. Baysinger (1984) 'Corporate strategy and legislative decision making: a review and contingency approach', *Sloan Management Review*, **25**(3), 53–61.

Khandwalla, P. N. (1983–4) 'Turnaround Management of Mismanaged Complex Organizations', *International Studies of Management & Organizational*, **13**(4), 42–62.

Levine, C. H. (1979) 'More on cutback management: hard questions for hard times', *Public Administration Review*, **39**(2), 179–83.

Lindblom, C. E. (1959) 'The science of muddling through', *Public Administration Review*, **19**, 91–9.

Lyles, M. A. and R. T. Lenz (1982) 'Managing the planning process: a field side of planning', *Strategic Management Journal*, **3**, 105–118.

Melin, L. (1985) 'Strategies on managing turnaround', *Long Range Planning*, **18**(11), 80–6.

Miles, R. H. and K. S. Cameron (1982) *Coffin Nails and Corporate Strategies*, Prentice-Hall, Englewood Cliffs, N.J.

Mortimer, K. and M. L. Tierney (1979) *The Three 'R's' of the Eighties: Reduction, Reallocation and Retrenchment*, Washington, D.C.: American Association for Higher Education.

Parker, B. (1987) *Discriminants for Recovery from Decline*, paper presented at the Annual Meeting of the Association for the Study of Higher Education, San Diego, Feb.

Parker, B. and R. Zammuto (1986) *Institutional Responses to Enrollment Decline: The Role of Perceptions*, paper presented at the Annual Meeting of the Association for the Study of Higher Education, San Antonio, Texas, Feb.

Pearson, M. (1986) *Managing for Excellence or Walk the Jarratt Way*, paper presented at the 8th European Forum of the Association of Institutional Research, Loughborough.

Pettigrew, A. M. (1973) *The Politics of Organizational Decision-Making*, Tavistock, London.

Pettigrew, A. M. (1976) 'Conference review: issues of change', in P. Warr (ed.), *Personal Goals and Work Design*, Wiley, London.

Pettigrew, A. M. (1984) *Some Limits of Executive Power in Creating Strategic Change*, paper presented at the Symposium on the Functioning of Executive Power, Case Western Reserve University, Cleveland, Oct.

Pettigrew, A. M. (1985) *The Awakening Giant: Continuity and Change in ICI*, Basil Blackwell, Oxford.

Pfeffer, J. (1981) *Power in Organizations*, Pitman, Marshfield, Mass.

Pfeffer, J. and G. R. Salancik (1978) *The External Control of Organizations*, Harper & Row, New York.

Quinn, J. B. (1978) 'Strategic change: logical incrementalism', *Sloan Management Review*, **19**, 21–7.

Quinn, J. B. (1980) 'Managing strategic change', *Sloan Management Review*, **21**(4), 3–20.

Randall, R. (1973) 'Influence of environmental support and policy space on organizational behaviour' *Administrative Science Quarterly*, **18**, 236–47.

Schendel, D. G. and G. R. Patton (1976) 'Corporate stagnation and turnaround', *Journal of Economics and Business*, **28**(3), 236–41.

Schendel, D. G., G. R. Patton and J. Riggs (1976) 'Corporate turnaround strategies: a study of profit decline and recovery', *Journal of General Management*, **3**, 3–11.

Skolnik, M. L. and N. S. Rowen (1984) *Please Sir, I Want Some More: Canadian Universities and Financial Restraint*, Toronto: Ontario Institute for Studies in Education.

Tierney, W. G. (1988) 'Organizational culture in higher education', *Journal of Higher Education*, **59**(1), 2–21.

Walford, G. (1987) *Restructuring Universities: Politics and Power in the Management of Change*, Croom Helm, London.

Weick, K. E. (1976) 'Educational organizations as loosely coupled systems', *Administrative Science Quarterly*, **21**, 1–19.

Zammuto, R. F. (1988) 'Organizational adaptation: some implications of organizational ecology for strategic choice' *Journal of Management Studies*, **25**(2), 105–20.

Zammuto, R. F. and K. S. Cameron (1985) 'Environmental decline and organizational response', *Research in Organizational Behavior*, **7**, 223–62.

CASE STUDY
6

The role of internal consultants: managing resistance to change

Vicky Russell

The company and its culture

RV Winkle was the UK operating base of a successful European company which had been a leader over many decades in a mature industry. Formerly it had been able to remain indifferent to external economic and political pressures due to its sheer size and its domination of dependent and passive markets. But now these markets were experiencing economic and political turbulence which were having a knock-on effect on Winkle's buying capabilities. In relation to industrial competition, the company could also be described as being in a somewhat uncomfortable ostrich-like position, pretending not to see the larger and obvious potential overseas. In addition there were increasing difficulties in obtaining the raw material of the product. These were leading the company into pioneering engineering developments, and thus new organizational processes, which were risky to implement (and which cut down profit margins).

Possible changes in management strategy and style had not been addressed, however, and the company continued to emphasize bureaucratic and centralized control procedures together with an authoritarian and paternalistic management style. This no longer appeared to be appropriate given the many changes which were rapidly taking place. There were a handful of new senior managers appearing in the company who were more sympathetic to newer and more flexible ways of doing things, but they were trying to work alongside the old-style authoritarian managers who still made up the majority of the company's management. Since the resulting conflicts were suppressed by the predominant organizational culture in favour of a rather elegant and gentlemanly style of surface consensus and compromise, the result was tension and unacknowledged dysfunctions. The organization was hamstrung by its conformity to established ways of doing things, and by its strong emphasis on 'followership' and not rocking the boat.

The situation

At this time, the Winkle Board, the company's strategic team, had briefed Lesley Biven, an internal organizational development consultant, to manage a change process. Her area of expertise was the development of innovative and entrepreneurial capabilities in mature, bureaucratic industries, particularly those facing technological and environmental change.

The consultancy process was heralded by a New Year message from the MD to every one of the 3000 or so staff, encouraging a change 'from our traditional bureaucratic culture to an entrepreneurial one more in keeping with the company's present day challenges'. Views on what was meant by 'entrepreneurial' varied widely, although everyone agreed that the present culture was certainly bureaucratic. Lesley picked up from the confidential interpretations of both managers and directors that although the MD's wishes would of course be supported and respected, there was some bewilderment at the suggestion that things should somehow be done differently—other than perhaps a shift or two in the reward system. One line manager unconsciously put the company's dilemma into words: 'Of course, we're all a hundred per cent behind entrepreneurial change in this company, as long as we don't have to do anything differently.' After all, this was not only a cradle to grave employer, but it was a company where any deviation in established practice was made very difficult by the detailed instructions of the company manual which was to hand in every office and operating area.

Lesley Biven wondered seriously whether such institutionalized and unchallenged resistance to change would prove impossible to overcome. She knew that you could take a horse to water, but might not be able to get it to drink. But the Board had been enthusiastic in obtaining her services, and the consultancy brief included an expectation that she would run a survey throughout the company over the coming year to provide a diagnosis of its present social and technical condition, and that this was to be discussed by all members of staff. She had also agreed to use the survey process to mirror back to the company its style and culture so that people could get a picture of how they behaved in their day-to-day operations. She thus began the New Year with a succession of separate meeting with her two main clients, the directors of the large and influential Personnel and Engineering departments, both of whom were Board members.

The Personnel Department

The previous Director of Personnel had been trying to introduce new ways of working for some time, but had been forced to resign over a year ago due to a nervous breakdown caused, according to some people in the department, by lack of support at senior levels for the changes he was trying to implement. Two middle managers had held the fort for almost a year until the arrival of Tim Jones as Director, a lively and articulate high-flyer brought in from an overseas posting to lift the Personnel Department by its bootstraps. He was independent of mind and hence cautiously regarded by his new colleagues on the Winkle Board, but he and the Director of Engineering already had a sneaking regard for each other's capability. Tim Jones's management style was unusual for RV Winkle. He walked the shop floor, he communicated with people at all levels and sought their opinions on present practices and future changes. He exuded a sense of energy and commitment to raising both his department and the company out of the slough of complacency and inertia as he saw it.

He expressed himself ready to work developmentally with the consultant for an initial year on the agreed company survey and produce a diagnosis of the Department's present condition and a plan for proposed change. So keen was Tim Jones to enable the MD's wish for a more entrepreneurial company to come about, that a memo from him asking for a meeting was on Lesley Biven's desk on her first morning of this assignment.

Over the months that they worked together, Lesley Biven saw him gain the trust and commitment of his new department, who described him as 'different from the usual kind of manager and because of that inspiring'. He obtained survey results which particularly highlighted the lack of trust and respect that the majority of staff had for managers in the department. His management team, which included the two caretaker managers, were obviously surprised and bewildered by the survey results but he gave them time and opportunity to talk this through with himself, all the rest of the staff and the consultant. A capable and senior personnel officer with some thirteen years' experience in the company explained to Lesley Biven why her commitment to the company had been draining away:

> Apart from Tim Jones no manager has ever taken any notice of my opinions. I'm working for clients in the Engineering function who are working long shifts in hostile and difficult locations which I'm supposed to be facilitating, yet I'm expected to deal with them by the book as if they're still doing regular nine-to-five office jobs. That's too slow and inflexible and only suitable for the most routine cases—it ends up with these new type of engineers thinking I'm the slow and inflexible one who had caused all the delays and paperwork. Certainly the Personnel Department has a name in the company for being inflexible and bureaucratic, but my suggestions to senior management to make fairly simple changes in our systems are either ignored or ruled out. I've been thinking seriously of leaving the company to be honest, and I'm not the only one, but I'll stay to see what Tim Jones can achieve.

This senior employee had been refused any help by senior managers in the previous couple of years to follow a professional development course. Instead, she had funded herself for both evening and correspondence courses to obtain post-experience qualifications which were not being used in her work with the company.

Tim Jones could see he needed to make fundamental changes if his department was going to develop from its present position of low morale and poor service. At the end of the year, having thoroughly concluded all but the implementation of the survey project, he invited Lesley Biven to agree a further year's contract to help him manage a cultural change process in his department and to advise on management development. He confided to her, 'This UK part of the company is so inert, it's like a headless corpse. I'm not impressed by the fact that, at management levels at least, ways of doing things seem to be reverted and unquestioned despite the evidence that they are actually tying us down unnecessarily. The MD is right. We do need to be far less bureaucratic and more entrepreneurial and adventurous, but we can't let go of the old ways it seems.'

The Engineering Department

The Engineering Director, Nigel Shaw, was an experienced and urbane operator with a number of years international management in the company. He confessed himself 'more of a technical than a management expert' to Lesley Biven, but showed genuine interest and curiosity in any new approaches to organizational management. After a number of useful conversations about the proposed process and content of the survey, they agreed a written contract in which his two operational managers also participated. Nigel Shaw was a clear and decisive line manager, and specified what he did and didn't want done in his department. Due to his frequent commitments overseas, he delegated line-management responsibility to George Hackett, one of his two operational managers.

Although just past retirement age, George Hackett had been asked by the Winkle Board to stay on in his management post for a further two years. This was much resented throughout the engineering function since he was seen to be blocking the career path of a number of equally good younger men. Although he was respected technically, there was an awareness that his degree qualifications were some thirty-five years old and that the pace of technological change made this an important factor for the department. One of the blocked younger men complained, 'Although George Hackett is technically respected, there are others equally good who haven't got as far. He's a member of the old school of management which persists around here. He only tolerates "yes-men" around him and has been known to scapegoat fellow professionals and consultants if they looked like getting in his way.'

His management activities, once Nigel Shaw was out of the way, made it clear that he intended to use the consultant and the survey project to obtain his own political goals. He made it clear to Lesley Biven that he intended to work to a revised contract to include certain of the things that Nigel Shaw had specifically proscribed. He attempted in his regular Reports to the Director and others to provide only partial and edited information about the project's progress and to ensure that meetings of the project team were only held at times when the Director was overseas. He made it clear to the consultant that he expected her to work to his personal brief which contradicted the fundamentals of the contract she and Nigel Shaw had agreed. When she explained that she could not ethically change from the agreed contract (unless George Hackett was able to influence Nigel Shaw to change it) he reacted with anger and threats and made it clear that he expected her to concede to his demands and instructions as if she were a member of his own staff.

He began setting up numerous meetings with the consultant and the project team—always making sure that Nigel Shaw was unable to attend—to which he invariably arrived late, hostile and unbriefed. And although he himself had chosen the project team, he began to chop and change its membership and its brief so that commitment and team development were prevented. At this time he was also beginning to show signs of deep hostility in relation to the Personnel Director, Tim Jones, who was by now making an impact at Board level with the support of fellow directors such as Nigel Shaw.

It was now nearly Christmas, and the Engineering survey project was already a couple of months behind schedule due to George Hackett's unwillingness to run the survey as agreed with Nigel Shaw. Lesley Biven knew that Nigel Shaw would call her on his return to the UK before Christmas for a report on how things were going.

The dilemma   Lesley Biven was unsure how she should proceed in a way that would meet her own professional standards by serving the needs of the Winkle business and yet not breach the confidences of Nigel Shaw and his deputy, nor involve her in a collusive alliance with George Hackett. While considering the dilemma and the management dysfunction it represented, she turned for a second opinion to a consultancy colleague, to ask what he would do in the circumstances. John Maitland did not mince his words:

'Consultancy work is difficult to get and even more difficult to keep. George Hackett would make a formidable enemy to us as consultants if we don't play along with him. My view is that it was a mistake to make a contract with Nigel Shaw—you should have left yourself free to manipulate a contract with clients—that way no one knows what you're actually expected to do and you don't upset anyone.'

If Lesley Biven was perturbed by these comments, she was even more perturbed when she shortly learned from another senior member of the Engineering Department that John Maitland had been secretly approached by George Hackett with a deal to replace her as consultant in the Engineering Department, and that he had already agreed to this. There were also strong rumours around that Nigel Shaw was imminently to be appointed to a senior post overseas, and would probably be replaced for the time being by George Hackett.

Lesley needed to ponder the comments and behaviour of her fellow consultant, John Maitland. She remembered her early doubts whether there was any real possibility of making an unwilling horse drink water. There was additional reason for concern about RV Winkle since prices for their product were plummeting in the world market due to political factors in the Middle East and elsewhere, but this was a topic which no one seemed willing to raise at senior levels of the company.

A further worrying factor in recent weeks had been an accident at one of the engineering plants which had killed over 30 employees and which indicated equipment failure and poor communications. She decided to seek an interview with the MD to test out his commitment to the vision of 'an innovative and entrepreneurial company'.

Questions

1 In which ways does Tim Jones personify and model a more 'entrepreneurial' style in the company, and how important is he to the MD's commitment to cultural change?

   Is there any significance in the fate of his predecessor in the Director role?

2 In which ways does George Hackett represent resistance to change in this company? Why do you think the Board is keeping him on at senior level after his retirement date while at the same time the MD is advocating change from the traditional culture that George Hackett personifies?

3 Is there dysfunction at the managerial level? If so, what are its main features and how do you think they are impacting on the operational levels of the Engineering Department — on factors such as quality, safety and communications, for example?

4 How far do you think that an ethical approach by business managers and by consultants, is important?

5 If you were Lesley Biven (OD consultant), how would you approach the consulting brief of managing a change process which will develop innovative and entrepreneurial capabilities in RV Winkle Ltd? How would you have handled things differently and why?

6 Would you experience different constraints if you were in the role of an external as opposed to an internal consultant to this company? What would these be? Assess the strengths and weaknesses of both internal and external change efforts?

Electronic Components Ltd: strategies and change[1]

Hugh Gunz

Introduction

Electronic Components Ltd (ECL) is typical of thousands of small-to-medium sized engineering companies in the UK. A wholly owned subsidiary of Intertron Ltd, a diversified multinational manufacturing firm, it has a turnover of £20 million per annum and operates from four sites: its headquarters on the South Coast, two others in the UK and a fourth on the Continent (Figure CS7.1).

Although ECL is entirely profit-responsible under its managing director, Arnold Gresham, it is subject to strong central control from Intertron. The parent company's board must approve any capital expenditure above quite trivial sums, and it is not unknown, for instance, for Intertron's managing director to turn up in person without warning at some remote location demanding to know why stock levels are as high as they are.

Historically, ECL has been involved in the electronics entertainment industry. It designs and makes a particular range of components supplied under sub-contract to manufacturers of consumer electronics products. It has been very successful, with a high share of the UK market. The components themselves are specific to consumer electronics (CE) products. It has been the policy of ECL's customers, the UK manufacturers, not to make these particular components themselves, nor to standardize on their designs. ECL thus had a steady stream of orders coming in for components for many years, each order with its own specific requirements.

Within the UK each incoming order went first to the R&D laboratory, located on the headquarters site, whose job it was to turn the order into a set of working drawings and specifications for the production departments. Although the theoretical principles of the work were simple it had never proved possible to reduce the design work to a set of routine calculations; with each job there was always a large element of trial and error before an acceptable design was produced.

As well as this design work the R&D laboratory was responsible for providing

Figure CS7.1
ECL before reorganization

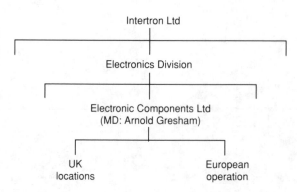

Intertron Ltd

Electronics Division

Electronic Components Ltd
(MD: Arnold Gresham)

UK locations

European operation

a technical service to the production departments, chiefly troubleshooting. This could at times become quite a significant part of the R&D workload, not least because the trial-and-error nature of the technology meant that when problems arose it could take no little skill and time to sort them out. The laboratory was not large, with 30–40 staff, and was often badly stretched to meet the conflicting demands of design and troubleshooting.

The UK R&D laboratory serviced all three UK production facilities, although most of its time was taken up with the one on the same site which was by far the largest. The European operation was self-contained, with its own R&D laboratory producing its own designs for its own production facility.

In the mid 1970s, however, ECL management became concerned at the company's almost total dependence on the CE market. Diversification was clearly needed, and Arnold Gresham set the objective of reducing the firm's dependence on CE to 50 per cent within five years, while retaining its existing share of the CE business. Very soon ECL spotted an opportunity for using its existing technology in an entirely different sector of the domestic appliances market, and New Products group was set up within the R&D laboratory in order to build a range of products to exploit this.

By the mid 1980s ECL had succeeded in reducing its dependence on the CE business to 70 per cent by adopting an aggressive 'first-to-market' strategy with its new products. It was realized from the outset that the company could not rely on patent protection in a new, fast-expanding market, so that it became vital that the R&D engineers developed new products as quickly as possible and that the process of putting them into production should be speedy and troublefree. The self-contained European operation was in Mr Gresham's view conspicuously better at this, and he lost few opportunities to make the point to his local R&D staff.

With the UK CE manufacturing business coming under increasing threat from imports (chiefly Japanese) pressure on ECL's diversification programme progressively increased. In order to improve the effectiveness of the company's innovation programme, Mr Gresham reorganized the business functions, creating five executive posts reporting to him. Each of these was responsible for all activities within a given business function across all locations (Figure CS7.2).

The head of the UK R&D Department, Oliver Smith, was promoted to Technical Director, and his place was taken by a young, highly-successful manager called Simon Davies. A well-qualified engineer, Davies had not worked in R&D before, but had been moved between a number of locations of the parent company, Intertron, in order to develop him for eventual senior management posts.

Figure CS7.2
ECL after reorganization

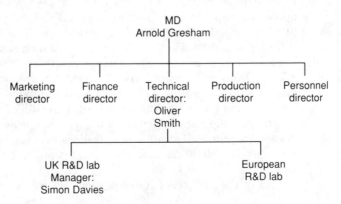

Meanwhile, the diversification programme was running into trouble. New products were taking too long to emerge from the R&D laboratory, in Mr Gresham's opinion. On more than one occasion he became exasperated at the engineers' tendency to continue to 'tinker about' with the design of a new product long after they had produced something which was in fact at the point where it could be manufactured and sold. He had been forced into arbitrarily stopping development of the products in question, telling the engineers that once the design was in production and earning cash they could carry on improving it to produce a Mark Two, which could supersede the first model. As a former production manager Mr Gresham was critical of the unrealistic view the R&D engineers took at the time they needed for their work, and was glad that Davies was making it his business to change this.

In this already difficult situation management became seriously alarmed to find that R&D engineers were beginning to leave the firm in large numbers. In one year alone turnover (excluding natural wastage) almost reached 25 per cent, with serious consequences for the morale and work of the laboratory. Something had to be done if ECL's diversification programme was not to be seriously threatened.

Technical management's diagnosis of the situation

The Technical Director, Oliver Smith, and his successor as R&D Manager, Simon Davies, were deeply worried by the high turnover amongst the R&D staff, although they could readily understand why it might have happened. Their explanation was as follows.

The parent company places tremendous stress on the financial performance of its subsidiaries, so that ECL feels itself under great pressure to be, in Mr Smith's words, a 'production-oriented cash generator'. This puts the laboratory under great pressure to provide a troubleshooting service as and when needed to the production department, generally seen as the key part of the company. Not only does this demand for service constantly interfere with the laboratory's work of developing new products, but it tends to devalue innovatory work in the eyes of everyone. As a result the engineers come to feel that their professional contribution has been downgraded by the company into merely that of the troubleshooter. This professional dissatisfaction is exacerbated by the nature of the main products (the CE components), which are subject to very tight design specifications. One component looks much like another, reinforcing the lack of innovative atmosphere in the laboratory. It is hard to feel that one's professional expertise is being put to good use under such circumstances.

The parent company holds a very tight control over ECL's capital investment programme. However Intertron's behaviour is sometimes apparently capricious, turning down plans to which it has previously agreed in principle and so increasing the general air of uncertainty in the company. A further manifestation of centralized control is rigid salary grades, which limit the material and status rewards management can give the engineers. With no freedom to award 'perks' for good performance there is reduced flexibility for motivating staff to work hard to respond to the changing demands on ECL. This situation is made more difficult to change by the insistence of the trades unions on job evaluation principles covering all grades. Sometimes the only way a good engineer can be paid more is by rewriting this job description, a lengthy, tedious and often unsuccessful procedure.

Finally, the engineers have no particularly exciting career prospects to compensate for these shortcomings. Unless they changed disciplines and ceased to be engineers there is no promotion route open for them other than laboratory line management, culminating in Mr Smith's job. The parent company does not, on the whole, regard engineering skills as transferable between its different businesses, cutting off another promotion route. When engineers go on Intertron courses and find out about attractive career opportunities elsewhere in the Group, they resent the implication that they are thought of as only capable of working in ECL and become suspicious that viable career possibilities are being deliberately withheld from them.

The best engineers are not prepared to put up with these conditions of work, and in due course leave. Their vacancies are filled by less able engineers, blocking the promotion paths for good junior staff, increasing the frustrations of the juniors and making it more likely that in turn they will leave as well.

Although salaries are low by comparison with other employers neither Mr Smith nor Mr Davies feel that this is a major factor. Bad business conditions mean that the labour market is very tight, and anyway, given the parent company's salary policies, there is nothing they can do about it.

The engineers' diagnosis of the situation

Many of the engineers disagreed with the views of top technical management concerning the importance of salary levels as a factor in the turnover of R&D engineers at ECL. The younger staff felt themselves particularly hard done by, and found that their only real chance of a rise was to leave for a better-paid job (so-called 'leap-frogging'). They did not seem to think that the labour market was nearly as tight as did their senior management. The more senior engineers did not feel the money problem nearly as acutely, and rarely gave it as an important reason for their (or their peers') leaving.

While the engineers resented the way they were treated by the production department, they found the engineering content of their work very satisfying. It provided variety and interest, and a change to work in a small, tightly knit organization where personal relationships were friendly and cooperative. Promotion prospects were not on the whole a serious concern. Apart from anything else, there was a widespread feeling that the technical expertise necessary to do Mr Smith's or Mr Davies's job took many years to acquire, and very few of the staff felt technically competent to manage at such a level.

The engineers were concerned about the commercial success of their designs. On one occasion Mr Smith had given a presentation to the laboratory staff on ECL's business plans, but although they had found this very interesting it had not been repeated. A constant source of irritation had always been the way in which projects would be stopped without anyone knowing why, and then perhaps restarted some months later just when people had forgotten where they had got to.

Their difficulties with the production department were put down largely to the ignorance of the production staff about what it took to develop a new product. This ignorance was amply demonstrated by the way in which, although production management complained about the speed at which the laboratory was able to work, they usually refused to allow production equipment to be used for essential test runs, claiming that this interfered with production schedules. What, the engineers asked, did the production department think they were going to be making in the future if they constantly prevented new products from being tested? The engineers agreed that the European operation was because advanced production techniques were being used which the UK production management refused point blank to consider.

The real problem, however, was nothing to do with these issues. For many years Mr Smith had run the laboratory in the style of, in his words, 'the involved engineer'. Deeply respected as an engineer among his staff, he kept closely in touch with staff at all levels and was always ready to discuss technical problems with them and provide advice when it was wanted. Although there was a line-management structure under Mr Smith, nobody put a great deal of emphasis on it. Good working relationships were based on a shared interest at all levels in the technical nature of the work, and engineers often referred back to the laboratory in those days as having a 'family atmosphere'.

When Simon Davies took over the management of the laboratory the atmosphere changed dramatically. As an outsider to the laboratory he came like a bolt from the blue, ordering a complete cleanout of everything that was not going to be used for the next six months—a job which stopped all other work for three days. Systems were tightened up, and communication, to everyone's consternation, became strictly through the line. Suddenly engineers found that the laboratory manager was not keeping in touch with them on their work. When he did, it was usually in formal meetings which he was usually too busy to be able to arrange at short notice. The same often applied when people wanted to see him about personnel matters. It became harder to find out what was going on: there seemed to be a much greater tendency to restrict information on a 'need-to-know' basis.

There were exceptions to this rule, however. Mr Davies took a particular interest in the work of the New Product group, and in one instance took over the role of project leader himself since there was no one else available. Unfortunately some events which flowed from this only increased the resentment of the laboratory staff at his managerial style, since at one point he used his authority to stop all other work going on in the drawing office in order to progress his project. Although he was well informed technically on the New Products work, it was clear, however, that on the CE component side of the laboratory's work his technical knowledge was comparatively weak. It was generally known that although he was seen by the company as a rising star, his previous job had been managing a routine testing laboratory, and his attempts to pick up technical know-how about CE components emphazied to the engineers a serious weakness in his ability to do his job effectively.

It was not long before resentment was beginning to build up. Another of Mr Davies's early moves had been to force out two engineers who, by common consent, were low performers. Although the staff agreed with the decision, it meant that other personnel changes he made were often interpreted as directed towards easing others out of the laboratory. His remoteness (by comparison with Mr Smith's style) exacerbated this problem. Other staff began to leave, and staff turnover began to climb dramatically. Looking back on events, both those who left and those who stayed agreed that a major reason for the resignations was the change in the way the laboratory was managed.

Note   1. The people and events in this case study are real, although names have been altered to preserve confidentiality.

Questions   1 Comment on the apparent lack of success in achieving and sustaining the change process of diversification. Were any parts of the change agenda successful? Why?

2 To what extent do you think the diversification strategy was appropriate to ECL's continued performance and operation in the engineering industry? What are the relationships between strategy and structure in this case? What other alternative strategies were open to ECL?

3 Explain why technical management and the engineers see the problems differently. What could cause this? What are the most and least important causal factors in your list?

4 You are called in as an external consultant. Detail your agenda for handling the situation in ECL. How will you address, for example, high labour turnover, lack of interfunctional knowledge and trust as well as the different internal organizational cultures? What would be your strategy for detailing proposed changes to Intertron Ltd?

Organizational structures and change: a case study of Compo

Diana Winstanley and Arthur Francis

The organization

Compo is a large British unionized multinational corporation. It produces electrical and mechanical components for a range of industries in the world market. Its main market is the automotive industry. This market had once been relatively secure, demand led, and with average growth rates of about 6 per cent per annum. It had now reached maturity and Compo was experiencing a decline in market share. In response to this the company was moving into different sectors of the automotive market, and developing systems rather than just components. It employs 65 000 people worldwide, 45 000 of them in the UK. Its turnover is over £1.5b a year with pre-tax profits somewhat below the industry average. This case study concentrates on one of its British operating units, Compo LEC, within the context of corporate level change at Compo.

The problem identified

Senior managers at the corporate level believe there is a serious problem related to increasingly stiff competition in the marketplace. Compo's profits have been spread patchily across its areas of business and some of its main areas of business have declined in turnover and profitability. Organizational changes have been brought in against a backdrop of contraction in size. A corporate level taskforce was set up to investigate Compo's competitive position. This produced a number of recovery achievement strategies where each part of the business was compared to the best competition in that area. The taskforce found that although Compo compared favourably on product quality and had a strong emphasis on manufacturing competence, it was very vulnerable in its manufacturing costs and product lead-times and costs. Costs and lead-times were intricately linked, partly because bad organization of the design process resulted in the lengthening of lead-times which increased costs. This was both because of the length of time costs were incurred and the inefficiencies which ensued as money was thrown at problems in the run-up to launch dates to recover lost time.

At the same time as setting up the taskforce two key powerful managers were recruited. One was an influential figure in education who had developed new methodologies in manufacturing, Chris Kent, and the other, Roger Moore, was from a company which had recently undergone many organizational changes in which he had been closely involved. Chris Kent was put in charge of pioneering the manufacturing changes and he introduced just-in-time and modular production among a number of other changes. Roger Moore was put in charge of the changes in the design area, and he was very keen on introducing methods and organizational arrangements which had become standard in his last company and which he believed reflected a move towards 'Japanese practices'. He was particularly interested in shaking up the organization of the design process and to introduce the 'multi-functional engineer'.

This case study is about how Roger Moore devised and implemented organizational changes in the design area as a solution to the company's competitiveness problem, high costs and long lead-times.

A history of organizational change in design at Compo LEC

Traditionally the company had operated using a functional organization structure. Compo LEC, however, was set up as the model for the future development of the organizational structure and was the most advanced British operating unit in pioneering organizational changes recommended by both the taskforce and Roger Moore. The taskforce had recommended setting up a loosely coordinated matrix structure. At Compo LEC designers and development engineers were all based in their functional areas and discipline departments and worked on projects within these departments. Design and development work was done by teams but these teams had part-time members drawn from a number of functions. Each team was led by a project engineer who had responsibility for time and costs but technical accountability remained in the functions. This proved to be very successful and as a result a more 'balanced' matrix structure was set up. The functions remained intact but technical accountability moved over to the project engineer who now had responsibility for all aspects of the project within the engineering context—cost, time and technically. Project engineers were supplemented by project planners and managers. This was found to work very well.

Roger Moore now proposed to pursue this route further with a totally new organization called 'the Business Management Organization'.

The new Business Management Organization (BMO)

Changes in organizational structure at Compo and particularly Compo LEC, the flagship of the operating units in this area, came from above. The ideas were sown by the taskforce and cultivated by Roger Moore. He took the findings of the taskforce and his experiences from his previous company and became the champion in developing and implementing the Business Management Organization. What had begun as an enquiry into problems of competitiveness became Moore's crusade to change the organizational structures and culture. He had strong views on organizational change and its role in solving lead-time and cost problems in the design and engineering area. He believed that 'the British desire to rush into hardware is the Achilles heel of British industry'. He wanted to overturn the design-and-build experimental methodology by creating more teamwork up at the front end of the design process in order to reduce the number of design iterations later on and costly change to the hardware. To do this required a move away from a functionally-based philosophy and towards a team or project based one. This idea being developed at the top had then to be sold to those in the operating units.

Some organizations resisted this change and were reluctant to adopt Moore's ideas. At Compo LEC they had already adopted a matrix structure and they decided to move a step further in adopting the new Business Management Organization. In this, each team had a team leader who reported directly to the General Manager. Each team member was either a full-time, part-time or contract member of the team, with most sitting and working in the teams. Team members were therefore taken out of the functions and these remained in a more limited fashion and also reported direct to the General Manager (see Figure CS8.1(a)(b)).

In association with this Roger Moore was pushing the move towards the 'multinational engineer' (MFE). At the time of the change all those listed in Figure CS8.2 were involved in project teams. His first move towards the

Figure CS8.1
Organizational
structure at Compo
(a) Before change
(b) After change:
introduction of BMO

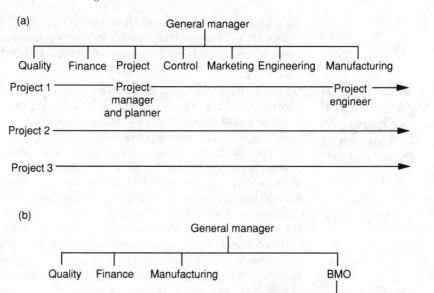

MFE was to propose a gradual merging of the conceptual engineers (designers) and the experimental engineers (development).

Figure CS8.2
Business
management team
representation

Staff	Full-time members	Part-time members	Sub-contract
Buying		*	*
Conceptual design	*	*	*
Cost estimating		*	
Customer engineering	*	*	
Experimental design	*	*	*
Fitters/testers	*	*	
Industrial engineers			*
Manufacturing development		*	*
Marketing		*	
Materials engineering			*
Quality engineers		*	*
Sample manufacture			*
Service		*	

Note: Sub-contract means services bought from elsewhere inside the organization and not outside the organization.

Questions   Imagine you represent the senior management team at Compo LEC and are currently introducing the new BMO into your organization. You have been asked to develop a position paper to report to Roger Moore and Compo Corporate on the implementation of the new BMO. You will be presenting this paper at a seminar for all the senior managers of all the British operating units of Compo. You have been picked as the flagship for the new organizational changes and Roger Moore looks to you to provide guidance to the other units on how to implement these changes. In particular you are asked to report on the following areas:

1 The benefits of moving towards this BMO to improve company competitiveness.

2 Potential pitfalls and drawbacks with the new BMO and how to overcome these.

3 Propose a detailed plan for implementation, and comment on issues and problems raised.

Part V
The Environment

The British business environment

Introduction

In Part V, we examine the interrelationships between organizations and their environments. To do this, we shall look at the role of the manager as an individual 'translator' of environmental events (such as market trends or changes) for his or her organization. We shall also look at how we might best describe and classify different environments (Chapter 17).

Part V will also cover some of the key events in the business environment, such as the OPEC oil crisis, the development and continuation of a market economy under Margaret Thatcher's administration, with privatization and deregulation as key parts of this process.

Translating the environment into corporate action

The role of the manager

The traditional role of the manager as detailed by Fayol (1949), Urwick (1943) and Barnard (1938) is fourfold:

1 planning—creating a framework for future decisions
2 organizing—getting the right resources together and developing an appropriate organizational structure to divide up the tasks
3 directing—achieving tasks either individually or through delegation to others
4 controlling—maintaining performance levels by monitoring and evaluation

This is also how many managers see the essence of their role. However, a substantial number of studies in Sweden, England and North America point to the manager's actual behaviour as being very different from the four elements described above. This research includes Carlson's (1951) study of Swedish managers (the very first of the 'diary' studies of what managers actually do); Stewart's (1967) study of British managers (using the same diary method); Sayles's (1964) and Mintzberg's (1973) studies of American managers, which both used a method of observation rather than asking managers to keep a record of their daily lives.

The most noticeable feature of this research is its high level of agreement over what managers actually do. Putting together the findings, managers:

- *work long hours*   The number of hours worked increases with seniority and when managers have more general rather than functional responsibility.
- *are highly interactive*   A typical day contains several hundred brief interactions. Working on one item for more than half an hour is very rare. As rank increases, the number of interactions increases, but the fragmented nature of the job remains.
- *have to cope with highly variable tasks*   Managers have to cope equally well with paperwork, meetings (both scheduled and unscheduled), telephone calls, visits, ceremonial functions and managing by walking about.
- *communicate mostly by word*   Around 75 per cent of communication is verbal. Many managers actually prefer verbal data such as hearsay, gossip or general feelings. Such data are immediate, accessible and can be acted upon before it is too late and gossip becomes fact. Information by post, or by

written reports comes very much in second place in informing the manager about what is going on internally and externally to the business.
- *use lots of contact points to gather information*   Managers continually exchange verbal information with others. Most of this occurs within the organization, although as rank increases the number of verbal information points outside the organization increase. Information is traded across all levels of the hierarchy, with superiors, peers and subordinates. Most managers spend more time collecting and trading information than they do making decisions.

Even this short list should convince you that managers really do not spend their time in ways that are significantly different from their predecessors years before the genesis of managerial sciences. Managers do not scan the environment, collect structured batches of information, evaluate alternative courses of action and then make decisions. Instead, they collect information 'on the hoof', in a haphazard and mostly informal way. They make decisions quickly, often on the basis of hearsay rather than fact. Finally, managers do not know themselves how they spend their time! According to Mintzberg (1973), managers think that they spend more time than they actually do scrutinizing technical reports, assessing special projects and making thoughtful and reflective decisions.

Significant events in the British business environment in the last ten years

Knowing how the manager acts in practice is one part of the jigsaw. We also need to know what are the major stimuli and events which surround that action and how they may have shaped it to some extent. Managers constantly operate in ambiguous and imprecise contexts. It is hardly surprising that we see a heavy predisposition towards verbal and 'soft' data for translating what is happening in the wider environment into concrete organizational decisions. The number of major events in Britain over the last ten years have created a very different environment for most managers of most organizations. Certainly, it is an environment which managers of fifteen or twenty years ago would find both strange and fast-changing.

The following description is not meant to be exhaustive. That is a task for business historians. The key events described here, however, are picked for the immediacy of their impact upon managers. They demand that active decisions are taken internally in most organizations to cope with and adapt to the changing conditions these events dictate. The key to many of the significant events (although by no means all of them) lies in the election of a Conservative government in 1979 which was to last throughout and beyond the next ten years. The nature of the operating environment was radically changed over this period.

Significant events which can be directly related to government actions and policies include:

1 The deregulation of many industries, allowing the entry of competitors and the operation of free market rules, often for the first time. This also occurred for the first time in the money markets with the deregulation of the British stockmarket.
2 Ownership changes of key industries from public monopolies and services to private enterprise, a process known as privatization.
3 A continuation of a focus towards European markets, culminating in the single European market in 1992. Trade has seen a shift towards Europe (rather than towards North America) although ideologically the Thatcher

administration has more parallels with the USA than with most countries in Europe.

4 A steady decline in the power of trades unions. The failure of union representation in the Civil Service and the inability of the coal miners to effect a stranglehold as tight as the one they had in 1973 are two examples. Others can be found in the printing industry as resistance to the adoption of new technology in newspaper production was ineffective in stopping it going ahead.

Events still related (but less directly) to government policies include:

5 The rapid adoption of new technologies across a wide range of manufacturing and service organizations. In particular this includes the increasing use of computers, information systems, expert guidance systems for business decisions and for military operations.
6 The OPEC oil crises, which signalled problems in the guaranteed continued production of oil in the long term, effected a massive price rise for the fuel and prompted many organizations to look for substitute energy supplies.
7 Fiscal crises, especially the stockmarket crash in October 1987, referred to as 'Black Monday'.
8 The publicizing of allegedly illegal insider deals between companies (the Guinness/Distillers takeover is one example) and the apparent increase in insider trading of stocks and shares by unscrupulous dealers in the now deregulated market.

All of the above have had a direct impact on individual organizations and their managers. Some are more obvious than others. Financial institutions are among the most obvious, having had to cope with massive changes in their environment. Many have become much more market-oriented, selling their services in competition with other financial institutions. For many managers in these organizations, this was the first time they had been forced to consider competitive markets, selling their wares and wooing the customer. Broking houses in the City have suffered. The volume of share trading has fallen almost by half since the crash. On 7 December 1988, 466.4 million shares were traded. Before the crash, almost 800 million was the norm. Organizations such as Morgan Grenfell, the investment banking group with a history spanning 150 years, have been forced to withdraw from key areas of their business (gilts and equity). Pre-tax profits for Morgan Grenfell, for example, were £82.2 million in 1986. In the first half of 1988, they had fallen to £21.9 million. Table 16.1 shows the number of job losses in the City following Black Monday.

Privatization and deregulation have also brought with them great changes in the environments facing managers. Certainly, markets have become more

Table 16.1
Job losses in the City: 1987–88 (end)

Morgan Grenfell	479	Hoare Govett	150
EF Hutton	300	Lloyds Bank	150
Standard Chart'd	267	Chemical Bank	150
Lloyd's of London	200	Merrill Lynch	150
County NatWest	181	Sheppards	140
Orion Royal	150	Canadian Imperial	137
Shearsons Lehman	165	HK & Shanghai	120
Salomon	150	Fidelity	100

Source: Banking, Insurance and Finance Union (BIFU).

competitive as what was previously a nationalized organization becomes owned by private shareholders. Below are listed some of the key transitions which have occurred under the banners of privatization and deregulation:

1 The sale of nationalized organizations to their management or to the workforce (for example the National Freight Consortium) or to private shareholders (for example British Telecom, British Steel).
2 The sale of assets from nationalized companies (such as British Rail's hotels).
3 Joint ventures between public and private sectors (such as Allied Steel and Wire, a private company jointly created by Guest, Keen and Nettleford and the British Steel Corporation, and the venture between Hoverlloyd and British Rail's Hovercraft service).
4 Giving access to private competition where none previously existed due to a public company's protected monopoly rights. Key examples here are the 1980 Transport Act which allowed competition for express coach routes and the 1981 British Telecommunications Act which similarly allowed competition for British Telecom.
5 Planning for and encouraging private contractors to bid competitively to provide services for parts of the public sector. Examples can be found in the National Health Service, for catering and cleaning, and in the private provision of a refuse collection service across a number of local authority areas.

(Adapted from Hastings and Levie, 1982: 12–14)

All of these events have significant implications for managerial control and ownership of organizations. They also raise obvious ideological and political issues over the role of the state in organizational activities. For those interested in following these arguments see, for example, Clegg and Dunkerley (1980), Clegg, Dow and Boreham (1983) and O'Connor (1973; 1974; 1984).

Going into Europe: the next ten years

The creation of an arguably single European market in 1992 will also have a substantial impact upon all organizations. The most obvious will be an increase in the level of uncertainty faced by managers and all individuals over a wide range of organizational problems. What will the market be like? What is its scope? How different will it be from currently familiar practice? What will happen to wage rates and current bargaining practices? Who will be the major players, organizations or nations? What level of change is likely to be needed to operate effectively in a single market and how soon will those changes have to take place?

All these questions will have to be faced by managers. The level of uncertainty will be enormous for most industries. Implementing necessary changes will also demand a high level of skill from all managers. Some sectors will have to implement changes almost immediately. Motor manufacturers will certainly be in this category. Other sectors will have longer to plan and adapt. Insurance companies will be unlikely to reach a stage of free trade in European insurance until 2001 at the earliest (*The Economist*, July 1988). Prices for premiums, scope for growth and regulations vary greatly between countries. Life policies cost three times as much in Italy as they do in England. Much variation is due to lack of competition within countries and the formation of large groups or cartels of insurance companies.

The creation of a single market will also mean that organizations which currently occupy a distinctive national niche will have to compete on the same terms. Car producers typify this problem. A more open market will have tremendous significance for Fiat and Volkswagen (VW), who are battling it out for number one position for European bestseller of cars. Table 16.2 shows the current league table for new car registrations in Europe for the first quarter of 1988.

Table 16.2
Car manufacturers' market share in Europe (% new car registrations)

Fiat	16.0	Japanese	10.5
VW	13.9	Renault	10.5
Peugeot	12.8	Mercedes	3.6
Ford	11.4	Rover	3.6
GM	10.7	BMW	2.4

Source: Drivers and Registrations Index, Europe.

Traditionally, Fiat has been heavily dependent upon home sales in Italy (around 60 per cent in 1987) while VW is only around 30 per cent dependent on its home market. We already know that an imbalance in dependencies leads to power differentials between players (see Chapter 11). As the single market develops, Fiat will not only have to face the threat of the Italian domestic market being open to overseas car manufacturers, but also its dependency ties on the domestic market will have to be reduced if the current level of competition is to be sustained.

The single market will also force managers to make strategic decisions over legislative practices which have, until now, been wholly domestic. Ranging from policies on taxation to the content of advertising slogans, this aspect of the Euromarket is immensely complex. In advertising, for example, the following two extracts illustrate both cultural and legislative barriers which currently preclude homogenization of advertising:

Television ads in France ooze with sexual innuendo—a woman in a negligée purrs to a man holding a new camera very close to her: 'Will this be the first time for you?' Roquefort cheese has a cheeky boy-and-girl theme, while even a biscuit commercial has a pretty thing falling on to a sofa bed with a young man after taking a nibble.

However . . . the really erotic days of French advertising are over, and the emphasis is swinging towards Beauty, a classy approach ('like Benson and Hedges ads', said one French account executive) and even British humour.

The 'humour' of a . . . Prudential Assurance ad in which a man throws a cat from a window—and then wonders whether it was the stuffed or the real version—is lost on the French. To look or sound silly is the worst social or intellectual stigma in France

(R. Mgadzah, *Sunday Times*, 11 Dec. 1988).

Thus, both legislation over 'decent' advertising and what is thought to be culturally acceptable in different countries will give marketing and advertising managers a hard time in 1992 and beyond. So, what is the likely compromise?

In many cases, a hit American tune, strong visual presentation and a short slogan. All right for the cat food Sheba, made by Mars. Yet even in this spot, showing a nice woman with a nice cat, the slogans are different from country to country.

In France, the message was—you've guessed it—l'amour. (*Pour dire je t'aime* was the reason for giving Sheba), in Germany *Ein Fest fur Katzen* (the word Fest being associated with those times in the year when the Germans have a party), and in Britain a terribly straightforward 'To your cat it's home cooked'. So there you have pan-Europeanism: love here, a celebration there, and good English homeliness.

(R. Mgadzah, *Sunday Times*, 11 Dec. 1988)

Sykes and Crabtree (1988) provide a useful summary of some of the challenges facing organizations in 1992. They cover 26 industrial sectors, 18 service sectors, and 7 social affairs sectors (broadcasting, education and labour relations, for example). Purely at the level of making the single economy work, questions of harmonizing investment policies, mergers and acquisitions, taxation, trade barriers and public ownership of companies will have to be resolved.

From our advertising example above, we also know that national culture is also likely to be a dominant feature in enhancing or blocking change towards a single harmonized market. Finally, changes in dependencies (on other organizations, on single nation markets, on regulation and domestic economic policies) will signal shifts in the balance of power in the wider political economy.

Maintaining coherence in organizational strategy will be very difficult. Sykes and Crabtree's (1988) report certainly indicates that all the rules will change (p. 18) for most organizations. Implicit in their report is that different functions in any single organization will also face variation in demands upon their specialism in the single market. Research and design, finance and marketing are likely to become key functional areas for some manufacturing organizations. Furniture and household goods manufacture are examples. The internal balance of power is thus likely to shift significantly as different functions become more strategically contingent (Hickson *et al.*, 1971). The danger here is not solely a change in power balance. The organizational infrastructure of rules, administration and procedure are unlikely to be designed with the 'new' scenario in mind. Organizations will have to adapt their infrastructure if fragmentation between functions is to be avoided.

Successful organizations: are there any lessons for the future?

Grinyer, Mayes and McKiernan (1987) examined twenty-six British companies over a ten year period (up to 1981) and concluded that 'sharpbenders' (those organizations which had successfully gone through major changes) were characterized by two main stimuli; either there had been *intense external pressure to change*, or there had been *the internal pressure of a change in chief executive*. In some cases, both pressures had occurred. Sharpbends occurred in periods of general economic difficulty such as the recession of 1980–81 and the oil crisis of 1974. The companies which had been successful are shown in Table 16.3.

These companies represent the middle-of-the-road companies. They are not those facing extreme external pressures such as liquidation or takeover. These companies had changed and adapted through the decisions of their managements to volunteer to change. There are no easy lessons to learn here. If there were, then all companies would be able to change easily. Some of the key aspects of the above firms have been:

1   Actions by shareholders, banks or other public institutions had little if any impact on driving change. This contrasts sharply with countries such as West Germany where these institutions had explicitly helped to achieve efficiency.
2   Luck seemed to play a major part. However, greater levels of timely luck came to those organizations which were already seeking to change and seize new opportunities.

Table 16.3
Successful British
companies: those
which have turned
around their
performance and
have maintained
success

Arthur Bell & Sons	Macallan-Glenlivet
Associated Book Publishers	McCarthy & Stone
Associated Paper Industries	Pringle of Scotland
Collins Publishers	Rotaflex
Countryside Properties	Sidlaw Group
Dawson International	Sirdar
Don & Low	TI Group
Ellis and Goldstein Holdings	UDI Group
Ferranti	Ward White Group
Fisons	Whatman Reeve-Angel
Glaxo Holdings	John Wood Group
Low & Bonar	

Source: adapted from Grinyer, Mayes and McKiernan (1987)

3 Investment in people and technology for the future was crucial. Along with tight controls on costings, the hallmark of the above successful firms was investing the spare resources into the future (explicitly on humans and machinery). Investment, training and quality were part of the corporate mission.

4 The whole pace of life and daily rhythm of the organization had to be changed. Often this involved changing the culture of the entire organization (see Pettigrew, 1985 for an analysis of cultural change in ICI: see Wilson, 1980 and Watzke, 1971; 1972 for an analysis of pace).

5 Achieving change was costly and largely irreversible. But these companies were not the chaotic arenas described so fondly by Peters (1987).

6 There are no guarantees. Subsequent difficulties will always occur. Lasting success is as big a dream as lasting stability and equilibrium.

On the last point, consider the Jaguar car company, which has been hailed as one of the great successes of turnaround and change in recent UK business history. Sold off from British Leyland in 1984, the company became increasingly successful under its Chairman Sir John Egan. Investing heavily in human resources (massively increased training budgets as well as in-house changes to salaries, promotions, etc.) and in technology (a £55 million plant at Whitley, Coventry), output rose in October 1987 to 48 020 cars. Jaguar was held as the keynote example of successful privatization. Companies could and would be profitable once they were free of the constraints of state ownership.

Yet Jaguar's fortunes have not remained stable. A heavy reliance on currency markets, especially the United States, and some labour relations difficulties coupled with problems in selecting and recruiting top-rate engineers have created further disequilibria. The removal of the state's restriction on share ownership (no stakeholder could own more than 15 per cent of the company) has resulted in predictable takeover bids from other car companies. In the autumn of 1989, Jaguar was taken over by Ford.

During the 1980s many British companies have experienced massive dislocations to their business which have also had the effect of acting as a spur to change. Over the last fifteen years, employment in manufacturing industries has dropped by over 20 per cent. Some of the deepest wounds have been in the motor industry and associated companies. See for example Table 16.4.

The above accounts might be interpreted as deterministic. What can the manager do? The environment and external events seem to be the dominant triggers for change and for success. Since these are outside the direct control of

Table 16.4
Reduction in
employment in motor
industry and other
industries (%)

Motor manufacturers	% reduction in employment
Talbot [later Peugeot-Talbot]	67.6
British Leyland/Austin Rover	40.0
Vauxhall	30.0
Associated industries	
Guest, Keen and Nettlefold	30.0
Lucas	20.0
Dunlop	30.0
Other industrial areas of high employment reduction	
Philips	50.0 (UK workforce)
ICI	30.0 (moving out of areas of production such as bulk fibres altogether)
Courtaulds	39.0 (again chopping out areas of manufacturing activity)
British Steel	52.0 (some linked to the motor trade)

Source: Financial Times 1000.

managers, there is really little point in trying to manage the environment. It determines what happens in the firm. This interpretation is, of course, only partially valid. Managers *do* have an element of choice despite sometimes intense environmental pressures. We explore these arguments in the next section.

Strategic choice and enactment: counterweights to environmental determinism

Strategic choice, a term coined by Child (1972), refers to the range of options which are available to managers despite external factors. The arguments surrounding strategic choice can be summarized in three major points. The reader is encouraged to read the original article to savour the full flavour of the debate. In summary:

1 Decision-makers have a range of autonomy open to them which is greater than that argued by authors who subscribe to the dominance of environmental, technological and other external forces.
2 Organizations sometimes can influence and exercise some level of control over their immediate environments.
3 The perceptions of managers are the key intervening link between organizational action and external factors.

(Child, 1972)

Child's argument is that most managers most of the time have a range of alternative actions open to them despite the constancy and the seeming inevitability of external pressures. Firms can (and do) enter new markets or new areas of service provision. Managers are not constrained to continue to do what their organization has always done in the past. Of course, having such autonomy does not mean that managers will always exercise it.

Lobbying, joint ventures, vertical integration and contracts of all kinds ensure that any organization has a degree of control and influence over its immediate environment. At the very least, this control would be manifested in managers being able to predict fairly accurately over a given time frame what is likely to happen in terms of competition levels, continuity of supply, fiscal policies of the state and so on.

Managers do not always perceive external events accurately. However, even inaccurate perceptions of external factors are likely to lead to some form of organizational adaptation even if this is inappropriate. Managers also 'enact' their immediate environment, since they define which of the multitude of external factors are important enough to require attention by the organization (Weick, 1969). Enactment is the process through which managers make sense of the world external to their organizations. It results in a manageable collection of factors which can then receive attention.

The process of enactment can be illustrated by imagining the manager wearing a coal miner's helmet which has an inbuilt light unit at the top. As the manager stares into the 'blackness' of the external environment, the cone of light projected from the helmet picks out a certain area in stark relief. The rest remains in the dark. The manager will act upon what is seen by the light, even though it is equally probable that elements in the environment which are not illuminated are really key influences upon the organization.

Two key points emerge from both strategic choice and enactment. First, the environment is not a fixed set of factors. It is what managers perceive it to be. Second, managers will act upon their perceptions (and not anyone else's). This may mean that factors which are 'actually' influencing the organization are both not recognized and not given any attention.

Summary

In this chapter we have discussed the key role of the manager as an interpreter of the external environment into action within the organization. Studies by Mintzberg and others tell us what managers actually do in this process (rather than what they are supposed to do by rational prescription). The management task is fluid, ill-defined, hectic and energy-sapping. It requires equal levels of skills in the interpretation of information and in handling people.

We have also looked at the relative impact upon an organization of the environment and the manager, asking the question—which makes most difference, external events or the manager? The answer appears to be—a bit of both. External factors weigh heavily on most organizations and managers must respond to the immediate environment. Equally, managers should not assume that they have no control over this process. The set of external factors is not fixed. It is also open to a degree of influence. Managers can exercise choice over how they interpret events and how they act towards them. As part of perceiving the environment, managers must also make sense of external factors. They often do this by classifying the environment, describing it broadly and as a 'type' which can be discussed and communicated to other managers. This classification forms the topic of the next chapter.

References

Barnard, C. I. (1938) *The Functions of the Executive*, Harvard University Press, Mass.

Carlson, S. (1951) *Executive Behaviour*, Strombergs, Stockholm.

Child, J. (1972) 'Organizational structures, environments and performance: the role of strategic choice', *Sociology*, **6**, 1–22.

Clegg, S., G. Dow and P. Boreham (eds) (1983) *The State, Class and the Recession*, Croom-Helm, London.

Clegg, S. and D. Dunkerley (1980) *Organization, Class and Control*, Routledge and Kegan Paul, London.

Fayol, H. (1949) *General and Industrial Management*, transl. C. Storrs, Pitman, London.

Grinyer, P., D. Mayes and P. McKiernan (1987) *Sharpbenders: the Secrets of Unleashing Corporate Potential*, Blackwell, Oxford.

Hastings, S. and H. Levie (eds) (1982) 'Privatisation?', Spokesman, Nottingham.

Hickson, D. J., C. R. Hinings, C. A. Lee, R. E. Schneck and J. M. Pennings (1971) A strategic contingencies' theory of intraorganizational power', *Administrative Science Quarterly*, **16**(2), 216–29.

Mintzberg, H. (1973) *The Nature of Managerial Work*, Harper & Row, New York.

O'Connor, J. (1973) *The Fiscal Crisis of the State*, St Martin's Press, New York.

O'Connor, J. (1974) *The Corporations and the State*, St Martin's Press, New York.

O'Connor, J. (1984) *Accumulation Crisis*, Blackwell, Oxford.

Peters, T. (1987) *Thriving on Chaos*, Harper & Row, New York.

Pettigrew, A. M. (1985) *The Awakening Giant: Continuity and Change in ICI*, Blackwell, Oxford.

Sayles, L. R. (1964) *Managerial Behavior*, McGraw-Hill, New York.

Stewart, R. (1967) *Managers and Their Jobs*, Macmillan, London.

Sykes, D. and C. Crabtree (eds) (1988) *Towards 1992*, University of Warwick Business Information Service, Warwick Research Institute.

Urwick, L. (1943) *The Elements of Administration*, Harper, New York.

Watzke, G. E. (1971) 'Pace of life as an environmental influence upon organizations', Ph.D. dissertation, University Graduate School of Business, Stanford, California.

Watzke, G. E. (1972) 'Pace in organizations and the community pace of life', *Preprint Series*, International Institute of Management, Berlin.

Weick, K. (1969) *The Social Psychology of Organizing*, Addison-Wesley, Reading, Mass.

Wilson, D. C. (1980) 'Organizational Strategy', Ph.D. thesis, University of Bradford Management Centre, Bradford, West Yorkshire.

Classifying organizational environments

Introduction

The previous chapter has outlined how managers scan and perceive the wider environment. Information from the external domain is filtered through both perceptive and cognitive processes by individual managers. They think differently; they see different things; and they act in different ways depending upon their interpretations.

This would seem at first sight to be a recipe for extreme complexity. The environment is all things to all individuals depending upon how they see it. Yet it is possible to classify parts of the environment of an organization, even if the distinctions between the parts are often blurred and overlap. Figure 17.1 outlines the major external factors which all organizations face.

Starting from the notion that the environment is everything that is external to an organization's boundary, we can split this undifferentiated definition into four broad categories (Hall, 1972; Jurkovich, 1974; Radford, 1978):

1 the general or societal environment;
2 the specific or task environment;

Figure 17.1
The organizational
environment

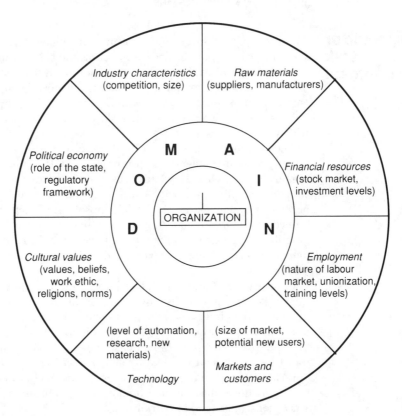

3 the inter-organizational environment;
4 the political and economic environment.

The general or societal environment

The general environment facing organizations is characterized by a number of key elements which are separable analytically and which can have separate and different impacts upon organizations. The unifying theme is that they all affect all organizations all of the time.

Economic characteristics   include the overall economy of a nation, the profile of ownership (public or private), the extent to which the economy is planned and centralized, levels of investment and consumption.

Technological characteristics   include the level of advancement of knowledge and equipment in society (or in specific countries), and the rate of development and application of such knowledge.

Educational and cultural characteristics   include the general literacy level of a country, the number of people with specialized knowledge or training, the beliefs, attitudes, values and norms of the country as well as its historical background.

Demographic and sociological characteristics   include class structure and mobility, the nature of available human resources of working age, distributions throughout the general population of sex, age and geographical concentration and dispersion.

Natural resource characteristics   include the availability of resources such as water, fuels, climate and topography.

The specific or task environment

This is the part of the general environment which directly concerns managers, since it impacts upon the decision-making and transformation processes of the organization (Dill, 1958). At any point in time, it will be the part of the environment which managers emphasize the most. While the general environment is roughly the same (for organizations in the same country or industrial sector for example) the task environment of each is likely to differ widely.

The task environment comprises (typically) customers, suppliers, trades unions, government agencies and competitors. It can be quite large. Some organizations such as Hewlett Packard are in contact with around 5000 suppliers. Combine this with a large customer base, and the task environment becomes extremely large indeed. Thompson (1967) refers generally to this immediate environment as the 'organizational domain'. This domain not only describes the task environment but also refers to the relative emphasis placed by managers on its component parts. It describes the *niche* of products and services offered.

Firms can be in the same industrial sector, but occupy distinctively different niches. For example, Rolls-Royce, Jaguar and Rover are all UK motor manufacturers, but their niche is self-evidently different. They have largely mutually exclusive customer bases and different groups of customers. Changes in niche size, niche shape or emphasis will also mean commensurate changes in the task environment. The nature of dependencies and the sources of uncertainties will change quite markedly. Managers will then be faced with redefining the immediate environment and will begin to emphasize different sets of constraints and opportunities.

Inter-organizational relations: networks

Rather than be a set of discrete factors, the environment of many organizations is rapidly becoming one which is composed of *networks* of other organizations. Managing the task environment becomes more a process of handling inter-organizational relations than it does attending to its separate components (Evan, 1966). Management strategies towards handling this network are thus quite different in emphasis from those which deal with its separate parts. Thompson (1967) and Thompson and McEwen (1958) have identified five strategies for managing the inter-organizational network. More recently, Hickson *et al.* (1986) and Butler and Wilson (1989) have empirically demonstrated these strategies in use in British organizations. Taken together, these two studies examined the strategies of 15 public organizations (service and manufacturing), 15 private organizations (service and manufacturing) and 31 voluntary organizations. There seems considerable support for the following five strategies:

1 *Contracting*   Organizations can enter contracts with either suppliers or customers to reduce uncertainty. Fixed price supply contracts for twelve months would be an example. Agreeing to give money to a charity for a fixed period would be another example. Charities such as the Royal National Lifeboat Institution and the Royal National Institute for the Blind actively seek to secure this kind of funding rather than rely on unpredictable levels of income from individual donors. Irrespective of your opinion on how they cook them, McDonald's the worldwide burger chain contracts for an entire crop of russet potatoes to ensure supply and quality.

2 *Co-opting*   Managers may choose to absorb uncertainties by encompassing elements in the network. For example, inviting an environmental lobbyist or a merchant banker to sit on the board of your organization is likely to reduce resistance from environmentalists and could lead to easier access to money markets.

3 *Coalescing*   A management strategy of combination. Joint action through pricing agreements, market shares and joint ventures, etc. While mostly legal, some practices under this strategy such as unwritten reciprocity or price agreements can become highly illegal. They are nevertheless attractive strategies since they achieve stability, especially in concentrated industrial sectors.

4 *Use of third parties*   Occurs when managers of one organization use the services of another organization to negotiate on their behalf. Professional and trade associations are obvious examples. Statutory regulations such as codes of practice in medical spheres are less obvious, since here the medical practitioners are effectively restricting entry and regulating competition via a third party agreement with government agencies. Depending upon your ideological persuasion, you could view this as generally beneficial (it protects the interests of the consumer and maintains standards) or as untenable (it protects and sustains monopoly provision of goods and services).

5 *Advertising*   Is successful when it gains differential advantage to one organization in the network. A good example of this is the generic term for the vacuum cleaner — the Hoover (and its associated verb 'to hoover') which comes from one manufacturer among many others. They still manufacture 'hoovers' however.

The political and economic environment

Under this category we refer to the constitutional, institutional and political tenor of the environment for the organization. The nature of national political organization, the devolution or centralization of power nationally and the nature of the economy (not forgetting laws which refer to taxation and corporate activities) will all colour both the task and the specific environments.

Many managers understandably have a difficult time responding to all the demands imposed by this aspect of the environment since they are both vague and, often, conflicting. For example:

On one hand	On the other
Government research agencies suggest weight-adding safety equipment for cars.	The Department of Transport insists on lighter vehicle weight to conserve petrol.
The Department of the Environment suggests restrictions in the use of pesticides.	The Department of Agriculture promotes pesticides for agriculture and forestry.
Energy departments try to keep rail haulage rates for coal at a cheap level, to encourage coal usage.	Transport departments try to keep rail rates high to bolster the declining rail industry.
Occupational health and safety suggests keeping exposure levels to hazardous substances at the lowest possible, short of bankrupting the company.	Departments of the Environment and Trade suggest flexible standards taking cost and risk level into consideration.

In addition, the state will differ from nation to nation in its tolerance and support of managerial practices. For example, in Russia, Albania and Romania, it is an environmental 'given' that entrepreneurialism and management are always subject to centralized government control despite recent changes toward greater democracy in Russia and Romania. In England and North America, they are virtually (and relatively) an autonomous category of actors.

Rojek and Wilson (1987) also pointed to the overlaps which occur between different political economies. Taking Yugoslavia as an example, they argue that self-management as a planned socialist ideal is impossible to achieve fully. One of the main reasons for this is that Yugoslavia trades with (and is dependent upon) a number of Western capitalist countries for trade and tourism.

> Large sections of the Yugoslav economy have been developed to tender more or less exclusively for the needs of the Western customer. The hotel and catering industries are examples. Other sections produce goods under licence from Western firms. These are made according to Western design principles and their manufacture and sale adds to the profits of Western shareholders.
>
> (Rojek and Wilson, 1987: 304–5)

Thus the wider political economy exerts an influence both within and between countries. Such influences may be ambiguous, but they are especially strong given their development throughout national histories. It is one of the key factors which could stand in the way of integration following the creation of a single European market post-1992.

Corporate social responsibility

Over the past century, business organizations have emerged as major actors. They are politically potent, important economically and, probably because of both of these, are key agents of stability and social change. Often viewed solely as inherently conservative and as supporters of the status quo, business organizations have also brought about radical changes in society.

The current development and implementation of new technologies is one example of this radical shake-up. Changes will be both for the good and the worse, depending upon your perspective. Perhaps as a previously skilled worker, you would not welcome the rapid advent of computer-controlled machines which have changed your role from operator to that of 'babysitter' for the machine. Customers who now receive better quality and more consistent products from the new technology would welcome the change.

The key to analysing such diametrically opposed views lies in the notion of control. If organizations have the power to effect changes of huge proportions, then what are the mechanisms by which control is achieved? Who monitors and checks corporate progress? Regulations, laws and standards all play their part, of course, but recently there has been a move to alerting managers of all types of organizations to the idea of corporate social responsibility (CSR).

CSR is a *voluntary* commitment by managers to a wider range of responsibilities than to shareholders and to corporate and labour laws (Carroll, 1981; Jones, 1980). Managers are required to conform to the latter, but are not required to conform or contribute to any wider social values. In particular, CSR focuses on an organization's *ethical* and *discretionary* responsibilities. Ethical responsibilities include fairness to customers and employees, honesty and integrity in all dealings, and a responsibility to ensure that the general public are kept informed about corporate issues and developments. Discretionary responsibilities include providing monies for charities (often for urban renewal where previous generations of industry have left their marks and scars), supporting training programmes for the long-term unemployed, as well as protecting degradation of the natural environment and helping in its renewal.

Since CSR is voluntary, it is not surprising that many managers see this attempt at control as misplaced and inappropriate. They argue that the organization is purely responsible to stockholders and that any practices beyond securing maximum profits will be detrimental. It is for others to pursue more altruistic goals. In addition, the CSR firm is placed at a competitive disadvantage in relation to those which do not practise upholding wider issues. Others argue that organizations are not just economic instruments. The problem is that many managers are not trained to deal with CSR when they make decisions, yet the social impact of their actions is inevitable. Increasing the level of CSR awareness should lead to a better environment all-round for both organizations and individuals.

To what extent business takes CSR seriously across the range of its activities remains to be seen. Socially responsive action on the part of managers has not figured large in the development of the modern industrial enterprise (although there are notable 'benevolent' exceptions such as Joseph Rowntree, Titus Salt and William Cobbett).

Summary

This chapter has attempted briefly to categorize and to classify the various environments which face the managers of all organizations. Broadly falling into two categories, there are very general environments which reflect widely held societal norms and values, and very specific, task-related, environments which are very much focused at the level of the individual firm.

The predominance of other organizations in the environment was also discussed in relation to organizational networks. From this perspective, managers had to try and exert some control over their environment by managing the network rather than attend to individual factors (such as one customer, or the prevailing fiscal conditions). There are five broad ways in which networks can be managed: contracting, coopting, coalescing, using third parties and advertising.

Finally, the notion of corporate social responsibility introduced the idea that managing the environment included a wider brief than just profitability and accountability to stockholders. Questions of ethics and voluntary actions towards the wider community could legitimately be thought of as management's brief in coping with the environment. In the next chapter, we look at how organizations interact with the environments we have so far described.

References

Butler, R. J. and D. C. Wilson (1989) *Managing Voluntary and Non-Profit Organizations: Strategy and Structure*, Routledge, London.

Carroll, A. B. (1981) *Business and Society: Managing Corporate Social Responsibility*, Little, Brown & Co., Boston.

Dill, W. R. (1958) 'Environment as an influence on managerial autonomy', *Administrative Science Quarterly*, **2**(4), 409–43.

Evan, W. M. (1966) 'The organization set: toward a theory of interorganizational relations', in J. D. Thompson (ed.), *Approaches to Organizational Design*, Pittsburgh University Press, Pittsburgh.

Hall, R. H. (1972) *Organizations: Structure and Process*, Prentice-Hall, Englewood Cliffs, New Jersey.

Hickson, D. J., R. J. Butler, D. Cray, G. R. Mallory and D. C. Wilson (1986) *Top Decisions: Strategic Decision-Making in Organizations*, Blackwell, Oxford; Jossey-Bass, San Francisco,

Jones, T. M. (1980) 'Corporate social responsibility revisited, redefined', *California Management Review*, 1980, Spring, 59–60.

Jurkovich, R. (1974) 'A core typology of organizational environments', *Administrative Science Quarterly*, **19**(3), 380–94.

Radford, K. J. (1978) 'Some initial specifications for a strategic information system', *The International Journal of Management Sciences*, **6**(2), 139–44.

Rojek, C. and D. C. Wilson (1987) 'Workers' self-management in the world system: the Yugoslav case', *Organization Studies*, **8**(4), 297–308.

Thompson, J. D. (1967) *Organizations in Action*, McGraw-Hill, New York.

Thompson, J. D. and W. J. McEwen (1958) 'Organizational goals and environments: goal-setting as an interaction process', *American Sociological Review*, Feb. 23–31.

Understanding organizational systems

Introduction

We have seen in Chapter 12 how many authors argued the idea of organization–environment fit. Authors such as Burns and Stalker (1961) and Lawrence and Lorsch (1967) constructed contingency models of organizational design. The arguments that mechanistic structures seemed appropriate in relatively stable and predictable environments, and that organic structures were more effective in environments which are rapidly changing and are unpredictable, were empirically based and seductively simple.

Recently, however, there has been a growing body of disquiet over the simplicity of this contingent 'fit' between structure and environment. In Chapter 16 we described one study by Child (1972) in which he suggested that environmental characteristics did not wholly fashion organizational structures. Managers had 'strategic choices' within certain limits to carve out their own organizational designs and processes irrespective of environmental characteristics. Other authors such as Astley and Van de Ven (1983), Hrebiniak and Joyce (1985) and Schreyogg (1980) have argued that factors other than environmental determinism must be taken into account when studying organizational design, performance and survival. These include subjective managerial perceptions, the ways in which perceptions are modelled (and interpreted) and the relative weights that can be given to strategic choice and other environmental factors.

While these debates have focused upon the interaction of environment and the firm, other researchers have argued that this is an inappropriate level of analysis for examining the questions of organizational survival, adaptation and performance. These authors argue that to understand such processes we have to shift our perspective to one of viewing *the dynamics of environment–organization relations as a system*. Based on general systems theory, many theories and empirical studies have emerged, the most influential of which include the *population ecology* and the *life-cycle* perspectives. We discuss each in this chapter. First, we must explain the general elements of systems theory which acts as the framework and the basis for subsequent studies.

Systems theory

Systems theory, originally a theory of organism survival and adaptation in the biological sciences, has proved a very powerful analytical construct in the study of organizations. Put simply, systems theory says that:

In any organization, the multitude of parts and processes are so interrelated and so interdependent that a small change in one part necessitates changes and adaptations in other parts.

Systems can be *closed* or *open*. Examples of closed system models can be found in early theories of organizational behaviour, such as those of the scientific management or human-relations schools (Taylor, 1911; Mayo, 1949). In closed systems, only the interdependent parts of a single organization were considered.

The focus was very much upon the internal workings of the firm. Job design, management roles and group behaviour were assumed to be themselves related, but to be independent of outside influences. It was assumed that there was one best way of organizing efficiently and effectively and this could be achieved by concentrating on the microcosm of the single organization in isolation.

The open-systems approach views any one organization as an interdependent piece of a much larger whole. Its actions and characteristics are no longer just determined by the aspirations of its managers and founders, but by a wider environment with which the firm interacts. Common interactions occur between an organization and its suppliers, its customers and its peer organizations, sometimes on a daily basis. These actions and interactions form a pattern, the nature of which will impact upon internal organizational design and functioning (Katz and Kahn, 1966). Other external interactions are more remote but none the less significant. Government agencies, trade associations, banks and other nations all have some kind of input to any organization and are sometimes recipients of its outputs in the form of goods or services. This is the wider context in which the organization operates.

It is the patterning of these linkages and interdependencies which gave rise to open-systems theory. Based around the three aspects of *Inputs — Throughputs — Outputs*, open-systems theory is able to identify key aspects and principles of the system itself. Figure 18.1 gives an idea of how we might draw a map of an organization in an open system.

Given that the focal organization is the part of the system which effects the throughputs (transformation of raw material into goods or services) and that inputs and the output domain are external to it, then the open system has the following properties:

1 *equifinality*   Organizations and their managers have a choice over the design of internal organization. There is no one best way of doing things. There are

Figure 18.1
The basic open
system's map

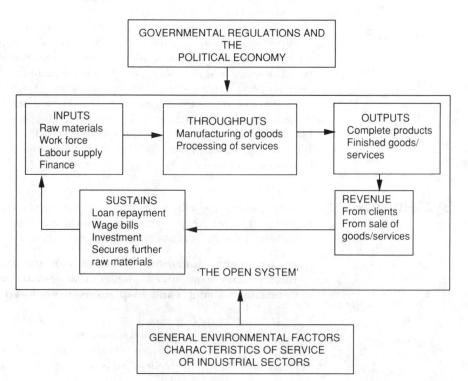

multiple, different ways to achieve the same goal. In closed systems, the same initial variables lead to the same end result. In open systems no such assumptions are made.

2 *negative entropy*   Entropy is the predisposition of objects to decay and to disintegrate (such as your car, or a building or other structure). In an open system, this tendency is halted or sometimes reversed (hence the term negative entropy). Organizations import more resources from their environment than they expend in producing outputs. They can 'store' energy in much the same way as some animals survive periods of lean food supply by some form of hoarding.

3 *steady state*   The balance between inputs, outputs and throughputs is characterized by always being in steady state. This is not a true equilibrium, for the steady state itself is subject to movement, but the balance of the exchanges taking place in the system remains steady.

4 *cycles and patterns*   The open system itself is cyclical. Reciprocal patterns can be identified. The most obvious is where the revenue from the sale of goods (outputs) is used to purchase further inputs. This would represent a single loop cycle. More complex cycles can occur where single loops interact, or where tangential factors come into the equation. Nevertheless, the open system itself remains open to identifying patterns (however complex) and is cyclical.

(von Bertalanffy, 1956; Emery and Trist, 1960)

The open-systems model has two benefits for the analysis of organizations:

1 It allows for explanation of variance which occurs *within* the firm to be explained by factors which lie *outside* it.
2 It facilitates the comparison of very different types of organization, since all organizations are argued to operate within an open system. This perspective gives us a common denominator, the language and means of comparison.

Understanding organizations as systems has become the basis for a very influential set of studies which take the properties of the open system as given and subsequently seek to explain other factors such as survival, adaptation and transformation. The first of these are population ecology models.

Population ecology models

These models combine elements of environmental determinism with open-systems theory. Population ecology models argue that organizational survival is akin to 'Darwinism' wherein extreme demands from the environment can result in the demise of 'weaker' organizations and 'select out stronger, more dominant organizational forms' (Bedeian, 1987: 9). Aldrich (1979) is a leading supporter of the population ecology model. The use of the term 'population' implies that an organization is one member of a larger set of similar entities (Aldrich, 1986). He writes:

From the population perspective, the distribution of organizational forms at any time is a result of three processes: the creation or birth of new organizations, the disappearance of existing organizations (through death, merger, bankruptcy, or whatever), and the transformation of existing organizations into new forms.

Organizational survival is dependent upon achieving and sustaining a position within the general population of organizations. According to Carroll

(1985), Hannan and Freeman (1977) and Harrigan (1985) this is achieved by examining *environmental niches* and *organizational strategies*.

Niches   These are characterized by the constellation of resources which impinge upon organizational action. Some resources (or, rather, lack of them) constrain action: others encourage and support action. Populations of organizations exist within each type of niche in a way similar to that described by Porter (1980) in his description of 'strategic groups'. These are groups of organizations within one industry or industrial sector which, faced with similar niches, adapt and adopt strategies at the level of the individual firm based upon the actions of others in the same domain. In the terminology of Grinyer and Spender (1979) such strategic responses are best described as 'recipes' which are shared throughout the sector.

Niches can be wide or narrow. Niche width (or narrowness) is determined by the combination of general resources and factors specific to a particular industrial sector, such as business cycles, product cycles, rates of innovation, union policies, the general economy, government policies and regulations and fiscal trends.

Organizations which have a broad environmental niche are generalists. They can transform or reproduce themselves with relative ease since they have a tolerance for handling changing conditions and for being able to handle competitors. Specialist organizations are those which have a narrow niche. They thrive in environments which are stable and which change slowly and predictably. They have specific resource requirements and usually have tightly defined markets. They can also build in to their structure a great deal of flexibility which also helps in the process of smooth adaptation to changing circumstances so long as change is neither too radical nor unpredictable.

Populations of organizations which are generalists are likely to find survival more difficult in environments which are stable. This is because they have to build in slack resources to cope with the broad niche and to fend off competition. These organizations are more likely to survive long term by continually transforming and by entering new populations and environmental states.

Organizational strategies   For a given population of organizations, the pursuit of certain strategies by some organizations can upset the equilibrium of the wider open system. These strategies are characterized either by more efficient use of the existing resource base or by exploiting new aspects of the niche (usually by exploiting and acting upon information to which other organizations in the population are not yet privy). Such strategies create temporary disequilibrium, which can lead to competitive advantage for the organization.

Aldrich (1986) proposed three areas of strategy where any single organization could achieve advantage over the others in its population. The first occurs through the entrepreneurial spirit of managers which is unlikely to be distributed evenly throughout organizations in the population. Actions by entrepreneurs in one organization can lead to 'first mover' advantages, particularly if this entails the identification of new and unique products and services. The extent to which first movers remain in disequilibrium with other organizations depends, of course, on how quickly (or whether) these actions can be copied.

The second strategy occurs through the particular mix of structure, processes and people in any organization which can give it a unique character of culture. So long as this remains inimitable, the organization should enjoy competitive advantage. A third strategy focuses on technology. Where a firm can employ technological innovations not available to others the firm will be in an advantageous position in the population. If success ensues from using this technology, then managers are likely to build on this, developing the technology so that other organizations find it difficult or impossible to catch up.

Since the population ecology perspective emphasizes groups of organizations (rather than individual firms) and is primarily concerned with births, transformations and deaths in the population, there must also be a way of examining organizations and their environments over time. Achieving this is one of the key questions in organizational behaviour. Longitudinal studies of single organizations are rare enough, never mind studies of entire populations of them. Authors such as Aldrich (1979; 1986) are making inroads to this field of study. They have studied the population of trade associations in the United States, concluding that the key factors in determining cycles of growth and contraction in their numbers are:

1 levels of complexity in industrial sectors which the associations represent;
2 the nature of government regulation;
3 economic health of the industry;
4 the propensity for systems to grow and to differentiate regardless of these factors.

Studies of other sectors are rare. In a review of seven articles which examined how organizations managed (or mismanaged competitively) in their sectors, Argyris (1987) argues that the propensity for managers to make 'errors' of judgement is a key factor in organizational survival and success in their niche. He identifies a number of misconceptions and lack of understanding by managers of the general population of organizations of which theirs is a part. So, it looks like we can add a fifth factor to the four outlined above: managers who have accurate interpretations of the structure and processes of the population are likely to make fewer strategic errors and thus achieve and retain competitive advantage.

Other studies which specifically examine the longitudinal aspects of organizational transformation are again firmly rooted in the open-systems tradition. These approaches may be discussed under the broad banner of 'organizational life-cycles'.

Organizational life-cycles

The life-cycle provides a framework for studying the patterns of birth, transformation and death in organizations (Kimberley and Miles, 1980). It is argued that all organizations go through a relatively predictable pattern of stages throughout their life-cycles. In each stage, we can identify various characteristics with which managers must cope in order to achieve transition to subsequent stages in the cycle. There are four broad stages:

1 entrepreneurial stage
2 collective stage
3 formalization stage
4 elaboration stage

The entre-preneurial stage

This is the very first stage of any organization's life. The organization is created and the first tasks to be achieved are those of creating a service or a product and surviving in the chosen domain of operations. Usually, the creators of this organization are entrepreneurs for whom the organization is their complete focus of attention. They work long hours, do most jobs in the organization and set the climate and the culture.

If this first stage is successful, the organization will grow. The pressing need now comes from the increased number of employees in the organization since they require managerial direction and the organization needs someone to handle the general issues of management. It is unusual for the initial entrepreneurs to be skilled in general management, so the immediate problem is one of deciding either to limit growth and remain small (but risk being unable to sustain competition) or to grow and recruit professional managers.

The collective stage

Assuming the successful recruitment of professional managers, the organization enters the collectivity phase. The organization begins to take 'shape'. Departments and functions begin to be defined and the division of labour is the dominant theme. The culture is still largely one of the collective or clan (see Chapter 15) and individuals are likely to feel committed to the organization and the goals of its managers. The professional managers recruited tend to be strong, often dominant leaders, who have a clear vision of where the organization should be heading.

As the organization continues to grow and to carve out with more precision its strategic niche, the need for management control and delegation arises. Strong leaders still want to lead. But the organization has begun to establish its position, and consolidating how internal tasks are allocated and who has responsibility and autonomy to carry them out becomes pre-eminent.

The formalization stage

Here, we see the implementation of control, information and communication systems. Communication and control become more formal. There is a division made explicit between the tasks of top management—to make strategic decisions and to implement policy—and lower-level managers, who are charged with carrying out and overseeing operational decisions.

A whole system of coordination and control emerges, including salary structures, reward and incentive schemes, number of levels in the hierarchy, reporting relationships and levels of discretion and autonomy for lower-level managers. The organization continues to grow, but more slowly. Structurally, it begins to resemble a bureaucracy, with pronounced functional specialization and differentiation. Towards the end of this stage, the organization can become over-burdened by the process of bureaucratization and the need for the structure to be 'freed up' becomes pressing. Retention of key staff is important. They are likely to leave the organization if they feel hemmed in, or impotent to influence or participate in wider organizational goals. One factor which contributes to this lies in the mechanism of formal control by management of roles (rather than individuals) which is characteristic of organizations in this stage of the life-cycle.

The elaboration stage

This is the stage during which the problems of over-formalization are addressed and solutions sought. The organization may have begun to 'plateau' in terms of growth and performance and may even show the first stages of decline. Managers used to handling bureaucratic structures and processes usually have to learn new skills or to unearth long forgotten notions of teamwork, self-assessment and problem confrontation. This stage of renewal can occur as soon as after ten years of operation, but more usually takes around fifteen to twenty years, during which time a number of other 'cures' may also have taken place such as the rapid turnover and replacement of senior managers (Greiner, 1972).

The idea of the life-cycle is also useful for drawing together some of the key management processes such as human-resource management, power and decision-making processes. At each stage in the life-cycle, the profile of management concerns will alter in the relative emphasis a manager needs to put on each. Table 18.1 summarizes some of these differences. To avoid over-complication, the table distinguishes three phases in the life-cycle corresponding to growth, stability and decline.

Table 18.1 Three stages of the organizational life-cycle: likely profile of selected factors in organizational behaviour

	Growth	Stability	Decline
Strategy	Competitive and innovative	Emphasis on consolidation. Aimed at securing efficiency or securing change through planned increments	Nearly always *reactive*. There is a strong tendency towards cooperation with other organizations in an attempt to secure stability. This can lead to serious organizational drift
Human resources	Focus on key individuals who have brought success	Focus on the *role* rather than upon the individual. Selection and appraisal schemes designed accordingly to accommodate role fulfilment	The focus returns very much towards the individual and not the role. Identification of 'problem' individuals (those who are assumed to have contributed to the decline) can lead to persecution. There is a tendency to sharpen stereotypes in the organization and to use these as justification for action
Power balance	Internal coalition very strong in relation to external coalition. Focus on the 'strong' few who are leading success. The organization 'enacts' its environment and tends towards niche management	Much less dominance internally. External interests play a large part in shaping decisions. There can be high levels of conflict between those in the organization who want to preserve the status quo and those who want to achieve change. This can bring with it the danger of slipping into decline through managing the politics rather than the organization	Usually externally dominated. Internal power is weak. Different parts of the organization begin to accrue power. Administration can become extremely powerful especially if its task is to monitor decline

Table 18.1 (cont.)

	Growth	Stability	Decline
Leadership	Style of leaders is determined largely by that which has brought success. There is general acknowledgement of this in the organization. Little attempt by individuals to try and change leaders' style. The only real alternative is to move organization if dissatisfied	Tends to be bound up with role description and behaviour expected. Style determined either by organizational culture, or by expected behaviours from subgroups (especially in bureaucracies)	Becomes crucial. Key people who can aid recovery and who can be effective when turnaround occurs must be retained. This is a real problem, since these are the very people most likely to 'jump ship' when decline begins. Style must be contingent on both group and individual needs
Motivation	Usually through resource acquisition which heralds better times ahead (certainty) or through team spirit, peer-group pressure and general group conformity	Might not appear to be a problem. A sense of no news is good news! Motivation cannot just be assumed. It needs active management in order to keep existing staff levels constant. Care must be taken not to demotivate staff through the pursuit of efficiency which can bring with it the need for pruning and/or role change/ redefinition	Declining morale. Conflict increases. Need for change increases. Individuals resist change. Must avoid leaving motivation until the onset of crisis. It's too late then!

Boundary spanning as a managerial activity

Open-systems theories provide us with a picture which is useful for understanding how organizations interact with their environments. A danger with concepts such as the population ecology models and life-cycles is that they can present an overly deterministic picture of the management process if each is taken in isolation. We already know that managers have a strategic choice in the way they interpret their environment and implement decisions (Child, 1972). Linked to this idea is the process of strategic management. It is through the process of strategy formulation that managers, at least in part, can exert reciprocal influences on the environment. Strategies have an impact. It is not just a one-way process with the environment being all determining.

Just to make matters more confusing, recent research evidence (Zammuto, 1988) indicates that there is a strong congruence between population ecology models and strategic choice approaches. They correspond in terms of the strategies adopted by the firms in Zammuto's sample. If this is true of a wide range of organizations, then distinguishing between proactive managerial action and the impact of the immediate environment will become virtually impossible. As yet, there is insufficient research evidence. However, it is likely that congruence is imperfect and that detailed studies of strategy formation processes and the strategic stances adopted by organizations will separate out the relative impact of proactive and reactive factors (see Chapter 19).

One of the key ways in which managers can achieve reciprocal impact on the environment occurs through boundary spanning activities. Boundary spanning refers to the role which sits astride the environment–organizational interface. It is a role, therefore, at 'the edge' of an organization. The role links and coordinates central parts of the organization, the 'technical core' (Thompson, 1967) with parts of the external environment (see Figure 18.2).

Figure 18.2
Monitoring and representing the organization: boundary spanning roles

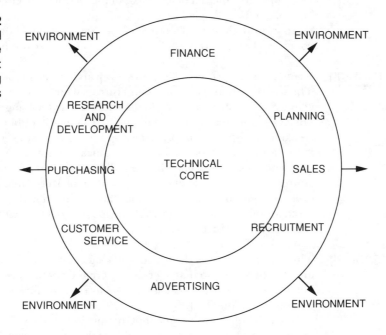

* This figure shows *external* boundary spanning roles. Examples of *internal* boundary spanning roles are: liaison departments, product group managers and some personnel departments.

There are two key functions for boundary spanning roles. The first is to *monitor the environment*, detect changes which are occurring and feed these into the organization. The second role is one of *representation* (Jemison, 1984). Monitoring protects the technical core of the organization. Production units, for example, do not have to worry about factors other than production. Any information they need about what technologies competitors are using, or developments in the field can be fed to them by the boundary spanning roles. They are thus protected from many influences and from multiple sets of often conflicting information, which might otherwise impinge upon their ability to carry out their central task.

The representative task is primarily one of sending information about the organization out into the environment and thus influencing others' perceptions. Individuals in this role act as the public face of the organization. Many outsiders form strong opinions about the nature of the organization on the basis of what its representatives do and say. Organizational image is created and maintained to a great extent by this role. In theory, the role has the capacity to influence the characteristics of the immediate external environment. Other individuals and organizations can be influenced in the way they perceive the organization and thus are likely to modify their behaviour towards it accordingly. In practice, the representative role often works this way. It can also spill over into 'impression management' in which representation is more a characteristic of the individual in the role. It can be, therefore, deceptive, misleading, calculated or dishonest (Goffman, 1959). For the reader interested in the psychology of public representation, Goffman's works should provide a wealth of detail. Our interest here is to show that, via this role, the organization can exert reciprocal influence on the external environment. It thus becomes an important part of the strategic management process, since strategic plans are likely to be formulated on the basis of the character of environmental–organizational linkages.

Apart from the representation of the organization, boundary spanning comprises two separable activities. These are: (1) scanning and (2) monitoring.

Scanning

Scanning is the process of information search in the immediate environment. The search is for opportunities and threats which may accrue from major changes which are occurring in the wider context. Changes in government policies (both fiscal and legislative) and changes in public tastes (such as anti-smoking, anti-pollution, pro-safety and swings of fashion) all provide information for the formulation of organizational strategy.

Their accurate and effective targeting is essential information for any strategic plan. It can lead to the prevention of over-bureaucratization in the life-cycle, for example, by ensuring that the organization does not become 'prematurely ossified and possibly no longer matched with [its] environment' (Aldrich and Herker, 1977: 219).

Monitoring

This aspect of the role deals with tracking environmental contingencies which are already known to managers in the organization. This activity is essential in helping to formulate plans based upon forecasting future scenarios for products and services (Adams, 1976).

It is also important to note that monitoring (and to a lesser extent, scanning) do not operate solely at the input side of the open-systems model. These roles also protect the organization at the output side. They monitor the characteristics of both supply and demand environments. Examples are protecting the organization from producing and selling products which might have unintended harmful side effects, from excessive and avoidable pollution, and from generally acting in a way which would be held corporately irresponsible.

Summary

In this chapter, we have introduced a general model for examining and understanding organization–environment relations and exchanges. This model, the open-systems perspective, allows us to analyse the particular processes through which organizations survive and grow in relation to their wider domain. The theory argues that the biological metaphor of the organization as an organism, constantly importing energy from its environment and exporting energy back into the environment, is both appropriate and useful.

Its utility largely lies in allowing the very general comparison of all organizational types (public or private ownership; manufacturing or service; large or small). These variables of organization simply do not apply at this level of analysis. According to open-systems theory, all organizations attempt to achieve an equilibrium or a balance between imports and exports. In a manufacturing organization, this would mean achieving a balance between buying in raw materials, processing them and exporting (selling) the final product in the market, at the same time taking into account the actions of competitor organizations and any fiscal or legislative regulations which might apply to the business.

Open-systems theory acts as the basis for two further theories: population ecology models and life-cycles. Population ecology models argue that all organizations operate within a framework of other organizations (a population) which co-exist in a particular industrial or service sector (a niche). It is this specific population which is important, rather than the wider system, which is the perspective of open-systems theory.

Organizations are born into populations and thrive and grow in line with characteristics of the population. For example, a population which is geared to supporting organizations which pursue generalist strategies is not going to provide much support for an organization which is pursuing a strategy of providing specialist goods or services. As the demands from the population change over time, generalists are able to transform and reproduce to a much greater extent than specialist organizations which are locked in to their particular niche. The population will inevitably not support organizations which do not 'fit' or adapt to its demands and changes. Thus, the population ecology model also accounts for organizational decline and death through this notion of 'bad fit'.

The life-cycle perspective again provides a general comparative model of organizations over time. Arguing that all organizations go through identifiable stages over time (growth, stability, maturation and decline or transformation) the model is able to show that particular characteristics of organization are associated with particular stages in the life cycle. For example, the structure and design of an organization is unlikely to be bureaucratic during its infancy. Ten years later, as stability becomes easier to achieve, it is unlikely that the organization will be anything other than bureaucratic. At the 'end' of the life-cycle, organizations which do not adapt and change will simply suffer a form of commercial arterio-sclerosis and seal their demise sooner or later. Those in which managers re-assess the situation and lead their organizations through renewal and regeneration will survive, beginning the life-cycle all over again.

Both theories are seductive in their generality and their seeming certainty about what will happen to all organizations. While they are useful analytical tools, all open-systems theories suffer from being overly deterministic. They portray the manager as powerless to do anything other than capitulate to the demands of the wider environment in which his or her organization resides. Of course, this is not the case. Managers and organizations have the power to interact with their environment on a reciprocal basis. They can influence, for example, how the organization is perceived by others, or can influence other environmental factors by cooperating with sister organizations rather than competing or by lobbying government for changes in legislation and so on. Most organizations have boundary roles in their design. These positions are explicitly created to allow the two-way transformation of knowledge, ideas and influences between organization and its environment.

The strategic management of an organization is thus a blend of environmental determinism and proactive managerial action. It is almost never just one or the other which is the engine of strategic decisions. Distinguishing between these two broad actions is often extremely difficult as we shall see in the following chapters. Defining what is deterministic and what is open to choice is sometimes impossible since managerial actions can combine both forces simultaneously. It is important, however, at this stage to recognize this dualism for it provides the platform for an understanding of organizational strategies which is the subject of the next chapter.

References   Adams, J. S. (1976) 'The structure and dynamics of behavior in organization boundary roles', in M. D. Dunnette (ed.), *The Handbook of Industrial and Organizational Psychology*, Rand-McNally, Chicago.

Aldrich, H. E. (1979) *Organizations and Environments*, Prentice-Hall, Englewood Cliffs, New Jersey.

Aldrich, H. E. (1986) *Population Perspectives on Organizations* (in collaboration with E. Auster, U. Staber and C. Zimmer), Acta Universitatis Upsaliensis, Uppsala, Sweden.

Aldrich, H. E. and D. Herker (1977) 'Boundary spanning roles and organization structure', *Academy of Management Review*, **2**, 217–30.

Argyris, C. (1987) 'Review essay: first- and second-order errors in managing strategic change: the role of organizational defensive routines', in A. M. Pettigrew (ed.), *The Management of Strategic Change*, Blackwell, Oxford.

Astley, W. G. and A. H. van de Ven (1983) 'Central perspectives and debates in organization theory', *Administration Science Quarterly*, **28**, 245–73.

Bedeian, H. (1987) 'Organization theory: current controversies, issues and directions', in C. L. Cooper and I. T. Robertson (eds), *International Review of Industrial and Organizational Psychology*, Wiley, New York.

Burns, T. and G. M. Stalker (1961) *The Management of Innovation*, Tavistock, London.

Carroll, G. R. (1985) 'Concentration with specialization: dynamics of niche width in populations of organizations', *American Journal of Sociology*, **90**, 1262–83.

Child, J. (1972) 'Organizational structures, environments and performance: the role of strategic choice', *Sociology*, **6**, 1–22.

Emery, F. E. and E. L. Trist (1960) 'Socio-Technical systems', in *Management Sciences Models and Techniques*, **2**, Pergamon, London.

Goffman, E. (1959) *The Presentation of Self in Everyday Life*, Doubleday, New York.

Greiner, L. (1972) 'Evolution and revolution as organizations grow', *Harvard Business Review*, **50**, 37–46.

Grinyer, P. and J.-C. Spender (1979) 'Recipes, crises and adaptation in mature businesses', *International Studies of Management and Organization*, **9**(3), 113–33.

Hannan, M. T. and J. Freeman (1977) 'The population ecology of organizations', *Sociology*, **82**, 929–64.

Harrigan, K. R. (1985) *Strategies for Vertical Integration*, Lexington Books, New York.

Hrebiniak, L. G. and W. F. Joyce (1985) 'Organizational adaptation: strategic choice and environmental determinism', *Administrative Science Quarterly*, **30**, 336–49.

Jemison, D. B. (1984) 'The importance of boundary spanning roles in strategic decision-making', *Journal of Management Studies*, **21**, 131–52.

Katz, D. and R. L. Kahn (1966) *The Social Psychology of Organizations*, Wiley, New York.

Kimberly, J. R. and R. H. Miles (and associates) (1980) *The Organizational Life-Cycle*, Jossey-Bass, San Francisco.

Lawrence, P. R. and J. W. Lorsch (1967) *Organization and Environment: Managing Differentiation and Integration*, Irwin, Homewood, Illinois.

Mayo, E. (1949) *Hawthorne and the Western Electric Company: The Social Problems of an Industrial Civilization*, Routledge, London.

Porter, M. E. (1980) *Competitive Strategy*, Free Press, New York.

Schreyogg, G. (1980) 'Contingency and choice in organization theory', *Organization Studies*, **1**, 305–26.

Taylor, F. W. (1911) *Principles of Scientific Management*, Harper, New York.

Thompson, J. D. (1967) *Organizations in Action*, McGraw-Hill, New York.

von Bertalanffy, L. (1956) 'General systems theory', in *General Systems, Yearbook of the Society for the Advancement of General Systems Theory*, **1**, 1–10.

Zammuto, R. F. (1988) 'Organizational adaptation: some implications of organizational ecology for strategic choice', *Journal of Management Studies*, **5**(2), 105–20.

Environments and managerial action: strategy and process

Introduction

In the previous chapter we described how the environment effects organizations and their managers and concluded that the environment was not all deterministic. Managers and organizations had a choice about the ways in which they responded to and interacted with their environments. In this chapter, we explore this scope for purposive action in greater detail.

To do this, we take the notion of organizational strategy. There are many definitions of strategy, but most of them are characterized by a number of prevailing themes. Strategic decisions:

1 are novel or have an element of novelty to the organization;
2 are organization-wide in their consequences;
3 are the stated future goals of senior management in the organization;
4 set precedents, which subsequent decisions are likely to follow;
5 are usually resource costly (time, money and people).

(Adapted from Wilson, 1980: 12)

Dror (1968) describes strategy as the 'major guidelines for action, directed at the future', while Chandler (1962: 13) says strategy is:

the determination of the basic long-term goals and objectives of an enterprise, and the adoption of courses of action and the allocation of resources necessary for carrying out these goals.

The result of much work in the field of strategy studies has been the evolution of a number of generalizable patterns. We shall be concerned with a specific set of these typologies in this chapter, since they allow the characterization of an organization as a single entity which displays a particular orientation towards its environment (Miles and Snow, 1978; Miller and Friesen, 1984).

The Miles and Snow typology is firmly based upon empirical research in 87 organizations (manufacturing and service as well as public, voluntary and commercial). The research identified *patterns* of strategy adopted by various organizations. The patterns included characteristics of organizational competences, structures and processes. The typology of Miller and Friesen is based upon 52 firms and is explicitly linked to organizational performance (successful and unsuccessful firms). Snow and Hrebiniak (1980) later took the Miles and Snow typology and related it to organizational performance. In this chapter, therefore, we shall look at broad strategic stances taken by organizations and the impact these are argued to have upon performance. First, we examine the work of Miles and Snow (1978) and Snow and Hrebiniak (1980).

Strategy and organizational domain

This approach to organizational strategy argues that all organizations are faced broadly with three problems which come from their immediate environment and from their position in the life-cycle (see Chapter 18 for details of organizational life-cycles). These domain-related problems are:

1 entrepreneurial problems
2 engineering problems
3 administrative problems

In general, the more mature an organization along its life-cycle, the more its managers will have to cope with all the above problems simultaneously. For analytical convenience, we describe each in turn.

Entrepreneurial problems   Describe the processes through which an organization gradually develops a firm portfolio of goods and services, coupled with a clear indication of target markets or market segments. For the organization in the initial phases of its life-cycle, this usually means shaping and refining the broad entrepreneurial vision of its founders into something more precise. In more mature organizations, these entrepreneurial problems are those which paradoxically define the organization clearly in a particular product or market niche, but which also can constrain innovative changes or modifications to overall strategies.

Engineering problems   Concern selecting the appropriate technology in order to achieve efficiency in the open system cycle of inputs, throughputs and outputs (see Chapter 18). Some organizations, such as Rover, have taken this set of problems very seriously and have installed extensive (and expensive) technological solutions to manufacturing efficiency. The installation of a computer integrated engineering system, which monitors and controls virtually everything from initial drawings to 'body-in-white' (the assembled, but unpainted car body) also integrates processes at Rover's three plants which are located at some distance from one another. Many other manufacturing organizations have already taken, or are contemplating taking, this route to achieving efficient throughputs. Of course, these solutions can also act as constraints to change should any factors of either organization or its domain shift markedly. Organizations can thus become locked in to their particular technology, which may be efficient in itself, but not if the outputs it produces are aimed at the wrong market or are otherwise inappropriate.

Administrative problems   Are those which focus on achieving stability for the organization. In order to make strategic decisions, managers require some level of predictability. Solving administrative problems allows this to happen. Reducing uncertainty is a key aspect here (Cyert and March, 1963; Thompson, 1967). The establishment of contracts with suppliers and customers, and the use of standard operating and control procedures internally are examples of reducing uncertainty. For organizations at an early stage in their life-cycle, the installation of an administrative system would represent a strategic response to the problems posed by domain uncertainty. More mature organizations must ensure that their internal processes are effectively monitored and controlled, but that, equally, these do not become dominant and ingrained so as to preclude future changes.

Miles and Snow (1978) developed four categories of strategic responses to the above domain issues. These strategies represent attempts to co-ordinate a response to all domain problems, engineering, entrepreneurial and administrative. Empirical research identified four broad strategies, *defenders*, *prospectors*, *analysers* and *reactors*. The brief characteristics of each strategy are described in Table 19.1.

Domain defenders	This strategy is one where management attempts to locate the organization in a stable niche. It is aimed at sealing off part of the market to secure a stable and predictable domain. Products and services are limited both in scope and in number but are aimed to be of consistently higher quality than those of competitor organizations. Organizational growth through more intensive market penetration is preferred to diversification. In the league of organizations, these are the consistent 'home players'.
Domain prospectors	This strategy allows failures as well as successes to be part of the strategic portfolio. The organization is usually operating in a broad domain for services and products, but managers are willing to experiment in an attempt to be first-to-market with new or revised products. Managers are early responders to changes which occur in the domain. Market entry is nearly always swift, though not necessarily sustainable in all areas.
Domain analysers	This strategy is aimed at concentrating on a limited range of products and services. Nevertheless, the strategy is a mixture of both defender and prospector, combining the efficient concentration of market operation with an open mind towards pursuing market opportunities which might prove to be profitable. It is a 'balanced' strategy, although one which is difficult to sustain in rapidly changing environments.
Domain reactors	This is not really a strategy at all in the strictest sense, since the organization is pulled this way and that by changes in its environment. There appears to be no consistent stance towards products and services or towards markets. These organizations are almost totally reactive in their strategies, unwilling to take risks or to exploit opportunities.

Domain defenders Achieving stability is the response of top management in these organizations when faced with any entrepreneurial demands from their domains. There is a deliberate setting of parameters in order to seal off sections of the market. As a corollary, a great deal of effort is put into achieving efficient inventory processing. Technology is often the key to sustaining success, since it is aimed at producing and supporting a limited number of products or services. These, in turn, are sustained in the market place by means of their image of prestige, quality, exclusivity or all three.

Typical defender 'industries' according to Snow and Hrebiniak's (1980) study are automobile production, airlines and plastics manufacturers. Consistently strong in the functions of general management and financial management, as well as being heavily biased towards production specialists, these organizations are structurally 'mechanistic' (Burns and Stalker, 1961) and strategically constrained. This is not surprising, since they all operate within industries which have relatively high set-up costs for manufacturing. Once established, the 'natural' tendency when faced with changes in the domain (such as increased competition, or greater numbers of foreign imports) is to look towards making the organization more efficient, keeping products relatively stable or as incremental additions to an existing range. Certainly, this strategy has characterized much of the British motor-car manufacturing industry over the past three decades or so. Whipp and Clark (1986) provide an insightful description of the strategy to launch the Rover SD1 motor car, arguing that such aspects as achieving manufacturing efficiency, ease of design production and over-zealous control mechanisms in the organization, took precedence over questions of markets and marketing of the product.

Domain prospectors

Prospecting is a relative term. It characterizes those organizations which, in a given industry, pursue a more dynamic and outward-looking strategy than others. While the defender is quite at home in a stable and predictable environment, the prospector consistently finds and exploits new markets, products and domains. Internally, the organization is constantly subject to change as some product lines flourish and others wither. This does not stop managers constantly trying to locate the organization in new areas. Failure and success are both at home in this dynamic strategy.

Snow and Hrebiniak (1980) show that organizations pursuing the prospector strategy are almost the reverse of defenders. In prospectors, technology is flexible. There are also likely to be multiple levels and types of technology in the same firm. Structurally, these firms are often represented by a grid or a project-based structure (see Handy, 1986). Domain prospectors also need to build into their structures plenty of environmental scanning departments or individuals. To thrive, these organizations rely on the accurate input of data concerning trends, changes and events in their domain. In terms of recruitment and selection, this means that such organizations may have to recruit individuals who currently appear not to fit with 'today's' business, but who have the potential to seek out and develop the business areas of tomorrow.

The matrix or grid structure provides a good basis for securing the essential flexibility which these organizations require. Both strategies of stability and new ventures occur simultaneously. Innovation and entrepreneurial strategies will have primacy. Administration in these organizations operates in the role of facilitator and support system rather than in the role of controller (as in defenders). Strong departments tend to be general management, product development and research units. It is here that the organization has distinctive competencies.

Domain analysers

Organizations pursuing this strategy fall between defenders and prospectors. This strategy is also a combination of some factors of both defenders and prospectors. The primary characteristic of analyser organizations is one of maintaining stability and at the same time being geared up for change. This parallels the 'loose-tight' orientation identified in Peters and Waterman's (1982) high-performing companies such as 3-M, Apple, Disney and MacDonalds. According to Miles and Snow (1978), domain analysers define their entrepreneurial problems as how to maintain a stable product and customer base while simultaneously identifying and exploiting new market opportunities.

Analysers tend to play safe. They are rarely first movers. Imitation or slight modification of what prospectors have done previously is the norm. In this way, the strategic risks are lessened, but then so too are the potential rewards of being first to market. Snow and Hrebiniak's (1980) study revealed two important characteristics of analysers. First, only 50 of 247 managers said that their organization pursued an analyser strategy. This is the least well represented category of the four strategic types. Second, the structures of analysers were extremely mixed. No single department (or group of them) was dominant, or contributed unambiguously to the distinctive competence of the firm (Selznick, 1957). The only consistent pattern found in the study was the high ranking of the finance function by respondents in all analyser organizations as contributing to success and continued good performance. It is likely that this reflects the centrality of finance in an organization which has to be both stable and flexible. Finance allows some measure of decision criteria to be examined when assessing competing bids for new projects, for example, and thus can act as a powerful control mechanism (see Burchell *et al.*, 1980; Jones, 1986).

Domain reactors

The key difference between reactors and the former three strategic types is that the reactor is never proactive in formulating strategies. The other three types can be either reactive or proactive. As their name implies, reactors spend most of their strategic life responding to one environmental change after another. As a result, they are strategically defined from without rather from within. Reactors often lack a clearly defined and articulated strategy within the ranks of their top management. We saw in the previous chapter how this situation might occur in an organization which is approaching maturity in its life-cycle (Kimberley and Miles, 1980). Having gone through a period of growth, led by a forceful entrepreneurial spirit (one person or a group), the organization enters a strategic void if the initial leaders leave or move on, and are not replaced with managers of equal or similar skills. It can sometimes be impossible for a new top manager to be brought in from outside the organization, to achieve a sense of strategic unity and purpose, particularly if his or her brief is to consolidate the previous eras of change and dynamism.

Decline can readily set in to reactor organizations. This is particularly evident in cases where management concerns largely focus on maintaining a particular configuration of organizational structure, to the neglect of scanning the immediate environment for changes, opportunities and trends. This can result in structural efficiency internally, but produce a structure which is largely inconsistent with the demands of the operating environment. The organization becomes ineffective and decline soon sets in unless quite radical changes occur to both strategy and structure.

Linking strategy and organizational performance

The work of Miller and Friesen (1984) follows and develops the themes outlined above of achieving fit or congruence between strategy, structure and environment. They argue that organizational performance is inextricably linked to the extent to which there is a match between these three factors. Many other authors have also pointed to this as the key aspect of organizing at the strategic level (see, for example, Chandler, 1962; Rumelt, 1974; Pettigrew, 1987).

Miller and Friesen (1984) attempt to forge a link between patterns of strategy and organizational performance (measured in terms of growth in profits and sales as well as return on equity in relation to competitor organizations). Their study covered 81 organizations, 52 of which were eventually selected to produce a comparison between successful and unsuccessful companies. Tables 19.2 and 19.3 summarize the major findings.

Strategy	Structure	Environment
Adaptive	Functional and monolithic with coordination by a strong leader	Firm adapts to environment. Power on a par with competition
Assertive	Functional, differentiated and integrated	Adaptive, but in the lead of competitors
Extra-polating	Hierarchical, control by committees, functional, technocratic	Proactive towards domain. Dominates competitors
Incremental	Decentralized, differentiated but with an elaborate and formal committee structure	Adaptive. Follows competitors
Expansion	Divisionalized, controlled from central HQ. Elaborate and formal collaborative mechanisms	Selects domain by process of diversification and aquisition
Niche	Functional, centralized	Creates a new segment of domain

Source: Miller/Friesen, *Organization: A Quantum View,* © 1984, pp 122–23. Reprinted by permission of Prentice–Hall, Inc., Englewood Cliffs, N.J.

Strategy	Structure	Environment
Over-extension	Divisionalized, centralized, differentiated, not integrated	Select environment via acquisitions
Ultra-conservative	Bureaucratic, mechanistic, formal. Monolithic, with centralized controls	Mostly ignore the environment
Muddle through	Leaderless, extremely decentralized, uncoordinated and fragmented. Political. Divisionalized	Each division has a different and unique relationship with the environment
Grafting and groping	Functional, centralized with few resources, differentiated	Adapt to environment in a piecemeal way

Source: Miller/Friesen, *Organization: A Quantum View,* © 1984, p 102. Reprinted by permission of Prentice–Hall, Inc., Englewood Cliffs, N.J.

Tables 19.2 and 19.3 show the ten archetypes of strategy and their relationship with organizational success. There are some obvious parallels with these archetypes and those outlined earlier by Miles and Snow (1978). For example, assertive strategies equate with domain prospectors, incremental strategies equate with analysers, and grafting and groping strategies reflect the domain reactor.

Miller and Friesen's work, however, tells us that the interrelationships between environment, structure and strategy are not simple. They are multi-variate and equifinal. That is, many different combinations can lead ultimately to organizational success. There are some patterns nonetheless which deserve mention since they fit the overall picture we have built up in this section of the book.

Strong individual leaders can lead to both success and failure

Strong, entrepreneurial leaders can succeed. We have ample evidence from firms which have turned round and escaped from the jaws of decline due to the tireless efforts of individual leaders (see, for example, Pettigrew, 1985). They can also lead to a strategy which will 'over-extend' the organization (see Table 19.3) with rapid growth followed perhaps by divisionalization, but which is uncontrolled or simply in the wrong strategic direction.

Decision-making is focused on the individual entrepreneur. Individual strategic decision processes are likely to be risky, impulsive and sporadic (Hickson *et al.*, 1986). There is no counterweight to the dominant power of the individual leader. The powerful chief executive remains unchecked by perhaps more cautious managers. So long as the decisions made by the leader are successful, the organization will survive. A series of false moves could secure organizational demise. There is an obvious parallel here with the 'power culture' described in Handy (1986) and outlined in Chapter 13 of this book.

We can also see that organizations themselves can be dynamic and innovative, populated by creative managers with multiple projects and ideas on the go all the time. Yet, a dominant leader (who is conservative and anti-risk) in these kinds of organizations will stifle innovation by 'constricting' decision-making processes (Hickson *et al.*, 1986). All major decisions will be made effectively by one person despite the potential corporate creativity over which he or she presides.

Incrementalism is not always a bad thing

In Chapter 10, we examined the debates over incrementalism in decision-making, concluding that there were those authors who described incrementalism as something to be avoided (Lindblom, 1959; Braybrooke and Lindblom, 1963), and those who suggested that incrementalism was normatively a strategy of playing safe (Quinn, 1980). According to Tables 19.2 and 19.3, both views are correct.

Providing incrementalism is a clearly thought through and well-articulated strategy among top management, then piecemeal adaptation can lead to success. Domain analysers do this, and so do the incremental strategists of Miller and Friesen's successful organizations. Incrementalism which results in muddling through, however, leads to failure. Very much like the domain reactors, the muddling-through strategists end up drifting, with a day-by-day focus on both the firm and its market. Coupled with poor communication and inadequate controls, this strategy almost inevitably results in strategic failure.

Dominate, adapt with purpose, or innovate

These seem to be the key patterns for sustained success. These three factors make up the harmonious chord of growth and success. They characterize all the organizations in Table 19.2. For those organizations which cannot dominate their industry or service sectors, the strategic choices for their managers are either to innovate or to adapt to selected trends and changes in the environment.

Unsuccessful firms appear to operate around different principles. Common factors here seem to be either a dominant concern with history and precedent (so firms continue to produce yesterday's product or service but more efficiently), or a lack of focused innovation (over-extension) or adaptation (muddling through).

Summary

There are no simple, easy answers to the question of fit between environment, structure and strategy, but it appears there are general patterns which we can isolate and identify. We have attempted to draw together these themes. The reader must be cautioned however. Relatively small sample sizes for research; investigations conducted mainly in North America; and at a different period of history, all raise a number of question marks over the validity of these findings in multiple contexts. Do these findings hold true for companies in Eastern Europe and the Far and Middle East, for example?

Studies are currently under way in the UK which will reveal to what extent the results apply to British enterprise (see Pettigrew, 1987; Johnson, 1987). At present, it looks as if the ability of managers continually to assess, amend and effect changes to organizational strategy is the key to sustained competitive and effective performance. It is unlikely that the typologies of Miles and Snow and Miller and Friesen will be wholly inapplicable to European organization. Just where any key differences lie will have to wait for the outcome of future investigations into this crucial area of organizational behaviour.

References

Braybrooke, D. and C. Lindblom (1963) *A Strategy of Decision*, Free Press, New York.

Burchell, S., C. Clubb, A. G. Hopwood and J. Hughes (1980) 'The roles of accounting in organizations and society', *Accounting, Organizations and Society*, **5**(1), 5–27.

Burns, T. and G. R. Stalker (1961) *The Management of Innovation*, Tavistock, London.

Chandler, A. D., Jr (1962) *Strategy and Structure: Chapters in the History of the American Industrial Enterprise*, MIT Press, Cambridge, Mass.

Cyert, R. and J. G. March (1963) *A Behavioural Theory of the Firm*, Prentice-Hall, Englewood Cliffs, New Jersey.

Dror, Y. (1968) *Public Policy Re-examined*, Chandler Publishing Co., San Francisco.

Handy, C. B. (1986) *Understanding Organizations*, Penguin, Harmondsworth.

Hickson, D. J., R. J. Butler, D. Cray, G. R. Mallory and D. C. Wilson (1986) *Top Decisions: Strategic Decision Making in Organizations*, Blackwell, Oxford; Jossey-Bass, San Francisco.

Johnson, G. (1987) *Strategic Change and the Management Process*, Blackwell, Oxford.

Jones, C. S. (1986) 'Organizational change and the function of accounting', *Journal of Business Finance and Accounting*, **13**(3), 283–310.

Kimberley, J. R. and R. H. Miles (and associates) (1980) *The Organizational Life-Cycle*, Jossey-Bass, San Francisco.

Lindblom, C. (1959) 'The science of muddling through', *Public Administration Review*, xix(2), 79–88.

Miles, R. E. and C. C. Snow (1978) *Organizational Strategy, Structure and Process*, McGraw-Hill, New York.

Miller, D. and P. H. Friesen (1984) *Organizations: A Quantum View*, Prentice-Hall, Englewood Cliffs, New Jersey.

Peters, T. and R. Waterman, Jr (1982) *In Search of Excellence: Lessons from America's Best Run Companies*, Harper & Row, New York.

Pettigrew, A. M. (1985) *The Awakening Giant: Continuity and Change in ICI*, Blackwell, Oxford.

Pettigrew, A. M. (ed.) (1987) *The Management of Strategic Change*, Blackwell, Oxford.

Quinn, J. B. (1980) *Strategies for Change: Logical Incrementalism*, Irwin, Homewood, Illinois.

Rumelt, R. P. (1974) *Strategy, Structure and Economic Performance*, Harvard University Press, Cambridge, Mass.

Selznick, P. (1957) *Leadership in Administration*, Harper & Row, New York.

Snow, C. C. and L. R. Hrebiniak (1980) 'Strategy, distinctive competence and organizational performance', *Administrative Science Quarterly*, **25**(2), 317–36.

Thompson, J. D. (1967) *Organizations in Action*, McGraw-Hill, New York.

Whipp, R. and P. Clark (1986) *Innovation and the Auto Industry: Product, Process and Work Organization*, Pinter, London.

Wilson, D. C. (1980) 'Organizational strategy', PhD Thesis, University of Bradford Management Centre.

Conceptualizing and managing the organizational environment

Roger Mansfield

To understand the nature and function of organizations requires an understanding of the environment in which an organization operates. Despite the importance of such an understanding, knowledge in this area is still limited. Despite knowledge being limited, it would be wrong to conclude that it is negligible. Organizational literature provides considerable insight and research evidence relating to the environment and how it may best be managed. Within this literature, there are three main approaches: (1) conceptualizing the environment in terms of global dimensions; (2) understanding the environment in terms of markets; and (3) examining the environment in terms of interlocking networks in which the organization is embedded.

Global environmental dimensions

Many organization theories have tended to view organizational environments in terms of a limited number of dimensions of the whole environment within which an organization operates. For example, the environment may be characterized in terms of its overall uncertainty, stability, or complexity. Although some researchers have considered as many as seven different dimensions simultaneously (e.g. Aldrich, 1972), most have concentrated on only two or three (e.g. Thompson, 1967; Child, 1972).

When employed on a large scale, comparative research can lead to useful conclusions about the nature of organization–environment relationships. However, they give a very simple picture of a very complex phenomenon. It is doubtful whether this approach can be taken much further. Many global concepts disguise the basic complexity of the environment and potentially give misleading or, at best, unhelpful results (Mansfield, Todd and Wheller, 1978).

Sectors of the environment will differ radically when assessed through concepts developed by organizational researchers to delineate environmental dimensions. Uncertainty may be greater in some sectors than in others. Complexity may differ in the market in which the organization sells its products to the one in which it hires its labour force.

The problem with this approach is that it does not seem to fit with current knowledge of the processes involved. It is rare to find a manager who reacts to the environment within which his organization operates in terms of global dimensions. His concerns are typically related to narrower problems linked to one or two environmental sectors. This suggests that to be useful, global concepts have to be 'unpacked' sector by sector. It is probably sensible to expect that each dimension will have a different value in each of the environmental sectors surrounding the organization.

Markets Economists have routinely considered the environment in which organizations operate in terms of markets and the forces of supply and demand. Such an approach makes intuitive sense to managers, whose actions are subject to market mechanisms. Many writers have argued that the concepts of markets and market transactions can be applied to all sorts of organizations—including the public sector. The application of the notion of markets, and its concentration on the economic elements of exchange relationships, means that only a limited view of the complexity of the organizational environment is taken. There is a strong tendency in this approach to undervalue the influence of long-term considerations and continuing relationships while concentrating attention on individual transactions.

Some elements of organizational behaviour can be explained in terms of organization–environment transactions of a marketplace type. Conventional versions of economic theories of the firm (Cohen and Cyert, 1965) are based on such concepts.

There can be no doubting the power of certain forms of economic analysis or their relevance to the subject in question. However, analyses based on the concepts of markets depend on a variety of limiting economic assumptions— starting with the assumption of perfect competition. Increasingly sophisticated analyses have attempted to take account of a wide variety of economic and non-economic assumptions; however the model still offers a limited view of the complexity of the environment. Most conventional economic analyses do not deal with understanding the internal management of organizations. Therefore, it is necessary to look at a combination of market analyses and other forms of organizational approaches (e.g. Williamson, 1967).

Networks The third approach to the study of organizational environments is referred to as inter-organizational analysis. This involves the study of networks of organizations. Evan (1966) developed the concept of the 'organization set' which refers to a focal organization and all the other organizations with which it has relationships. Although many of these relationships are mediated by market mechanisms, the emphasis has been on the variety of non-market factors which influence such organizational networks. The work of Evan and others (e.g. Pfeffer, 1976; Miles, Snow and Pfeffer, 1974) draws attention to the way the organizational environment and inter-organizational relationships are affected by the flow of personnel between organizations, interlocking directorships, legal and quasi-legal factors, long-term contracts, mergers and acquisitions, and third-party organizations such as trade associations and government agencies.

Such analyses conceptualize individual organizations as parts of larger social systems and draw attention to the variety of the linkages that hold such larger systems together. Research has demonstrated the variety of linkages that can occur at a number of different hierarchical levels. Although this approach appears to offer considerable promise it has not, in most cases, been carried far enough to provide clear indications of the implications of such networks for the focal organization.

Attempts to provide the needed theoretical framework has led to the development of ecological theories of organization (e.g. Aldrich, 1979; Mansfield, 1984). This approach emphasizes the flow of resources and information between the organization and other parties in its environment. It has not yet been developed to a point where it is typically likely to be useful for functional managers in most situations.

Managerial views

Independently, the three approaches outlined above are unable to deal with the complexity of the environmental circumstances faced by most organizations. There must also be considerable doubt about the extent to which any one of them approximates the approaches used by managers. The last point is not just relevant to an assessment of the practical utility of the ideas; it also has major theoretical implications.

As organizations are run in accordance with decisions taken by individuals, it is important that the conceptualization of the environment takes account of the way individuals perceive and react to it. If this cannot be achieved, it is hard to see how both the *nature* of organizations and the *processes* involved in organizational behaviour can be understood within a single theoretical perspective.

Importance must be attached to the difficulties with the approaches outlined. They do not seem to fit with the problems confronted by individual managers, or the perspective they adopt. Most managers will not conceive of the environment as a whole but rather in terms of the different sectors relating to the different activities of the organization in question. This suggests that it is essential to examine the environment in sectors corresponding to the different functional activities carried on within organizations and in terms of the sectors identified by managers themselves.

Within each sector, the different approaches would have some utility but, on their own, seem unlikely to provide a framework within which all the relevant environmental factors can be considered. It is probably most useful if the environment is seen in different ways for different purposes, and that if any overall framework is to be developed for the understanding of organizational environments, it must encompass elements from each of the three approaches.

Boundaries and systems

Organization–environment interactions can only be fully comprehended when the boundary of the organization is understood. The question of organizational boundaries is subsidiary to the question of organizational identities. This latter question may be resolved by recourse to socio-legal concepts, as many organizations are legally identified within the social system in which they operate. However, it is also to look at a social system which is not a legally identifiable organization. For example, one that is part of a larger legal entity — such as a division or department.

It is very rare for this to cause any significant problem as most organizations tend to have a well-accepted formal existence even if they have no clear legal identity. In this respect, they tend to differ from other forms of social groupings whose existence may be problematic and ephemeral.

Open-systems theory suggests that organizational boundaries should be seen as analogous to semi-permeable membranes. This is most obviously relevant when one looks at the flow of people and information, into and out of, organizations. In the large majority of cases, organizational members have a clear existence outside their organizational role as well as within it. Under these circumstances the question of boundary definition is often a difficult one. The question of membership may itself be problematic. Although it would seem to be agreed that organizational employees are members of their employing organization, the relationship of such groups to shareholders or trade unions is ambiguous. It has to be accepted that organizational boundaries are conceptual divisions between internal and external factors rather than physical boundaries. Even in these terms there are problems and, in many cases, the 'informal organization', as it is often described, relates perhaps in part to extra-organizational activities brought into an organizational context.

Although the nature and position of organizational boundaries may be difficult to define, across these boundaries flow physical resources, services, information, people and money in varying mixtures and for varying reasons. Relationships which flow across boundaries carry with them influences between the parties. When consideration is given to these boundary-crossing relationships, the simple exchange models of such transactions are inadequate. There are many other elements involved which cannot easily be conceptualized within such a framework. It is reasonable to argue that these cross-boundary relationships are organized in somewhat similar ways to intra-organizational relationships. Logically, they depend on administrative or legal arrangements (Simon, 1957; Mansfield, 1984) and moral parameters. Such an argument implies that the market model is a special case of the general network approach to organization–environment interactions—applicable in circumstances where other aspects of the relationships become relatively unimportant.

The organizational environment and organization–environment interactions can be conceptualized in both static and dynamic terms in the same way as an organization itself. The approaches mentioned thus far suggest that the global dimensions approach is particularly geared to describing the static characteristics of the environment at a particular point in time. The network approach may also provide a definition of the static relationships that exist between an organization and elements of its environment. Within this framework it is easier to envisage an integration of static and dynamic aspects of the situation. Within the organization–environment networks, transactions of a variety of sorts can continue to take place, leading to the flow of goods, services, information, people and money across national organizational boundaries. These flows and the ways in which they change may be described as the dynamic characteristics of the environment and the organization–environment interactions.

Simplifying assumptions

The main problem in conceptualizing and managing the organizational environment is its enormity and complexity. Taken literally, the environment encompasses everything external to the organization and as such is too huge and complex to be comprehended. It is therefore essential, whether one is looking for a means of describing the environment or of understanding it or controlling it, that one or a variety of simplifying assumptions are utilized. In some cases these may be consciously calculated; in others, merely adopted without further thought.

The first set of assumptions that is routinely used are those relating to the *selective ignoring* of large areas of the environment on the grounds that they are or seem to be irrelevant to the day-to-day functioning of the organization. Such a set of assumptions depends on the identification of strategic contingencies which are reckoned to be of vital relevance to the welfare of the organization and the ignoring of other factors. This sort of assumption is utilized by anyone analysing a situation in an organization to exclude the large majority of external events that have no obvious impact upon the organization in question.

The second set of assumptions which are routinely used involve *globalization*. Here, characteristics are assumed to represent the whole environment or significant sectors of it where they are actually only characteristic of some limited set of phenomena within it. The use of global dimensions of organizational environments is a clear example of this. In these cases simplicity is achieved by assuming a simplified version of the environment based on the assessment of certain aspects of it or on estimates of what they might actually be.

The third set of assumptions are those suggesting *excessive homogeneity* and are commonly employed in many forms of economic analysis based on the theory of markets. Economic theories simplify the environment by inventing methods of aggregation of a large number of phenomena via theories of supply and demand in the marketplace. Thus, it is assumed that, on average, potential customers will modify their demand for so much of a product at a particular price and other conditions of sale in a similar way when these parameters are changed without the necessity for analysing the behaviour of every individual in the marketplace. The same style of assumption can be utilized on the supply side with a similar simplification.

The fourth set of assumptions that are routinely used adopt a notion of *temporal consistency* where current environmental circumstances are assumed to continue into the future without significant change. Here the influences of environment change are likely to be ignored or downgraded. A more complex variant on this theme is to assume a continuation of current trends rather than a continuation of the status quo.

The fifth set of assumptions that are routinely used relate to a *proximate focus* where the closest parts of the environment are examined carefully and it is assumed that they represent the whole environment of relevance to the organization.

The sixth set of assumptions are similar in kind but take the *'typical' case* and generalize from it. Thus, relatively few well-understood instances are assumed to be generalized to the overall market sector or even the overall environment.

The last set of assumptions that will be examined here relate to the exaggeration of the effects of dependence. Thus, an assessment of the environment is made in terms relating to the greatest *dependencies* that the organization has on outside organizations or agencies, thus focusing heavily on the areas of dependence and largely ignoring other aspects of the environment.

Any of these assumptions may be useful in particular circumstances to provide an approximation to the overall environmental situation — thus allowing it to be described or understood, or even controlled or managed. There are great dangers in these assumptions if they are entered into blindly. They may lead to major environmental phenomena and changes being ignored with catastrophic potential results for the organization in question. Despite the dangers inherent in making simplifying assumptions, managers have no alternative but to move along this route in order to deal with the full complexity of the environment rather than let it paralyse them into inaction.

A conceptual approach

Given all the problems of conceptualizing the organizational environment and the nature of organization–environment interactions, it is obviously difficult to find a conceptual model to advance our understanding in this area. In order to move forward, it is useful to examine three different aspects of the environment which encompass their static and dynamic properties. First, it is necessary to examine the *structure of the environment* and of organization–environment interactions. Second, is to chart the *flow of resources, information and influence* between the organization and its environment and between different parts of that environment. Third, it is necessary to examine the ways in which the structure and the flows are *changing over time*, both in terms of the nature of the changes and the rates of change involved.

Each of the three aspects noted above must be charted for each of the different sectors with which the organization relates. In examining the structure of the environment and of organization–environment interactions, it would seem useful to combine the market approach with that which isolates particular dimensions of the environment. Thus, in addition to market structure, concepts like dependence, uncertainty and complexity would seem particularly useful. In charting the flows from the organization to the environment and between different sectors of the environment, the network or ecological approach would seem especially useful, particularly if allied with the dynamic aspects of the market approach. In examining change, it is necessary to consider all these aspects over time and develop a model of temporal change and rate of change.

Managing the environment

In a general sense, managing the environment or the organization–environment interface has the same logic to it as managing anything else. That is to say, the first step must involve the collection of information, followed by some form of planning process which will lead to action, with the action and its consequences being monitored. In organizations, the collection of information relating to the environment and the monitoring of the consequences of actions will be carried out within functional areas relevant to the particular environment sector in question. Increasingly, this process is aided by the utilization of management information systems based on modern information technology. Improved communication and computational facilities allowed the data to be handled at high speed and processed to aid the decision making processes relating to planning and action within the organization.

Of course managing the environment is merely one aspect of both strategic and operational management. It should take place within an overall strategic framework which allows the linking of different functional areas of overall organizational strategy. This is a key factor which is necessary in order that the managing of different environmental sectors can be interlinked in pursuit of corporate objectives.

The key to appropriate cross-boundary control can be based on a variety of strategic approaches such as acquisition, vertical integration or diversification, which attempt to encompass aspects of the environment and spread the organization's ownership. However, there are a variety of other techniques which have been routinely employed, short of gaining ownership (such as long-term contracts, franchising, interlocking directorships, etc.) through which significant control of aspects of the organization's environment can be achieved across the boundary.

Weick (1969) suggested that the organizational environment could be enacted rather than reacted to by a process of definition of the relevant aspects of the environment and the movement of the organization within the available environmental space. Three different approaches to managing the environment or particular environmental sectors can be developed. First, there is the reactive approach which depends on an accurate assessment of environmental forces. The second approach is proactive, which involves taking initiative to change or control the environment rather than merely react to it. The third approach is one of enactment, which involves a strategic approach encompassing both reactive and proactive elements but within a moving relationship between the organization and its environment. Clearly managers can become victims of environmental forces, masters of circumstances or creators of opportunities depending on which of the three postures they are able or prepared to adopt.

References   Aldrich, H. E. (1972) 'An organization–environment perspective on co-operation and conflict between organizations and the manpower training system', in A. R. Negandhi (ed.), *Conflict and Power in Complex Organizations*, Kent State University, Kent, Ohio.

Aldrich, H. E. (1979) *Organizations and Environments*, Prentice-Hall, Englewood Cliffs, New Jersey.

Child, J. (1972) 'Organization structure and performance: the role of strategic choice', *Sociology*, **6**, 1–22.

Cohen, K. J. and R. M. Cyert (1965) *Theory of the Firm: Resource Allocation in a Market Economy*, Prentice-Hall, Englewood Cliffs, New Jersey.

Evan, W. M. (1966) 'The organization-set: toward a theory of interorganizational relations', in J. D. Thompson (ed.), *Approaches to Organizational Design*, University of Pittsburgh Press, Pittsburgh.

Mansfield, R. (1984) 'Formal and informational structure', in M. Gruneburg and T. Wall (eds), *Social Psychology and Organizational Behaviours*, Wiley, London.

Mansfield, R., D. Todd and J. Wheller (1978) 'Structural implications of the company–customer interface', *Journal of Management Studies*, **17**, 19–33.

Miles, R. E., C. C. Snow and J. Pfeffer (1974) 'Organization–environment: concepts and issues', *Industrial Relations*, **13**, 244–64.

Pfeffer, J. (1976) 'Power and resource allocation in organizations', in B. M. Staw and G. R. Salencik (eds), *New Directions in Organizational Behavior*, St Clair Press, Chicago.

Simon, H. (1957) *Models of Man*, Wiley, New York.

Thompson, J. D. (1967) *Organizations in Action*, McGraw-Hill, New York.

Weick, K. (1969) *The Social Psychology of Organizing*, Addison-Wesley, Reading, Mass.

Williamson, O. E. (1967) *The Economics of Discretionary Behavior*, Markham, New York.

READING 11 The political economic environment of organizations

Monir Tayeb

Introduction

Following Pennings (1975), it is useful to group the organizational environment into three broad categories. The first, the technical environment, consists of factors which have immediate relation with organizations and are directly relevant to what they do and what they want to achieve. These include technology, market share, competitors, suppliers, customers, and employees. The second category is the intermediary environment, made up of social, political and economic institutions with which organizations interact, such as education system, trade unions, pressure groups, and government. The third category comprises the cultural characteristics of the society within which organizations operate. This reading will examine the political aspects of national cultures.

Socialism versus capitalism

Relatively few studies have been carried out to examine the influence of the two major forms of economic system of production, namely capitalism and socialism, on organizations. The two systems stand in sharp ideological and institutional contrast. There are at least five major aspects on which capitalist and socialist societies differ fundamentally from one another, and which have significant implications for work organizations. These are: ideology and value systems, characteristics of class structure, ownership and control of means of production, management of the economy, and the role of the state.

Dominant ideology and value systems

The dynamic of state socialist societies is a form of ideological activism, whereas that of the capitalist societies is a form of 'instrumental activism' (Bell, 1966; Lane, 1977). In socialist societies, the pattern of industrialization is derived from the overriding value system of Marxism–Leninism and cannot be understood independently of ideas of historical materialism which legitimate the forms of development pursued. Capitalist ideology appeals to the notion of economic betterment through individual initiative and self-help. Although it has clearly become modified with the rise of large, bureaucratic corporations, and perhaps never took deep root in more corporatist societies, capitalist ideology stands in stark contrast to its socialist counterparts. Socialist ideology emphasizes the collective. The party is seen to play the role of representing the interests of the working class as a general collective.

Class structure

Capitalist societies are characterized by an antagonistic class structure with an inherent conflict of interests and inequality between the dominant owning and/or controlling class and the working class. A distinctive feature of the former is the extraction of surplus from the latter in a capitalist form of economy having capital and commodity market operating to maximize profit.

Socialist societies, as Lane (1977) argues, are not classless, but they are not antagonistic class societies either. They are single-class societies or workers' states. The working class is the dominant class for whom the state rules. This is not to say that in socialist societies, where the state owns and controls the means of production, profit is not sought. Rather, the extraction of surplus value is to maintain a high level of investment to ensure all-round industrialization. At the same time, however, they have an essentially inegalitarian or 'bourgeois' system of unequal distribution of commodities — expressed through the price and wage system and in other forms of market relationships.

Ownership and control of means of production

In capitalist societies, there is both private and state ownership and control of means of production. Under socialism, the means of production is formally socialized in the hands of the state (Giddens, 1973). The means of production is not owned, in the sense of exclusive rights to enjoy and to dispose of assets, by any social class: no identifiable group of persons may enjoy a source of income from the proceeds of ownership. Investment, production and the appointment of leading personnel of industrial enterprises in state socialist societies are firmly controlled by industrial ministries, and the possibilities of any group consistently extracting an economic surplus as a factor source of profit are extremely limited (Mandel, 1969).

Management of the economy

In capitalist societies, the market economy operates to maximize profit, which in turn maintains a bourgeois class. A distinctive feature of socialist societies is the absence of a market economy. Economy is planned and controlled by the state. The centralization of planning and control in most socialist countries contrasts with the decentralization inherent in the use of market mechanisms.

The role of the state

Under capitalism the type of activity performed by the government must of necessity be limited, whereas this is not the case under socialism. In the latter, the formal political apparatus is responsible to a much wider extent in determining who gets what, when and how: the political process decides the distribution of resources between various social groups and interests (Lane, 1977).

Organizations in capitalist and socialist societies

The debate continues as to whether the development of both capitalist and socialist societies is eroding the differences between them, and whether it would be more accurate to distinguish several variants of capitalism and socialism. Nevertheless, as Child and Tayeb (1983) put it, so long as each system rests upon intrinsically different functions it is to be expected that their organized units will reflect the different basis and dynamic of each system.

The model of capitalist objectives and its implications for organizational relations appear generally to hold in practice. However, the socialist alternative does not. The avoidance of tensions in the relation of production by means of planning oriented towards social objectives has not been achieved in socialist societies. The low productivity of labour has been a long-standing concern in countries like the USSR, and there are many complaints about poor discipline (Lampet, 1984; Pietsch, 1984). Although socialism is expected to promote a sense of collective identity within organizations, there is concern about worker motivation in socialist countries, together with evidence of considerable job dissatisfaction and illegal informal practices (Haraszti, 1977; Grancelli, 1984). In Yugoslavia, the workers' dissatisfaction can be judged, among other things, by the relatively high occurrence of strikes (see Rojek and Wilson 1987 for a discussion of worker dissatisfaction in workers' self-management schemes).

Ramondt (1979) estimates that probably there is on average a strike in Yugoslavia every two days. Table 1 compares salient characteristics of work organizations in socialist and capitalist countries.

Table R11.1
Organizations in capitalist and socialist economies

Organizations in capitalist countries
- profit, growth and market power as primary objectives
- objectives set by the organization (owners, managers)
- decentralized approach to planning, resource allocation, control and other strategic decisions
- market-allocation mechanism for resources and employment
- independent trade unions' action and voice in enterprise policy-making, where it affects them
- investment fund-raising in private sector is the organization's responsibility
- single-hierarchy structure
- structure and leadership style decided by managers and other employees within the organization
- employees' participation in decision-making is not institutionalized to any significant degree, especially in strategic areas
- bureaucratic and non-bureaucratic forms of structure

Organizations in socialist countries
- full-employment, welfare, redistribution of wealth as primary objectives
- objectives are set by the central state
- centralized approach to planning, resource allocation and control, direct state investment and control
- state is responsible for raising investment funds
- major decisions taken above organization
- dual-hierarchy structure, party parallel hierarchy
- workers' participation is institutionalized to a great degree, e.g. worker director, workers'committee
- bureaucratic structure

Convergence or divergence?

The implications of capitalism and socialism for organizations can easily be contrasted in terms that are both too sharply drawn and static. Capitalist and socialist systems place many similar requirements upon management and organization and share many organizational problems. Both systems are evolving, and may in certain respects become more similar, particularly in relations between the state and large corporate bodies in economic and social management (Child and Tayeb, 1983).

Tinbergen (1961) observes the changes that have occurred in the socialist system since the Russian Revolution: the belief that 'workers' could take care of management functions is decreasing in prevalence. There is recognition that management is a specialized set of activities. Attempts to equalize incomes did not work. Wages are now dependent on productivity. For some time planning was done in terms of physical quantities and not money values. Gradually the use of money and the significance of prices and costs were increasingly recognized. Additional changes in the Soviet system include the introduction of the concept of interest, the increase in emphasis on consumption, the use of mathematical methods associated with capitalists, and changing concepts of international trade to include trade between socialist and capitalist economies.

In the mean time, as Perlmutter (1977) argues, the capitalist economies have also undergone changes: the public sector is now considerably larger than it was in the nineteenth century—especially in Western Europe. Taxes have been used to redistribute wealth. Free competition has been limited. Education has gradually been made available to an increasing portion of the population. Market forces have been eliminated or modified in some cases (although Britain is perhaps currently an exception), reflected, for example in international commodity agreements. Planning has been given a larger role in industry and government.

Many factors may explain convergence between the two systems. Industrialization is one such factor. In the two 'camps' there are both highly advanced industrialized countries and those which are in the process of becoming industrialized. As Harbison and Myers (1959) argue, there is a central logic to industrialization which derives from the imperatives of machine technology and economic development. Industrialization brings about certain changes in the fabric of organizations, particularly their size and complexity. These changes in turn are seen as necessitating certain developments in organization structuring: greater specialization, reliance upon rules, and decentralization. Management becomes more professionalized and authority relationships tend to shift from autocratic to formalized and more participative modes. The logic of industrialization prevails whatever the social and cultural setting, although these factors can impinge on the process and may govern its speed.

Kuc *et al.* (1981) observed that in many ways the Polish factories have characteristics similar to their counterparts in Western societies. Highly structured, they are specialized, formalized administrative control systems, operating under efficiency norms in ways predicted by Weber (1947). They operate with technological processes requiring certain skills from the workforce and subject to the constraints of rationality or bounded rationality (see Chapter 10).

The so-called contingency variables and task environmental factors with which organizations have immediate relationships, such as size, market share, competition, production technology, and dependence on other organizations, pose similar opportunities and threats to organizations regardless of the socio-political setting within which they operate (Hickson *et al.*, 1974). In both capitalist and socialist systems there have been somewhat comparable experiments in organizational design intended to reduce the top-level overload that accompanies centralized decision-making in large organizations, and also to devolve responsibility for the performance of diversified operations. These look rather like similar responses to the contingencies of scale and diversification commonly experienced by organizations in both systems (Child and Tayeb, 1983).

Kuc, Hickson and McMillan (1981) found that the relationships between size, inter-organizational dependence and major structural characteristics of Polish firms were much the same as elsewhere. Reading in a causal argument, Polish organizations in a communist-controlled centrally planned economy are subject to the same pressures and constraints for growth and inter-organizational dependence as those which appear in more market-oriented economies. The bigger they get the more bureaucratic they become; the more dependent they are on others, the more centralized their decision-making becomes (and they lose autonomy).

There is also a danger of exaggerating the differences in, say, planning, resource allocation, and control between organizations in capitalist countries and those in the socialist countries. Although the authorities in socialist countries find it difficult to accept decentralization in the sense of fostering a relatively high degree of autonomy among lower-level subsidiary units, experiments have been under way for some time with forms of 'deconcentration' (Glinski, 1979). This has been described by Schwartz (1974: 154) as 'an administrative device in a hierarchical system which involves the shifting of decision making from an overloaded centre to lower levels of the hierarchy'.

Moreover, the degree of autonomy permitted to lower-level units in capitalist societies should not be overestimated. The so-called 'semi-autonomous' divisions or subsidiaries of a capitalist enterprise normally remain subject to strategic planning and expenditure approval from the top, and certain types of performance are expected of them. In Britain, for example, central control and monitoring of local units have recently increased even in the sphere of democratically elected local government (Child and Tayeb, 1983).

In recent years there has been a growing tendency in many socialist countries to give more autonomy to business organizations, as a means of increasing their efficiency and ability to respond to their environment. China's experimental enterprises scheme 1978–80 (Lockett and Littler, 1983) is a good example of such tendencies. From 1978 various pilot schemes expanding enterprise autonomy began in the state sector. There were considerable regional variations in the form of experiments; however, the key features were similar and included:

Profit retention   At the heart of the experiments was the right of enterprises to retain and utilize part of their profits. Previously state enterprises' profits were handed over to the state. The experimental enterprises were able to keep a percentage of their profits for re-investment in production and technical innovation, and for workers' and staff individual bonuses and collective welfare. The implication of these schemes is that enterprises have increased incentives to raise profits and hence to improve efficiency in the use of both human and natural resources.

Extension of planning and marketing rights   Once enterprises have met the targets of the state plan, they can also decide what to produce next. Alongside these extended production planning power have come more rights to market an enterprise's products, which entails greater freedom in production planning. Parallel to these changes came greater rights to conduct foreign trade and to retain a proportion of foreign-exchange earnings for importing foreign machinery, etc.

Increased flexibility in labour management   Theoretically, enterprises were given greater rights to recruit, promote and demote both cadres and workers as well as the power to sack workers on disciplinary grounds and to determine their own pay and incentive schemes. However, this new policy of restricting job security has met with resistance from government departments, economists and workers (White, 1983). The result is that actual dismissals appear to have been rare.

There are also plans for the party to be separated from enterprise management in order to give more independence to the latter. So the enterprise system will in future comprise thousands of separate, relatively independent enterprise hierarchies each with a top manager who, it is planned, will be elected by the employees (Laaksonen, 1984).

References

Bell, D. (1966) 'The "end of ideology" in the Soviet Union?', in M. Drachkovitch (ed.), *Marxist Ideology in the Contemporary World—Its Appeals and Paradoxes*, Praeger, New York.

Child, J. and M. H. Tayeb (1983) 'Theoretical perspectives in cross-national organizational research', *International Studies of Management and Organization*, xii, 23–70.

Giddens, A. (1973) *The Class Structure of the Advanced Societies*, Hutchinson, London.

Glinski, B. (1979) 'System of central management of the socialist economy and its evolution', *Oeconomica Polona*, **4**, 45–61.

Grancelli, B. (1984) 'Managerial practices and patterns of employee behaviour in Soviet enterprise', paper presented to the Third Workshop on Capitalist–Socialist Organizations, Helsinki, August.

Haraszti, M. (1977) *A Worker in Workers' State*, Penguin, Harmondsworth.

Harbison, F. and C. A. Myers (1959) *Management in the Industrial World*, McGraw-Hill, New York.

Hickson, D. J., C. R. Hinings, C. J. McMillan and J. P. Schwitter (1974) 'The culture-free context of organization structure: a tri-national comparison', *Sociology*, **8**, 59–80.

Kuc, B., D. J. Hickson and C. J. McMillan (1981) 'Centrally planned development: a comparison of Polish factories with equivalents in Britain, Japan and Sweden', in D. J. Hickson and C. J. McMillan (eds), *Organization and Nation*, Gower, Farnborough.

Laaksonen, O. (1984) 'The management and power structure of Chinese enterprise during and after the Cultural Revolution', *Organization Studies*, **5**, 1–21.

Lampet, N. (1984) 'Job security and the law in the USSR', paper presented to the Conference on Employment and Labour Policy in USSR, Birmingham, June.

Lane, D. (1977) 'Marxist class conflict analyses of state socialism', in R. Scase (ed.), *Industrial Society: Class, Cleavage and Control*. Allen & Unwin, London.

Lockett, M. and C. R. Littler (1983) 'Trends in Chinese enterprise management, 1978–1982', *World Development*, **11**, 683–704.

Mandel, E. (1969) *The Inconsistencies of State Capitalism*, International Marxist Group Pamphlet, London.

Pennings, J. (1975) 'The relevance of the structural-contingency model for organizational effectiveness', *Administrative Science Quarterly*, **30**, 393–410.

Perlmutter, H. W. (1977) 'Emerging East–West ventures: the transideological enterprise', in T. D. Weinshall (ed.), *Culture and Management*, Penguin, Harmondsworth.

Pietsch, A-J. (1984) 'Shortage of labour and motivation problems of Soviet workers', paper presented to the Conference on Employment and Labour Policy in USSR, Birmingham, June.

Ramondt, J. (1979) 'Workers' self-management and its constraints: the Yugoslav experience', *British Journal of Industrial Relations*, xvii, 83–94.

Rojek, C. and Wilson, D. C. (1987) 'Workers' self-management in the world system: the Yugoslav case, *Organization Studies*, **8**(4), 297–308.

Schwartz, D. V. (1974) 'Decision making, administrative decentralization, and feedback mechanisms: comparisons of Soviet and Western models', *Studies in Comparative Communism*, **7**, 146–83.

Tinbergen, J. B. (1961) 'Do communist and free economies show a converging pattern?', *Soviet Studies*, April.

Weber, M. (1947) *The Theory of Social and Economic Organization*, Free Press, New York.

White, G. (1983) 'Urban employment and labour allocation policies', in S. Feuchtwang and A. Hussain (eds), *The Chinese Economic Reforms*, Croom Helm, London.

Change and restructuring at the Royal Oak Building Society

David A. Preece

The organizational problem

During the 1980s major changes have taken place in the external contexts of building society operations. Historically, however, building societies have become accustomed to working within a relatively stable (and, hence, predictable) and only slowly changing environment.

The particular forms of organizational structure, job design, culture management style, social processes and institutional arrangements which became established in the latter context over a number of years have become increasingly inappropriate to the very different situation of the 1980s. The Royal Oak Building Society therefore found it necessary to make internal innovations and changes in the broad range of its structural, institutional and processual arrangements, in order to remain competitive and viable. The 'organizational problem' concerns how it meets this challenge through these internal adaptations.

The case study, which is based on the actual experiences of a medium-sized building society (the name has been changed to provide anonymity) consists of three main elements—a brief description of the organization; an overview of the key contextual changes of the 1980s; and the social and cultural processes as they existed at the beginning of the 1980s.

The study concludes with a number of questions for the reader about how the organization might be advised to respond to the challenges of the 1990s.

The organization

The Royal Oak Building Society was founded in 1849, and has since grown steadily in terms of business volume, the number of branch offices and the number of people employed. Its head office is in the West Midlands, where it also has its highest concentration of branch offices; however it operates across a much wider area—having offices as far apart as West Wales, Northamptonshire, South Yorkshire and Hampshire.

In terms of size, measured in business volume, it ranks around twentieth among UK building societies. There has been some tendency in recent years for branch offices in the outer ring of its network to be altered to agencies. Nonetheless, transactions at head office in the branches still account for the great majority of its business, and it is here that the focus will be placed in the case study. The number of branch offices grew steadily during the 1970s, and up to 1984, since when the total has settled at around eighty.

Table CS9.1 shows how the number of people employed by the society has fluctuated over recent years, both at head office and in the branch network.

Between 1981 and 1986 numbers employed at head office showed little increase, while in the branch office network, numbers had increased annually

Table CS9.1
Royal Oak Building
Society: staff
employed in head
office and branch
offices, 1978–87

| | Head office | | | Branch offices | | | The society |
	Full time	Part time	Total FTE*	Full time	Part time	Total FTE*	Total FTE*
1978	86	3	87.5	186	24	198.0	285.5
1979	105	2	106.0	222	25	234.5	340.5
1980	119	2	120.0	233	37	251.5	371.5
1981	132	3	133.5	226	55	253.5	387.0
1982	139	2	140.0	247	65	279.5	419.5
1983	131	1	131.5	263	71	298.5	430.0
1984	119	1	119.5	271	85	313.5	433.0
1985	127	5	129.5	258	79	297.5	427.0
1986	134	5	136.5	253	78	291.0	428.5
1987	175	5	177.5	254	81	294.5	472.0

*FTE=full time equivalent

from 1978 to 1984, whereafter there had been a slight reduction and, at least for the moment, a plateau appears to have been reached. The main explanations for the above are as follows:

1 In head office, the notable increase in the number of staff between 1986 and 1987 is due to three main factors:
   (a) a significant expansion in business, particularly in mortgage lending;
   (b) the recruitment of additional computer specialists;
   (c) the lifting of a ban on recruitment to most head-office posts (the ban had lasted for two years).
2 In the branch offices, the number of staff employed had increased essentially in line with the opening of new offices. Since 1984 there has been no such net increase. Seven branches were disposed of during 1985/86 (all being relatively low on business volumes, and concentrated at the boundaries of the Royal Oak's geographic area. *Some* of these branches, however, became agencies, but were now owned and run, of course, by other companies such as estate agents).

It is now pertinent to outline the organization structure of the Royal Oak's head office. For reasons of brevity I have only indicated 'top-down' roles from the chairman to departmental manager level (see Figure CS9.1).

One aspect of structure which is indicative of the way in which the organization has changed and developed recently is that there are no separate mortgage and investment departments, as there have historically always been in the majority of building societies—not least, the Royal Oak. During 1985 the new department of Members' Accounts was created out of the old Mortgage and Investment departments. The rationale for the change emerged from two separate processes which had taken place during 1984:

1 The Management Services department, which had been analysing the work and structures of the mortgage and investment departments, had concluded that there were similarities between the two departments, and had therefore asked the question: 'Why not have one department?'
2 A software house was developing new specialist programs for the society. The basic unit of the software is that of a *customer*. It was realized by managers that the new information system (including the new software) would much

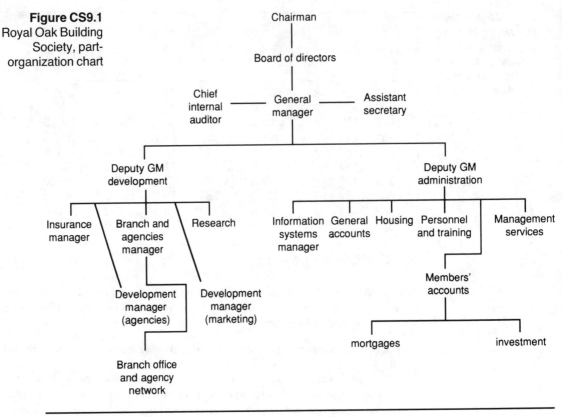

Figure CS9.1
Royal Oak Building
Society, part-
organization chart

Notes:

1.   The General Manager (previously called Chief executive) is not on the Board.
2.   All the Board are non-executive.

more readily and effectively fit into an organization structure which was also
based on the customer (who in turn, could have a mortgage with the society,
and/or some investment or other affiliation).

Key contextual changes during the 1980s

The context has altered from one which was essentially stable, unchanging,
and, therefore, predictable, to one where there is a good deal of turbulence, with
more intensified competition, a burgeoning of new services and initiatives, and
a proliferation of new technology. These developments will be discussed in more
detail below, following some introductory caveats. Expansion in business
volume and the number of branch offices is *not* taken to be a distinguishing
feature of recent years, neither is a reduction in the number of societies in the
UK, for both were already well-established trends by the 1970s. At the same
time, during the 1980s, the *rate* of increase in branch office numbers has slowed
down, mainly as a result of mergers of building societies and a renewed interest
in agencies as sub-branches. Merger activity has intensified in the 1980s,
particularly where two larger societies have come together, as well as smaller
ones merging with each other or with a larger society. Between 1975 and 1985
the total number of societies fell from 382 to 167, while the number of branches
increased from 3375 to 6926. Many of these developments are, of course, closely
connected. For example, the intensified merger activity has often led to a newly
merged society having two branches very close to each other in the same street,

with the result that one closed down. Total staff numbers continued to increase from the 1970s, through the 1980s, but predictions are that they will increasingly stabilize (see Table CS9.2).

Table CS9.2
UK building societies
1975–85

Year	Number of societies	Number of branches	Number of staff Full-time	Part-time	Total assets (£)
1975	382	3375	32 485	2 464	24 204
1976	364	3969	34 673	2 704	28 202
1977	339	4130	37 876	3 213	34 288
1978	316	4595	40 870	4 062	39 538
1979	287	5147	43 963	5 207	45 789
1980	273	5684	46 418	6 309	53 793
1981	253	6162	47 716	7 661	61 815
1982	227	6480	49 102	9 047	73 033
1983	206	6643	50 761	10 431	85 869
1984	190	6816	51 660	11 454	102 689
1985	167	6926	53 172	12 519	120 763

Source: Annual Reports of the Chief Registrar of Friendly Societies.

There has developed a highly competitive market for mortgages, investments, and other financial services. This has occurred both *within* the building-society sector itself and *across* the wider financial sector, of which they have become a central part. Competition between the societies intensified following the formal abandonment of their cartel in 1985, up to which time rates were fixed centrally by the Building Societies Association. Although there was no strict requirement to stick to these rates, there was a closer adherence to them than has been the case subsequently. A form of 'balancing act' is necessary, in the sense that if, for example, a society reduces its mortgage rate, and hence attracts more applications in this area, it has to be attuned to attracting sufficient funds from savers in order to support this level of activity—with the consequent implication for rates of interest on savings/investments. Further, all this needs to be done in the context of base rates, shifts and competitors' actions.

The *nature* and *scope* of the societies' competitors has also dramatically changed during the 1980s. There are more competitors from among non-building-society organizations, to such an extent that the distinction between banks and building societies has become blurred. If some of the large societies, under the new legislation, move to corporate status, any remaining distinctions may well become virtually meaningless. This 'non-building-society' competition has come in the main from UK and foreign banks and insurance companies. These organizations are attacking the traditional mainline business of societies, that is mortgage provision and investments. However, the new picture is not entirely a strict competitive one, for some alliances have been formed—for example, between a society and bank, allowing, *inter alia*, the former to provide conventional banking services. *Within* the building-society sector, cooperation between typically the medium-to-larger organizations has developed through the sharing of common ATM[1] networks.

Building societies have been able to provide a much-enhanced range of activities following the Building Societies Act which came into force on 1 January 1987. These services include cheque books, insurance, personal loans not secured on a house, estate agency, surveying and conveyancing.

Additionally, a society can now become a publicly quoted company, but strict qualifying provisions have to be met. Many of the above possibilities will only be open to certain societies, given the legislative requirements. For example, to take advantage of the wider lending powers, societies must have commercial assets in excess of £100 million. This appears to restrict such opportunities to the fifty or so largest societies.

It could be argued that the building society sector of the future will consist of three main groupings—a few very large national societies offering a full range of services, a few medium-sized regional ones with a more restricted range, and a limited number of small localized societies just providing the traditional mortgage and investment facilities.

Aspects of the Royal Oak Building Society's organizational culture and social organization at the beginning of the 1980s

The predominant management style at this time can be described as paternalistic/autocratic. The General Manager likened the society to a family of which he was the head, emphasizing his personal interest and approachability on staff matters, and taking pride in the belief that staff had ready access to him on their individual problems. It was 'autocratic' in the sense that staff, on the whole, would tend to take their concerns to their immediate boss, having an attitude of fear, rather than affection towards the General Manager. Control was centralized in the General Manager's office, and there was little delegation to deputies, or to managers lower in the hierarchy. Senior managers and executives had invariably spent their whole working lives in the sector and in the same society, and many had achieved a long service record, going back over 30 to 40 years. It was almost unknown for senior managers to move between societies (a high value was placed on the confidentiality of the information they were privy to, and a 'gentleman's agreement' about non-poaching of other societies' managers was reputed to be in existence), and for younger staff to be promoted to higher management, or for specialists to be recruited from outside the sector.

Underlying this organization and structuring of managerial positions is a division of labour by gender. Although females constitute around two-thirds of the total labour force, they hold only one-fifth of the managerial jobs. There is a strong patriarchal ideology, both within the Royal Oak Building Society and the sector itself.

Administration according to the established rules and regulations and, above all, financial considerations were the focus of activity throughout the society. There was no new technology, and corporate planning and market research were non-existent. It was not until 1976 that a personnel specialist (in the form of Personnel Officer) was appointed, and the main reason for the appointment is indicative of the corporate culture and management style at the time: it was not so much a result of the recognition of the need for an overall personnel policy (although this *was* becoming necessary by that time, in view of the size of the organization), but, rather, of the wish to formulate a strategy to defeat a recognition claim by the National Union of Bank Employees (NUBE; now known as the Banking, Insurance and Finance Union—BIFU). A key element of management's strategy here was the formation of a Staff Association which would be granted sole negotiating rights.

The strategy was successful, and a Staff Association came into existence in 1977. It fulfilled a consultative and negotiating role, although it had limited bargaining rights. It had little real power or influence within the society, and only managed to rebut subsequent attempts by BIFU to gain recognition with the active support of management.

The first task of the Staff Association was to help management produce a staff grading structure for the society, although management decided upon the form and content of the structure. Two schemes were produced—one for head office, and one for branch office staff. In 1978 these two structures were combined into one common scheme, with seven grades, but, as before, there had been little formal analysis to ensure its suitability and accuracy (de facto, it was job ranking).

Branch management structure is shown below (with numbers of managers in brackets)

Branch and agencies
manager
(Head Office)

Area managers
(4)

Regional managers
(30)

Branch managers
(70)

The structure was constituted on a geographical basis. The regional managers had two main responsibilities: to oversee their branches, and to develop business at the regional level. However, many of them were not very good at administration and/or marketing and selling. Most had had little or no formal training, and, as the Personnel Manager put it in 1985: 'They went to visit the people they knew and felt comfortable with.' The area managers worked as a team with the Branch Agencies Manager at head office. As for the branch managers, they were essentially 'glorified cashiers', who had administrative responsibilities for their branch, but no development or marketing/selling responsibility.

Note   1. Automated teller machines, which dispense cash, usually from the outside wall of the branch office, but also provide statements, receipts, and other information—all on a '24-hour' a day, seven-days a week, basis.

Questions   1 What are the main innovations and changes which the Royal Oak Building Society needs to make in order to remain viable and competitive in the later 1990s?

2 What would you advise the society to do about the following aspects of its operations:

(a) organization structuring,
   (i) at head office?
   (ii) in the branch office network?
(b) work organization and job design?
(c) training and management development?
(d) job grading and recruitment?

Realigning internal and external environments: organizational change at Pilkington

Ken Starkey and Alan McKinlay

Pilkington Brothers is one of the world's largest producers of glass and related products such as insulation material. The company entered the 1980s with a growing number of problems. Its privileged position of near-monopoly command of the glass market had been drastically eroded by competition, so much so that by the end of the 1970s its market share had dropped from a high of 80 per cent to 50 per cent of the UK glass business. It was also experiencing production-cost problems associated with inefficient and non-competitive working practices in its other core business—insulation material manufacture. 1980–82 saw two years of steady losses in the UK. Major readjustments were obviously necessary in management practices to meet changing market conditions and, because the company has lost the technological edge it once enjoyed with the elapsing of its float glass licensing rights, changes in working practices were also needed to make the most efficient use of a technology it now shared with its major competitors.

The company had to come to terms with the reality of new competition and the steady deterioration in its market share. Pilkington's problems reflected those of the British economy generally in a time of acute recession. Two major external forces have influenced the rate of change. The decline of the British motor industry has had major repercussions on its glass business and the loss of government financial support for home insulation programmes has profoundly affected the insulation business. The effects of the changes—in management strategy, structure, culture and in working practices—initiated in the first half of the 1980s are still working their way through the company but are already reflected in significant steps back to competitiveness. Improved results reflect the effects of cost reduction and productivity gains in traditional manufacturing areas due to rationalization and manpower reduction, cost cutting, and strict control on capital expenditure, limiting it to essential projects and working capital.

This has been achieved despite over-capacity in traditional markets, strong competition and the continuing depressed state of the building industry and the British car industry. In all business areas manufacturing capacity is now better matched to market demand. The focus of attention throughout the company is now on improving plant yields, plant utilization, and margins in highly competitive market environments.

Changes in work organization have been accompanied by major managerial changes. There has been significant reshaping of the Group both through acquisition and internal reorganization. This saw major changes of strategic direction in the diversification away from traditional products and markets and geographical diversification most notably into the USA. There have been important developments in the downstream side of the glass business with a new emphasis on value-added products as opposed to the previous concentration on flat glass. Business policy now aims at retaining two-thirds of the Group's activity in its core glass and insulation businesses while expanding new growth areas in electro-optical and ophthalmic glass.

A key element of the change process has been the attempt to inculcate a new managerial culture. One result of pre-1980s attitudes in management had been a high degree of bureaucratization and functionalization, the major dysfunctional consequence of which, in the markedly different market environment of the 1980s, was a lack of business focus. Managerial expertise was mainly concentrated on technical facets of the business — technical excellence for its own sake. Actual business expertise, in the 'entrepreneurial, cutting costs, getting things done' sense was low. The development of this expertise was a key element in the change strategy. The company emphasized the importance of a marketing focus — that making and selling are its 'life-blood'.

> Now the only way to get an edge on the competition is to emphasise the marketing end. But that is easier said than done if you have a company with a long tradition that based its success on operating complex plants. We almost need to grow a new breed of person.   (*Financial Times*, 12 June 1985)

The company has become much more flexible to react quickly to customer requirements. This was reflected in a major restructuring of managerial responsibility with a reorganization of Group and board responsibilities and a new emphasis on decentralization. Operational and profit responsibility for budgeting, manufacturing, marketing, dividend policies and industrial relations was delegated to divisional chief executives. Most of the Group central committee structure was dismantled and decisions devolved to the operational level. Divisional reliance on the centre was minimized.

The need for cultural change was reflected in a major concern with personnel policy. The Chairman, Antony Pilkington, emphasized the need to get 'our people situation right'. This was recognized as a business need. In its traditional operations Pilkington has always had a reputation for being a highly centralized company. In the 1980s centralization came to be associated with an over-reliance on the centre. A new departure was the decision to negotiate differently. New working practices negotiated at a greenfield site in the glass division could not be fitted into a central bargaining mould. Manning levels, for example, were to be very different to those in force at traditional plants. The principles underlying the negotiation of new working practices formed the basis of a change disseminated throughout the group. The central plank in all future negotiations was not to be the national agreement but an agreement based on the needs of particular sectors of the business analysed and responded to at the local level.

Personnel directors in the various divisions were offered a unique opportunity to make fundamental changes by negotiating according to their own particular market needs which were to be explained to their workforces in terms of that particular division's market position and not Pilkington Group's generally. The directive to divisional management from the board was that they relate whatever changes they thought necessary in work organization to their own particular business circumstances and not to the Group as a whole. The effort here was aimed at 'trying to break the culture thing they've had for years' (Personnel Director) — the recourse to the centre to solve all divisional problems and the reliance on central initiatives. For the Pilkington Board, the changes were associated with more realistic responses to market situations interpreted at the appropriate local level and also a different managerial culture, 'a different style of management, one in which the ball is pushed right down so that divisional managers became more accountable and responsible' (Personnel Director).

The company set itself the task of introducing innovations in working practices throughout the group. In particular, wage bargaining was decentralized. This decentralization initiative met with resistance from the unions. Despite prolonged negotiation and management's strong desire to negotiate the introduction of the new way of organizing and resistance remained strong so that, ultimately, in 1983, decentralization of bargaining was imposed unilaterally over the unions' heads. An unintended consequence and major benefit of the prolonged negotiation and communication process involved in the attempt to arrive at agreement was that the understanding of the need for decentralization was accepted by the workforce despite union advice to the contrary. The main union argument against decentralization had been that it was a policy aimed at 'divide and rule'. The workforce, though, 'could see that they weren't just being divided or left. They could see the business starting to move away from them' (Personnel Manager) and consequently accepted the need for major changes. Key agents in the practice of implementation were line managers and shop stewards at site level who took responsibility for the negotiation and implementation of the new arrangements. Personnel managers took on the role of advisers, providing an enabling function, rather than an industrial-relations function.

The effects of this broader work reorganization can be clearly seen in the experiences of the Pilkington Insulation Division. What was exceptional here was the introduction of practices pioneered at a greenfield site into long-established factories with traditional working and pay-bargaining practices. Pilkington Insulation Division's business is predominantly UK-based principally because exporting insulation materials composed of trapped air is bad economics because it involves huge volumes for very little weight. The business is strongly affected, therefore, by the vagaries of the UK economy. There was rapid growth in the insulation market throughout the 1960s and 1970s with, at the end of the 1970s, an exponential scale of growth fuelled by the oil crisis arising from the policies of the OPEC cartel which caused energy costs to escalate. The UK government reacted with intervention in the insulation business by providing central grant aid for home insulation and, more important, finance for local authorities to embark on a major programme of insulation of local-authority properties. The insulation market at this time was characterized by under-capacity. Pilkington, as market leaders, sold their products at highly profitable prices.

In response to strong government pressure to expand capacity, a new plant was opened on the Ravenhead site. With such favourable market conditions, two new UK competitors arrived in the market, setting up operations on greenfield sites, which meant that they had new working practices with low overheads and low-cost structures. But, in the short term, this did not pose a major threat to Pilkington.

However, in 1980, there was complete change around. As one senior manager put it: 'the world went mad'. The effects of oil-price stabilization and the deepening recession were exacerbated by a radical change in government policy. With the success of a Conservative government in the UK in the 1979 General Election the attitude to the public financing of energy conservation changed. Interventionism gave way to market forces. Grant aid was drastically reduced with the result that local authorities either dropped or greatly reduced their insulation progammes. The result was a massive slump in demand with huge overcapacity in the industry and heightened competition from the two new competitors who had to justify their high capital-intensive investments in terms of market share. Overcapacity, intense competition and a massive slump in demand led to intense downwards pressure on prices.

In 1979/80 the division made £20 m in profit, almost doubling profits from the year before. Over the next 18 months it plunged to a dramatic loss of £12/13 m. Standard responses aimed at reducing costs in energy and raw materials were implemented. Scope for these changes was soon exhausted. The next area to be examined was working practices. The fat times of the 1970s had bred overmanning to a large extent and a 'fairly soft' managerial approach. For instance, extensive demarcations had been allowed to develop with, in the craft area, large numbers of different mechanical trades without flexibility between them.

Three main measures were taken to reduce manufacturing costs: *capital investment* to transfer manually intensive processes on to continuous-process lines and investment in automatic handling technology; *rationalization* to bring capacity and costs more in line with the level of demand; and '*belt-tightening*' to reduce overmanning. At the main insulation works these measures led to a halving in numbers from 1800 to 900 over three years with the major reduction in the unskilled process workers. This rationalization was done by voluntary means.

These actions on manufacturing costs did not solve the division's problems. The issue turned out to be not just one of cost and capacity reduction. Major gains in this area were offset by a steady loss of market share. The company had tried to hold on to its market leadership posture and to keep prices high through marketing quality and service in an attempt to minimize the conflict in the industry so that competitors did not damage each other through a price-competition spiral. Its goal had been to keep prices stable rather than allowing them to drift down with competitive pressures. This strategy, in terms of market share, proved a marked failure. Pilkington market share fell from around 60 per cent down to just over 40 per cent, caused by the new competition establishing a position in the market, but also by competition generally exploiting the new market conditions to get share because Pilkington's were artificially trying to hold on to a high-price leadership posture.

1983 was a watershed for the division because it clearly could not go on losing market share to the extent it had been. The company decided that the only strategy still open was to exploit what impact it still had in the market and to engage in an outright price war. It adopted a much more aggressive marketing posture, the result of which was the beginning of an unrestricted price war. Prices fell by 30 per cent in a six-month period in a high-asset industry with huge fixed costs. Finally prices stabilized when there was no longer a premium on undercutting. Pilkington market share started to pick up. The issue then became which company could support the lower prices best, which could adapt best to permanently lower realization from insulation manufacture.

Pilkington found that it was not them. Despite halving numbers employed, its sales revenue per employee was only £35 000 per year whereas its competitors' sales revenue per employee was between £55 000 and £65 000. It was clear that, despite all that had been accomplished in productivity, the company still had a long way to go in achieving efficiency.

The company's problems can be summarized as:

1 static-to-declining market demand, so no possibility of generating a bigger market;
2 unrelenting pressure on prices so that going for more share in an aggressive way was really just re-stimulating the price spiral;
3 it needed £6 million of operating costs to achieve parity with its competitors; and it had already pursued the obvious remedies open to it (capital investment, plant/process rationalization and belt tightening). 'The only route left was a much more fundamental approach to people costs — structural solutions in other words, rather than simple trimming solutions' (Personnel Director).

The window of opportunity to introduce a fundamental restructuring of its operations opened with the Pilkington Group decision to decentralize collective bargaining. This presented the Division with a major opportunity to overcome the inertia caused by central negotiations. The Division decided to mount a major restructuring of jobs, working practices and rewards with which to compete against companies that had all the advantages of greenfield sites with highly efficient working practices and low-cost structures in its own brownfield sites with their long-entrenched methods of working.

The broad objectives of the Insulation restructuring programme were: to establish employment structures, systems and working practices aimed at increased cost effectiveness in the use of human resources, based on a stronger sense of site and business identity; to facilitate team-based commitment to the objectives of the business and the elimination of artificial divisions between employee groups; and to improve the quality of industrial relations by changing attitudes.

The architecture for these changes was made up of: new job definitions to enable optimum flexibility and mobility of employees; a single, integrated pay structure for all employees below middle management based on common job evaluation arrangements, participatively managed, and multi-union negotiations on pay and conditions; a simple grading structure with proper differentials and relativities. The basis for attitude change was to be a commitment to a broad range of tasks in return for which the company offered an annual salary without per occasion payments, harmonization of terms and conditions, a pay structure that is simple to understand, common to all groups and low on administration costs, computerized attendance recording for all in order to support flexible working-time arrangements, and a pay increase of 12 per cent.

There were also three structural changes: fewer but bigger jobs with greater responsibility and accountability; an emphasis on 'back to the line' with fewer specialists; and fewer levels of accountability. 'Back to the line' was critical as a means of reintroducing accountability for product quality and for process conditions at the point of production and thus reducing the need for indirect labour. It was also seen as a means of promoting individual commitment. It also contributed to the overall goal of a leaner organization with fewer levels and maximum flexibility and mobility of employees.

Flexibility was a key concept. It fell into three dimensions:

1 *tackling the obvious*   the development of mechanical/electrical craftsmen, the elimination of craftsmen's assistants and a simple three-level process structure (process operator, senior process operator and service attendant) to replace the multiplicity of jobs;

2 *addressing the not-so-obvious*   the elimination of quality inspectors and the development of maintenance supervision to run the process to eliminate on-line inspection and invest it back into the process operators, and the development of a multi-functional office structure (the introduction of an administrative job structure which transcends the functional specialism of such roles as supplies clerk, accounts clerk or salaries clerk);

3 *enabling the future*   the goal of a multi-disciplined process craftsman, the development of process workers in routine maintenance roles, using tools which had hitherto been the prerogative of craftsmen, and the elimination of craft supervision so that craftsmen become a self-supervising group.

The choice of implementation method for these new working practices is now seen as crucial in gaining acceptance for them by the workforce. The company saw itself faced with a choice:

> whether to just whack an enormous package deal on the table, you know, Fawley, and recent versions of, or to actually do something more creative, to actually take our people and trade unions [and] sit round a table and develop the organizational changes and develop job structures as far as we could with them. . . . we wanted people to open, to be open to the new structures. Perhaps most of all we wanted a process that was based on understanding business needs. If you say to somebody, 'Here's a package of changes and here's what you have to do and here's the extra money for them' you might well get them to do it but you don't get the understanding of why it's important. The understanding of why it was vital to us was the key for us . . . if we wanted to continue . . . and have it work and have it dynamic (Personnel Director).

The division entered into what it called its multi-union discussion plan. The focus of this centred upon the business plan rather than on changes in the forms of work organization that the company thought necessary. A major consultation exercise throughout the division focused on achieving cost competitiveness in enormous detail, so that a fundamental understanding of the economic problems was communicated to the workforce. The workforce gained an understanding of the necessary changes and the company gained outline agreement on a starting point for its change initiative and an objective.

Following this, discussions about the actual organization of work began. The unions were informed that the projected size of the workforce was to be around 600. Job structures were then analysed over a 5-month period which included extensive discussion with the whole workforce. Job structure planning concentrated on the definition of the categories of jobs that the new principles of work organization required; 250 different jobs with their own job profiles were reduced to a final total of 60 new job definitions.

Having agreed a new framework the next stage was job analysis and job evaluation to flesh out the concept of the new work roles. Job-analysis teams were set up. They included one trade unionist and one manager responsible for translating the new job ideas into job definitions in consultation with the shopfloor. In hindsight, these teams came to be construed as a vital element in affecting change. They 'preached the gospel, effectively selling this to the workforce and it was getting from the workforce a sense of realism too' (Personnel Director). Following this, job evaluation (also using multi-union-management teams and a team of management consultants) was used to match job to reward structures and create a new grading scheme. Between 7 and 8 per cent of the workforce were actually members of the job-analysis teams or the job-evaluation panel and at various stages in this process the company stopped work to spend time (up to a week in total) briefing the whole workforce.

Payback was dramatic. Following the agreement in 1984, numbers reduced by the end of 1985 from 800 to 550. The target then was to reduce to 500 by the end of 1985/86. The actual reduction achieved was 470. Within 12 months there was recovery from £3.5 m loss to £3.8 m profit. A positive basis for future changes had also been established with the new negotiations structure providing a framework for ongoing change and establishing a style of operating and a receptivity to that form of involvement which the company believes will allow it to develop positive changes in the future. The process of implementation has forged a relationship with the workforce which is now far more aware of the impact of the organization's external environment. For labour there is the dual pay-off of enhanced job security and the extra pay that has accompanied the increase in productivity.

Questions

1 What were the environmental pressures affecting Pilkington?

2 Discuss the interrelationships between strategy, structure, culture and work organization that this case illustrates.

3 Discuss the changes in managerial orientation that changes in the company's external environment necessitated in Pilkington's search for renewed competitiveness.

4 What were the key elements of the company's strategy of getting 'its people situation right'?

5 Can you compare the changes at Pilkington to changes in other companies? What common features, if any, does such a comparison illuminate?

6 To what extent was change in corporate performance at Pilkington internally or externally determined?

Company responses to youth unemployment

Caroline Clark and Sheila Rothwell

Walsall is one of the cities in the huge conurbation at the heart of the West Midlands in Britain. Its economy has, for over a hundred years, been heavily dependent on traditional metal manufacturing and engineering, and until the early 1970s, local unemployment ran at only 2 per cent. It was a prosperous area.

However, the recession of the late 1970s and early 1980s hit Walsall hard and fast. Between 1980 and 1981 unemployment rose from 6.7 per cent to 14.1 per cent as the engineering industry collapsed. By 1983, unemployment was 18.6 per cent.[1] In a relatively short period of time, the area became one of the worst hit in the whole country. The local workforce has been predominantly in skilled and semi-skilled manual jobs: even if new industries had grown up quickly in the region, the local skills base would have been appropriate for their needs. Walsall and the engineering industry were highly interdependent, and both slumped together.

In the mid 1980s, unemployment in the West Midlands area stabilized at an above-average level of about 13.6 per cent. By 1987, unemployment as a percentage of the working population of Great Britain was 11.8 per cent for the West Midlands, in comparison with a national average of 10.4 per cent. However, the figures for young people were considerably worse throughout the period. In 1984, young men of 16–19 were experiencing an unemployment rate of 22.1 per cent and young women a rate of 20.1 per cent. In 1987, these figures had dropped only slightly to 19.4 per cent and 15.5 per cent. In the West Midlands, as elsewhere, it was young people who experienced the worset effects of the recession as the numbers of job opportunities available to them dried up.[2]

Acme Engineering can trace its roots back to the early nineteenth century. It was bought up by a British multinational in the early 1960s, but has retained a high degree of autonomy from its parent, except in terms of investment. It is a heavy engineering company, specializing in hydraulic components and electrical heat and cooling systems, with customers in the aerospace, electronics, electrical, transport and defence industries.

Acme's brochure points out that many of its staff have long service records with the company and that it prides itself on harmonious industrial relations 'based on a tradition of good employee consultation and good conditions of employment'. It has, however, lost some employee confidence over the last eight or nine years due to redundancies and early retirements, occasioned by the recession of the early 1980s. In the late 1970s, it employed about 1350 people. By 1987, there were 840 employees left. Though—in keeping with the company's 'caring' tradition—there were no compulsory redundancies or early retirements, the morale of employees did suffer during the period.

The nature of Acme's markets means that it is constantly having to innovate and update facilities and technology. The US aerospace market, to which it is a recent newcomer, demands greater stringency of standards for components and so quality is all-important. Because technology in the aircraft industry advances so quickly, the technical skills of its engineers need to be of the highest standards. Engineers outnumber production workers by 2:1.

Introduction of computer-aided design and computer-aided manufacture (CAD/CAM) also puts a new emphasis on the skills on the shop floor and Acme uses its brochure to publicize its 'high levels of operator skill and integrity'.

Recruitment and training are based on two-year manpower forecasts, and it is company tradition to 'move people up the hierarchy and replace them from the bottom with teenagers'. However, 1981 and 1982 were critical years for the company, and the Board made the decision to stop training apprentices and to close the computer training centre. Previously, up to half a dozen teenagers were taken on as apprentices each year, a modest contribution to the West Midlands skills base, but sufficient for Acme's own skills needs. This break with tradition caused concern to the Managing Director, who asked the Training Department to investigate alternatives, so that Acme could continue some skills training.

As a result, the company took part in a Youth Training Scheme (YTS) pilot, and took on nine teenagers who would subsequently use YTS 'credits' as contributions towards craft apprentice training. After two years, Acme applied for and was accepted as a Managing Agent by the Manpower Services Commission. At the same time it extended the scheme to take on 30 teenagers, and drew about 20 other local employers into a consortium who would provide work experience and subsequently employ the trainees.

At the beginning of each year, Acme's Training Manager goes around consortium members helping them to identify their skills needs. He and his staff interview fifth-formers in local schools and offer places to those who can achieve the appropriate academic grades. He liaises with the YTS tutor at the local college of further education who will then devise and organize the relevant off-the-job training for that year's intake of trainees.

In 1987, Acme itself was to take 5 teenagers of the 30 on the scheme. Two or three of these would go on to do full apprentice training afterwards, necessitating a further two years under an Engineering Industry Training Board Scheme. YTS has not been used to take on more trainees than in earlier years, but has allowed Acme to get 'a better spread of trainees across departments'.

Senior management are concerned for the image of the company in its community, especially after the redundancies of the early 1980s, and the scheme enables Acme to begin to redress local opinions about the viability of the engineering industry. Senior management of the company do regard it as an integral part of the local community: the effects of any downturn in the engineering industry seriously affect the economy in the area. Management is therefore very aware of the ramifications of its decisions on the world outside its gates.

Numbers of trainees vary each year, according to the needs of the consortium. If a company drops out (either temporarily because of its manpower situation, or occasionally permanently when it is discovered that trainees are being abused), another organization will be invited to join the collective. The scheme can be selective about the trainees who are recruited. Acme's Training Manager puts this down to the high quality of the scheme which attracts a high volume of applications. It is not advertised because its reputation has spread by word of mouth. The training is designed so that all trainees can subsequently enter formal skills training schemes and gain nationally recognized qualifications. A training schedule is agreed with each company and each trainee at the outset of training, and the teenagers are sent to college for an initial six months off-the-job tuition.

Many companies in the collective do not guarantee jobs at the end of the course. Acme's Training Manager said, 'a job at the end is a bonus. Engineering is so fickle, it's utopia if we can get all of them jobs. Otherwise we give them training so they can get a job elsewhere, so we say a job is not guaranteed, but look at the figures.' However, part of the success of the scheme is the virtual guarantee of a job at the end of it. Acme's Training Manager acts as an unofficial job agency to place any trainees in alternative companies should their training and work experience placement fail to offer them a job at the end of the apprenticeship period.

Initial suspicion on the part of both companies and trainees about the quality of YTS training has been allayed by the success of this particular scheme, which has offered skills training with the virtual guarantee of a job at its conclusion for up to 30 school-leavers a year for the past three years. As a result of its good reputation, local schools often write to Acme, drawing its attention to potential candidates. Though other local engineering companies also have apprentice schemes, Acme's is 'the only scheme which is absolutely full'.

Acme's Training Manager considers that there are many practical advantages to running this scheme, despite the fact that it is so labour-intensive for his department, but some query its need once the recession appears to have ended.

Notes
1. K. Roberts, S. Dench and D. Richardson, 'The changing structure of youth labour markets', Department of Employment, Research Paper No 59, 1986.
2. These figures are taken from the Labour Force Survey 1987, given in the March 1988 Employment Gazette and are therefore based on 1987 criteria for assessing unemployment levels.

Questions

1 Discuss the balance between self-interest and concern for the future of local young people displayed by Acme in its YTS programme. What else did Acme get out of participating other than a supply of potential recruits? Is it possible for Acme to serve its own interests while answering a need of its local community? What are the tensions which might grow out of an attempt to reconcile these two objectives?

2 What other alternatives are open to Acme? Why do so many companies not participate in YTS or in 'charitable' activities?

3 What characteristics of company 'culture' would you expect to find in companies that do participate in such activities? What would ensure such involvement was 'successful'?

4 What kind of contributions can a company such as Acme make to the resolution of problems like unemployment, in its local community? Are its managers appropriately placed to take action on societal issues which they think need resolution? Should they do so?

5 Would this scheme be appropriate at a time of 'youth shortages'?

6 How far does national culture shape a company's response to a social problem such as youth unemployment? How was the problem tackled in other countries with different traditions of dealing with the transition from school to work?

Part VI
International
Management

**The national cultural
environment**

Introduction

The impact of *national culture* upon organizations is becoming of increasing concern for virtually all staff. Many single societies have become multicultural, and trade now regularly extends across a number of different countries. The advent of the single European market in the 1990s will also bring the question of national culture high on the agenda of managers around the world. So what is national culture? What is it like to work in a French or an Arab State organization? What are the similarities and differences to working in Britain, for example? How can managers cope with cross-national trade?

**Identifying
national culture**

To answer these questions really requires that the elements of national cultures are identified precisely, giving us the means of comparison between countries. This is no easy task. Reading 12 by Geert Hofstede is one large study of some factors on which nations appear consistently to differ. Nancy Adler's reading (13) fits well alongside Hofstede, since it describes graphically the very personal impact of working in other countries for the wives of ex-patriate managers. Weinshall's (1977) collection of papers on culture give an overview of the key issues. Some of the factors contributing to the national cultural environment of organizations are shown in Figure 20.1 (drawn generally from Hofstede, 1980; Tayeb, 1989).

Figure 20.1
The cultural
environment of
organizations

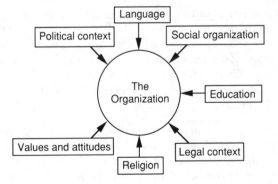

**Convergence
and divergence**

There are two broad debates between researchers concerning the impact of national culture upon organizations. These deal with *convergence and divergence* (see Lammers and Hickson, 1979). The convergence view argues that organizations are becoming increasingly alike (in terms of structure, technology levels of bureaucratization, etc.) Thus, the *context* of business operates independently of national culture and predominates over it. The divergence view gives primacy to the differentiating effects of national culture (the residual effects of history, beliefs, values and attitudes held in each nation or society).

There is empirical support for both views, but there are no definitive studies which can strongly support one or the other. Of course, it is likely that both views are correct. Business pressures will certainly influence the common shaping of organizational structures and processes. Yet, such organizations are also staffed by individuals who hold very different beliefs attitudes and values. These will obviously have an impact on motivation, satisfaction, group working and so on. Key differences in orientation towards *time* (linear clock time, or personal time), *working* (as a means to an end or as an end in itself), the accumulation of *wealth* (as a primary concern or not), and towards *change* (open to change or resistant) can be identified across different national cultures.

Many of the Aston researchers and their associates (see Chapter 12) conducted cross-national research using the variables of size, technology, formalization and specialization (see Hickson and McMillan, 1981). One conclusion of this work is that there appears to be a common industrial logic across different nations. Despite differences in political and ideological thought, organizations are *converging* around the common imperatives of economics, competition and technology (see Galbraith, 1967).

Other studies support divergence. They argue that organizational structures and processes are culture specific. Ruedi and Lawrence (1970) and Sorge and Warner (1986) conclude that national cultural factors specific to Germany accounted for differences between English and German organizations. These differences included *education levels* (higher in Germany), *power* (German managers have a more significantly culturally ingrained view of organizations as authority structures), and *autonomy* (British managers experience more decentralization).

Categories of national cultures

Building on Hofstede's (1980) research, Ronen and Shenkar (1985) have produced a clustering of nations based upon certain commonalities in *geographical position* in the world, common *language* and similar *religions*. Table 20.1 summarizes these results.

Since each category is based upon key cultural values and attitudes, we can predict that organizational behaviours generally should be more similar within categories than between them. A British manager would thus find not too much difficulty in recognizing and adapting to the structures and processes of firms in Ireland, New Zealand, Canada, etc. A more difficult cultural transition would be between managing in British and Colombian or Greek organizations.

One example of difficulties arising from cultural differences is provided by Giddy (1978: 102):

> The managers of one Amercian firm tried to export the 'company picnic' idea into their Spanish subsidiary. On the day of the picnic, the U.S. executives turned up dressed as cooks, and proceeded to serve the food to their Spanish employees. Far from creating a relaxed atmosphere, this merely embarrassed the Spanish workers. Instead of socializing with their superiors, the employees clung together uneasily and whenever an executive approached their table, everyone stood up.

In societies which value and expect formal, authority relationships between individuals, informal management styles may be inappropriate as the illustration above indicates. Research also indicates that French managers view organizations as political networks, whose main purpose is to support the social order (and the prior distribution of power). North American managers view organizations as instrumental. They are designed primarily for task accomplishment (Laurent, 1983).

Table 20.1
Groupings of
national cultures
clustered by
language, geography
and religion

Anglo	*Latin-European*
Australia	France
Canada	Belgium
New Zealand	Italy
Ireland	Portugal
South Africa	Spain
USA	
United Kingdom	
Latin-American	*Far-Eastern*
Argentina	Malaysia
Venezuela	Hong Kong
Chile	Singapore
Mexico	Philippines
Peru	South Vietnam
Colombia	Indonesia
	Thailand
	Taiwan
Near-Eastern	*Germanic*
Turkey	Germany
Iran	Switzerland
Greece	Austria
Arab	*Nordic*
Bahrain	Sweden
United Arab Emirates	Denmark
Kuwait	Norway
Saudi Arabia	Finland
Oman	
Abu-Dhabi	
Unclassified	
Brazil	
Japan	
India	
Israel	

Source: Ronen and Shenkar (1985: 449).

Even within categories, there can be differences (which are of course not as great as those *between* categories). Ali and Al-Shakhis (1989) found significant differences in perceptions between 132 Saudi and 203 Iraqi managers. While both are Arab cultures, Iraqi managers showed a greater predisposition to consensus, egalitarianism and humanistic beliefs. Saudi managers were found to be more individualistic:

> Iraqi managers believe more in hard work and independence, enjoy challenging work, and are more oriented toward teamwork and group success and the organization's collective norms. On the other hand, Saudi managers believe more in the free enterprise system, and that rich people should not exploit others and that workers should get a fair share and are more dubious about increasing leisure time (Ali and Al-Shakhis, 1989: 177).

One of the countries not represented in Table 20.1 is the People's Republic of China. Partly this is because of the difficulty of classifying a country in which the whole context of the political economy has undergone massive changes in the last three decades. As Lansbury, Ng and McKern (1984) note, China has swung violently and rapidly from extremely centralized control to highly decentralized anarchy.

In 1989 the world witnessed the Chinese government re-establish centralized control over what it considered to be overly anarchistic student protesters. Violence and death were the result. It is thus difficult to classify China in terms of national culture other than to indicate its instability since the death of Chairman Mao. Warner (1986) indicated that China was likely to need massive investments in management training, professionalization and specialization. Largely it seemed these would be based on Western models of decentralization, apprenticeships, promotion and training. Following the events of 1989, it is unclear whether this will still take place.

Japan, unclassified on Table 20.1, is discussed in more detail in Part VII (see especially Chapter 24). In this chapter, the twin themes of *language* and *religion* which underpin the categorization in Table 20.1, are explored in more detail in the following sections.

Language

Language and national culture

While beliefs and attitudes form the basis of cultural differences, the first expression of national culture is found in language. Language can act as a mirror reflecting both the content and nature of the culture it represents. Despite attempts to create a universal language such as Esperanto, it seems unlikely to succeed until a universal culture is in place to support it. Language reflects the 'deep structure' of national culture.

There are over 3000 different languages in the world. Since the number of nations in the world numbers less than 200, it is obvious that culture, as reflected by language, rarely adheres to political boundaries. For example, it is estimated that in India alone some 1000 different languages are spoken.

There are many countries which share the same official language. English, French and Spanish are the national languages in about 20 countries each. Arabic is the national language in a further dozen or so countries.

A common feature of linguistic diversity within a country is both cultural and political fragmentation. In many such countries, language bridges or *lingua francas* have been used to aid communication. In countries which have previously been controlled by a large colonial power, the colonists have usually imposed their own mother language as the bridge. For example, in India, it is English. In Zaire, it is French. In many former French and British colonies, the imperial language linked all parts of the country. Initially, few natives spoke the language. Gradually, it has become an important and widely spoken language. Such languages sometimes have a prestige value attached to them. English or French is often viewed as the language of higher education, economics and senior government.

Language and business

The wide variety in languages in the global economy presents an enormous challenge to a manager in organizations which wish to operate beyond their domestic markets. International business depends on communication and consists primarily of language. Every time a language barrier is crossed, a potential communication problem could result. To operate successfully in foreign cultures, effective communication must be achieved at virtually every level of analysis, the individual, the group, the organization and between societies.

As technology improves the speed of international communication, the ability to converse in a number of different languages becomes increasingly important. Within any large foreign subsidiary, parent company–subsidiary communications take place on a variety of levels (e.g. the managing director, financial, marketing and technical staff).

Multinational organizations have two options when deciding how to deal with this problem. First, they could put home-country nationals in key managerial positions. This strategy reduces the communication difficulties with the head office, but correspondingly may increase communication problems in the foreign subsidiaries. The second option relies upon local nationals assuming key managerial positions. The communication advantages within the foreign subsidiary must be viewed alongside the potential misunderstandings which can result from poor coordination between the head office and its various subsidiaries.

Communicating with a 'local' workforce requires a special understanding of the role of language. In many instances, this requires bilingual managers who can communicate between the subsidiary and its foreign owners. This situation is complicated by a workforce which may speak more than one language. In some African nations, where employees may be drawn from several tribes, a lingua franca may be used. In Canada, where there is some hostility between the French and English-speaking segments of the population, both languages may have to be used appropriately. Because language reflects national culture, it may be impossible to find language equivalents for particular terminology the firm wishes to introduce. For example, in many developing countries, to train an individual in such activities as computer operating requires some familiarity with English or French as a prerequisite.

A unique approach to overcoming this language barrier has been attempted by Caterpillar Tractor Company. The company had been experiencing a problem with communicating its parts, service and repair manuals across the wide range of language areas in which their machinery operated. Local independent dealers and repair shops did not have the means to train their employees in the appropiate language skills as well as mechanical skills.

Caterpillar developed a simple system of printed communication called 'Caterpillar Fundamental English' (CFE). Essentially, CFE is a one-way communication system which does not require the pronunciation of any words. Employees acquire an understanding of only 800 words, even though they may not be able to pronounce them properly. All words not necessary to service Caterpillar tractors are omitted. Over the past few years, several thousand individuals have taken the CFE course throughout the world.

This kind of simplication cannot be used when dealing with governments or customers for example. With customers, it is important that the seller can speak the customer's language fluently. Marketing across language groupings can require expensive and sometimes difficult changes to advertising, packaging and labelling. With governments, it is usually a matter of protocol which requires communication with foreign governments to be undertaken in their own national language. In the 70 or so nations where English, Spanish or French are the official languages, difficulties should not be insurmountable. However, in countries such as Saudi Arabia and Japan, it becomes much more important to employ local managers to represent the company's interests. Many organizations have discovered that it pays to hire the very best local people rather than attempt to provide bilingual foreign managers.

Only 10 per cent of the world's population use English as their primary language. Despite this, English is currently the world's major language. The dominance of English is not solely the result of imperialism. Although the

English language would not have achieved its position if the British Empire had not been such a powerful trading nation in the eighteenth and nineteenth centuries, it was the rise of the United States as a major world force which has further established English as an international language (Pei, 1965). The ubiquitous American tourist, films and television have spread the language much further than global conquest ever could:

- around 700 million people use English as their second language;
- English is spoken, written and broadcast on every continent;
- about 75 per cent of the world's post is written in English;
- one half of the world's newspapers are written in English;
- English is the language of over half of the world's radio stations;
- English is the most widely studied language in countries in which it is not the native language;
- SKF of Sweden and Philips of the Netherlands both have adopted English as an official company language.

Religion

Religion and national culture

Radcliffe-Brown, the British anthropologist, defined religion as 'an expression . . . of a sense of dependence on a power outside ourselves, a power of which we may speak as a spiritual or moral power' (Radcliffe-Brown, 1945). The potency of this belief system cannot fail to have been noticed virtually anywhere in the world. An example has been the attempts on a global scale to ban the novel *The Satanic Verses* by Salman Rushdie, resulting in the author having to go into hiding following death threats.

The values and attitudes of religious belief systems shape individual behaviour. From the perspective of organizational behaviour, religion may be viewed as reinforcing the 'culture-bound' thesis. People behave differently and for different reasons because the values of their religion differ widely. We outline briefly below some of the core values and beliefs of some major religious groups.

Differences in religious beliefs

Five indicative religious belief systems are:

1 Animism
2 Hinduism
3 Buddhism
4 Islam
5 Christianity

The descriptions which follow are not intended to be comprehensive. Instead, the focus is to highlight some of the potential points of contact between religion and economic behaviour.

Animism

Major features include:

Ancestor worship   The animist respects and fears ancestors and seeks to please and appease them. In practice, this means that the animist is encouraged to behave along traditional lines in order to please the ancestors. The effect of such beliefs is very strong conservatism and an overwhelming orientation towards maintaining traditional ways.

Spirit worship   This goes beyond the respect given to ancestors. It attributes spiritual power not only to the departed, but also to non-human objects such as animals, trees and rocks. Magic is a key element of animism. It represents the 'science' through which unknown cause and effect relationships are made. In some developing countries, there have been marketing campaigns to introduce new products which either directly or indirectly imply that the possession of the products will give some sort of magical quality to the owner.

Taboos   Where belief in magic exists, there is usually a taboo against the use of an object or against engaging in a particular practice. Taboos are associated with almost every aspect of life (e.g. childbearing, housebuilding and farming). Taboos also instil conservative values and traditional behaviour among its adherents.

Hinduism   No religion is more difficult to define than Hinduism. It has no recognized creed or dogma which can identify its followers. Despite such difficulties, there are some broad identifiable themes. First, though practices are important, statements of dogma are not. Second, Hinduism is an ethnic religion. Hindus are born into this faith and partly for this reason, Hinduism is almost exclusively identified with the Indian subcontinent. Third, Hinduism has existed for 4000 years largely through its ability to embrace rival philosophical beliefs, animist beliefs and a colourful mythology. Even today, there are elements of Christianity, Islam and Buddhism evident in some of the beliefs and practices of Hindus.

Some of the elements of Hinduism which have most impact upon organizational life are:

The caste system   Though originating as a colour bar, it has gradually become tied with vocational/occupational restrictions. In total, there are some 3000 castes and sub-castes. *Varna* describes the national caste system: *jati* the localized systems. Membership in each caste is determined by birth. The word caste implies more than social class. It is more closely aligned to the European notion of 'species'. *Dharma* (duty) is the system of conduct appropriate to each caste. The caste hierarchy has been argued to be the main force in controlling the economy, in sustaining social structure (especially the constraints on women) and in being a major force against change (see Liddle and Joshi, 1986).

Baradari   Hindu ethics aim to uphold the preservation of the extended family unit. In economic terms, the strong family bonds have meant large numbers of family-owned and operated businesses, with organizational hierarchies based on family relationships. Such potential nepotism does not have the negative connotation which it has in the West.

Veneration of the cow   Though there is some dispute, this is the one belief common to all Hindus. In practical terms, it means there is a total ban on the killing of cows. This has also meant that no animal husbandry can be effectively carried out.

Buddhism   Emerging out of Hindu beliefs in India, Buddhism is an international religion with a following in many countries, though particularly in South-East Asia and Japan. Buddhism is much easier to describe than Hinduism. Essentially, it was a reformation against Hinduism. One important practical difference between the two religions is that no caste system exists in Buddhism. The growth of the Buddhist religion is derived from its contemplative ethical system. Though it demands a high ethical standard of its adherents, there exists in Buddhism a greater sense of unity among its adherents than in many other religious groups. Essentially Buddhist beliefs focus on wantlessness and contemplation rather than upon consumption and work. It is an all-encompassing lifestyle involving spiritual, cultural and political identity.

Islam   Islam is the religion of about 500 million people in about 30 countries.
Compared to many other religions, Islam has spread rapidly. One factor aiding
this dissemination was the absence of racial discrimination. Islam actively
promotes and practises the equality of every Muslim, regardless of race or
colour. The term 'Islam' is an Arabic verb meaning to submit. The word
'Muslim' is the present participle of the same verb. The term *inshallah* means
'god willing'. This stems from the Muslim belief that everything proceeds
directly from the divine will. Some aspects of Islam relevant to organizational
behaviour include:

1 *a ban on the payment of interest on loans*   In some Muslim countries, interest
   payments are referred to as commissions to circumvent religious objections.
2 *religious holidays*   In Muslim countries, the normal weekend is Thursday
   afternoon and Friday. When combined with the Western weekends of
   Saturday and Sunday, this leaves only three and half days for business
   activity. In addition, the month long celebration of 'Ramadan'—involving
   fasting during daylight hours—can cause dramatic drops in productivity.
3 *inshallah*   In many Muslim countries, the view that nothing will happen
   unless Allah wills it makes it difficult for Western organizations to do
   business. For instance, insurance policies are seen by some Muslims as an
   attempt to defy Allah's will.

Christianity   The two major branches of Christianity—Catholicism and Protestantism—
have both had a significant impact on economic life in areas where they have
predominated. Within the Protestant sects, there was a downgrading in the role
of the Church and the priest. The emphasis was placed upon individuals to be
in charge of their own salvation. Consequently, individualism has become a
major characteristic of Protestantism (Weber, 1952).

Weber was clear that individual entrepreneurs created capitalism, but that
Protestantism was only one of many variables supporting this process. Thus,
religion did not cause the economic structure of capitalism, but contributed to
its continuity. Calvinism, for example, values method and rationality highly.
Such desire for efficiency encouraged accounting, controlled investment and
general record-keeping behaviours. In turn, this has arguably led to the
development and the continuance of capitalist enterprises.

Within Christianity, it has been argued that the impact of its religious creed
has been diminishing with respect to its social and economic significance. This
process is called secularization (Wilson, 1966). Whether or not this is really
occurring is open to debate since data are unreliable. Recently, Griffiths (1982)
has argued the case for the setting up of a market economy in Britain along the
lines of Christianity as he interprets them:

- accountability and judgment are central to sustaining the economy;
- materialism (personal) is counter-productive to the economy;
- the relief of poverty has primacy over securing equality;
- private property ownership is preferable to state of collective ownership;
- individual families should all have a stake in the economy;
- the creation of wealth is of central importance, and allows the subsequent
  relief of poverty;
- the role of the government is that of economic arbiter. It has a free hand.

Griffiths argues that the development of capitalism was underpinned by
Christian values and that these should be the central theme for its continuation.
Capitalism thus becomes synonymous with Christianity. It relies on the

creation of wealth to sustain the economy and relieve poverty. Personal greed and materialism are not part of this Christian capitalism. Whether the impact of equating the morality of capitalism with Christianity sustains its potency into the 1990s remains to be seen. It is certain, however, that Islam, Buddhism and Hinduism will continue to be a large influence in the area of cross-national trade and relations (Myrdal, 1968).

Judaism remains a paradox in the living religions. It was the progenitor of two religions, Islam and Christianity whose followers now total over 60 per cent of the world's population. Yet Judaism itself has remained relatively small over the centuries. Despite this, Judaism is practised widely throughout the world. One of the noble tenets of Judaism is the emphasis on education. This has led to a relatively high profile of people of the Jewish faith in professional occupations.

In addition to language and religion, two further aspects of cross-national analysis have a direct impact upon the study of organization behaviour. These are the political and legal contexts in which organizations operate.

The political context

For organizations operating internationally, the political context becomes an important variable. International organizations may operate in many, sometimes conflicting, political environments simultaneously. To operate in such conditions requires a heightened sensitivity by all staff towards political issues. In this section, four concepts are outlined briefly to illustrate the important implications of variations in political context. They are:

1 the nation-state
2 nationalism
3 business–government relationships
4 geopolitics

The nation-state

In its most simple form, a nation-state may be identified by its ability to exert political control over a discrete territory. A nation-state is thus a political unit which defines geographical boundaries, establishes citizenship requirements, controls the movement of goods and people across its borders, settles internal disputes and protects the nation against outsiders.

An alternative view identifies a nation-state in its social context. A nation can be said to exist in terms of its geography, history and culture. At least in theory, a nation can be identified as a community of individuals who share a common ethnic identity and history. However, many countries including Canada, Belgium, Nigeria and India do not meet such a definition particularly well. The borders of many nation-states indicate the degree of arbitrariness in assigning lines on a map to imply a common community of individuals.

The goals and objectives of nations are derived from their expressed national interests. Though the national interest may be used to imply a wide variety of objectives, there are at least five common themes:

1 *Self-preservation* is the prime goal of any state.
2 *Security* is of paramount concern and is exercised through efforts made at the minimization of threats to their continued existence.
3 In order to maintain the cohesive nature of a nation, attempts must be made to improve the *collective well-being.*
4 Nation-states seek *prestige* as a means of achieving recognition for their sovereignty.

5 Nations desire to increase their economic and political *power* relative to others.

Nationalism

Nationalism applies to individuals, not to nations. It is a state of mind in which the individual places loyalty to the nation-state providing a basis for social and eonomic cohesion. Nationalism can range from rather mild feelings of 'belonging' to absolute and unswerving commitment and loyalty.

Current debates about the unification of Europe as a single market are beset with arguments based upon nationalism for example. Each nation appeals to its individuals to preserve what is 'typically British', or 'typically French', and much time is spent by politicians assuring various populaces the nationalism will not disappear under the banner of the single market. Of course, nationalism at its extreme has figured large in in the history of warfare.

Managers of organizations operating internationally ignore the potency of nationalism at their peril. Individuals in the host country can perceive expansionist moves by overseas organizations as threatening their national culture and will become defensive or aggressive towards the perceived threat.

In countries which have been formed as a consequence of some form of geographical division, nationalism can unite different tribes, racial origins and languages. In some instances, nationalism can serve as an ideological basis for behaviour. Governments commonly exhort their citizens to consider nationalism in their individual economic decisions (for example 'Buy British' slogans for consumers).

Business–government relationship

The relationship between the state and business varies greatly between countries. At one extreme, the planned socialist economies do not distinguish between government and commercial enterprises. In the Western capitalist economies, the distinction is very clear. In between lie a wide range of possibilities. The nature of the interaction between state and enterprise colours the ways in which economic goals of the state are coordinated with organizational goals. For example, the close business–government relationship in Japan is credited with much of the success of the Japanese economy since the 1950s. It is also associated with the lack of economic development in China.

As the internationalization of business continues, the state–business relationship becomes important. Conflicting objectives can easily emerge between the multinational company and the home and host-country governments. For the host country, the placement of a multinational company raises important issues of control over their economic destiny. The objectives of the multinational firm and host state may differ considerably. For the multinational company, the purpose of locating in a particular country lies in allocating and utilizing resources so as to maximize its competitive position on a global basis. The nation-state has a different view. Its interests lie in such concerns as domestic growth, employment, and social and economic stability. The two views are unlikely to coincide since that of the multinational is largely exploitative, with economic benefits accruing to the home base without significantly contributing to the economic welfare of the host countries. There are exceptions of course, but in both directions. Some multinationals have arguably contributed to a decrease in overall welfare for the host nation. (The case of Nestlé is a good but not unique example, where powdered baby formula milk with insufficient nutrients was used by mothers in the Third World: see Chapter 21 for details.)

Geopolitics   So far, the assumption has been that of a simple two-country model, home and host country. Difficulties multiply when multinational firms get caught up in international political issues which may involve many countries. For example, in the long-standing conflict in the Middle East between Israel and its Arab neighbours, many Arab countries have adopted a policy of boycotting those firms which have maintained a relationship with Israel or Israeli firms. Though many multinationals have gone to elaborate lengths to circumvent such political actions, it does raise complex legal and moral issues for the managers of multinationals. Many multinationals have been caught up in scandals of bribery, for example, where conduct considered ethical (or necessary) in the host country has contravened laws in the home country.

The need to understand the political context of host countries is an important issue. In response to such concerns, the field of 'political risk analysis' has emerged. Political change can be difficult to anticipate, particularly if little is known about the variety of host-country contexts in which multinationals operated. For international investment decisions, the need to assess the potential political uncertainty of a country is crucial. These risks can arise out of the internal domestic political context as well as a result of international relationships. Results of political uncertainty include: restrictions on market shares, limits on the repatriation of profits and in extreme cases, expropriation.

Legal context

The laws of a society are one dimension of its culture. They are the rules established by authority, society, or custom. The laws of a nation are a manifestation of its attitudes and cultural norms; thus it is not surprising to find diversity among them. As societies differ in their attitudes towards the behaviour of individuals and institutions, then they will have different laws which regulate their behaviour. A common problem in international trade is that companies often do not understand key differences between legal systems. Briefly, three distinct bodies of law are relevant. They are:

1 laws of host countries
2 international law
3 laws of home countries

Laws of host countries   Though it is safe to say that the laws of one nation will differ from the laws of any other nation, there is *some* similarity. The semblance between the various legal systems can be attributed to three factors. First, many laws are based on religious beliefs and practices. Consequently, countries with similar religious cultures would tend to reflect this in their legal codes. Second, the imperialist and colonial history of much of the modern world has served to impose a rough model of a legal system on the colonies. Such colonialism does not just derive from the more recent British and French colonial empires. The effects of the Roman Empire are still evident in those countries which use a codified set of laws. Third, the creation and recognition afforded to international law have mediated between differences among countries. As international law has grown from agreements between two or more countries, it implies an effort at reducing international legal difficulties. Nevertheless, sufficient differences exist in host-country legal systems to make managing cross-national business an intricate and complex process.

International law   International law is different from the laws of nations for three reasons. First, there is no international legislative body which makes the laws. They exist solely through agreements, treaties and conventions between two or more nations. Second, there are relatively few ways in which international laws can be enforced. For example, the World Court may make rulings, but relies entirely on nation-states for enforcement. Third, the jurisdiction of international law covers only relations between nations. Topics covered include: international trade and investment, taxation, patents, the international flow of labour, etc.

Laws of home countries

A surprising number of domestic laws have an impact on the international operations of a firm. The concerns of government over the foreign activities of firms covers a wide range of issues. Three particular areas of concern can be highlighted. First, there is exporting. Many countries have restrictions. For example, the United States has maintained a complete ban on trade with North Korea, Vietnam and Cuba among others. Controls also exist regarding the types of products which can be exported. For example, the United States and its Western European allies maintain restrictions exist on the sale of products which use computer technology to the Soviet Union and its allies. A second area of concern to home-country legislators lies in the area of potential monopolistic practices. For example, if a domestic company were to acquire a foreign competitor, it could be assumed that the domestic competitor may have lessened competition. A consequence could be a legal ruling to divest of its holding to ensure the firm's market share does not rise disporportionately. The third area of influence of home-country laws is in the area of taxation. The means by which foreign income is taxed can have serious consequences upon the economic viability of investing abroad. Tax incentives for exporters or reducing the taxes paid on foreign earnings can aid foreign investment.

Summary

Organizational behaviour can no longer assume homogeneity in organizational structures and processes. What happens in one firm in one country is likely to be very different from another. The key factor at play is national culture. Organizations and their constituent individuals reflect differences in national culture. Although difficult to define and to measure, national culture can be classified on a number of dimensions (such as tolerance for ambiguity among its people, preferences for individual or collective decision-making, or the pervasity of religious thought).

Given the continued increase of international markets and trade, it seems a clearer understanding and analysis of national cultural differences and their impact upon organizational behaviour are necessary. As Roberts and Boyacigiller (1983) argue, key issues lie in the management of human resources, legal differences between countries, differential development rates of economies, the impact of new technologies, storage and retrieval of data and the general coordination and control of cross-national business.

References

Ali, A. and M. Al-Shakhis (1989) 'Managerial beliefs about work in two Arab states', *Organization Studies*, **10**(2), 169–86.

Galbraith, J. K. (1967) *The New Industrial State*, Hamilton, London.

Giddy, I. (1978) 'Social Organization' in V. Terpsta (ed.) *The Cultural Environment of International Business*, Southwestern Publishing, Cincinatti, Ohio.

Griffiths, B. (1982) *Morality and the Market Place: Christian Alternatives to Capitalism and Socialism*, Hodder and Stoughton, London.

Hickson, D. J. and C. J. McMillan (eds) (1981) *Organization and Nation: The Aston Programme IV*, Gower, Farnborough.

Hofstede, G. (1980) *Culture's Consequences: International Differences in Work Related Values*, Sage, London.

Lammers, C. J. and D. J. Hickson (eds) (1979) *Organizations Alike and Unlike*, Routledge, London.

Lansbury, R., S. H. Ng and B. McKern (1984) 'Management at the enterprise level in China', *Industrial Relations Journal*, **15**, 56–63.

Laurent, A. (1983) 'The cultural diversity of Western conceptions of management', *International Studies of Management and Organizations*, **13**, 1–2, 75–96.

Liddle, J. and R. Joshi (1986) *Daughters of Independence: Gender, Caste and Class in India*, Rutgers University Press, New Jersey and Zed Books, London.

Myrdal, G. (1968) *Asian Drama: An Inquiry into the Poverty of Nations*, Twentieth Century Fund, New York.

Pei, M. (1965) *The Story of Language*, J. B. Lippincot, Philadelphia.

Radcliffe-Brown, A. (1945) *Structure and Function in Primitive Society*, Free Press, New York.

Roberts, K. and N. Boyacigiller (1983) 'A survey of cross-national organizational researchers: their views and opinions', *Organization Studies*, **4**(4), 375–86.

Ronen, S. and O. Shenkar (1985) 'Clustering countries on attitudinal dimensions: a review and synthesis', *Academy of Management Review*, July, 445–54.

Ruedi, A. and P. R. Lawrence (1970) 'Organizations in two cultures', in J. W. Lorsch and P. R. Lawrence (eds), *Studies in Organization Design*, Irwin-Dorsey, Homewood, Illinois.

Sorge, A. and M. Warner (1986) *Comparative Factory Organisation: An Anglo-German Comparison of Management and Manpower in Manufacturing*, WZB Publications, Wissenschaftszentrum, Berlin.

Tayeb, M. H. (1989) *Organizations and National Culture: A Comparative Analysis*, Sage, London.

Warner, M. (1986) 'Managing human resources in China: an empirical study', *Organization Studies*, **7**(4), 353–66.

Weber, M. (1952) *The Protestant Ethic and the Spirit of Capitalism*, Allen & Unwin, London.

Weinshall, T. D. (ed.) (1977) *Culture and Management*, Penguin, Middlesex.

Wilson, B. (1966) *Religion in a Secular Society*, Watts and Co., London.

Managing the international organization

Introduction

There is little agreement on, or definition of, what is and is not an international (or multinational) organization. This difficulty is because there are many different types of organizations which operate, to some extent, across national boundaries (see Aharoni, 1971). In general, an international organization is one which operates directly managed investments in more than one country, has a number of foreign subsidiaries which employ a number of expatriate managers.

Though it is difficult to generalize, most companies which are considered international became so through a slow incremental process. Export orders received may have led to the licensing of a sales agency abroad. If successful, this then led to the creation of a dedicated foreign sales force, perhaps leading to foreign production sites and a divisional structure reflecting its global ambitions (see Chapter 12).

The international firm is likely to present very specific problems and opportunities from the perspective of organizational behaviour. Key (but not exhaustive) areas are:

1 conflict between head office and subsidiaries;
2 conflict within head office;
3 conflict between the various subsidiaries and their host countries;
4 communication difficulties between head office and subsidiaries (and between subsidiaries);
5 appropriate human-resource strategies to cope with the added complexity of international operations.

Conflict in the international firm

The international division

When domestic business firms begin developing regular business with foreign purchasers, a typical problem they face is a lack of management expertise in international matters. Their managements have not had any experience in operating under foreign conditions. The firm's managers have made their mark in the domestic setting. Conflict can occur at a number of levels. It is difficult for an organization to rectify this shortage of international skill in the short term. They cannot replace all their domestic managers by those more experienced in international business. Similarly, retraining the entire set of managers in a short period of time would also be expensive. The option which many firms adopt is to centralize all of the bits and pieces of international expertise that the firm does possess or can hire and to create a separate organizational unit in which to house it. From this 'international division' the scarce skills are then rationed out to the various operating divisions on the basis of their relative need.

Conflicts primarily occur over priorities in decision-making. Should production levels or sales volumes be the key criteria? How closely should the international division work with subsidiaries? Should head office decide corporate policy globally, or should the divisions (including the international division) have a say? How should resources be allocated across the organization and upon what criteria?

Decisions over structure

Decisions concerning organizational structure present a considerable challenge to the managers of international firms and they can also be the source of intense conflict. Do managers organize on product lines, or should the firm be structured largely according to its geographical markets? Should they create a separate international division to handle 'multinational' problems centrally, or should decentralization be the hallmark of the operating subsidiaries? These are key questions which cannot always be easily resolved since mediating factors such as technology, maturity of the firm, specific global areas of operation and levels of competition will all confound apparently simple solutions.

Product structures

Firms which have adopted a product structure have generally done so due to the differing technologies associated with each product. Each division is required to master a significantly different product technology. In such a structure, management power is usually rooted in its knowledge of a technologically complex product. In product structures, an international division may cause difficulties since there is a tendency to regard the international division as a source of administrative expertise for handling letters of credit, invoices, customs duties, the translation of foreign documents, etc. The various product divisions tend to reserve all policy decisions pertaining to international operations for themselves. This reduces the influence of the international division's managers on overall strategies and policy decisions and interdivisional conflict becomes inevitable.

Territorial structures

Companies which have structured themselves along territorial lines tend to lend primacy to policy decisions about markets rather than to considerations of technologies or specific products. This could be due to the relatively simple product technologies involved, the complexity of the markets, or both factors combined. In whichever case, the primary function of the line manager is to observe and develop the market.

The international division is essentially a variant of the territorial principle. Therefore, an international division will generally fit more easily into an organization structured along territorial lines than it would along product lines. Conflicts over policy are less likely, although questions of which subsidiaries get scarce resources will remain a source of friction.

Companies which have adopted such a geographically based structure tend to share two characteristics (Prasad and Shety, 1976). First, the bulk of their sales revenue is derived from markets which all have similar end-uses for the goods produced. This minimizes the need for greater intensity of development, production and marketing expertise for particular product lines. Second, an understanding of local-marketing requirements is critical to maintaining demand for the products. In other words, though the product may require only minimal alterations to be suitable for particular markets (labelling, etc.) the techniques for penetrating local markets demand greater managerial attention.

Territorial structures can also be places of conflict. Because of the relative independence of the geographical groups, it is often difficult to transfer new ideas and experiences across territorial boundaries. Subsidiaries, once created, can become pressure groups for maintaining the status quo. This can result in conflicts between subsidiaries and head office, inter-subsidiary conflict, and conflict between the needs of production and markets. One typical example is the desire by the territorial management to have the products altered to correspond with their market requirements. This can affect the potential benefits of economies of scale by reducing the efficiency of the production processes.

Decisions over production

One solution to the conflicts described above is the decision to expand production capacity through facilities in other countries. International production facilities can be incorporated as part of either a territorial, a product-oriented structure or a mix of the two.

The decision to create an internationally dispersed range of production facilities marks a change of perspective for senior management. Rather than view foreign markets as adjuncts to domestic markets, foreign production capacity implies a decision to engage in international competition through the entire transformation process from raw materials to finished goods.

The challenge of international production facilities lies in the need to understand the implications of variations in the economic, social and political environment of the countries in which it produces goods as well as in those in which the products are sold. A lack of appreciation here can lead to intense conflict over raw materials, labour and capital. All these inputs can be scarce, variable in quality, and cost, as well as being difficult to procure. These differences can directly affect the transformation process through the choice of technology, the scale of operations, equipment, maintenance and manufacturing techniques.

Many firms which consider expanding their production facilities internationally do so because of potential cost savings either from raw materials or labour inputs. In particular, there has been a flow of production capacity to those countries which offer substantial savings on labour costs. Though such cost efficiencies can be attractive, they are in many cases outweighed by the supply conditions for the entire range of manufacturing inputs.

Many international firms which have chosen to locate production in developing countries for cost-saving reasons have found that the procurement of resources is one of their most critical problems (Brooke, 1984). In their efforts to manage production facilities, managers are frequently required to grapple with problems such as chronic late delivery of materials, high cost of raw materials, or shoddy quality. Other restrictions which can be imposed by the local government include: domestic content requirements and local procurement rules. By having to source their raw material requirements from within the host country, the manufacturer may not be able to take advantage of foreign-based potential suppliers who have achieved greater economies of scale. The potential for conflict at all levels in these cases is particularly high.

Communication problems in the international firm

The extent of global operations

The complexity of the structure of the international firm will have a marked effect on the ease or difficulty which which information is transmitted across the organization. However, it is difficult to determine precisely when an organization becomes truly 'international'. Managers of international organizations speak of 'degrees of multinationality', although quantifying this degree is almost impossible. An alternative approach is to consider the assumptions which lie beneath an organization's strategy. Perlmutter (1969) suggests that the key to understanding communication is to examine the relationships between headquarters and its international operations. Though they may never appear in pure form, four general types are proposed: ethnocentric, polycentric, regiocentric and geocentric. These are shown in Table 21.1.

Communication difficulties

The levels of decentralization, the extent to which the international organization operates globally, and the structure of the firm will all create potential problems for communication. In extreme cases, head office can be

Table 21.1
Four 'ideal types' of
head office-
subsidiary
relationships

1   *Ethnocentric*
Focused on the home-country. Home-country nationals are considered
superior in skill and performance to foreigners either at head office or in
the subsidiaries. Performance criteria and decision rules are usually
based on home-country standards and there is great resistance to any
change.

2   *Polycentric*
The opposite of ethnocentricism. The assumption is that local people know
what is best and can inform organizational strategy. Subsidiaries should
be as local in identity and behaviour as possible. Structurally, a polycentric
organization is similar to a loose confederation of quasi-independent
subsidiaries.

3   *Regiocentric*
Managers are recruited, developed and assigned on a regional basis. An
example would be an organizational structure which lumps together
operations concentrating in European countries. The assumption
underlying this approach is that greater economies of scale can be
achieved than with a polycentric approach, but without resorting to the
more centralized focus of an ethnocentric perspective.

4   *Geocentric*
Both head office and local subsidiaries see themselves as important parts
of the global organizational entity. Such a worldwide approach considers
subsidiaries neither as satellites nor as independent operations.
Managerial efforts are directed towards increasing collaboration among
subsidiaries and head office to establish universal standards as well as
permissible local variations.

unaware of critical information, or can misunderstand completely information
coming from subsidiaries (Robock and Simmonds, 1983).

Despite the attractiveness of the geocentric perspective, it holds a number of
difficulties in the added costs and efforts expended on communication.
Managers tend to spend more time travelling between the various worldwide
operations in order to train personnel, communicate objectives and achieve
consensus. An associated communication cost is the relatively slow decision-
making process associated with increased efforts to reach consensus. To make
such an open system operate (see Chapter 18) also requires an adequate supply
of managers at all levels who are sufficiently globally oriented to understand
fully the dynamics of international business.

Communication in the ethnocentric perspective can suffer from both
blinkered thinking and from the exercise of power. A truly global perspective is
unlikely to be achieved since the views and experience of those with local
operating conditions in international operations do not carry sufficient weight
in head-office strategic decision-making. Head-office strategies become in
danger of institutionalization, with the preclusion of certain attitudes and
behaviours (see Chapter 11 on non-decision-making).

In polycentrics and regiocentrics, communication difficulties can arise from
the duplication of effort between subsidiaries and from the inefficient use of
head-office experience (Heenan and Perlmutter, 1979).

Choosing an effective and efficient structure

There is no perfect organizational structure for undertaking international business. There are examples of successful companies which use a variety of the above organizational forms. Although there do not seem to be standard configuration requirements for multinational organizations, the choice of organizational structure can be informed by considering a small number of key variables. Robock and Simmonds (1983) and Stopford and Wells (1972) have highlighted six broad factors which influence the choice of organizational structure:

1 Senior management perceptions regarding the relative importance of foreign and domestic markets both now and in the future.
2 The way in which the organization has evolved and the process by which it has become involved in international operations.
3 The nature of the organization's business and its competitive strategy.
4 The underlying philosophy and skills of the senior management of the organization.
5 The availability of sufficient numbers of internationally experienced managers.
6 The ability of the organization to undergo major structural changes.

All the above factors act as constraints in designing an 'ideal type' international organization in which host-country and home-country needs and values are balanced, and where levels of conflict are at a minimum, given effective communication channels. Many international organizations are prisoners of their own history. This can include the prevailing attitudes and beliefs of senior management as well as the characteristics of the foreign economies in which the organization operates (see Chapter 20).

Communication with local economies

So far, we have looked at communication strictly within the structure of the international firm. Of course, many communication difficulties arise from the interactions of firms with their local environments.

For the managers of an international organization, the relationships between the home country and the host country can be bewildering. The range of environmental factors faced by a manager of a foreign subsidiary does not normally fit with the established perceptual framework which was appropriate for head-office assignments. Managers of foreign subsidiaries are generally put in the role of go-between for the international company and the host country. The pressures arising from this role provide a formidable challenge, given the often-conflicting demands from home and host sources.

International organizations may provide a force for change in the host country's economy. This can occur through technology transfer, or more generally through economic and social development. This is particularly true in developing countries. Despite the potential benefits such development can bring, many host countries are concerned by the side effects of such foreign direct investment.

These can have a substantial impact on long-standing social networks as well as upon levels of environmental pollution, for example. The primary concern in many developing countries is the potential contribution international business can have on their economic, social and political development. To foreign firms, the attractiveness of doing business within a particular country may differ from the country's longer term development goals.

To be successful over the long term, international companies must try to remain flexible to the differing requirements of the host country. The need to be flexible to national requirements can, in many instances, run counter to the company's desire to create a clear and consistent global strategy. Where the interests of the firm differ from the interests of the host-country, conflict and poor communication will be the inevitable result (Doz, Bartlett and Prahalad, 1981). Two concrete examples of this lie in *product image* and in *operations throughout developing countries*.

Images, nationality and products

One issue which many international companies continually debate is whether it is best to create a local or a foreign image for their products. In some countries, imports from certain countries are seen as being of higher quality than domestic products. Consequently, advertisements for particular products in these markets may choose to accentuate the national origin of the product rather than the domestic source (Ronen, 1986).

The market perception of the goods from a particular country can vary significantly over time. For example, in the 1950s and 1960s, Japanese goods were perceived to be of poor quality and were characterized by low levels of technical innovation. The term 'Made in Japan' was used as an indication of cheap, but shoddy merchandise. By the late 1980s, the image of Japanese goods had changed completely. Japanese electronics producers such as Sony, Panasonic and Sharp have established international reputations for high quality, innovative products. The turnround by Japanese producers has been so successful that non-Japanese producers of electronic goods have taken to using 'Japanese' names to market their product.

Operating and communicating in developing countries

The relationship between multinational companies and developing countries has sometimes becomes quite tense. There have been many occasions when the product strategies of some multinationals have placed them in direct confrontation with the governments involved. In Zambia, the government banned advertising for Fanta soft drinks after they discovered that mothers were weaning their children on the glamorous, but less than nutritious beverage. Another case involved the high-pressure promotion of powdered baby food formula in developing countries (Turner, 1974).

Although Nestlé of Switzerland are usually remembered in this context (the World Health Organization published a paper in 1974 called 'Nestlé kills babies'), other international firms were also involved. These included Borden, Cow & Gate, American Home Products and Glaxo among others. The firms were alleged to have sold powdered milk products to mothers in developing countries without providing sufficient instructions for their use. Small babies suffered health damage when mothers over-diluted the milk, or used unsterilized water which was all that was available. The milk provided none of the immunity found in natural mother's milk. High-pressure selling involved using radios, distributing free products via sales-people dressed in what looked like nurse's uniforms.

The problem for the international firms was a little more complex than this, however. Had they chosen *not* to sell to developing countries, criticism would also have inevitably followed. The sales promotion itself was expensive (given the difficulty of organizing such campaigns in poor countries) and this was reflected in a relatively highly priced product. The firms argued that the whole affair had been blown out of all proportion and that much benefit to health had occurred from using the milk (which was rarely voiced). Rectifying the situation was relatively easy, since misusing the product was the prime cause of ill health rather than the product itself.

Nevertheless, the controversy over Nestlé's continued sale of the product has stirred the emotions of many people and a number of boycotts of Nestlé products have been mounted (*Wall Street Journal*, 1976).

Human resource issues in international organizations

Staffing international operations

International firms commonly categorize managers as 'locals' (i.e. citizens of the country in which they are working) or 'expatriates' (non-citizens). Expatriates can be further sub-categorized as home-country or third-country nationals. Home-country nationals are citizens of the country where the firm has its head office. Third-country nationals are citizens of any other country. Simply at the level of who to choose (local or expatriate) to staff an organization, multiple factors have to be borne in mind. The major ones are listed below.

1 *Knowledge of the local operating conditions*   Under ideal conditions, a firm should hire managers who understand the local environment as well as having the appropriate technical knowledge and business acumen. This combination is not always available. The trade-off which has to be made in terms of local knowledge or technical expertise will depend on a number of factors. The greater the difference in operating environment with the home country, the greater is the need to have managers skilled in local conditions. In contrast, where the need is great to maintain worldwide standards of production and close coherence to corporate directives, then it will be more critical to have in place a team of managers who are well-rehearsed in the usual methods of the firm. They act as preservers of coporate culture (Kotter, Schlesinger and Sathe, 1986).

2 *Incentives to local personnel*   One of the arguments for giving preference to local personnel is that if incentives for advancement or increased pay are given, the potentially high turnover of skilled managerial personnel may be reduced. Another perspective is that the organization should only promote the best qualified people—regardless of national origin. Staffing with local managers can help promote a local image if this is sought. This can backfire, however, if the occasion should arise when local managers are no longer wanted or needed. There may be legal or social restrictions which could affect the firm's operations. The likelihood of such a situation arising could lead the organization to consider a risk-avoidance strategy of using predominantly expatriate managers.

3 *Cost*   A strong argument for the use of local managers is the cost of transferring expatriate managers around the world. Aside from moving and settling-in expenses, many multinational firms will purchase homes for their executives in order to ease the transition. In many cases, the executive's own furniture and household goods may be inappropriate for the new environment and will have to be put into storage.

4 *Legal restrictions*   Every government has laws which favour employment of its own citizens. Such rules restrict foreign entry to take up employment. These restrictions are usually much more stringent for lesser-skilled jobs because unemployment rates are usually much higher. The process by which permission is obtained to import personnel can be very time-consuming, and delays of up to one year in obtaining the appropriate entry and permit requirements are not uncommon.

5 *Control*   One strategy used by many multinational organizations to control their far-flung operations is by frequently transferring staff from head office to the foreign operations. The result is that those who have been 'acculturated' in the ways things are done in head office are likely to try and achieve the same procedures in the foreign subsidiaries (see Galbraith and Edstrom, 1976). Subsidiary benefits include the experience gained by those who are transferred around the world. Given the increased latitude of action provided to managers of foreign subsidiaries, when these individuals are returned to head office, their managerial experience is much greater than those who remained at home.

6 *Long-term focus* Most multinational organizations will transfer their personnel for only a few years to any particular subsidiary. Managers therefore tend to focus their attention on projects which will have a 'result' during their tenure. Though the satisfaction of seeing a successful result completed may be important to satisfy the personal advancement needs of the individual manager, it may not be best for overall corporate objectives. Employing local individuals as managers, who are expected to stay in situ for longer periods, may facilitate a longer-term perspective on organization objectives.

7 *Management development* Many multinational organizations transfer their personnel through a variety of countries. One objective of this process is to train them in understanding the overall corporate system. Another benefit is their increased ability to adapt to differing social systems. By learning the means of managing in different, sometimes difficult environments, these managers are likely to be well prepared for ultimate corporate responsibility.

Global mobility of personnel

While nationality plays an important part in determining the staffing policies of foreign operations, there are other factors to consider. When moving across national cultures, there are countless variables which can affect the likely success and effectiveness of individual employees. Among these are:

1 *Local prejudice* In some circumstances, individuals may have to be excluded from consideration for a particular cross-cultural assignment. This may have very little to do with the individual's aptitude for a particular job. For example, unlikely staffing policies would be a black manager operating in South Africa, a Jewish manager in Syria or a very young manager in Japan.

2 *Technical competence* Multinational companies must ensure that those awarded foreign assignments must be technically proficient in the tasks they are to be assigned. It is natural to expect that local employees may resent someone coming in from abroad, particularly if they feel that the newcomer can do the job no better than themselves. Managers also need to be able to adapt to local technical conditions. When moving to areas with different levels of economic and industrial development, the expatriate must be able to cope with often scaled-down plant and equipment, varying standards of productivity, a poor internal distribution system, and financial restrictions.

3 *Repatriation* Some of the difficulties encountered during repatriation are: (a) financial—many of the benefits provided in foreign assignments are taken away on return; (b) head office corporate structure—despite claims that assignments overseas will improve subsequent career prospects, this does not always occur. Returning expatriates can find their peers have been promoted while they were away and that they now have less autonomy in their current job; and (c) personal re-acclimatization—the needed readjustment back to new schools and new lifestyles for families after a long period away can be just as difficult as the initial move abroad.

Recruitment, selection and training

The most appropriate strategy for international organizations would seem to be one of staffing operations at all levels with 'truly' international managers. Recruitment should transcend nationality and the location of any specific job consideration. Very few organizations have been able to adopt this strategy, although some international companies such as Royal Dutch-Shell, Unilever and Nestlé have tried to develop an international cadre of managers.

The long-term success of any multinational organization depends upon its ability to locate and tap sources of managerial manpower. One way of obtaining personnel for foreign operations is to buy an existing firm operating in the local markets and to use their stock of human resources. The difficulty in quickly attracting sufficient workers in foreign markets has been a major reason why many multinational firms prefer to expand through acquisition rather than by setting up their own facilities from scratch (see Perlmutter and Heenan, 1974).

1 *Recruitment*   For an international organization, the ideal employee is one who has: (a) a high level of expertise in the job required; (b) a good understanding of local operating conditions; (c) an ability to understand and fulfil head-office demands. Unfortunately, such individuals are seldom easy to find. Multinationals have devoted much effort to identifying suitable recruitment forums in which to select likely candidates. Many have made an effort to seek out foreign graduates of the major Western universities. The reasoning is that such recruits, who are familiar with Western ways, may wish to return to their home countries. A growing source of international management personnel has been the international business schools such as INSEAD and IMD. As the demand for multinational managers increases, more business schools are becoming sensitive to these needs. This response to the demands of businesses can be seen in the increasing numbers of courses which relate to the international dimension of business studies.

2 *Cross-cultural ability*   The international transfer of personnel requires special qualities of intercultural flexibility if the move is to be a success. Unfortunately, many organizations are unable accurately to gauge the ability of their personnel to adapt to a different culture. As the needs of multinational organizations have become more acute in the 1980s, more attention has been given to developing assessment procedures which purport to identify the likelihood of cross-cultural adaptability. Training consultancy organizations have emerged which provide such assessments as well as briefing courses for managers who are moving internationally. The large multinational organizations such as Exxon and Mobil Oil have incorporated the assessment of a potential expatriate's family to try to identify potential problems in advance.

3 *Training*   Environmental training for an international assignment is an important part of the staffing process. An orientation programme which covers the country, its people, and its culture will facilitate the adjustment of an employee to a foreign environment. Living in a foreign country without adequate orientation may lead to 'culture shock'. To overcome this, multinational companies provide training in language skills, along with a basic knowledge of the host country, its people and its culture. Aside from such rudimentary topics such as job characteristics, compensation and general information on housing, climate, education and health, a wide number of other issues must also be reviewed. These can include: (a) the mechanics of the relocation process; (b) foreign social structure; (c) communication links; and (d) personal and family security precautions.

4 *Compensation* The compensation system of an international organization should effectively support the broad human-resource objectives of the company. People performing relatively similar jobs in different countries may receive very different amounts and forms of compensation. These tend to reflect the diversity in productivity level of the countries involved, costs of living, tax rates, and the supply and demand of certain skills. International organizations must meet the local competitive labour-market conditions or risk either not hiring sufficiently qualified people or incurring labour costs that are too high compared to the local competition. The issues which surround the international transfer of personnel are complex and sensitive. For example, if a French company transfers its British-based finance manager (who is earning £20 000 per year) to Italy (where the going rate is £29 000 per year) what should the salary be? Similarly, if the Italian-based finance manager was to be transferred to Britain, what salary should be offered? Non-monetary issues are also involved. In Britain, a holiday of four weeks per year may be the norm. In Italy, the holiday entitlement is likely to be six weeks. Similar questions also apply when considering fringe benefits such as pensions, health care, company car, etc.

To entice qualified managers to move abroad generally requires consideration of three components to the existing compensation package. First, there is the variation in cost-of-living between the countries. Second, is the need to align compensation packages with the equivalent job-status in the host country. If the status and compensation accorded particular skills or position in the host-country is higher than back home, then the individual may feel maltreated if his or her compensation package is not upgraded accordingly. Third, is the issue of hardship allowances. In a foreign country certain brands of food and drink will not be available; the quality of children's schooling is likely to differ and television programmes will be in a 'foreign' language, etc. The amount of hardship allowance offered is dependent upon the perceived desirability of living in a particular location. Postings in cities like London, Paris, New York and Hong Kong arguably present less 'hardship' than in Lima, Nairobi and Riyadh, although there will be individual differences in preferred location.

Comparative industrial relations

In every country in which it operates, the international organization must deal with its workers through some kind of systematic procedure. The relationship between the organization and its employees is determined by many variables. Two of the more important factors are the socio-political environment and trade-union structure.

Whether or not a workforce is unionized, the organization must come to terms with the socio-political environment in which it draws its employees. One of the characteristics which distinguish national labour–management relations is how the two sides traditionally view each other. In societies where traditional delineations between labour and management remain strong, there may be relatively little effort towards cooperating to reach overall corporate objectives. This is particularly true if there is a marked class difference between management and labour. Many observers (see, for example, Gallie, 1981) have argued that many of the labour difficulties in Britain are due to the perception among management and labour leaders that they are involved in a class struggle.

Trade-union structure also varies by country. In some countries, unions may represent workers in many different companies (as in Britain). In other countries, unions may represent workers only in one company. In the United States and Canada, trade unions tend to represent certain types of workers (coal miners, automobile workers, university academics) on a national basis. In Japan, a union typically represents all the workers in a particular company, with only very loose ties to any national body.

In other countries, a process of co-determination exists between management and labour. The concept of co-determination or *Mitbestimmung* (literally, 'having a voice in') is a process whereby management and labour jointly assume the responsibility for the determination of corporate policy. Co-determination was first introduced on a large scale in West Germany shortly after World War Two, when the steel and coal trade unions were given 50 per cent representation on the industry boards. It proved to be popular and was subsequently extended to include all corporations with over 500 employees. Other countries in Europe and Scandinavia have also moved towards similarly 'democratic' procedures which are usually protected by government legislation.

Multinational trade unions

As multinational companies continue to grow and prosper, many trade unions have become concerned about the impact such a development may have on their ability to look after the interests of workers. The power of multinational organizations to shift their operations from one country to another is seen as a highly effective strategy to reduce trade-union bargaining power.

Trade unions also claim that the ability of the multinational to use transfer pricing strategies for goods and services flowing between its various subsidiaries can also seriously affect labour negotiations. By portraying a misleading picture of profitability for a particular subsidiary, the firm can argue against local wage demands.

Yet another disadvantage of local trade unions when dealing with a multinational is the tendency to decide on global-relations policies at head office without regard to local issues and problems. The consequence is that local union negotiators will not be able to meet with the ultimate corporate decision-makers. It is exceptionally difficult for a trade union, which is confined to one country, to exert any influence on management that is located in another country and which oversees operations in a number of other countries as well.

In response to these problems, many trade unions have been stressing the need to coordinate their action with their corresponding trade unions in other countries. These activities are aimed at building the strength and ability of the unions when confronting multinational organizations. Such activities include an international exchange of information, international consultation and the coordination of policies and tactics.

Coordinated bargaining is also being sought by many trade unions. This would involve the simultaneous bargaining with all or most of a multinational's subsidiaries (either throughout the world or in a given region). Trade unionists feel that such an arrangement would result in direct access to the top decision-makers in the multinational organization and provide them with greater influence over decisions affecting employee relations.

Summary

Organizational-behaviour concepts, originally developed in single-country organizations, become especially relevant when applied to firms operating internationally. In particular, questions of organizational design, coordination and control take centre stage. Also in the spotlight, however, are the factors attributable to national differences in culture. These underpin the beliefs, attitudes and values of individuals within many of the subsidiaries of international firms. Differences here, between home and host country nationals, can create tensions, misunderstandings and conflict.

In many respects, the problems facing international organizations are similar to those described in Chapter 13 of this book when we examined corporate culture. Establishing a holistic culture (or a *modus vivendi*) for an international firm and its subsidiaries is the ultimate goal. This is both difficult to achieve and slow to develop. Other integrating devices are thus employed, including the careful selection and transfer of managers, designing around products, designing around markets and putting into place an explicit human-resource strategy to cope with the challenges of international operations. It is assumed that business organizations will continue to develop an international focus, so these issues will become even more pressing as we enter the final decade of the twentieth century. We explore the challenges and opportunities of the future in Part VII.

References

Aharoni, Y. (1971) 'On the definition of a multinational corporation', *Quarterly Review of Economics and Business*, Autumn, 27–37.

Brooke, M. Z. (1984) *Centralization and Autonomy: A Study in Organization Behaviour*, Holt, Rinehart & Winston, London.

Doz, Y. L., C. A. Bartlett and C. K. Prahalad (1981) 'Global competitive pressure and host country demands: managing tensions in MNCs', *California Management Review*, **23**(3), 72–84.

Galbraith, J. and A. Edstrom (1976) 'International transfer of managers: some important policy considerations', *Columbia Journal of World Business*, Summer, 100–12.

Gallie, D. (1981) 'Managerial strategies, the unions and the social integration of the work force', in M. Zey-Ferrell and M. Aiken (eds), *Complex Organizations: Critical Perspectives*, Scott, Foresman, Glenview, Illinois.

Heenan, D. A. and H. Perlmutter (1979) *Multinational Organization Development*, Addison-Wesley, Reading, Mass.

Kotter, J. P., L. A. Schlesinger and V. Sathe (1986) *Organization: Text, Cases, and Readings on the Management of Organizational Design and Change*, 2nd edn, Irwin, Homewood, Illinois.

Perlmutter, H. (1969) 'The tortuous evolution of the multinational corporation', *Columbia Journal of World Business*, Jan.–Feb., 9–18.

Perlmutter, H. and D. Heenan (1974) 'How multinational should your managers be?', *Harvard Business Review*, Nov.–Dec., 129.

Prasad, S. B. and Y. K. Shety (1976) *An Introduction to Multinational Management*, Prentice-Hall, Englewood Cliffs, New Jersey.

Robock, S. H. and K. Simmonds (1983) *International Business and Multinational Enterprises*, 3rd edn, Prentice-Hall, Homewood, Illinois.

Ronen, S. (1986) *Comparative and Multinational Management*, Wiley, New York.

Stopford, J. and L. T. Wells (1972) *Managing the Multinational Enterprise*, Basic Books, New York.

Turner, L. (1974) 'There's no love lost between multinationals and the Third World', *Business and Society Review*, Autumn, 74.

Wall Street Journal (1976) 'Nestlé wins libel case, is ordered to revise some sales practices', 25 June, 30.

The cultural relativity of organizational practices and theories

Geert Hofstede

Introduction: management and national cultures

A key issue for organization science is the influence of national cultures on management. Twenty or even ten years ago, the existence of a relationship between management and national cultures was far from obvious to many, and it may not be obvious to everyone even now. In the 1950s and 60s, the dominant belief, at least in Europe and the US, was that management was something universal. There were principles of sound management, which existed regardless of national environments. If national or local practice deviated from these principles, it was time to change local practice. In the future, the universality of sound management practices would lead to societies becoming more and more alike. This applied even to the poor countries of the Third World, which would become rich as well and would be managed just like the rich countries. Also, the differences between management in the First and Second World (capitalist and socialist) would disappear; in fact, under the surface they were thought to be a lot smaller than was officially recognized. This way of thinking, which dominated the 1950s and 60s, is known as the 'convergence hypothesis'.

During the 1970s, the belief in the unavoidable convergence of management practices waned. It was too obviously in conflict with the reality we saw around us. At the same time supranational organizations like the European Common Market, which was founded very much on the convergence belief, had to recognize the stubbornness of national differences. Even within existing nations, regional differences became more rather than less accentuated. The Welsh, the Flemish, the Basques, the Bangladeshi, the Quebecois defended their own identity, and this was difficult to reconcile with a management philosophy of convergence. It slowly became clear that national and even regional cultures do matter for management. The national and regional differences are not disappearing; they are here to stay. In fact, these differences may become one of the most crucial problems for management—in particular for the management of multinational, multicultural organizations, whether public or private.

The importance of nationality

Nationality is important to management for at least three reasons. The first, very obviously, is political. Nations are political units, rooted in history, with their own institutions: forms of government, legal systems, educational systems, labour and employer's association systems. Not only do the formal institutions differ, but even if we could equalize them, the informal ways of using them differ. For example, formal law in France protects the rights of the individual against the state much better than formal law in Great Britain or Holland. However, few French citizens have ever won court cases against the state, whereas this happens quite regularly in Holland or Britain. Such informal political realities are quite resistant to change.

The second reason why nationality is important is sociological. Nationality or regionality has a symbolic value to citizens. We all derive part of our identity from it; it is part of the 'who am I?'. The symbolic value of the fact of belonging to a nation or region has been and still is sufficient reason for people to go to war, when they feel their common identity to be threatened. National and regional differences are felt by people to be a reality—and therefore they are a reality.

The third reason why nationality is important is psychological. Our thinking is partly conditioned by national culture factors. This is an effect of early life experiences in the family and later educational experiences in schools and organizations, which are not the same across national borders. In a classroom, I can easily demonstrate the process of conditioning by experience. For this purpose I use an ambiguous picture: one that can be interpreted in two different ways. One such picture represents either an attractive young girl or an ugly old woman, depending on the way you look at it. In order to demonstrate the process of conditioning, I ask one half of the class to close their eyes. To the other half, I show for 5 seconds a slightly changed version of the picture, in which only the young girl can be seen. Then I ask the other half to close their eyes, and to the first half I show, also for 5 seconds, a version in which only the old woman can be seen. After this preparation, I show the ambiguous picture to everyone at the same time. The results are amazing: the vast majority of those 'conditioned' by seeing the young girl first, now see only the young girl in the ambiguous picture; and most of those 'conditioned' by seeing the old woman first can see only the old woman afterwards. (See Chapter 3, Figure 3.4).

Mental programming

This very simple experiment shows that; as a teacher, I can in 5 seconds condition a randomly taken half of a class to see something else in a picture than would the other half. If this is so, how much stronger should the differences in perception of the same reality be between people who have been 'conditioned' by different educational and life experiences not for a mere 5 seconds, but for 20, 30, or 40 years? Through our experiences we become 'mentally programmed' to interpret new experiences in a certain way. My favourite definition of 'culture' is precisely that its essence is *collective mental programming*: it is that part of our conditioning that we share with other members of our nation, region, or group but not with members of other nations, regions, or groups.

Examples of differences in mental programming between members of different nations can be observed all around us. One source of difference is, of course, language and all that comes with it, but there is much more. In Europe, British people will form a neat queue whenever they have to wait; not so, the French. Dutch people will as a rule greet strangers when they enter a small, closed space like a railway compartment, doctor's waiting room, or lift; not so, the Belgians. Austrians will wait at a red pedestrian traffic light even when there is no traffic; not so the Dutch. Swiss tend to become very angry when somebody—say, a foreigner—makes a mistake in traffic; not so the Swedes. All these are part of an invisible set of mental programmes which belongs to these countries' national cultures.

Such cultural programmes are difficult to change, unless one detaches the individual from his or her culture. Within a nation or a part of it, culture changes only slowly. This is the more so because what is in the minds of the people has also become crystallized in the institutions mentioned earlier:

government, legal systems, educational systems, industrial relations systems, family structures, religious organizations, sports clubs, settlement patterns, literature, architecture, and even scientific theories. All these reflect traditions and common ways of thinking, which are rooted in the common culture but may be different for other cultures. The institutions constrain and reinforce the ways of thinking on which they are based. One well-known mechanism by which culturally determined ways of thinking perpetuate themselves is the self-fulfilling prophecy. If, for example, the belief is held that people from a certain minority are irresponsible, the institutions in such an environment will not admit these people into positions of responsibility; never being given responsibility, minority people will be unable to learn it, and very likely they will actually behave irresponsibly. So, everyone remains caught in the belief— including, probably, the minority people themselves. Another example of the self-fulfilling prophecy: if the dominant way of thinking in a society is that all people are ultimately motivated by self-interest, those who do not pursue self-interest are considered as deviant. As it is unpleasant to be a deviant, most people in such an environment will justify whatever they want to do with some reference to self-interest, thereby reinforcing the dominant way of thinking. People in such a society cannot even imagine motives that cannot be reduced to self-interest.

National character

This reading is limited to national cultures, excluding cultural differences between groups within nations; such as, those based on regions, social classes, occupations, religion, age, sex, or even families. These differences in culture within nations, of course, do exist, but for most nations we can still distinguish some ways of thinking that most inhabitants share and that we can consider part of their national culture or national character. National characters are more clearly distinguishable to foreigners than to the nationals themselves. When we live within a country, we do not discover what we have in common with our compatriots, only what makes us different from them.

Statements about national culture or national character smell of superficiality and false generalization. There are two reasons for this. First, there is no commonly accepted language to describe such a complex thing as a 'culture'. We meet the same problem if we want to describe someone's 'personality': we risk being subjective and superficial. In the case of 'personality', however, psychology has at least developed terms like intelligence, energy level, introversion–extroversion and emotional stability, to mention a few, which are more or less commonly understood. In the case of 'culture', such a scientific language does not exist. In the second place, statements about national character have often been based on impressions only, not on systematic study. Such statements can indeed be considered false generalizations.

A research project across 50 countries

My own research into national cultures was carried out between 1967 and 1978. It has attempted to meet the two objectives I just mentioned: to develop a commonly acceptable, well-defined, and empirically based terminology to describe cultures; and to use systematically collected data about a large number of cultures, rather than just impressions. I obtained these data more or less by accident. From 1967 to 1971 I worked as a psychologist on the international staff of a large multinational corporation. As part of my job I collected data on the employee's attitudes and values, by means of standardized paper-and-pencil questionnaires. Virtually all employees of the corporation were surveyed, from unskilled workers to research scientists in many countries around the globe. Then from 1971 to 1973 the surveys were repeated once more with the same group of employees. All in all the corporation collected over 116 000 questionnaires which were stored in a computerized data bank. For 40 countries, there were sufficient data for systematic analysis.

It soon appeared that those items in the questionnaires that dealt with employee values rather than attitudes showed remarkable and very stable differences between countries. By an attitude I mean the response to a question like 'How do you like your job?' or 'How do you like your boss?' By a value I mean answers to questions of whether people prefer one type of boss over another, or their choice of factors to describe an ideal job. Values indicate their desires, not their perceptions of what actually went on. These values, not the attitudes, reflect differences in mental programming and national character.

These differences, however, were always statistical in nature. Suppose people were asked whether they strongly agreed, agreed, were undecided, disagreed, or strongly disagreed with a certain value statement. In such a case we would not find that all employees in country A agreed and all in country B disagreed; instead we might find that 60 per cent of the employees in country A agreed, while only 40 per cent in country B agreed. Characterizing a national culture does not mean that every individual within that culture is mentally programmed in the same way. The national culture found is a kind of average pattern of beliefs and values, around which individuals in the country vary. For example, I found that, on average, Japanese have a greater desire for a strong authority than English; but some English have a greater desire for a strong authority than quite a few Japanese. In describing national cultures we refer to common elements within each nation, but we should not generalize to every individual within that nation.

In 1971 I went as a teacher to an international business school, where I asked the course participants, who were managers from many different countries, to answer the same values questions we used in the multinational corporation. The answers revealed the same type of pattern of differences between countries, showing that we were not dealing with a phenomenon particular to this one company. Then in my later research, from 1973 to 1979, at the European Institute for Advanced Studies in Brussels, I looked for other studies comparing aspects of national character across countries. I found about 40 such studies comparing 5 or more countries which showed differences confirming the ones found in the multinational corporation. All this material together forms the basis for my book *Culture's Consequences* (Hofstede, 1980). Later, supplementary data became available for another 10 countries and 3 multi-country regions, thereby raising the total number of countries to 50 (Hofstede, 1983).

Four dimensions of national culture

My terminology for describing national cultures consists of four different criteria which I call 'dimensions' because they occur in nearly all possible combinations. They are largely independent of each other:

1 individualism versus collectivism;
2 large or small power distance
3 strong or weak uncertainty avoidance; and
4 masculinity versus femininity.

The research data have allowed me to attribute to each of the 40 countries represented in the data bank of the multinational corporation an index value (between 0 and about 100) on each of these four dimensions.

The four dimensions were found through a combination of multivariate statistics (factor analysis) and theoretical reasoning. The cases analysed in the factor analysis were the 40 countries; the variables were the mean scores or answer percentages for the different value questions, as produced by the multinational corporation's employees within these countries. This factor analysis showed that 50 per cent of the variance in answer patterns between countries on the value questions could be explained by three factors, corresponding to the dimensions 1+2, 3 and 4. Theoretical reasoning led to the further splitting of the first factor into two dimensions. The theoretical reasoning meant that each dimension should be conceptually linkable to some very fundamental problem in human societies, but a problem to which different societies have found different answers. These are the issues studied in primitive, nonliterate societies by cultural anthropologists, such as, the distribution of power, or the distribution of roles between the sexes. There is no reason why such issues should be relevant only for primitive societies.

Individualism–collectivism

The first dimension is labelled 'Individualism versus collectivism'. The fundamental issue involved is the relation between an individual and his or her fellow individuals. At one end of the scale we find societies in which the ties between individuals are very loose. Everybody is supposed to look after his or her own self-interest and maybe the interest of his or her immediate family. This is made possible by a large amount of freedom that such a society leaves individuals. At the other end of the scale we find societies in which the ties between individuals are very tight. People are born into collectivities or in-groups which may be their extended family (including grandparents, uncles, aunts, and so on), their tribe, or their village. Everybody is supposed to look after the interest of his or her in-group and to have no other opinions and beliefs than the opinions and beliefs in their in-group. In exchange, the in-group will protect them when they are in trouble. We see that both the individualist and the collectivist society are integrated wholes, but the individualist society is loosely integrated, and the collectivist society tightly integrated.

All 50 countries studied can be placed somewhere along the individualist–collectivist scale. On the basis of the answers obtained on the questionnaire in the multinational corporation, each country was given an individualism index score. The score is such that 100 represents a strong individualist society, and 0 a strongly collectivist society: all 50 countries are somewhere between these extremes.

It appears that the degree of individualism in a country is statistically related to that country's wealth. Figure R12.1 shows the list of countries used, and Figure R12.2 shows vertically the individualism index scores of the 50 countries, and horizontally their wealth, expressed in their gross national product per capita at the time the surveys were taken (around 1970). We see evidence that wealthy countries are more individualist and poor countries more collectivist. Very individualist countries are the US, Great Britain, the Netherlands; very collectivist are Colombia, Pakistan, and Taiwan. In the middle we find Japan, India, Austria, and Spain.

Power distance

The second dimension is labelled 'Power distance'. The fundamental issue involved is how society deals with the fact that people are unequal. People are unequal in physical and intellectual capacities. Some societies let these unequalities grow over time into inequalities in power and wealth; the latter may become hereditary and no longer related to physical and intellectual capacities at all. Other societies try to play down inequalities in power and

Figure R12.1 The
countries and
regions

ARA	Arab countries (Egypt, Lebanon, Libya, Kuwait, Iraq, Saudi-Arabia, UAE)	JAM	Jamaica
		JPN	Japan
		KOR	South Korea
		MAL	Malaysia
ARG	Argentina	MEX	Mexico
AUL	Australia	NET	Netherlands
AUT	Austria	NOR	Norway
BEL	Belgium	NZL	New Zealand
BRA	Brazil	PAK	Pakistan
CAN	Canada	PAN	Panama
CHL	Chile	PER	Peru
COL	Colombia	PHI	Philippines
COS	Costa Rica	POR	Portugal
DEN	Denmark	SAF	South Africa
EAF	East Africa (Kenya, Ethiopia, Zambia)	SAL	Salvador
		SIN	Singapore
EQA	Equador	SPA	Spain
FIN	Finland	SWE	Sweden
FRA	France	SWI	Switzerland
GBR	Great Britain	TAI	Taiwan
GER	Germany	THA	Thailand
GRE	Greece	TUR	Turkey
GUA	Guatemala	URU	Uruguay
HOK	Hong Kong	USA	United States
IDO	Indonesia	VEN	Venezuela
IND	India	WAF	West Africa (Nigeria, Ghana, Sierra Leone)
IRA	Iran		
IRE	Ireland	YUG	Yugoslavia
ISR	Israel		
ITA	Italy		

wealth as much as possible. Surely, no society has ever reached complete equality, because there are strong forces in society that perpetuate existing inequalities. All socieites are unequal, but some are more unequal than others. This degree of inequality is measured by the power-distance scale, which also runs from 0 (small power distance) to 100 (large power distance).

In organizations, the level of power distance is related to the degree of centralization of authority and the degree of autocratic leadership. This relationship shows that centralization and autocratic leadership are rooted in the 'mental programming' of the members of a society, not only of those in power but also of those at the bottom of the power hierarchy. Societies in which power tends to be distributed unequally can remain so because this situation satisfies the psychological need for dependence of the people without power. We could also say that societies and organizations will be led as autocratically as their members will permit. The autocracy exists just as much in the members as in the leaders: the value systems of the two groups are usually complementary.

In Figure R12.3 power distance is plotted horizontally and individualism–collectivism vertically. The Philippines, Venezuela, India, and others show

Figure R12.2
The position of the 50 countries on their individualism index (IDV) versus their 1970 national wealth: individual index (IDV) versus 1970 national wealth (per capita GNP) for 50 countries

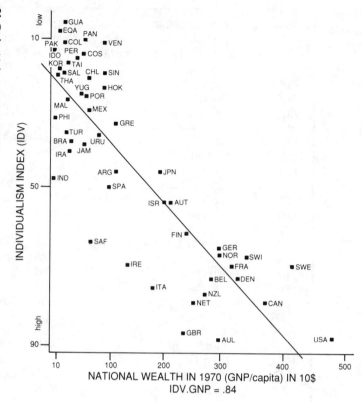

Figure R12.3
The position of the 50 countries on the power distance and individualism scales: A power distance ×individualism–collectivism plot for 50 countries and 3 regions

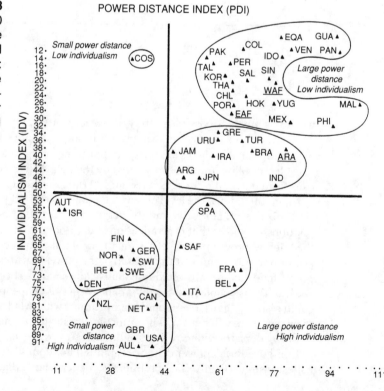

large power distance index scores, but also France and Belgium score fairly high. Denmark, Israel, and Austria score low. We see that there is a global relationship between power distance and collectivism: collectivist countries always show large power distances, but individualist countries do not always show small power distances. The Latin European countries—France, Belgium, Italy, and Spain, plus marginally South Africa—show a combination of large power distances plus individualism. The other wealthy Western countries all combine smaller power distance with individualism. All poor countries are collectivist with larger power distances.

Uncertainty avoidance

The third dimension is labelled 'Uncertainty avoidance'. The fundamental issue involved here is how society deals with the fact that time runs only one way; that is, we are all caught in the reality of past, present and future, and we have to live with uncertainty because the future is unknown and always will be. Some societies socialize their members into accepting this uncertainty and not becoming upset by it. People in such societies will tend to accept each day as it comes. They will take risks rather easily. They will not work as hard. They will be relatively tolerant of behaviour and opinions different from their own because they do not feel threatened by them. Such societies can be called 'weak uncertainty avoidance' societies; they are societies in which people have a natural tendency to feel relatively secure.

Other societies socialize their people into trying to beat the future. Because the future remains essentially unpredictable, in those societies there will be a higher level of anxiety in people, which becomes manifest in greater nervousness, emotionality, and aggressiveness. Such societies, called 'strong uncertainty-avoidance' societies, also have institutions that try to create security and avoid risk. We can create security in three ways. One is technology, in the broadest sense of the word. Through technology we protect ourselves from the risks of nature and war. We build houses, dikes, power stations, and ICBMs which are meant to give us a feeling of security. The second way of creating security is law, again in the broadest sense of the word. Through laws and all kinds of formal rules and institutions, we protect ourselves from the unpredictability of human behaviour. The proliferation of laws and rules implies an intolerance of deviant behaviours and opinions. Where laws cannot be made because the subject is too fuzzy, we can create a feeling of security by the nomination of experts. Experts are people whose word we accept as a kind of law because we assume them to be beyond uncertainty. The third way of creating a feeling of security is religion, once more in the broadest sense of the word. This sense includes secular religions and ideologies, such as Marxism, dogmatic capitalism, or movements that preach an escape into meditation. Even science is included. All human societies have their religions in some way or another. All religions, in some way, make uncertainty tolerable, because they all contain a message that is beyond uncertainty, that helps us to accept the uncertainty of today because we interpret experiences in terms of something bigger and more powerful that transcends personal reality. In strongly uncertainty-avoiding societies we find religions which claim absolute truth and which do not tolerate other religions. We also find in such societies a scientific tradition looking for ultimate, absolute truths, as opposed to a more relativist, empiricist tradition in the weak uncertainty-avoidance societies.

The uncertainty-avoidance dimension, thus, implies a number of things, from aggressiveness to a need for absolute truth, that we do not usually consider as belonging together. They appear to belong together in the logic of culture patterns, but this logic differs from our own daily logic. Without research we would not have found that, on the level of societies, these things go together.

Figure R12.4 plots the uncertainty-avoidance index for 50 countries along the vertical axis, against the power-distance index on the horizontal axis. We find several clusters of countries. Thee is a large cluster of countries with strong uncertainty avoidance and large power distance. They are: all the Latin countries, both Latin European and Latin American; Mediterranean countries, such as, Yugoslavia, Greece, and Turkey; and Japan plus Korea.

Figure R12.4
The position of the 50 countries on the power distance and uncertainty avoidance scales: A power distance ×uncertainty avoidance plot for 50 countries and 3 regions

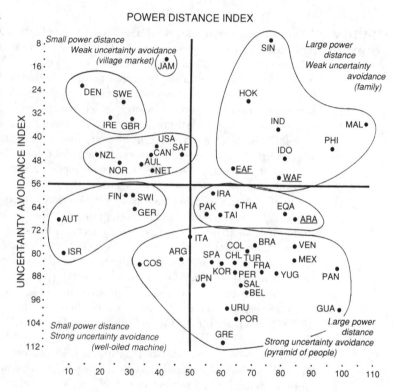

The Asian countries are found in two clusters with large power distance and medium to weak uncertainty avoidance. Then we find a cluster of German-speaking countries, including Israel and marginally Finland, combining small power distance with medium to strong uncertainty avoidance.

Both small power distance and weak uncertainty avoidance are found in Denmark, Sweden, Great Britain, and Ireland, while the Netherlands, US, Norway, and the other Anglo countries are in the middle.

Masculinity–femininity

The fourth dimension is labelled 'Masculinity versus femininity'. The fundamental issue involved is the division of roles between the sexes in society. All societies have to deal with the basic fact that one half of mankind is female and the other male. The only activities that are strictly determined by the sex of a person are those related to procreation. Men cannot have babies. Human societies, however, through the ages and around the globe, have also associated other roles to men only, or to women only. This is called social, rather than biological, sex role division.

All social-role divisions are more or less arbitrary, and what is seen as a typical task for men or for women can vary from one society to the other. We can classify societies on whether they try to minimize or to maximize the social sex role division. Some societies allow both men and women to take many different roles. Others make a sharp division between what men should do and what women should do. In this latter case, the distribution is always such that men take the more assertive and dominant roles and women the more service-oriented and caring roles. I have called those societies with a maximized social sex-role division 'maculine' and those with a relatively small social sex-role division 'Feminine'. In masculine societies, the traditional masculine social values permeate the whole society—even the way of thinking of the women. These values include the importance of showing off, of performing, of achieving something visible, of making money, of 'big is beautiful'. In more feminine societies, the dominant values—for both men and women—are those more traditionally associated with the feminine role: not showing off, putting relationships with people before money, minding the quality of life and the preservation of the environment, helping others, in particular the weak, and 'small is beautiful'. In a masculine society, the public hero is the successful achiever, the superman. In a more feminine society, the public sympathy goes to the anti-hero, the underdog. Individual brilliance in a feminine society is suspect.

Following the procedure used for the other dimensions, each of the 50 countries was given an index score on the masculinity–femininity scale: a high score means a more masculine, a low score a more feminine country. Figure R12.5 plots the masculinity index score horizontally and the uncertainty avoidance index again vertically. The most masculine country is Japan; also quite masculine are the German-speaking countries: Germany, Austria, and Switzerland. Moderately masculine are a number of Latin countries, such as

Figure R12.5

The position of the 50 countries on the uncertainty avoidance and masculinity scales: A masculinity–femininity × uncertainty avoidance plot for 50 countries and 3 regions

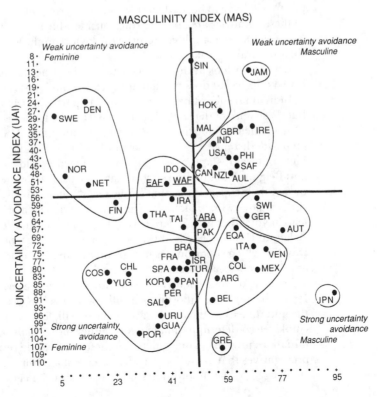

Venezuela, Mexico, and Italy; also the entire cluster of Anglo countries including some of their former colonies: India and the Philippines.

On the far end towards the feminine side we find the four Nordic countries and the Netherlands. Some Latin and Mediterranean countries like Yugoslavia, Chile, Portugal, Spain, and France are moderately feminine.

Some consequences for management theory and practice

The naive assumption that management is the same or is becoming the same around the world is now tenable in view of these demonstrated differences in national cultures. Consider a few of the ideas about management which have been popularized in the Western literature in the past 15 years; in particular, about leadership, about models of organization, and about motivation. These theories were almost without exception made in the US; in fact, the post-Second World War management literature is entirely US dominanted. This reflects the economic importance of the US during this period, but culturally the US is just one country among all others, with its particular configuration of cultural values which differs from that of most other countries.

Leadership

The most relevant dimensions for leadership are individualism and power distance. Let us look at Figure R12.3 again. We find the US in an extreme position on the individualism scale (50 out of 50) and just below average on the power distance scale (16 out of 50). What does the high individualism score mean? US leadership theories are about leading individuals based on the presumed needs of individuals who seek their ultimate self-interest. For example, the word 'duty', which implies obligations towards others or towards society, does not appear at all in the US leadership theories.

Leadership in a collectivist society—basically any Third World country—is a group phenomenon. A working group which is not the same as the natural in-group will have to be made into another in-group in order to be effective. People in these countries are able to bring considerable loyalty to their job, providing they feel that the employer returns the loyalty in the form of protection, just like their natural in-group does.

Let us now look at the power-distance dimension, in terms of participative leadership. What does participative leadership US style mean?

Individual subordinates are allowed to participate in the leader's decisions, but these remain the leader's decisions; it is the leader who keeps the initiative. Management prerogatives are very important in the US. Let us remember that on power distance, the US is more or less in the middle zone. In countries with higher power distances—such as, many Third World countries, but also France and Belgium—individual subordinates as a rule do not want to participate. It is part of their expectations that leaders lead autocratically, and such subordinates will, in fact, by their own behaviour make it difficult for leaders to lead in any other way. There is very little participative leadership in France and Belgium. If the society is at the same time collectivist, however, there will be ways by which subordinates in a group can still influence the leader. This applies to all Asian countries.

Let us take some countries on the other side, however: Denmark, Sweden, or Israel. In this case, subordinates will not necessarily wait until their boss takes the initiative to let them participate. They will, for example, support forms of employee co-determination in which either individuals or groups can take initiatives towards management. In these cultures there are no management prerogatives that are automatically accepted; anything a boss does may be challenged by the subordinates. Management privileges in particular are much more easily accepted in US than in some of the very low power distance countries. A similar difference is found in the ratios between management compensation and subordinate compensation.

Organization

In organizations the decisive dimensions of culture are power distance and uncertainty avoidance. Organizations are devices to distribute power and they also serve to avoid uncertainty, to make things predictable. So let us look at Figure R12.4 again. My former colleague, Professor James Stevens from INSEAD, once gave the same description of an organizational problem to separate groups of French, West German, and British managment students. The problem described a conflict between two departments. The students were asked to determine what was wrong and what should be done to resolve the problem. The French in majority referred the problem to the next higher authority level. The Germans suggested the setting of rules to resolve such problems in the future. The British wanted to improve communications between the two department heads, perhaps by some kind of human-relations training. My colleague concluded that the dominant underlying model of an organization for the French was a pyramid, a hierarchical structure held together by the unity of command (larger power distance) as well as by rules (strong uncertainty avoidance). The model for the Germans was a well-oiled machine; the exercise of personal command was largely unnecessary because the rules settled everything (strong uncertainty avoidance, but smaller power distance). The model for the British was a village market: no decisive hierarchy, flexible rules, and a resolution of problems by negotiating (small power distance and weak uncertainty avoidance). These models left one corner in the diagram of Figure R12.4 unexplained, but a discussion with an Indian colleague led me to believe that the underlying model of an organization for the Indians is the family: undisputed personal authority of the father-leader but few formal rules (large power distance and weak uncertainty avoidance). This should also apply in the Chinese culture city-states of Hong Kong and Singapore (see Figure R12.4).

The US is close to the centre of the diagram of Figure R12.4 and so are the Netherlands and Switzerland. This may explain something of the success of US, Dutch, and Swiss multinationals in operating in a variety of cultures; in the US literature and practice, all four models of organization—the pyramid, the well-oiled machine, the village market, and the family—can be found, but none of them can be considered dominant.

Motivation

The theories of motivation (what makes people act) and the practices of motivating people can both be related to the indivualism–collectivism dimension. In the US the highest motivation is supposed to stem from the individuals' need to fulfil their obligations towards themselves. We find terms like 'self-actualization' and 'self-respect' on the top of the list of motivators. In a more collectivist society, however, people will try primarily to fulfil their obligations towards their in-group. This may be their family, but their collective loyalty may also be directed towards some larger unit: their enterprise, or their country. Such people do not seek self-actualization or self-respect, but they primarily seek 'face' in their relationships with in-group members. The importance of face as a motivator does not appear in the US motivation literature at all. The distinction between 'face' cultures and 'self-respect' cultures is similar to the distinction between 'shame' and 'guilt' cultures identified by the anthropologist Ruth Benedict (1974).

Other dimensions relevant to motivation are uncertainty avoidance and masculinity–femininity. Let us look at Figure R12.5 again. The dominant theme of the US literature of the past 20 years is that people are basically motivated by a desire to achieve something. We should, therefore, allow our people to achieve: give them challenge, and enrich their jobs if they do not contain any challenge. The idea of 'achievement' and 'challenge', US style, implies two things: a willingness to take some risks (weak uncertainty avoidance) and a need to perform, to assert oneself (masculinity). It is therefore no wonder that in the diagram of Figure R12.5 we find the US in the weak uncertainty avoidance, masculine corner. It shares this position with the other Anglo countries. Let us take the case of some other countries, however: Japan or Germany. These are also masculine countries but with stronger uncertainty avoidance. This means that in these countries there is less willingness to take risks: security is a powerful motivator. People are very willing to perform if they are offered security in exchange. Interestingly, these security-seeking countries seem to have been doing better economically in the past 20 years than the risk-takers; but the management theories that tell us that risk-taking is a good thing were made in the US or Great Britain, not in Japan or Germany.

If we go to the other corner of Figure R12.5, we find the Netherlands and the Nordic countries combining weak uncertainty avoidance with a more feminine value system. Here, the maintenance of good interpersonal relations is a strong motivator, and people frown at competition for performance. In these countries we meet a powerful interpersonal motivation which is missing in the US theories. There is striking difference in the forms of 'humanization of work' proposed in the US and in Sweden: a stress in the US on creating possibilities for individual performance, but a stress in Sweden on creating possibilities for interpersonal solidarity. In the fourth corner of Figure R12.5, we find both security and interpersonal motivation; Yugoslav worker self-management contains both elements. We are far away here from the motivation to achieve according to the US style.

Conclusion: the cultural relativity of management and organization practices and theories

Both management practitioners and management theorists over the past 80 years have been blind to the extent to which activities like 'management' and 'organizing' are culturally dependent. They are culturally dependent because managing and organizing do not consist of making or moving tangible objects, but of manipulating symbols which have meaning to the people who are managed or organized. Because the meaning which we associate with symbols is heavily affected by what we have learned in our family, in our school, in our work environment, and in our society, management and organization are penetrated with culture from the beginning to the end. Practice is usually wiser than theory, and if we see what effective organizations in different cultures have done, we recognize that their leaders did adapt foreign management ideas to local cultural conditions. This happened extremely effectively in Japan, where mainly US management theories were taken over but in an adapted form. This adaptation led to entirely new forms of practice which in the Japanese case were highly successful. An example is the quality control circle, originally based on US impulses but adapted to the Japanese uncertainty-avoiding, semicollectivist environment. The quality control circle has been so effective in Japan that now the Americans are bringing it back to the US; but it is doubtful whether most of its present US protagonists realize the role that Japanese educational and social conditions play in the ability of Japanense workers to function effectively in a quality control circle.

Not all other countries have been as fortunate as Japan in that a successful adaptation of American management theories and practices could take place. In Europe but even more often in Third World countries, foreign management methods and ideas were indiscriminately imported as a part of 'technology transfer'. The evident failure of much of the international development assistance of the 1960s and 1970s is at least partly due to this lack of cultural sensitivity in the transfer of management ideas. It has caused enormous economic losses and human suffering. Free market capitalism as practised in the US, for example, is an idea which is deeply rooted historically and culturally in individualism. 'Everybody for himself' is supposed to lead to the highest common good, according to Adam Smith (1970). If this idea is forced upon a traditionally collectivist society, it means that work organizations will be created which do not offer to employees the protection which they expect to get in exchange for their loyalty. The system itself in such a society breeds disloyal, irresponsible employees. Japan has not taken over this aspect of capitalism and has maintained a much higher level of protection of employees by their organization. Many US managers and politicians have great problems with recognizing that their type of capitalism is culturally unsuitable for a more collectivist society. It is for good cultural reasons that various forms of state capitalism or state socialism are tried in Third World countries.

Most present-day management theories are ethnocentric', that is, they take the cultural environment of the theorist for granted. What we need is more cultural sensitivity in management theories; we could call the result 'organizational anthropology' or 'management anthropology'. It is unlikely to be the product of one single country's intellectual effort; it needs by definition a synergy between ideas from different sources. The fact that no single country now enjoys a degree of economic dominance as the US once did will certainly help: economic power is all too often related to intellectual influence. In a world in which economic power is more widely spread, we can more easily hope to recognize truth coming from many sources. In this process, the contribution of Japanese and Chinese scholars, for example, will be vital, because they represent sources of practical wisdom and ideas which complement practices and ideas born in Europe and the US.

The convergence of management will never come. What we can bring about is an understanding of how the culture in which we grew up and which is dear to us affects our thinking differently from other people's thinking, and what this means for the transfer of management practices and theories. What this can also lead to is a better ability to manage intercultural negotiations and multicultural organizations like the United Nations, which are essential for the common survival of us all.

References

Benedict, R. (1974) *The Chrysanthemum and the Sword: Patterns of Japanese Culture*, 1st edn, 1946, New American Library, New York, p. 222.

Hofstede, G. (1980) *Culture's Consequences: International Differences in Work-Related Values*, Sage Publications, Beverly Hills/London.

Hofstede, G. (1983) 'Dimensions of national cultures in fifty countries and three regions'. J. Deregowski, S. Dziurawiec, and R. C. Annis (eds), in *Expiscations in Cross-Cultural Psychology*, Swets and Zeitlinger, Lisse, Netherlands.

Smith, A. (1970) *The Wealth of Nations*, 1st edn, 1776, Penguin, Harmondsworth.

A portable life: the expatriate spouse

Nancy J. Adler*

In an international move, the spouse has the most difficult role of any family member. While employees have the basic company and job structure that continues from the home to the foreign country, and children have the continuity and routine of school, spouses often must give up their friends and activities. More and more frequently today, spouses must also leave a job or career in order to follow their partners to the foreign country. Spouses lose both the structure and the continuity in their lives (D'Orazio, 1981; Priestoff, 1976). The spouse's dissatisfaction, which often leads to early return, is the single most important reason for failure on an overseas assignment—nearly half of 300 surveyed companies have brought families home early due to the unwillingness or inability of the spouse to adapt. The average cost to the company of repatriating an executive and the family exceeds $100 000 (Baker, 1975).

The experience of an international employee differs quite markedly from that of his or her spouse. The spouse becomes more immersed in the culture than the employee, and the challenges for successful adjustment are both different and greater. This reading focuses on the most common spouses: the wives of international managers. The reason is not that all spouses are wives, but that, to date, very few married women have been sent overseas and even fewer have been accompanied by a husband (Adler, 1984).

This reading looks at the expatriate experience through the eyes of wives who have been moved from country to country in order to follow their husbands' careers. What challenges does she face in moving overseas? How does she adapt to the foreign culture? How does she create a meaningful, 'portable' life for herself—one that works in whatever situation she encounters? This reading will discuss her expatriate cycle: her initial reaction to the move overseas, her arrival in the foreign country, her ways of creating a new lifestyle, and her return to the home country. This cycle takes place concurrently with the employee's international career cycle, but may or may not be recognized by the couple or the organization.

One hundred and ninety-seven wives of managers sent overseas by American and Canadian multinational corporations and by a government agency (the Canadian International Development Agency) described their international experiences in interview and on questionnaires (Adler, 1980). The women had been sent to Asia, Africa, Europe, and Latin America. Some had lived in urban centres and others in rural areas; some in economically developed countries and others in extremely poor regions; some in linguistically similar areas (e.g. English- or French-speaking) and some in areas in which the language was totally foreign. The ages and family situations also varied. While the diversity of their backgrounds and overseas situations is noteworthy, the challenges they faced in attempting to survive the transition and create meaningful portable lives overseas are amazingly similar.

*Reproduced by permission from: *International Dimensions of Organizational Behaviour*, Kent Publishing, Boston, 1986, pp. 219–38.

Moving overseas: pre-made decisions

Companies' involvement in overseas operations takes many forms, including exporting, licensing, joint ventures, turnkey projects, and subsidiary operations. Companies therefore transfer employees for a wide variety of reasons, including staffing, management development, and organization development (Edstrom and Galbraith, 1977). Companies make staffing transfers when they lack sufficient local personnel to fill a given position, often in economically underdeveloped areas of the world which lack technological and managerial expertise. They design management development transfers to give managers overseas experience as well as to staff overseas positions. Organization development transfers remain the least common of the three transfer types. Companies design organization development transfers to allow managers from different countries to (1) learn thoroughly the organizational's operation, procedures, and culture worldwide; (2) get to know each other personally and thus develop an effective communication network; and (3) develop the high level of flexibility and adaptability necessary to succeed in the wide range of environments encompassed by the organization.

By contrast, a wife is sent overseas because the company transferred her husband (Wederspahn, 1980). Many wives are unaware of the possibility that they might move to a foreign country. At times, they initially react with surprise or shock:

Argentina   I just didn't have any idea. I was thoroughly settled in Toronto. We were going to live there the rest of our lives. Our family and friends were all around us and everything was very comfortable . . . I just didn't have any idea of what was ahead of me. I looked it up on the map and I knew it was an awful long way from Toronto. I remembered a little bit in school about Argentina—that Buenos Aires was the capital. But beyond that, it was just like stepping into oblivion. I had no idea what to expect.

Can a wife turn down an overseas transfer? Although the company and the employee usually believe that the wife has a role in the decision to move overseas, she rarely does in actuality. By the time the company identifies the employees they want to transfer and announces its decision, it has made a large investment in their acceptance. Subtle pressure discourages open discussion of the pros and cons of the move. An employee often feels he would disappoint the company if he did not accept; the wife feels that she would disappoint her husband. An employee often feels he would hinder his career by saying no; his wife is reluctant to disagree. Concerns that they could discuss and resolve prior to departure are never mentioned. At a time when communication is critical, open communication is often absent.

Venezuela   Bill came home in November and asked me what I thought about moving overseas. I was silent. Then he told me about what a big promotion it would mean for the rest of his career. I told him that I was delighted. The company told us about the things to take and the name of an international school. And we were made busy with the preparations. We left.

Cross-culture transitions

Expatriates must not only go through a gruelling physical move overseas, they must adjust to the foreign culture and create a meaningful life as well. Much attention is generally given to the logistics of the transfer itself: what should be packed, which shipper used, where to stay upon arrival, and so on. Less attention is given to the skills necessary for adjusting to the foreign country: good language training, a knowledge of the culture and its people, and an awareness of culturally based differences in values, attitudes, and behaviours. Least attention is paid to assisting the spouse in creating a meaningful portable life overseas. While not recognized as a potent issue by either the employee or the children, the structureless role of the spouse demands explicit attention: if she is to have a fulfilling life overseas, she must design it. First the transition itself and the initial adjustment issues confronting the spouse will be discussed, then the broader and more fundamental issue of creating a meaningful life overseas will be investigated.

It's harder for the spouse

As mentioned earlier, when a wife moves overseas, she comes into more direct contact with the 'foreignness' of the new culture than her husband. The husband generally works in the most internationally sophisticated strata of society: he meets people who speak English and have met foreigners before. The wife meets less sophisticated people. Whether in caring for the family's daily living needs or in arranging for servants to perform household tasks, she meets people who do not always speak English and have rarely met foreigners. Whereas an employee often has a secretary and colleagues to translate the language and explain the foreign customs, the wife must depend on her own skills and ingenuity. Whereas an employee works in an office filled with other expatriates to answer his questions and share his frustrations, the wife often finds herself isolated in her home world. She must confront the differences on her own.

Many wives feel unprepared for their move. They know little about the country, the culture, or the specific location. Their expectations and the foreign reality have little in common. Upon arrival, they often react with surprise and excitement mixed with bewilderment and fear. Below, three expatriate wives describe their arrival in Africa:

> Well, my expectations were very, how would I say, very large. For me, Africa was . . . totally unknown . . . except that I could equate it with wild animals, missionaries, nice black people, and a very different way of life than in Canada . . . I didn't question anything. I was very young, just married, and very happy to discover a new country. I could imagine that they had modern cities, that Conakry would be a modern city with all the amenities, asked no questions and just left.

> Finally arrived at . . . this hazy airport . . . I got off the plane, and there were . . . all of these black faces which I wasn't really used to in such mass. So I said, 'It's good to be here and I am so looking forward to getting into my house.' . . . [My husband] didn't know how to say it, but he said, 'But we don't have a house.' So I burst into tears. I guess it was just the whole stress of thinking that finally I was going to be in a house, and the jet lag, and just being in a completely different culture and a completely different colour.

> Well, it was very different from what I had imagined. My first shock was in Dakar, where we had to change planes . . . I was very surprised to see all the white people left aside while the black people boarded the plane. The white people were like second-class citizens. I could understand that later on, when I realized that Guinea had only been independent for a year.

Culture shock: the initial period overseas

Culture shock is the reaction of expatriates to entering a new, unpredictable and therefore uncertain environment. During the first few months in a foreign culture, expatriates often find that other people's behaviour does not make sense, and even more disconcerting, that their own behaviour does not produce expected results. The wives, being in more direct contact with the foreign culture than the employees, describe some of their initial reactions as surprise, bewilderment, and disorientation:

Guinea   Well, then we went into our building, a very modern building. We were on the ninth floor, and the building had no elevators. So we had to walk the nine floors. And then we arrived in this beautiful, huge apartment, with three bathrooms and no water.

Argentina   Everything I was comfortable with in a North American suburban setting, like my shopping, and the schools, and my daily routine, just was drastically different in Argentina. Perhaps the thing that struck me the most was when I set out to do my grocery shopping (which is something that we take for granted with our big supermarkets here), I found myself in the biggest supermarket in Argentina, which was just a filthy little dump really, and as I looked around to fill my grocery cart, the only thing I recognized was a box of Quaker Oats. Everything else was packaged differently, everything had Spanish names on it, and I couldn't tell salt from icing sugar.

Hong Kong   Before I went to Hong Kong, I'd read a lot of books. I expected the Chinese to be dignified and very courteous. The Cantonese in Hong Kong are the opposite of that. They are very noisy and . . . very pushy. In Argentina I expected the romantic Latin. Instead, I was annoyed at the 'macho-ness' of the men. The reality . . . was disappointing.

Frustration   The first few months in a foreign culture are rarely easy. The constant frustration of not understanding and not being able to get simple things done follows the initial surprise.

It's the constant minor frustrations . . . the phone never works, the electric power is variable, and, oh yes, filling the water bottles at 4.00 am, just to be sure that we'd have some water.

I had my new Electrolux vacuum cleaner and I tried to show the help how to use it . . . The next thing I knew they were vacuuming the patio and the grass. They just had no concept of what this [vacuum] was.

We were not aware of the fact that everything seems to be done through a bribe. We were insulted when it was suggested. I think we just didn't understand the culture. So we waited from January until May before our furniture was sprung from customs.

Things can be very difficult . . . [say] you have to put on a dinner party: dinner parties are very important because there is not very much entertainment, so you have to make your own entertainment. You have ten people coming, and there is no electricity, and you have just put the roast in the oven. Right, what do you do? And it's pouring with rain outside so you can't make a barbecue. So you raid the cupboard and find a tin of ham, and you find some tomatoes, and then you find this and that, and you all have a good giggle. You know, really there is no other way of doing it. You can't get depressed about these things.

I like it . . . but things don't work and it's frustrating. I didn't expect things not to work in Europe. In a developing country, yes, but not in Europe.

While the newness of the environment in large part causes the difficulties, they are exacerbated by insufficient language competence, loneliness, boredom, and a sense of meaninglessness.

Foreign language illiteracy   While most employees have less immediate need for foreign language competence than do the wives, many organizations only offer language training to employees. They expect the wife to enrol in language courses if she so desires, and often not at company expense. Consequently, many women never become fluent in the foreign language and therefore have little possibility of becoming fully comfortable living in the culture.

Italy   I think the most difficult thing when you arrive in a country is not being able to communicate. You feel very isolated because you don't speak the language. So everything becomes very difficult; all small details, everyday life is difficult because you don't know how to communicate.

Mexico   The only foreign language I learned is Spanish . . . and I didn't find it easy. I was embarrassed to speak in case I didn't have it right, and this became a big problem . . . I would pretend I hadn't been there very long, even when I had been there several months. And I'd have the children speaking for me in the taxi because they could speak far better Spanish than I could.

Argentina   I think the thing that bothered me the most was just my inability to express myself in Spanish. It was a while before I was able to take lessons, and I never did become fluent in the language. I could get by in English in most situations, but it was a little disappointing to see my husband learning Spanish through the office and my children learning it in school and yet I just could never seem to find the time or the concentration to sit down and master this thing.

Loneliness   The lack of intimate friendships causes a major part of the difficulty of the initial period abroad. Most wives leave their family and friends at home and experience a void upon arrival overseas. The loneliness expresses itself in a number of ways:

I spent more time alone than anywhere ever . . . It's hard to spend so much time alone.

We had a lot of acquaintances, few good friends . . . You can't make friends until you've learned the language.

Loneliness is the biggest problem with all the moves. I can remember moving from Mexico to the United States very worried about what we would find there. Looking down at the little family that was in just a shack in Mexico City and envying them because they had the whole family there. And I thought, they are better off than I am . . . In Hong Kong, not long after we arrived, our daughters were going back to school, my husband was going back with them on a business trip, and I felt, well, this is ridiculous. I am the only one here, and the rest of the family is on the other side of the world . . . I think that every country and every move has its low point and then you start going up . . . I think loneliness is probably the low point.

When you live abroad and you suffer loneliness, you have to . . . be your best friend.

So I was very alone, very lonely and my husband was not going through the same problems as I . . . And I felt more lonely because I couldn't share my problems with him. It was very difficult for . . . at least a year, a year and a half.

Boredom and meaninglessness   Many of the wives describe themselves as having hours and hours on their hands with nothing to do. They describe themselves as living in gilded cages: they have nice homes and servants to do the work but they do not have a meaningful role to fulfil. They no longer feel needed to perform many of the duties that they had previously fulfilled for their families, and, in addition, most are barred from working or continuing careers outside the home.

> I was like a prisoner in my own apartment. I had nothing to do. I had no books with me, except for one or two and that's very quickly gone through . . . I had absolutely nothing to do. So I started to write letters. This was my only contact with the outside world; and I don't like writing letters!

> I felt useless. I was a fifth wheel. There was a maid to do the work and no children that needed my attention.

> I was going to be a nurse, but I had to have a work permit . . . so I threw myself into the women's club . . . bridge and golf, empty activities, but they filled my time.

> Time . . . trying to find things to do with my time. I spent time sewing and I *hate* to sew . . . We got together to crochet and talk. Blah!

> After the novelty wears off, you have to find something to do with your time. I worked in a hospital, cooked, gardened . . . I want to work again.

Separation and a lack of support

The employee's frequent absence compounds the difficulties present in adjusting to the new environment. Having just started a new job, the employee often works long hours. Exacerbating the situation further, many foreign assignments include regional responsibilities and a great amount of travel. Whereas the wife has just given up her friends, activities, and in many cases a job or career to follow her husband and family overseas, the husband continues and increases his major involvement in the job, often to the near exclusion of his wife. Separation and lack of support cause numerous complaints:

> My husband wasn't there to help me. He did nothing on the move. He works and travels.

> My husband was always away; never available. The men are so busy and the women have nothing to do.

> Well, I expected him to travel a little, but I didn't expect it to be so long or so often.

> My husband, as well as most of the men in the company, was away probably two weeks out of four. We knew before we left that there was going to be a lot of travelling, but it didn't really make its impact until he was actually doing it.

As shown in Figure R13.1, the husband's work often leaves him least available during the few months abroad, exactly when the wife needs him the most to help with the logistics of settling in and to provide companionship and support. Unfortunately, the pattern of absent husbands and isolated wives reinforces itself in a vicious cycle. As more problems build up at home, many employees have less desire to spend time at home. By their own admission, many employees spend more time in the office and travelling than is necessary or required by the job. As the wife's situation becomes more difficult, the husband, often feeling guilty at the realization than his career caused the situation in the first place, increasingly avoids home.

Figure R13.1
The availability gap

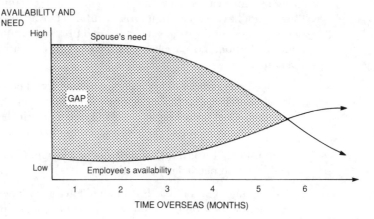

AVAILABILITY AND NEED

Creating a meaningful portable life

Following the initial period of adjustment, the wife faces the hardest task of all: creating a meaningful life overseas. She must identify what she wants to do and find a way to do it in the foreign country. For women who follow their husbands from country to country, it becomes the search for a meaningful *portable* life.

> Being a transient, I tried to develop those things because . . . it is very difficult for me to have a career. And luckily, I am not a particularly career-minded person. I want to take experiences and opportunities as they come. I want to learn different things, and I want to try different things. I mean, I only have one life. So a career and stepping up the ladder isn't important to me personally, it isn't. But it is important for me to take skills that are portable because, being transient, you have to have something that you can grasp hold of, that you can take with you, that can be a certain continuity.

Creating a meaningful life overseas remains the most neglected aspect of the spouse's overseas move. People talk about the initial culture shock, learning a foreign language, and adjusting to the new culture. But adjustment is only half of the challenge; it brings a potentially negative situation to neutral, not to positive. Adjustment only brings the wife to the point where the foreign environment no longer constantly frustrates her; it does not provide motivation, direction and a meaning to daily life overseas. Introspection and life planning remain necessary for the spouse to answer the questions: What do I really want to do? What would I be happiest having accomplished during my years in this country? How can I continue doing the things that I find most important even while I am no longer living at home?

The answers to these questions vary. One woman becomes an artist, another becomes a counsellor to expatriate families, a third teaches English to immigrant children, a fourth does extensive volunteer work, and a fifth starts her own business. Many simultaneously remain very involved in raising a family. One woman, who focused on learning the history, literature, and culture of the foreign country, described her growing sense of purpose:

> you start to understand the people around you . . . They are different, but

very often the difference is not so evident. But slowly, you go into knowing these differences, and it is a new world that opens up to you . . . You discover the arts, and the folklore, and how the folklore is lived in the modern world. It is not so evident that there is always something that stays from these roots. You start to see all the small differences that you wouldn't notice if you were just a tourist for a month or so in the country. When you live there, slowly you get to know the people much more, the civilization, how they are and why they are like that and then I think it is very enjoyable. You are gaining something, it is not just giving.

Today, more and more frequently, the questions centre on identifying ways to continue a career while overseas.

Returning home

Expatriates often remember their home country as a more wonderful and perfect place than it actually is. As things get rough overseas and they experience culture shock and the difficulties in adjusting to a foreign culture, they dream of how easy and good life will be when they get back home. However, in reality, re-entry often presents more difficulties than the initial move overseas. One woman, who had lived in a number of foreign countries, captured the difficulty and the disillusionment of returning home:

> Coming back was . . . the most difficult move of all. Why was it so difficult? Because . . . you change, the country changes, the people change. You are expecting . . . that you are coming back to your place and that you will feel good right away . . . It is not true. You come back and you feel like a foreigner in your own country . . . People deal with you as if . . . you are different. Even your way of speaking the language. So you feel cut off completely and it is your own country. The roots that you were not really consciously, but somehow, dreaming with. You know everybody needs some kind of roots and you come back to these roots and you don't feel well with them.

A British woman said:

> I was in England recently. I was sitting in the train and I watched two English mums coming from the corner shop, standing and talking. And I said to my husband, 'I know exactly what they are going to do, they are going to go home, have little lunch, have a little sleep, and then they will watch a little bit of tele [television] and maybe do some ironing, then they will get dinner.' It is a pity that I am not able to do that any more. I'm wanting more from life. I am pleased that I have changed, that I have matured, that I have developed, but sometimes it would be easier if I had stayed content with that life. We don't feel we can go back to England. We have been gone too long . . . They have changed and we have changed.

Recommen-dations

Expatriate wives have a range of suggestions for coping with cross-cultural transitions and creating a meaningful portable life overseas. The strongest recommendations include: know yourself and what you want out of life, and take responsibility for creating the type of life that you want to live. It is also important to treat the move as permanent, no matter how temporary. Perserve and be patient. Some recommendations focus on what the wives must do for themselves, others require the assistance of the organization and the husband. For example, wives must ask themselves what they really want out of the move; the company needs to include the spouse in a pre-departure site visit and, if possible, in selecting a house; employees, to the extent possible, need to limit their travel during the first one to three months overseas. Most recommendations work best if all three—the organization, employee, and spouse—commit themselves to making the transition successful.

Many companies now interview the employee and spouse prior to an international move (*Business Week*, 1979; Karras and McMillan, 1971; Labovitz, 1977). They screen out couples with high probability failure, including couples with excessive alcohol and drug use, indications of rigid and inflexible personalities or lifestyles, lack of communication among husband, wife and children, and inappropriate or inadequate coping and stress-management mechanisms. Research has shown that the worlds of work and family overlap (Culbert and Renshaw, 1972; Renshaw, 1976). Companies that screen couples recognize that the quality of home life will affect the employee's ability to perform at work, and similarly that the very nature of an expatriate assignment will strongly influence the family's daily life.

While many organizations do an excellent job of handling the physical logistics of the move, few facilitate the spouse's creation of a meaningful life overseas. Companies usually leave it to the couple and, unfortunately, frequently to the wife alone, to identify those aspects of her life that she finds most important and to develop ways of incorporating them while overseas. This search, rarely being an easy task, is better addressed explicitly by both members of the couple than left to chance. Perhaps creating a meaningful portable life is the one area in which the most can be done to improve the overseas move from the perspective of the spouse, the employee, and the company.

Summary

The spouse's role is the most difficult of all family members. The spouse must adjust to the foreign culture and create a meaningful life for herself in the foreign country. Her adjustment is made more difficult by her interaction with the least internationally sophisticated strata of society. Her ability to lead a meaningful life is challenged by the lack of structure of her overseas life and compounded by all of the activities and friends that she has had to leave behind in the home country. Successful management of the transition abroad and the creation of a meaningful life in the foreign country demand the involvement of the husband and the company.

References

Adler, N. J. (1980) *Managing International Transitions*, Alcan Aluminium Ltd, Montreal.

Adler, N. J. (1980) 'Reentry: a study of the dynamic coping processes used by repatriated employees to enhance effectiveness in the organization and personal learning during the transition back into the home country', dissertation, UCLA, June.

Adler, N. J. (1984) 'Women in international management: where are they?', *California Management Review*, xxvi (4), June, 122–32.

Baker, J. C. (1975) 'An analysis of how the U.S. multinational company considers the wives of American expatriate managers', *Academy of Management Proceedings*, **35**, 258–60.

Business Week (1979) 'Gauging a family's suitability for a stint overseas', 16 April, 127–30.

Culbert, S. and J. Renshaw (1972) 'Coping with the stresses of travels as an opportunity for improving the quality of work and family life', *Family Process*, **11**(3), September, 321–37.

D'Orazio, N. (1981) 'Foreign executives' wives in Tokyo', Institute of Comparative Culture Business Series, Bulletin No. 82, Sophia University, Tokyo.

Edstrom, A. and J. Galbraith (1977) 'Transfer of managers as coordination and control strategy in multinational organizations', *Administrative Science Quarterly*, **22**, June, 248–63.

Eliot, T. S. (1968) *Four Quartets*, Harcourt Brace Jovanovich, New York.

Karras, E. J. and R. F. McMillan (1971) 'Interviewing for a cultural match', *Personnel Journal*, April, 276.

Labovitz, G. (1977) 'Managing the personal side of the personnel move abroad',
    Advanced Management Journal, **43**(3), Summer, 26–39.
Priestoff, N. (1976) 'The Gaijin executive's wife', *The Conference Board Record*, **13**(5), May,
    51–64.
Renshaw, J. R. (1976) 'An exploration of the dynamics of the overlapping worlds of work
    and family', *Family Process*, **15**(1), March, 143–65.
Wederspahn, G. M. (1980) 'The overseas wife: excess baggage', *The Bridge*, **5**(4), Winter,
    16.

International personnel planning pressures at Mogul Oil

Paul R. Sparrow

Organizational setting

Mogul Oil is one of the world's largest oil companies. It is the most 'international', operating in over 100 countries with refineries in 34 of these. Yet at the same time it is also seen as being distinctly 'national'. As a result of a strategy of strong decentralization by the organization, people in Britain, Europe and the US feel the company is their own. Mogul Oil employs over 138 000 people worldwide (see Figure CS12.1), more than two-thirds of whom work outside their home countries. Since the late 1970s the number of people employed has been shrinking.

Mogul Oil had a turnover of £55.5 b in 1986—about the same as the GDP of Denmark—but this was a bad year for the company! Oil prices had fallen from an average of $28 a barrel in 1985 to a low of $8 a barrel in July 1986. Falling oil prices had hit hard, reducing profits by over 16 per cent and wiping £830 m off the value of its oil stocks. However, the price of refined oil products had fallen more slowly, providing all the oil companies—Mogul included—with a buffer. While 'upstream' profits (from the exploration and production businesses) had fallen by a massive 50 per cent, profits from the 'downstream' business (refining and marketing) had risen by nearly 60 per cent. Cheaper feedstocks had also helped increase the profits coming from the chemicals business (see Figure CS12.2).

However, in the long term even profits from refinery activities were under pressure. Oil companies had closed down 37 per cent of their capacity since

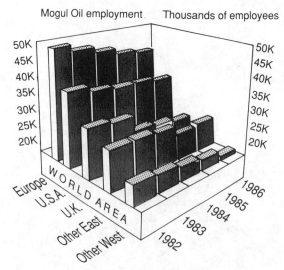

Figure CS12.1
Mogul Oil
employment

Mogul Oil employment.   Thousands of employees

Figure CS12.2
Mogul Oil profits

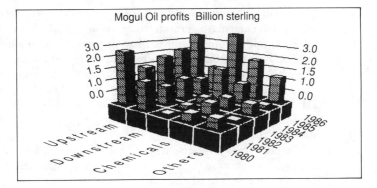

1980, and although technological advances and more flexible production now allowed twice as many different types of crude oil to be refined, and more lighter, higher value products to be produced from crude oil, by early 1987 Mogul Oil was earning at best only $1 a barrel from its downstream activities.

The human resources management context

Ian Moran, the Personnel Director, knew that he was going to have to change the way his function managed employees. Mogul Oil had managed on the basis of a cradle-to-grave workforce, but contraction meant that there were fewer senior-management positions. High levels of recruitment twenty years ago had created a large number of managers who expected to reach their potential by international promotion, but the openings were not there. Moreover, the changing nature of the business created uncertainty about the type of workforce Mogul Oil needed anyway.

Ian knew that Mogul Oil owed much of its success to two strengths—decentralization and long-term planning. General managers in each of the operating companies (which were organized along a triple matrix of geographical region, function and business centre) had a lot of local discretion. Mogul Oil had several hundred operating companies around the world engaged in various branches of oil and natural gas, coal, chemicals, metals and other businesses. The organizational culture placed a strong emphasis on consensus building, usually on slow, conservative capital-justification grounds. It also placed a strong emphasis on understanding the environment through business planning. While operating companies were generally self-sufficient and had the resources to cope with most problems, they were provided with global scenarios describing economic, social and technological trends and their implications for energy supply. Mogul Oil had not anticipated exactly when the oil crash would come, but it had been quick to respond to it when it came.

Because the company was decentralized the central personnel function formed part of the 'service' company. International operating companies paid for their existence, and as part of the response to falling oil prices central support functions like Ian's had been cut by 20 per cent a couple of years ago. As a result, he had lost a lot of people who had been working on career planning and assessment centres. However, a coherent system of international career placement, job evaluation and merit appraisals was still run centrally by Ian's function for around 10 000 mainly British and European managers.

Personnel planners

These managers were the 'glue' that held the company together, and they were held together in turn by a key group of his staff—the personnel planners. The personnel planners had to coordinate the moves of around 400 or so managers each. Central to this process was the concept of *estimated potential* — a rating assigned to each manager indicating the hierarchical job grade which it was currently felt he could achieve. Most managers had made their career moves within a broad function such as exploration, production, marketing and so on. The personnel planners acted as parents for the managers they had initially recruited into their function, assuming a special responsibility for finding them a suitable international placement. As most managers moved every two to three years, Ian's personnel planners were making a couple of international placements every week.

The personnel planners advised function management about these placements and were responsible for implementing their decisions. Although they reported into Ian's central personnel function, the business function (operating company) they operated in was their major client. The operating company did not have a totally free choice in career moves, and so there was a process of lobbying and prioritizing. Personnel planners therefore acted as *job brokers* — relying on their negotiating skills and career planning systems to fill jobs successfully and develop managers.

Career planning system

About once every three years a personnel review was carried out by the various operating companies which would outline the business environment, organization, broad personnel resourcing considerations and a management succession chart. However, the detailed planning system started with an annual manpower review conducted by the general manager of the operating company. This was quantitative and not qualitative. It would detail how many people were needed in the function one year in advance. The personnel planner would then act as a clerk, adding up figures and determining how many people needed recruiting. The recruitment was done by a local personnel function, as was any subsequent training.

A staff report was written annually for every manager who was on the central planning list. The personnel planners coordinated the system. The report detailed both performance and development actions and would form the basis on an annual merit review for pay awards. The operating company general manager would visit central personnel once a year and bring with him up to 200 of these reports as part of a formal staff discussion process. As a result of this each manager would have a paragraph about them which set out their broad career path and an agreed *estimated potential*. The development actions were collected and a planning sheet produced to match 'men for jobs and jobs for men'. This indicated when people were due for a move and where they were to go. If a planned move could not be made — as was often the case for operational reasons — then a provisional move was made.

A good personnel planner did not fulfil his or her role in isolation. To place people into new jobs they needed to know what level it should be created at, salary structures and details of job content. For this, good working relationships with the local line managers and the local personnel function were important.

New pressures

Ian knew, however, that the personnel function was about to be reorganized, and he felt this was an ideal time to get to know just what business changes were influencing the activities and role of his personnel planners, and what tools and techniques they were using to manage the development of their reports. He ran a workshop to find this out. It left him a worried man, because many of his worst suspicions were confirmed. He had noted a number of important changes:

1 There was a group policy that every international management team had at least one ex-patriate on it. But the increasing pressure on costs in central office meant that any ex-patriate assignment had to be looked at very closely, because they were expensive. There were also moves towards *regionalization* in many parts of Mogul Oil's empire, with local management teams wanting to place more of their own managers in their top teams. He could see a problem emerging in Brunei, Oman and South Africa. Just recently he had heard how one operating company managing director had issued a statement to say he was going to increase the number of local citizens in his organization. Foreign residents were not to be promoted or replaced once they left. The intention had been good, but the process had happened too quickly and as foreign residents left there had not been enough local staff of high enough quality. This had complicated the technical retraining that was going on for the production supervisors because they had had to be pulled off their training course to cover for the shortages. How could his personnel planners influence such regionalization processes and make sure that next time things happened more smoothly?

2 Beyond that, how was this going to affect his UK and European based managers anyway? In a few years' time his planners would have more and more British and European managers in the systems waiting for career placements, and there might be fewer international openings. How would he be able to meet their career expectations if there were to be fewer development moves? His personnel planners and the system was geared up to develop people by these placements. How good were they at developing people on the job?

3 Like many major international companies, Mogul Oil was increasingly entering joint ventures. His personnel planners had told him he needed different people to run these operations—managers not just with the right intellectual abilities (for which their current estimated potential rating had always been a good guide)—but with the right personal characteristics as well, such as adapability, good human relations skills, and a tactful leadership style. Were his operating company managers thinking like this, or were they still appointing people just on their current estimated potential rating?

4 Studies of competitive positioning had shown that Mogul Oil needed more people of high quality who were computer literate. Mogul Oil needed more marketeers—MBAs as opposed to PhDs. His personnel planners needed to encourage the line managers to be more aggressive in the recruitment market. He wanted them to find the funds for a sponsorship scheme to take on twenty MBAs, but he also knew that the oil industry wasn't as glamorous as it had been when he joined. What could he do to make the image of Mogul Oil more attractive to graduates?

5 Mogul Oil had been acquiring companies on a large scale. Not only was it acquiring new companies to expand its empire into new business areas such as coal and bitumen, but many nations—he could think of at least five or six in Africa alone—who had nationalized Mogul Oil's operations twenty years back were now eager to sell them back to Mogul Oil. He would need even more managers with good marketing and general management skills pretty soon. His personnel planners would need to find replacements for these managers and for this they would probably have to look outside their own functions. They were going to have to enter some very delicate negotiations for the release and return of staff.

The problem

What worried Ian was that while he had found out what the pressures on his international personnel planning would be, there didn't seem to be any strong sense of concern about them in the field. Mogul Oil was still comfortable financially. There was still plenty of investment money around, in some of the international operating companies there were no competing oil companies, and in general there was no sense of impending business crisis to make managers feel they should start doing things differently. Yet change they must, and with an impending reorganization, Ian didn't want to waste the opportunity to build new roles and activities into his organization.

Ian was also worried about the 'historical baggage' that his personnel planners carried. While they had become sophisticated negotiators and job brokers, they operated a very formal and inflexible career planning system. He suspected many of his planners were stuck in a bureaucratic, administrative and reactive mode. He needed to get them involved in helping to formulate the operating company business plans to make sure that they could address some of the worrying changes he had now listed. How was he going to get these issues on the agenda? Were the personnel planners the people to influence, or should he try and influence the senior line managers instead? What was he going to do next?

Questions

1 Is there a need to change the way the personnel function is organized? If so, why, and under what pressures?

2 What sort of strategy would you adopt to manage and organize the process of change in your function?

3 How would you develop the developers? What new roles and activities do the personnel planners need to become engaged in?

4 How would you try and get more line 'ownership' of the HRM pressures the workshop had identified?

5 What would you try and do about future selection and training in the operating companies?

6 Is the current career planning system capable of dealing with future international placement needs? If not, how should it be developed?

Group behaviour in French business: quality circles à la française

Jean-Louis Barsoux

I graduated ten years ago from one of the big French engineering schools (l'Ecole des Arts et Metiers) and joined my present company, a large French cosmetics firm, last year. After about six months' learning the ropes I was named head of production, and that was how I came to participate in the residential weekend seminar on quality circles.

The twelve of us, all heads of department, together with the plant manager, Monsieur Ansart, met up for dinner on the Friday evening at our luxury hotel in Deauville. Quality circles were not on the menu for that first meal. Instead, the conversation centred around the old days—the boss and the 'old guard' (particularly the commercial director) exchanging stories about the showdowns they used to have with the unions and about the jerks at head office in Paris.

Several of the older heads were on familiar '*tu*' terms with each other which made it impossible for newcomers like myself to break into their conversation. Fortunately, I was able to speak to old Prouvot, the head of purchasing and a fellow '*Gadzarts*' some years my senior ['*Gadzarts*'—contraction of '*gars des Arts et Metiers*'—an alumni of l'Ecole des Arts et Metiers—which is one of the number of dominant grandes écoles in the French educational landscape).
Normally we would have been on familiar terms, through our collegiate ties, but in front of the others I had to show a little more respect, so I addressed him deferentially as '*vous*'. There was also Mme Bertillon, the head of research, with whom I got on well; had the two of them not been there I would have felt rather left out.

The following morning we set about the serious business of discussing quality circles. We gathered round the conference table, with M. Ansart, the boss, at the head of the table, surrounded by his cronies. Mme Bertillon and myself were at the far end. The boss kicked off the meeting by reminding those who had not been around two years ago (that is, me) that this was our second attempt at launching quality circles. The first attempt had failed after one year.

He then handed over to the head of training, Tourneur, to set the scene. Tourneur had prepared a list of 'irrefutable' principles to justify the reintroduction of quality circles and lay the foundations for our discussion.

'I think we all agree', he started, 'that each worker is an expert in his work.'

This raised an immediate objection. A protracted discussion ensued about the validity of the statement and the outcome was a redefinition which did away with the word 'expert'. This struck me as pretty typical of our meetings, definitional exactitude passing for progress.

Tourneur was allowed to proceed until he made the mistake of uttering another statement implying faith in worker aptitudes.

'There are untapped reserves of intelligence in our workforce,' he declared.

Once again the meeting hit a sticking point—the heads of department felt they could not let the proposition pass unchallenged and suggested that 'reserves of intelligence' be replaced by 'resources'.

One of them chipped in with, 'I think if the workers were so smart we would probably have realized that by now.'

After this inauspicious start, M. Ansart suggested we go round the table and give our impressions as to why the initial attempt had failed.

Nice prototype: shame about the follow-up

The head of personnel set the ball rolling by pointing out that the launch of the quality circles had taken place in very different conditions from its subsequent expansion. The launch had identified a favourable group (a small, stable, autonomous unit), with a good team spirit and an enthusiastic facilitator. All the conditions had combined to favour a successful outcome—in the hope that this would provide the necessary publicity to encourage subsequent circles.

The head of maintenance, whose quality circles had been among the first to flounder, added that the pilot group had also benefited from the psychological boost of being under public scrutiny. They had derived pride from being recognized as the most likely candidates for success—and had often been congratulated by the boss for their pioneering efforts. Under these circumstances, he suggested, it was hardly surprising they had made a go of it—concluding, with a note of satisfaction—at the start at least.

The head of quality control, in whose section the experiment had started, felt that part of the reason for his own group's decline, after a promising start, was that rewards had not been forthcoming. The quality circles were not officially integrated into the appraisal system. Consequently, the anticipated recognition in the form of promotion or salary had not materialized—in spite of considerable personal efforts on behalf of many of his staff.

Inter-departmental friction

M. Ansart turned to the administrative head and asked him if that was why his section's quality circles had failed to take off. The head of administration did not think so. Instead he attributed their failure to the fact that the concept of quality circles was seen as related to production rather than administrative activities. He added that as far as most of his staff were concerned, quality meant product quality, full stop. This drew antagonistic jibes from the head of maintenance who suggested that the real reason for the failure of quality circles in the offices was that administrative staff were all too 'stuck up' and inhibited to express themselves frankly in open meetings.

The boss moved on swiftly and was about to pass me by, assuming I would have nothing to say, but I caught his eye and was invited to speak. I started by justifying my contribution, explaining that although I had not been there first time round, I'd done a fair amount of legwork among my own staff and felt I could pass on some of their comments.

One particular group of highly skilled workers from my department had refused outright to operate a quality circle. Eventually they had been forced to do so, but their circles proved unproductive.

'As I see it,' I explained, 'these were workers involved in the finishing of costly components, who were already at the summit of the shopfloor hierarchy—they felt they had nothing to gain from revealing the tricks of the trade to lesser skilled workers in group discussions. I think they were opposed to quality circles on the grounds that it would force them to divulge and formalize their methods—not for the economic reasons they put forward at the time.'

My interpretation of events seemed to strike a chord with my peers (I seemed to be on safe ground with criticism of the workers), so I carried on with a little more confidence.

'On a more general level though,' I resumed, 'there seems to have been a problem in the way the circles were introduced.' I explained how the supervisors I had spoken to felt they had had little say in the decision to introduce the circles.

I was interrupted at this point and asked in no uncertain terms to refrain from commenting on things I knew nothing about. The personnel manager put me straight, saying that the entire management group right down to supervisory level had attended numerous meetings to keep them informed of what was going on. I could have retorted that today's seminar was further proof of their exclusion, but refrained from further antagonizing him.

Instead, I tried to retrieve my situation by making another point regarding production, which was that the production managers saw a contradiction between quality circles and production imperatives. On the one hand they are told to stick to deadlines and cut costs; on the other hand, the quality circles were costing both time and money. Arranging meetings during the work hours would be virtually impossible. As one supervisor put it to me, 'It's difficult enough to get them to stop the machines to carry out preventive maintenance, never mind stopping them to hold a mothers' meeting.'

This merely laid me open to criticism from the staff functions, which never had any trouble scheduling meetings and sticking to them without disrupting their day-to-day work. The administrative head tried to tell me how production would have to sort its act out and make time for meetings—how it was all a matter of organization. I responded angrily that it was fine for them, they wouldn't have to worry about shutting down a production line for two hours just to hold a meeting.

The boss tried to cut short the political points-scoring before it degenerated further and turned to the head of purchasing (a self-taught man): 'What about you, Herault, what do you think went wrong last time?' Like me, he had not yet made the transition to those whom the boss deigned to call by their first name.

Herault, with his usual frankness, suggested that we were all being a bit hypocritical—that there were secret objections to the circles which no one dared mention. He explained that he thought the circles upset the traditional flows of information around the organization. They require people to surrender information which is part of their power, privileges and expertise. The circles, like the unions used to be before them, constitute a parallel hierarchy, which circumvents the formal chain of command. It leaves everyone, including all of the managers, in a state of uncertainty.

Herault's comments drew impassioned reactions from the departmental heads who resented the idea that they derived their power from the possession of information. 'That's rubbish,' exclaimed the head of finance, 'our authority is based on our education and intellectual apparatus.'

Herault was asked to be more constructive in his contributions, so he resumed, but this time stayed on an impersonal level. 'Let's face it, we French are individuals at heart—and we're trying to implement a technique emanating from an obsessively collectivist country.' Carried away by his own oration, he went on: 'A Frenchman is not an industrial animal; he is an artisan, an individualist.'

Perhaps unwisely, I jumped to Herault's support, on the basis of my experience in production. At best a French worker will consider himself responsible for his work—but certainly not for the product. He regards that as the problem of the bosses and designers. I concluded, 'French workers have no tradition of personal investment in the work—if anything they look upon the factory as a locus of manipulation—they still think of productivity as a weapon used to exploit the working class.' Aware that Herault and I might be undermining the whole seminar, the boss cut us short.

He moved swiftly on to the commercial director, who made the valid point that the circles seemed to fall outside normal management activities. The quality circles were seen as an additional burden, in parallel to their daily activities. 'Indeed', he suggested, 'it is a view we have inadvertently encouraged by failing to reward achievements in that field.'

'That's spot on, Thierry', said M. Ansart approvingly, and on that point the boss decided to wrap up what he considered a fruitful morning's activities in order to break for lunch. There was the usual competition to claim seats next to the boss. I did not join in—there was little point in my jockeying for position, since it would not go down very well with the others.

In the afternoon, M. Ansart suggested we split up into three groups and have a brainstorming session about the lessons we could learn for the relaunch. The boss himself opted out, but the three groups divided instinctively in line with hierarchical pecking order. Naturally, I was in the third group.

Mme Bertillon took the notes for our group. Herault, the head of purchasing, started by complaining that all we'd done this morning was talk.

'We're wasting time,' he said. 'I've been using my own brand of quality circles every day for twenty years—I don't need them to work any better.'

Mme Bertillon responded with an impatient, 'Well, that's very positive I must say, M. Herault—I'll just note it as one of our points shall I?'

'That's half the problem,' I suggested. 'It strikes me we're not really convinced of the need for them. Intellectually we know that they should lead to better work relations, better economic performance and all that, but I don't know if we're really committed to implementing them. It's typical of this country,' I rounded off, 'we like conceptualizing but can't be bothered with execution.'

Mme Bertillon told me I was as bad as Herault. There was no point in questioning the need for quality circles at this stage, the problem was how to put them into practice. 'For instance', she suggested, 'maybe the word quality is too restrictive in the concept it evokes. Besides, there may still be negative connotations among some of the workers who have been through it all before. Maybe we could call them progress groups,' she suggested.

This concrete suggestion aside, we came up with a series of platitudes, which we hoped would satisfy the boss. We outlined what a change of mood there had been among the workforce in the last two years—how the ground was well prepared to sow the seed of quality circles—how the management team were sensitized to the problems and knew it would be a continuous struggle, not a one-off effort.

Each group then took turns to present their findings to the other groups. The boss seemed quite pleased with our contribution. He felt it was a very positive note on which to round off the seminar. He then went on to sum up the day's events, saying that he thought he could detect in our ruthless self-criticism a real determination to make the circles work this time. 'I'm not sure that the workers and middle management are equally convinced, but it's our job to persuade them, and like it or not, we'll persist with it this time—by God, they make economic and social sense—how can anyone possibly object to them?'

He then outlined his plans to send all of us on quality circle training courses—followed by the middle managers, foremen and finally the workers, if the training budget stretched that far. He closed the seminar by saying he thought we'd cleared the air and were on a firm footing to introduce 'Progress Groups Mk. II'.

We all went up to the boss to bid him a good end of weekend. I hung around for a while waiting for him to stop chatting and proffer his hand. He eventually did so in a distracted sort of way which bore little relation to the solid handshake reserved for some of my senior colleagues. It sometimes made me wish I hadn't bothered, but that was out of the question.

As I walked to my car, I mulled over the day's events. I couldn't help feeling it had been something of a charade. All the linguistic nitpicking and definitional hair-splitting seemed part of a deeper problem. There was a lack of confidence in the workforce and a lack of collective spirit which really didn't auger well for the implementation of quality circles. I recalled the boss's closing speech about imposing participative management. 'Talk about a contradiction in terms', I thought, and drove off.

Questions

1 How would you suggest implementing quality circles in this company? Describe the processes by which you would introduce the ideas for implementation. Write a report to M. Ansart explaining your suggestions for the future use of quality circles.

2 Identify any aspects of national 'French culture' you have observed from the case. To what extent do you think these hinder or help the adoption and implementation of quality circles. Would the meeting have been different in character if the topic had been something other than quality circles?

3 What alternative strategies are open to you to suggest to this French company? How else could you achieve participation, decentralization and responsible autonomy? Assess the likelihood of success of your suggestions using evidence from the case and from your readings on national and organizational cultures.

---

14 The Carpenter case

Foulie Psalidas-Perlmutter*

Tom and Jane Carpenter are a young couple living comfortably in a New England town in the United States. They have three children, Mary (aged 11), Jerry (aged 6) and Ann (aged 3).

Tom works in the headquarters of a manufacturing company as an executive in the engineering department. He has an excellent salary and up until now has been satisfied with his job. A quiet, handsome man about thirty-six years old, he is intelligent, sensitive, ambitious and known as 'a good family man'. He has the respect of his colleagues and subordinates. The upper echelons of management regard him as a promising candidate for senior management in this company. Tom is considered a practical man, able to take the changes in life with a basic optimism and adaptability that appear to have given him a maturity beyond his years. He likes the material wealth and comfort that his years of conscientious work have produced. He enjoys the status in his company which has an excellent name in its field, being considered one of the most progressive and future-minded of US companies of this type.

If Tom is the practical member of the family, Jane is the 'dreamer'. She is a pretty, energetic woman of 30, a good wife and mother and an active member of several committees and voluntary groups. She is strongly attached to both her family and her parents who are in their sixties and live in a nearby town. She is sincerely interested in many good causes and always finds the time and energy to devote to them. While she is not a very practical woman by nature, her enthusiasm for her projects is admired by her many friends.

Tom and Jane married early and struggled together for several years until they were able to achieve the comfortable life they now have. Their marital life has been happy and more or less undisturbed, and through the struggle of their earlier years they were able to develop between themselves a rewarding relationship. Although they have travelled to several parts of the US with and without the children, neither Tom nor Jane have travelled abroad until two years ago. At that time Tom, together with three other executives, was sent to Latin America to explore the possibilities of setting up four new plants in different countries in Latin Amercia.

Both Tom and Jane have been feeling more and more relaxed in the past years, since many of their dreams have realized. They have a good family, financial security and many friends. They are especially proud of their new home, recently finished. Jane has worked hard to find the furniture and the internal decorations they wanted and now her dream house seems completed. They have both been so far generally satisfied with their children, who are well adjusted to their present environment. There have been certain problems with Mary, who is a very sensitive and shy girl, and with Jerry who has had some

*Reproduced by permission; originally published in Adler, N. (1986) *International Dimensions of Organizational Behavior*, Kent Publishing, Boston.

difficulties adapting to school. But these were very minor problems and they have not seriously disturbed the otherwise happy family life.

Despite their very satisfactory picture of family life, there have recently been more and more occasions when Tom and Jane have felt (each one without admitting it to the other) that something is 'missing'.

More and more, Tom thinks that life has become a comfortable routine. The new tasks he is given have less 'challenge' and 'adventure'. For a long while he has been satisfied that his career has developed steadily. The time of anxiety and uncertainty has passed, but also with it the time of excitement and the inner feeling of searching and moving. Then, quite unexpectedly, his company sent him to Latin America for four months. Tom felt that this trip was going to be one of the most interesting and rewarding events of his whole life.

Being away for the first time from his family for such a long period, he missed them and he was disappointed because the wives were not allowed to accompany their husbands on that trip. But the prospects of building up their company in Latin America have been attractive and he found that he liked to travel, to meet new people, to become acquainted with different ways of living, to be more a part of the 'world' and of events outside their home town. The three other executives who took the trip with him felt the same as he had. Each seemed to be a little 'weary' of being 'a little fish' at headquarters. The possibility of being a pioneer in the new Latin Amercia division was an exciting prospect. Tom somehow felt reluctant to communicate to Jane all his satisfaction and his thoughts about that trip, as well as the fact that he was hoping to be chosen from among the executives to be responsible for setting up the plants in Latin America.

In a different way, but with the same feeling of restlessness and discontent, there are times now that Jane feels that the pleasant, well-organized life she has is lacking the excitement of unpredictability. She divides her time between many activities, but finds herself at times dreaming about the world outside her home town. She wonders at times, like Tom, whether their life has not become too settled, an almost unaltered routine, but unlike Tom, she checks herself by asking the simple question that, after all, isn't this what life really is?

When Tom came home with the news that Mr Abbott, the president of the company, had offered him the key position in the Latin America operation, she was pleased to hear of the high esteem his superiors had for Tom. Actually, Jane too had been wondering for some time what could be the result of Tom's trip to Latin America. Although she would have liked to have been able to go with him, the idea that they would have had to leave the children for such a long time ruled out the possibility of her going, even had executives' wives been allowed to accompany them. After that, she used to wonder whether the company would choose him if the decision was made—the idea of moving to a new environment was not an unpleasant one.

But now that there was a firm offer with a high salary, cost of living expenses and opportunity to travel throughout Latin America, she began to have some fears. As Tom talked excitedly about the challenging tasks he faced, these fears increased. More and more she felt that they had little to gain from this experience in terms of their family and their life. It was a big step forward in Tom's career, to be sure, but Jane felt that Tom would be successful wherever he was. In his present job, Tom and she shared so much time together, while in the new job, as she understood it, Tom would have to travel a great deal. She was very unhappy and ashamed about her fears, but Tom was enthusiastic and obviously willing to go ahead with the move.

One evening she tried to sit down by herself and decide why this new job was not so attractive to her. There was some urgency for Tom had to make up his mind within a week, and she needed to understand what moving abroad meant for her and for her family.

She tried to be honest with herself. Naturally she had fears about moving to a new environment which was strange and where people spoke another language. She knew that the climate was very different and she believed that the living conditions were likely to offer fewer comforts. She would be far away from her friends and her parents. Their furniture would have to be stored, and their new house rented or sold, since it was not clear how many years Tom would need to get the four new plants going.

She imagined she would be isolated, with little close contact with the local people. What she has heard so far about the personality of Latin Americans made her fear that close friendships would be difficult to achieve, at least for some time: she had the impression that the people were rather temperamental and unstable. Although she admitted to herself that this impression was based on hearsay and fiction, she somehow could not avoid believing it. She had also heard that there was a great deal of anti-American feeling in the country where they would first live. Furthermore, she wondered whether the sanitary conditions would be dangerous to the health of the children. The company had little experience in Latin America, so it would be likely that the would have to find their own way and learn, probably by hard experience, how to get along in these countries.

She realized that what disturbed her more than anything else was probably that Tom was going to travel a lot. She would probably have to face a great deal of the problems of their adaptation there alone, while up until this time they had always shared whatever problems they had to face and supported each other in finding solutions. Tom would see more places, meet more people, and get more satisfaction out of the whole experience than she and the children would. She was distressed to realize that she was already resentful towards him and angry because she could sense that, although he was discussing the problem with her, he had already made up his mind.

Jane kept these fears more or less to herself, but she did tell Tom of her reluctance to go and of her worry about the effect of the move on the education of their children as well as on their health.

Tom sensed most of Jane's fears and reacted to her expressed doubts by saying that he thought that the children would adapt after a while and that the experience would be a good one for them. They could learn a new language and make new friends after a while. As for themselves, he had the best of memories from his own trip and he believed that they were both going to find this new experience an enriching and rewarding one. He did not underestimate the difficulties involved, but he expressed the belief that they were capable of overcoming them, while enjoying all the advantages that living abroad would offer them. Inwardly Tom was disappointed with Jane's negative reactions and the difficulties she seemed to be having. He had always believed her to be a woman of courage, curiosity and interest for the world outside. In previous times of crisis she had always proved to be strong and supportive and she had always shown a spirit of adventure and willingness to go ahead. It was a painful surprise for him to realize that this spirit would operate only in the security of a familiar environment, while such a change as this presented itself to Jane as a threat to herself and her family. He had hoped that she would back him in a decision which was so important to his career. Nevertheless, he maintained his confidence in her and believed that she would change her mind in time. He called a Berlitz school nearby and made plans for both of them to take Spanish lessons.

When Jane's parents came to visit during this period, Jane told them of the company's offer to Tom. Her father, who had been ailing for some time, was visibly depressed by the news. Her mother said that this was going to be a great experience for them, 'a chance of a lifetime', as she put it. Jane knew that her mother had always regretted not being able to travel abroad. Now she was thrilled that the children were being given the opportunity and promised to come and visit them in Latin America if Tom accepted the job.

Dinner with Mr Abbott

A few days later, Tom's boss, Mr Abbott, invited Tom and Jane for dinner, saying that he always talked over a new job abroad with both husband and wife because he felt that it was very important to take how the wife felt into consideration. Jane had many fears about this dinner. First, she resented being 'looked over' by Mr Abbott who, until now, had not really spent much time with them socially. Second, she did not want to reveal her doubts to Tom's boss, who had a reputation for making quick judgements about people, often not very favourable.

But the dinner turned out to be very pleasant. Mrs Abbott helped to put everyone at ease, talking about the pleasant experience abroad when Mr Abbott was managing director of a subsidiary branch in Europe. Mrs Abbott had enjoyed Paris and Rome, but admitted that she knew little about life in cities like Buenos Aires and Rio.

Mr Abbott finally turned to Jane and said: 'Well, we are very glad you are taking the news of this new assignment for Tom so well. I know you realize what an opportunity this job will be for him. It is a real challenge for him, far greater than what he can get here, you know.'

Tom hurriedly answered for Jane, who was about to reply to Mrs Abbott: 'Jane is really a born traveller. I know she's looking forward to this. She's already found out about taking lessons in Spanish.'

Mr Abbott seemed pleased. He said, 'That's really good. You know, Tom, we're becoming an international company. There'll be few opportunities for executives with limited overseas experience at headquarters. Our policy is to create a management team which could base its decisions on actual experience abroad. Of course, having the kind of wife who is willing to take the risk of going off to the jungle is quite an asset. You are a lucky man, Tom.'

While Jane joined in the spirited conversation, she was inwardly angry. That night, she and Tom had a quarrel which continued for the next few days. Jane resented the fact that the whole discussion was conducted as though Tom had already accepted the job, as well as the fact that she was not given a chance to talk about Tom's work with Mr Abbott. Tom insisted that Mr Abbott was not the kind of man to whom one could reveal any doubts about a company decision. Discussing the problem the next day with the children confused Tom and Jane more, because the children's reaction was not clear. Mary was unwilling to go, Jerry and Ann seemed excited, but it was more because of the thrill they felt than because they really understood the issue. By now Jane was finding it difficult to sleep, and Tom said that a formal decision was required by next Monday.

They had a long weekend to think over the decision and give a final answer to Mr Abbot on Monday.

Questions

1   Do you think it is the responsibility of a multi-national corporation to 'culturize' the spouses of expatriate employees, in order to help them build meaningful lives overseas?

2 This morning you have been approached by a senior vice president concerning a job in Nigeria, and as you ride home you are considering how to discuss the topic with your spouse. What are some of the approaches you could take, and what are the pros and cons?

3 How would you, as an expatriate employee, ensure that your spouse is happy in the new cultural experience? What type of balance would you try to strike between office and home.

Part VII
Managing in the Future

CHAPTER 22 The new worker

Introduction

One of the key considerations for the future is the changing profile of the population which, in turn, will radically alter the composition of the available labour force and will bring fresh challenges to the process of managing people. Demographic research in Britain indicates that:

1 There will be a shortage of 16–24 year olds in the labour force. As a direct result of the fall in birth rate during the 1970s, there will be a drop of 1.2 million individuals in this category by 1995 (a decline of a fifth); 16–19 year olds will see a 23 per cent reduction in number over the same period.

2 The total civilian labour force in Britain is increasing. By 1995, it is estimated that the labour force will increase by almost a million people. However, over 80 per cent of the increase will be among women (often returning to work after having a family). The labour force is also consistently getting older. Around 60 per cent of the labour force fell into the band 25–54 years old in 1987. In 1995, this is likely to be over 70 per cent.

3 Despite the above population increase, it is estimated that the number of people in full-time employment in Britain will fall during the 1990s from the present figure of 16 million out of 24 million in some form of paid work to 12 million. The implication of this forecast is that 50 per cent of the UK workforce will either be self-employed, working on temporary contracts, or in part-time occupations.

(NEDO/Training Commission, 1988; Handy and Lloyd, 1988)

Leaving demographics aside, other key considerations for the future include rapid changes in new technologies, the greater internationalization of work (particularly among Europeans), and changing attitudes towards work. Reading 15 by J. Martin Corbett explores one set of views on the role of technology in the future. Reading 14 by Elizabeth Chell argues that managers will need particular skills and attitudes if they are to steer their organizations successfully into the future.

This chapter looks at some of the issues which currently and in the future will drastically change the nature of work and workers. By looking into the future, it is of necessity speculative and incomplete. Yet, it highlights key human resource considerations which will have a substantial impact on managing the transition from today's to tomorrow's organizations.

Changing views about work

The meaning of work is changing constantly. To the Ancient Greeks and Romans, work was associated with drudgery. To the Calvinists, work was regarded as an act of religious salvation. The Protestant work ethic was derived from this view. The reason for the Protestant label is simply because it was derived from the dogma followed by the Reformation movement which ultimately created the Protestant Church. This much-discussed work ethic defined work as important, virtuous and a source of dignity. Work was seen as inherently good and should be continued even if the individual's financial position did not require it (see Weber, 1976). The potency of the work ethic varies both over time within populations and between different populations (see Part VI).

Researchers in the United States have detected a decline in the prevalence of the work ethic over the past twenty years, at least in the male population. Among female workers, there are more conflicts with other equally important ethics: e.g. the *homemaker* ethic or the *mothering* ethic. In Sweden, high levels of absenteeism have been attributed to the erosion of the work ethic, since workers appear to 'go sick' with increasing frequency. They prefer to absent themselves from work, even though Swedes enjoy fewer working hours per week than almost any other nation (less than the 35 hours per week currently sought by unions across Europe). According to Lennart Sunden, deputy managing director of Electrolux, 'a belief in work has deteriorated among the young' (*Financial Times*, 30 August 1989).

A 'decline' in the strength of the work ethic is often associated with adverse economic and social events (especially in the popular press). The loss of a nation's competitive position as well as any alleged decline in morality have, on various occasions, been blamed on the decline in people's desire to work hard. However, closer analysis reveals that it is highly unlikely that something as socially complex as a decline in the desire to work can be seen as a cause for a society's problems (see Barbash *et al.*, 1983).

It is possible to link workers' attitudes to work with the levels of complexity and affluence in any one society. Motivation theories (see Chapter 5) would predict that organizations are faced with at least two dilemmas:

1 *Competition for attention*   In relatively affluent societies, individuals have a wide range of activities which compete for their time. They no longer have to work long hours in tough and dirty jobs just to survive. Although some of these jobs will always exist, they are in the minority in affluent societies. Individuals can consider pursuits other than work (unlike their Dickensian counterparts at the beginning of this century). Another perspective is the degree of satisfaction which people receive from various activities. Once an individual has risen above the immediate need of having to work in order to survive, then a modified pain-avoidance strategy may be followed. This means that individuals may prefer to undertake those activities which can provide them with the most pleasure (least pain) and this may be in activities other than work.

2 *Expectations of work*   As part of the educational process in our society, individuals are taught to anticipate a relatively high degree of choice in how they manage their lives. Unfortunately, most organizations have not been structured to allow them the freedoms or alternatives which they may have expected. In itself, this is a very complex, emotive issue. A variety of organizational factors impinge on this: job content, supervision styles, motivation and control systems, formal rules and structures, etc. If workers have been conditioned to expect considerable freedom in their lives, it is not surprising that they are disillusioned spending great amounts of their time in an organization which explicitly seeks to control or to deskill their knowledge. The reading by Martin Corbett discusses how new automated technologies can reduce workers' skill requirements to those of machine minding. In a challenging book, Cooley (1987) also argues that technology will play the largest part in shaping future expectations of work. He draws a pessimistic view of a future which deskills and demotes workers to drones in the service of automated technologies, thereby losing a great deal of craft and innovative skills.

These two dilemmas bring into question many fundamental current organizational practices. There is a need for organizations continually to update their cultures, structures and human-resource strategies in line with the changing context of the future. In the light of predicted demographic changes it is likely that those organizations which stand still in these respects will put their continued survival at risk. They will neither be able to attract nor retain workers. The implication is that the presumed decline in the work ethic has less to do with moral decay and more to do with the modern management practices. The methods of managing people must keep pace with the increasing complexity and expectations of individuals in order to ease the conflict between the individual and the organization.

The balance between work and leisure

The concept of more leisure time itself has become well-accepted. The long working hours of previous generations has evolved into a 5-day, and perhaps even a compressed 4-day working week. Currently, European trade unions are pressing for a standard 35-hour working week. More people are opting to choose part-time work opportunities or job-sharing, especially women who are returning to work having had their families.

Strictly, the distinction is not between work and leisure, since working mothers who job share and work flexitime will look after the home and family at other times. This is work, of course, but it occurs away from the formal place of employment. To organizations, the net result is the same. They will have to cope with very different attitudes towards work and non-work activities. Workers are likely to see working in formal organizations as only a part of their total lives. Expanding vacation times and paid sabbaticals are all part of the increasing amounts of time people can devote to non-work activities.

There is a potential problem looming on the horizon. If we can envisage a future where organizations are capable of producing all the goods and services which are required with a workforce of only 75 per cent of those able to work — what happens to the other 25 per cent? This remaining quarter of the population available for work would have the opportunity to do whatever leisure activities they wanted. However, this situation raises important questions about such a society:

1 How should the unemployed 25 per cent obtain their 'title to consumption', i.e. money? If their input is truly not required by society's economic apparatus, should the provision of unemployment benefits be seen as degrading? What alternatives are there to providing support? How should the decisions be made concerning who is in formal employment and who is not?

2 If a substantial proportion of the population continues to want to work, and continues to be excluded from this activity, why should they continue to support the existing economic and social system? Revolt and anarchy could be the outcomes of a process which is primarily aimed at increasing general welfare and promoting fairness. To make such a future society work, societal values will have to change substantially.

The quality of working life approach

One solution of the above dilemmas has already been tried. The quality of work life (QWL) programmes argue that formal work organizations are able to fulfil the important personal needs of their employees as well as remain economically viable within a dominantly capitalist system of production. In organizations which have undertaken QWL programmes, efforts are generally concentrated in eight areas:

1 *Compensation*   The primary concern is that rewards for doing the job are equitable and also meet a minimum standard level.

2 *Health and safety*   An important element in improving the QWL of a work environment is to seek to reduce the physical and mental adverse conditions which are present. This includes occupational hazards, noise, air pollution, visual annoyances, etc.

3 *Job design*   This must allow workers to fulfil their needs as well as to ensure consistent levels of production. The autonomous working group approach (made famous by Volvo) is one such approach (see Chapter 2).

4 *Job security*   An improvement in QWL may also require that more attention is paid to needs of individuals to know that their jobs are secure and that their future is taken into account by the organization.

5 *Social integration*   This includes the eradication of all forms of prejudice, the development of supportive work groups and encouraging openness between individuals.

6 *Protection of individual rights*   The clear communication of individuals' rights. This includes explicit facilities for due process in considering grievances, appeals, etc.

7 *Respect for non-work activities*   Organizations which desire the benefits of QWL programmes must also consider the effects of work on the personal lives of individuals. The effects of job changes and moving homes are substantial and should be taken into account.

8 *Social relevance of work*   For individuals to align their own personal objectives with those held by the organization, it requires some degree of satisfaction with the commercial mission of the firm. The external perception of the organization in terms of its ethics, the social value of the product line and its responsiveness to community needs can influence the perception of the individual in maintaining his or her association with that organization.

(Walton, 1973)

Is QWL the answer for the future? It looks attractive and certainly early empirical research supports reduced levels of worker dissatisfaction, reduction in absenteeism and improved productivity (see Emery, 1972). More recently, many organizations have been frustrated in their attempts to seek its implementation (see, for example, the findings of the DIO International Research Team, 1983).

One implementation difficulty lies in the 'systems effect'. To achieve long-lasting improvements in QWL requires the integration of many different aspects of organizational life—not all of which are under the organization's control. External expectations must be considered alongside internal demands if organizations desire to improve the QWL. Social values, beliefs and attitudes are fundamental.

Paradoxically, the 'home' of many previously successful QWL programmes—Sweden—has become the focus of much discontent and dissatisfaction among its workforce. There appear to be two 'systemic' reasons for this. One is the apparent reduction in the work ethic (see the beginning of this chapter); another is the system of payment for sick leave which pays at full net-income rates from the first day of illness. For shift workers, sickness benefits can often exceed gross pay because of the system whereby payment is calculated. There was a 46 per cent increase in numbers of workers becoming ill in forestry shift work in 1988. In the same year, Swedish workers averaged 23.4 days of sick pay per worker; in 1983 it was 18.4 days. The British average is around 10 days per worker per year (one of the lowest absentee rates in Western Europe).

Taken alone, QWL programmes appear to be short-lived remedies for future changes. They rely for the most part upon stability in values, attitudes and beliefs among workers. They also rely upon support from the general environment since changes here can upset any number of initiatives taken by individual organizations. QWL is also susceptible to international differences in social attitudes (see Table 22.1).

Table 22.1
A comparison of attitudes to work for men and women between Italy and Britain

Equal confidence in both sexes for jobs as:	% answering 'yes'		
	Italy	*UK*	*European average*
Bus or train driver	54	61	63
Surgeon	56	70	64
Barrister	55	66	63
Member of Parliament	59	75	67

Differences in such perceptions will greatly affect the efficacy of human-resource programmes such as QWL. For example, in Europe, differences in perceptions over equal treatment for the sexes are highly varied. In Denmark, there is a high confidence in both sexes to carry out a wide range of jobs. In a study by OECD (1987) 84 per cent of Danish respondents perceived no difference in ability between the sexes. In Ireland, only 51 per cent thought that men and women had equal ability to perform the same range of jobs. The European average for equal sex ability (12 member states) was 64 per cent. Luxembourg respondents indicated the lowest preference for their partners to work (29 per cent), while in Greece over 60 per cent of respondents preferred that their partners should work. Given the coming emphasis on women in the labour force (from demographic and equal-opportunity pressures) such differences are fundamental to the success of any human-resource programme aimed at 'democratizing' the workplace.

Nevertheless, an organization which cannot or will not pay attention to QWL issues will generally have many employees who feel unfulfilled in their careers and view their jobs as simply a means to subsidize other activities. A consequence is that such individuals may show little loyalty to their employer and may also engage in sabotage. Poor QWL often manifests itself through high levels of absenteeism, alcohol and drug abuse, personal stress, boredom on the job and labour–management conflicts.

The knowledge worker

Advances in technology can potentially enhance or erode the nature of work (see Reading 15 by J. Martin Corbett). Beyond this, one result has been the continuing increase in demand for what has become known as 'the knowledge worker' (see Drucker, 1977).

Traditionally, workers have been stereotyped into two broad classifications: white-collar and blue-collar. Over the past thirty years, the proportion of white-collar workers has grown rapidly. However, the changing workplace has caused the knowledge worker to emerge which, though more closely aligned to white-collar working environments, also includes activities formerly undertaken by blue-collar workers. Included in this group are engineers, computer programmers, accountants, teachers and nurses. The value of such employees does not lie in their manual dexterity. It lies in their ability to apply their knowledge to specific situations. They tailor their skills to the context of the job, which is likely to be highly varied. Such employees are flexible and knowledgeable.

Though one might think that managing such individuals would be easy—given the challenge and rewards associated with their jobs—many organizations have found it difficult to retain such valued employees. The problem lies in the old-fashioned human-resource strategies still practised by many organizations. As a throwback to the days when managers had to dominate their workers through fear (of being fired), organizations have found it difficult to cope with individuals who, if disillusioned with one employer, can get another job elsewhere relatively easily. In general, knowledge workers tend to prefer far more open operating environments and consequently resent traditional styles of control. Their specialized knowledge is usually so highly in demand that their tolerance of an unfavourable working atmosphere can afford to be slight.

Though it is difficult to generalize, knowledge workers tend to be achievement-oriented. They also prefer working environments which provide adequate recognition for their achievements. Among their personal goals, knowledge workers aspire to growth and personal satisfaction which are derived from challenging tasks. Data from a number of studies suggest that the following human resource strategies are favoured by this section of the labour force (see Sisson, 1989).

1 *Regular feedback*   Knowledge workers prefer to operate in an environment which shares information about their organization and how their job relates to the whole.
2 *Management by objectives*   By jointly developing goals and objectives with knowledge workers, and then following them up with supportive control and recognition, knowledge workers are more likely to remain committed to their role.
3 *Eliminating unnecessary activities*   Most organizations tend to restrict individual action through the use of meetings, reports and paperwork. It is important for managers to be aware of how such activities may impede the work of knowledge workers and to seek ways of reducing them.
4 *Challenging work*   Knowledge workers stand a greater chance of leaving from boredom if they are under-employed. Managers of such individuals therefore must ensure a constant supply of challenging, non-routine work activities.
5 *Opportunities for creativity*   Aside from providing challenging work, knowledge workers also prefer to see their work as creative. Therefore, some latitude has to be built in which allows individuality to emerge.
6 *Averting low morale*   For most organizations, the investment made in attracting and training knowledge workers is substantial. If problems which lead to low morale are not caused early enough, valuable human resources may leave the organization—seriously threatening the organization's competitive position.
7 *Careful selection and placement*   To get the most out of knowledge workers, organizations must seek to match the most appropriate people with particular jobs. Any mismatch is likely to result in low morale and high employee turnover.

Summary

The future holds immense challenges for human-resource management. Attitudes towards work itself, towards working hours and towards the place of work in the wider social context are changing. Such perceptions differ significantly between countries such as Italy, France or Britain, despite their geographical proximity.

The composition of the labour force is also not stable over time. Demographic trends mean that the profile of available labour will be very different in the 1990s compared with the 1980s. In particular, the number of available young people will be severely reduced. Technological advances have deskilled (and removed) some jobs as well as enhancing others and have created a range of new knowledge-based occupations.

Strategies to cope with these changes are varied. Those based upon QWL programmes would appear to be suitable in relatively stable environments, but may not be suitable for more rapidly changing human-resource contexts. Some solutions to the changing profile of the 16–24 year old labour force in Britain are outlined in Table 22.2.

Whether or not such strategies are successful, only time will tell. It is certain, however, that organizations which do not confront the issues of the new worker in the future are unlikely to survive very long. It would seem that sustaining a

Table 22.2 Some alternative strategies to the changing profile of the 16–24 year old labour force in Britain

Strategy	Objective	Some policy approaches	Comments
Alternative labour sources	Reduce demand for young persons through substituting other sources of recruits 1 internal substitution 2 external substitution	*Internal substitution:* ● Retraining or cross-training programmes to reduce demand for young trainees ● Ditto for qualified young entrants (graduate entry, technician and intermediate skills, management trainees) by upgrading training of existing employees	Special training programmes and aptitude assessment needed; knock-on benefits in retention, job satisfaction, etc.
		External substitution: Direct or indirect labour substitution through: ● married women and other returners ● students seeking part-time work ● long-term unemployed ● former employees (e.g. maternity leave) ● more mature recruits (mid-career change, early retired, other retired)	Need to support by appropriate changes to training, induction, career planning and to work organization
Widening the recruitment catchment	Maintain numbers of young persons recruited and recruitment standards	● Changes to geographical catchment for local recruitment	Valuable where local youth unemployment differences exist
		● Targeting recruits of the under-represented sex ● Overseas recruitment	Restricted application, use mainly confined to qualified recruits

Table 22.2   (cont.)

Strategy	Objective	Some policy approaches	Comments
Improving the competitive position (for young recruits)	Improve organization's ability to recruit similar numbers of school leavers at same or similar standards	• Establish or improve procedures for schools/colleges liaison • Improvements to training or career prospects for young people; • Improvements to image of organization (to stimulate applications) • Improvements to pay or benefit systems for young recruits	Protecting the share of recruits attracted by individual recruiters (at the expense of others); quick benefits but often only short-term gains and knock-on effects may be a major problem
Modifying recruitment or selection criteria	Maintain similar number of young recruits but reduce the average entry standards	• Lower or abolish qualification filters/screens for young recruits	Maintain similar standard of recruits albeit with reduced academic attainment
		• Substitute qualified young entrants with lower or unqualified entrants or trainees • Combining both approaches	Appropriate skills needs are decreased and/or supplemented with top-up training/development programmes
Retention of existing staff	Reduce demand for young recruits as trainees or replacements through improvements to rates of employee turnover	Improvements to: • Induction training procedures • Recuitment/selection procedures • Wastage management (e.g. career breaks) • Employee awareness of company benefits • Work organization/job satisfaction • Procedures for human-resource aspects of change management	Substantial benefits to those organizations with relatively high levels of employee turnover in relevant activities; benefits in organizations with low turnover rates may be marginal
Other adjustment strategies	Reduce effects of demographic changes by work organization or positive locational changes	• Changes to organization of work • Targeted productivity improvements • Relocation to less tight local labour markets	Could be high cost options

Source: NEDO/Training Commission (1988).

competitive edge in the future will depend as much upon successful human-resource management as upon product or service innovations.

We have hinted in this chapter that such strategies for dealing with the future will require changes both to the nature of the manager and managerial activities, and to the design and rationale of organizations. We explore these questions in the following chapters.

References

Barbash, J., R. J. Lampman, S. A. Levitan and G. Tyler (1983) *The Work Ethic: A Critical Analysis*, Industrial Relations Research Association, Madison, Wisconsin.

Cooley, M. J. E. (1987) *Architect or Bee?: The Human Price of Technology*, Hogarth Press, London.

DIO International Research Team (1983) 'A contingency model of participative decision-making: an analysis of 56 decisions in three Dutch organizations', *Journal of Occupational Psychology*, **56**(1), 1–18.

Drucker, P. F. (1977) *People and Performance: The Best of Peter Drucker on Management*, Harper & Row, New York.

Emery, F. E. (ed.) (1972) *Systems Thinking: Selected Readings*, 3rd Edition, Penguin, Harmondsworth.

Handy, C. B. and B. Lloyd (1988) 'Careers for the 21st century', *Long Range Planning*, **21**(3), 90–8.

NEDO/Training Commission (1988) *Young People and the Labour Market*, NEDO, London.

OECD (1987) *Men and Women of Europe*, OECD, Paris.

Sisson, K. (ed.) (1989) *Personnel Management in Britain*, Blackwell, Oxford.

Walton, R. E. (1973) 'Quality of working life: what is it?', *Sloan Management Review*, **15**(1), 11–21.

Weber, M. (1976) *The Protestant Ethic and the Spirit of Capitalism*, 2nd Edition, Allen & Unwin, London.

The new manager

Introduction

Organizations are changing, the attitudes of individuals towards work is changing; therefore it should be no surprise that managers themselves will have to adapt as well. The population of managers is changing all the time. The tendency to promote internal candidates to middle- and senior-management positions is crumbling. The educational level and aspirations of managers are continually increasing. The demographics of managers are changing: managers are getting more responsibility at earlier stages of their career and an increasing number of managers are female.

According to Drucker (1988) current managerial activities will be entirely inappropriate for the organizations of the 1990s. He argues that currently, managers:

- do not like to create a climate which encourages change;
- spend too much time protecting their own limited territory;
- are good at complaining, but poor at making good proposals;
- rarely question the services they provide;
- spend too much time organizing their activities, without checking whether or not they are doing the right thing.

Since organizations are changing rapidly towards becoming dencentralized, information-based, task-force dominated institutions (see Chapter 24), the new manager will need to possess a significantly different repertoire of skills and abilities. Certainly, he or she cannot operate as above. Attention will be centred upon flexibility, the possession of a general/corporate vision rather than a functional specialism, an ability to work easily in teams coupled with highly developed communication skills.

To cover all the potential changes for the managers of future organizations would be an impossible task in the short space allotted. Therefore, we concentrate on three main areas in which changes have already begun to take place and which are aimed at securing and developing managers' skills for organizations of the future. They are:

1 *educating managers*
2 *modern management techniques*
3 *appropriate management styles*

Educating managers

It has been put forward by many commentators that a key component of a nation's ability to compete economically is the educational quality of the managerial resource which the country has available. Management training is, however, rather less than homogeneous or standardized between different nations. For example: (1) 85 per cent of senior managers in the US and Japan have university degrees compared to approximately 24 per cent in the UK; (2) US business schools produce 70 000 MBAs per year, the UK produces 1200, Japan 60 and West Germany, none; (3) the UK has over 120 000 qualified accountants, while Japan has 6000 and West Germany has only 4000 (Handy *et al.*, 1988). Though it is interesting to consider the differences which emerge from numerical comparisons (see Table 23.1), it is not yet clear whether one approach is better or worse than any other.

Table 23.1
International comparisons of managers and MBAs

Country	Top managers with degrees %	Number of qualified accountants ('000s)	MBAs per year
UK	24	120.0[a]	1 200[b]
US	85	300.0	20 000
W. Germany	62	3.8	0
France	65	20.0	0[c]
Japan	85	6.0	60

Notes:
[a]Accountants working in UK—combined estimates of six professional bodies.
[b]British nationals only.
[c]Does not include INSEAD graduates as it is not part of French system.

Source: Handy *et al.* (1988).

The educating and training of managers has always received a great deal of lip-service. In quite a few organizations, the reality is that development is seen as an 'on-the-job' activity. Time-off for attending courses is hard to negotiate, particularly in an organization trying to control its costs.

An important distinction which is not always made clear is the difference between 'business education' and 'management development'. In an attempt to define the two terms, Handy *et al.* (1988) allocate business education to the responsibility of each individual. Generally, business education is provided through some sort of course presented by an educational institution, though it could also include reading and updating of knowledge by individuals. Management development is seen as much more the responsibility of the organization which employs the individual. The assumption is that the benefits which are derived from management development accrue both to the individual as well as the organization. Among the activities which can be considered as management development there are: experience through job rotation, on-the-job training, as well as bespoke courses to upgrade particular skills or knowledge areas.

One reason why management development has, until recently, been overlooked is the long-time scale involved. It takes time for a manager to gain experience and it is often necessary to look at events over a 5–10 year period in order to put his or her development into proper perspective.

In the UK, the drive to upgrade the education and training of managers has recently been undertaken by what has become known as the Management Charter Initiative. The idea is to provide a recognized professional qualification to managers in much the same way as there are professional accountancy or other qualifications. Behind this undertaking lies the Council for Management Education and Development. They have called upon large and small organizations in the private and public sectors to subscribe to a code of practice on management development. The code calls on companies to:

1 improve leadership and management skills throughout the organization;

2 provide managers with support and time-off to enable them to pursue learning opportunities;

3 review progress annually;

4 set new targets for the organization and the individual manager;

5 publicize both the review and the targets.

Though not part of the code itself, there is also a desire to raise the profile of management development so that it becomes a board-level responsibility. In terms of the amount of time which organizations should grant managers to undertake development activities, one number suggested is that ten days per year should be seen as the average. This contrasts sharply with the fact that in 1987 British managers received, on average, only one day's formal training, and that the majority received no training at all (Keep, 1989).

The ability to reward employees with promotion and responsibility (rather than provide management education) may decline in the future. Byrne and Konrad (1983) noted that many organizations that had established a management 'fast track' when business was expanding have begun to slow the process as business stabilizes. Instead, these organizations are emphasizing higher-quality management development in job assignments for young managers with potential rather than highly visible and rapid advancement up the hierarchy. So advancement up the hierarchy is likely to become less common. The new manager is mobile, trained and self-developed and is likely to seek rewards by moving from organization to organization as a promotional route (Drucker, 1988).

Educating organizations to employ more female managers

The future manager is also more likely to be female than is the current, male-dominated, practice (NEDO/Training Commission, 1988). Over ten years ago, both Bem (1975) and Henning and Jardim (1977) were arguing that the future manager is going to be more markedly androgynous (i.e. display both male and female characteristics) than is currently the fashion. To date, many women have been discriminated against (wittingly or unwittingly) in selection for management positions and for attaining senior management positions because:

1 women have typically made career decisions later in life than their male counterparts;

2 women seem to be more passive in taking up career opportunities; there was a sense of 'waiting to be chosen' rather than actively seeking advancement;

3 males seem to be more concerned with 'winning' or 'scoring a goal' in their personal strategies; females tend not to think of their careers in such 'game-oriented' terms.

(Henning and Jardim, 1977).

To attract and retain female managers, organizations are being forced to become more conscious of their needs and tend towards human-resource policies which favour neither male nor female stereotypes. Many large firms have formed corporate policies designed to break down traditional areas of male dominance. Some of the tactics used in these strategies include:

1 regular checks to assess that salaries of males and females are equal;

2 early identification of female employees available for training and promotion;

3 revising established job descriptions to ensure they are not defined in a way which restricts female applicants;

4 regular surveys of female employees to increase awareness of their needs and aspirations.

Bem (1975) found that individuals who are not burdened by rigid sex roles are more able to adapt to diverse situations, show greater flexibility in what they can do and have a greater ability to express themselves and communicate with others. These are precisely the qualities argued to be the hallmark of successful managers in the future (Drucker, 1988). It seems that a breaking down of traditional sexual stereotypes will be an important part of the managerial challenge for the future. Since Bem identified that around 50 per cent of the population adhere to 'traditional sex roles' there would seem to be a great deal of room for improvement in this sphere of management (and social) education.

Management techniques—a help for the future?

Managers have always sought new techniques in an attempt to better both themselves and their organizations. Today, however, the number of available techniques is unsurpassed. Some are more fashionable than others, but in less than fifty years we have seen the emergence of Henri Fayol and Weberian bureaucracy (1930s), management by objectives (attributed to Peter Drucker) surfacing alongside programme evaluation and review techniques (PERT) in the 1950s, and management and leadership styles in the 1960s (especially Theory X and Y from Douglas McGregor and the managerial grid from Blake and Mouton). The 1970s and 1980s brought a more strategic emphasis, particularly on zero-based budgeting (Robert McNamara), the Boston Consulting Group's portfolio management (market share and growth), followed by small groups, team building, quality circles (making decisions in small groups through consensus and cooperation), to the 'one-minute manager' (make decisions alone but quickly) of Blanchard and Johnson (1982) and the market-led, close-to-the-customer, 'excellent' organizations of Peters and Waterman (1982) and many others.

A spin-off effect has been for managers also to look towards Japan's management techniques for lessons to improve their own performance. The belief was that the key to the success of Japan since the end of the Second World War was their managerial system (particularly of group decision-making and quality circles).

Despite the cultural differences, many authors have argued that Western managers can learn from the Japanese. Perhaps the most widely recognized term which epitomizes this process is 'Theory Z' (Ouchi, 1981). According to his research, Ouchi argued that American firms (Theory A) are characterized by:

1 short-term employment;
2 rapid evaluation and promotion;
3 specialized career paths;
4 individual responsibility and decision-making.

In contrast, Japanese firms (Theory J) stress:

1 lifetime employment;
2 slow evaluation and employment;
3 non-specialized career paths;
4 collective responsibility and decision-making.

Ouchi suggested the compromise—Theory Z as:

1 decision-making and problem-solving devolved to groups, teams and committees;
2 development of cohesiveness and teamwork through matrix organizations, the elimination of status barriers and, where feasible, company uniforms;

3 seek out areas to implement employee participation;
4 move towards lifetime employment for certain employees;
5 flatten the organization to reduce the emphasis on hierarchies towards a greater stress on 'clans'.

There has been much discussion concerning the ability of Theory Z to overcome Western cultural barriers. There have been highly publicized success stories of Japanese management techniques in the West. Similarly, there have been just as many attempts which have quietly been removed. There are many appealing attributes to a Theory Z organization. To individuals who have experienced the sometimes short-term perspective of Western organizations, the prospect of lifetime employment and a more paternal working environment are attractive attributes. Other aspects of Japanese 'style' organizations are less appealing. These include: (1) very slow promotions; (2) employees are expected to be loyal to the organization and consider the organization's needs before their own; and (3) a lack of status symbols to indicate position—this may include: employee uniforms, common eating facilities, open-plan offices, etc.

For organizations which are considering the use of Japanese management techniques, some of the attractions include: (1) the creation of autonomous work groups which require less formal direction from above; (2) by offering 'guarantees' of permanent employment, employees may be more willing to accept organizational change; and (3) the emphasis on creating a workforce of generalists could increase informal communication and reduce interdepartmental conflict.

The real questions are first, do any of the above techniques really work and, second, will any of them be applicable for the future? We present very briefly views for and against these techniques in the following sections.

A management style for the 1990s: is it identifiable?

Drucker (1988), Peters and Waterman (1982) and Kanter (1982) are among those authors who believe management thought has currently reached a state where particular management styles will be appropriate for the future. Their arguments are:

1 Organizations of the future will be staffed predominantly by professionals (Drucker).
2 Organizations of the future will have to be more responsive to the needs of clients and customers (Peters and Waterman; Kanter).

Managing professionals

A growing problem for many organizations is the need for specialists in a wide variety of disciplines. As the role of the generalist wanes (at least until senior management levels), the need to attract and retain the very best skills and knowledge has risen. At the same time, more and more people are working for 'professional' organizations such as accountancy firms, consultancies and high-technology companies. In organizations where high levels of expertise are the firm's most valued asset, great care must be taken regarding how people are managed.

The conventional approach is to take the best individual and appoint him or her as manager. The problem with such an approach is that the organization may lose their professional contributions and may make individuals dissatisfied in time. Many professionals have spent years studying to achieve a professionally recognized status. For such individuals, their own identities are derived from their work. They choose their careers because they found the work exciting and challenging—not because they wanted to be managers. In many cases, the nature of managerial work conflicts with the very things which makes professional work exciting. According to Lorsch and Mathias (1987), some of the characteristics of the professional employee are:

1 *Professionals enjoy their work since it provides rapid and measurable results*   As a group, professionals tend to have a greater need for quick feedback from their action. Examples include: a consultant working on a project for a client and getting immediate feedback from the client, or a merchant banker working on a merger deal for a client. Managers, on the other hand, usually achieve results gradually and even then there may be no concrete outcome. A good example is the need to develop new people in the organization.

2 *Professionals enjoy the content of their work*   Usually, they have chosen their profession because of its intellectual challenge and stimulation. Being a manager normally involves the control of small details which may lack the glamour of their profession. While managerial issues can be as complex as any professional task, they don't necessarily have to interest the specialist.

3 *Professionals often prefer working alone or in small teams of colleagues*   People who focus all of their energies on project assignments value the freedom that such work entails. Given their objective, individuals or small project teams of specialists can do whatever they can to accomplish their task. Managers rarely find life so simple. They are forced to deal with the complex set of relationships with superiors, peers and subordinates, which all require some of their attention.

The dilemma for organizations which employ many specialists is clear. Do you leave your top specialists in the job which they are best at and choose the less able professionals to be managers? If so, the organization runs the risk of confirming the traditional specialists complaint about management: that they are second-rate. An alternative which some organizations are trying is to bring in managers from outside. The difficulty with this approach is that the new managers may lack the necessary expertise to understand fully the tasks they are asked to oversee.

Management styles for flexible, responsive firms

Beyond the challenge of managing professionals lie the questions of appropriate management styles for the 1990s. Linked into the market-led, customer-driven culture (see Chapter 13) are some fairly evangelical statements about the qualities of the future manager. Table 23.2 summarizes some of these key qualities (from Peters and Waterman, 1982).

Table 23.2
Management styles
for the future

Traditional management based upon role culture and bureaucratic structures:	Future management based upon task cultures and flexible decentralized structures:
Policeman	Guide
Disciplinarian	Cheerleader/coach
Paper-shuffler	Enthusiast
Office-bound	Verbal communicator
Allocates jobs	Delegates tasks
Focus on control	Focus on quality
Focus on markets	Focus on customers
Maintains bureaucracy	Sheds bureaucracy and creates a vision

Evidence for whether these styles work is mixed. Certainly, some of Peters and Waterman's companies turned in rather less than excellent performance in the late 1980s (although others such as 3M and Disney managed to sustain their success). Companies in Britain such as Eagle Star, Barclays Bank, STC ICL which have emphasized quality and customer service are currently successful. Yet others manage well without total quality programmes and the like. Fads and corporate cure-alls are not new of course and it is likely that the future manager could add 'healthy scepticism' to his or her list of necessary knowledge for the future, at the same time acknowledging that these techniques do work for some organizations some of the time.

A management style for the 1990s: fads will not help

Two authors who argue that the above management styles are founded on little other than fads and fashion and therefore will be of little use for the future are McGill (1988) and Gunz (1989). McGill (1988) argues that every style and approach has worked for some organizations in the past and the tendency is to view these organizations as role models for the rest. He declares that the marketing of management-style packages for the future has become itself big business with acronyms (such as LEAD—Leader Effectiveness and Adaptability Description) abounding, and often taking precedence over rigorous, academic content.

Gunz (1989) disagrees with the notion of an appropriate management style based upon a mixture of individual knowledge, skills and traits. Based upon empirical evidence from executives in the British operations of four large manufacturing organizations, he argues that successful management for the future seems to depend largely upon the organization rather than the individual. Specifically, organizations create the conditions in which particular management styles will flourish. The conditions are called 'command-centred', 'evolutionary', 'constructional' and 'turnaround'.

The *command centred* organization consists of managers who have advanced through commanding a succession of bigger and bigger business units, but where the actual management process remains substantially the same. Retail banks are examples. Management style is inflexible (they are good at a narrow range of skills) and resistant to change. The *evolutionary* organization is one where management style is predominantly achieved through expanding a particular part of the business (their own) and growing with it. The problem here is often that efficiency of existing operations suffers in the quest for diversification.

The *constructional* organization is one which appoints managers deemed to have the 'right' qualities to run very different sections of the business at short notice. Such styles develop political and procedural skills above all else, but detailed understanding of the business or its customers is lacking. The *turnaround* organization favours management styles which favours fast-track, well-reputed managers who grasp the nettle and effect change quickly and sometimes brutally. The problem is that management skills here often become focused on manipulating the grapevine, so that reputations are made (often without any supporting evidence).

Gunz (1989) argues that specific styles are appropriate for each of the four organizational contexts. It is a case of horses for courses. Change the organizational context and most managers will not be able to adapt. From his evidence, it seems that management styles are not easily transferable.

Summary

So, the question of whether we can identify a specific set of factors for an appropriate future management style remains not only unanswered, but the subject of polarized debate. As a student of organizational behaviour, you would have been suspicious of any other finding! We can, however, say some relatively concrete things about the future.

While it is difficult to say whether the environment facing managers will be any more or less challenging in the future, there is no doubt that it will be different. Managers will not only have to respond to the pressures of change, but also be the agents of change themselves.

As more organizations realize the value of an educated workforce, the gap between management development and business education may narrow. Recent efforts in the UK such as the Management Charter Initiative are aimed at achieving this although the precise identification of management skills is likely to remain a problem. Forecasts for the future growth of organizations indicate an extended period of stabilization. This implies that fewer promotions will be able to be offered as rewards for top performers. In its place, increased learning opportunities may be offered to retain key staff.

A long overdue change in organizations is the attempt to remove the traditional barriers which have restricted females from senior managerial positions. More organizations than ever before are offering flexible working arrangements so that women can better cope with the often conflicting demands of work and family life. In addition, the increasing number of females in managerial ranks is having an effect on organizational behaviour generally. The result is likely to be an organization in which masculine and feminine values are regarded as equally significant.

Japanese management principles are only now beginning to lose some of the stigma which was attached to them during the highly publicized days of the early 1980s. If nothing else, the lessons derived from Japan's style of management will encourage managers to consider the effectiveness of what they are presently doing. Managers are likely to become more self-reflective in the future.

As the service economy grows and organizations become more specialized, the assumptions of a flexible workforce must be reconsidered. The complexity of many tasks—computers, law, accounting, etc.—means that organizations will have to value the amount of expertise which an individual brings to the organization. To attract and retain such people, the organization will have to construct a work environment which allows the individual to maximize his or her utility, while at the same time permitting the organization to monitor and direct the energy of its human resources. We approach the question of the organization in the future in the next chapter.

References

Bem, S. L. (1975) 'Androgeny vs. the tight little lives of fluffy women and chesty man.' *Psychology Today*, Sept. 58–62.

Blanchard, K. and S. Johnson (1982) *The One-Minute Manager*, Prentice-Hall, Englewood Cliffs, New Jersey.

Byrne, J. A. and W. Konrad (1983) 'The fast track slows down', *Forbes*, 18 July, 77–8.

Drucker, P. (1988) 'The coming of the new organization', *Harvard Business Review*, Jan.–Feb., 21–7.

Gunz, H. (1989) *Careers and Corporate Cultures*, Blackwell, Oxford.

Handy, C., C. Gordon, I. Gow and C. Randlesome (1988) *Making Managers*, Pitman, London.

Henning, M. and M. Jardim (1977) *The Managerial Woman*, Doubleday, New York.

Kanter, R. M. (1982) *The Change Masters: Corporate Entrepreneurs at Work*, Allen & Unwin, London.

Keep, E. (1989) 'A training scandal?, in K. Sisson (ed.), *Personnel Management in Britain*, Blackwell, Oxford.

Lorsch, J. W. and P. E. Mathias (1987) 'When professionals have to manage', *Harvard Business Review*, July–Aug., 78–83.

McGill, M. E. (1988) *American Business and the Quick Fix*, Henry Holt & Co., New York.

NEDO/Training Commission (1988) *Young People and the Labour Market*, NEDO, London.

Ouchi, W. (1981) *Theory Z: How American Business Can Meet the Japanese Challenge*, Addison-Wesley, Reading, Mass.

Peters, T. and R. Waterman, Jr (1982) *In Search of Excellence: Lessons from America's Best Run Companies*, Harper & Row, New York.

The new organization

Introduction

The nature of organizations is changing all the time. Living and observing them in the present, we find it difficult to pick out trends in the ways in which organizations function. Unlike businesses in the past, which were characterized by manufacturing oriented towards the domestic economy, organizations in the future are likely to be information-based, operating in a global economy. The people who inhabit these organizations also have changing expectations about their employment relationship and about the broader role of the firm in society.

To provide a final perspective on the attributes which organizations may have in the future, five potential issues are presented:

1 intrapreneurialism
2 the growth of diversified conglomerates
3 the growth of the small business sector
4 globalization of business
5 the increasing importance of business ethics

The list is of necessity incomplete. The role of organizations in our society is as complex as the people which populate them. The study of organizational behaviour in the future will have to cope with an even greater diversity of views and objectives. The challenge will be, as always, to try and seek coherence out of such diversity.

Intra-preneurialism

The traditional dichotomy between being an employee of an organization and an entrepreneur (who founds his or her own organization) is crumbling. The first signs of this lay in the introduction of individual profit centres within large organizations. By allocating financial and product/market decisions to distinctive groups, the intent was to create a sense of ownership and responsibility among the profit centre managers. They could be their own entrepreneurs under the larger corporate banner.

In an attempt to achieve both innovation and a sense of ownership in large organizations, many firms have adopted policies of 'corporate venturing' or *intrapreneurialism* to remain competitive. Corporate venturing is a practice by which 'venture capital' is provided by the company to a set of its employees for them to set up a business on their own. As an alternative to seeking venture-capital funding from outside the organization, corporate venturing offers budding entrepreneurs a staged withdrawal from the firm. In many cases, the start-up company is provided with cheap accommodation and access to many of the company's resources. In return, the company would own a percentage of the share capital of the new company. The argument is that if the firm were not willing to accept this proportion of control, then the potential for the innovation succeeding would be lost forever.

Most people are familiar with the term 'entrepreneur'. It generally refers to the founder(s) of a start-up company who have risked their financial livelihood on their confidence that their business idea can succeed. The term 'intrapreneur' was created in the United States by Gifford Pinchot III, a management consultant. Pinchot argued that organizations can retain creativity and innovation within by creating an infrastructure which rewards entrepreneurial behaviour and yet protects such people from the financial ruin which a failure can bring.

To encourage the potential of creating an organization of intrapreneurs requires the entire organization to reconsider its culture and processes of assessing performance. The rewards and punishments for success or failure have to be reconsidered. Many intrapreneurial projects are likely to fail and potential innovators must see that such setbacks will not unduly harm their careers. Similarly, the organization will also have to be more flexible in determining the appropriate rewards for successful innovation. One approach could be to create separate subsidiaries for successful innovations and to allow the intrapreneurs an equity share of the business as well as the opportunity to run the new operation. Atterhed (1985) illustrates the required change in attitudes between the traditional cultures of large firms and an intrapreneurial culture (see Table 24.1).

Table 24.1
The corporation and the intrapreneurial cultures

Big corporation culture values	Intrapreneurial culture values
Control	Trust
Meddling	Protection
Boss	Mentor
Instructions	Visions
Planning	Flexibilty
Orders	Viewpoints
Alienation	Participation
Fragmentation	Wholeness
Rules	Customers

Source: Atterhed (1985: 81).

One of the key aspects of the intrapreneurial culture will be that of 'adding value' to the existing organization. This can occur on a number of levels, from adding value by creating new profitable firms in which the mother firm has a stake, to adding value in specific product lines and services. Either way, the future organization is likely to face some or all of the following 'rethinking' if added value is to take place:

- assess strengths and weaknesses
- transform from bureaucracy into leadership and flexibility
- achieve effectiveness rather than efficiency
- always ask: why are we doing this?

The growth of diversified conglomerates in the future

One question which every student of organizational behaviour and every senior manager faces is—what business is this organization in? It is a relatively simple question, designed to elicit some understanding of the primary business purpose of an organization, but the answer is rarely straightforward. The increasing number of diversified conglomerates is a perfect illustration of this difficulty. Essentially, conglomerate diversification is a growth strategy that involves adding new products or services significantly different from the organization's present products or services. Though such diversification can be achieved internally through growing an operation in-house, it is more often undertaken through mergers, acquisitions and joint ventures.

Current trends seem to indicate that these diversification strategies will continue well into the 1990s. For example, in their 1981 Annual Report, the Chairman of the General Electric Company of the United States, Jack Welch, stated that GE was 'in the business of creating business'. In Britain, the classic conglomerate is Hanson plc (formerly Hanson Trust). Operating throughout the world, Hanson Trust has acquired companies as diverse as Imperial Tobacco, British Ever Ready (batteries), Allders Department Stores, SCM (Smith Corona typewriters, US) and Kaiser Cement (US) to name but a few. In the period 1983–87, Hanson's turnover has jumped from £1484 m to £6682 m.

Though conglomerates are often criticized for their aggressive, acquisitive nature, they are not always so profitable as Hanson. Nevertheless, the number of conglomerates continues to increase, with a commensurate decrease in the number of single businesses (see Table 24.2).

Table 24.2 Composition of the top 200 British companies by type (percentage of companies)

	1950	1960	1970	1980
Single businesses	35	21	11	9
Dominant businesses	41	41	30	26
Related businesses	20	31	50	47
Conglomerates	4	7	9	18

Note:
Single business gets no less than 95 per cent of its sales income from one basic business; dominant business gets 71–95 per cent from any single business; related business gets no more than 70 per cent of its sales turnover from any single business; conglomerates get no more than 70 per cent of its sales income from any one series of related businesses.

Source: Kidron and Segal (1987: 42).

During the past thirty years, there have been periodic waves of 'merger mania' as giant companies have acquired large numbers of small firms. Many of these conglomerates have been criticized for showing little concern for the employees of the acquired companies and for not being as profitable as might be expected. Even so, there is little sign that the continued growth of large multinational conglomerates will decrease. They will become a dominant form of organization in the 1990s.

The growth of the small business sector

A contrasting trend to the increasing dominance of conglomerates in the Western economies is the rise of the small business sector. Though small firms account for only 13 per cent of total sales turnover in the UK, they have provided 31 per cent of all new jobs created between 1971 and 1981.

In the UK, the Conservative government under Margaret Thatcher has consistently encouraged the small-business sector through a variety of means. Though the government would undoubtedly accept some (if not all) of the credit for the resurgence of small businesses, there are also a variety of social and economic pressures which have helped to nurture the entrepreneur.

One social factor which seems to be encouraging the small business is the increasing recognition in the workforce that the job security offered by the larger organizations can be matched by many smaller firms. Profit-sharing schemes, share options and company pension-plans can be offered just as easily by most small businesses. Similarly, the recognition which one can receive in a small business for work well done can be more immediate than in many large, impersonal organizations.

Economic factors are also providing opportunities for the small business. The continual demands of investors in large organizations for adequate returns means that they must pay closer attention to short-term profit targets. Small businesses are generally privately held and can, subject to the agreement of the directors, forgo short-term profits to create a market presence. The expense and risk involved with starting up a new business has also been reduced. The government, through a variety of local and national programmes, offer grants and loan guarantees to help the entrepreneur with finding the financial backing required. The increasing popularity of franchising is another route to creating new businesses. By agreeing to pay a royalty on future sales, a franchisee can take advantage of the larger company's brand image, marketing, production and management expertise.

Globalization of business

A major advantage which the Western societies have had since the 1900s has been a relatively affluent domestic market, characterized by ever-increasing levels of consumer demand. Industries in other countries have found it difficult to produce goods of equal quality or sophistication. The competitive advantage enjoyed by Western firms was largely based on the domestic market which they served.

The dominance of Western firms in serving their own domestic markets has been thrown into doubt by the spectacular rise of the Japanese since 1960. Though many Western firms have taken the lead in becoming multinational, very rarely do these firms think in truly global terms. Naisbitt (1984) has estimated that by the year 2000, Third World countries will be the source of 30 per cent of the world's manufactured goods.

The potential effect of the relaxation of trade and customs barriers within the European Community in 1992 is frequently discussed, but rarely completely understood. Most countries have, over the years, erected substantial legal and procedural barriers to restrict foreign companies entering domestic markets. The proposals for 1992 offer to sweep away many of these restrictions.

The effect is likely to be profound, though not immediately apparent. Pan-European mergers and acquisitions are likely as firms try to gain market share. Previously heavily controlled sectors such as financial services will be opened up to allow for new competitors. The possibility of a Continental financial services firm purchasing one of the major UK clearing banks is conceivable.

One likely effect of 1992 will be the increasing competitive pressure for companies to operate in as many of the EC countries as possible. Mitchell (1989) says that those organizations which will be more competitive in post-1992 Europe will evolve new structures to take advantage of national markets as well as European economies of scale. The 'Euro Network' organization predicted by Mitchell will contain the following attributes:

1 dividing the company up into identifiable business units with clear business objectives;
2 implementing an organizational control system which minimizes the need for referral across the structure or above;
3 a recognition that duplication of support services is preferred over the greater complexity of centralization;

4 management must adopt the vision of a single European market before it is a reality;

5 increasing the span of control at all levels of the organization to allow for fewer organizational levels and for greater delegation;

6 a central services function which exists to serve the various operating units rather than supply the centre with resources

In terms of human-resource concerns, the increasingly global outlook of organizations may mean that managerial careers will be more likely to require some time spent abroad. Managers will have to exhibit cross-cultural qualities. For firms which operate globally, its managerial resource base will also have to be assessed in terms of its ability to function globally. One potential effect of this shift will be to increase the numbers of managers who speak more than their native language. Many academic institutions such as business schools have recognized this need and encourage students to improve their understanding of at least one European language.

The predicted shortfall in graduate recruits will have an important effect on European organizations' recruitment drives. It has been reported that Olivetti has concluded that the total output of *all* of Europe's universities is likely to be less than its own requirements in key disciplines (Skapinker, 1988). The implication is that the market for university graduates will increase remarkably through the entrance of more European firms into the job 'milk round'. Conversely, some British schools are seeking to employ English-speaking Europeans to try and shore up the shortfall in supply of domestic teachers in some cities. Skapinker also reports that UK graduates may be in greater demand than their Continental counterparts. He attributes this to five reasons:

1 For historical reasons, UK universities have a better organized recruitment procedure and actively seek to market their graduates.

2 Compared to other European countries, the UK sends a lower proportion of their population through the university system. In practice, this means that the relative standard of UK graduates is high.

3 As English is now accepted as a universal language of international business, firms are eager to acquire fluent speakers—particularly if they can supplement English with other European languages.

4 British students are more likely to have lived away from home when attending university than students in Europe. Therefore, the experience of uprooting and travelling will not be as great a shock as it may be for others.

5 Lastly, salaries in the UK have tended to be lower than those offered on the Continent.

One of the effects of 1992 may be the creation of a truly international labour market. Organizations will have to offer compensation and working conditions which will meet or better the inducements of work elsewhere in Europe. Perhaps the most important result of 1992 will be the changes it brings to the human-resource management practices of European companies.

Business ethics

Increasing social and some governmental pressure is being placed upon organizations to consider their contribution to wider social objectives. It is likely that the future will bring even stronger expectations that businesses must consider social issues alongside the pursuit of profit. Shareholders of the future are likely to have to become used to a lower return on their investment as firms attend to being corporately socially responsible (see Chapter 17).

Business is being held increasingly accountable for improving the quality of

the environment, making safe products, providing for worker health and safety
and seeking to advance broad social objectives such as equal opportunity
programmes. Many of the larger organizations have begun to recognize this
trend and have initiated public-relations campaigns which highlight their
public-spiritedness. Others, such as the British automobile industry, are more
tardy particularly in their lack of response to cutting down the levels of exhaust
pollution from cars. In this case, it seems that pressure from the British and
European governments will have to be exerted on car manufacturers, rather
than its being a voluntary decision.

One reaction many large firms have taken to this growing pressure to have a
social conscience has been to issue 'corporate codes of conduct' (Chatov, 1980).
These codes represent an effort to specify behaviour that the organization does
or does not sanction. The behaviours which are most commonly frowned upon
include:

1 extortion, gifts and kickbacks
2 conflicts of interest
3 illegal political payments
4 violation of laws in general
5 use of insider information
6 bribery

Though these may not sound particularly innovative, for many firms,
particularly those operating in many different national contexts, they represent
a major challenge. The difficulties emerge where the local views on what is
appropriate business behaviour differs from that proposed by the codes.
Nevertheless, the movement towards an ethical approach to doing business is
gaining momentum and it deserves to succeed.

Despite the increasing expectations about the role of organizations in
fulfilling social objectives, Naisbitt (1984) argues that general confidence in
large organizations is decreasing. The ability and desire of the government to
satisfy the basic needs of citizens and provide for their welfare seems to be
declining. Decentralization and greater emphasis on the role of the individual is
the replacement.

Business leaders have done little in the past to modify the misconceptions and
prejudices held by the general public regarding their activities. Too often
managers have been overly defensive or have placed excessive attention on how
good everything is. Because businesses have been reluctant to talk about their
problems openly, the public can frequently feel that there is something to hide.

Managers must become more adept at convincing a sceptical public that the
organization and its members maintain high ethical standards. To achieve this
recognition, business leaders must establish long-term commitments to social
action. In many cases, the programmes adopted in a blaze of publicity have
been ill-conceived, hastily adopted and lack the long-term commitment of all
parties.

Some observers of the past records of businesses in ethical behaviour remain
sceptical. Many people argue that the only effective way to get businesses to pay
attention to social issues is continually to mount aggressive attacks on
companies. To convince the public otherwise, organizations will have to display
sincere concern for the well-being of society. Most definitely, it is a long-term
objective.

Summary

The kind of organization which will be operating successfully in the future seems to be one which incorporates either the small-business orientations, or the global conglomerate approach, or is the bustling, innovative organization crammed full of intrapreneurs. How realistic is this picture? Of course, it is impossible to be sure. We speak from our own perspective of today. The way we currently view organizations effectively places parameters on the way we think about them in the future.

It is unlikely, however, that none of the foregoing characteristics will be present. Summarizing the arguments so far, we can construct some predictions for the future characteristics and values of organizations, even if we cannot accurately predict their size or structure (see Table 24.3).

Table 24.3
Characteristics of the future organization

In the short term	In the long term
An emphasis on quality	Establishing a 'vision' for future strategies ('Imagineering')
High degree of customer orientation and a concern for the client	Developing the notion of effective service provision both internally between functions and externally between the organization and its clients
Organizing around existing markets rather than products	Creating and developing new markets
Human-resource strategies based on coaching and counselling, progress reviews, and personal goal-setting	Human-resource strategies oriented towards people development and the reassessment of goals
Flexibility and an ability to respond to change	An appetite for change driven by flexibility

Perhaps the issue of greatest long-term importance will prove to be the social conscience of organizations. As concern over protecting our environment grows, the call for organizations to regulate their own actions has grown. The frequently conflicting pressures between maximizing shareholder returns and preserving the greater good of society will have to be addressed, confronted and resolved. The role of organizations as fellow citizens of our global society will have to be resolved very quickly, otherwise organizations may still be profitable, but to what end?

References

Atterhed, S. G. (1985) 'Intrapreneurship: the way forward', in D. Clutterbuck, *New Patterns of Work*, Gower, Aldershot, Hants.

Chatov, R. (1980) 'What corporate ethics statements say', *California Management Review*, **22**(4), 22.

Kidron, M. and R. Segal (1987) *Business, Money and Power*, Pan Books, London.

Mitchell, D. (1989) '1992: the implications for management', *Long Range Planning*, **22**(1), 32–40.

Naisbitt, J. (1984) *Megatrends: Ten New Directions Transforming Our Lives*, Warner Books, New York.

Skapinker, M. (1988) 'A European market for managers', *Financial Times*, 28 Oct., 21.

READING
14

New managerial behaviour

Elizabeth Chell[1]

In the 1990s, the job of management will still comprise the threefold function of managing the business, managing people and managing work (Drucker, 1955). Management is about change, anticipation, responsiveness, flexibility and adaptiveness. The key to progress will be the ability of managers to think and act strategically. It is trite to suggest that strategy is a function of management. However, strategy formulation and development has long been perceived as a responsibility of top management; survival and growth will depend upon middle and lower management's perception of, and commitment to, strategy. No longer can their roles be concerned solely with day-to-day issues. Middle- and lower-level managers must appreciate and have a commitment to the goals, direction and strategy of the organization.

A general model of managerial behaviour

Business context

Assessing the roles and performance of managers in the future cannot be successful without understanding the situational context. Writers on organizations have typically associated terms such as 'dynamic', 'heterogeneous' and 'hostile' with 'environment' (Miller and Friesen, 1984). Such conditions are said to create 'turbulence', 'uncertainty' and severe 'competition' (see Figure R14.1).

Changes in financial markets or the political situation can produce dramatic shifts to a company's viability. Competition from less advanced countries has blighted the mature industries in the advanced industrialized countries (AICs) (Grant, 1987). The concern has been to re-establish competitiveness against such apparently unfavourable international trends and to maintain and restore

Figure R14.1
A general social
model of managerial
behaviour

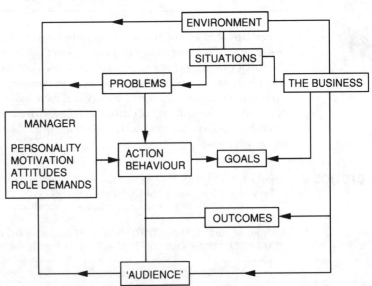

Source: Miller/Friesen, *Organization: A Quantum View*, © 1984, pp. 102, 122–21.
Reprinted by permission of Prentice–Hall, Inc., Englewood Cliffs, N.J.

a competitive edge against rival companies. Such a comparative advantage must be created by firms investing in strategic change.

In addition to international sources of competition, another major threat is technological change. To increase the efficiency of their operations, firms will need to update their technological base. Radical product developments may threaten the firm more rapidly than changes in process technology. Despite this, evidence suggests that many firms are unable to make dramatic shifts—even when faced with such large discontinuities in technology. It has been suggested that this is because the new technology poses a problem of 'business definition' (Abell, 1980)—managers being unable to reconceive the nature of their business and change accordingly. Such inertia might also be explained by the specific nature of the distinctive competences of the firm. The dramatic shift in technological regimes may mean that the firm does not possess the technical know-how to effect the required change (Metcalfe, 1985).

The management of change

Businesses change and develop. However, the rate of change varies, not only due to the nature of the industry, but also in relation to its culture, and the willingness of management to implement change and adopt consonant strategies. The various routes by which change comes about are: the proactive, where the manager foresees the need for change; the reactive where change is in some sense 'forced' upon the firm; and evolutionary where change occurs naturally, slowly and in a more manageable, predictable way. In practice, most firms will blend such routes together. The balance is likely to depend upon the innovative or entrepreneurial nature of the firm (Miller and Toulouse, 1986).

Change invariably produces novel situations which need to be handled. Situations, while constraining action, may also provide opportunities. The manager who is aware will pursue the opportunities which arise and strive to overcome the constraints. For the task-oriented manager this will mean focusing on business goals and the strategies for achieving them. The encouragement and development of such behaviours is, in effect, an invitation for the manager to become more entrepreneurial. Implicit in the decision processes of managerial activity at such a time is an assumption of the level of acceptable risk which may be associated with this particular opportunity. The old tactic may have been to 'hedge one's bets' and take an incremental approach. On the other hand, for the new manager, opportunities may create the circumstance for a major shift in the business's strategic position.

The implications of all this are the needs for the manager to: (1) actively seek information and foresee change; (2) be responsive and prepared to initiate change; and (3) develop a strategy to offset the possible impact of externally imposed change.

Situations, roles and the parameters of decisions to be taken are likely to become blurred until there is a redefinition of the problem, the goals and the means of achieving them. Once a transition has been made, the next stage is likely to be defined by a new and different set of problems. This suggests that the nature of the problems facing the manager are determined by:

1 recognition and awareness of the need for change;
2 action to bring about the desired change;
3 the motivational structure of the individual and the collective management team;
4 the stage of development of the business and its size;
5 externally imposed conditions.

Table R14.1 delineates a four-stage model of business development: stage 1 comprises the creation and establishment of the new venture; stage 2, its expansion; stage 3, increased professionalization of the business; and stage 4, its consolidation. The duration of each stage varies depending upon the nature of the business, but more particularly the entrepreneurial flair of the owner/manager.

The goals of the business are in part defined by its stage of development. Management's primary task is to create an ethos whereby personal goals will coincide with those of the business. Different managers will approach this task from different perspectives, but the new manager must be both entrepreneurial and professional in his or her management practices. This dual set of expectations and skills is outlined diagrammatically below:

Key characteristics of the new manager

The role and associated expectations for a manager can exert a strong influence on their behaviour (Biddle, 1979; Katz and Kahn, 1966). This raises the issue of the nature and personality of the new manager as he or she must be capable to adapting to periodic and sometimes unanticipated change. Social learning theory allows for the growth and development of the person as a consequence of accumulated shifts in experience and circumstances (Rotter and Hochreich, 1975). The cognitive structure of the personality may be thought of in terms of five general categories: constructs (beliefs, knowledge base, etc.); competencies (abilities and skills); expectancies; values; plans, goals and strategies (see Chell, 1985; 1987; Mischel, 1973). The content of each of these categories shapes the personality of us all, but more pertinently that of the new manager.

As individuals we construct our reality for different dimensions of our world. In the world of work, the manager's reality will be shaped by his or her beliefs about the nature of the business, the marketplace, the aggressiveness of the competition—and what is considered to be 'best practice' in deciding upon appropriate courses of action. The belief structure of managers with respect to the environment and the firm's place within it serves to underpin key attitudes which may be identified. Such attitudes, once communicated, shape the organizational culture of the firm.

Managers are generalists (Minkes, 1987). Their competencies are geared to managing and controlling people with a view to directing the business towards achieving its goals. This means that the new manager's competencies must comprise the ability to: (1) work through other people and build effective teams; (2) think through where the business is going and execute plans; (3) tolerate uncertainty and risk; (4) develop self-awareness and insight; (5) be able to motivate others; and (7) solve problems, think laterally and formulate novel solutions. In small firms, there may be less to argue about over the allocation of resources. In medium to large organizations, such issues need sensitive handling and the exercise of political judgement. The new manager will need to develop such skills and maintain a balance between making concessions on political grounds and goal attainment.

Management is about anticipation and setting priorities. Within the cognitive structure of the manager, his or her expectancies regarding the business are fundamental. The expectations of the behaviour of others and of events arise from experience, but also from training. In order to develop tactical

Table R14.1 Stage models of business development compared

Stage	Flamholtz (1986)	Churchill (1983)	Problems	Orientation after (Kazanjian)
Stage 1	New Venture	Existence Survival	Develop customer base; deliver product in sufficient volume; market niche; develop products and services; cash generation	External relationships (customers); strategic positioning (market niche); sales/marketing
//
Stage 2	Expansion	–disengagement Success –growth	Stretching of resources and operational system; space; monitoring performance; hiring of appropriate personnel; changing strategy; cash for growth	Sales/marketing
//
Stage 3	Professional-ization	Take off	Delegation; decentralization; formalization; sufficient cash for planned growth; personnel with different skills; management control system—at appropriate level of sophistication	Organizational factors
//
Stage 4	Consolidation	Resource mature	Establishing corporate culture; socialization process; image; need for more formal communication process	Strategic positioning organizational factors

*Stages 1 and 2 entrepreneurial firm according to Flamholtz.

Key | /////////////// | transition

manoeuvres, manage industrial-relations affairs and 'second guess' the competition, the new manager must be perspicacious, observant and sufficiently clever to develop accurate expectations and be able to judge and predict successfully the likely outcomes of complex situations which arise. Expectations are thus part of the goal orientation and motivational structure of the manager.

Managing the expectations of others and being able to meet targets are facilitated by setting priorities and communicating them effectively. The ordering of priorities may arise as a matter of urgency due to externally imposed pressure or for idiosyncratic or expeditious reasons. The relative importance of some actions to the manager is a value judgement which shapes his or her attitudes and subsequent behaviour. Values, being so deep-seated, are difficult to change (Rokeach, 1973). The new manager will learn, assimilate and shape the values which underpin the organizational culture and ethos. Organizational values, such as maintaining standards, emphasizing quality and the importance of improving the firm's competitive position, are likely to represent the kind of cultural setting which will be faced by the new manager.

People develop sets of strategies for survival, personal growth and happiness. A typical managerial career strategy is intimately linked to the growth and prosperity of the company. Personal plans and goals which are consonant with such ends will therefore be acted upon. The new manager has this 'safe' option, but there are other options: considerable job mobility; intrapreneurial activities within the company; and the increasingly more respected option of self-employment.

The motivational forces driving the new manager are becoming clear: the recognition of a changing and challenging environment; the need to take the initiative and secure the company's position within that environment; the need to reward and be rewarded for business growth and success; and the need to develop a strategy whereby personal and business goals can be achieved.

The roles of change agent and intrapreneur present challenges to the new manager. No longer is a reactive stance appropriate: to be effective the new manager must be proactive. This means achieving a subtle blend of task and political contingency approaches (Child, 1984). To achieve desired ends, a manager needs the allegiance and support of his or her subordinates. Such commitment can only be attained if there is a shared vision of the goals and direction which is effectively transmitted by active and genuine methods of participation (Chell, 1985).

Strategic behaviour   The development and execution of a strategy is crucial to the new manager's behavioural repertoire. Strategy formulation is not necessarily a rational process of identifying and choosing between options. Typically it is incremental and adaptive (Lindblom, 1959; Mintzberg, Raisinghani and Theuret, 1976); organizations do not usually make large strategic shifts but test out strategic options. The strategy may not be explicit, known or consciously being pursued (Pennings, 1985), it may be implicit in the actions taken or rationalized after events have taken their course. Clearly the manager who knows what he or she is about will develop an explicit strategy and communicate it effectively.

Formulating a strategy and implementing it are two different activities. Borrowing Spender's term, 'strategic recipe', Johnson discusses competitive positioning as the adoption of a strategic recipe or 'set of beliefs and perceptions in which the strategy is rooted' (Johnson, 1984: 25). However, the strategic recipe contains two sets of beliefs: those concerned with the environment and the firm's competitive standing in the environment; and those concerned with how the company should operate to achieve that standing. Johnson defines these beliefs as:

1 strategic frames are those beliefs about the nature of the organization's environment and the organization's position within it;
2 strategic formulae are those beliefs about the modes of operation of the organization which managers perceive as bestowing beneficial competences and capabilities on the organization (i.e. 'best practice').

Figure R14.2 presents a summary of the key factors which shape the formulation and enactment of a competitive strategy. The belief structure of the new manager comprises two sets of mediating variables: those which broadly speaking are internal to the operations of the firm and as such form the belief set

Figure R14.2
A model of
competitive strategy
formulation by the
new manager

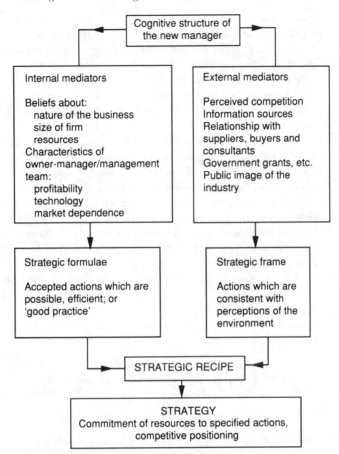

which most directly impinges upon the development of strategic formulae; and those external factors which make up significant parts of the firm's environment and which most directly shape the strategic frame.

The new manager's concern is with outcomes and with the achievement of set targets and goals. A person with such a need to achieve will develop performance measures to enable them to assess their progress and as such they will want regular feedback on their performance (McClelland, 1961). Such behaviour while personal to the manager will also be carried out with an 'audience' in mind. Audiences may comprise any combination of customers, clients, subordinates, suppliers, superiors, the bank manager, and so on. In this way the new manager will build up a reputation in the eyes of others (Chell, 1987).

Summary and conclusions

The new manager has to operate with a changing environment from which situations emerge and with which he or she has to deal. These situations are rule-governed in a social and business sense and underpinned by perceptions of the firm's competitive position in the environment and the beliefs about what is thought to be best practice. They new manager's key actions and behaviours are strategic. They are goal-directed and rely upon the development of well-thought-out objectives which are consistent with personal ambitions and the success of the business. These aims can only be achieved by more highly developed perceptions and sensitivity to the issues.

The model of managerial behaviour presented in this reading shows the manager in context: what the manager brings to the job in terms of his/her cognitive framework will shape and be shaped by external influences. This has implications for the assessment of managerial performance and it raises certain questions. Are the manager's skills, attitudes and motives compatible with delivering in a competitive world? What are and what should the manager's time horizons be? Has he or she vision and is he or she hungry to achieve? The model is general: it applies to all levels of management and to specialist and line functions.

The key lesson for management is to consider strategic thinking not simply as a boardroom level responsibility, but as the responsibility of all levels of management. From this flow other considerations: (1) the need for more effective communication and participation to convey clear role expectations; (2) to develop an organizational culture which looks forward to success; (3) to develop reward systems linked to the strategic performance of management thus motivating those who take initiative; (4) to shape the organizational structure in such a way that it enables the emergence and fostering of new ideas; and (5) constantly to seek out and utilize information and increase the awareness of environmental change. Management isn't simply about managing people; it is about directing the ship. If there is land in sight, we all want to see it; if there is an iceberg adrift we must take corrective action. Spending too much time in the engine room is not the answer!

Note   1. I would like to thank Ms Helga Drummond, Assistant Director of Personnel and Industrial Relations, Direct Works, the Greater Manchester Council, for her perspicacious comments on an earlier draft of this paper.

References

Abell, D. F. (1980) *Defining the Business: The Starting Point of Strategic Planning*, Prentice-Hall, Englewood Cliffs, New Jersey.

Biddle, B. J. (1979) *Role Theory-Expectations, Identities and Behaviors*, The Academic Press, New York.

Chell, E. (1985) *Participation and Organization: A Social Psychological Approach*, Macmillan, London.

Chell, E. (1987) *The Psychology of Behaviour in Organizations*, Macmillan, London.

Child, J. (1984) *Organization: A Guide to Problems and Practice*, 2nd edn, Harper & Row, London.

Churchill, N. C. (1983) 'Entrepreneurs and their enterprises: a stage model', in J. A. Hornaday, J. A. Timmons and K. H. Vesper (eds), *Frontiers of Entrepreneurship Research*, Babson Center for Entrepreneurial Studies, Wellesley, Mass., 1–22.

Drucker, P. F. (1955) *The Practice of Management*, Pan, London.

Flamholtz, E. G. (1986) *How to Make the Transition from an Entrepreneurship to a Professionally Managed Firm*, Jossey-Bass, San Francisco.

Grant, R. M. (1987) 'Business strategy and strategy change in a hostile environment: failure and success among British cutlery producers', in A. M. Pettigrew (ed.), *The Management of Strategic Change*, Basil Blackwell, Oxford.

Johnson, G. N. (1984) 'Managing strategic change—a frames and formulae approach', paper presented at the Strategic Management Society Conference, Philadelphia, October.

Katz, D. and R. L. Kahn (1966) *The Social Psychology of Organizations*, Wiley, New York.

Kazanjian, R. K. (1984) 'Operationalizing stage of growth: an empirical assessment of dominant problems, in J. A. Hornaday *et al.* (eds), *Frontiers of Entrepreneurship Research*, Babson College, Center for Entrepreneurial Studies, Wellesley, Mass.

Lindblom, C. E. (1959) 'The science of muddling through', *Public Administrative Review*, **19**, Spring, 79–88.

McClelland, D. C. (1961) *The Achieving Society*, Van Nostrand, Princeton, New Jersey.

Metcalfe, J. S. (1985) 'On technical competition', University of Manchester, Department of Economics, unpublished paper.

Miller, D. and P. H. Friesen (1982) 'Innovation in conservative and entrepreneurial firms: two models of strategic momentum', *Strategic Management Journal*, **3**, 1–25.

Miller, D. and P. H. Friesen (1984) *Organizations: A Quantum View*, Prentice-Hall, Englewood Cliffs, New Jersey.

Miller, D. and J. M. Toulouse (1986) 'Chief executive personality and corporate strategy and structure in small firms', *Management Science*, **32**(11), 1389–1409.

Minkes, A. L. (1987) *The Entrepreneurial Manager*, Penguin, Harmondsworth.

Mintzberg, H. (1979) *The Structuring of Organizations: A Synthesis of the Research*, Prentice-Hall, Englewood Cliffs, New Jersey.

Mintzberg, H., O. Raisinghani and A. Theuret (1976) 'The structure of unstructured decision processes', *Administrative Science Quarterly*, **21**, 246–75.

Mischel, W. (1973) 'Towards a congitive social learning reconceptualisation of personality', *Psychological Review*, **80**(4), 252–83.

Pennings, J. M. (ed.) (1985) *Organizational Strategy and Change*, Jossey-Bass, San Francisco.

Rokeach, M. (1983) *The Nature of Human Values*, Free Press, New York.

Rotter, J. B. and D. J. Hochreich (1975) *Personality*, Scott, Foresman, Glenview, Illinois.

The factory of the future

J. Martin Corbett

Popular wisdom within the production engineering and computer science fraternity has it that 'peopleless' production will have become a reality by 2010 (Wright and Bourne, 1988). Governments and large corporations are investing large sums in the factory of the future. Since 1982, the Commission of European Communities has invested £600 million of public money developing ideas for the factory of the future. In America, private industry spent nearly $50 billion on automated production systems between 1981 and 1986. By the mid 1980s, Japanese manufacturers were using more robots than American and European manufacturers put together.

The aim of this reading is to outline the social dynamics behind the well-publicized drive towards full automation. An alternative vision is then outlined. The reading ends with a brief discussion of the job-design implications of these two opposing visions, or scenarios, of the future. The reader is encouraged to consider the implications and ramifications of the information contained in the reading for, and within, the wider sphere of organizational behaviour and theory.

In order to examine the social dynamics of technological development, Kurt Lewin's (1952) 'fields of force' model of change will be employed. This model views the change process in terms of a dynamic equilibrium between 'driving' and 'restraining' forces. In any situation there are forces which push for change (driving forces) as well as forces that hinder change (restraining forces). Change occurs when one of these forces is stronger than the other.

Scenario 1: the fully automated factory

Figure R15.1 illustrates a number of driving and restraining forces which currently effect the drive towards the 'peopleless factory' of the future. These are discussed in more detail below.

Driving forces

Management desire for control

Writers have argued that the design of production jobs is heavily influenced by the desire of higher management and top organizational decision-makers to achieve greater control over the production process (Braverman, 1974; Noble, 1984). Tighter managerial control can be achieved by adopting higher levels of automation and centralized production control technology. This managerial strategy is an important driving force towards the 'peopleless factory'. Braverman and others argue that shopfloor and line-management tasks have become increasingly fragmented and simplified, which leaves their jobs ripe for automation at each successive step of an organization's technological development.

In a recent survey of UK manufacturing, 20 per cent of organizations cited the desire to increase management control as the main objective of their automation investment plan (Industrial Computing, 1987). Many suppliers of

Figure R15.1
Force field analysis
1—full automation as
desired state

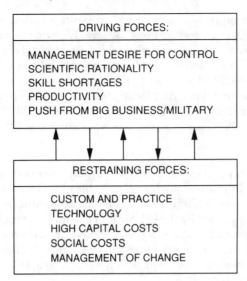

advanced manufacturing technology have used the predictability of machines as powerful marketing images to bolster this managerial perspective (e.g. 'Robots don't strike').

Scientific rationality   Since the turn of the century, science and technology have been ideologically linked with the idea of economic progress (Rose, 1979). It is indisputable that they have contributed to the economic prosperity of the industrialized world. Cottrell (1986) argues that the competitive nature of scientific and technological development is such that an advance in one country raises fears in other countries that they may be missing some great opportunity for the future unless they add it to their own national lists of scientific and technological activities. Hence, 'we have, in effect, a scientific and technological "Olympic Games" in which every technically advanced country can hardly resist the temptation to enter a candidate for every event' (Cottrell, 1986: 113). Within manufacturing, the pervasiveness of an 'automate or liquidate' philosophy adds poignancy to this process.

Skill shortages   In recent years, one of the most cited reasons for the need to automate has been based on the perception that traditional metal working and craft skills are in short supply. Given the cost of training employees to demanding standards, many companies have looked to technology to enable them to employ less skilled (lower-cost) operators. It was common for the vendors of the early numerically controlled (NC) machine tools to boast that 'even an idiot can operate them' (Noble, 1984).

   With the advent of the 'information technology revolution' (Forester, 1982), it not only became possible to embody craft skills into software and hardware, but also to integrate previously discrete stages of the production process— propagating the belief that automation can replace entire groups of skilled labour.

Productivity   The economic benefits of automation most frequently cited by manufacturers are: reduced throughput times; reduced inventory and work-in-progress; reduced labour costs; increased flexibility; increased quality; increased managerial control of the production process; and increased overall productivity.

These are impressive claims which are substantiated by the publicized experiences of large corporations. General Electric's factory of the future in Louisville, Kentucky has raised productivity levels of dishwasher manufacturing by nearly a third, cut warranty calls by a half and boosted the company's market share from 31 per cent to 43 per cent. Similarly at IBM's highly automated typewriter factory in Lexington, Kentucky, 2000 employees can now turn out 1.4 million units per year, where 6000 used to produce 0.7 million units. Not only that, the new typewriters cost $1000 less than the models they replace.

Push from 'big business' and the military

Both large corporations and the military have invested huge sums in the drive towards the fully automated factory. Noble (1984) shows how the development of NC—the basic building block of automated production systems—was driven by huge investments by the US Air Force to fulfil a technical need (machining helicopter rotor blades) and a political need (to place control of production in the hands of management). Other designs, equally viable in economic terms, found it impossible to compete with the NC design, primarily due to lack of comparable capital resources.

The role of large, often multinational, corporations in the development of full automation is considerable. Many of these companies (e.g. General Electric, General Motors, Yamasaki and Boeing) design, manufacture and service innovative technological products which are the basis for production process innovations for their customers (Roy and Wield, 1986). For example, General Motors in Detroit invested $40bn between 1979 and 1987 on automation. They are currently imposing their own 'manufacturing automation protocol' (MAP) on the rest of the industry. MAP is a significant development towards full automation as it consists of a set of rules which govern how different machines should communicate with each other to enable full integration of design, manufacture and sales.

Restraining forces

Custom and practice

Organizations—particularly long-established organizations—are not renowned for their ability to respond rapidly to change. Simply because certain avenues are open to organizational decision-makers does not guarantee that they will take them. Established patterns of behaviour can prove highly resistant to change (Mirvis and Berg, 1977).

There are cases of trade unions and management groups successfully redirecting executive implementation strategies when the process was seen to lead to labour displacement or loss of power or status (Clegg *et al.*, 1984; Wilkinson, 1984; Burnes, 1988). Hence, even if full automation *can* be achieved, there is no guarantee that it *will* be achieved.

Technology

The present levels of safety, integrity and reliability of advanced manufacturing and information technology are such that a number of commentators seriously question whether the fully automated factory of the future is a realizable goal (e.g. Brodner, 1986).

Documented cases of robotic homicide (e.g. Nagamachi, 1988), major software modelling errors (Wray, 1988), and computer-aided malpractice and misjudgement (Cooley, 1987) support this view. Proponents of full automation argue that the development of artificial intelligence (AI) and expert systems will enable 'intelligent' manufacturing systems to take contingent, as opposed to pre-programmed, actions to deal with unforeseen and unexpected occurrences reducing error and failure. Whether or not this argument is based on misplaced optimism is a matter for debate, although AI system designers openly profess

serious difficulty encapsulating human intelligence in a machine-readable form
(Wright and Bourne, 1988).

High capital costs   Full automation is capital-intensive and only the wealthiest of companies seem
prepared to enter the arena. With the number of small-to-medium-sized
companies increasing steadily (Brodner, 1987), full automation may be
restricted to large multinational corporations, while the smaller, less wealthy
companies stand aside evaluating the appropriateness of technological
developments for their particular needs.

Social costs   There has been much debate on the social effects of automation, particularly
with regard to labour displacement and job design. The literature offers a
cloudy picture of the social impact of automation, ranging from optimistic
(Forester, 1982) to pessimistic (Noble, 1984). As the drive towards the
peopleless factory continues, shopfloor jobs will start to disappear. If the
displaced employees fail to find alternative employment, the financial and
social costs to society will inevitably increase.

In a US case study of three shopfloor employees displaced by one robot,
Mital and Genaidy (1988) calculated that the loss of revenue to society
(through loss of income tax, the payment of unemployment benefits, etc.)
outweighed gains (increased tax levied on company profits and sales owing to
productivity gains, etc.) by a factor of two over a three-year period.

The dynamic productivity model proposed by Rosenbrock (1981) and
developed by Seliger (1984) demonstrates that such short-term productivity
benefits occasioned by labour displacing automation can lead to unfavourable
economic and social consequences in the long term. This analysis questions the
economic viability of full automation.

Management of change   The productivity increases which support the drive towards full automation
appear to be more a reflection of executive and managerial aspirations than of
the current reality in manufacturing organizations. Majchrzak (1988) argues
that American manufacturers are experiencing an estimated 50 to 75 per cent
failure rate when implementing advanced automated technology.

It is difficult to assess failure rates in organizations because companies are
reticent to publicize negative experiences. From what is known about the
management of technological change, researchers agree that successful
implementation of automation crucially depends on the development of human
resource and management practices which support, rather than undermine,
factory automation (e.g. Buchanan and Boddy, 1983; Wall, Clegg and Kemp,
1987; Majchrzak, 1988). The economic success of Japanese manufacturing
companies is often attributed to developments in organizational and managerial
techniques as opposed to any inherent properties of automation *per se*
(Schonberger, 1982).

Scenario 2: Hybrid factory automation

Hybrid factory automation refers to production systems which are designed to
facilitate shared, concurrent control between skilled human operators and
machines. The goal of hybrid automation is the design of systems which
encourage a synergy between the creativity, flexibility and skills of users on the
one hand, and the accuracy, data storage capacity and speed of new technology
on the other. Figure R15.2 illustrates driving and restraining forces which
currently influence developments towards the hybrid factory of the future.

Figure R15.2
Force field analysis
2—hybrid automation
as desired state.

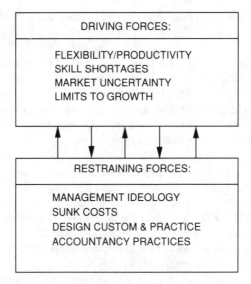

Driving forces

**Flexibility and
productivity**

This driving force towards hybrid automation has two components. First, the experience of many companies suggests that high levels of automation can reduce (or at best emulate) rather than increase productivity and flexibility levels associated with lower levels of automation. Hence a number of companies are now looking towards alternative hybrid automated systems.

At General Motors, their $500 m Hamtramck facility in Detroit contains 310 robots in a 'factory for the day-after-tomorrow'. Yet, the factory can only boast similar product quality and productivity as the ageing (less capital-intensive) General Motors factory in Fremont, California. Similarly, the $400m Buick City fully automated factory in Michigan can only achieve half the production throughput rate of the factory it superseded.

The second component of the driving force towards hybrid automation is the success of companies attempting to achieve human–technology synergy. Toyota's success in flexible manufacturing is based more on organizational practices and hybrid automation than on full automation. The company's famous 'Kanban' production technique—a key to the company's control of work-in-progress and inventory levels—is based on the very low technology of cards or chits which travel with containers of parts through the factory. The aim is to reduce the number of cards in circulation through removing bottlenecks in order to achieve just-in-time manufacturing. No cumbersome computer scheduling programs are involved—Toyota have concentrated their efforts on reducing waste and production bottlenecks and not on implementing increasingly sophisticated levels of automation. Toyota's success has driven many companies to re-assess their automation strategies.

Skill shortages

One of the key stumbling blocks to full automation is the inherent difficulty transferring production and craft knowledge from humans to machines. This is crucial as advanced manufacturing systems rely on skilled intervention for their operational performance. This human intervention is problematic in the monitoring and diagnosis of system error because machine 'minders' cannot develop the requisite skills simply from observing automated machinery in action (Bainbridge, 1983).

Hence, there is a two-fold skill shortage which hinders the development of full automation and promotes the embracement of hybrid systems. On the one hand, there is a growing shortage of shopfloor operators with the skills to manually control or override malfunctioning highly automated systems. On the other hand, there is a shortage of computer and social scientists with the skills to extract and codify the important craft knowledge of skilled operators. A number of commentators argue that such skill, by its very nature, cannot be codified into machine-readable form (e.g. Cooley, 1987).

Market uncertainty   The key word in the manufacturing world of the 1980s and 1990s is 'flexibility'. Companies no longer think in terms of mass production, but market niches, small batches and customized one-offs (Brodner, 1987). Manufacturers of advanced automation technology claim flexibility to be a key attribute of their products. Others argue (Brodner, 1986) that companies following strategies of full automation suffer from relative inflexibility with regard to batch changes and process innovation. Every change of a customer order or a piece of production equipment first needs to be modelled in a computer system. 'In the long run, the firm might even lose its innovative capability, since production knowledge and creativity on the human side would have been wasted away over time. All this is in contrast with market requirements' (Brodner, 1986: 147).

Limits to growth   The social costs outlined in the previous scenario are one example of the possible limits to the growth of full automation. Other limiting factors include ecological considerations such as energy resources and pollution.

Despite fierce controversy over the methods used to predict the likely effects of pollution and resource shortages in the future, it is becoming increasingly clear that there are real finite limits to material consumption. Dickson (1975) argues that 'it is physically impossible for the world to continue tracing out current patterns of industrial and technological growth without taking into account the physical limits imposed by the finite nature of the earth and its resources' (p. 21). An economy based on rapid growth demands a particular type of technology which is capable of producing the maximum innovation of new products with little consideration of real social need.

Restraining forces   A major obstacle to the development and diffusion of hybrid automation is management ideology—particularly management's desire for control of the

Management ideology   production process. Managers often resist changes (whether technological or organizational) which result in a reduction in this control even when such a change brings undisputed gains in performance.

Emery and Thorsrud (1976) report the instance of a Norwegian electrical company who experimented with semi-autonomous work groups. Within the first year of the experiment, productivity rose by 20 per cent, in the next year by a further 10 per cent. Yet management refused to extend these new methods of working to the main plant.

> The management argument was that the workers were not really interested and that the old system gave better management control. Individual piece rates were assumed to be necessary to keep up productivity. In retrospect one can easily see that what was really at stake was management's basic idea of work organisation (Emery and Thorsrud, 1976: 97).

Sunk costs   Investment in full automation is costly. For a large company to shift their emphasis to hybrid automation would involve writing off considerable investment.

It is also likely that large corporations which have invested heavily in the drive towards the 'peopleless factory' will attempt to regain control over the market if a shift towards hybridization became evident. Recent history shows that companies may attempt to manage their environments by suppressing the development and diffusion of competing technologies through patents and information manipulation (Dunford, 1987) or through influencing or 'tying in' customers to continue their present purchasing strategy (DeLamarter, 1988). This 'tying in' effectively excludes other competitors from supplying alternative manufacturing technology.

Design custom and practice

The design of hybrid automation which seeks to retain and develop the skills and knowledge of users is not unproblematic. Designers and production engineers (even when committed to developing hybrid automation technology) have great difficulty incorporating unpredictable human components into their design practice (Corbett, 1987a; 1990). Until new techniques and design methods are developed, this problem will restrain the development of exemplary hybrid systems. However, there are encouraging signs that the new methods which are now emerging can help overcome these problems (Clegg and Corbett, 1987; Corbett et al., 1989).

Accountancy practices

In many companies there is a tendency to justify investments in automation by forecasting substantial savings in direct labour cost. This practice is biased against investment in hybrid automation which does not explicitly aim to displace labour.

Management accountants generally experience great difficulty in quantifying the inherent flexibility of hybrid systems in monetary terms (Primrose and Leonard, 1984). Others argue that the unsophisticated nature of manufacturing accounting is directly connected with a falling off in relative competitive performance, particularly against Japan (Kaplan, 1983). Until accountants develop methods to appraise investments in advanced manufacturing technology in broader terms, strategic investment in hybrid automation will remain 'unjustifiable'.

Job design and the factory of the future

Research into the impact of automation on job design is dominated by case-study analyses from which generalizations are difficult to articulate. Recent research (Corbett, 1987b; Zuboff, 1988; Corbett et al., 1989) suggests that the centralized, highly integrated production systems (the precursors of full automation) are associated with stress and low motivation among operating personnel. The degradation of tacit craft skills may lead to a loss of innovative potential and an over-reliance on theoretical knowledge and systems analysis divorced from the production process itself. These findings are of crucial importance because an organization's technology choice today will carry over into the future.

Job designs associated with hybrid automation are less problematic since they are linked into the technical design process itself. The participation of company personnel in the design process enables job specific knowledge to be included into the system specification and thus allow a company to retain and develop its innovative capabilities.

Drucker (1988) argues that organizations of the future will be 'knowledge-based', with the knowledge resting in the minds and actions of employees at the lower levels of the organization hierarchy. Drucker forecasts that 'knowledge workers' will resist the command-and-control model that business took from the military a hundred years ago.

Full automation is incompatible with this new form of organization. It remains to be seen if organizations will develop a sufficiently broad vision of the future (encompassing technology and job design in its broadest context) into their strategic planning. This reading has briefly sketched out the fields of force which impinge on this vision of the factory of the future. It is for the new generation of management to convert such information into action.

References

Bainbridge, L. (1983) 'Ironies of automation', *Automatica*, **19**, 775–9.

Braverman, H. (1974) *Labor and Monopoly Capital*, Monthly Review Press, New York.

Brodner, P. (1986) 'Skill based manufacturing versus "unmanned factor"—which is superior?', *International Journal of Industrial Ergonomics*, **1**, 145–53.

Brodner, P. (ed.) (1987) *Strategic Options for New Production Systems*, CEC-FAST Publications, Brussels.

Buchanan, D. A. and D. Boddy (1983) *Organizations in the Computer Age*, Gower, Aldershot.

Burnes, B. (1988) 'New technology and job design: the case of CNC', *New Technology, Work and Employment*, **3**, 100–11.

Clegg, C. W. and J. M. Corbett (1987) 'Research and development in "humanizing" advanced manufacturing technology', in T. D. Wall, C. W. Clegg and N. J. Kemp (eds), *The Human Side of Advanced Manufacturing Technology*, Wiley, Chichester.

Clegg, C. W., N. J. Kemp and T. D. Wall (1984) 'New technology: choice, control and skills', in G. C. Van de Veer, M. J. Tauber, T. Green and P. Gorny (eds), *Readings on Cognitive Ergonomics: Mind and Computers*, Springer-Verlag, Berlin.

Cooley, M. J. E. (1987) *Architect or Bee?: The Human Price of Technology*, Hogarth Press, London.

Corbett, J. M. (1987a) 'Human work design criteria and the design process: the devil in the detail', in P. Brodner (ed.), *Skill Based Automated Manufacturing*, Pergamon Press, Oxford.

Corbett, J. M. (1987b) 'A psychological study of advanced manufacturing technology: the concept of coupling', *Behaviour and Information Technology*, **6**, 441–53.

Corbett, J. M. (1990) 'Human centred advanced manufacturing systems: from rhetoric to reality', *International Journal of Industrial Ergonomics*, **5**, 83–90.

Corbett, J. M., S. J. Ravden and C. W. Clegg (1987) 'The development and implementation of human and organizational criteria in computer integrated manufacturing systems', in K. Rathmill and P. MacConnaill (eds), *Computer Integrated Manufacturing*. IFS/Springer, Bedford.

Corbett, J. M., R. Martin, T. D. Wall and C. W. Clegg (1989) 'Technological coupling as a predictor of intrinsic job satisfaction: a replication study' *Journal of Organizational Behavior*, **10**, 91–5.

Cottrell, A. H. (1986) 'Technological thresholds', in R. Roy and D. Wield (eds), *Product Design and Technological Innovation*, Open University Press, Milton Keynes.

DeLarmarter, R. T. (1988) *Big Blue: IBMs Use and Abuse of Power*, Pan Books, London.

Dickson, D. (1975) *Alternative Technology and The Politics of Technical Change*, Fontana/Collins, Glasgow.

Drucker, P. (1988) 'The coming of the new organization', *Harvard Business Review*, **66**, 15–21.

Dunford, R. (1987) 'The suppression of technology as a strategy for controlling resource dependence', *Administrative Science Quarterly*, **32**, 512–25.

Emery, F. E. and E. Thorsrud (1976) *Democracy at Work*, Martinus Nijhoff, Leiden.

Forester, T. (1982) (ed.), *The Information Technology Revolution*, Blackwell, Oxford.

Industrial Computing (1987) 'Survey supplement', October, EMAP Publications, London.

Kaplan, R. S. (1983) 'Measuring manufacturing performance: a new challenge for management accounting research', *The Accounting Review*, October, 23–4.

Lewin, K. (1952) 'Group decision and social change', in G. E. Swanson, T. M. Newcomb, and E. L. Hartley (eds), *Readings in Social Psychology* (rev. edn), Holt, New York.

Majchrzak, A. (1988) *The Human Side of Factory Automation*, Jossey Bass, San Francisco.

Mirvis, P. H. and D. N. Berg (eds) (1977) *Failures in Organizational Development and Change*, Wiley, Chichester.

Mital, A. and A. M. Genaidy (1988) 'Automation, robotisation in particular, is always economically desirable. Fact or fiction?', in W. Karwowski, H. R. Parsaei and M. R. Wilhelm (eds), *Ergonomics of Hybrid Automated Systems I*, Elsevier, Amsterdam.

Nagamachi, M. (1988) 'Ten fatal accidents due to robots in Japan', in W. Karwowski, H. R. Parsaei and M. R. Wilhelm (eds) *Ergonomics of Hybrid Automated Systems I*, Elsevier, Amsterdam.

Noble, D. (1979) 'Social choice in machine design: the case of automatically controlled machine tools', in A. Zimbalist (ed.), *Case Studies on the Labour Process*, Monthly Review Press, New York.

Noble, D. (1984) *Forces of Production*, Knopf, New York.

Primrose, P. L. and R. Leonard (1984) 'Optimising the financial advantages of using CNC machine tools by use of an integrated suite of programs', *Proceedings of the Institute of Mechanical Engineers*, **198**, 147–51.

Rose, M. (1979) *Industrial Behaviour*, Penguin, Harmondsworth.

Rosenbrock, H. H. (1981) 'Human resources and technology', *Proceedings of the Sixth World Congress of the International Economic Association of Human Resources, Employment and Development*.

Roy, R. and Wield, D. (1986) (eds) *Product Design and Technological Innovation*, Open University Press, Milton Keynes.

Schonberger, R. J. (1982) 'The transfer of Japanese manufacturing management approaches to US industry', *Academy of Management Review*, **7**, 479–87.

Seliger, G. (1984) *Wirtschaftliche Planung automatisierter Fertigungssyteme*, Springer-Verlag, Berlin.

Wall, T. D., C. W. Clegg and N. J. Kemp (eds) (1987) *The Human Side of Advanced Manufacturing Technology*, Wiley, Chichester.

Wilkinson, B. (1984) *The Shopfloor Politics of New Technology*, Heinemann, London.

Wray, T. (1988) 'The everyday risks of playing safe', *New Scientist*, 8 September 1988, No. 1628, 61–5.

Wright, P. K. and D. A. Bourne (1988) *Manufacturing Intelligence*, Addison-Wesley, Reading, Mass.

Zuboff, S. (1988) *In the Age of the Smart Machine*, Heinemann Professional Publishing, Oxford.

The changing face of line management: the case of British Rail

Patrick Dawson

Case introduction

The management of a national railway freight service is a complex operation which requires the constant monitoring, scheduling and adjustment of resources (such as staff, wagons and locomotives) to meet daily fluctuations in customer demands and the regular occurrence of operating contingencies (such as derailments, staff accidents and equipment failures). The basic sequence of operations in freight transits comprise: planning and running local services to meet changing customer demands; sorting freight in marshalling yards and assembling wagons into train formation for outbound services (high-capacity yards can cover a geographical area of over 1 sq. mile with facilities to classify wagons into 80 or more separate sidings); monitoring and co-ordinating scheduled trunk services to ensure that the marshalled wagons are transferred to the appropriate destination freight terminal yard; and finally, arranging local services to dispatch wagons to customer unloading points.

Information is a key management resource in the control of these interdependent operations, and to improve service provision British Rail introduced a management information system known as TOPS (Total Operations Processing System). The TOPS system was first introduced in 1975 and currently provides accurate, up-to-date accounts of the movement and composition of freight trains over the entire national railway network.

During the early stages of computerization senior British Rail management attempted to devolve daily operations control freight transits to the local level through the creation of a new supervisory-managerial role, the Area Freight Assistant (AFA), whose job was designed to exploit the operational control potential of the new technology. The position of AFA was accredited senior supervisory status with increased managerial responsibility for making daily operating decisions on the running, cancellation and alteration of freight train services. While this enabled senior management to devolve some of the traditional elements of management decision-making from divisional headquarters to the local level, current variations in the recruitment, training, and career characteristics of AFAs indicate growing uncertainty over the nature of this position. This case sets out to examine this problem by briefly describing the emergence of the AFA position, the typical career path and defining personal characteristics of AFAs, and the routine operating practices of these supervisors-cum-managers of the future.

The creation of a new area freight operations manager

It was not until the initial operation of TOPS computer system that management's objective to devolve additional elements of freight transit control to the local level was fully realized. This new management information system enabled pre-planning on a scale that was inconceivable under the traditional manual system, and the potential for devolving operations control to the local level was recognized by the TOPS Project Manager. He advocated the need for a 'new supervisory concept' which demanded:

> A supervisor with organising ability . . . to act for the Area Manager round the clock over the whole area and not just over the yard in which the [computer] was located. With TOPS he has the means to control the whole area, and this is how the grade of Area Freight Assistant came into being (TOPS Project Manager).

TOPS provided accurate and comprehensive accounts of the current state of railway freight operations over the national railway network. The computer data base could be used directly at local as well as headquarters levels, so that real-time information was available at the point of operations. Consequently, there was no longer a need for a large, manual, hierarchical reporting and command structure and hence, British Rail management set about transforming the existing operational control organization.

The devolution of daily operating decisions to the local level went hand-in-hand with management's plans to centralize overall control of operations at regional and national headquarters, and their intention to contract divisional offices by reducing their role to round-the-clock intelligence centres. In response to the latter proposal, the rail unions mounted strong opposition, questioning the ability of TOPS to react to operating contingencies and emergencies. In the face of union objections, management agreed not to pursue a nationalization of the divisional control organization but to allow each region to proceed at its own pace with those changes it deemed necessary. This has created a situation in which the new local freight 'supremo' is formally constrained by the persistence of divisional offices to work in close liaison with them. In practice, however, it was clear that they could and did discharge their responsibilities largely independently of them. The coexistence of an outdated organization reporting and command structure with a more centralized and devolved computer-based operating system has created a certain amount of controversy and confusion over the responsibilities, authority and status that should be accredited to the position of AFA. This has been exacerbated by the uncertainty and mystique which surrounds the job and the conflicting perceptions on what makes a good AFA and what is the most appropriate career path to this position.

Managers, supervisors or clerks? The recruitment and training of AFAs

The AFA occupies a mixed managerial–supervisory position. He (there were no female AFAs) is concerned with planning, monitoring and correcting freight operations within a specified geographical area; namely, a TOPS Responsibility Area (TRA). He is officially defined as: a second-line supervisor with responsibility for the control of area freight operations.

The defining personal characteristics of the majority of AFAs correspond to traditional types of supervisory roles. They were predominantly of working-class origin; recruited from the shop floor; had knowledge based on years of practical experience; had little formal education and training. The position represented the end of their career progression. Typically, an AFA would have joined British Rail at an early age and worked his way up through the ranks. Consequently, the recruitment and training of AFAs centred on the career paths of traditional railway freight supervisors and, as such, continued to emphasize the importance of 'knowledge-through-experience'.

During the 1980s, however, a small number of AFAs were recruited via an alternative route, namely, as ex-management trainees. Unlike their colleagues they fitted more appropriately into a more modern type of supervisory role. In contrast to the conventional career path of railway supervisors these ex-management trainees were: of middle-class origin; recruited as a graduate entrant; acquired knowledge from formal education and 'in-house' training; held a position which represented one stage in their career development; and were relatively young.

These two very different career paths to the position of AFA reflected strategic management's confusion over whether the job of the AFA was predominantly supervisory or managerial. British Rail managers, interviewed as part of the study, also indicated a great deal of uncertainty about the nature of the job and the attributes required to make a 'good' AFA. This was particularly noticeable among area managers, who were uncertain as to whether it was the clerical aspect of the job, the operating element or managerial decision-making that was most important. For the most part, this uncertainty stemmed from management's confusion over what the job of the AFA actually involved. As one AFA put it:

> People don't understand now what it is, honestly, several managers have never quite grasped it and I'm not being unkind. It's just so intense a job.

Areas managers expressed a number of different views; some felt that it should remain a senior supervisor's job, others that it should be a junior management post, and one area manager felt that it should be open to senior clerical staff. From this diverse set of opinions, three distinct countervailing beliefs were identified: firstly, that ex-management trainees did not have enough operating experience; secondly, that first-line freightyard supervisors did not have sufficient clerical experience; and thirdly, that senior clerical staffs operating the computers did not have enough experience of making decisions under pressure.

Nevertheless, there was general agreement among area managers and AFAs that the job involved elements of management decision-making. This is illustrated in a typical reply made by one AFA who said:

> I've always believed that it should be a management grade and that it should have been from its earliest days. It's a very managerial job, you make endless managerial decisions . . . you do an awful lot of planning in the proper sense, things that actually involve a lot of people outside your own area of responsibility. I think it's much more managerial than a supervisory job and that's not trying to make more out of it than it is because I've got my feet on the ground don't worry. . . . But the trouble is you just can't, it would unbalance the area managers organization you see.

In addition, all the AFAs studied felt that it was important to have an understanding of the TOPS system. In fact, training in TOPS techniques was in every case evaluated as being more important to the job than general supervisory training. Typically, AFAs who had attended both a supervisory training course and a computer course claimed that the latter was far more relevant to their actual job. AFAs would normally support this claim by pointing out that the job involved little, if any, elements associated with the close supervision of labour. As one AFA put it:

> The clerks that I deal with, they hardly need any supervision. They don't really, they've got their own job and they just get on with it. There is no supervision. I call it an area freight assistant, it's dealing with the freight all the time. The supervision of men comes from the yard supervision to my mind.

So what does the actual job of the AFA involve and how far is it concerned with supervisory and/or managerial tasks and activities? To provide the reader with some insights into this question the final section briefly examines the routine working practices of a group of AFAs.

The job of the area freight assistant under TOPS

The job of the AFA involves the control and coordination of area freight operations. Their primary aim is to ensure the efficient utilization of resources in the provision of local and trunk freight train services. In order to achieve this objective, AFAs exploit the information generated from the TOPS computer system in assessing, planning, and coordinating freight-train movements within their operating area. Working within a local supervisory team, they will monitor area freight operations, deal with operating contingencies, and plan the future movements of freight in close liaison with other supervisors and senior yard staff. The AFAs main concern is with the control and coordination of railway resources in the provision of freight train services.

At the beginning of the AFA's turn of duty, monitoring and evaluating area freight operations is particularly intense. Before it is possible to plan local freight movements and correct and adapt trunk freight-train services, it is first necessary to evaluate the current state of area freight operations. The AFA will make two basic computer enquiries from his terminal which provide information on the current state of freight traffic on hand and en route, and a summary of all incoming trains and their destinations. There are a number of additional computer enquiries which AFAs can make if they require information other than that provided by these standard enquiries; for example, if an AFA is worried about the supply of locomotives he or she could make a locomotive enquiry. Essentially, the TOPS computer system provides the AFA with all the information he or she requires to make decisions on freight operations within his local operating area.

From the information generated by the TOPS computer system, AFAs will evaluate area freight operations. They will be particularly interested in finding out: what traffic is available for their various booked services; what resources are available; and what traffic is coming towards them. Once AFAs have managed to gain an accurate overview of the current state of the operating system under their charge, they are then in a position to plan a programme of action and direct the future movements of freight. Monitoring and evaluating freight-train services and planning a course of action, could take up to two to three hours of the AFA's turn of duty. During this time the AFA will also be directing the arrival and departure of freight-train services, and dealing with any operating contingencies which may arise.

A key function of the job of the AFA is directing operations and planning the future movements of freight. The 'bible' from which the AFA operates is the Working Time Table (WTT). This lists all outbound scheduled services, all inbound scheduled services, and all those services which are scheduled to connect on to other booked freight train services. Formal alterations to the

WTT are sent from regional headquarters in the form of weekly and daily freight-train notices. This official plan of freight-train services is the framework within which the AFA operates.

In the process of monitoring, evaluating, planning, and directing area freight operations, the AFA will correct and adapt operations to take account of any operating contingencies which may arise. Derailments, shortages of locomotive power and locomotive failures were consistently cited by AFAs as the most regular type of operating contingency which they would have to deal with. Typically, AFAs would cancel services and make new arrangements for the movements of local freight traffic to accommodate these and other types of operating contingencies.

The breakdown of a locomotive on the main line was generally viewed as the most difficult and frustrating type of operating contingency which could arise. According to AFAs, this was because: firstly, it is necessary to use valuable resources to deal with the problem; and secondly, a main-line failure makes it necessary for the AFA to reroute existing services, and alter, cancel and arrange future services. In dealing with this operating contingency the AFA will make a number of computer enquiries and plan the future movements of freight in close liaison with other operating staff. In addition, the AFA will deal with the immediate problem of clearing the main line and rerouting any services which were due to use that section of line. Thus, although there is a high degree of pre-planning in the form of the WTT, there is also a need to assess and replan freight-train services due to the regular occurrence of operating contingencies, such as machinery breakdowns, daily variations in the level of freight traffic and daily variations in the supply and demand of resources.

A key job task of the AFA is to exploit the information generated from the TOPS computer system, for the purpose of planning and directing these time-sensitive and interdependent cycles of freight operations in the course of dealing with any operating contingencies which may arise. As one AFA described the job when asked how much of his work he felt was routine:

> Well it's nearly all non-routine really. Alright we use those monitoring sheets but that's just to keep you fixed. You've got to have an overall plan because you could never start, you couldn't just kick-off off the top of your head.

The decision on whether to alter, cancel, or rearrange freight-train services is based on a number of operating considerations. The most important of these are: firstly, the priority of the service in question (for example, whether the traffic is mandated or not); and secondly, the consequence of change for the operating system as a whole (for example, whether, the freight traffic is due to connect with another service or whether the locomotive is allocated to run a mandated service elsewhere on the railway freight network). Such operating considerations are taken into account by AFAs in making alterations to the WTT in liaison with other operating staff. Moreover, as changes in the running of local services are less likely to affect the operating system than changes to national freight services, it is the local freight train services which are more frequently cancelled.

Essentially, the AFA will replan scheduled services and plan the future movements of freight with the aim of minimizing disruptions to the operating system as a whole. In this sense, the AFA attempts to steer area freight operations for the purpose of achieving optimum operating efficiency.

In making operating decisions, AFAs must be able to form a mental picture of the actual consequences of their decisions for the operating system, and estimate the timespan required for their implementation. The ability to conceptualize the practical outcome of decisions based on information provided by the TOPS computer naturally draws upon the individual's stock of knowledge and experience of railway operations. As one AFA described it:

> You need to be able to sit there and see in your mind's eye what's going on everywhere at a given moment, even though you were talking about it an hour before, or even though you're talking about something now, you've got to be able to imagine how the thing's going to hang together in two hours' time. And that involves how long it will take the engine to get from A to B, has it got to have relief, and all these multifarious little elements that are in it. I think that really to do the job well you've got to get all those things, and that's what I call an operating imagination.

Conclusion: who are the new information managers?

In the British Rail case study presented here, management decided against locating this new computer-oriented position within the existing management organization, and/or accrediting it with first-line managerial authority; instead, they decided to create a new second-line supervisory position with increased responsibility. This signalled the emergence of the position of AFA, whose job was designed explicitly to exploit the control potential of the information generated by the TOPS computer system in an attempt to secure the long-awaited strategic objective of devolving daily freight operations control to the local level. Through using the computer AFAs acquire information on: wagon stocks awaiting departure on scheduled outbound services; empty wagon resources on-hand; and the composition of approaching freight services. This information is used to plan the area movements of traffic in accordance with rail freight operations, which are themselves planned to meet the schedule of incoming and outbound services. To this extent, AFAs now hold a pivotal position in the day-to-day management of railway freight operations.

However, while the role of AFA remains formally defined as a senior supervisory post, many practising AFAs felt that it should be a management grade. As indicated by the case, much of the job is non-routine in making operating decisions in response to unforeseen human, technical and resource contingencies. Moreover, the job involves little if any people supervision, and yet AFAs continued to be trained in human-relations techniques. Perhaps, as one AFA noted, the reason for the position being defined as supervisory stems from the problems associated with locating AFAs within the existing management organization. Whatever the reason, they are clearly problems which need to be tackled with regard to work organization, recruitment policies and training programmes.

Questions

1 What changes in work organization are required to improve the future management of British Rail freight operations? Explain why the changes are needed and how you would bring them about.

2 What is the nature of the problem? Consider how the problem arose and critically assess the current operating difficulties associated with the creation of a new post.

Subject Index

Author Index